Hospitality Law

5th Edition

Hospitality Law

Managing Legal Issues in the Hospitality Industry

5th Edition

STEPHEN BARTH, J.D.
Conrad N. Hilton College of Hotel and Restaurant Management
University of Houston
Attorney and Founder of HospitalityLawyer.com

DIANA S. BARBER, J.D., CHE, CWP
Michael A. Leven School of Culinary and Sustainability and Hospitality
University College
Kennesaw State University

WILEY

VP AND EDITORIAL DIRECTOR	George Hoffman
EDITORIAL DIRECTOR	Veronica Visentin
ACQUISITIONS EDITOR	Elena Herrero
EDITORIAL ASSISTANT	Ethan Lipson
EDITORIAL MANAGER	Gladys Soto
CONTENT MANAGEMENT DIRECTOR	Lisa Wojcik
CONTENT MANAGER	Nichole Urban
SENIOR CONTENT SPECIALIST	Nicole Repasky
PRODUCTION EDITOR	Annie Sophia Thapasumony
COVER PHOTO CREDIT	© tanawat_c /iStockphoto; DNY59 /iStockphoto; AnthiaCumming /iStockphoto; sebastian-julian /iStockphoto

This book was set in Source Sans Pro 9.5/12.5 by SPi Global and printed and bound by Lightning Source, Inc.

Founded in 1807, John Wiley & Sons, Inc. has been a valued source of knowledge and understanding for more than 200 years, helping people around the world meet their needs and fulfill their aspirations. Our company is built on a foundation of principles that include responsibility to the communities we serve and where we live and work. In 2008, we launched a Corporate Citizenship Initiative, a global effort to address the environmental, social, economic, and ethical challenges we face in our business. Among the issues we are addressing are carbon impact, paper specifications and procurement, ethical conduct within our business and among our vendors, and community and charitable support. For more information, please visit our website: www.wiley.com/go/citizenship.

ISBN: 978-1-119-30504-0 (PBK)
ISBN: 978-1-118-98920-3 (EVALC)

Library of Congress Cataloging in Publication Data:

Names: Barth, Stephen C., author. | Barber, Diana S., author.
Title: Hospitality law : a manager's guide to legal issues in the hospitality industry / Stephen C. Barth, Diana S. Barber.
Description: Fifth edition. | Hoboken, NJ : John Wiley & Sons Inc., 2017. | Includes bibliographical references and index.
Identifiers: LCCN 2017004049 (print) | LCCN 2017005651 (ebook) | ISBN 9781119305040 (pbk.) | ISBN 9781119299134 (Adobe PDF) | ISBN 9781119299097 (ePub)
Subjects: LCSH: Hotels—Law and legislation—United States. | Hospitality industry—Law and legislation—United States.
Classification: LCC KF2042.H6 B368 2017 (print) | LCC KF2042.H6 (ebook) | DDC 343.7307/864794—dc23
LC record available at https://lccn.loc.gov/2017004049

The inside back cover will contain printing identification and country of origin if omitted from this page. In addition, if the ISBN on the back cover differs from the ISBN on this page, the one on the back cover is correct.

Contents

PREFACE **ix**
ACKNOWLEDGMENTS **xiii**

1 Prevention Philosophy 1

1.1 The Future Hospitality Manager and the Legal Environment **1**
1.2 The Hospitality Manager and Legal Management **2**
Legally Managing at Work: **Applying the STEM Process in Hospitality Management 5**
1.3 Ethics and the Law **6**
International Snapshot: **Mitigating Risks Associated with Legal and Ethical Compliance in International Business Transactions 12**
What Would You Do? **13**
What Did You Learn in this Chapter? **13**

2 Government Agencies that Impact the Hospitality Industry 15

2.1 Federal Regulatory and Administrative Agencies **15**
2.2 State Regulatory and Administrative Agencies **29**
2.3 Local Regulatory and Administrative Agencies **33**
2.4 Regulatory Interaction and Oversight Impacting Travel and Tourism **35**
2.5 Managing Conflicting Regulations **40**
Legally Managing at Work: **Recommended Steps for Responding to Inquiries and Complaints by Government Agencies 40**
2.6 Responding to an Inquiry **41**
2.7 Monitoring Regulatory Change **42**
International Snapshot **42**
What Would You Do? **43**
What Did You Learn in this Chapter **44**

3 Hospitality Business Structures 45

3.1 The Importance of Business Structure **45**
3.2 Common Hospitality Organizational Structures **46**
3.3 Common Hospitality Operating Structures **51**
3.4 The Agency Relationship **55**
International Snapshot: **A Comparative Overview of Business Entities in the Hotel Industry 58**
What Would You Do? **58**
What Did You Learn in this Chapter? **58**

4 Contract Basics 59

4.1 Introduction to Contracts **59**
4.2 Components of an Enforceable Contract **61**
4.3 The Uniform Commercial Code **64**
4.4 Preventative Legal Management and Contracts **65**
Legally Managing at Work: **Eight Steps to Follow When Entering into Contracts 67**
Legally Managing at Work: **Reducing No-Show Reservations 70**
International Snapshot: **International Contracts 71**
What Would You Do? **72**
What Did You Learn in this Chapter? **72**

5 Significant Hospitality Contracts 73

5.1 Specific Contract Clauses **73**
5.2 Franchise Contracts **80**
5.3 Management Contracts **84**
5.4 Conference Services Contracts **87**
International Snapshot: **A Comparison of Franchise Disclosure Requirements under U.S. Law and International Law 93**
What Would You Do? **94**
What Did You Learn in this Chapter? **94**

6 Legally Managing Property 95

6.1 Introduction to Property **95**
6.2 Purchasing Property **97**
6.3 Financing the Purchase of Property **102**
6.4 Leasing Property **105**
Legally Managing at Work: **Legal Considerations of Buying versus Leasing 109**
6.5 Respecting Intellectual Property Rights **110**
International Snapshot: **U.S. Hotel Companies' Options for Seeking Trademark Protection Abroad 114**
What Would You Do? **115**
What Did You Learn in this Chapter? **115**

7 Legally Selecting Employees 117

7.1 Employee Selection **117**
7.2 Discrimination in the Selection Process **126**
Legally Managing at Work: **Accommodating Disabled Employees 128**

7.3 Verification of Eligibility to Work 129
7.4 The Employment Relationship 134
International Snapshot: **Canadian Employment Laws** 137
What Would You Do? 138
What Did You Learn in this Chapter? 138

8 Legally Managing Employees 139

8.1 Employment Relationships 139
8.2 Workplace Discrimination and Sexual Harassment 141
8.3 Family and Medical Leave Act 148
8.4 Uniform Services Employment and Reemployment Rights Act 149
8.5 Compensation 149
Legally Managing at Work: **Calculating Overtime Pay for Tipped Employees** 154
8.6 The Patient Protection and Affordable Care Act of 2010 156
8.7 Managing Employee Performance 157
Legally Managing at Work: **Guidelines for Conducting Defensible Employee Terminations** 160
8.8 Unemployment Claims 161
8.9 Employment Records and Retention 164
8.10 Employment Posting 166
8.11 Workplace Surveillance 166
International Snapshot: **Managing Employees Abroad** 168
What Would You Do? 169
What Did You Learn in this Chapter? 169

9 Your Responsibilities as a Hospitality Operator 171

9.1 Duties and Obligations of a Hospitality Operator 171
9.2 Theories of Liability 172
9.3 Legal Damages 176
9.4 Anatomy of a Personal Injury Lawsuit 176
Legally Managing at Work: **The Manager's Role in Litigation** 180
9.5 Responding to an Incident 180
Legally Managing at Work: **Responding to an Accident** 181
International Snapshot: **Negligence** 184
What Would You Do? 184
What Did You Learn in this Chapter? 185

10 Your Responsibilities as a Hospitality Operator to Guests 187

10.1 Accommodating Guests 187
10.2 Guest Privacy 191
Legally Managing at Work: **Law Enforcement and Guest Privacy** 192
10.3 Facility Maintenance 193
Legally Managing at Work: **Five Steps to Facility Evaluation** 196
10.4 Responsibilities to Nonguests 197
10.5 Removal of Guests 198
Legally Managing at Work: **Responding to Guest Health Emergencies** 200
International Snapshot: **Should Foreign Governments Adopt Provisions from the USA PATRIOT Act to Combat Terrorist Acts against the Hospitality Industry?** 200
What Would You Do? 201
What Did You Learn in this Chapter? 201

11 Your Responsibilities for Guests' Property 203

11.1 Liability For Guests' Property 203
11.2 Bailments 205
11.3 Property with Unknown Ownership 209
Legally Managing at Work: **Disposing of Found Property** 211
International Snapshot: **Limited Liability of Innkeepers in Canada** 211
What Would You Do? 212
What Did You Learn in this Chapter? 212

12 Your Responsibilities When Serving Food and Beverages 213

12.1 Serving Food 213
Legally Managing at Work: **Steps to Take When a Guest Complains of Foodborne Illness** 215
12.2 Truth-in-Menu Laws 216
12.3 Serving Alcohol 221
International Snapshot: **Understanding Barriers to Entry and Regulatory Requirements for Foreign Producers of Alcohol Seeking to Import to the United States** 228
What Would You Do? 228
What Did You Learn in this Chapter? 229

13 Legal Characteristics of Travel and Tourism 231

13.1 Travel 231
13.2 Travel Agents and Tour Operators 235
13.3 Transportation and Common Carriers 240
13.4 Tourism 246
13.5 Online Travel Sales 251

Legally Managing at Work: **Internet Advertising Checklist 255**
International Snapshot: **Government Support of Tourism 255**
What Would You Do? **256**
What Did You Learn in this Chapter? **257**

14 Safety and Security Issues 259

14.1 The Importance of a Protected Environment **259**
14.2 Safety and Security Programs: Four-Step Safety and Security Management Method **262**
Legally Managing at Work: **Establishing an Effective Guestroom Lock Policy 266**
14.3 Crimes against Hospitality Businesses **268**
Legally Managing at Work: **Procedures to Reduce the Incidence of Skipping 269**
Legally Managing at Work: **Guidelines for Handling Credit Cards 270**
Legally Managing at Work: **Personal Check Verification 271**
14.4 Human Trafficking **273**
14.5 Crisis Management Programs **274**
Legally Managing at Work: **The Manager's Responsibilities in a Crisis 277**
Legally Managing at Work: **Guest Relations in a Crisis Situation 278**
Legally Managing at Work: **Guidelines for Dealing with the Media during a Crisis 279**
International Snapshot: **Legal Claims and Recovery for Injury under Mexican Law 281**
What Would You Do? **282**
What Did You Learn in this Chapter? **282**

15 Managing Insurance 283

15.1 Introduction to Insurance **283**
15.2 Types of Coverage **285**
15.3 Selecting an Insurance Carrier **289**
15.4 Selecting the Insurance Policy **289**
15.5 Policy Analysis **290**
International Snapshot: **Hotels Operating Internationally Need to Think Globally 292**
What Would You Do? **293**
What Did You Learn in this Chapter? **294**

GLOSSARY **295**
INDEX **301**

Preface

Hospitality Law: Managing Legal Issues in the Hospitality Industry, Fifth Edition, was written to help teach hospitality students what they need to know to manage a facility legally, safely, and securely.

In the day-to-day operation of a hospitality facility, it is the manager, not the company attorney, who will most influence the legal position of the operation. Rarely will you find a hospitality manager who is also a licensed attorney. However, professional hospitality managers (and, by extension, their staffs) make decisions every day based on their own interpretation of the law. The quality of these decisions will ultimately determine whether lawyers and the expense of fees, trials, and potential judgments may become necessary. A few examples will help illustrate this fact:

- A restaurant guest is unhappy with the quality of service provided during his meal. He complains to the manager and angrily demands his money back, but his meal has been eaten.
  - Is the guest legally entitled to a refund?
- A hotel guest maintains that a $50 bill she had left on her bedside table was gone when she returned to her room after going out for lunch.
  - Is the hotel required to replace the funds?
- A resort employee is arrested by the local police for driving under the influence of alcohol. He is employed by the hotel as a van driver but was not on duty at the time of the arrest.
  - Should the hotel suspend his employment?
- A hotel food and beverage director is presented a bottle of rare and expensive wine as a Christmas gift from her linen vendor.
  - Can she legally accept the gift without threatening her employment status?
- A franchise restaurant owner receives a letter from her franchisor stating that the "casual Friday" dress code policy recently adopted by the owner is in violation of the franchise agreement.
  - Must the owner change her policy?

These examples are just a few of the thousands of legal issues that daily confront hospitality managers. Obviously, it would be very expensive to consult an attorney each time a legal issue arises. It is also true, however, that making the wrong decision in any of these cases could result in tremendous costs in legal fees and settlements or in costly negative publicity. Because that is true, a hospitality student's and a professional manager's greatest need is to understand how they can act in ways to ensure that they are managing legally in the hospitality industry. ***Hospitality Law: Managing Legal Issues in the Hospitality Industry, Fifth Edition,*** will show them how.

New to This Edition

Organization: The ***Fifth Edition*** maintains the more logical flow that was developed in the prior editions. Throughout the book, changes to the law have been updated and revised to ensure that the most current information is presented.

Web exercises: Each of the Search the web exercises have been updated to ensure accuracy and enrich the learning experience. Strategic links have also been added to ensure they are current as the law changes between editions.

Access to actual legal cases: Summaries of actual legal cases are now a part of the instructor's manual and will be useful in a class setting to further illustrate and practically apply the law. In addition, faculty and students are able to access an annual case summary of over 100 of the most significant hospitality case decisions made during a particular year by logging into Solutions at http://hospitalitylawyer.com/solutions/find-academic-resources/hospitality-law-textbook-support/, then the Find Academic Resources section, and then clicking on the blue highlighted text Hospitality Law Textbook Support, and finally Referenced Cases on **hospitalitylawyer.com**, where you will also find downloadable PowerPoints and links to the cases cited in the book.

International Snapshots are included for each chapter to give the instructor and students a different perspective on legal issues. Each of these was contributed by practicing attorneys or professionals in their field and describe the differences between U.S. law and the international arena in general or as it compares to a particular foreign country.

Travel and tourism: Continuing the trend on globalization, Chapter 13, "Legal Responsibilities in Travel and Tourism," has an added dimension, including medical tourism and corporate travel risks. Chapter 15, "Managing Insurance," has added information on cyber insurance.

Additionally, information on relevant recent events and trends has been added throughout, including:

- Evolving laws on the use of cannabis
- Obamacare (The Patient Protection and Affordable Care Act)
- Do's and Don'ts of media interaction

- Human Trafficking concerns
- Sharing Economy (ex. Airbnb and Uber)
- Trade secrets used by former employees
- Data privacy and security breaches
- Allergy, nutrition, and all new food labeling concerns in the food and beverage arena
- Terrorist attacks, travel warnings, and the PATRIOT ACT
- Employment discrimination including pregnancy and genetic information
- USERRA update

The Conceptual Developmental Process

After teaching hospitality law for several years, we recognized the need for a different kind of resource that could be used to teach hospitality students what they need to know about managing in today's litigious environment. Accordingly, this book is built around *interactive pedagogy*, which *exposes readers to realistic scenarios*.

Before developing the first edition of ***Hospitality Law: Managing Legal Issues in the Hospitality Industry,*** a survey of attorneys and human resource directors at the top 100 U.S. hospitality organizations was completed. The participants were asked to identify the primary areas they felt were critical to a hospitality student's legal education and training. The most significant areas of interest focused on the ability to manage correctly and, thereby, reduce the potential for legal liability.

Thus, **preventing liability through a proactive management of the law** is the dominant theme of this textbook. In all cases, where issues of content, writing style, and design were involved, the touchstone for inclusion was simply: "Does this add to a student's ability to do the right thing?" If so, it was considered critical; if not, it was quickly deemed superfluous. For that reason, this book will look and read very differently from any other hospitality law textbook on the market. The legal information in it has been carefully selected and classroom tested to be clear, understandable, and easy to apply. This book exposes the reader to many realistic scenarios that hospitality managers regularly face.

Creating an Interactive Learning Environment

This textbook has been designed as a necessary tool for a hospitality law course that will foster an attitude of *compliance and prevention* in work ethics and personal management philosophy. Compliance and prevention means gaining an understanding of how to prevent or limit your legal liability by complying with legal norms. Instead of approaching the topic of hospitality law from a traditional case study viewpoint, this book provides a necessary understanding of the basic foundations and principles of the laws affecting the hospitality industry. Following the presentation of basic principles, the text goes on to provide guidelines and techniques that show how to manage preventively and apply a practical legal awareness prior to taking action.

Much of the book's effectiveness as a learning tool relies on participating in an interactive learning process. Several different types of learning features and exercises intended to help develop a pattern of behavior are included. Their purpose is to teach you to consider the legal implications of day-to-day management activities. Finally, in recognition of the importance of technology, a number of activities showcase the value of the computer as a lifelong learning tool.

Chapter Outline. Each chapter begins with an outline that helps demonstrate how topics fit together in the context of the overall subject.

In This Chapter You Will Learn. This section is more than just a list of learning objectives. This feature identifies concrete skills and necessary information that will have been gained after studying the chapter. This demonstrates how the information will be useful in management careers.

Legalese. Legal definitions are provided, written in simple language to help develop the vocabulary and understanding needed to follow the law.

Analyze the Situation. These hypothetical but realistic scenarios illustrate how a legal concept just encountered in the textbook is relevant to situations that are likely to arise in the hospitality industry. In many cases, we have intentionally made the facts ambiguous to present a challenge and encourage thinking through the situation and fostering discussion in the classroom.

Search the Web. Every chapter includes interactive Search the Web exercises, which provide URLs to a carefully chosen collection of Internet sites that hospitality managers can use to find guidelines, access information, or learn more about the hospitality industry and the law.

Legally Managing at Work. These sidebars contain practical legal guidelines for managers, covering a variety of situations that directly relate to restaurant and hotel operations. Topics range from recommended steps for managers when responding to guest injuries or health emergencies, legal guidelines for drawing up contracts, and dealing with the media during an emergency situation.

In this section, checklists, step-by-step procedures, and written forms will demonstrate how to create policies and respond to situations in a manner that will help ensure compliance with the law and protect businesses.

International Snapshot. An attorney or industry professional has compared U.S. legal practices with the same practices in the international community at large or a specific country. This section will create an enhanced perspective.

What Would You Do? These realistic decision-making scenarios ask readers to put themselves in a situation that requires them to apply the legal principles they have learned in the chapter. Many include a concrete activity, and all contain questions that require a personal decision in a set of circumstances that may be faced in future careers.

What Did You Learn in this Chapter? The main ideas and objectives of each chapter are briefly summarized here. The summary can be used as a supplement to, but not as a substitution for, a thorough review of the chapter material.

Instructor's Materials

To help instructors manage the large number of exercises, activities, and discussion questions posed in this textbook, an *Instructor's Manual* is also available to qualified instructors on the Wiley website at www.wiley.com/college/barth. This site also includes PowerPoint slides and an updated Test Bank.

Instructors who adopt ***Hospitality Law, Fifth Edition,*** can download the Test Bank for free.

Stay in touch with Stephen Barth. Follow him on Twitter @hospitality_law!

Acknowledgments

Please welcome Diana S. Barber to the 5th Edition of Hospitality Law.

Diana is the consummate Hospitality Lawyer, having focused on the industry in her private practice, serving as in-house counsel for Ritz-Carlton, all the while researching, publishing, and teaching to assist the industry and its customers.

This edition, like the four before it, was truly a community effort. It would be impossible to thank everyone who over the years has provided me, and now us, with insight or ideas that made this book possible. Accordingly, for those of you we fail to mention personally, please know that it was not an intentional oversight.

First, many thanks to David Hayes for his contributions to ***Hospitality Law***, and for helping to make this book a success.

Thanks, also, to the attorneys and industry professionals who devoted their time and expertise in providing content and the international snapshots. The book is much better due to their efforts.

Weili Cheng
Sarah Hawk
John Vernon
San San Lee
Robert Zarco
Himanshu M. Patel
Robert Cumbow
Irv Sandman
Alan Wells
Allison DiCesare
David Comeaux
Perrin Rynders
Rick Barrett-Cuetara
Dominic Mochrie
Andraya Firth
Elizabeth DeConti
Neville Bhada
David Samuels
Elizabeth Demaret
Souwei Ford
Kenneth Winkler

Special thanks go to Annie Sophia Thapasumony and JaNoel Lowe of Wiley and Marilyn Faz for their exceptional assistance in keeping us organized and on track.

This edition is dedicated to Diana S. Barber. Welcome aboard!

STEPHEN BARTH, J.D.
Professor of Hospitality Law & Leadership
Conrad N. Hilton College of Hotel and Restaurant Management
University of Houston
Attorney and Founder of HospitalityLawyer.com, the Hospitality Law Conference Series, and the Global Congress on Travel Risk Management

DIANA S. BARBER, J.D., CHE, CWP
Assistant Professor of Hospitality Law and Liability
Michael A. Leven School of Culinary and Sustainability and Hospitality
University College
Kennesaw State University

CHAPTER 1

Prevention Philosophy

1.1 The Future Hospitality Manager and the Legal Environment

"Hospitality law is a legal and social practice related to the treatment of a person's guests or those who patronize a place of business. Related to the concept of legal liability, hospitality laws are intended to protect both hosts and guests against injury, whether accidental or intentional."[1] In other words, hospitality law is the body of law relating to the foodservice, travel, and lodging industries governing the specific nuances of transportation, hotels, restaurants, bars, spas, theme parks, country clubs, conventions, events, and more.

Hospitality managers must be multitalented individuals. In addition to knowledge of their own designated area of expertise, such as food and beverage, marketing, accounting, or rooms management, hospitality managers are often called on to assume specialized roles, such as employee counselor, interior designer, facility engineer, or computer systems analyst. Given the complexity of the modern business world, it is simply a fact that the skill level required for success today in this field is greater than it was in the past.

Hospitality management has always been a challenging profession. Whether in a casino, a school lunch program, a five-star hotel, a sports stadium concession program, or myriad other environments, hospitality managers are required to have a breadth of skill not found in many other areas of management. Hospitality managers are in charge of securing raw materials, producing a product or service, and selling it—all under the same roof. This makes them very different from their manufacturing counterparts (who are in charge of product production only) and from their retail counterparts (who sell, but do not manufacture, the product). Perhaps most important, the hospitality manager has direct contact with guests, the ultimate end users of the products and services supplied by the industry.

Additionally, hospitality managers are called on frequently to make decisions that will, in one manner or another, impact the legal standing of their employers. Robert James, founder of one of the largest hotel contract management companies in the United States, once estimated that 60 to 70 percent of the decisions he made on a daily basis involved some type of legal dimension. This is not to say that a hospitality manager

CHAPTER OUTLINE

1.1. The Future Hospitality Manager and the Legal Environment

1.2. The Hospitality Manager and Legal Management

1.3. Ethics and the Law

IN THIS CHAPTER, YOU WILL LEARN

1. Why the study of laws related to hospitality is important.
2. The historical origins of the law and its evolutionary nature.
3. A philosophical framework to help prevent legal difficulties before they begin.
4. How to evaluate management actions on an ethical basis.

[1] https://en.wikipedia.org/wiki/Hospitality_law

needs to be an **attorney**. He or she does not. However, the decisions made may or may not increase the organization's chance of needing the services of an attorney.

Consider the situation in which a hospitality manager is informed that a guest has slipped and fallen in an area of the dining room containing a salad bar. It appears that the guest had been serving himself and slipped on a piece of lettuce dropped by a previous guest. Was this a simple accident? Could it have been prevented? Is the restaurant responsible? What medical attention, if any, should the manager be prepared to provide? What if the injuries are severe? Should the restaurant be held responsible? Can the restaurant manager be held personally responsible? Most important, what should the manager actually do when the incident is brought to his or her attention? What, if anything, should the employees do? Who is responsible if the employees were not trained in what to do?

From this example, it is clear that the hospitality manager is in a position to profoundly influence the legal position of the operation. Day after day, in hundreds of situations, the actions of hospitality managers will influence the likelihood of the business or the manager becoming the subject of **litigation**.

There is a unique body of law relating to the foodservice, travel, and lodging industries. These laws have developed over time as society and the courts have sought to define the relationship between the individual or business serving as the host and the individual who is the guest. This textbook will give you up-to-date information on the most important of those special laws and relationships. That is not to imply, however, that this book is designed to make you a lawyer. What it will do, if you use it properly, is train you to think like one. It will teach you to consider carefully how the actions taken by you and those you work with will be viewed in a legal context. The industry's very best legal educators, hospitality managers, writers, and reviewers have created this book especially for you. They all speak with one voice when they say, "Welcome to the exciting world of hospitality management!" As an industry, we need your skill, ability, and creativity. This textbook, if studied carefully, will help you become the hospitality manager you deserve to be and that our industry and guests require you to be.

1.2 The Hospitality Manager and Legal Management

Jack P. Jefferies, who served for more than 20 years as legal counsel for the American Hotel and Lodging Association (AH&LA), has stated: "Over 135,000 new federal and state laws are issued annually, as well as hundreds of thousands of federal and state administrative rules."[2] With this much change in the **law**, some believe that the topic is too complex to learn in an introductory course or from one book. In addition, they would argue that because the law is constantly changing, even if an individual learned the law today, his or her knowledge would be out of date in a very short time.

Although these positions are understandable, they argue for, not against, the future hospitality manager's study of legal management.

Although the law is indeed complex, certain basic principles and procedures can be established that will minimize a manager's chances of encountering legal difficulty. Since it is possible to prevent legal difficulty by anticipating it beforehand, it is less important to know, for example, the specific rules of food safety in every city than it is to know the basic principles of serving safe food. No one, not even the best lawyer, can be expected to know everything about every area of the law. In the same way, hospitality managers are not required to have a comprehensive knowledge of every law or lawsuit that impacts their industry. What they must know is how to effectively manage their legal environment. To begin this journey, it is important to grasp three key concepts:

1. Laws have historical origins, and managers need to know them.
2. Laws have an evolutionary nature, based on changes in society.
3. It is possible to use a philosophy of preventative management to manage the legal environment and minimize the chances of litigation.

Historical Origins of the Law

Common law and **civil law** are the two major systems of law in place in the Western world. Common law is the body of law that has descended from the law created in Great Britain and is used in the United States and most countries in the British Commonwealth. Civil law is descended from the law created in the Roman Empire and is used by most Western European countries, as well as Latin America, Asia, and Africa. Although both legal systems certainly defy oversimplification, it can generally be said that common law comes from reviewing past litigation that has been decided by the courts. It is greatly

[2] Jack P. Jefferies, *Understanding Hospitality Law*, 3rd ed. (East Lansing, MI: The Educational Institute of the American Hotel and Lodging Association, 1995).

LEGALESE

Attorney: Any person trained and legally authorized to act on behalf of others in matters of the law.

Litigation: The act of initiating and carrying on a lawsuit, often used to refer to the lawsuit itself.

Law: The rules of conduct and responsibility established and enforced by a society.

Common law: Laws derived from the historical customs and usage of a society and the decisions by courts when interpreting those customs and usages.

Civil law: The body of law (usually in the form of codes or statutes) created by governmental entities that are concerned with private rights and remedies, as opposed to criminal matters.

interested in precedent or what has been decided in previous court cases with similar situations or facts.

In civil law, decisions evolve based on written laws or codes. Judges in civil law feel less bound by what others have decided before them and more compelled by the law as it has been established by government bodies. Given the nearness of countries within Europe and the influence of the British Empire, it is no wonder that these two great legal systems frequently operated in close proximity, which has often blurred their distinctions. Interestingly, the term *civil law* is actually used in the common law system to refer to private law (or private disputes), as opposed to public or criminal matters.

Common law developed in England following the Norman Conquest. In common law, the principle of **stare decisis** is followed. A decision made by a higher court must be obeyed by all lower courts. In this manner, citizens know which actions are legal and which are punishable. Essentially, the purpose of the common law was to interpret and enforce rules related to the granting of land by the British monarchy to those subjects deemed worthy of such land grants. The barons who received this land would often grant parts of it to those they felt were deserving. The courts that were created at this time were charged with overseeing the peaceful resolution of disputes regarding land, inheritance, marriage, and other issues related to land grants.

Between 1765 and 1769, an Englishman, Sir William Blackstone, wrote four volumes he titled the *Commentaries*. In these books, Blackstone sought to compile a general overview of all the common law of his time. Blackstone's work formed the basis for much of the law in the New World, as his work migrated there with the English colonial settlers. Laws related to those in the hospitality industry were, of course, included.

Despite the anger against Britain that resulted in the Revolutionary War, the colonists of the soon-to-be United States embraced the common law as their favored rules of conduct and responsibility. Blackstone's work was widely used as a textbook in the law schools of the new country, and it influenced many of its early law students, including Thomas Jefferson, John Marshall, James Monroe, and Henry Clay. Inevitably, succeeding generations throughout the history of the United States have taken the common law as they have found it and modified it to meet the needs of their ever-changing society.

Evolutionary Nature of Common Law

It should come as no surprise that a rapidly changing society will often revise its rules of conduct and responsibility. This is true in society as a whole and in how society views the hospitality industry. In the United States of the 1850s, obviously, one would not have been expected to find a law requiring a certain number of automobile parking spaces to be designated for people with disabilities seeking to enjoy an evening meal at the town's finest restaurant because the world in that era contained neither the automobile nor the inclination of society to grant special parking privileges to those who were disabled. In today's society, we have both. What changed? First, the physical world changed. We now have automobiles along with the necessity of parking them. More significant, however, is the fact that society's view of how people with disabilities should be treated has changed. Parking ordinances today require designated "disabled" parking spaces, generally located close to the main entrances of buildings to ensure easy access. Not only is it good business to have such spaces, but current laws also mandate that the hospitality manager provide them.

Another example of evolving law is that certain state laws now allow their citizens to use cannabis oil, hemp oil, and other related substances that have historically been and are still on the federal list of prohibited drugs for consumption. Consumption is sometimes regulated and restricted to medicinal purposes, but some states have legalized or decriminalized the use of cannabis or marijuana for personal recreational purposes. Hospitality managers need to be familiar with their own state's laws and how these laws affect operations and employment situations.

In this case, parking requirements grew out of a law created at the federal government level. The law is called the **Americans with Disabilities Act** (ADA). This act, and its many applications to hospitality, will be discussed in greater detail in Chapters 7 and 10, "Legally Selecting Employees" and "Your Responsibilities as a Hospitality Operator to Guests." It is mentioned here to illustrate that laws evolve just as society evolves. Changes in society lead to changes in the law.

Search the Web 1.1

Go to the Internet. Search for categories related to laws regulating tobacco use and sales in your state, city, and/or county.

Assignment: Draft a one-paragraph essay summarizing the laws governing tobacco use in your state. Are there any special stipulations that a hospitality manager would especially want to be aware of (such as the designation of smoking and nonsmoking areas in a restaurant or public lobby)?

LEGALESE

Stare decisis: The principle of following prior case law.

Americans with Disabilities Act: Federal legislation (law) that protects the rights of people with disabilities so that they may be treated fairly in the workplace and have access to places of public accommodation, such as hotels, restaurants, and airplanes.

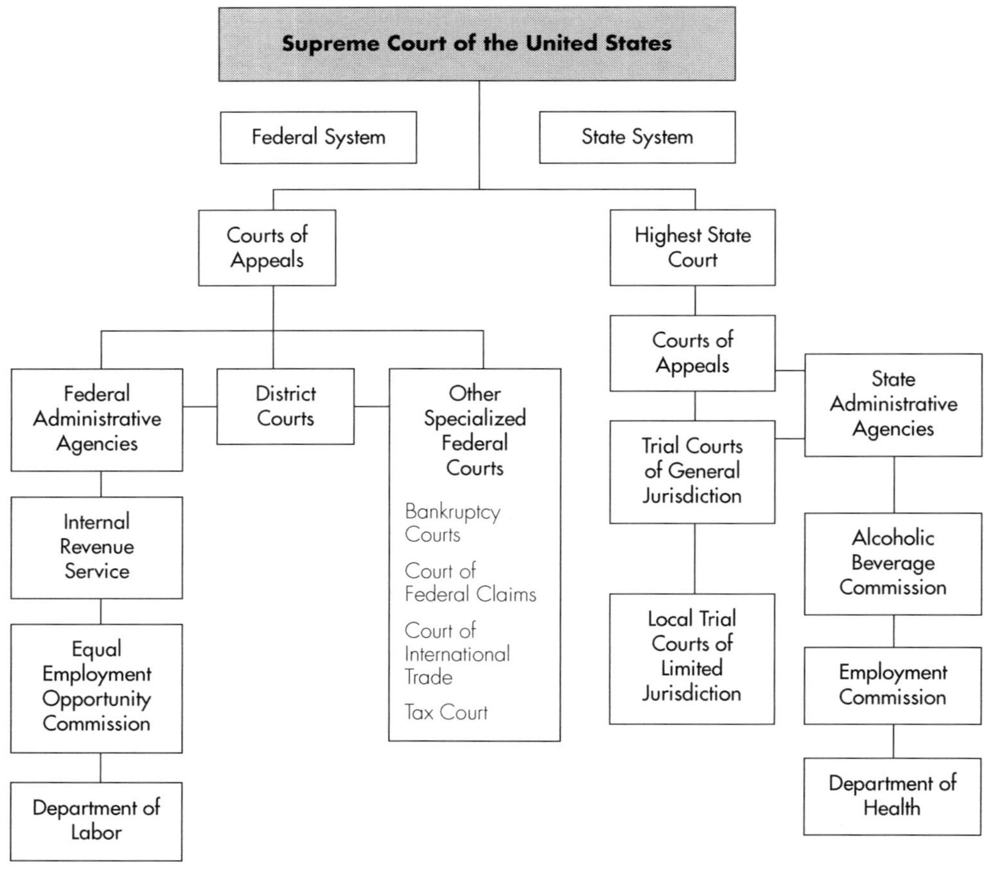

FIGURE 1.1 **The U.S. legal system.**

Laws in the United States may be enacted at the federal, state, and local levels (see Figure 1.1).

At each of these levels, the laws reflect the changing desires of the citizens and their elected officials. Because society includes members who operate hospitality facilities, **hospitality laws** created and modified by society impact those who work in the hospitality industry.

Preventative Legal Management

Future hospitality managers will encounter laws that do not currently exist. How, then, can they be expected to operate their facilities in full compliance with the law throughout their career? Just as important, how can they be expected to manage these facilities in a way that will minimize their chances of doing something illegal? The answer is not to attempt to monitor every legislative body empowered to enact law. The answer is to operate hospitality facilities in a way that combines preventative legal management with sound ethical behavior and smart judgment.

LEGALESE

Hospitality law: Those laws that relate to the industry involved with the provision of food, lodging, travel, meetings, events, and entertainment services to its guests, employees, vendors, and clients.

Lessons from the Medical Field In the medical field, it is widely agreed that it is better to prevent a serious illness beforehand than to treat it after the fact. For example, doctors advise that it is preferable to prevent a heart attack through proper diet, exercise, and the cessation of smoking than for a patient to have a bypass operation after a heart attack has occurred. In the case of prevention, the doctor advises the patient, but it is, in large measure, up to the patient to put into practice the recommendations of the physician.

In a similar vein, it is far better for hospitality managers to operate their facilities in a way that minimizes the risk of litigation, rather than in a manner that exposes their operations to the threat of litigation.

STEM the Tide of Litigation As noted, the law is not static; in fact, it changes frequently. Managers must stay abreast of these changes so that ultimately, on a daily basis, they integrate their acquired knowledge and awareness of the law into a personal style of management and decision making. The acronym STEM was coined as an easy way to remember the steps in a decision-making process that can assist managers in getting started. It stands for select, teach, educate, and manage. It is presented here as a way of beginning to "STEM" the tide of litigation. The details of how STEM works are included in the box on page 5.

Legally Managing at Work

Applying the STEM Process in Hospitality Management

A process can be implemented that will help reduce employee errors and omissions and, therefore, litigation and liability. The process is called STEM, for *select, teach, educate,* and *manage.* It works like this:

1. *Select:* Managers can begin reducing litigation by selecting the right employee for the right job. Managers cannot hire "just anyone" at the last minute. Employees must be selected based on specific job qualifications, written job specifications, and information derived from a thorough investigation of the candidate for the position, whether the employee to be hired is a bus person, waitperson, hostess, door supervisor, or line supervisor.
2. *Teach:* Managers must develop proper training methods for employees, including feedback devices such as competency testing, to ensure that the training is effective.
3. *Educate:* Managers must continuously educate themselves so that they know which topics and procedures must be passed on to employees through effective teaching methods. Effective managers stay on top of all current happenings in the hospitality industry. One useful tool is the industry news and newsletters from www.smartbrief.com. You can sign up for free daily e-newsletters on most industry segment topics. For hotels, see www.smartbrief.com/ahla; and for restaurants, see www.smartbrief.com/nra.
4. *Manage:* Effective managers know that if you consistently do things the right way, the chances for mistakes—and, therefore, for litigation—will diminish. Management has been defined as consisting of four functions: planning, organizing, controlling, and motivating. Although all four have legal implications, the STEM process focuses almost exclusively on the motivating function. A manager who creates a supportive work environment will gain the trust and respect of employees, who will then be motivated to do their best work and thus avoid making errors that could result in litigation.

On any given day, the general manager of a hotel or restaurant in the United States will make decisions about hiring, firing, and/or providing benefits to employees. Other daily tasks might include approving a meeting space contract for a major event to be held on the property, an event that involves the service of alcohol. Decisions regarding if and when to add a lifeguard to the pool area, whether to subcontract parking services to a local valet company, and even the uniform requirements of staff, will all be made by the manager. All of these seemingly independent decisions have a significant common denominator—they all have legal implications.

Whether it is opening a restaurant, operating a country club, or hiring a housekeeper, hospitality managers must be aware of the legal implications of each and every decision they make. It is of vital importance that managers resolve to be fair, to operate within the law, and to manage preventatively. On occasions when they do not and a lawsuit results, the courts may hold managers **liable** for their inattentiveness.

This philosophy of preventative management becomes even more important when one considers that a great many litigation matters encountered by hospitality operators have a common denominator: a poorly prepared employee. Injuries and the resulting damages, whether financial, physical, or mental, are usually a consequence of an employee who has not been sufficiently taught to perform his or her duties. He or she might make an omission, such as not cleaning up a spill near a salad bar, or might pursue an activity outside the scope of his or her duties, such as sexual harassment or arguing with a customer.

The recent increasing number of lawsuits is not caused solely by employees, of course. The legal system and some attorneys certainly share the blame. Managers, however, bear most of the responsibility for what has been occurring. When an employee makes a mistake, often it is the result of management error. The wrong person was hired for the job, the duties of the job were not effectively communicated to the employee, the employee was not properly trained, or the employee was not effectively supervised or motivated to do the job properly.

To create an environment conducive to motivation, you must first establish trust and respect. When managers make a commitment to employees or guests, they must follow through. They also must be willing to accept responsibility for their mistakes and to apologize for them when appropriate. Managers must set an example: If managers ask employees to be on time, then managers must also be on time; if managers expect employees to pay for food, beverages, and services, then he or she must also pay for food, beverages, and services. In current parlance, managers must walk the talk!

Finally, all of the planning, organizing, controlling, and motivating in the world will not help if management cannot effectively communicate its vision and plan to the employees who will carry out that vision. The ability to communicate with skill and grace is a critical component of being a successful manager.

Today's culturally diverse workforce will require diverse motivating techniques. Remember that different people are motivated by different incentives. Money is a perfect example. To some, it is a strong motivating factor; others would prefer more time off instead of additional pay. Managers must know their employees and determine—by asking them, if need

LEGALESE

Liable: To be legally responsible or obligated.

be—what will motivate them, both as individuals and as a work team. Examples of possible motivational efforts include the following:

- A sales contest with a significant prize
- A parking space with recognition for the employee of the month
- A 50 percent discount on meals at the restaurant
- A card on their birthday
- A written "pat on the back" for a job well done
- Taking the time to ask employees how their day was
- Involving employees in setting goals
- Seeking employee input in developing work schedules
- Listening to their concerns

All of those listed and others are the types of activities a manager should undertake to build the trust and loyalty of employees. If a consensus can be reached on what to do and how to do it, the motivating task becomes much easier.

The goal of STEM is to reduce employee mistakes. By continually encouraging and rewarding good performance, managers can create an environment that will, in fact, reduce the number of times employees make mistakes. Remember that even if a goal may is reached, the efforts of the individual or group still might merit praise. In other words, managers should try to catch their employees doing something right instead of trying to catch them doing something wrong.

It is not possible to manage effectively while sitting behind the desk. Effective managers know that "management by walking around" is alive and well, particularly in a service industry such as hospitality. Of course, an important part of managing is the ability to motivate employees. As much as managers would like all employees to come to the job every day brimming with enthusiasm, the fact is, too often, just the opposite is true. A significant number of employees may dislike coming to work, their jobs, their situation in life, and much more. They must be motivated to perform at the level management has targeted in order to exceed management's own expectations, and, more important, those of the guest.

To recap the STEM process: Select, not just hire, the right employee for the right job; continuously teach employees while creating a training trail; educate management; motivate staff in a positive and nurturing manner. All these efforts will help foster loyalty and goodwill, while reducing the likelihood of litigation.

Analyze the Situation 1.1

A fellow supervisor confides in you that he has been arrested for a second time in two years for driving under the influence of alcohol. His current case has not yet gone to trial. This supervisor is responsible for the late-night closing of the restaurant in which you both work.

1. Should you discuss this situation with the restaurant's general manager?
2. After reading the next section on Ethics, has your answer changed?
3. Which aspect of STEM is relevant here?

1.3 Ethics and the Law

It is not always clear whether a course of action is illegal or simply wrong. Put another way, an activity might be legal but still be the wrong thing to do. As a future hospitality manager who seeks to manage his or her legal environment and that of other employees, it is important that you be able to make this distinction.

Ethics refers to the behavior of an individual toward another individual or group. Ethical behavior refers to behavior that is considered "right" or the "right thing to do." Consistently choosing ethical behavior over behavior that is not ethical will go a long way toward avoiding legal difficulty. This is true because hospitality managers often will not know what the law requires in a given situation. In cases of litigation, juries may have to make determinations of whether a manager's actions were ethical or deliberately unethical. How juries and judges decide these questions may well determine their view of a manager's liability for an action or inaction.

Although it is sometimes difficult to determine precisely what constitutes ethical behavior, the following seven guidelines can be very useful when evaluating a possible course of action:

1. *Is it legal?* Does the law or company policy prohibit this activity?
2. *Does it hurt anyone?* Will this action negatively affect any stakeholders?
3. *Is it fair?* Is it fair to all the stakeholders?
4. *Am I being honest?* Are you being honest with yourself and with the company?
5. *Would I care if it happened to me?* Would it bother you if you were the recipient of the action?
6. *Would I publicize my action?* Would you be embarrassed if stakeholders became aware of your action?
7. *What if everyone did it?* Could the business effectively operate in an equitable fashion?

LEGALESE

Ethics: Choices of proper conduct made by an individual in his or her relationships with others.

Consider the hospitality manager who is responsible for a large wedding reception in a hotel. The bride and groom have selected a specific champagne from the hotel's wine list to be used for their champagne punch. The contract signed by the bride and groom lists the selling price per gallon of the punch but does not specifically mention the name of the champagne selected by the couple. In the middle of the reception, the hotel runs out of that brand of champagne. A less costly substitute is used for the duration of the reception. Neither the bride and groom nor the guests notice the difference. Using the seven ethical guidelines just listed, a manager could evaluate whether he or she should reduce the bride and groom's final bill by the difference in selling price of the two champagnes.

How an individual determines what constitutes ethical behavior may be influenced by his or her cultural background, religious views, professional training, and personal moral code. A complete example of the way someone would actually use the seven ethical guidelines is demonstrated in the following hypothetical situation.

An Ethical Dilemma: Free Champagne

Assume that you are the food and beverage director of a large hotel. You are planning for your New Year's Eve gala and require a large amount of wine and champagne. You conduct a competitive bidding process with the purveyors in your area and, based on quality and price, you place a very large order (in excess of $20,000) with a single purveyor. One week later, you receive a case of very expensive champagne, delivered to your home with a nice note from the purveyor's representative stating how much it appreciated the order and that the purveyor is really looking forward to doing business with you in the years ahead. What do you do with the champagne?

Ethical Analysis Your first thought might be the most obvious one—that is, you drink it. But, hopefully, you will first ask yourself the seven questions of the ethical decision-making process.

1. Is it legal?

   From your perspective, it might not be illegal for you to accept a case of champagne. However, there could be liquor laws in your state that prohibit the purveyor from gifting that amount of alcoholic beverage. You must also consider whether it is permissible within the guidelines established by the company for which you work. Many companies have established gift acceptance policies that limit the value of the gifts that employees are eligible to accept. In this case, violation of a stated or written company policy may subject you to disciplinary action or even the termination of your employment. Accordingly, you need to be extremely familiar with the ethics policy that has been adopted by the company you are working for. Assuming that it does not violate a law and/or company policy, go to question 2.

2. Does it hurt anyone?

   Well, it probably would not hurt you unless you drank all of the champagne at once; but, realistically, are you really going to be fair and objective when you evaluate next year's bids, or is your mind going to be thinking back to the case of champagne that you received? Assuming that you do not think that it is hurting anyone, go on to question 3.

3. Is it fair?

   Before answering this question, you have to recognize who the stakeholders are in this particular situation. How might others in your company feel about the gift you received? After all, you agreed to work for this firm at a set salary. If benefits are gained because of decisions you make while on duty, should those benefits accrue to the *business* or to *you*? Assuming that you have decided that it is fair for you to keep the champagne, go to question number 4.

4. Am I being honest?

   This question gives you the opportunity to second-guess yourself when you are answering questions 2 and 3. Do you really believe that you can remain objective in the purchasing aspect of your job and continue to seek out the best quality for the best price, knowing that one of the purveyors rewarded you handsomely for last year's choice and may be inclined to do so again?

5. Would I care if it happened to me?

   If you owned the company you work for and you knew that one of the managers you had hired was given a gift of this magnitude from a vendor, would you question the objectivity of that manager? Would you like to see all of your managers receive such gifts? Would you be concerned if they did?

6. Would I publicize my action?

   If you have trouble remembering the other questions, try to remember this one. Would you choose to keep the champagne if you knew that tomorrow morning the headlines of your city newspaper would read: "Food and Beverage Director of Local Hotel Gets Case of Champagne after Placing Large Order with Purveyor"? Your general manager would see it, other employees would see it, all of the other purveyors that you are going do business with would see it, and even potential future employers would see it.

7. What if everyone did it?

   If you justify your choice of keeping the champagne, consider: Does this process ever stop? What would happen if the executive housekeeper had a bed delivered to her home every time she ordered new bedding for the hotel? What would happen if every time she ordered new washers and dryers, she received a matching set at home?

Alternative Options What are some of the realistic alternatives to keeping the champagne?

- Return it to the purveyor with a nice note stating how much you appreciate it but that your company policy will not allow you to accept it.
- Turn the gift over to the general manager to be placed into the normal liquor inventory (assuming that the law will allow it to be used this way).
- Donate it to the employee Christmas party.

Use the seven questions to evaluate each of these three courses of action. Do you see any differences?

Codes of Ethics

Some hospitality managers feel it is important to set their ethical beliefs down in a code of ethics or core values. Figure 1.2 is the code of core values developed by Meeting Expectations, an award-winning event management and association management company with headquarter offices located in Atlanta, Georgia.

In some cases, a company president or other operating officer will relay the ethical philosophy of a company to its employees in a section of the employee handbook or through a direct policy statement, as illustrated in the ethics statement presented in Figure 1.3, which was created by Hyatt Hotels.

Notice that in both the Meeting Expectation's core values and in Hyatt's corporate policy, reference is made to the importance of complete honesty and integrity as well as following the law and legal rules. Laws do not exist, however, to cover every situation that future hospitality managers will encounter. Society's view of acceptable behavior, as well as of specific laws, is constantly changing. Ethical behavior, however, is always important to the successful guidance of responsible and profitable hospitality organizations.

Meeting Expectations Core Values

CORE VALUES

At Meeting Expectations, our team lives and works according to the following values:

1. We are customer driven. We will take action and feel a sense of urgency on matters related to our customers.
2. We respect the individual employee and believe that people treated with respect and given responsibility will respond by giving their best. We treat others as we would like to be treated.
3. We require complete honesty and integrity in everything we do. We insist on open and honest communication. Hidden agendas and gossip will not be tolerated.
4. We make commitments with care, and live up to them. When we discover a problem, we own that problem until it is resolved, even if it involves someone else doing the work.
5. We expect continuous improvement in our journey towards excellence.
6. We challenge ourselves and each other as it brings out the best in us. We look for others doing the right thing so that we can celebrate success along the way.
7. We insist on giving our best effort toward everything we do and take responsibility for our actions. We understand that even despite our best efforts, bad results may sometimes occur. Bad results are unacceptable if they are the consequence of sloppiness or lack of effort.
8. We are financially responsible with company and client funds and guard them with the same vigilance that we use to guard our own.
9. Clarity in understanding our mission, goals, and what we can expect from each other is critical to our success.
10. Work is an important part of life and should be enjoyed by striking a balance between fun and seriousness.

FIGURE 1.2 Meeting Expectations Core Values.
(Reprinted with permission from Meeting Expectations.)

Hyatt Hotels Corporation

Code of Business Conduct and Ethics 2013

INTRODUCTION

This Code of Business Conduct and Ethics (this "Code") is designed to reaffirm and promote Hyatt Hotels Corporation's compliance with laws and ethical standards applicable in all jurisdictions in which Hyatt Hotels Corporation and its subsidiaries (collectively referred to herein as "Hyatt") conduct their business.

FIGURE 1.3 Corporate policy for Hyatt Hotels.
(Reprinted with permission by Hyatt Hotel's General Counsel.)

This Code is applicable to all directors and officers of Hyatt, and all associates, including, without limitation, General Managers, members of the Management or Executive Committees and other persons (collectively, "associates") who work in or are affiliated with any hotel, residential or vacation ownership property that is owned, leased, managed or franchised by Hyatt and operated under or in association with the "Hyatt," "Hyatt Regency," "Grand Hyatt," "Park Hyatt," "Andaz," "Hyatt Place," "Hyatt House," "Hyatt Residence Club," "Hyatt Zilara", or "Hyatt Ziva" trademarks, or such other trademarks owned by Hyatt (individually referred to herein as a "Hotel" and, collectively, as the "Hotels").

References in this Code to "you" and "your" refer to the officers, directors and associates of Hyatt. Similarly, references in this Code to "we" and "our" refer to Hyatt and the Hotels.

Hyatt operations and Hyatt associates are subject to the laws of many countries and other jurisdictions around the world. Associates are expected to comply with the Code and all applicable government laws, rules and regulations. If a provision of the Code conflicts with applicable law, the law controls.

Because Hyatt Hotels Corporation is incorporated in the United States, our associates around the world often are subject to U.S. laws. Other countries may also apply their laws outside their borders to Hyatt operations and personnel. If you are uncertain what laws apply to you, or if you believe there may be a conflict between different applicable laws, consult Hyatt's General Counsel or any Associate General Counsel of Hyatt's Legal Department, whose contact details are attached at the end of this document.

Seeking Help and Information

This Code is not intended to be a comprehensive rulebook and cannot address every situation that you may face. There is no substitute for personal integrity and good judgment. If you feel uncomfortable about a situation or have any doubts about whether it is consistent with Hyatt's ethical standards, we encourage you to contact your supervisor. If your supervisor cannot answer your question or if you do not feel comfortable contacting your supervisor, contact the General Counsel or any Associate General Counsel of Hyatt's Legal Department.

Reporting Violations of the Code

You have a duty to report any known or suspected violation of this Code, including any violation of the laws, rules, regulations or policies that apply to Hyatt. If you know of or suspect a violation of this Code, immediately report the conduct to your supervisor or in the event of a violation of Section 12, directly to the General Counsel or Vice President of Internal Audit. Your supervisor will contact the General Counsel or any Associate General Counsel of Hyatt's Legal Department, who will work with you and your supervisor to investigate your concern. If you do not feel comfortable reporting the conduct to your supervisor or you do not get a satisfactory response, you should contact the General Counsel, any Associate General Counsel of Hyatt's Legal Department, or Vice President of Internal Audit directly. All reports of known or suspected violations of the law or this Code will be handled sensitively and with discretion. Your confidentiality will be protected to the extent possible, consistent with applicable law and Hyatt's need to investigate your concern.

We also have a website, www.hyattethics.com, and a dedicated toll-free number for those of you in the United States, 1-866-294-3528, available 24 hours a day, seven days a week, to provide you and vendors a way to anonymously and confidentially report activities that potentially may involve criminal, unethical or otherwise inappropriate behavior in violation of applicable law, and Hyatt's established policies, including this Code. International toll-free numbers and specific reporting instructions and limitations for those reporting from outside the United States may be found on the website at www.hyattethics.com. In the event an international toll-free number is not available, you may call us collect at 503-726-2412.

Policy Against Retaliation

Hyatt prohibits retaliation against anyone who, in good faith, seeks help or reports known or suspected violations of this Code. Any reprisal or retaliation against anyone covered by this Code because such person, in good faith, sought help or filed a report will be subject to disciplinary action, which may include suspension or termination of association with Hyatt.

Amendments to and Waivers of the Code/Enforcement

This Code may be amended or modified only by the Board of Directors of Hyatt Hotels Corporation.

Waivers of this Code for associates may be made only by Hyatt's General Counsel. The General Counsel will provide quarterly reports to the Audit Committee of such waivers. Any waiver of this Code for directors, executive officers or other principal financial officers of Hyatt Hotels Corporation may be made only by the Audit Committee of the Board of Directors or the Board of Directors of Hyatt Hotels Corporation, and will be disclosed to the public as required by law or the rules of the New York Stock Exchange.

Violations of this Code will be addressed promptly and, subject to compliance with applicable law or regulation, may subject persons to corrective and/or disciplinary action.

This Code supplements and does not supersede or replace the terms and conditions of any agreement signed by you and Hyatt. If you believe the terms of this policy conflict with any such agreement, you should contact Hyatt's General Counsel.

FIGURE 1.3 *(continued)*

Policy Statement

Standards of Conduct/Compliance with Applicable Laws

It is the policy of Hyatt to conduct its business and to cause the business of all Hotels to be conducted in accordance with all applicable laws and regulations of the jurisdictions in which such business is conducted and to do so with honesty and integrity and in accordance with the highest moral and ethical standards.

Conflicts of Interest

A conflict of interest can occur when the private interest of a person who is covered by this Code interferes, or reasonably appears to interfere, with the interests of Hyatt or any Hotel, as the case may be. You should avoid any private interest that influences your ability to act in the interests of Hyatt or any Hotel or that makes it difficult to perform your work objectively and effectively. Conflicts of interest may also arise if you (or any member of your family) receive personal benefits as a result of your position with Hyatt.

Situations involving a conflict of interest may not always be obvious or easy to resolve. If you suspect that you have a conflict of interest, or something that others could reasonably perceive as a conflict of interest, you should report it to your supervisor or the General Counsel or any Associate General Counsel of Hyatt's Legal Department. Your supervisor and the Legal Department will work with you to determine whether you have a conflict of interest and, if so, how best to address it.

Corporate Opportunities

You are expected to advance the interests of Hyatt and the Hotels when the opportunity to do so arises. You may not take for yourself business opportunities that arise through either the use of our property or information or your position with Hyatt or any Hotel. You are also prohibited from using either our property or information or your position for personal gain and competing in any way with Hyatt. Competing with Hyatt may involve engaging in the same line of business as Hyatt, or any situation where you take away from Hyatt opportunities for sales or purchases of services, products, property or interests. Your service as a director or an officer of a company, organization or association in a related business, if timely disclosed to Hyatt and approved or ratified by the Audit Committee, is not deemed to be a violation of this Code.

Confidential Information

You have access to a variety of confidential information while employed at Hyatt or a Hotel, as applicable. Confidential information includes all non-public information that might be of use to competitors, or, if disclosed, harmful to Hyatt or such Hotel or our customers. Examples of such confidential information include, without limitation, brand standards, operating manuals, data processing systems, programs, procedures, databases, data, sales and marketing information, marketing strategies, and financial information. Respect the property of Hyatt, including its intellectual property (such as trademarks, logos, brand names and computer systems) and confidential information. You are expected to safeguard all confidential information of Hyatt, the Hotels or third parties with which Hyatt or the Hotels conduct business, except when disclosure is authorized or legally mandated.

Competition and Fair Dealing

You should compete fairly without collusion or collaboration (whether express or implied, formal or informal, oral or written) with competitors to divide markets, set prices, restrict production, standardize terms of trade (including such matters as hours of operation, service charges, hotel check-out times, or hotel reservation policies), allocate customers or otherwise restrain competition or to boycott any individual or entity. You should also endeavor to deal fairly with customers and suppliers of Hyatt and the Hotels, as applicable. You should not take unfair advantage of anyone through manipulation, concealment, abuse of privileged information, misrepresentation of material facts or any other practices that may violate the laws designed to prevent unfair competition or anti-competitive practices.

Protection and Proper Use of Corporate Assets

You should protect the assets of Hyatt and the Hotels, as applicable, and ensure their efficient use for legitimate business purposes only. No funds, assets, services or facilities of Hyatt or of any Hotel (including, for the purposes hereof, without limitation, complimentary items, discounts and amenities) may be used, directly or indirectly, for any unlawful or unethical purpose. Use the property of Hyatt only for legitimate business purposes, as authorized in connection with your job responsibilities. You should not share or use computer access information of other Hyatt or Hotel personnel, such as passwords. Any question as to the legality or ethics of any contemplated use of our funds, assets, services or facilities shall be referred to the General Counsel or any Associate General Counsel of Hyatt's Legal Department.

FIGURE 1.3 *(continued)*

Prohibition Against Bribes or Kickbacks

You are prohibited from using or promising to use the funds, assets, services or facilities of Hyatt or of any Hotel to secure or retain business where such use is in violation of any applicable law or regulation. Without limiting the foregoing, you are prohibited from engaging in any form of bribery or kickbacks and from using the funds, assets, services or facilities of Hyatt or of any Hotel to improperly influence or corrupt the action of any government official, agent or employee or of any private customer, supplier or other person. In addition, Hyatt and/or its employees may be held liable for bribery or kickbacks by third parties working on behalf of the company (such as consultants, advisors, distributors, and other intermediaries) where Hyatt and/or its employees knew or reasonably should have known of the third party's unlawful action, given the circumstances.

Gifts and Entertainment

The giving and receiving of gifts is a common business practice. Appropriate business gifts and entertainment are welcome courtesies designed to build relationships and understanding among business partners. However, gifts and entertainment should not compromise, or appear to compromise, your ability to make objective and fair business decisions. It is your responsibility to use good judgment in this area. As a general rule, you may give or receive gifts or entertainment to or from customers or suppliers only if the gift or entertainment would not be viewed as an inducement to or reward for any particular business decision and if the expenditure is for a legitimate business purpose, reasonable, not lavish, and reflects an amount that is customary and proportionate in the relevant jurisdiction and appropriate for the particular occasion. You are expected to properly account for expenses related to gifts and entertainment on expense reports. In the event that you are offered a gift or entertainment that exceeds the limits set by Hyatt's Gift Policy applicable to your position, you should contact the General Counsel or any Associate General Counsel of Hyatt's Legal Department and obtain approval prior to accepting such gift or entertainment.

Prohibition Against Taking Commissions or Referral Fees

You are prohibited from accepting anything of value in exchange for referring third parties to any person, organization or group doing business or seeking to do business with Hyatt or any Hotel.

Prohibition Against Using Corporate Assets for Political Purposes

Hyatt encourages you to participate in the political process as an individual and on your own time. However, you are prohibited from using the funds, assets, services or facilities of Hyatt or of any Hotel, directly or indirectly, for the purpose of aiding, supporting or opposing any political party, association, organization or candidate where such use is illegal or improper under the laws or regulations of the relevant jurisdiction. Please contact the General Counsel or any Associate General Counsel of Hyatt's Legal Department if you have any questions about this policy.

Compliance With Insider Trading Laws

Associates are prohibited from trading in the stock or other securities of Hyatt Hotels Corporation while in possession of material, nonpublic information about Hyatt. In addition, associates are prohibited from recommending, "tipping" or suggesting that anyone else buy or sell stock or other securities of Hyatt Hotels Corporation on the basis of material, nonpublic information. Associates who obtain material nonpublic information about another company in the course of their association with Hyatt are prohibited from trading in the stock or securities of the other company while in possession of such information or "tipping" others to trade on the basis of such information. Violation of insider trading laws can result in severe fines and criminal penalties, as well as disciplinary action by Hyatt, up to and including termination of association or employment with Hyatt. The laws against insider trading are specific and complex. Please refer to Hyatt's Insider Trading Compliance Program for more information. If you have any questions about this policy, please contact the General Counsel or any Associate General Counsel of Hyatt's Legal Department.

Accuracy of Company Records and Financial Reports

Accurate and reliable records are crucial to our business. Our records are the basis of our earnings statements, financial reports, public filings and other disclosures to third parties and guide our business decision-making and strategic planning. Our records include booking information, customers' personal data, payroll, timecards, travel and expense reports, emails, accounting and financial data, measurement and performance records, electronic data files and all other records maintained in the ordinary course of our business.

FIGURE 1.3 *(continued)*

All of our records must be complete, accurate and reliable in all material respects. Undisclosed or unrecorded funds, payments or receipts are inconsistent with our business practices and are prohibited. You are expected to act in good faith, responsibly, with due care, competence and with common sense in a timely manner. You may not misrepresent material facts or allow your independent judgment or decisions to be improperly influenced or biased by others or by other factors such as operating unit or individual performance or objectives, plans, forecasts or financial commitments. If you believe someone is asking or directing you to violate these obligations, report the situation promptly. You are responsible for understanding and complying with our record-keeping policy. Ask your supervisor if you have any questions.

Hyatt's financial officers and other associates serving in a finance, accounting, corporate treasury, tax or investor relations role (the "Finance Team") have a special responsibility to ensure that all of our financial disclosures with respect to Hyatt and the Hotels are prepared and reported in a full, fair, accurate, timely and understandable manner. These associates must understand and comply with applicable law, Hyatt's accounting policies and U.S. generally accepted accounting principles. You are expected to comply with the internal controls, disclosure controls and procedures and other policies and procedures established by Hyatt from time to time.

Any action (direct or indirect) to force, manipulate, mislead or fraudulently influence any person, including a financial officer or other member of the Finance Team, in the performance of their duties with respect to the financial books and records is a violation of this Code. This includes situations involving the recording or authorization of any financial transactions that are incorrect or improper or not adequately supported. Any action (direct or indirect) to force, manipulate, mislead or fraudulently influence Hyatt's independent auditors in the performance of their audit or review of Hyatt's financial statements is prohibited. Any violation of this Section 12 should be reported directly to the General Counsel or Vice President of Audit Services.

Certification

After reading this Code, all (i) directors and officers of Hyatt Hotels Corporation; (ii) employees working at Hyatt's corporate headquarters, divisional offices, service centers and sales offices; (iii) members of the Management and Executive Committees at the Hotels; (iv) associates with the title of Manager and above; and (v) associates who work in Hotels in materials management, finance and human resources shall acknowledge in writing that he/she has read and understood this Code of Business Conduct and Ethics, and understands that he/she is responsible to abide fully with all of the obligations contained herein. The Acknowledgement of Code of Business Conduct and Ethics form attached at the end of this Code may be executed via an electronic acknowledgement or by returning a signed copy of the Acknowledgement to Hyatt's General Counsel.

FIGURE 1.3 *(continued)*

International Snapshot

Mitigating Risks Associated with Legal and Ethical Compliance in International Business Transactions

A legal and ethical compliance program is critical to the success of a multinational company. Such a program reduces reputational risk and the risk of legal liability, both civil and criminal. Most countries and jurisdictions have enacted prohibitions against bribery and corruption. While such laws may not be consistently enforced, particularly in developing countries, the risk of enforcement proceedings may be higher for a U.S. company, depending on the status of diplomatic relations. The U.S. Foreign Corrupt Practices Act and the U.K. Bribery Act are well known and yet many companies have run afoul of these laws and other laws when doing business outside the United States.

Nevertheless, even a comprehensive legal and ethical compliance program is not enough to adequately shield a company from risk.

Legal and ethical compliance policies are meaningless without the support of a company's chief executive officer. A culture of compliance begins with the CEO's full and continuing commitment to ethical compliance as a core value. This is far more effective at reducing risks than any program championed solely by a company's law department.

And yet, outside the United States, a corporate culture that supports a comprehensive legal and ethical compliance program is still not adequate to mitigate risks arising from legal and ethical lapses. The following actions should also be taken.

1. Conduct Due Diligence. Transactions outside the United States mean doing business with local, foreign entities. Know your counterparty. A business venture will succeed only if the local "partner" shares ethical core values. Law firms, accounting firms, the U.S. Embassy or Consulate and others can provide accurate and reliable information about local entities and individuals.
2. Communicate Ethical Values. Once a local entity has been selected, it is important to communicate your company's values and policies regarding legal and ethical compliance to the entity's key individuals. Better still is documenting your company's policies. Initially and periodically discussing and providing written information about company policies will educate and set expectations.

(continued)

3. Develop Personal Relationships. A personal relationship with a local business partner is often more important to the success of a transaction than a strong contract. A written agreement is useful but often difficult to enforce, especially in a developing country. A local business partner may view a contract merely as an indication of the parties' intent at the time of signing and so may repudiate contract terms if circumstances change. Personal relationships will help resolve disputes involving legal or ethical problems. Such relationships require significant time and effort to nurture. American executives doing business outside the United States are often criticized for failing to invest such time and effort. Developing business relationships internationally is subject to certain key caveats. First, while a relationship with the local partner's representative is helpful, it is no substitute for a personal relationship with the local partner's most senior executive, usually its CEO or chairman. Second, one should be alert to local politics. The local partner may have close ties to the government's party in power but could, after a coup or vote or the passage of time, lose all political influence or even be viewed as toxic in the local business community.

In sum, due diligence, personal relationships and the communication of strong ethical corporate values will, in addition to a corporate culture supporting a comprehensive compliance program, mitigate the risks of legal and ethical lapses when doing business outside the United States.

Provided by J. Weili Cheng, former Sr. VP and Deputy General Counsel of The Ritz-Carlton Hotel Company, LLC currently with a business consortium known as Laguna Strategic Advisors; www.lagunastrategicadvisors.com.

WHAT WOULD YOU DO?

Assume that your local municipality is considering the passage of a law that would prohibit the sale of all tobacco products from the interiors of bars and restaurants but not grocery stores. The restaurant you manage has a cocktail lounge, and cigarettes are both consumed and sold in that section of your restaurant. There is no current effort to prohibit smoking in cocktail lounges such as the one you operate. You are considering whether to address the local government body charged with creating such legislation:

1. What are the major considerations you will think about before you decide to support or oppose the proposed legislation?
2. Will the fact that you do or do not smoke influence your position?
3. Which ethical issues are in play here?

WHAT DID YOU LEARN IN THIS CHAPTER?

As a manager, you will be called on to make many decisions that have legal consequences. It is unrealistic to expect a manager to know all of the laws that could potentially impact his or her operation. Because litigation is prolific in the hospitality industry and laws change frequently, it is imperative that you develop and practice a management philosophy of prevention, such as STEM.

Just because a law does not prohibit a particular activity does not make it the right thing to do. Accordingly, you should also follow a process that will assist you in determining the ethical implications of a decision, as well as the legal implications, such as the one described in the chapter.

CHAPTER 2

Government Agencies that Impact the Hospitality Industry

CHAPTER OUTLINE

2.1. Federal Regulatory and Administrative Agencies
2.2. State Regulatory and Administrative Agencies
2.3. Local Regulatory and Administrative Agencies
2.4. Regulatory Interaction and Oversight Impacting Travel and Tourism
2.5. Managing Conflicting Regulations
2.6. Responding to an Inquiry
2.7. Monitoring Regulatory Change

IN THIS CHAPTER, YOU WILL LEARN

1. How federal governmental agencies are involved in regulating the hospitality industry.
2. How to analyze the various roles of state governmental agencies that regulate the hospitality industry.
3. How to identify local governmental agencies involved in regulating the hospitality industry.
4. How to recognize those national and international agencies and departments charged with monitoring and regulating the travel industry.
5. How to manage conflicting regulations.
6. How to properly respond to an official inquiry or complaint from a regulatory entity.
7. How to keep abreast of regulatory changes.

2.1 Federal Regulatory and Administrative Agencies

The hospitality industry is regulated by a variety of federal, state, and local governmental entities. Hospitality managers must interact with these agencies in a variety of different ways and observe all applicable procedures and regulations established by government. Managers must fill out forms and paperwork, obtain operating licenses, maintain their property to specified codes and standards, provide a safe working environment, and open up their facilities for periodic inspection. The purpose of this chapter is to help you understand the scope of the regulatory process and be able to respond to questions from these regulatory agencies in a way that is both legally correct and sound from a business perspective.

With thousands of federal, state, and local agencies, departments, offices, and individuals regulating business today, it is simply not possible for a hospitality manager to be knowledgeable about all the requirements that may apply to his or her operation. It *is* possible, however, to take these four actions:

1. Be aware of the major entities responsible for regulation.
2. Understand how to resolve conflicting regulations.
3. Be aware of the process for responding to an inquiry or complaint from a regulatory entity.
4. Stay abreast of changes in regulations that affect your segment of the industry.

Internal Revenue Service (IRS)

The Internal Revenue Service (www.irs.gov), founded as far back as 1862, is a division of the United States Department of Treasury. The stated mission of the IRS is to "Provide America's taxpayers top-quality service by helping them understand and meet their tax responsibilities and enforce the law with integrity and fairness to all." Although it is unlikely that the agency responsible for collecting taxes will be popular in any country, the right of the IRS to charge an individual with a criminal act makes it deserving of a manager's thoughtful attention.

In the hospitality industry, managers perform two separate roles when interacting with the IRS. A manager is both a taxpayer to the federal government (by paying income tax on the profits of a business) and a tax collector for the federal government (by withholding individual employee taxes on income). (Circular E), Employer's Tax Guide will assist businesses in properly withholding and paying taxes to the IRS. See https://www.irs.gov/pub/irs-pdf/p15.pdf.

The IRS requires businesses to:

- File quarterly income tax returns and make payments on the profits earned from business operations (Form 941). Taxes must be filed on or before the last day of the month following the end of each calendar quarter.
- File an Income and Tax Statement with the Social Security Administration on or before the last day of January (Forms W-2 and W-3).
- Withhold income taxes from the wages of all employees and deposit them with the IRS at regular intervals.
- Report all employee income earned as tips (Form 4070) and withhold taxes on the tipped income; however, no report is required for months when tips are less than $20.
- Record the value of meals charged to employees when the meals are considered a portion of an employee's income; but if the meals are provided for the convenience of the employer, then the meals are not subject to federal income tax withholding or employment taxes.
- Record all payments to independent contractors, and file any forms listing those payments (Forms 1096 and 1099).
- Furnish a record of withheld taxes to all employees on or before January 31 (Form W-2).

The IRS ensures that businesses pay their taxes through periodic examinations of their financial accounts and tax records. These examinations are called audits. A hospitality manager must respond if the IRS notifies him or her of a forthcoming audit. The manager should also consult a certified public accountant (CPA) or an attorney that specializes in tax audits as soon as possible to ensure that the appropriate documents are prepared and in order.

It would be an oversimplification to state that federal tax laws are complex—they are hugely complex. As a hospitality manager, you may be responsible for submitting or filing the taxes owed by a business, so it is important that you understand the role that you play in ensuring your company's compliance with federal tax laws.

For example, the IRS considers tips and gratuities given to employees by guests of the business as taxable income. As such, this income must be reported to the IRS, and taxes, if due, must be paid on that income. In addition, employers are responsible for assisting the IRS in this reporting process by collecting tip-reporting forms from employees and forwarding the information to the IRS.

Figure 2.1 is a copy of IRS Publication 531. This publication explains the regulations related to an employee's reporting of tipped income. It is a good example of the instructions the IRS gives an individual taxpayer. Note that the IRS explains what is required and how the requirements can be met.

Just as employees have specific responsibilities for reporting tipped income, the employer also has responsibilities imposed by the IRS. For a complete list of a business's tax responsibilities and to obtain copies of various tax forms, visit the IRS website at www.irs.gov/businesses and look up employment. Search the Web 2.1 will guide you as you examine these requirements.

Search the Web 2.1

Go online to **www.irs.gov**

1. Select: Forms and Publications.
2. Select: List of Current Forms & Pubs.
3. Select: Publication 15.

Read the portion of Publication 15 that refers to an employer's responsibilities related to the reporting of tip income by employers.

Occupational Safety and Health Administration (OSHA)

OSHA (www.osha.gov) is an agency established in 1971 in the United States Department of Labor and was created after the passage of the Occupation Safety and Health Act of 1970. The purpose of the act was "to assure safe and healthful working conditions for working men and women by setting and enforcing standards and by providing training, outreach, education and assistance." Despite criticism from many in business, OSHA has taken an aggressive role in protecting workers' rights.

All businesses, including hospitality operations, must comply with the extensive safety practices, equipment specifications, and employee communication procedures mandated by OSHA. Specifically, businesses are required to:

- Provide a workplace free from serious recognized hazards and comply with standards, rules, and regulations issued under the OSH Act.
- Examine workplace conditions to make sure they conform to applicable OSHA standards.
- Make sure employees have and use safe tools and equipment and properly maintain this equipment.
- Use color codes, posters, labels or signs to warn employees of potential hazards.
- Establish or update operating procedures and communicate them so that employees follow safety and health requirements.

Keeping a Daily Tip Record

Why keep a daily tip record.

You must keep a daily tip record so you can:

(1) Report your tips accurately to your employer,
(2) Report your tips accurately on your tax return, and
(3) Prove your tip income if your return is ever questioned.

How to keep a daily tip record.

There are two ways to keep a daily tip record. You can either:

(1) Write information about your tips in a tip diary; or
(2) Keep copies of documents that show your tips, such as restaurant bills and credit or debit card charge slips.

You should keep your daily tip record with your tax or other personal records. You must keep your records for as long as they are important for administration of the federal tax law. For information on how long to keep records, see How Long to Keep Records in chapter 1 of Pub. 17, Your Federal Income Tax.

If you keep a tip diary, you can use Form 4070A, Employee's Daily Record of Tips. To get Form 4070A, ask IRS or your employer for Pub. 1244, Employee's Daily Record of Tips and Report to Employer. Pub. 1244 is also available at www.irs.gov/pub1244. Pub. 1244 includes a 1-year supply of Form 4070A. Each day, write in the information asked for on the form.

In addition to the information asked for on Form 4070A, you also need to keep a record of the date and value of any noncash tips you get, such as tickets, passes, or other items of value. Although you do not report these tips to your employer, you must report them on your tax return.

If you do not use Form 4070A, start your records by writing your name, your employer's name, and the name of the business (if it is different from your employer's name). Then, each workday, write the date and the following information.

(1) Cash tips you get directly from customers or from other employees.
(2) Tips from credit and debit card charge customers that your employer pays you.
(3) The value of any noncash tips you get, such as tickets, passes, or other items of value.
(4) The amount of tips you paid out to other employees through tip pools or tip splitting, or other arrangements, and the names of the employees to whom you paid the tips.

https://www.irs.gov/pub/irs-pdf/p531.pdf

FIGURE 2.1 **Reporting tip income.**

- Employers must provide safety training in a language and vocabulary workers can understand.
- Employers with hazardous chemicals in the workplace must develop and implement a written hazard communication program and train employees on the hazards they are exposed to and proper precautions (and a copy of safety data sheets must be readily available). See the OSHA page on Hazard Communication.
- Provide medical examinations and training when required by OSHA standards.
- Post, at a prominent location within the workplace, the OSHA poster (or the state-plan equivalent) informing employees of their rights and responsibilities.
- Report to the nearest OSHA office all work-related fatalities within 8 hours, and all work-related inpatient hospitalizations, all amputations and all losses of an eye within 24 hours. Call our toll-free number: 1-800-321-OSHA (6742); TTY 1-877-889-5627. [Employers under federal OSHA's jurisdiction were required to begin reporting by Jan. 1, 2015. Establishments in a state with a state-run OSHA program should contact their state plan for the implementation date].
- Keep records of work-related injuries and illnesses. (Note: Employers with 10 or fewer employees and employers in certain low-hazard industries are exempt from this requirement.)
- Provide employees, former employees and their representatives access to the Log of Work-Related Injuries and Illnesses (OSHA Form 300). On February 1, and for three months, covered employers must post the summary of the OSHA log of injuries and illnesses (OSHA Form 300A).
- Provide access to employee medical records and exposure records to employees or their authorized representatives.
- Provide to the OSHA compliance officer the names of authorized employee representatives who may be asked to accompany the compliance officer during an inspection.

- Not discriminate against employees who exercise their rights under the Act. See our "Whistleblower Protection" webpage.
- Post OSHA citations at or near the work area involved. Each citation must remain posted until the violation has been corrected, or for three working days, whichever is longer. Post abatement verification documents or tags.
- Correct cited violations by the deadline set in the OSHA citation and submit required abatement verification documentation.
- OSHA encourages all employers to adopt an Injury and Illness Prevention Program. Injury and Illness Prevention Programs, known by a variety of names, are universal interventions that can substantially reduce the number and severity of workplace injuries and alleviate the associated financial burdens on U.S. workplaces. Many states have requirements or voluntary guidelines for workplace Injury and Illness Prevention Programs. Also, numerous employers in the United States already manage safety using Injury and Illness Prevention Programs, and we believe that all employers can and should do the same. Most successful Injury and Illness Prevention Programs are based on a common set of key elements. These include: management leadership, worker participation, hazard identification, hazard prevention and control, education and training, and program evaluation and improvement. OSHA's Injury and Illness Prevention Programs topics page contains more information including examples of programs and systems that have reduced workplace injuries and illnesses (https://www.osha.gov/as/opa/worker/employer-responsibility.html).

OSHA monitors workplace safety with a large staff of inspectors called compliance safety and health officers. Compliance safety and health officers visit workplaces during regular business hours and perform unannounced inspections to ensure that employers are operating in compliance with all OSHA health and safety regulations. In addition, compliance safety and health officers are required to investigate any complaints of unsafe business practices. Figure 2.2 is an excerpt of the Occupational Health and Safety Act codified at 29 U.S. Code § 657 that gives the agency authority to enter a business to investigate worker safety.

Hospitality managers have the right to accompany OSHA compliance officers during an inspection, and managers should make it a point of doing so, for two reasons. First, the manager may be able to answer questions or clarify procedures for the compliance officer; and second, the manager should know what transpired during the inspection. Afterward, the manager should discuss the results of the inspection with the compliance officer and request a copy of any inspection reports filed. Generally, inspections are not announced, although the compliance officer must state a specific reason for the inspection.

The penalties for violating OSHA regulations can be severe and costly. These penalties can be found at 29 U.S. Code § 666. Because of the stringent penalties for noncompliance, it is important that hospitality managers ensure that their workplace is safe. As stressed in this book several times, the best way to avoid accidents, lawsuits, and penalties is to adopt a philosophy of preventative management. Where worker safety is concerned, this may be as simple as providing information or as complex as developing an employee training program.

One example of the type of information OSHA requires to be posted or provided is the Safety Data Sheets (SDS, formerly known as Material Safety Data Sheets). An SDS is a manufacturer's statement detailing the potential hazards and proper methods of using a chemical or toxic substance. The SDS is intended to inform workers about the hazards of the materials they work with so that they can protect themselves and respond to emergency situations. The law states that employees must have access to SDS and be assisted in reading and understanding them. OSHA inspectors are responsible for ensuring that SDSs are placed in areas accessible to workers.

Section 8, Title: INSPECTIONS, INVESTIGATIONS, AND RECORDKEEPING

In order to carry out the purposes of this Act, the Secretary, upon presenting appropriate credentials to the owner, operator, or agent in charge, is authorized:

(1) to enter without delay and at reasonable times any factory, plant, establishment, construction site, or other area, workplace or environment where work is performed by an employee of an employer; and

(2) to inspect and investigate during regular working hours and at other reasonable times, and within reasonable limits and in a reasonable manner, any such place of employment and all pertinent conditions, structures, machines, apparatus, devices, equipment, and materials therein, and to question privately any such employer, owner, operator, agent or employee.

FIGURE 2.2 OSHA inspection provisions.

Analyze the Situation 2.1

Carlos Magana was a Spanish-speaking custodian working in a health-care facility kitchen. Bert LaColle was the new food and beverage director. Mr. LaColle instructed Mr. Magana to clean the grout between the red quarry kitchen tile with a powerful cleaner that Mr. LaColle had purchased from a chemical cleaning supply vendor. Mr. LaColle, who did not speak Spanish, demonstrated to Mr. Magana how he should pour the chemical directly from the bottle to the grout and then brush the grout with a wire brush until it was white.

Because the cleaner was so strong, and because Mr. Magana did not wear protective gloves, his hands were seriously irritated by the chemicals in the cleaner. In an effort to lessen the irritation to his hands, Mr. Magana decided to dilute the chemical. He added water to the bottle of cleaner, not realizing that the addition of water would cause toxic fumes. Mr. Magana inhaled the fumes while he continued cleaning, and later suffered serious lung damage as a result.

Mr. LaColle was subsequently contacted by OSHA, which cited and fined the facility for an SDS violation. Mr. LaColle maintained that SDS statements, including the one for the cleaner in question, were in fact available for inspection by employees.

1. Did the facility fulfill its obligation to provide a safe working environment for Mr. Magana?
2. What should Mr. LaColle have done to avoid an OSHA violation?

An OSHA Hazard Communication provides a guide for what a standard SDS should include:[1]

1. Identification
2. Hazard(s) Identification
3. Composition/Information on Ingredients
4. First-Aid Measures
5. Fire-Fighting Measures
6. Accidental Release Measures
7. Handling and Storage
8. Exposure Controls/Personal Protection
9. Physical and Chemical Properties
10. Stability and Reactivity
11. Toxicological Information
12. Ecological Information (nonmandatory)
13. Disposal Considerations (nonmandatory)
14. Transport Information (nonmandatory)
15. Regulatory Information (nonmandatory)
16. Other Information

Figure 2.3 shown on the next page is an excerpt example of an SDS. The specific product detailed is Jet Dry, a trademarked item distributed by Economics Laboratories for use in commercial dishwashers. The point here is that all hospitality managers must be aware of the sometimes very specific requirements that federal agencies place on them. The requirements can be numerous, and they change frequently. One way to stay current with your obligations as an operator is to log on to OSHA's website (www.osha.gov) and click on What's New.

Environmental Protection Agency (EPA)

The EPA (www.epa.gov) is an independent agency of the federal government. Established in 1970, the EPA's mission is to "protect human health and the environment."[2] In the hospitality industry, the EPA serves as a regulator of pesticides, as well as water and air pollution. Care must be taken when discharging waste, particularly toxic waste such as pesticides or cleaning chemicals from laundry areas. In 1996, new amendments were added to the Safe.

Drinking Water Act (SDWA) of 1974 is a federal law that empowers the EPA to set standards for drinking water quality and to oversee the states, towns, and water suppliers that implement and enforce those standards. The EPA also monitors indoor air-quality issues (such as smoking in commercial buildings). The SDWA was amended in 2002 pursuant to the Public Health Security and Bioterrorism Preparedness and Response Act of 2002 and continues to be updated due to ongoing public concerns for safe drinking water.

Many EPA directives are carried out or implemented by state and local governments, such as state recycling laws and municipal ordinances for trash disposal. Thus, while you, as a hospitality manager, may have little contact with the federal agency, it is important to be fully aware of your state and local laws in these areas.

[1] https://www.osha.gov/Publications/OSHA3514.html

[2] https://www.epa.gov/aboutepa/our-mission-and-what-we-do

SAFETY DATA SHEET

JET DRY

Section 1. Chemical product and company identification

Product name	:	JET DRY
Recommended use and restrictions	:	Rinse additive Use only for the purpose on the product label.
Product dilution information	:	Up to 5.6 oz/100 gal in water
Supplier's information	:	Ecolab Inc. Institutional Division 370 N. Wabasha Street St. Paul, MN 55102 1-800-352-5326
Code	:	914598-01
Date of issue	:	**22 Oct 2013** EMERGENCY HEALTH INFORMATION: 1-800-328-0026 Outside United States and Canada CALL 1-651-222-5352 (in USA)

Section 2. Hazards identification

		Product AS SOLD	**Product AT USE DILUTION**
GHS Classification	:	SERIOUS EYE DAMAGE/ EYE IRRITATION - Category 2B	Not classified.
GHS label elements			
Signal word	:	Warning	No signal word.
Hazard statements	:	Causes eye irritation.	No known significant effects or critical hazards.
Precautionary statements			
Prevention	:	Wash hands thoroughly after handling.	Wash thoroughly after handling.
Response	:	IF IN EYES: Rinse cautiously with water for several minutes. Remove contact lenses, if present and easy to do. Continue rinsing. If eye irritation persists: Get medical attention.	Get medical attention if symptoms appear.
Storage	:	No other specific measures identified.	No other specific measures identified.
Disposal	:	See section 13 for waste disposal information.	See section 13 for waste disposal information.
Other hazards	:	None known.	None known.

Section 3. Composition/information on ingredients

Substance/mixture : Mixture

Product AS SOLD

Hazardous ingredients	Concentration Range (%)	CAS number
oxirane, methyl-, polymer with oxirane	1 - 5	9003-11-6
alcohols, c10-16, ethoxylated	1 - 5	68002-97-1

FIGURE 2.3 An SDS for Jet Dry.

JET DRY **22 Oct 2013**

Section 3. Composition/information on ingredients

Product AT USE DILUTION

Within the present knowledge of the supplier, this product does not contain any hazardous ingredients in quantities requiring reporting, in accordance with local regulations.

Section 4. First aid measures

	Product AS SOLD	Product AT USE DILUTION
Eye contact	: Rinse cautiously with water for several minutes. Remove contact lenses, if present and easy to do. Continue rinsing. Get medical attention if irritation persists.	No known effect after eye contact. Rinse with water for a few minutes.
Skin contact	: No known effect after skin contact. Rinse with water for a few minutes.	No known effect after skin contact. Rinse with water for a few minutes.
Inhalation	: No special measures required. Treat symptomatically.	No special measures required. Treat symptomatically.
Ingestion	: Get medical attention if symptoms occur.	Get medical attention if symptoms occur.

Protection of first-aiders : No action shall be taken involving any personal risk or without suitable training. It may be dangerous to the person providing aid to give mouth-to-mouth resuscitation.

Notes to physician : Treat symptomatically. Contact poison treatment specialist immediately if large quantities have been ingested or inhaled.

See toxicological information (section 11)

Section 5. Fire-fighting measures

Product AS SOLD

Suitable fire extinguishing media : Use water spray, fog or foam.

Specific hazards arising from the chemical : In a fire or if heated, a pressure increase will occur and the container may burst.

Hazardous thermal decomposition products : Decomposition products may include the following materials:
carbon dioxide
carbon monoxide

Specific fire-fighting methods : Promptly isolate the scene by removing all persons from the vicinity of the incident if there is a fire. No action shall be taken involving any personal risk or without suitable training.

Special protective equipment for fire-fighters : Fire-fighters should wear appropriate protective equipment and self-contained breathing apparatus (SCBA) with a full face-piece operated in positive pressure mode.

Section 6. Accidental release measures

	Product AS SOLD	Product AT USE DILUTION
Personal precautions	: Use personal protective equipment as required.	Use personal protective equipment as required.
Environmental precautions	: Avoid contact of large amounts of spilled material and runoff with soil and surface waterways.	Avoid contact of large amounts of spilled material and runoff with soil and surface waterways.
Methods for cleaning up	: Use a water rinse for final clean-up.	Use a water rinse for final clean-up.

FIGURE 2.3 *(continued)*

JET DRY **22 Oct 2013**

Section 7. Handling and storage

	Product AS SOLD	Product AT USE DILUTION
Handling	: Avoid contact with eyes, skin and clothing. Wash thoroughly after handling.	Wash thoroughly after handling.
Storage	: Keep out of reach of children. Keep container tightly closed. Store between the following temperatures: 0 and 50°C	Keep out of reach of children.

Section 8. Exposure controls/personal protection

Control parameters

Ingredient name	Exposure limits
None.	

	Product AS SOLD	Product AT USE DILUTION
Appropriate engineering controls	: Good general ventilation should be sufficient to control worker exposure to airborne contaminants.	Good general ventilation should be sufficient to control worker exposure to airborne contaminants.
Personal protection		
Eye protection	: No protective equipment is needed under normal use conditions.	No protective equipment is needed under normal use conditions.
Hand protection	: No protective equipment is needed under normal use conditions.	No protective equipment is needed under normal use conditions.
Skin protection	: No protective equipment is needed under normal use conditions.	No protective equipment is needed under normal use conditions.
Respiratory protection	: A respirator is not needed under normal and intended conditions of product use.	A respirator is not needed under normal and intended conditions of product use.

Hygiene measures : Wash hands, forearms and face thoroughly after handling chemical products, before eating, smoking and using the lavatory and at the end of the working period. Appropriate techniques should be used to remove potentially contaminated clothing. Wash contaminated clothing before reusing.

Section 9. Physical and chemical properties

	Product AS SOLD	Product AT USE DILUTION
Physical state	: Liquid.	Liquid.
Color	: Green [Dark]	Clear
Odor	: Odorless	Odorless
pH	: 2.61 (100%)	7 to 8
Flash point	: > 100°C Product does not support combustion.	> 100°C
Explosion limits	: Not available.	
Flammability (solid, gas)	: Not available.	
Melting point	: Not available.	
Boiling point	: Not available.	
Evaporation rate (butyl acetate = 1)	: Not available.	
Vapor pressure	: Not available.	
Vapor density	: Not available.	
Relative density	: 1.01 (Water = 1)	

FIGURE 2.3 *(continued)*

JET DRY **22 Oct 2013**

Section 9. Physical and chemical properties

Solubility : Not available.

Partition coefficient: n-octanol/water : Not available.

Auto-ignition temperature : Not available.

Decomposition temperature : Not available.

Odor threshold : Not available.

Viscosity : Kinematic (room temperature): 0 cm^2/s (0 cSt)

Section 10. Stability and reactivity

Product AS SOLD

Stability : The product is stable.

Possibility of hazardous reactions : Under normal conditions of storage and use, hazardous reactions will not occur.

Conditions to avoid : No specific data.

Materials to avoid : Not available.

Hazardous decomposition products : Under normal conditions of storage and use, hazardous decomposition products should not be produced.

Section 11. Toxicological information

Route of exposure : Skin contact, Eye contact, Inhalation, Ingestion

	Product AS SOLD	Product AT USE DILUTION
Symptoms		
Eye contact	: Adverse symptoms may include the following: irritation watering redness	No specific data.
Skin contact	: No specific data.	No specific data.
Inhalation	: No specific data.	No specific data.
Ingestion	: No specific data.	No specific data.
Acute toxicity		
Eye contact	: Causes eye irritation.	No known significant effects or critical hazards.
Skin contact	: No known significant effects or critical hazards.	No known significant effects or critical hazards.
Inhalation	: No known significant effects or critical hazards.	No known significant effects or critical hazards.
Ingestion	: No known significant effects or critical hazards.	No known significant effects or critical hazards.

Toxicity data

Product/ingredient name			
oxirane, methyl-, polymer with oxirane	LC50 Inhalation Dusts and mists	Rat	0.147 mg/l
	LD50 Dermal	Rabbit	>2000 mg/kg
	LD50 Oral	Rat	>2000 mg/kg
alcohols, c10-16, ethoxylated	LC50 Inhalation Dusts and mists	Rat	>50 mg/l
	LD50 Dermal	Rat	>2000 mg/kg
	LD50 Oral	Rat	>1000 mg/kg

Chronic toxicity

FIGURE 2.3 *(continued)*

JET DRY **22 Oct 2013**

Section 11. Toxicological information

Carcinogenicity	: No known significant effects or critical hazards.
Mutagenicity	: No known significant effects or critical hazards.
Teratogenicity	: No known significant effects or critical hazards.
Developmental effects	: No known significant effects or critical hazards.
Fertility effects	: No known significant effects or critical hazards.

Section 12. Ecological information

Product AS SOLD

Ecotoxicity : This material is toxic to aquatic life.

Aquatic and terrestrial toxicity

Product/ingredient name	Result	Species	Exposure
oxirane, methyl-, polymer with oxirane	Acute LC50 >100 mg/l	Fish	96 hours
alcohols, c10-16, ethoxylated	Acute EC50 >0.1 mg/l	Daphnia	48 hours

Other adverse effects : No known significant effects or critical hazards.

Section 13. Disposal considerations

	Product AS SOLD	Product AT USE DILUTION
Disposal methods	: Diluted product can be flushed to sanitary sewer. Discard empty container in trash.	Diluted product can be flushed to sanitary sewer. Discard empty container in trash.

Section 14. Transport information

Certain shipping modes or package sizes may have exceptions from the transport regulations. The classification provided may not reflect those exceptions and may not apply to all shipping modes or package sizes.

DOT

DOT Classification **Not regulated.**

IMO/IMDG

IMO/IMDG Classification **Not regulated.**

For transport in bulk, see shipping documents for specific transportation information.

Product AT USE DILUTION
Not intended for transport.

Section 15. Regulatory information

Product AS SOLD

U.S. Federal regulations

TSCA 8(b) inventory : All components are listed or exempted.

SARA 302/304/311/312 extremely hazardous substances: No listed substance

SARA 302/304 emergency planning and notification: No listed substance

SARA 313	**Product name**	**CAS number**	**Concentration**
Form R - Reporting requirements	: No listed substance		

California Prop. 65 : No listed substance

FIGURE 2.3 *(continued)*

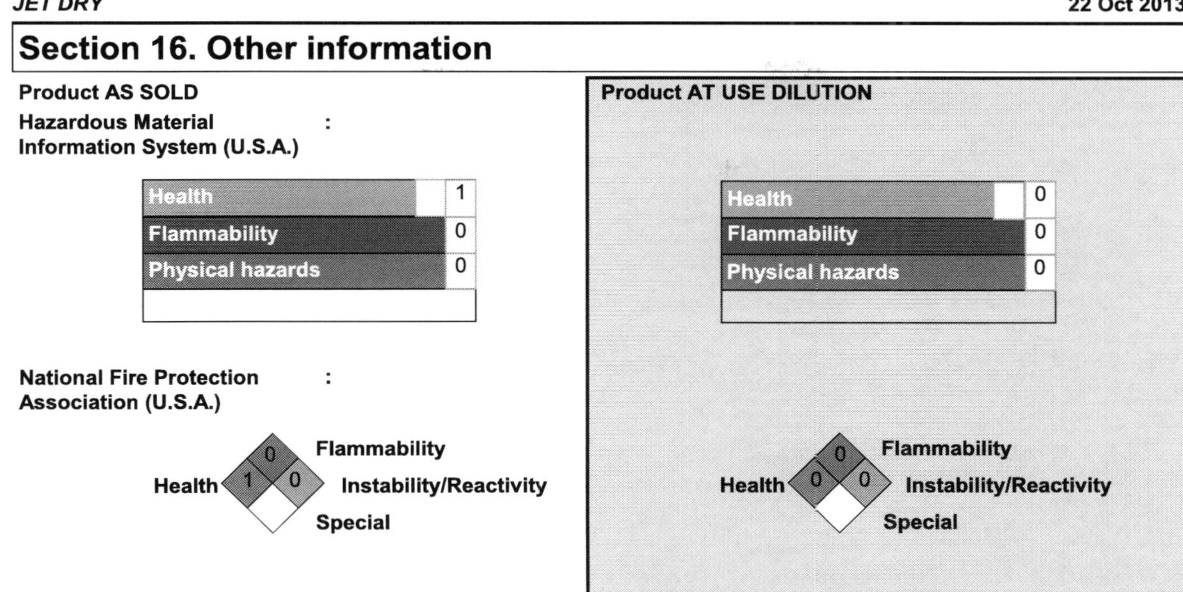

JET DRY 22 Oct 2013

Section 16. Other information

Product AS SOLD

Hazardous Material Information System (U.S.A.) :

Health	1
Flammability	0
Physical hazards	0

National Fire Protection Association (U.S.A.) :

Product AT USE DILUTION

Health	0
Flammability	0
Physical hazards	0

Date of issue : **22 Oct 2013**

Prepared by : Regulatory Affairs
1-800-352-5326

Notice to reader

The above information is believed to be correct with respect to the formula used to manufacture the product in the country of origin. As data, standards, and regulations change, and conditions of use and handling are beyond our control, NO WARRANTY, EXPRESS OR IMPLIED, IS MADE AS TO THE COMPLETENESS OR CONTINUING ACCURACY OF THIS INFORMATION.

FIGURE 2.3 *(continued)*

Food and Drug Administration (FDA)

The FDA (www.fda.gov) is one of the oldest consumer protection agencies in the federal government and began with the passing of the Pure Food and Drugs Act in 1906. The FDA plays an important role in the hospitality industry. It is responsible for ensuring the proper labeling of food and the safety of food. As a foodservice manager, you will encounter the work of the FDA whenever you purchase food that has a mandatory FDA nutrition label. In addition, the FDA's Model Food Service Sanitation Ordinance is used by many state and community health departments as a basis for their own foodservice inspection programs. You can find the 2013 FDA Ordinance online at *http://www.fda.gov/Food/GuidanceRegulation/RetailFoodProtection/FoodCode/ucm374275.htm*.

Or, if you wish to view a state-adopted Food Service Sanitation Ordinance, you can view the ordinance recently adopted by Montgomery County, Illinois, and Chester County, Pennsylvania, at:

- www.montgomeryco.com/health/Environmental%20Health/Food%20Service%20Sanitation%20Ordinance.pdf
- http://chesco.org/2880/FDA-Food-Code-Update

Foodservice operators also need to be aware of the FDA's precise definitions governing the use of nutritional and health-related terms. A restaurant that prints phrases such as "low-calorie," "light," or "cholesterol-free" in their menus must make sure that the recipes for those dishes meet the FDA's requirements for those statements. These and other menu-labeling requirements will be discussed more fully in Chapter 12, "Your Responsibilities When Serving Food and Beverages."

Equal Employment Opportunity Commission (EEOC)

The Equal Employment Opportunity Commission was established by Title VII of the Civil Rights Act of 1964 and went into effect on July 2, 1965. Essentially, this agency enforces laws against discrimination in employment. Figure 2.4 shown on the next page lists the specific laws that are enforced by the EEOC. The following general areas fall under the jurisdiction of the EEOC:

- Sexual harassment
- Race/color discrimination
- Age discrimination

Title VII of the Civil Rights Act of 1964
Equal Pay Act of 1963
Age Discrimination in Employment Act of 1967 (ADEA)
Rehabilitation Act of 1973, Sections 501 and 505
Titles I and V of the Americans with Disabilities An of 1990 (ADA)
Civil Rights Act of 1991
The Pregnancy Discrimination Act of 1978
The Genetic Information Nondiscrimination Act of 2008 (GINA)

FIGURE 2.4 **Laws enforced by the Equal Employment Opportunity Commission.**

- National origin discrimination
- Pregnancy discrimination
- Religious discrimination
- Portions of the Americans with Disabilities Act
- Sex discrimination
- Equal Pay/Compensation discrimination
- Genetic Information discrimination
- Retaliation discrimination

Some of these areas will be discussed in detail in Chapter 8, "Legally Managing Employees." The impact of the EEOC on the daily tasks of the hospitality manager is obvious. Consider, for example, the hotel manager who seeks to schedule a Christian to work on Christmas Day. The hotel is, of course, open. The question that might arise is whether the needs of the manager, who must staff the hotel, should take precedence over those of the worker, who desires a day off on the basis of his or her religious convictions.

Title VII of the Civil Rights Act of 1964 prohibits employers from discriminating against individuals because of their religious beliefs when hiring and firing. The act also requires employers to reasonably accommodate the religious practices of an employee or prospective employee, unless doing so would create an undue hardship on the employer. Flexible scheduling, voluntary substitutions or swaps, job reassignments, and lateral transfers are examples of accommodating an employee's religious beliefs. The question of whether a manager could "reasonably" accommodate the request of a Christian worker to be off on Christmas Day is complex. The point to be remembered, however, is that managers are not free to act in any manner they desire, but the federal government, through the requirements of the EEOC, also plays a role in the actions of management.

The EEOC also investigates complaints by employees who think they have been discriminated against. Businesses that are found to have discriminated against employees can be ordered to compensate the employee(s) for damages, such as lost wages, attorney fees, and punitive damages or possibly reinstate the employee to the workplace, which can be challenging in itself.

Bureau of Alcohol, Tobacco, Firearms and Explosives (ATF), and Alcohol and Tobacco Tax and Trade Bureau (TTB)

The Bureau of Alcohol, Tobacco, Firearms and Explosives (www.atf.gov) is responsible for enforcing all federal laws and regulations governing the manufacture and sale of alcohol, tobacco, firearms, and explosives as well as for investigating incidents of arson. Formerly, the entire ATF was housed within the U.S. Department of Treasury, just as the IRS is, because it enforces the payment of federal taxes on the production of alcohol and the sale of alcoholic beverages. However, on January 24, 2003, pursuant to the creation of the Department of Homeland Security, the law enforcement functions of the ATF were transferred to the Department of Justice, but the tax and trade functions of the ATF stayed with the Treasury Department under the newly created Alcohol and Tobacco Tax and Trade Bureau (www.ttb.gov). The ATF's roll is to target, identify and dismantle criminal enterprises associated with violent crime and to prevent their encroachment into legitimate alcohol businesses. The TTB role, under the Federal Alcohol Administration Act, is to ensure that only qualified businesses engage in the alcohol beverage industry. The TTB does not enforce laws in connection with the retail sales of alcohol products; that is left up to the state enforcement agencies. The TTB does regulate permits for those who are producers, importers, or wholesalers of alcohol and ensures that labeling and advertising of alcohol provides information to protect consumers from deception.

Hospitality managers will interact with the TTB in the following ways:

- Retail sellers of alcohol—including bars, restaurants, and hotels—must comply with certain requirements of federal laws and regulations including registration.

- Bar, restaurants, and hotels must keep detailed records showing the date and quantity of all distilled spirits, wine, and beer received on their premises and from which distributors as well as keep a record of all sales.
- Operators must properly dispose of empty liquor bottles and may not reuse or sell them.

In its publication "P-5170.2, Liquor Laws & Regulations for Retail Dealers," published in 1995, updated in August 29, 2012, the TTB specifically dictates the way liquor retailers should handle empty liquor bottles. An excerpt from P-5170.2 is presented in Figure 2.5. Note the severe penalties assessed against businesses that do not comply with this regulation. The TTB enforces these regulations with its own officers who conduct inspections during an operation's regular hours of business. Additional information on the regulations covering the sale of alcohol is included in Chapter 12, "Your Responsibilities When Serving Food and Beverages."

Department of Labor (DOL)

The U.S. Department of Labor (www.dol.gov) was established in 1913 to "foster, promote, and develop the welfare of the wage earners, job seekers, and retirees of the United States; improve working conditions; advance opportunities for profitable employment; and assure work-related benefits and rights."[3]

Today, the department is charged with preparing the U.S. workforce for new and better jobs and for ensuring the adequacy of America's workplaces. It is responsible for the administration and enforcement of more than 180 federal laws, which govern the protection of workers' wages, health and safety, employment, and pension rights; equal employment opportunity; job training; unemployment insurance and workers' compensation programs; collective bargaining; and collecting, analyzing, and publishing labor and economic statistics. Following is a brief description of some of the principal federal labor-related regulations most commonly applicable to hospitality businesses.

Wages and Hours The Fair Labor Standards Act (FLSA) prescribes standards for wages and overtime pay, which affect most private and public employment. The act is administered by the Wage and Hour Division, created in 1938. It requires employers to pay covered employees the federal minimum wage and overtime of one-and-one-half times the regular wage. It restricts the hours that children under 16 can work and forbids their employment in certain jobs deemed too dangerous. On May 18, 2016, the rules updating overtime regulations were signed into law, effective December 1, 2016, with the intention to extend overtime wages to over 4 million workers within the first year (https://www.dol.gov/whd/overtime/final2016/).

This agency also establishes guidelines for tip credits, meal credits, and uniform purchases. In Chapter 8, "Legally Managing Employees," we will look at specific provisions of the FLSA that hospitality managers must keep in mind. In addition, the Wage and Hour Division also enforces laws that apply to aliens authorized to work within the United States under the Immigration and Nationality Act of 1990.

[3] https://www.dol.gov/100/timeline/alternate.version.timeline.html

(a) Refilling or reusing liquor bottles - Any retail dealer, or agent or employee of such dealer, who refills any liquor bottle with distilled spirits, or who reuses any liquor bottle by adding distilled spirits or any substance (including water) to the original contents is subject to a fine of not more than $1000 or imprisonment for not more than 1 year, or both.

(b) Disposition of liquor bottle - The possession of used liquor bottles by any person other than the one who emptied the contents thereof is prohibited, except that this prohibition shall not:

(1) prevent the owner or occupant of any premises on which such bottles have been lawfully emptied from assembling the same on such premises

(i) for delivery to a bottler or importer on specific request for such bottler or importer;

(ii) for destruction either on the premises on which the bottles are emptied or elsewhere, including disposition for purposes which will result in the bottles being rendered unusable as bottles; or

(iii) in the case of unusual or distinctive bottles, for disposition as collectors' items or for other purposes not involving the packaging of any products for sale;

(2) prevent any person from possessing, offering for sale, or selling such unusual or distinctive bottles for purposes not involving the packaging of any product for sale; or

(3) prevent any person from assembling used liquor bottles for the purpose of recycling or reclaiming the glass or other approved liquor bottle material.

Any person possessing liquor bottles in violation of law or regulations is subject to a fine of not more than $1000, imprisonment for not more than 1 year, or both.

FIGURE 2.5 Refilling, reusing, and disposing of liquor bottles.

Employee Benefit Security The Employee Retirement Income Security Act (ERISA) of 1974 regulates employers who offer pension or welfare benefit plans for their employees. This area of the Department of Labor is also responsible for reporting requirements for the continuation of health-care provisions, required under the Comprehensive Omnibus Budget Reconciliation Act of 1985 (COBRA) and the Health Insurance Portability and Accountability Act (HIPAA) of 1996. Other laws include the Newborns' and Mothers' Health Protection Act (1996), the Mental Health Parity Act (1996), and The Mental Health Parity and Addiction Equity Act of 2008.

In addition, the Patient Protection and Affordable Care Act (ACA, also known as Obamacare) was passed and signed into law in March of 2010 in order to make medical and hospital health insurance available to all Americans and to increase the quality and affordability of insurance coverage. This reform of the American health care insurance system has created much controversy among Americans and continues to be discussed in political arenas.

Plant Closings and Layoffs Hospitality businesses that are changing operators and will be laying off employees even for a short period of time before being rehired by the new operator may be subject to the Worker Adjustment and Retraining Notification Act (WARN). WARN protects employees by requiring early warning of impending layoffs or plant closings. WARN is administered by a special division of the Department of Labor.

Employee Polygraph Protection Act This law, enacted in 1988 and administered by the Wage and Hour Division, bars most employers under most circumstances from using lie detectors on employees or prospective employees. However, the law does permit employers to request that an employee undertake such a test in connection with any ongoing investigation into an incident that resulted in loss to the employer. Results of the lie detector test are not to be shared with anyone except the examiner, the employer, or those so ordered by the courts.

Family and Medical Leave Act This law, the FMLA, administered by the Wage and Hour Division, requires employers with 50 or more employees to grant up to 12 weeks of unpaid, job-related leave to eligible employees for the birth or adoption of a child and for the serious illness of the employee, a spouse, or a family member. In 2015, the term "spouse" was amended to include eligible employees in legal same-sex marriages in furtherance of the United States Supreme Court's landmark decision in *United States v. Windsor* (699 F.3d 169), which struck down Section 3 of the Defense of Marriage Act as being unconstitutional. These provisions and others that relate to hiring and managing employees are discussed in Chapter 7, "Legally Selecting Employees," and Chapter 8, "Legally Managing Employees."

It is important to note that other federal agencies besides the Department of Labor also enforce laws and regulations that affect employers. As discussed earlier in this chapter, laws that ensure nondiscrimination in employment are generally enforced by the Equal Employment Opportunity Commission. The Taft-Hartley Act of 1947, which regulates a wide range of unionization issues, is enforced by the National Labor Relations Board.

Department of Justice (DOJ)

In the United States, the Department of Justice (www.usdoj.gov) is headed by the U.S. attorney general. Although the position of attorney general has existed since the founding of the republic, it was not until 1870 that a separate Department of Justice was created, bringing together under the authority of the attorney general the activities of U.S. attorneys, U.S. marshals, and others. The Justice Department investigates and prosecutes federal crimes, has thwarted multiple terrorist plots against the United States, represents the United States of America in court, manages the federal prisons, and enforces the nation's immigration laws.

The Department of Justice also enforces Title III of the Americans with Disabilities Act (ADA), which states that hospitality operations must remove barriers that can restrict access or the full enjoyment of amenities by people with disabilities. The requirements for complying with this section of the ADA are discussed in Chapter 10, "Your Responsibilities as a Hospitality Operator to Guests."

U.S. Department of Homeland Security

Most hospitality managers will interact with the U.S. Citizenship and Immigration Service, a component of the U.S. Department of Homeland Security (www.dhs.gov) (DHS), through its regulation of illegal immigrants. Formerly, these duties were handled by the Immigration and Naturalization Service (INS) under the purview of the Department of Justice, but on March 1, 2003, pursuant to the Homeland Security Act, the INS was dismantled and separated into three component agencies under the Department of Homeland Security. These agencies are the Immigration and Customs Enforcement (ICE), Customs and Border Protection (CBP), which handle immigration enforcement and border security, and the U.S. Citizenship and Immigration Service (USCIS), which handles the administration of benefit applications. The mission of the DHS is "With honor and integrity, we will safeguard the American people, our homeland, and our values." These agencies are important to keep in mind when hiring employees because hospitality managers are required to secure identification documents from all those they hire. This is mandated so that jobs will be given only to those legally able to secure them. The precise method of verifying employment eligibility will be discussed in Chapter 7, "Legally Selecting Employees." Penalties for noncompliance in this area can be severe, so it is a good idea to stay well versed in the applicable regulations.

As you have already noticed, in response to the unfortunate incidents occurring on September 11, 2001, the federal government made sweeping changes to many agencies, combining a number of them under the Department of Homeland Security umbrella. This agency is discussed more thoroughly in Chapter 13, "Legal Responsibilities in Travel and Tourism."

2.2 State Regulatory and Administrative Agencies

Just as the federal government plays a regulatory role in the hospitality industry, so too do the various state agencies. It is important to understand that the states serve both complementary and distinct regulatory roles. The roles are complementary in that they support and amplify efforts undertaken at the federal level, but they are distinct in that they regulate some areas in which they have sole responsibility. Let's take a brief look at some of the state entities that play a significant regulatory role in the hospitality industry. The administrative structure or specific entity name may vary by state, but the regulatory process will be similar.

It is important to note that state and/or local regulations may affect the actions of hospitality managers more often than federal regulations. Codes and ordinances established at the state or local level can often be very strict and may require investment in equipment or to pay extra diligence in the operation of a facility. The penalties for violating these laws can be just as severe as those at the federal level.

Employment Security Agency

Each state regulates employment and employee/employer relationships within its borders. Generally, items such as worker-related unemployment benefits, worker safety issues, and injury compensation will fall to the state entity charged with regulating the workplace. In addition, in most states, this entity will also be responsible for areas such as providing employment assistance to both employees and employers.

Consider the case of Virgil Bollinger. The hotel where Mr. Bollinger works is purchased by a new owner, who states that Mr. Bollinger's sales manager position is no longer needed. In Mr. Bollinger's state, an employer's account is not charged for **unemployment benefits** if an employee is let go as a result of staff reductions. However, Mr. Bollinger believes that his employment has been terminated for other reasons, none of which relate to his work performance. It would be the role of the Employment Security Agency to determine to which, if any, unemployment compensation benefits Mr. Bollinger is entitled.

Workers' compensation is an area of great concern to most hospitality managers. Worker injuries are expensive, in terms of both money and disruption to the workplace. As a hospitality manager, it is important for you to know and follow the state regulations related to workplace safety and the method for properly documenting and reporting any work-related injury. In each state, worker safety will usually be monitored by a workers' compensation agency, commission, or subdivision of the employment security agency.

Alcoholic Beverage Commission (ABC)

Although the sale of alcohol is not a requirement for a foodservice or lodging operation, many facilities do offer it for their guests' enjoyment. The nature of alcohol and its consumption, however, subjects the hospitality manager to intense regulation. Generally, this regulation takes place at both the state and local levels. A state's alcoholic beverage commission (ABC) will be responsible for the following areas of control:

- License issuing
- Permitted hours of sales
- Advertising and promotion policies
- Methods of operation
- Reporting of sales for tax purposes
- Penalties and revocation of licenses

As a hospitality manager, failure to abide by the regulations required to sell alcoholic beverages lawfully may subject you to criminal prosecution, as well as a civil proceeding (an administrative hearing) before the regulatory body of your state's ABC. In addition, the enactment of **dram shop act** legislation could make a hospitality manager, or the business itself, liable to guests or third parties and their families should significant violations of the alcohol service regulations result in injury to an intoxicated guest or to persons harmed by an individual who was illegally served. Simply put, providers of alcoholic beverages can be held responsible for the acts of their intoxicated patrons if those patrons were illegally served. Specific techniques related to the proper selling of alcoholic beverages will be fully discussed in Chapter 12, "Your Responsibilities When Serving Food and Beverages."

States are very careful when granting licenses to sell liquor, and they are generally very aggressive in revoking the

---

LEGALESE

Unemployment benefits: A benefit paid to an employee who involuntarily loses his or her employment without just cause.

Workers' compensation: A benefit paid to an employee who suffers a work-related injury or illness.

Dram shop acts: Legislation passed in a variety of forms and in many states that imposes liability for the acts of others on those who serve alcohol negligently, recklessly, or illegally.

licenses of operations that fail to adhere to the state's required procedures for selling alcohol. In most states, license revocation can be the result of any of the following:

- Frequent incidents of fighting, disorderly conduct, or generally creating a public nuisance
- Allowing prostitution or solicitation on the premises
- Drug and narcotic sales or use
- Illegal adult entertainment, such as outlawed forms of nude dancing
- Failure to maintain required records
- Sale of alcohol to minors

Hospitality operators are also responsible for reporting all sales of alcohol to their state's alcoholic beverage commission (ABC). The ABC will perform random audits to determine the accuracy of the information received. Other enforcement tools used by the ABC are to conduct unannounced inspections of the premises where alcohol is sold and/or, usually in connection with a sting operation from local law enforcement, to intentionally send minors into an establishment to test whether the operator will serve them.

Treasury Department/Controller

A state's treasury department is responsible for the collection of taxes levied by that state. For those in the hospitality industry, this can include liquor taxes, sales taxes, occupancy taxes, bed taxes, and a wide array of use taxes.

An excellent example of the diversity displayed by the various states in regard to taxation is the document in Figure 2.6, published in 1987 by the State of Georgia. It demonstrates the importance of a thorough understanding of the laws regarding taxation in the state where you will manage a hospitality facility.

A relatively recent development in the United States has caused an expansion of duties for many state treasury departments. In addition to the collection of taxes, these departments or agencies are often responsible for the regulation of their state's lottery and gaming operations. As this segment of the hospitality industry expands, so too will the regulatory efforts of the various state treasury departments. Typical areas of gaming and lottery regulation by treasury departments include licensing, lottery ticket sales, winnings disbursement, and casino operations. Figure 2.7 is an excellent example of the procedures that treasury regulators can mandate in the operation of gaming facilities. In this document, the Michigan Treasury Department identifies some of the written procedures for money handling that must be filed with the department prior to the granting of a casino license.

Attorney General

The state's attorney general is the chief legal officer of the state. In Chapter 3, "Hospitality Operating Structures," you will learn that one responsibility of the attorney general's office is to specify the franchise information required for disclosure in that state. If, for example, an entrepreneur were interested in purchasing a franchise, the attorney general's office would regulate the franchisor and franchisee relationship.

Public Health Department

The public health department is generally responsible for the inspection and licensing of facilities that serve food. This department may be self-standing, but it is often associated with or housed in a state department of agriculture.

ATTENTION: GEORGIA HOTEL AND MOTEL OPERATORS

On April 2, 1987, Act Number 621 amending Official Code of Georgia Annotated Section 48- 13- 51 became effective. This Act provides that Georgia State or local government officials or employees traveling on official business should not be charged county or municipal excise tax on lodging.

Sales tax is not exempted under the current sales tax law, since the payment of hotel/motel bills by an employee is not considered to be payment made directly by a State agency from appropriated funds. Upon verification of the identity of the State official or employee identified below, Georgia hotel and motel operators are authorized to exempt the individual from any applicable county or municipal lodging excise tax. Sales tax, however, should continue to be charged.

A copy of this certification should be maintained with your tax records to document the individual's status as a state official or employee traveling on official business. If you have any questions, please contact the accounting or fiscal office of the Department or agency employing the individual identified below.

STATE OF GEORGIA CERTIFICATE OF EXEMPTION OF LOCAL HOTEL/MOTEL EXCISE TAX

This is to certify that the lodging obtained on the date(s) identified below was required in the discharge of my official duties for the State and qualifies for exemption of the local hotel/motel excise tax under Official Code of Georgia Annotated Chapter 48- 13 (as amended by Act 621, Georgia Laws 1987).

Signature of Official or Employee____________________________

Date ________________

FIGURE 2.6 **Tax-exempt notice.**

Analyze the Situation 2.2

Trixie Mitchell managed The Dusty Cellar, a bar near a college campus. She was active in her business community and served on the college's Presidential Advisory Board for Responsible Drinking. All servers and bartenders in her facility were required to undergo a mandatory 4-hour alcohol service training program before they began their employment and to take a required refresher course each year. Each server was certified in responsible alcohol service by the national office of Ms. Mitchell's hospitality trade association.

On a busy Friday night during the fall football season, one of Ms. Mitchell's servers approached a table with four female patrons. Since all appeared to be near 21 years old but well under the 35-year-old limit Ms. Mitchell had established for a mandatory identification (ID) check, the server asked to see a picture ID from each guest.

The server checked each guest's ID—verifying the age, hair color, general likeness, and absence of alterations to the ID card—and then requested—in a practice unique to Dusty's—the mandatory recitation by each patron of the birthday and address printed on the ID. Since all four guests passed their ID checks, the server served the patrons. Each guest had three glasses of wine over a period of 90 minutes.

The next day, Ms. Mitchell was contacted by the state ABC and an attorney for the parents of a teenager whose car was involved in an accident with one of the four patrons served the prior night. It had been established that one of the patrons, whose ID had been professionally altered, was 20 years old, not 21. This patron was involved in the auto accident after she left the bar and drove back to her dorm room. The ABC began an investigation into the sale of alcohol to minors, while the attorney scheduled an appointment with Ms. Mitchell's attorney to discuss a settlement based on the potential liability arising from the dram shop act legislation enacted in Ms. Mitchell's state.

1. Did Ms. Mitchell break the law by serving alcohol to an underage student?
2. Are Ms. Mitchell and her business liable for the acts of the underage drinking if her state has enacted dram shop legislation?

DEPARTMENT OF TREASURY, MICHIGAN: GAMING CONTROL BOARD

CASINO GAMING: (By authority conferred on the Michigan Gaming Control Board by section 4 of Initiated Law of 1996, as amended, being § 432.204 of the Michigan Compiled Laws)

PART 9. INTERNAL CONTROL PROCEDURES R 432.1901 Rule 902.

The procedures of the internal control system are designed to ensure all of the following:

(a) That assets of the casino licensee are safeguarded.

(b) That the financial records of the casino licensee are accurate and reliable.

(c) That the transactions of the casino licensee are performed only in accordance with the specific or general authorization of this part.

(d) That the transactions are recorded adequately to permit the proper recording of the adjusted gross receipts, fees, and all applicable taxes.

(e) That accountability for assets is maintained in accordance with generally accepted accounting principles.

(f) That only authorized personnel have access to assets.

(g) That recorded accountability for assets is compared with actual assets at reasonable intervals and appropriate action is taken with respect to any discrepancies.

(h) That the functions, duties, and responsibilities are appropriately segregated and performed in accordance with sound practices by competent, qualified personnel and that no employee of the casino licensee is in a position to perpetuate and conceal errors or irregularities in the normal course of the employee's duties.

(i) That gaming is conducted with integrity and in accordance with the act and these rules.

History: 1998 MR 6, Eff. June 26, 1998.R 432.1903 Board approval of internal control system. Rule 903.

(1) A licensee shall describe, in a manner that the board may approve of require, its administrative and accounting procedures in detail in a written system of internal control. A written system of internal controls shall include a detailed narrative description of the administrative and accounting procedures designed to satisfy the requirements of these rules. Additionally, the description shall include separate section for all of the following:

(a) An organizational chart depicting appropriate segregation of functions and responsibilities.

(b) A description of the duties and responsibilities of each position shown on the organizational chart.

FIGURE 2.7 **Lottery control.**

(c) A detailed, narrative description of the administrative and accounting procedures designed to satisfy the requirements of these rules. Additionally, the description shall include a separate section for all of the following:

- **(i)** Physical characteristics of the drop box and lip box.
- **(ii)** Transportation of drop and tip boxes to and from gaming tables.
- **(iii)** Procedures for table inventories.
- **(iv)** Procedures for opening and closing gaming tables.
- **(v)** Procedures for fills and credits.
- **(vi)** Procedures for accepting and reporting tips and gratuities.
- **(vii)** Procedures for transporting chips and tokens to and from gaming tables.
- **(viii)** Procedures for shift changes at gaming tables.
- **(ix)** Drop bucket characteristics.
- **(x)** Transportation of drop buckets to and from electronic gaming devices.
- **(xi)** Procedures for chip and token purchases.
- **(xii)** Procedures for hopper fills.
- **(xiii)** Procedures for the transportation of electronic gaming devices.
- **(xiv)** Procedures for hand-paid jackpots.
- **(xv)** Layout and physical characteristics of the cashier's cage.
- **(xvi)** Procedures for accounting controls.
- **(xvii)** Procedures for the exchange of checks submitted by gaming patrons.
- **(xviii)** Procedures for credit card and debit card transactions.
- **(xix)** Procedures for the acceptance, accounting for, and redemption of patron's cash deposits.
- **(xx)** Procedures for the control of coupon redemption and other complimentary distribution programs.
- **(xxi)** Procedures for Federal cash transactions reporting.
- **(xxii)** Procedures for computer backups and assuring the retention of financial and gambling operation.

(d) Other items as the board may require.

(2) Not less than 90 days before the gambling operation commences, unless otherwise directed by the board, a licensee shall submit, to the board, a written description of its internal control system that is designed to satisfy the requirements of subrule (1) of this rule.

(3) If the written system is the initial submission to the board, then a letter shall be submitted from an independent certified public accountant selected by the board stating that the licensee's written system has been reviewed by the accountant and is in compliance with the requirements of . . . this rule.

(4) The board shall review each submission required by subrule (2) of this rule and shall determine whether it conforms to the requirements of subrule (1) of this rule and whether the system submitted provides adequate and effective controls for the operations of the licensee.

If the board finds any insufficiencies, then the board shall specify the insufficiencies, in writing, and submit the written insufficiencies to the licensee. The licensee shall make appropriate alterations. A licensee shall not commence gambling operations until a system of internal controls Ii approved.

FIGURE 2.7 *(continued)*

Hospitality operators must comply with a variety of health codes and regulations that govern many aspects of their business. The most common areas of state health regulation include the following:

- Standards for the cleanliness of food and proper procedures for storing, handling, preparing, and serving food
- Standards for the storage and handling of food supplies
- Mandated health procedures for employees working with food
- Standards for the proper care and washing of food equipment, utensils, glasses, dishware, etc.
- Standards for the proper care and washing of hotel bedding and towels and specified quantities to be furnished to guests
- Standards for the supply and use of water for guest use (faucets, showers, swimming pools) as well as for cleaning and dishwashing
- Standards for water and sewage discharge
- Display of procedures for helping choking victims
- Regulations for smoking in public places

Penalties for violating state health ordinances vary widely. Sometimes it is a fine, but in other cases, an operation could be shut down entirely. In minor cases, if an operator can correct the violation within a specified time frame, no penalty will be imposed. And, at the end of that time period, the inspector will come back to verify that the appropriate corrections have been made.

Some state or local health departments occasionally furnish a list of health violators to local newspapers or television stations, which could result in unwanted negative publicity for a hospitality operator. This is an added incentive for managers to make sure they are always in compliance with state and local health ordinances.

Department of Transportation

The states' departments of transportation are responsible for a variety of areas that directly impact hospitality managers. Too often, regulators are viewed only as inspectors rather than allies. This should not be the case. Consider the situation of a restaurant owner who operates a facility on a busy street in a midsized town. The street itself is maintained by the state highway department. During lunchtime, the restaurant's guests have a hard time turning into the restaurant parking lot from the opposite side of the street because traffic is so heavy that there are few breaks in the traffic stream. The speed limit on the street is relatively high, so the crossing can be dangerous. This manager should approach the state department of transportation with the problem in an effort to fashion a solution. It may well be that traffic patterns are so heavy that a reduced speed limit or even a turn lane could be justified. Typically, departments of transportation are also responsible for regulating driveways, exits and approaches, and traffic signage, including billboards on highways.

2.3 Local Regulatory and Administrative Agencies

Much of the regulatory process you will face as a hospitality manager will take place at the local level. This is a positive situation because it allows local inspectors to personally get to know both you and your facility.

Health and Sanitation

Often, the health and sanitation department is responsible for the local inspection and licensing of facilities that serve food and beverages. Local inspectors may check for compliance with state health and sanitation codes, as well as municipal ordinances. Additional duties may include the mandatory certification of foodservice workers and managers, issuing and revoking licenses, establishing standards for restroom facilities, and certifying a safe water supply.

Building and Zoning

Building and zoning departments issue building permits and inspect the building prior to, during, and after any construction. They regulate both new building construction and additions or renovations. Standards for lighting, ventilation, restrooms, elevators, and public corridors and entryways may be established by state or local agencies. (In addition, your insurance company may have its own requirements for lighting levels and ventilation systems.) Local zoning ordinances may also regulate outside land use, such as parking spaces and permits for sidewalk or patio dining. Local inspectors will make sure that facilities are in compliance with all state and local building codes, including laws that require disability accessibility.

In addition, these departments often regulate the type of businesses that can be located in specified areas. This regulation is called zoning, and though this process can be contentious, it is generally accepted as necessary for the greater good of communities. Most hospitality professionals would agree, for example, that a bar or nightclub should not be operated in a building adjacent to a school or house of worship.

Zoning officials regulate land use in ways that can benefit hospitality managers, for example, by prohibiting negative businesses from locating next to land reserved for restaurants, hotels, and other commercial use. Imagine your concern, for example, if you were to learn that a private landfill operator had just purchased the vacant lot next to your four-star restaurant and was to begin accepting deposits in 30 days!

In addition to their role in regulating the placement and construction of businesses, local building and zoning officials are typically responsible for the construction and placement of signs outside a business. The regulations controlling the size of, number of, and construction materials required for signs can be quite extensive. Figure 2.8 shown on the next page is an example of a local sign ordinance that you might encounter as a hospitality manager. Note, in particular, the specificity of information required by the business prior to the granting of a sign permit.

Inspectors randomly visit businesses to ensure compliance with building and safety codes. Violators can be fined, and if guests or employees injure themselves as a result of a violation, it may result in a lawsuit.

Courts and Garnishment

In most communities, some agency of the court, sometimes called a "friend" of the court, will have the responsibility of assisting creditors in securing payment for legally owed debts. These debts can include a variety of court-ordered payments, such as child support payments. In cases like these, a hospitality manager may be ordered by the court to **garnish** an employee's wages.

LEGALESE

Garnish: A court-ordered method of debt collection in which a portion of a person's salary is paid to a creditor.

Sign Permits, Delta Township

The provisions of this chapter shall be administered by the township building official who shall have the authority to issue sign permits, without which it shall be unlawful to erect or replace any sign, whether free-standing, or mounted on, applied to or painted on a building or other structure.

Sign permits required. No person shall erect, place, structurally alter, or add to any sign without first obtaining a permit to do so in the manner hereinafter provided.

Application procedure. Application for a permit to erect, place, structurally alter or add to a sign shall be made to the township building official, by submission of the required forms, fees, exhibits and information by the owner of the property on which the sign is to be located, or by his agent or lessee. The application shall contain the following information:

1. The property owner's name and address.
2. The applicant's name and address
3. Address and permanent parcel number of the property on which the sign is or will be located
4. Identification of the type of sign (ground, pole, wall, etc.)
5. Name of business or name of premises to which the sign belongs or relates
6. Plans drawn to an accurate, common scale, depicting the following:
7. Dimensions and display area of the proposed sign, based on the definition of display area contained in this chapter
8. For ground signs and pole signs, the setback of the sign from the nearest public or private road right-of-way
9. For ground signs and pole signs, the height of the sign
10. For wall signs, the height and width of the building wall or tenant-controlled portion of building wall to which the sign will be attached.
11. The proposed graphic images and text to be displayed on the sign.

Scope. Sign permits issued on the basis of plans and other information submitted as part of the permit application authorize only the design and construction set forth and described in the permit application, and no other design or construction.

FIGURE 2.8 **Sign permit ordinance.**

Historical Preservation

In some communities, historical buildings, their use, and renovation may be regulated by an agency charged with historical preservation. If you manage a hospitality facility in a historic building, city zone, or community, you might face regulation from the governmental entity charged with preserving the historical integrity of your facility. This might limit the types of alterations or improvements you may make to your facility or require you to maintain your property in a manner that is consistent with the historical nature of the area.

Fire Department

The local fire department is a critical part of the safety net that hospitality managers offer their guests. Whether it is for a hotel or restaurant, dependable fire safety departments can assist a manager in limiting potential liability through careful adherence to all local fire codes and procedures. Fire departments will normally conduct routine facility inspections, assist local building departments in reviewing plans for new or renovated buildings, ensure that emergency lighting and sprinklers are installed and maintained properly, and offer fire safety training for managers and employees. As a hospitality manager, it is important to know your local fire codes and to make sure that your operation always includes the required number of fire extinguishers, smoke detectors, sprinklers, fans and ventilation ducts, emergency lights, and emergency exit signs. This equipment should be tested periodically to make sure that it is in good working order. The National Fire Protection Association (www.nfpa.org) has established national standards for ventilation systems and automatic fire protection systems in commercial kitchens. Insurance companies also have regulations that will determine the type and amount of fire protection equipment you will need for your operation.

Another important role of the fire department is to regulate the number of individuals who are allowed in a particular space at a given time. For example, it would be the fire department that would determine the maximum number of patrons who could be in a hotel ballroom at one time. The capacity of bars, nightclubs, dining rooms, and sleeping rooms are all examples of areas regulated by the local fire department. You have probably noticed signs that indicate the maximum number of people who can safely be in a public space. Often, local laws require these signs to be prominently displayed. It is up to the hospitality manager to liaison with the local fire department to find out the appropriate regulations.

Law Enforcement

Although local police do not generally serve a regulatory role for business, some communities do have local laws or codes that are enforced by the police department in a city or by the sheriff's department in a more rural community. As we have seen, liquor laws, for example, are sometimes enforced by the local police. Other areas of interaction may be parking enforcement, ongoing scams in the area or community, and the removal of disorderly guests.

Tax Assessor/Collector

Local municipalities obtain a significant portion of their tax revenues from businesses. These taxes may be levied on the basis of property value, sales revenue, or a combination of both. The tax assessor or collector is responsible for the prompt collection and recording of these taxes.

Increasingly, communities are looking to the hospitality industry as a vehicle for raising tax revenue. One such source of tax revenue is the local occupancy, or bed, tax. Essentially, the occupancy tax is a tax on the sale of hotel rooms. It typically will range from 1 to 15 percent of gross room revenue. This tax may be assessed at the state level, local level, or both. In any case, there are typically few waivers for the tax, and its collection is aggressively enforced by the taxing entity.

2.4 Regulatory Interaction and Oversight Impacting Travel and Tourism

The travel industry is heavily regulated, and because it is so large and diverse, the number of groups and organizations responsible for the legal oversight of travel activities is considerable. From the perspective of the hospitality manager, some of the most significant of these include governmental agencies, both at the federal and state levels, and nongovernmental groups that operate internationally to coordinate travel policies, which are discussed later in this section.

U.S. Government Agencies

You have been introduced to federal agencies that have responsibility for regulation and oversight in the hospitality industry. In the following subsections, you will learn about other federal agencies involved in regulation and policy development for the travel industry. The list is long and represents the most significant of the federal groups responsible for monitoring travel activities, but it is not exhaustive. In fact, travel-related activities impact nearly every federal agency. The agencies and departments identified here will, however, give some indication of the many ways in which travel professionals interact with the federal government in the course of their managerial duties. In addition to federal monitoring and control, states, counties, and local governments may all have agencies, departments, and code enforcement professionals that combine to provide additional regulatory oversight.

Federal Trade Commission (FTC) The Federal Trade Commission (www.ftc.gov) is charged with ensuring that the nation's markets are free of restrictions that could potentially harm consumers. In addition, it works to ensure that competition among firms is fair and results in the availability of lower prices and better goods and services. A further role of the FTC is the dissemination of information that consumers can use to make better purchase decisions. To ensure the smooth operation of the free market system, the FTC enforces federal consumer protection laws that prevent fraud, deception, and unfair business practices. The commission also enforces federal antitrust laws that prohibit anticompetitive mergers and other business practices that restrict competition and could harm consumers.

With regard to the travel industry, the FTC has increasingly devoted its attention to protecting consumers by investigating false, misleading, or deceptive advertising, telemarketing fraud, and Internet scams. Although the FTC does not seek to resolve individual consumer problems, it does use information from individual complaints to investigate fraud and initiate law enforcement actions. The FTC also shares information by entering Internet, telemarketing, identity theft, do-not-call registry violations, sweepstakes, lotteries, prizes, and other fraud-related complaints into the Consumer Sentinel, an online cyber-tool database available for use by civil and criminal law enforcement agencies worldwide.

Search the Web 2.2

One of the most popular services offered by the CDC is its online "Travelers' Health" information. It seeks to inform travelers about the health risks they may encounter when traveling in various parts of the world. To view a sample of the information provided, go to **www.cdc.gov/travel**. Under the "Destinations" tab, select a region to find out about the health risks you might encounter in an area of the world you would someday like to visit.

Centers for Disease Control and Prevention (CDC) The Centers for Disease Control and Prevention (CDC) (www.cdc.gov) is the major federal agency operating to protect the health and safety of individuals at home and abroad as well as to provide information to enhance health decisions. The CDC, located in Atlanta, Georgia, is an agency of the Federal Department of Health and Human Services. Its official mission is to keep Americans safe and healthy where they work, live, and play.

Becoming seriously ill or having a major accident while traveling, especially in a country where the traveler does not

Analyze the Situation 2.3

An elderly couple from Canada, traveling in Central/South America, goes on a shopping trip to a local produce market, where the couple buys and consumes some locally grown fruit. Upon returning that evening to the international hotel in the area, which you manage, the husband falls ill and his wife calls your front desk seeking assistance.

1. What is the likely cause of the man's illness?
2. Based on what you know about reasonable care for guests, what action would you expect your management team to take relative to the man's illness?
3. What would your position be if your hotel was later sued by the couple, claiming you had failed to warn them of local health risks?

speak the local language, is one of many tourists' greatest fears. Travelers may also face health risks of which they are unaware because they simply do not know about travel-related threats to their health and safety in places they have not previously visited, such as Ebola, Legionnaires' Disease, and the Zika virus. In many cases, some of these threats could be avoided or minimized if the traveler were aware of them. The CDC makes available, on a region-by-region basis, information about health and safety risks for travelers worldwide. In addition, this information includes recommendations for addressing or minimizing these travel-related threats to health and safety.

Department of Commerce

The U.S. Department of Commerce (www.commerce.gov) is dedicated to the improvement of business, including tourism. It houses the Census Bureau (www.census.gov), which collects economic data on the hotel and restaurant industries, as well as other service businesses. It also houses the National Travel & Tourism Office (www.tinet.ita.doc.gov), which was established by the National Tourism Policy Act of 1981. This agency gathers statistics on travel activity and promotes tourism. In February 25, 2010, the Travel and Promotion Act of 2009 was created and established the Office of Travel Promotion within the Department of Commerce. It encourages the growth of domestic and international travel. On February 20, 2003, the Omnibus Appropriation Act for FY 2003 became law. Included in this appropriation was Section 210, which authorized the U.S. Department of Commerce to award grants and make lump-sum payments in support of an international advertising and promotional campaign to encourage individuals to travel to the United States. The Department of Commerce is advised by its Travel and Tourism Promotion Advisory Board, which includes some of the travel industry's most notable businesspeople.

Search the Web 2.3

The National Park Service is in the tourism business. To view its website, where visitors can book tours, go to **www.nps.gov/findapark/index.htm**.

It is also possible to find information about national parks and nearby communities at **www.nationalparkreservations.com**.

Department of the Interior (DOI)

In 1849, Congress passed a bill to create the Department of the Interior (www.doi.gov). Over the course of its history, the DOI has played a changing role in its mission of managing the country's internal affairs. As a result, it has had, at various times, responsibility for the construction of the national capital's water system, the colonization of freed slaves in Haiti, exploration of the western wilderness, oversight of the District of Columbia jail, regulation of territorial governments, management of hospitals and universities, management of public parks, and the basic responsibilities for Native Americans, public lands, patents, and pensions. In one way or another, all of these roles had to do with the internal development of the nation or the welfare of Americans.

In 1916, President Woodrow Wilson signed legislation creating the National Park Service. The act assigned to the new bureau the 14 national parks and 21 national monuments then under the DOI and directed it "to conserve the scenery and the natural and historic objects and the wildlife therein and to provide for the enjoyment of the same in such manner and by such means as will leave them unimpaired for the enjoyment of future generations."[4] The national monuments, generally smaller than the parks, included prehistoric Native American ruins, geologic features, and other sites of natural and cultural significance reserved by presidential proclamations under the Antiquities Act of 1906. Today, this agency sets policy for the National Park Service, which includes some the country's most significant tourism destinations.

Search the Web 2.4

An important service provided by the Department of State is that of issuing travel advisories and warnings to Americans planning to travel outside the United States. Travelers can access these warnings at **https://travel.state.gov/content/passports/en/alertswarnings.html**.

Department of State

The executive branch and Congress have constitutional responsibilities for U.S. foreign policy. Within the executive branch, the Department of State is the

[4] National Park Service, "Organic Act of 1916," www.nps.gov/grba/parkmgmt/organic-act-of-1916.htm. Last accessed June 8, 2016.

The Department of State is updating the Worldwide Caution with information on the continuing threat of terrorist actions and violence against U.S. citizens and interests throughout the world. Current information suggests that ISIL, al-Qa'ida, Boko Haram, al-Shabaab, and other terrorist groups continue to plan terrorist attacks in multiple regions. Recent terrorist attacks, whether by those affiliated with terrorist entities, copycats, or individual perpetrators, serve as a reminder that U.S. citizens need to maintain a high level of vigilance and take appropriate steps to increase their security awareness. This replaces the Worldwide Caution dated July 29, 2015.

In August 2014, after the United States and regional partners commenced military action against ISIL, ISIL called on supporters to attack foreigners wherever they are. Authorities believe there is a continued likelihood of reprisal attacks against U.S., Western, and coalition partner interests throughout the world, especially in the Middle East, North Africa, Europe, and Asia.

U.S. citizens continue to be at risk of kidnappings and hostage events as ISIL, al-Qa'ida, and their affiliates attempt to finance their operations through kidnapping-for-ransom operations. U.S. citizens have been kidnapped and murdered by members of terrorist and violent extremist groups. ISIL, al-Qa'ida in the Arabian Peninsula (AQAP), and al-Qa'ida in the Islamic Maghreb (AQIM) are particularly effective with kidnapping for ransom and are using ransom money to fund their activities.

Extremists may use conventional or non-conventional weapons and target both official and private interests. Examples of such targets include high-profile sporting events, residential areas, business offices, hotels, clubs, restaurants, places of worship, schools, public areas, shopping malls, and other tourist destinations both in the United States and abroad where U.S. citizens gather in large numbers, including during holidays. In the past year, major extremist attacks occurred in countries including Tunisia, France, Nigeria, Turkey, Egypt, and Mali.

U.S. citizens are reminded of the potential for terrorists to attack public transportation systems and other tourist infrastructure. Extremists have targeted and attempted attacks on subway and rail systems, aviation, and maritime services.

U.S. citizens considering maritime travel also should review information at the websites of the National Geospatial Agency, the Maritime Administration, and the U.S. Coast Guard for information related to maritime and port security globally. Current areas of concern include the Caribbean, Gulf of Guinea, Horn of Africa, and the Straits of Malacca and Singapore as a result of maritime crimes including smuggling, human trafficking, and piracy.

FIGURE 2.9 U.S. State Department Travel Worldwide Caution.
Last updated March 3, 2016.

lead U.S. foreign affairs agency, and the secretary of state is the president's principal foreign policy adviser. The Department of State advances U.S. objectives and interests in shaping a safer and freer world through its primary role in developing and implementing the president's foreign policy. The State Department also supports the foreign affairs activities of other U.S. government entities, including the Department of Commerce. In addition, it provides a variety of important services to U.S. citizens traveling abroad, including the issuing of passports and providing travel warnings. Figure 2.9 is an example of the type of warning developed by the Department of State and is available to those traveling internationally.

Department of Homeland Security (DHS)

In the months following the terrorist attacks against America on September 11, 2001, 22 previously separate domestic agencies were merged into one department to protect the nation against terrorist threats. This merger created the Department of Homeland Security (DHS) (www.dhs.gov). It has a sixfold agenda:[5]

1. Increase overall preparedness, particularly for catastrophic events.
2. Create better transportation security systems to move people and cargo more securely and efficiently.
3. Strengthen border security and interior enforcement and reform immigration processes.
4. Enhance information sharing with our partners.
5. Improve DHS financial management, human resource development, procurement, and information technology.
6. Realign the DHS organization to maximize mission performance.

More specifically, the department is composed of these divisions:[6]

National Protection and Programs Directorate works to advance the Department's risk-reduction mission. Reducing risk requires an integrated approach that encompasses both physical and virtual threats and their associated human elements.

Science and Technology Directorate is the primary research and development arm of DHS. It provides federal, state, and local officials with the technology and capabilities to protect the homeland.

Directorate for Management is responsible for budget, appropriations, expenditure of funds, accounting and finance; procurement, human resources and personnel, information technology systems, facilities, property and

[5] Homeland Security, "Department Six-point Agenda,"2011. https://www.dhs.gov/department-six-point-agenda (Last Accessed June 8. 2016).

[6] Homeland Security, "Department Subcomponents and Agencies," www.dhs.gov/xabout/structure/ (Last modified on May 31, 2011. Accessed July 5, 2011).

equipment, other material resources, and the identification and tracking of performance measurements relating to the responsibilities of the Department.

Office of Policy serves as the department's principal source of thought leadership, policy development, and decision analysis for DHS senior leadership, secretarial initiatives, and other critical matters that may arise in a dynamic threat environment.

Office of Health Affairs provides medical, public health, and scientific expertise in support of the department of Homeland Security's mission to prepare for, respond to, and recover from all threats.

Office of Intelligence and Analysis equips the Homeland Security Enterprise with the timely intelligence and information it needs to keep the homeland safe, secure, and resilient.

Office of Operations Coordination is responsible for monitoring the security of the United States on a daily basis and coordinating activities within the department and with governors, Homeland Security advisers, law enforcement partners, and critical infrastructure operators in all 50 states and more than 50 major urban areas nationwide.

Federal Law Enforcement Training Center (FLETC) provides career-long training to law enforcement professionals to help them fulfill their responsibilities safely and proficiently.

Domestic Nuclear Detection Office works to ensure a coordinated response to nuclear threats and prevent nuclear terrorism by continuously improving capabilities to deter, detect, respond to, and attribute attacks in coordination with domestic and international partners.

Transportation Security Administration (TSA) protects the nation's transportation systems to ensure freedom of movement for people and commerce.

U.S. Customs and Border Protection (CBP) is one of the largest and most complex components of the Department of Homeland Security with a priority mission of keeping terrorists and their weapons out of the United States. It also has a responsibility for securing and facilitating trade and travel while enforcing hundreds of U.S. regulations, including immigration and drug laws.

U.S. Citizenship and Immigration Services (USCIS) secures America's promise as a nation of immigrants by providing accurate and useful information to our customers, granting immigration and citizenship benefits, promoting an awareness and understanding of citizenship, and ensuring the integrity of our immigration system.

U.S. Immigration and Customs Enforcement (ICE) promotes homeland security and public safety through the criminal and civil enforcement of federal laws governing border control, customs, trade, and immigration.

U.S. Coast Guard is one of the five armed forces of the United States and the only military organization within the Department of Homeland Security. The Coast Guard protects the maritime economy and the environment, defends our maritime borders, and saves those in peril.

Federal Emergency Management Agency (FEMA) supports our citizens and first responders to ensure that as a nation we work together to build, sustain, and improve our capability to prepare for, protect against, respond to, recover from, and mitigate all hazards.

U.S. Secret Service (USSS) safeguards the nation's financial infrastructure and payment systems to preserve the integrity of the economy and protects national leaders, visiting heads of state and government, designated sites, and National Special Security Events.

The policies put in place by the DHS now and in the future will have a significant impact on the way Americans travel, as well as how America receives travelers.

Treasury Department The U.S. Treasury Department (www.treasury.gov) is entrusted with a variety of duties and functions. In addition to collecting taxes and managing currency production and circulation, this department oversees functions in law enforcement, economic policy development, and international treaty negotiation. Travelers are affected by the department's participation in negotiations to reduce barriers to international trade and finance by working through the World Trade Organization (UNWTO) (www.wto.org), the Organization for Economic Cooperation and Development (www.oecd.org), and other international trade negotiating teams. In addition, it houses the Office of Foreign Assets Control (OFAC), which administers and enforces economic and trade sanctions, including travel bans, based on U.S. foreign policy and national security goals against targeted foreign countries, terrorists, international narcotics traffickers, and those engaged in activities related to the proliferation of weapons of mass destruction.

Department of Transportation (DOT) Congress established the Department of Transportation in 1966, and its first day of operation was April 1, 1967 (www.transportation.gov). Its mission is to serve the United States by ensuring a fast, safe, efficient, accessible, and convenient transportation system that meets our vital national interests and enhances the quality of life of the American people today and into the future. The DOT consists of several individual operating administrations:

1. Federal Aviation Administration
2. Federal Highway Administration
3. Federal Railroad Administration
4. National Highway Traffic Safety Administration
5. Federal Motor Carrier Safety Administration
6. Federal Transit Administration
7. Maritime Administration
8. Saint Lawrence Seaway Development Corporation
9. Office of the Secretary of Transportation
10. Pipeline and Hazardous Materials Safety Administration

Analyze the Situation 2.4

Ted Flood had a reservation at the Sleep Right hotel for the night of October 15. According to the reservation policy explained to Mr. Flood at the time he reserved the room from Sleep Right's national reservation system, the nonguaranteed reservation was to be held until 4:00 P.M. the afternoon of Mr. Flood's arrival.

Unfortunately, Mr. Flood's flight to the city where the Sleep Right was located was delayed because the plane had to spend four hours on the airport runway because of mechanical difficulties. Mr. Flood was unable to contact the hotel and, as a result, his room was released by the hotel at 4:30 P.M. and sold to another guest at 5:00 P.M. Consequently, the hotel had no rooms available when Mr. Flood, tired and frustrated, arrived at the front desk at 8:00 P.M.

1. What could Mr Flood have done to avoid his difficulty?
2. What responsibility, if any, does the hotel now have to Mr. Flood?
3. What role did the FAA likely play in this situation?

Tourism Policy Council (TPC) As is clear by now, there are many federal agencies whose policymaking affects travel in the United States. The TPC is an interagency, policy-coordinating committee composed of the leaders of nine federal agencies and the president of the U.S. National Tourism Organization (USNTO). The TPC members work cooperatively to ensure that the national interest in tourism is fully considered in federal decisions that affect tourism development. The TPC also coordinates national policies and programs relating to international travel and tourism, recreation, and national heritage resources that involve federal agencies. The council works with the private sector and state and local governments on issues and problems that require federal involvement.

International Organizations

The United States is not, of course, the only government interested in promoting safe travel for its citizens, for many countries count on tourism for significant financial contributions to their economies; hence, they, too, are concerned with traveler safety. That means that there are a large number of international groups and organizations whose goal is to improve and promote the travel industry worldwide. The result is the creation of travel procedures, policies, and agreements. The following three organizations direct or control some of the most important of these international cooperative efforts.

World Tourism Organization (UNWTO) The World Tourism Organization is the leading international organization in the field of travel and tourism. It serves as a global forum for tourism policy issues and as a practical source of tourism know-how and statistics. Its membership includes 157 countries, 6 associate members, and over 480 affiliate members representing the private sector, educational institutions, tourism associations, and local tourism authorities.

The UNWTO promotes tourism as a driver of economic growth, inclusive development, and environmental sustainability and offers leadership and support to the travel and tourism sector in advancing knowledge and tourism policies worldwide.

International Civil Aviation Organization (ICAO) The International Civil Aviation Organization is one of the least known but most important of the many international groups that affect travel policy and procedure. Established in 1944, this UN specialized agency works with 191 member states and industry groups to reach an agreement on international civil aviation standards and recommend practices to support a safe, efficient, secure, economically sustainable, and environmentally responsible civil aviation sector.

World Health Organization (WHO) The World Health Organization, the UN's specialized agency for health, was established in 1948. The objective of WHO is the attainment

Analyze the Situation 2.5

Sharon Alexander operated The Texas Saloon, a steakhouse restaurant that also served beer and wine. Its average menu item sold for $10. Employees were allowed to eat one meal during their shift. For those who voluntarily elected to eat this meal, Ms. Alexander would deduct $0.25 per hour ($2 per eight-hour shift) from the federal minimum wage rate she paid her entry-level dishwashers, which reflected the reasonable cost of the meal.

Ms. Alexander relied on the Fair Labor Standards Act (FLSA) Section 3(m), which states that employers can consider, as wages, "reasonable costs . . . to the employer of furnishing such employees with board, lodging, or other facilities if such boards, lodging, or other facilities are customarily furnished by such employer to his [or her] employees." She interpreted this regulation to mean that she could pay the entry-level dishwashers a rate that, when added to the $0.25 per hour meal deduction, equaled the federal minimum wage.

One day, Ms. Alexander was contacted by her state department of employment, which charged that she was in violation of the state minimum wage law. The law stated that "total voluntary deductions for meals and uniforms may not decrease an employee's wages below the federal minimum wage on an hourly basis." Ms. Alexander maintained that because she was in compliance with the federal law, she was allowed to take the meal credit against the wages paid to her entry-level dishwashers.

1. Is Ms. Alexander in compliance with the compensation laws of her state?
2. Do federal laws, in this case, take precedent over state law?

by all peoples of the highest possible level of health. "Health" is defined by WHO as a state of complete physical, mental, and social well-being—not merely the absence of disease or infirmity. International travelers are affected by the work of WHO, especially when visiting nations challenged to provide their own citizens and thus visitors with the basic components of healthy food and water supplies.

2.5 Managing Conflicting Regulations

Given the large number of legislative bodies daily creating new policies, there are surprisingly few instances where regulations are in direct conflict. As a rule, local legislators and public officials will review state guidelines prior to implementing new regulations, just as state regulators will review federal guidelines. In fact, where there are agencies at each governmental level, the federal agency may create model regulations that will then be adopted in whole or in part at the state level, just as the state may take the role of creating model regulations for possible use at the local level.

Consider the case of A. J. Patel. Mr. Patel is the regional manager for a hotel company that operates properties that provide a free continental breakfast to all registered guests. His properties operate in three different states. Mr. Patel must be familiar with the public health codes of three different state and local governments, which means that he must stay abreast of the changing health code regulations of all six entities. His task has been made easier, however, because the federal Food and Drug Administration (FDA) created the Model Food Service Sanitation Ordinance, which is followed, with varying degrees of specificity, by many state and local communities.

There will be times when the requirements placed on a hospitality manager will be in conflict with one another. For example, a federal requirement may conflict with a local one. Although this can sometimes be frustrating, it is important to know what you, as a manager, should do in such a situation.

A conflict between regulatory restrictions occurs when one entity sets a standard higher or lower than another. If, for example, a local sanitation code requires all shelving in a kitchen to be 12 inches above the floor, yet the state code allows shelving to be within 6 inches of the floor, the more restrictive regulation will prevail. This is true because, in this case, a shelf 12 inches above the floor satisfies both regulatory bodies. The principle to remember is this: When regulatory demands conflict, the "most restrictive" regulation should be followed.

In some cases, a regulatory agency will influence a hospitality manager's operation in an indirect, but intentional, manner. One example is the Hotel and Motel Fire Safety Act of 1990. The federal government enacted this law because it was hesitant to require many older hotels to incur the expense of adding in-room sprinkler systems to their rooms, yet it still wanted to influence the safety of the traveling public.

The Hotel and Motel Fire Safety Act of 1990 aims to increase the level of fire safety in hotels and motels by discouraging federally funded travel to hotels and motels that do not meet certain minimum fire protection standards. These standards require the installation of automatic sprinkler systems in hotels and motels over three stories in height, and the installation of hard-wired (not battery-operated) smoke detectors in every room of each and every hotel and motel.

In general, the act prohibits federal funding of a meeting, conference, convention, or training seminar that is conducted in a place of public accommodation that does not meet the fire safety requirements of the act. Under the act, states are responsible for submitting data to the U.S. Fire Administration regarding which hotels and motels meet those specified standards. Note that, in this case, the regulatory body, Congress, did

Legally Managing at Work

Recommended Steps for Responding to Inquiries and Complaints by Government Agencies

1. Upon notification of a complaint or violation, you or your clerical staff document the date and time that all paperwork was received, and are sure to check correspondence for required deadlines.

   Upon receipt of correspondence from a government agency, the first thing that you or your clerical staff must do is to note on the correspondence itself the date that it was received. This can be done manually but preferably with a small mechanical stamping device. Be sure that you include the day, month, and year of receipt. This is important because many governmental agencies require you to respond within a certain number of days from the date you received the correspondence.

   As you read the correspondence, be on the lookout for the due dates of responses. Some due dates are measured from the date of receipt; other due dates are measured from the date mailed. For instance, a letter might state, "If you do not respond within 10 days of your receipt of this correspondence, then we will assume that the claimant's position is true and act accordingly." This is known as an automatic default provision. It is imperative that if you intend to respond, you do so within the time frame specified in the correspondence. There is rarely a remedy to missing a deadline for an initial response.

2. Assess the severity of the complaint. Determine if legal consultation is necessary.

As you read the correspondence, you will need to decide if legal counsel should be consulted in order to deal with the complaint raised in the correspondence. Additionally, you will need to decide if the issue raised needs to be referred to your insurance carrier. It may be a good idea to scan and email or fax the correspondence to your insurance agent to get his or her opinion as to whether or not there might be coverage for the particular concern raised.

In the event you do forward this matter to your insurance carrier and the carrier determines that you are covered, ordinarily as part of your coverage, the carrier will provide an attorney to defend the claim. If the carrier denies you coverage, you will need to hire your own counsel. In the event that this occurs or in the event that you determine on your own that you need legal counsel when dealing with a government agency, you may want to consult with, or retain, an administrative law specialist, an attorney who devotes a significant part of his or her practice to handling complaints for alleged violations of government regulations and/or prosecutions by the government.

3. Develop a plan of action.

How you as a manager should respond to a complaint or violation will vary based on whether you have determined that legal assistance is needed.

Without an Attorney

- Calendar all response dates, and be sure to allow yourself enough time for mailing.
- Identify all the people who need to be involved in the response, and contact them in a timely fashion to solicit their input.
- Always keep clear, legible copies of anything that you forward as a response to a complaint. In any response that you give, if it is not true or you cannot prove it, do not state it in your response.
- Follow the instructions on the correspondence exactly. If it says that you have only one page to respond, then use only one page. If it says that the response must be typed, then make sure it is typed. If your response needs to be signed and a notary public must notarize your signature, be absolutely certain that it gets done, and make sure that the copies that you keep are copies of the responses after you have signed them and had them notarized.

With an Attorney

- Forward the correspondence immediately to your attorney, together with any supporting documentation that the attorney might need to understand the situation completely. Also, include a list of people who might have knowledge of the situation raised in the correspondence. It is a good idea to include contact information for the attorney. You want to facilitate communication between the attorney and any witnesses who can help present a positive response on your behalf.
- Stay in direct communication with your attorney until the matter is resolved. Just because you have given it to an attorney does not mean it is off of your plate. It is still crucial that you keep up with time deadlines and potential witnesses. For instance, if you know that certain people are going on vacation or you yourself are going on vacation, let the attorney know so that he or she can plan accordingly in the event he or she needs statements of additional information from you or the witnesses.

not implement a restriction on operating hotels without sprinkler systems; it simply prohibited funding, by the federal government, of any travel to such a hotel. It is worthy to note that a portion of the law was repealed in 1996 that required federal employees to stay in fire safe hotel rooms by eliminating the General Accounting Office's responsibility to ensure that all federal agencies complied with the law, but the general policy still states that travelers must give first consideration to hotels that include these fire safety requirements.

2.6 Responding to an Inquiry

Despite the best efforts of management, it is not uncommon for a facility to be found in violation of a regulation. Consider the case of Gerry Monteagudo. He has, for many years, heavily decorated the lobby and public areas of his hotel during the Christmas season. This year, shortly after the decorations had been put in place, Mr. Monteagudo received a letter from the local fire chief citing the hotel for three violations of the local fire code. An inspector noticed that some of the holiday lights were illuminated via the use of extension cords. These extension cords are not allowed, by ordinance, in the township where Mr. Monteagudo operates the hotel. In this case, the problem could be quickly rectified by replacing the extension cords with surge protector cords that are allowed by the local ordinance.

At the other extreme, consider the case of the hospitality manager who is notified that the IRS will be conducting an audit of tip-reporting compliance in her facility. The IRS auditors plan to trace the last three years of tips to all employees and verify that the required employment taxes were paid on those tips. The manager, in assembling three years of paperwork, discovers that not all taxes were paid during the first year, before she had assumed management of the facility. A penalty may still be assessed.

As can be seen, some regulatory violations can be very serious. Because that is true, it is a good idea to follow a standard set of procedures anytime a governmental agency raises the question of regulatory noncompliance. Comply with the governmental agencies' requests, but limit the information to what is being requested.

As a manager, you should never willingly violate a legitimate regulation. In most cases, noncompliance is unintentional, and the governmental agency has, as its responsibility, the duty to inform management of violations. Because many of these agencies can have a significant effect on the facility and, in some cases the manager personally, it is best to respond quickly and professionally to any charge of noncompliance.

2.7 Monitoring Regulatory Change

It is simply not possible to know every governmental regulation that could affect the hospitality industry, and some laws change on a regular basis. Although changes in major federal law are rather well publicized, you cannot be sure that the policies of all federal agencies, state regulators, and local governments will be made known to you. Sources such as www.HospitalityLawyer.com and your local trade association can be very helpful in keeping you current. Reading about the hospitality industry will not only make you a better manager but will also enable you to keep up with changing regulations.

For those managers employed by a national chain or management company, the parent company can be an excellent source of information on changing regulations. Indeed, one valuable service provided by franchisors to franchisees is regular updates on regulatory agencies and their work.

Because the federal government can play such a major role in regulating the hospitality industry, it is important to have current and rapid access to the actions taken by each of the federal regulatory agencies. Accessing the website addresses provided in each section of this book is a good way to keep up-to-date on any changes in the law in that particular area.

As a hospitality manager, it is important to stay involved in the hospitality trade association that most closely represents your industry segment. The National Restaurant Association (NRA), the American Hotel and Lodging Association (AH&LA), and others regularly provide their memberships with legislative updates and have lobbying efforts designed to protect the interests of owners and operators. Many of these organizations have state, regional, or local chapters that can be invaluable sources of information.

On a local level, chambers of commerce, business trade associations, and personal relationships with local police, fire, and building officials can help a manager stay up-to-date with municipal changes.

As a hospitality manager, it is critical that you take an active role in shaping the regulations that affect the industry. Governments, on the whole, attempt to pass regulations that they believe are in the best interests of the communities they represent. The problem arises, however, when the cost in dollars or the infringement on individual rights will far exceed the societal value of implementing a proposed regulation. For example, some consumers feel that it would be a good idea to have 24-hour video surveillance cameras placed in hotel corridors, even if the cost of installing them resulted in higher room rates. Such a camera might be a deterrent to crime and would make them feel safer; however, other guests object to the cameras as an invasion of their privacy. Hotel managers caught in the middle agree that the safety of their guests is a major concern, but they also know that there are less intrusive ways to make people feel safe while respecting their privacy. Without input from the hospitality industry, however, regulators may not be aware of those alternatives and could pass a law that is ultimately not in the best interests of the hotel guest, the lodging industry, or society.

It is only by staying aware of regulatory changes and being committed to proactive participation in the regulatory process through education and leadership that the hospitality industry will continue to flourish.

International Snapshot

Immigration

Globalization of the world's economy and labor markets continues to impact companies in the United States and worldwide. Employers need to be aware of immigration and security issues because they affect the hiring needs of a global workforce. For the hospitality industry, employers are challenged by complicated immigration and compliance laws and regulations. Hospitality companies must fill critical staffing positions at all levels, from management to specialty-skilled workers, and at the same time remain compliant in this labor-intensive and growing industry.

Throughout the world, companies hiring noncitizens must be familiar with the immigration laws of any given country, as each country typically will require sponsorship of a work permit and a certain level of responsibility from the local employer. However, there is the advantage for European Union (EU) countries, which recognize work authorization for nationals from other EU countries. Most countries have common types of work authorization permits that affect highly skilled professionals, entrepreneurs, investors, managers/executives, and corporate-level international transferees. While these work permits are limited and temporary in nature, many countries allow permanent residence after certain criteria, including lawful residence in that country for a specific period of time, are met.

The U.S. immigration system, like many other countries, is based on the admission of immigrants under different categories and limited by eligibility standards and quotas. The two main immigration categories include family-based immigration and employment-based immigration with many different types of work visa options, especially for those with skills that are valuable to the U.S. economy. The remaining categories of immigration include refugee/asylum status, a diversity visa program, and certain forms of humanitarian relief including Temporary Protected Status (TPS).

Employment—Temporary Visas

Under the employment-based immigration category, there are more than 20 types of visas for temporary or nonimmigrant workers. These visas are specific to the employer/sponsor and are limited to a defined

(continued)

period of time, a work location and specific job responsibilities. The U.S. Citizenship and Immigration Services (formerly known as INS) decides whether to approve nonimmigrant and immigrant petitions.

One of the most common visa categories is H-1B, which is for specialty-occupation positions that require at least a bachelor's degree. H-1Bs are subject to a statutory numerical limit each year of 85,000 visa numbers, and cases are selected under a "lottery system." For companies that need short-term or seasonal workers (such as the hospitality industry), the H-2B visas are available for lesser-skilled employees for companies that can demonstrate the unavailability of U.S. workers through a labor market test. H-2Bs are also subject to a "cap" of 66,000 per year with 33,000 for workers for the first half of the year and 33,000 for the second half of the year.

The L-1 intracompany transferee visa is popular for multinational companies to transfer employees from one of its affiliated foreign offices to one of its U.S. offices. These employees must have worked at least one year out of the past three years at an affiliated office abroad either as "managers/executives" or "specialized-knowledge" employees. Many large hotel chains utilize the L-1 category, and under certain circumstances, very large companies have an "L-1 blanket petition program" to prequalify and establish the required intracompany relationship for its worldwide entities for easier transfer of its L-1 employees.

Other visas include the TN classification for citizens of Canada and Mexico for certain professional positions under the North American Free Trade Agreement (NAFTA) and the O-1 visa category for individuals with extraordinary ability in science, arts, education, business, or athletics who have been recognized nationally or internationally for their achievements. Hospitality groups and restaurants have often utilized the O-1 for a special niche of essential culinary artists including executive chefs, sous and pastry chefs, sommeliers, and even mixologists.

Permanent Immigration

The Immigration and Nationality Act (INA) governs current U.S. immigration policy and provides for an annual worldwide limit of 675,000 permanent immigrants. Under the family-based immigration category, there are 480,000 family-based visas available each year, subject to a "family preference system" broken down by different levels depending on the family relationship to a U.S. citizen or lawful permanent resident sponsoring that family member including certain age and financial requirements.

For employment-based permanent immigration, the limit is set at 140,000 visas per year, divided into five preferences, each of which is subject to numerical limitations and per country ceilings. Most permanent residence cases require the employer to prove there are no qualified U.S. workers willing and able to fill the position through a testing of the labor market, called a "labor certification." Some exceptions are made for advanced or extraordinary individuals that allow them to skip the labor certification process to obtain permanent resident status or what is more commonly known as "green card" status.

I-9 Compliance

The Immigration Reform and Control Act (IRCA) was passed in 1986 and addressed concerns of illegal immigration and employment, making it illegal for U.S. companies to knowingly hire or continue to employ persons who are unauthorized to work in the U.S. and requiring employers to check identity and employment eligibility for all new hires with review of original documents and the completion of the Form I-9. Failure to comply may result in both civil and criminal liability with substantial fines currently ranging from $110–$1100 per employee, as well as possible imprisonment for a pattern or practice of noncompliance. In addition, IRCA prohibits discrimination on the basis of immigration status in hiring, firing, and recruitment of individuals. The Department of Homeland Security (DHS) and specifically the Immigration and Customs Enforcement (ICE) is responsible for I-9 compliance enforcement, and the Office of Special Counsel (OSC), located within the Civil Rights Division of the Department of Justice is responsible for enforcement of the antidiscrimination provisions. Audits and worksite investigations of U.S. companies' I-9 compliance have increased significantly under the Obama administration, targeting employers who hire unauthorized workers.

Provided by Sarah J Hawk of Ogletree and Deakins Law Firm, Atlanta, Georgia and Raleigh, North Carolina. www.ogletreedeakins.com.

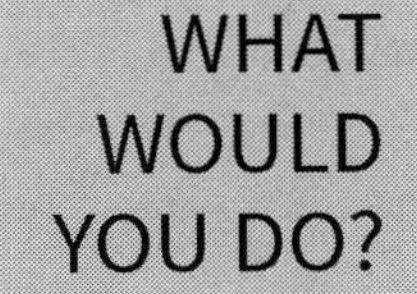

After the highly publicized death of a college student, a local sports bar in your town lost its liquor license for 60 days. The student had consumed 21 shots of alcohol on his birthday and later died in his dorm room from alcohol poisoning. The bar was crowded and because the shots had been purchased by a variety of friends of the victim, the bar manager and staff were not aware of the impending problem. Subsequently, the college's student newspaper published editorials warning against the perils of binge drinking and accused the management of the facility of negligence or indifference.

Sorrow in the community and outrage in the local press prompted the mayor of the city in which you operate your own Italian restaurant/pizzeria to propose a local ordinance banning the sale of more than three drinks per day to any individual. A drink, under the ordinance, would be defined as a 12-ounce beer, a 4-ounce glass of table wine, and a 1-1/2-ounce shot of liquor. Violators would face a fine of $5,000 per incident. Enforcement would fall to the local police. It is widely known in the community that the mayor, generally a strong promoter of business, is a nondrinker, and support for the ordinance is strong because of the accident.

As the elected president of your local restaurant association, you have been asked to address the proposed ordinance at the next meeting of the city council. Develop a plan of action and outline for your address to the city council. In your plan, answer the following five questions:

1. What issues will you consider as you prepare your statement to the city council?
2. What message do you believe the majority of citizens in your community will support?
3. Where will you turn for advice and counsel in preparing your statement?
4. Will it make a difference to you if you know that the local television station will cover the council meeting?
5. How will social media play into your plan?

WHAT DID YOU LEARN IN THIS CHAPTER

Federal, state, and local governments all pass laws and regulations that can potentially impact a hospitality operation. These laws and regulations are enforced by administrative agencies at all three levels of the government. Hospitality managers need to be familiar with the most common agencies and the areas of the industry that they regulate. In order to comply with these regulations, hospitality managers may be required to file forms, submit to inspections, apply for licenses, operate their business in a specified manner, and maintain their facilities and equipment in good working order.

Many government and nonprofit agencies publish guidelines for managers that can help you take the necessary steps to keep your facility in compliance with various regulations. In situations where federal, state, or local laws conflict with one another, the most restrictive regulation is the one that must be followed.

If you receive a complaint from a government agency, it is important that you take the appropriate steps to respond to the complaint in a timely fashion, respond in the manner requested, and develop a satisfactory plan of action. You may also choose to consult with an attorney or your insurance company, depending on the nature and severity of the complaint.

Government publications and websites, industry trade associations, and local community groups are common sources of information that hospitality managers can turn to for information on changing laws and regulations.

CHAPTER 3

Hospitality Business Structures

3.1 The Importance of Business Structure

One of the most appealing aspects of the hospitality industry is the opportunity for people to have their own business. Whether they are interested in owning restaurants or hotels, one establishment, or a whole chain, self-ownership is a strong factor in many people's excitement about the field of hospitality.

When individual entrepreneurs elect to start their own business, they face a variety of decisions about brands, location, product offerings, and financing, to name but a few elements. An extremely important decision, and one that will affect the future success or failure of the business, is that of its **organizational structure** and its **operating structure**. In this chapter, you will learn about the most common types of organizational and operating structures used in the hospitality industry.

Organizational structure refers to the legal formation of the business entity. It represents the relationship between the business owner(s) and the outside world. This legal formation is important because the courts and all levels of government treat businesses and their owner(s) differently based on their organizational structure. Therefore, it is important to select an organizational structure that works to the advantage of both the business and its owner(s).

Operating structure refers to the relationship between a business's owners and its management. The composition of a business entity's management can be just as important as its type of structure. Operating structures of different hospitality organizations vary greatly. For example, the individual owner of a restaurant may, in fact, manage it on a day-to-day basis. In another operating structure, however, a hotel may actually be owned by one legal entity, be managed by another legal entity, and have contractual relationships about precisely how it is to be managed with yet another legal entity.

To understand better the importance of structure, consider the case of John Graves, an individual who, after years of working for a national restaurant chain, wishes to open his own restaurant. Depending on the type of organizational structure Mr. Graves selects, the income tax he must pay on profits will vary considerably. In addition, the limits of his

LEGALESE

Organizational structure: The legal entity that owns a business.

Operating structure: The relationship between a business's ownership and its management.

CHAPTER OUTLINE

3.1. The Importance of Business Structure

3.2. Common Hospitality Organizational Structures

3.3. Common Hospitality Operating Structures

3.4. The Agency Relationship

IN THIS CHAPTER, YOU WILL LEARN

1. The importance of selecting the proper organizational and operational structures for a hospitality business.
2. The various organizational business structures used in the hospitality industry.
3. The most common operational business structures used in the hospitality industry.
4. The responsibilities and obligations created by an agency relationship.

personal liability for the debts of his business will be directly influenced by the organizational structure he chooses.

Banks and other sources of capital will often make decisions on the worthiness of lending to a business venture based on the organizational structure. In addition, investors may make investment decisions based on the organizational structure selected by a business entity's owners. Vendors may also determine whether to extend credit to a business based, in part, on its organizational structure.

Equally as important, an individual's ability to sell or transfer ownership of the business will be affected by the organizational structure selected. As you have learned, the organizational structure selected for a business is important, and a variety of organizational structures are available to an entrepreneur. The most common ones are discussed in Section 3.2.

It is also important to determine where the business will be formed in order to get the most benefit out of the laws available to businesses. Generally speaking, business entities are governed by state law, and these requirements often vary from state to state. Thus, it is important to know which state law governs the requirements of a business entity.

The applicable law that governs a business entity is determined by which state the entity is formed in, which in most cases is easily determined by where that entity—say, a corporation—has filed its creation documents. A corporation has the ability to choose the state in which it will be incorporated, which does not necessarily have to be the state in which it is physically located, and a corporation has the ability to incorporate in multiple states.

Some uniformity does, in fact, exist among the state laws as a result of the overwhelming number of business entities that decide to incorporate in the state of Delaware. In order to attract revenue, Delaware has created a set of laws that is extremely favorable to business entities that decide to incorporate in that state. In fact, a significant amount of Delaware's state revenue directly comes from business entity incorporation filings and fees. Thus, the Delaware business laws have become a sort of model standard that most states adopt as their own state laws, and business owners should be aware of this standard in not only choosing which type of business entity to create but also choosing exactly where to create it.

3.2 Common Hospitality Organizational Structures

Sole Proprietorship

A **sole proprietorship** is the simplest of all organizational structures. In this structure, a single individual owns all of the business and is responsible for all of its debts. The majority of small businesses in the United States are sole proprietorships. Examples in the field of hospitality could include a food truck, local hot dog stand, an event planner, or perhaps a small bed and breakfast. In a sole proprietorship, the personal assets of the owner can be used to pay any losses, taxes, or damages resulting from lawsuits against the business. There is no personal legal protection from any of the risks associated with owning a business. Put another way, the sole proprietor has unlimited liability for the indebtedness and liability of his or her business.

Profits in a sole proprietorship are taxed at the same rate as the owner's personal income tax. Each year, the owner files a tax return listing the proprietorship's income and expenses. Any profit or loss is reported on the individual owner's tax return. If the owner has income not directly related to the business, losses from the business can be used to reduce the overall amount of income subject to taxation.

Should the owner of a sole proprietorship wish to sell the business or pass his or her ownership rights on to others, he or she is free to do so.

Sole proprietorships can be started simply by opening a bank account to keep track of the business's income and expenses. Because the owner will have unlimited liability, lenders to a sole proprietorship evaluate the financial position of the owner carefully before providing capital to the business.

If the owner of a sole proprietorship is operating under an "assumed name" or "trade name," a name other than his or her own, an assumed-name certificate should be filed with the local government. Thus, if David Daniels began operating a diner and called it Davey's Diner, the term Davey's Diner would be the trade name. Accordingly, the assumed-name certificate filed with the local government would let anyone know that when they do business with Davey's Diner, they are actually doing business with David Daniels, or, put another way, they are doing business with David Daniels d/b/a (doing business as) Davey's Diner.

Any entity operating under an assumed name—not just sole proprietorships—should file a certificate disclosing the ownership and ownership structure of the operation. In many states, filing this certificate is required by law.

General Partnership

A **general partnership** is similar to a sole proprietorship except that it consists of two or more owners who agree to share the responsibility for the operations, financial performance, and liability of the business. Partnerships are formed through oral or written contracts. Generally, these agreements will specify the contributions and responsibilities of each partner:

- How much money each partner will contribute to the business?
- How much time each partner will contribute to the business?

LEGALESE

Sole proprietorship: A business organization in which one person owns and, often, operates the business.

General partnership: A business organization in which two or more owners agree to share the profits of the business but are also jointly and severally liable for its debts.

- Who will make decisions on how the business is operated?
- How profits will be divided?
- How losses will be shared?
- A procedure for transfer of ownership, if one or more partners wishes to sell his or her portion of the business or becomes unable to participate as a partner.

In hospitality, partnerships are occasionally used to begin small operations; but as the risk of liability increases, the operations are better served by converting to one of the limited liability structures discussed later in the chapter.

As in a sole proprietorship, the partners in a general partnership have unlimited liability for the indebtedness of the business. Additionally, the partners are liable jointly and severally for the partnership's debt; that is, they are liable jointly as partner/owners, but they are also liable severally, meaning that one partner alone could be liable for the entire amount (100 percent) of the debt. Thus, even if the partnership is owned on a 50–50 basis, should one partner be unable to pay his or her portion of the debt, the other partner will be liable for the entire amount of the debt. If loans are needed to establish the business, potential lenders will evaluate the personal assets of each partner. Profits from the business are distributed to the partners and taxed at the same rate as the owners' personal income tax.

Partnership agreements can be simple or complex, but as described in Chapter 4, "Contract Basics," because they are complex contracts, they are best documented in writing. This is particularly important when addressing the transfer of ownership rights by one or more partners.

Consider the case of Greg Larson and Mike Haley, who have been equal partners for 20 years in a business that operates a ski run and lift for a resort hotel in Wisconsin. This year, at age 50, Greg would like to sell his portion of the partnership to his daughter. If there were nothing in the partnership agreement prohibiting such a sale, Greg would be free to transfer his half of the business to his daughter. If, however, there is language in the partnership agreement that allows the remaining partner the right of first refusal, Mike would be able to purchase the other half of the business himself, should he so desire, before Greg has the right to sell it to anyone else.

Limited Partnership (LP)

While a sole proprietorship has only one owner and a general partnership may consist of several owners, a **limited partnership (LP)** consists of two classes of owners: the **limited partner** and the **general (or managing) partner**. The limited partner is simply someone, whether an individual or a company, who invests money in the partnership. The general partner may or may not be an investor but serves as the business's operating and financial manager.

Many successful hotel chains began as limited partnerships. A limited partnership is so named because of the "limits" it places on the limited partner's liability. As a general rule, liability will be limited if a partner is not directly involved in the day-to-day managerial decision making of the business. The legal principle involved is one of control. A general partner exercises control over day-to-day operations but as a result bears unlimited liability for any debts or damages incurred by the business. A limited partner risks only his or her investment in the business but must give up the control of that investment in exchange for a limitation on the amount of liability. In fact, if a limited partner becomes actively involved in the business's managerial decision making, the state may revoke the limited partnership's protected status, which would then subject the limited partner to potential unlimited liability for the debts of the business.

The taxation on the profits of a limited partnership is similar to the taxation requirements of general partnerships. The profits are distributed to the partners and taxed at the same rate as the owner's personal income tax.

The limited partnership is a special type of business arrangement provided for by state law. Most states require specific forms to be filed with the secretary of state or some other government official in order for a business to be granted limited partnership status. A limited partnership is closely regulated by the state in which it operates, and it is the state that permits limited partners to invest in a business and be exempt from a large share of the liability should the business fail. Most states require a written limited partnership agreement to be filed as well. Even in a state where it is not required, it is a good idea to have an attorney draw up an agreement prior to the start-up of the business.

C Corporation

A C corporation, often referred to simply as a **corporation**, is formed when groups of individuals elect to band together to achieve a common purpose. When they do, the corporation has a legal identity completely separate from that of its individual owners. A corporation is empowered with some but not all legal rights that are usually reserved only for individuals,

---

LEGALESE

Limited partnership (LP): A business organization with two classes of owners. The limited partner invests in the business but may not exercise control over its operation, in return for protection from liability. The general or managing partner assumes full control of the business operation and can also be held liable for any debts the operation incurs.

Limited partner: The entity in a limited partnership relationship who is liable only to the extent of his or her investment. Limited partners have no right to manage the partnership.

General (or managing) partner: The entity in a limited partnership relationship who makes the management decisions and can be held responsible for all debts and legal claims against the business.

Corporation: A group of individuals granted a charter, legally recognizing them as a separate entity with rights and liabilities distinct from those of its individual owners.

Analyze the Situation 3.1

Nicholas Kostanty formed a limited partnership with his father-in-law, Ray Sweeney, to open an upscale French restaurant in a Midwestern town. Mr. Kostanty was the general partner and owned 75 percent of the business. Mr. Sweeney, with 25 percent ownership, was the limited partner and invested $100,000. After one year, difficulties in the restaurant's operation caused business to drop off, and Mr. Kostanty called Mr. Sweeney for advice.

After hearing of the difficulties and concerned with the security of his investment, Mr. Sweeney traveled from Arizona to Indiana to visit the operation. Upon observing the operation for two days, the two partners decided to launch a large and expensive television ad campaign to increase flagging sales. Mr. Sweeney designed the campaign with the help of Seelhoff Advertising and Video, a local advertising agency specializing in television commercials.

Despite an immediate increase in sales, over time, volume continued to decline, and finally, three months after the ad campaign was launched, the restaurant closed its doors. Total debts at the time the restaurant closed equaled $400,000 with assets of the partnership totaling only $200,000. Included in the debt was $150,000 owed to the advertising agency. The agency sought payment directly from Mr. Sweeney. Mr. Sweeney, claiming that his liability was limited to the $100,000 he had previously invested in the business, refused to pay any additional money. The Seelhoff Advertising Agency sued the limited partnership, as well as Nicholas Kostanty and Ray Sweeney individually.

1. By hiring the advertising agency, did Mr. Sweeney forfeit his limited partner status?
2. Is Mr. Sweeney liable for the outstanding debts of the limited partnership?

such as the right to sue and be sued, own property, hire employees, and loan and borrow money. This empowerment is known as corporate personhood. Corporate personhood was expanded in 2010 to allow corporations to participate in campaign finance pursuant to a U.S. Supreme Court ruling in *Citizens United vs. Federal Election Commission,* 558 U.S. 310 (2010). A corporation is different from a sole proprietorship or a partnership in that it is the corporation itself, rather than the individual owners, that is liable for any debts incurred. This is a powerful advantage. Accordingly, as an operation becomes more complex and the risk of liability becomes greater, incorporating becomes a sound business practice. Today, many of the major hotel and restaurant companies are incorporated (e.g., Marriott, McDonald's, Hilton, Hyatt, and Yum! Brands).

The actual owners of a corporation are called shareholders because they own **shares**, or portions, of the business. Legally, shareholders have the power to determine a corporation's direction and the way it is managed. In reality, though, in many cases, individual shareholders may have little influence on the way a corporation is run. Shareholders elect directors who oversee the business and hire managers for day-to-day operations (many of these directors and managers may be shareholders themselves). A shareholder is not liable for the debts or other obligations of the corporation except to the extent of any commitment that was made to buy its shares. Shareholders also have a right to participate in the distribution of any residual assets of the corporation if it is ever dissolved once all liabilities have been paid off.

A C corporation gets its name from Chapter C of the United States Internal Revenue Code (IRC). Although C corporations eliminate individual liability, they also have a significant disadvantage. Profits from a C corporation are taxed twice. The first tax is levied on the profits the corporation earns. After those taxes are paid, the after-tax profits that remain can be distributed to the corporation's shareholders in the form of **dividends**. The individual owners are then required to pay income taxes on those dividends. It is important to note that the corporation must pay taxes on its profits even if those profits are not distributed to the corporation's owners.

Corporations are taxed at different rates from those of individuals, and the taxes they pay may be affected by special rules that allow certain business expenses to be deducted from revenues prior to establishing the corporation's taxable income.

Consider the case of Michelle Rogen, an entrepreneur who wishes to establish a company providing part-time security guards for restaurants and nightclubs. Ms. Rogen has an inheritance of $1 million that she holds in her name in various bank accounts. She would like to use $100,000 of her funds to begin her business. Because of her concern for potential liability, Ms. Rogen selects her business structure carefully. A sole proprietorship or a general partnership would not provide any liability protection for her. A limited partnership would also be ineffective because Ms. Rogen, as the business manager, would have to take on the general partner's role, and thus her liability would still be unlimited.

Ms. Rogen selects a C corporation structure, which will limit her liability to only the assets of the corporation. If the company is successful, however, it will pay a corporate tax (at a higher rate than Ms. Rogen would have to pay as an individual on those profits), and then Ms. Rogen must pay her own

LEGALESE

Shares: Fractional portions of a company in which the owner of the portion(s) has voting rights and rights to a respective fraction of the assets of the company.

Dividends: Profits received by a shareholder, usually in relation to his or her ownership (shares) of a corporation.

individual tax on any profits she removes from the business. This double taxation is a powerful disadvantage of the C corporation structure.

C corporations are ordinarily more costly to establish and administer than sole proprietorships and general partnerships, but their ability to limit liability makes them very popular. To establish a corporation, the officers of the business must file "articles of incorporation" with either the secretary of state or a corporate registrar's office in the state in which the business will be incorporated. These articles will disclose the officers and board of directors of the corporation as well as the number of shares the company is authorized to sell initially.

S Corporation

There is a type of corporation that avoids the double taxation inherent in a C corporation. This is known as an **S corporation**, and it also gets its name from the U.S. tax code. An S corporation is also known as a subchapter S corporation.

The S corporation format makes good sense for many hospitality businesses, such as family-owned operations. There are several requirements for establishing and maintaining an S corporation status:

- Be a domestic corporation
- Have only allowable shareholders
  - May be individuals, certain trusts, and estates
  - May not be partnerships or corporations and not have nonresident alien shareholders
- Have no more than 100 shareholders
- Have only one class of stock
- Not be an ineligible corporation (i.e., certain financial institutions, insurance companies, and domestic international sales corporations)[1]

An S corporation provides the same liability protection offered by a C corporation but must be established with the agreement of all shareholders. This is done by filing a form with the Internal Revenue Service that has been signed by all of the corporation's shareholders to signify their agreement to elect S status.

In an S corporation, any profits from the business are distributed directly to the shareholders in proportion to their ownership of the corporation. The profits are reported on the individual owners' income tax returns and are taxed at the individuals' taxable rates, which are similar to the favorable taxation treatment of a partnership; however, shareholders also receive the liability protection of a corporation.

It is also important to remember, however, that income from an S corporation is taxable even if it is not distributed to the shareholders. For example, assume two brothers open a microbrewery and select the S corporation structure. Profits from the bar in the first year are $50,000. The brothers decide they want to use all of the profits from the first year to expand their marketing efforts in the second year. The brothers still, however, must pay individual taxes on the first year's profits in proportion to their ownership in the S corporation.

In addition to filing the S election form with the federal government, in some instances, the state in which the business operates may also require notification. Some states do not recognize the S corporation for state income tax purposes but do recognize it for liability purposes. Generally speaking, the restrictions on an S corporation make it most suitable for smaller companies, especially those in which the owners are also the employees and managers.

Limited Liability Company (LLC)

The **limited liability company (LLC)** is a form of legal entity created under state (rather than federal) law. To fully understand the LLC, let's first recall the disadvantages of the business structures examined so far. If someone starting a new business chooses to establish it as a partnership, it is taxed only once but obligates the owners to part or all of the liability and risk involved in operating the business. A limited partnership is also only taxed once, but the liability of the general partner is unlimited A corporation offers liability protection but features double taxation and complex administrative regulations. An S corporation could be selected to avoid double taxation, but the restrictions on an S corporation can be significant.

The limited liability company is a fairly new type of entity created by some states to combine the best features of a corporation with the simplicity of a partnership. Under the typical LLC statute, the members (similar to shareholders in a corporation or partners in a partnership) are all protected from the company's debts unless they undertake personal responsibility for a debt, such as personally guaranteeing a loan for the business. Thus, a member can serve as the company's owner or manager yet still protect his or her personal assets from liability.

The LLC is governed by an operating agreement, which is similar to a partnership agreement. It sets the rules for managing the company, as well as the rights and responsibilities of the members.

If formed properly, the Internal Revenue Service will treat the LLC as a partnership for tax purposes; thus, there is no

[1] www.irs.gov/businesses/small-businesses-self-employed/s-corporations

LEGALESE

S corporation: A type of business entity that offers liability protection to its owners and is exempt from corporate taxation on its profits. Some restrictions limit the circumstances under which an S corporation can be formed.

Limited liability company (LLC): A type of business organization that protects the owners from liability for debts incurred by the business without the need for some of the formal incorporation requirements. The federal government does not tax the profits of LLCs; however, some states do, but others do not.

double taxation. However, in some states, the LLC will have to pay state income taxes on its profits. If the LLC is not formed properly or within the guidelines established by the state in which it does business, the IRS may consider the LLC to be a corporation for tax purposes.

Depending on the state in which it does business, the LLC may have to pay a filing fee or an annual registration fee. The LLC has become the preferred type of organizational structure in the hospitality industry, particularly for independent operators and many franchisees. Its characteristics and advantages are well suited to hospitality operators who are able to elect such a structure.

Like all organizational structures, the limited liability company should be selected only after seeking the advice of a business attorney and tax adviser.

Another entity is available in most states. Known as the limited liability partnership (LLP), it provides limited liability for its partners, as well as retaining the tax advantages of a general partnership. However, this particular entity is more often used for professional partnerships, such as doctors, lawyers, or engineers, rather than for individuals seeking to enter into a general business operation.

Figure 3.1 summarizes the important differences among the most well-known types of organizational structures.

	Sole Proprietorships
Liability	Unlimited personal liability.
Tax Liability	Owner pays.
Tax Rate	Individual.
To Transfer Ownership	No restrictions.
Number of Owners	One.
	General Partnerships
Liability	Unlimited personal liability.
Tax Liability	Partners pay, even if profits are not distributed.
Tax Rate	Individual.
To Transfer Ownership	Per partnership agreement.
Number of Owners	At least two.
	Limited Partnerships (LP)
Liability	General partner has no limited liability protection. Limited partners have limited liability protection unless provided otherwise.
Tax Liability	Partners pay, even if profits are not distributed.
Tax Rate	Individual.
To Transfer Ownership	Per partnership agreement. Generally, an assignee cannot become a limited partner without majority consent.
Number of Owners	At least two.
	C Corporations
Liability	All shareholders have limited liability protection unless otherwise provided.
Tax Liability	Corporation taxed on profits, shareholders taxed on dividends.
Tax Rate	Corporate rate on profits, individual rate on dividends.
To Transfer Ownership	No restrictions for transferring shares.
Number of Owners	All shareholders share limited liability.
	S Corporations
Liability	All shareholders have limited liability protection unless otherwise provided.
Tax Liability	Shareholders pay, even if profits are not distributed.

FIGURE 3.1 **Organizational structures summary chart.**

Tax Rate	Individual.
To Transfer Ownership	There are no transfers to an ineligible shareholder. Cannot exceed 100 shareholders.
Number of Owners	All shareholders have limited liability.
	Limited Liability Companies (LLC)
Liability	All members have limited liability protection from the debts of the LLC unless otherwise provided. Some question exists as to whether states that do not have the LLC form will respect the limited liability of members.
Tax Liability	Members pay, even if profits are not distributed.
Tax Rate	Individual.
To Transfer Ownership	Generally, an assignee cannot become a full member without majority consent.
Number of Owners	No restrictions, but at least two members to gain partnership level taxation. May be taxable as a corporation if it has more than 500 members.

FIGURE 3.1 *(continued)*

3.3 Common Hospitality Operating Structures

Now that you understand the manner in which ownership of hospitality operations can be structured, it is equally important to understand the varied manner in which these businesses are managed and operated.

Owner–Operator

Assume that you wished to start your own restaurant. If you proceeded to do so, it is very likely that, regardless of the organizational structure you select, you will also want to manage your restaurant. If you do select an **owner–operator** structure, you would join the ranks of literally thousands of hospitality businesses operated under this model.

Owner–operators may own a single small business, or they may own multiunit facilities in several geographic areas. In many cases, the owner–operator structure is used by families that pass restaurants or lodging facilities on to new generations of hospitality managers. In fact, most towns and cities are home to one or more "family-run" businesses that have served their communities for multiple generations.

The actual organizational structures used by owner–operators may vary from single proprietorship to various forms of partnerships and corporations. As the independent owner–operator of your own business, you will have freedom to implement any policies, procedures, and products you feel are appropriate. Drawbacks, however, include the possible insufficiency of marketing influence or public recognition, reduced purchasing power, and a lack of operational support (something that business owners without a lot of experience may find valuable or necessary). In many cases, independent business operators who start businesses experience markedly lower expenditures on both initial investment and promotion than do some other operational structures; however, their long-term survival rate is typically lower than with some other operational structures.

Franchise

When customers see facilities with well-established business names such as Hilton, Zaxby's, Subway, Marriott, and the like, they may assume that the company that owns these businesses is also its operator. In fact, however, in most cases, the owners of these businesses are not owner operators, but rather, they have elected to enter into a **franchise** relationship.

According to the International Franchise Association, a franchise is the agreement or license between two legally independent parties that gives a person or group of people (franchisee) the right to market a product or service using the trademark or trade name of another business (franchisor). One of the earliest franchisors was the Singer Sewing Machine Company, which set up dealers shortly after the Civil War to sell and repair its sewing machines. McDonald's is a present-day classic

---

LEGALESE

Owner–operator: A type of operating structure in which the owners of a business are directly responsible for its day-to-day operation. Also known, in some cases, as an "independent."

Franchise: A contract between a parent company (franchisor) and an operating company (franchisee) to allow the franchisee to run a business with the brand name of the parent company, as long as the terms of the contract concerning methods of operation are followed.

Analyze the Situation 3.2

After five years of effort, you develop a unique style of roasting pork that is extremely popular in your hometown. You own and operate five units called Porkies that sell this product. Each unit costs $175,000 to develop. Total sales of each unit average $600,000 with a net profit margin of 10 percent per unit.

A friend of yours discusses your success with you and suggests the possibility of opening five new stores in the friend's hometown. Your friend wants to know what you would charge to sell your recipe and your standard operating procedure (SOP) manual, as well as the use of the name Porkies.

1. How would you determine a fair price for your experience?
2. If your friend is successful, causing the name of Porkies to be even better known, thus resulting in greater demand for franchises, should your friend share in future revenue from franchise sales?
3. What are the ethical issues at play here?

example of how, without tremendous personal wealth, an entrepreneur named Ray Kroc could take an idea and quickly spread it coast to coast and then around the world. Many companies turn to franchising as a system for expansion because they can do so rapidly with a minimum amount of capital and with the assistance of top-notch operators. However, in return, the company must be willing to share its revenues with those operators.

In a franchise operating structure, the actual owner of a hospitality facility (the **franchisee**) agrees to operate that facility in a specific manner in exchange for the franchise rights. A franchise can take many forms, but, as stated previously, it generally involves the right to use the name, trademark, and procedures established by the **franchisor** for the sale of a product or service in a specific geographic area.

In a typical franchise operating structure, an owner (a franchisee) gives up part of his or her freedom to make operational decisions in exchange for the franchisor's expertise and the marketing power of the franchisor's brand name. The owner of a doughnut franchise, for example, gives up the right to make doughnuts according to any recipe she chooses but gains the national recognition of a well-known "name" for her doughnut products. The use of the franchise as an operating structure is extremely common in the hospitality industry.

If a business owner elects to operate a franchise, he or she can gain the marketing support of an established trademarked name: credibility with potential investors, lenders, customers, and vendors; and, in many cases, assistance with operational problems that are encountered. Of course, these advantages come with a price. Typically, the franchisor will charge the franchisee an initial fee plus a percentage of gross revenue. In addition, both parties will sign a legal agreement, which outlines the duties and responsibilities of both the franchisor and franchisee. This franchise agreement is often referred to as a **licensing agreement** because the franchise company (**licensor**) is granting the right, or **license**, to operate as one of its franchisees (**licensee**).

The operating agreement requirements and other legal aspects of buying and utilizing the franchise operating structure are complex. In Chapter 5, "Significant Hospitality Contracts," we will look closely at those mandatory disclosures and arrangements that relate to franchising. Here, what is important to remember is that operating a business as a franchise is simply one of several operating structures available to a hospitality business owner.

The primary advantage to buying a franchise is that doing so allows the owners of a business to acquire a brand name with regional or national recognition. In many cases, affiliation with a strong brand name will increase the sales of a business and thus its profitability. However, the charges for using the name of the franchisor's brand increase as the perceived quality of the brand name increases. The total fees paid by the business owner to the brand owners are related to the strength of the brand name and the revenue that the name will likely bring. Although the fees related to a franchise agreement are sometimes negotiable, they will, on average, equal 3 to 15 percent of a business's gross sales revenue.

In addition to increased sales levels, affiliation with a brand affects the ability of a business's owner to secure financing. When owners seek financing from banks or other lending institutions, they often find that these lenders will look more favorably on those businesses that elect this operating structure than those that do not. Additional advantages, depending on the franchisor selected, may include assistance with on-site training, advice on purchasing items for sale, and reduced operating costs resulting from vendors who give brand operators preferred pricing. Due to obvious conflicts of interest, legal assistance is generally not provided by franchisors to franchisees.

LEGALESE

Franchisee: The person or business that has purchased and/or received a franchise.

Franchisor: The person or business that has sold and/or granted a franchise.

Licensing agreement: A legal document that details the specifics of a license.

Licensor: One who grants a license.

License: Legal permission to do a certain thing or operate in a certain way.

Licensee: One who is granted a license.

The greatest advantages to a franchisor of entering into a franchise agreement with a business owner are the increases in growth of the brand and fee payments to the brand that will result from the agreement. Like all businesses, franchise companies desire growth. The higher the number of businesses that operate under a single brand name, the higher, in general, is the value of the name—and, thus, the fees that can be charged for using that name. In addition, each additional business that affiliates with a brand helps to pay for the fixed overhead of operating that brand. Therefore, additional properties operating under the same brand name result in greater profits for the franchise company.

For a business owner, there are also disadvantages associated with purchasing a franchise. Although there is no question that consumers often prefer the consistency associated with buying a franchised product or service, the manager of such a facility may be hampered by franchisor rules and regulations that do not take into account local needs and tastes. For example, having grits on a breakfast menu may make tremendous sense for an operation in a southern state but may make no sense at all for the same type of unit in the northeastern section of the United States. If a franchisor is not sensitive to the needs of local clientele, the franchisee may have a difficult time achieving success. In addition, religious preferences for some franchisees may require franchisors to make menu adjustments. For example, some franchisees may, for religious reasons, not agree to serve pork on the standardized breakfast menu. It is important for the success of the brand for franchisors to listen to the franchisees' concerns and come to a mutual agreement on how best to operate the franchise.

Local conditions can affect more than menu items. Returning to the example of McDonald's as a franchise model, in his book *Grinding It Out,* Ray Kroc speaks of the difficulties he encountered persuading the McDonald brothers to allow the modifications he required to adjust his building design from one that was successful in California to one that could survive the frigid winters of Illinois.[2] The best franchisors allow their franchisees to make adjustments for local conditions while maintaining the integrity of the franchise concept. Thus, business owners who select this operating structure should be very familiar with the operating procedures of their franchisors.

Management Contracts

In many cases, those who own a business are not the same individuals as those who want to manage a business. Either these nonoperating business owners can hire individual managers to operate their businesses, or, if they desire, they can select a **management company** with the desired expertise to do so. When they do, nonoperating business owners will enter into a **management contract** with the chosen management company.

In some cases, investors who are not experienced in hospitality management simply elect to hire a qualified company to run their businesses. In other cases, the owners of a business have absolutely no interest in managing or even in the continued ownership of it. For example, assume that a bank has loaned money to a restaurant owner to start a business. The owner opens the restaurant but, over time, fails to make the required loan repayments. As a result, the bank is forced to repossess the business. In a case such as this, the bank, which is now the restaurant's owner, will likely close it, or, if it feels it is best, seek a company to manage the restaurant until it is put up for sale and purchased by a new owner.

The hotel industry, because it is cyclical, sometimes experiences falling occupancy rates and revenues. Sometimes these cycles result in properties that fall into receivership and lenders who face the consequence of becoming involuntary owners. In cases such as these, effectively managing a hotel may simply mean optimizing the property's value while offering it for sale.

Interestingly, the operating relationship that exists when a hotel owner signs a management contract with a hotel management company is very different from that of a restaurant owner who does not wish to operate the restaurant. Typically, in the restaurant business, the owner of a restaurant who elects not to operate it but wishes to continue ownership will often lease the space to another restaurateur. In that situation, the business entity that leases the restaurant pays the restaurant's owner an agreed amount and assumes responsibility for all the expenses associated with operating the business. If the restaurant makes money, the benefit goes to the person(s) who leased the space. If the restaurant loses money, the same person(s) is (are) responsible for the loss.

Unlike the restaurant business, in most cases, hotel owners find they cannot lease their properties to management companies. Rather, it is the management company that receives a predetermined monthly fee from the hotel's owners in exchange for operating the property, and it is the owners who assume a passive position regarding operating decisions, while at the same time assuming responsibility for all operating expenses, and debt service. The fees charged by management companies to operate a hotel vary, but commonly range between 1 and 5 percent of the hotel's monthly gross revenue. Thus, regardless of the hotel's operating performance, the management company is paid the fee for its services and the hotel's owners receive the profits (if any) after all expenses are paid. Just as the legal agreements governing franchises can be complex, so too can be those related to management contracts and leases. As a result, these also will be examined in more detail in Chapter 5.

LEGALESE

Management company: An entity that, for a fee, assumes responsibility for the day-to-day operation of a business.

Management contract: The legal agreement that defines the responsibilities of a business owner and the management company chosen to operate the owner's business.

[2] Ray Kroc, *Grinding It Out: The Making of McDonald's* (Chicago: Contemporary Books, 1977).

REITs

Some ownership and operating structures are quite unique. One of these is the real estate investment trust **REIT**. A REIT is a form of business ownership that, in many cases, expressly forbids the owner of a business from operating it. Thus, for example, an individual REIT could own 300 hotels but not be allowed to serve a customer breakfast in any of them!

As a REIT, a company can own hotel properties but in most cases must lease them to operating companies. A real estate investment trust is a private or public corporation (or trust) that enjoys special status under the U.S. tax code. That status allows the REIT to pay no corporate income tax as long as its activities meet statutory tests that restrict its business to certain commercial real estate activities. Most states honor this federal treatment and, as a result, do not require REITs to pay state income tax.

The REIT is a popular ownership model for hotels because the Real Estate Investment Trust Act of 1960 set up three key provisions when it created REITs:

1. Owners that operate as REITs pay no tax on corporate income.
2. In order to get that tax break, REITs must pay out at least 90 percent of their taxable income to their shareholders in the form of dividends.
3. Companies can pass the tax savings from the dividend deduction on to shareholders, making REITs an attractive investment.

The Tax Reform Act of 1976 had an impact on REITs by allowing them to be established as corporations in addition to business trusts. Although the details of how a REIT is established (there are actually several varieties of REIT) are beyond the scope of this text, it is important for hospitality managers to understand that, especially in the lodging industry, the REIT is a common business structure.

Condo Hotels/Shared Services

A popular hotel structure, and thus a common hotel organizational/operating structure, is the **condominium** or "condo" hotel (sometimes also referred to as a mixed-use property or a contel).[3] A "condo" hotel can refer to many types of hotel operating structures ranging from a traditional hotel with residential condominiums next door or on the top few floors, to properties where some or all of the hotel rooms have actually been turned into condominiums and are then sold to individual owner/investors. The units are typically found in major cities using high-rise buildings developed and operated as upper-tier lodging units. These owners may own their condominium units entirely, or they may have purchased **fractional ownership**.

Condo hotels differ from traditional condominium complexes in that, in a condo hotel, owners who are not staying in their units on a given night have the option of placing the unit in a rental "pool." Under such a pooled rental program, the condo owner's unit is sold as a traditional hotel unit. Revenue from the sale is then shared, according to a previously agreed upon formula, between the unit's owner and the entity responsible for administering the rental program.

It is easiest to understand the increased popularity of condo hotels when they are viewed from the perspective of the hotel's developer. In contrast to a traditional hotel developer who normally faces many years of operation before a significant return on capital can be expected, a condo hotel developer expects to sell some or all of the guest rooms constructed to individual unit owners prior to, or immediately upon, completion of the hotel. As a result, the condo hotel developer is able to realize significant financial returns several years earlier than the developer of a traditional hotel is. As well, construction loans for condominiums are often less expensive and easier to obtain than traditional hotel construction loans. In summary, the condo hotel developer expects, and thus far has been achieving, higher rates of return than those rates achievable by traditional hotel development.

In completed condo hotel projects, the business operating structure employed typically takes one of two forms. One is that the project's developer retains ownership of, and typically manages, the revenue-generating areas such as restaurants, lounge, meeting space, and the like. In such an arrangement, the operating structure employed may be that of an owner–operator, a management contract, or even a franchise. In the other case, all of the hotel's commercial areas are turned over to and operated by a **condominium homeowners' association (CHOA)**.

Although CHOAs are usually elected in a democratic manner, it may also be true that the condo owners elected simply are not experienced in hotel operations management.

[3] "The Condo Hotel Boom," *Global Hospitality Advisor* (January 2006), p. 1. Available at http://articles.jmbm.com/2006/01/01/global-hospitality-advisor-the-condo-hotel-boom. Accessed June 10, 2016.

LEGALESE

REIT: Short for "real estate investment trust," a very special form of business structure in which the owners of a business are generally prohibited from operating it.

Condominium: A multiple-unit complex (i.e., hotel, apartment house, office building), the units of which are individually owned with each owner receiving a recordable deed to the individual unit purchased, including the right to sell that unit and sharing in joint ownership of all common grounds, hallways, and on-site facilities.

Fractional ownership: A purchase arrangement in which a condominium owner purchases the use of his or her unit for a portion (fraction) of a year. The fraction may be defined in terms of the number of days per year (e.g., 30, 60) or very specific days and/or months (e.g., January 1 through March 31). Individual units purchased under such an arrangement are commonly known as fractionals.

Condominium homeowners' association (CHOA): A group of condo owners elected by all of the condo owners in a project to interpret, develop, and implement the policies and procedures required to effectively manage their condominium complex.

This is true for both revenue-generating areas, such as room rental and restaurant and bar operations, and the basic maintenance of the facility.

Shared services is the term used to refer to a sharing economy in which services and/or assets, such as lodging reservations, are provided between private individuals and are arranged via a smartphone or other Internet-connected device. This shared service is a not a hotel structure but offers a popular tool for customers to list, find, and book reservations for lodging in places all over the world, including private homes. Airbnb is part of the sharing economy. The company (www.airbnb.com) was founded in 2008 and is privately owned and operated. Another type of shared service for lodging reservations is known as VRBO owned by HomeAway.com, Inc. (www.vrbo.com). It allows private owners to list their vacation properties/homes for short-term rentals to other private individuals, usually in beach areas. It has over 1 million listings in 190 countries. Airbnb and VRBO are mentioned here because due to the recent development and popularity of these styles of lodging, some may be confused about their place within the lodging industry. More information on the sharing economies is provided in Chapter 13.

3.4 The Agency Relationship

As you have learned, the ownership of hospitality businesses can be maintained utilizing a variety of organizational structures. As well, these businesses are managed under a variety of operating structures. Sole proprietorships, partnerships, and corporations are all subject to the federal and state laws governing employer–employee relationships.

It is also true that owner–operators, franchisors, franchisees, and management companies are subject to the laws governing employer–employee relationships. This is important to understand because the conduct of a business entity's employees, regardless of organizational or operating structure, will directly affect its liability (or potential liability). Hospitality owners need to keep laws regarding employee relationships in mind when deciding on an organizational or operating structure for their business and then choose the structure that will best allow them to absorb any liabilities incurred by the employees of the organization.

In the United States, regardless of the business structure selected, the relationship between businesses and their hired help usually takes the form of one of three concepts:

1. Master–servant
2. Agent–principal
3. Independent contractor

Figure 3.2 summarizes the characteristics of each relationship.

The Master–Servant Relationship

Returning to the previous example of John Graves, the man who wanted to begin his own restaurant, we can examine these relationships and the special rights and responsibilities they involve. It is highly unlikely that Mr. Graves will be able to operate his new restaurant entirely by himself. He would more than likely need to hire bartenders, wait staff, and kitchen help. When he hires people to fill these positions, he is creating a master–servant relationship: Mr. Graves is the master and his employees are the servants. Traditionally, in the law, the term *servant* was used to describe employees who performed manual labor. They were not generally in a position to act and/or make decisions on behalf of the master or employer when dealing with third parties. The master–servant relationship implies that the employee is under the direct control of the employer, and since the employers are presumed to be in control of their employees, employers are generally held responsible for the behavior of their employees when they are working. To illustrate, assume that a groundskeeper was directly hired by Mr. Graves to maintain the grassy areas, parking lots, and landscaping around his restaurant. This employee would likely be assigned a variety of groundskeeping tasks, including cutting grass.

Relationship	**Characteristics**
Master-servant	Also known as the employer-employee relationship, where the servant is the employee whose performance is controlled by the employer.
Agent-principal	An agent is empowered to act on behalf of or for the principal, with some degree of personal discretion, and the principal is ordinarily responsible for the conduct and obligations undertaken by the agent.
Employer-independent contractor	The employer has very little control, if any, over the conduct of the independent contractor; accordingly, the independent contractor is not an employee and usually not an agent (however, one could hire an independent contractor specifically to be an agent, such as a real estate agent or an attorney).

FIGURE 3.2 **Three types of employer–employee relationships.**

Assume further that, while mowing, the worker inadvertently ran the mower over a rock and that the rock was discharged, with great force, into the parking lot where it struck the side of a parked car, resulting in significant damage to that customer's car. Mr. Graves, as this groundskeeper's employer, will be directly responsible for the actions of this employee and the damage he or she has caused.

The Agent–Principal Relationship

Mr. Graves could also hire someone to act as his general manager. In this instance, some of the general manager's work might be under the direct control of Mr. Graves, but the general manager might also be empowered to make decisions on behalf of the restaurant and to enter into contracts on behalf of the restaurant. When employees act on behalf of the **principal**, they are usually referred to as **agents** of the principal. Agents have a fiduciary duty (responsibility) to act in the best interests of the principal. In this instance, the agent would be the general manager, and the principal would be Mr. Graves and his restaurant business. In general, a contract is used to specify the specific terms of a principal–agent relationship.

In many cases, the distinction between the agent–principal relationship and the master–servant is quite blurred. As empowerment becomes more widespread in hospitality workplaces, this distinction may fade altogether. Servants who are given more discretion and more authority will be more frequently categorized as agents. The distinction becomes important when you are trying to assess the responsibility of the employer for the acts of the employee. For example, assume that a restaurant customer becomes violently ill from food poisoning that is later linked to unsanitary practices by a kitchen employee in Mr. Graves's restaurant. If the relationship is considered a master–servant relationship, he could be held legally responsible for the guest's injuries under the legal concept of **respondeat superior**.

In this example, the servant in the master–servant relationship does not have the ability to speak on behalf of Mr. Graves or the restaurant and thus will not be considered an agent. However, if the servant did have independent decision-making capabilities, then the employee could be classified as an agent. In the agent–principal relationship, the principal is ordinarily responsible for the behavior of the agent, as well as for any significant, or even insignificant, promises or obligations undertaken by the agent on behalf of Mr. Graves (the principal) or the restaurant. Thus, if the general manager of the restaurant (the agent) enters into a long-term contract to purchase meat from a particular purveyor, Mr. Graves and the restaurant will be responsible for fulfilling the obligations undertaken by the contract (assuming that the contract is in proper form, as discussed in Chapter 4, "Contract Basics.")

Because principals are held responsible for the actions of their agents, agents have a **fiduciary responsibility** to act in the best interest of their principals.

The agent generally has five duties:

1. *Utmost care:* The agent is bound to a very high standard to ensure the maximum protection of the principal's interest.
2. *Integrity:* The agent must act with fidelity and honesty.
3. *Honesty and duty of full disclosure:* The agent must make honest and full disclosure of all facts that could influence in any way the principal's decisions, actions, or willingness to follow the advice of the agent.
4. *Loyalty:* The agent is obligated to refrain from acquiring any interest adverse to that of a principal without full and complete disclosure of all material facts and obtaining the principal's informed consent. This precludes the agent from personally benefiting from secret profits, competing with the principal, or obtaining an advantage from the agency for personal benefit of any kind.
5. *Duty of good faith:* The agent must act with total truthfulness, absolute integrity, and total fidelity to the principal's interest.

Because of the master–servant and agent–principal relationships, it is very important that hospitality operators carefully select and train their employees. If you, as a hospitality owner or manager, are responsible for selecting employees who will represent or make decisions on behalf of your operation, you must trust the decision-making capability of those individuals as well as their integrity to act in the best interests of the operation when they are making decisions and/or entering into contracts.

In Chapters 7, "Legally Selecting Employees," and 8, "Legally Managing Employees," you will learn how to properly select and manage employees under current federal and state employment laws and to see some ways that you can minimize the risk of liability by using effective employee selection and training techniques.

LEGALESE

Principal: Employer, the person hiring and directing employees (agents) to perform his, her, or its business.

Agent: A person authorized to act for or to represent another, usually referred to as the principal.

Respondeat superior: Literally, "let the master respond," a legal theory that holds the employer (master) responsible for the acts of the employee.

Fiduciary responsibility: The requirement that agents act in the best interest of their principals.

Analyze the Situation 3.3

The Great Fox Waterpark and Resort, located in the Wisconsin Dells area of Wisconsin, has received an invoice from Lion Distributing of Reisterstown, Maryland. The invoice is for 10 cases of pool chemicals delivered to the resort two weeks ago. The invoice states Mr. Mark Bell, the resort's head lifeguard, ordered the chemicals. The price on the invoice is three times the normal price paid for chemicals of this type (which are normally purchased from a local vendor).

When questioned by the hotel's accounting office about the purchase, Mr. Bell stated that all he recalls is that he was working one day and received a telephone call in which the caller asked for the "right" shipping address for the resort. The confirmation of address was needed, the caller maintained, because an office mix-up had resulted in some shipments of products purchased by its customers being misdelivered. Mr. Bell provided the caller with the hotel's correct shipping address.

Despite the obvious overcharge, the vendor refuses to accept the shipment back, claiming Mr. Bell, as an agent of the resort, had authorized the purchase of the chemicals. The vendor threatens a lawsuit if its invoice is not paid. Upon investigation, it is determined that 1 of the 10 cases of product has, at this time, already been used.

1. Assume that Mr. Bell did not ordinarily purchase pool chemicals for the resort. Is the resort responsible for paying the invoice?
2. Assume that Mr. Bell did in fact ordinarily purchase pool chemicals for the resort. Is the resort then responsible for paying the invoice?
3. What steps would you suggest that the resort's owners take to prevent being victimized by potential invoice frauds of this type?

The Independent Contractor

Back to Mr. Graves, our restaurant owner. From time to time, he may need to hire individuals or other companies to come in and perform specialized tasks that are outside the day-to-day operations of his restaurant. For instance, he may need to repaint the exterior walls of the building that houses the restaurant. Mr. Graves could hire an individual painter or a company that provides painting services. This type of relationship would involve an **independent contractor** relationship.

Usually, employers are not liable for the behavior of independent contractors, and independent contractors cannot ordinarily bind employers to obligations that they have made. The general rule is that the more control that the worker retains, the more likely that the worker will be characterized as an independent contractor. Misclassification of a worker as an independent contractor versus an employee is a serious problem facing hospitality businesses. Such misclassification can result in an employer being liable for unpaid wages and benefits, as well as penalties. It is important to note that in 2015, the U.S. Department of Labor updated its standards for determining whether a worker is classified as an employee or an independent contractor. The Department of Labor uses a test known as the "Economic Realities Factors."

Figure 3.3 displays the Department of Labor's six factors used to determine whether the worker is truly an independent contractor. No one single factor is determinative, and all factors need to be considered together.

To illustrate the importance of understanding the differences in employer–employee relationships, return to the previous lawn-mowing example. This time, however, assume that Mr. Graves hired a lawn service company to care for the grass around his restaurant. In this case, John's relationship with the lawn service company would be that of an employer–independent contractor. As a result, if an employee of the lawn service company inflicted the same damage to a customer's car that was described earlier, it would be the lawn service, not Mr. Graves's restaurant, that would be liable for repairing the damages to the customer's vehicle.

Chapters 9 through 13 examine the different types of circumstances under which hospitality operations may be held liable in a court of law, and they identify some preventive measures that managers can take to minimize the risk of litigation. Although we strive throughout this book to emphasize managerial practices that will promote safe and legal operations (and prevent the possibility of a lawsuit), accidents or misunderstandings will invariably occur, and at those times, a well-chosen business structure may provide the hospitality owner with a higher degree of protection against liability than one that was poorly chosen.

1. Is the work an integral part of the employer's business?
2. Does the worker's managerial skill affect the worker's opportunity for profit or loss?
3. How does the worker's relative investment compare to the employer's investment?
4. Does the work performed require special skill and initiative?
5. Is the relationship between the worker and the employer permanent or indefinite?
6. What is the nature and degree of the employer's control?

FIGURE 3.3 Department of Labor's Economic Realities Factors.
https://www.dol.gov/whd/workers/Misclassification/AI-2015_1.htm (Accessed June 10, 2016).

LEGALESE

Independent contractor: A person or entity that contracts with another to perform a particular task but whose work is not directed or controlled by the party retaining the person to do the task.

International Snapshot

A Comparative Overview of Business Entities in the Hotel Industry

United States

Traditional hotels in the United States operate as various types of entities under a variety of models. Most often, they take the forms of corporations or limited liability companies rather than partnerships. Limited liability companies offer added protection for officers and directors above that of a normal corporation. Among these entities, the majority of the larger hotel companies are publicly traded companies, such as Hilton and Hyatt.

There is a greater variety among the operation structures of hotels. The major distinction can be drawn between a traditional hotel model and a condo hotel model. Traditional hotels have many different forms of management and franchise agreements, but all follow the basic model that there is one central owner for the entire property. Condo hotels, which have become significantly more popular in recent years, have many units owned by many people but typically are managed by one entity. A third group, hybrid hotels, has made a larger footprint in the market recently. Some of hybrid hotel units are condos, typically full-time residences, and the remaining units are traditional hotel rooms. Both the W Hotels and Ritz-Carlton Hotels have properties with this new hybrid structure. Finally, the newest trend in the hotel market involves home-sharing websites, such as those of Airbnb and HomeAway, that allow people to rent out their own residences to travelers. These nontraditional hotels are generally operated by the home owner and represent a rapidly growing segment of the industry, although they face regulatory challenges in some cities, such as Santa Monica, California.

China

From 2010 through 2016, the hotel industry in China has enjoyed an 8.0 percent average growth to an estimated $58.6 billion-dollar industry, according to IBISWorld. A particularly remarkable year for hotel expansion was in 2010 due to the Shanghai Expo and the Guangzhou Asian Games and the tourism those events brought to China. However, growth slowed since the boom in 2010 as tourism declined and the overall Chinese economy has stagnated since 2014. Foreign enterprises greatly affected the hotel industries development in China with the introduction of top global brands, chain management concepts, and higher service standards to China. This is particularly true with the higher-end hotels, but the mid-to-lower range hotels and brands have also seen recent expansion in China. *Hotel News Now* reports that the biggest cities in China, including Beijing, Shanghai, Guangzhou, Shenzhen, Sanya, and Wuhan, and even the medium-sized cities have continued to exhibit strong performance. However, the tertiary cities, such as Tianjin, Chengdu, Qingdao, Dalian, and Xi'an face intense challenges, especially the ones with oversupply issues. Generally, there appears to be a drop in international hotel demand as the domestic demand for hotels becomes more dominant.

Chinese companies are increasingly interested in acquisitions of United States real estate and large hotel chains. Chinese investors appear to be especially attracted to the top brand names, especially in the luxury hotel market, such as Four Seasons, Ritz-Carlton, InterContinental, and Loews brands.

Provided by John Vernon, managing partner of The Vernon Law Group, PLLC.

WHAT WOULD YOU DO?

Assume that you are responsible for approving commercial loans at a bank where you are the senior lending official. You are approached by two hospitality management college graduates, each with three years' management experience acquired after they completed their studies. They are seeking a loan slightly in excess of $1 million to establish a restaurant in the community. The funds will be used to lease land, facilities, and equipment, as well as for renovation, inventory, salaries, and other start-up costs.

Write an essay that answers the following questions:

1. Will the organizational structure selected by the partners have an impact on your decision to extend the loan?
2. Will the operating structure selected by the partners have an impact on your decision to extend the loan?
3. What other factors would influence your decision?
4. Would it make a difference to you if the partners were requesting the loan to complete a franchise agreement with an established and successful franchisor?
5. What additional information might you request if the partners were seeking the loan to operate as an independent restaurant? Would it matter if the loan were for an existing restaurant as opposed to a start-up?

WHAT DID YOU LEARN IN THIS CHAPTER?

Establishing the appropriate business structure for a hospitality operation is a decision that requires owners or managers to consider the amount of liability risk they are willing to absorb, their willingness to pay taxes on the operation's profits, and the degree of control they wish to exercise over the business. There are a variety of business structures to choose from, each offering different benefits to the business operator. Your business may not fit within the parameters established for particular structures, so your choices may be limited.

However you choose to operate your business, you will rely on others to represent the interests of your business. To varying degrees, you will be responsible for the decisions and acts they select. Determining the types of employees and agents that will be needed for your business operation and the degree of control they will have are important liability considerations that must be factored into your choice of organizational structure.

CHAPTER 4

Contract Basics

4.1 Introduction to Contracts

In any society, the members of the society choose to abide by rules designed to enhance the quality of life of that group. Violations of the rules are typically met with some form of negative consequence imposed by group members. In some cases, rules of conduct are passed down to successive generations by societal customs and mores. In other cases, the rules are expressly stated in the written laws governing the society. One important job of the courts is the enforcement of societal laws. It is also the job of the courts to enforce **contracts**.

Business Contracts

Generally speaking, litigation in the hospitality, or any other, industry arises because the **plaintiff** believes one of the following to be true:

- The **defendant** did something he or she was not supposed to do.
- The defendant did not do something he or she was required to do.

Surprisingly, it can sometimes be perplexing for hospitality managers to know precisely what is expected of them when serving guests. It can also be just as difficult to know what should reasonably be expected of the vendors and suppliers with which the manager interacts. Business contracts, and the laws surrounding them, have been established so that both parties to an agreement can more clearly understand exactly what they have agreed or promised to do. This is important for many reasons; however, one of the most important, as the majority of participants in lawsuits (regardless of their outcome!) will attest, is avoiding legal difficulties, which is very much preferable to settling those difficulties in court.

Verbal and Written Contracts

Hospitality managers, in the course of their normal duties, make a great number of promises and enter into a multitude of agreements on a daily basis. Although effective managers enter into these agreements in good

---

LEGALESE

Contract: An agreement or promise made between two or more parties that the courts will enforce.

Plaintiff: The person or entity that initiates litigation against another, sometimes referred to as the claimant, petitioner, or applicant.

Defendant: The person or entity against which litigation is initiated, sometimes referred to as the respondent.

CHAPTER OUTLINE

4.1. Introduction to Contracts
4.2. Components of an Enforceable Contract
4.3. The Uniform Commercial Code
4.4. Preventative Legal Management and Contracts

IN THIS CHAPTER, YOU WILL LEARN

1. The two basic types of valid business contracts.
2. The four essential components that must be present to create a valid contract.
3. The purpose of the Uniform Commercial Code (UCC).
4. The consequences of breaching an enforceable contract.
5. How to avoid legal difficulties related to contracts before they arise.

Analyze the Situation 4.1

In response to a telephone inquiry, Vincent's Tree Service offered to trim an apple tree on the lawn outside the front lobby of the Olde Tyme Prime Rib restaurant, for a fee of $500. Mr. Wilbert, the restaurant's manager, agreed to the price and a start date of Monday. At noon on Monday, Vincent's informed Mr. Wilbert that the job was completed. The tree trimming went fine, but a large quantity of branches and leaves from the tree were left neatly piled near the tree's base. When Mr. Wilbert inquired about the removal of the debris, Vincent's stated that removing it had never been discussed and was not included in the quoted price. Mr. Wilbert agreed that the topic of removal was never discussed but stated that it is generally assumed that when a company trims a tree, it will remove the brush it generates; therefore, he refused to pay until the brush was removed.

1. Which party's position seems most valid to you? Why?
2. How would you suggest the issue be resolved between these two contracting parties?

faith, any number of problems or misunderstandings can arise that may prevent promises from being fulfilled.

Valid and legally enforceable contracts may be established either in writing or verbally. In most cases, written contracts are preferred over verbal contracts because it is easier to clearly establish the precise responsibilities of each party when those responsibilities are completely spelled out. In addition, time can cause memories to fade, businesspeople may change jobs or retire, and recollections, even among the most well-intentioned of parties, can differ. All of these factors can create discrepancies in verbal contracts.

Interestingly, despite the fact that written contracts have many distinct advantages over verbal agreements, in the hospitality industry, most transactions with guests are established orally rather than in writing. For example, when a potential customer calls a restaurant to order a pizza for home delivery, a contract is established via telephone. The guest agrees to pay for the pizza when delivered, just as the restaurant agrees to prepare and deliver a high-quality product. It simply would not be practical to get such an agreement in writing. Likewise, the guest who calls a restaurant and makes a reservation for eight people at 7:30 P.M. on a Friday night does not usually get a written agreement from the restaurant stating that it accepts the responsibility to provide a table for that group. The guest simply makes a verbal request, and that request is either accepted or denied based on the space available at the restaurant.

There are many cases in which transactions with guests or other businesses are actually confirmed in writing. In Chapter 5, "Significant Hospitality Contracts," you will review, in detail, some of the most important types of written contracts used in the hospitality industry.

Perhaps the most common example of a written, ordinarily enforceable, contract related to hospitality guests is the registration card, which is signed by guests when they stay at a lodging facility. Today, many hotel companies are using electronic forms of guest registration, personalizing the registration card for the individual guest that will indicate the guest name and contact information, the dates of stay, and the rates to be charged for the stay. Note that, while most written contracts are actually signed by both contracting parties, only the guest signs this type of contract. Also, the responsibilities of the hotel are not clearly stated on the registration card, although they have been clearly established over time by common law. These responsibilities will, however, be discussed fully in Chapter 9, "Your Responsibilities as a Hospitality Operator."

When dealing with vendors, suppliers, and others who provide services to the hotel, verbal contracts are quite common. When a hospitality operation does business with a vendor that

Analyze the Situation 4.2

Jeremy Moss's credit card was billed $450.00 by the Langford Inn.

The charge was a "no-show" charge that resulted from Mr. Moss not arriving at the hotel on a night that "he" had reserved, via the hotel's website, two rooms (at $225.00 each). The hotel had been sold out that night, and the rooms, in keeping with hotel policy, had been held for Mr. Moss until 4:00 A.M. the next morning.

Mr. Moss contacts the hotel when he receives his credit card statement and protests that he never made the reservations. The reservation data collected on the website lists Mr. Moss's actual address and his home telephone number, as well as the credit card number billed by the hotel.

Mr. Moss, however, still maintains that he did not make the reservation, and thus demands that the "no-show" billing be removed from his card.

1. Do you believe the hotel is justified in charging Mr. Moss for the no-shows?
2. How could this hotel prevent such misunderstandings in the future?

has an excellent reputation, a typical verbal contract can be established in as simple a manner as a telephone call. If, for example, the manager of a restaurant is required by state or local law to have the fire extinguisher system above the deep-fat fryers inspected twice a year, the agreement to do so may not be committed to writing each time an inspection is made. Perhaps the same company has been performing the inspection for several years. Indeed, it may be that in order to efficiently schedule its staff, the inspection company, rather than the restaurateur, decides on the exact day of inspection. In this case, the presence of the inspector, access provided to the facility, the invoice for services performed, and a written inspection report all serve as indications that a verbal agreement to inspect the restaurant was in existence even if no written agreement exists.

4.2 Components of an Enforceable Contract

All contracts, whether verbal or written, must include specific components that will make them legally **enforceable** in a court of law. If any of the components are missing, the courts will consider the contract unenforceable.

To be enforceable, a contract must be legally valid, and it must consist of an offer, consideration, and acceptance.

Capacity and Legality

Not all agreements or promises made between two or more parties are legally valid. If, for example, a child who is 10 years old "agrees," even in writing, to host 100 of his friends at the local amusement park, the park owner would have no recourse if the 10-year-old subsequently neglected to arrive with his friends and pay the admission fees. The reason, logically, is that society requires a party to a contract to be of a minimum age before he or she can legally commit to the promises made in the contract. In most cases, minors do not meet the minimum age requirement; therefore, any contract they enter into would be considered unenforceable by the courts. In addition, an individual who does not have the mental capacity to understand what the terms of the contract entail will not be able to enter into an enforceable contract. This incapacity could be due to a variety of reasons, from mental illness to drug use or inebriation.

Even if the parties to a contract are considered legally capable, the courts will not enforce a contract that requires the breaking of a law. If, for example, a gourmet restaurant contracts with a foreign supplier to provide an imported food product that has not entered the country with the proper inspections, the courts will not enforce the contract because the activity involved—that is, the selling of uninspected food products—is itself illegal. Agreements to perform illegal acts are not enforceable. Thus, to be considered legally enforceable, a contract must be made by parties who are legally able to contract, and the activities specified in the contract must not be in violation of the law.

In addition, to be enforceable, some contracts must be in writing and cannot be verbal. This law is called the "statute of frauds." An example includes the purchase and sale of real estate in connection with a restaurant business. The transfer of title must be in writing.

Offer Given that two or more parties are legally capable of entering into a contract and that the contract involves a legal activity, the second component required in a legally enforceable contract is an offer.

The **offer** simply states, in as precise a manner as possible, exactly what the offering party is willing to do and what he or she expects in return. The offer may include specific instructions for how, where, when, and to whom the offer is made. The offer may include time frames or deadlines for acceptance, which are either clearly stated or implied. In addition, the offer will generally include the price or terms of the offer.

When a guest enters a restaurant and reads the menu, he or she is reading a series of offers from the restaurant manager. While the menu may state, "16-Ounce Roast Prime Rib of Beef, $22.95," the contract offer could be stated as, "The restaurant will provide prime rib, if you, the guest, will agree to pay $22.95 for it."

When a school foodservice director places an order for produce with a vendor, the offer is similar. The foodservice director offers to buy the necessary products at a price quoted by the vendor. The reason that an offer is a required component of a contract is clear. The offer sets the term and responsibilities of both parties. The offer states, "I will promise to do this, if you will promise to do that."

Returning to the tree-trimming case referred to in Analyze the Situation 4.1; you can see why the offer is so important in a contract. In that example, the restaurateur and the tree service had differing ideas on precisely what constituted the offer. In fact, a great deal of litigation today involves plaintiffs and defendants who seek the court's help to define what is "fair" in regard to a legitimate offer when that offer has not been clearly spelled out. It is important to note also that the courts will enforce contracts that have reasonably identifiable terms, even if those terms are heavily weighted in favor of one of the parties. Because of this, it is a good idea to clearly understand all of the terms of an offer prior to its acceptance. By doing so, the effective hospitality manager can help minimize his or her potential for litigation.

LEGALESE

Enforceable contract: A contract recognized as valid by the courts and subject to the court's ability to compel compliance with its terms.

Offer: A proposal to perform an act or to pay an amount that, if accepted, constitutes a legally valid contract.

Consideration An important part of the contract is **consideration**, which can best be viewed as something of value, such as the payment or cost of the promises of performance agreed to in a contract. For a contract to be valid, consideration must flow both ways. In the case of the prime rib dinner just mentioned, the consideration by the restaurant is the prime rib. The guest, by ordering the prime rib, is agreeing to pay $22.95 as consideration. Similarly, an airline that offers to transport a passenger round trip does so for a specific fare, which, in this case, is the consideration. The airline provides the trip and the guest pays the fare.

Consideration may be something other than money. If a restaurant agrees to host an employee Christmas party for a professional decorating company in exchange for having the company decorate its restaurant for Christmas, the consideration paid by the restaurant would be the hosting of the employee Christmas party, while the consideration paid by the decorator would consist of the products and services required to decorate the restaurant.

Another type of consideration often employed in the hospitality industry is the temporary or permanent use of property. When a hotel advertises a specific rate for the rental of a room, that rate is the consideration to be exchanged for the overnight use of the room.

When that same hotel company purchases a piece of land to build a new property, it will likely exchange money for the right to build on or own the property.

Consideration can also be the promise to act or not act. When the board of directors of a country club agrees to employ a club manager for a certain annual salary, the club provides consideration in the form of money, while the club manager's consideration consists of the work (acts) that he or she will do while managing the club. In some cases, consideration requires that one of the contracting parties does not act. Suppose that a couple buys an established restaurant from its current owner. The restaurant's name, as well as the original restaurant owner, is well known in the local area. Consideration in the sales contract may well include language that prohibits the original owner from opening a restaurant with a similar name in the immediate vicinity for a specified period of time. In this case, the consideration requires the original owner not to act in a specific manner. Another example is an executive who is going through a separation of employment and may agree to waive certain rights or claims against the employer in exchange for a settlement cash amount—an agreement to not sue the employer.

A hotel may rent a room for $25, $250, or $2,500 per night should it so choose. The guest has a right to agree or not agree to rent the room. As long as both parties to a legitimate contract are in agreement, the amount of the consideration is not generally disputable in court. Indeed, should an individual who is competent wish to sell a piece a land he or she owns for $1 (perhaps to a charitable group), the courts will allow it, regardless of the appraised value of the land. The important point here is that the courts will ordinarily not deem a contract unenforceable simply because of the size of the consideration. It is the agreement to exchange value that establishes mutual consideration, and thus the contract's enforceability, not the magnitude of the value exchanged.

Acceptance Because it takes at least two parties to create a contract, a legal offer and its consideration must be clearly accepted by a second party before the contract comes into existence. It is important to note that the **acceptance** must mirror exactly the terms of the offer in order for the acceptance to make the contract valid. If the acceptance does not mirror

Analyze the Situation 4.3

JoAnna Hart was offered a position as director of foodservice for the independent school district of Laingsford. She received a written offer of employment on the first of the month with a stipulation that the offer would be in effect until the 15th of the month. If Ms. Hart were to accept the employment offer, she would have to sign the employment contract and return it to the Laingsford superintendent of schools before the offer expired on the 15th. Upon reading the details of the contract, Ms. Hart felt that the salary identified in the letter was too low, and thus she adjusted it upward by $5,000, initialing her change on the contract copy. She then returned the offer letter to the school superintendent with a cover letter, stating she was pleased to accept the position as detailed in the contract. The contract arrived by mail in the office of the superintendent on the 14th of the month, at which time, the superintendent called Ms. Hart to express his regret that she had rejected the employment offer. During the telephone call, Ms. Hart realized that the superintendent would not accept her salary revision proposal, so instead, she verbally accepted the position at the original rate of pay. The superintendent, however, declined her acceptance, stating that the original employment offer no longer existed.

Does the school have the legal right to withdraw its offer of employment? Why or why not?

LEGALESE

Consideration: The payment/value exchanged for the promise(s) contained in a contract.

Acceptance: Unconditional agreement to the precise terms and conditions of an offer.

the offer, it is considered a **counteroffer** rather than an acceptance. When an acceptance that mirrors the offer is made, an **express contract** has been created.

An offer may be accepted orally or in writing unless the offer itself specifies the manner of acceptance. In both cases, however, it must be clear that the terms of the offer were in fact accepted. It would not be fair, or ethical, for a wine steward to ask if a diner would like an expensive bottle of wine, and then, because the diner did not say no, assume that the lack of response indicated an acceptance of the offer. In that circumstance, the diner should not be required to pay for the wine. In the same manner, a contractor who offers to change the light bulbs on an outdoor sign for a restaurant cannot quote a price to the restaurant manager and then proceed to complete the job without a clear acceptance by the manager.

Legal acceptance may be established in a variety of ways. In the hospitality industry, these generally take the form of one of the following:

1. *Verbal or nonverbal agreement.*

   In its simplest form, acceptance of a contract offer can be done verbally, with a handshake, or even with an affirmative nod of the head. If, for example, a guest in a cocktail lounge orders a round of drinks for his table, he is verbally agreeing to the hotel's unspoken, but valid, offer to sell drinks at a specific price. If, when the drinks are consumed, the guest is asked if he would like another round, and he nods his head in an affirmative way, he will be considered to have accepted the offer of a second round. Acceptance may also be implied by conduct. If a guest at a delicatessen stands in line to order coffee, and while doing so sees a display of breakfast muffins that are clearly marked for sale, unwraps a muffin and begins to eat it while waiting in line, her actions would imply the acceptance of the deli's offer to sell the muffin.

2. *Acceptance of a deposit.*

   In some cases, a hospitality organization may require a deposit to accompany, and thus affirm, the acceptance of an offer. If, for example, a hotel is offering a two-night package over New Year's weekend, it may decide that the offer to rent a room for that period specifies an acceptance that must be made in the form of a nonrefundable guest deposit.

3. *Acceptance of partial or full payment.*

   In some cases, full or partial prepayment may be required to demonstrate acceptance of an offer. This concept of payment prior to enjoying the benefits of the contract is not at all unusual. Theaters, amusement parks, and quick service or fast-food restaurants are all examples of contracts that are affirmed via prepayment. It is the right of hotels and restaurants to make full or partial prepayment a condition of their contracts. It is the right of the guests, however, to refuse this contract offer and take their business elsewhere should they wish to do so.

4. *Agreement in writing.*

   In many cases, the best way to indicate acceptance of an offer is by agreeing to the offer in writing. As mentioned previously, a large number of management/guest contracts in the hospitality industry are made orally. Dinner reservations and hotel reservations made over the telephone or through the Internet are quite common. When the sum of money involved is substantial, however, even these reservation contracts should be confirmed in writing if at all possible. In most cases, the confirmation of an offer in writing provides more than just proof of acceptance. Because most people are more cautious when their promises are committed to paper, a written contract acceptance is often accompanied by a summary of the terms of contract. This helps prevent confusion. For example, when a hotel guest asks the hotel to send written confirmation of a room reservation, that confirmation document would include such information as:

   Name of the guest
   Date of arrival
   Date of departure
   Room rate
   Type of room requested
   Smoking or nonsmoking preference
   Number of guests in room
   Type of payment agreed to (e.g., cash, credit card, and debit card)
   Hotel cancellation policy

It is generally one or more of the preceding elements of a reservation that are in dispute when guests claim that the hotel has made an error in their reservation. It is clear that the number of disputes over hotel-guest contract terms would be greatly reduced with the increased use of written documentation of acceptance.

In today's business environment, agreement in writing can take several forms. Electronic mail (email) is quite popular as a quick and effective way to accept contract terms in writing. Email has the advantage of allowing both parties to revise documents directly as they are passed back and forth. As well, a record (the email string) is maintained of the changes and revisions as they occur. Last, the U.S. Postal Service has traditionally been recognized as a legally binding method of providing written acceptance of contracts.

To illustrate the importance of this concept, consider, for example, the food vendor that is promoting a special sale on boneless hams for the Christmas holidays. The vendor sends an email to all of its clients. In the email, an offer for the sale of the hams is made that includes a 20 percent price reduction if orders of the hams exceed $100,000 and "payment is made by November 1."

LEGALESE

Counteroffer: Conditional agreement to the terms and conditions of an offer that includes a change to those terms, creating a new offer.

Express contract: A contract in which the components of the agreement are explicitly stated, either orally or in writing as opposed to an implied contract.

A cafeteria chain's purchasing agent receives the email and decides to take advantage of the offer. The agent prints the email, fills in the email order form's blank spaces to indicate the amount of product to be purchased, and places it in an envelope, along with a check for the full purchase amount (including the discount). The printed email form and check are mailed, and the envelope is postmarked on November 1 by the postal service. The purchasing agent will be considered to have met the terms of the contract and to have responded within the prescribed time frame because the acceptance was postmarked on the first of the month. However, if the vendor had stated, "Acceptance must be received in our offices by November 1," then the acceptance would not have been in time. Again, this points out the importance of clarity and specificity when agreeing to any contract terms.

Search the Web 4.1

Go to **www.yahoo.com**

1. Under Search, type: "hospitality contracts."
2. Search for stories related to contracts and contract negotiations that are making headlines in the news, nationally, or in your area.
3. Print out one of the articles, and be prepared to summarize it in class.

4.3 The Uniform Commercial Code

Although hospitality managers encounter a wide variety of business contracts, two of the most common are those related to buying the goods and services needed to operate their businesses (purchase agreements) and those related to selling goods and services to their customers (sales contracts).

It is important that the hospitality manager become familiar with purchase agreements and sales contracts for two reasons: because they are used frequently in the industry and because a very special code of laws exists to help facilitate business transactions that are carried out using sales contracts. The **Uniform Commercial Code (UCC)** was developed to simplify, modernize, and ensure consistency in the laws regulating the buying and selling of personal property (as opposed to land), any loans granted to expedite those sales, and the interests of sellers and lenders. The rules of the UCC, first developed in 1952, were designed to add fairness to the process of transferring property, to promote honesty in business transactions, and to balance the philosophy of **caveat emptor** by giving buyers, sellers, and lenders a measure of protection under the law.

The main purposes of the UCC are:

1. To simplify, clarify, and modernize the law governing commercial transactions.
2. To permit the continued expansion of commercial transactions.
3. To provide for consistency in the law regarding the sale and financing of personal property in the various jurisdictions (municipalities, counties, and states).

The UCC comprises 11 articles, or topic areas:

Article 1	General Provisions
Article 2	Sales
Article 2A	Leases
Article 3	Negotiable Instruments
Article 4	Bank Deposits and Collections
Article 4A	Funds Transfers
Article 5	Letters of Credit
Article 6	Bulk Transfers and Bulk Sales
Article 7	Warehouse Receipts, Bills of Lading, and Other Documents of Title
Article 8	Investment Securities
Article 9	Secured Transactions

The UCC governs many aspects of the hospitality manager's work, including the selling of food and drink, the buying and selling of goods (personal property), and the borrowing and repayment of money. Accordingly, you need to become familiar with its basic concepts. For example, when purchasing goods under contract, the UCC has three basic requirements:

1. Sales of more than $500 must be in writing and agreed to by both parties.
2. The seller has an obligation to provide goods that are not defective and that meet the criteria and terms set forth in the contract.
3. The buyer has an obligation to inspect the goods that were purchased, to make sure they conform to the terms of the contract, and to notify the seller immediately of any discrepancies.

The important thing to keep in mind about the UCC is that it is a law that requires you to fulfill any promises made in a purchasing or sales contract. If a restaurant enters into an agreement to buy 50 heads of lettuce from a food wholesaler on or before a specified date, then that wholesaler is obligated

LEGALESE

Uniform Commercial Code (UCC): A model statute covering such issues as the sale of goods, credit, and bank transactions.

Caveat emptor: A Latin phrase meaning "let the buyer beware." The phrase implies that the burden of determining the relative quality and price of a product falls on the buyer, not the seller.

Analyze the Situation 4.4

The Smoking Bones BBQ restaurant serves an excellent spinach salad as an accompaniment to its popular chicken and rib dishes. Michelle Brennan, the restaurant's manager, purchases all of her produce, including fresh spinach used in the salads, from a local vendor.

Unfortunately, one of Ms. Brennan's guests becomes ill after eating at her restaurant. The source of the illness is traced directly to the fresh spinach used in the restaurant's salads. In fact, upon further investigation, it is determined that the spinach, when delivered to the restaurant's produce vendor, was already infected with E. coli bacteria that matched a strain identified in cattle manure used to fertilize the spinach field.

1. According to the UCC, a seller has a responsibility not to sell defective products. Who, in this example, is the seller?
2. Assume that you were the guest sickened by the bacteria. Who do you believe should be held responsible for the damages you incurred?
3. What specific steps could Ms. Brennan take to help prevent incidents such as the one described here from reoccurring in her restaurant?

to deliver 50 heads of lettuce on time, and the restaurant is obligated to pay for it.

The UCC protects the interests of buyers by requiring that goods or products offered for sale be fit for use and free of any known defects. In other words, the food wholesaler cannot deliver 50 heads of spoiled lettuce to the restaurant, or it will not have fulfilled the terms of the sales contract. Likewise, the UCC also protects the interests of sellers by requiring that buyers inspect all goods after receiving them and inform the seller immediately of any defects. Thus, the restaurant cannot claim three months after the fact that the lettuce it received was spoiled and then refuse to pay the outstanding bill. It must notify the food wholesaler immediately of the spoiled lettuce or live with the consequences.

The UCC is a very complex law with many requirements that hospitality managers must be aware of. In Chapter 6, "Legally Managing Property," we will look closely at Articles 2 and 9 when we discuss the legal aspects of buying and selling property. Then, in Chapter 12, "Your Responsibilities When Serving Food and Beverages," you will learn how the UCC regulates the wholesomeness of the food and beverages that are sold in restaurants and other hospitality operations.

4.4 Preventative Legal Management and Contracts

Breach of Contract

In some cases, the agreements and promises made in a contract are not kept. When this happens, the party that has not kept its agreement is said to be in **breach of**, or to have breached, the terms of the **contract**.

Sometimes, it is simply not possible to fulfill the obligations set forth in a contract. Guests who stay past their previously agreed-on departure dates may make it difficult for a hotel to honor upcoming room reservations. Diners who stay longer than anticipated may do the same to other restaurant guests who hold dinner reservations. Events of **force majeure** such as acts of nature (sometimes referred to as acts of God), or war, government regulations, disasters, strikes, civil disorder, the curtailment of transportation services, and other emergencies may make keeping the promises of a hospitality contract impossible. This can happen to either party. A hotel that is closed because of a hurricane, as sometimes happens on the southern and eastern coasts of the United States, may well be unable to service the guests it had planned to host. Likewise, if an air traffic controllers' strike closes all major airports, guests flying to a convention in Las Vegas may be unable to arrive in time for their room reservations. Adding a force majeure clause to a contract allows the parties to both specify what will happen should a force majeure event occur and identify some types of force majeure events that will trigger the clause.

Voluntary breach of contract occurs when management elects to willfully violate the terms of the contract. There are times when a voluntary breach of contract is financially feasible so long as the party affected by the breach is made whole and thereby agrees to the change. In most cases, however, it is unwise to voluntarily breach a contract. When it is done, it usually means that the breaching party should not have agreed to the contract terms in the first place.

There can be a variety of reasons for breaching a contract, and the consequences of such a breach can be very serious even if the breach was unavoidable. Consider the case of the hotel that contracts to cater a couple's wedding reception. The contract to provide dinner, a cash bar, and a room with a dance floor is agreed upon in January for a wedding that is to take

LEGALESE

Breach of contract: Failure to keep the promises or agreements of a contract.

Force majeure: Greater force; a natural or human-induced disaster through no fault of the parties to the contract that causes a contract to not be performed.

place in early June. In late May, the hotel is sold, and the new owner immediately applies to the state liquor control board for a transfer of the liquor license. The control board requires a criminal background check of the new owner, which will take 60 days to complete. As a result, the hotel must operate for that period of time without a liquor license. The contract to provide a cash bar for the wedding is now breached, and the wedding party threatens litigation for the hotel's failure to keep its agreement. It may be that the breach just described could not have been avoided, but the negative effect on the wedding party is real as is the threat of litigation and loss of customer goodwill.

Remedies and Consequences of Breaching an Enforceable Contract

If a contract's terms are broken, and the contract is enforceable, the consequences can be significant. The plaintiff can pursue a variety of options when it is clear that the other party has breached a contract.

Suit for Specific Performance When this option is selected, the party that broke the contract is taken to court with the plaintiff requesting that the court force the defendant to perform the specific contract terms that have not been performed or to refrain from engaging in some activity that is prohibited by the contract. A simple example is a franchisee that has met all the terms and conditions of a franchisor and has signed a franchise agreement but at the last minute is told that he or she will not be granted the franchise because the franchisors themselves wish to build and operate on the designated site. In this case, the potential franchisee could bring legal action to force the franchisor to keep its promise and grant the franchise.

Liquidated Damages Often, the language of a contract will call for a specific penalty if the contract terms are not completed on an agreed-on date. If, for example, a building contractor has agreed to complete the repaving of an amusement park's parking lots by the beginning of the park's season, penalties may be built into the contract itself if the job is not finished on time. Indeed, the contractor may have offered the penalty option as an incentive to win the contract. Liquidated damages refer to these penalty payments. When a contract is breached, liquidated **damages** could be imposed.

Economic Loss When damages have not been specifically agreed on in the terms of the contract, the party that has created the breach may still be held responsible for damages. Consider the plight of the travel agency that contracts with a hotel for 100 sleeping rooms during the Christmas season for a tour group traveling to Hawaii. Upon arrival, the group finds that the hotel is oversold and thus the reserved rooms are not available. Because the hotel has breached the contract, the travel agency may bring litigation against the hotel claiming that the reputation of the agency itself has been damaged due to the hotel's contract breach. In addition, the agency may be able to recover the costs required to provide alternative housing for its clients. Few would argue that angry vacationers are good for business, and thus the agency may stand a good chance of recovering significant economic damages. These damages, if awarded, would be the responsibility of the hotel to pay as a direct result of the contract breach.

Alternative Dispute Resolution Often, there is honest disagreement over the meaning of contract terms. When this is the case, it may be difficult to determine which, if either, of the parties is in breach of the contract. When that occurs, the parties, or in some cases the courts, will elect to use dispute resolution techniques aimed at clearing up confusion or resolving the situation. Dispute resolution may also be used in other controversies, such as those involved with personal injury, employment, or labor disputes.

The two most common types of dispute resolution techniques are **arbitration** and **mediation**. In arbitration, the arbitrator is an independent, unbiased individual or a panel of individuals who works with the contracting parties to understand their respective views of the contract terms. The arbitrator then makes a decision that may or may not be binding on each party, depending on what the parties agree to prior to the arbitration hearing. A party to a dispute may want the arbitrator's decision to be nonbinding in order to have a glimpse at what a jury might do in the event the case proceeds to litigation and trial. In mediation, the mediator, who is again an independent, unbiased reviewer of the facts, helps the two parties come to an agreement regarding the issues surrounding the contract terms. If an agreement is reached between the parties, then the agreement is binding on all parties. Mediation can be an extremely effective way to bring a contract dispute to resolution.

Statute of Limitations

It is important to understand that if you intend to use the courts to enforce a contract, you must do so in a timely manner. There are specific laws that set out maximum time periods in which the courts are legally permitted to enforce or settle contract

---

LEGALESE

Damages: Losses or costs incurred due to another's wrongful act or omission.

Arbitration: A process in which an agreed-on, independent, neutral third party (the arbitrator) renders a resolution to a dispute. The decision of the arbitrator is known as the "award."

Mediation: A process in which an appointed, neutral third party (the mediator) assists those involved in a dispute to resolve their differences. The result of mediation, when successful, is known as the "settlement."

Legally Managing at Work

Eight Steps to Follow When Entering into Contracts

1. *Get it in writing.*

   The single most important thing a hospitality manager can do to avoid contract breach is to get all contracts in writing whenever possible. Many hospitality contracts are, by their nature, verbal contracts. Generally speaking, however, the verbal contracts for dining reservations or food delivery tend to be rather simple ones. When the relationsship between the contracting parties is more complex, it is nearly impossible to remember all the requirements of the contract unless the contract is committed to writing. For example, the standard contract for a hotel to provide sleeping rooms to airline crews staying overnight may run 50 typed pages or more. Obviously, it would not be possible to recall all the details of such an agreement without having that agreement in writing. A manager and his or her staff can only fulfill the terms of a contract if those terms are known and readily available for review.

   Because many contracts are complex, it is sometimes advisable to have these contracts reviewed by an attorney before agreeing to their terms. This can best be done if the contract is a written one. Changes, corrections, and improvements can be made only if the attorney can see the terms of the agreement and read what will truly be required of the client.

   Last, it is a simple fact that the representative parties to a contract may change, but the contract can still be used. For example, the contract between a waste hauler and a hospital to provide trash removal service to the hospital's foodservice facility will continue even if the manager of that facility is transferred, quits, or retires. In such a situation, the terms of the trash removal contract need to be established in writing, both as a professional courtesy to the incoming manager and as a service to the foodservice facility itself.

2. *Read the contract thoroughly.*

   The number of individuals and hospitality managers who sign contracts without thoroughly reading them is surprising, given that it simply is not possible for the managers or staff of a hospitality organization to fulfill all of their contractual responsibilities unless they know exactly what those responsibilities are. Just as important, it is not possible to hold vendors and suppliers accountable for the full value of their products and services unless contract language is known and understood.

   Consider the case of the hotelier who plans a beach party during a spring break weekend. This manager contracts one year in advance with a talent agency to provide a popular and expensive band that will play at the hotel during the two-day party. A fee is agreed on and the agent sends the hotelier a standard performance contract. Upon reading the contract carefully, the hotelier discovers the following paragraph:

   The agent, on behalf of himself and the entertainers, hereby authorizes the hotel and its advertising agency to use all publicity information, including still pictures, and biographical sketches of any and all entertainers supplied by the agent. These pictures and information may be used in any media, including television, radio, newspapers, and the Internet, that are deemed appropriate by the hotel. Agent further agrees that all such publicity information will be made available to the hotel no later than 30 days before the first performance.

   It is the hotelier's opinion that 30 days is not nearly long enough to advertise the event. In fact, at least six months of lead time is required to advertise in some of the spring break magazines that will be distributed on college campuses across the country. In this case, a single sentence in a much longer document could have a tremendous impact on the economic success of the entire spring break event. It is highly likely that the talent agent will, under the circumstances, agree to provide the publicity material in a time frame acceptable to the hotel. It is important to note, however, that it required a careful reading of the entire contract and the hotelier's experience in the field of advertising to detect this potential difficulty.

   Reading a written contract thoroughly before signing it is an important activity that must be undertaken to prevent contract breach. If it is determined that the hospitality manager simply does not have the time to read a complex contract in its entirety, then the contract should be referred to an attorney for review. Many managers refer any contract that exceeds a specific dollar amount or length of time to an attorney. The important concept to remember, however, is that all contracts must be read carefully. It is the manager's responsibility to see that this is done.

3. *Keep copies of all contract documents.*

   When agreements proceed as planned, contract language causes little difficulty. When there is disagreement or failure on the part of either party, however, contract language can be critical. It has been said, tongue in cheek, that "the large print giveth and the fine print taketh away." Because it is never possible to determine whether a contract will be trouble free, it is a good idea to keep a copy of all contracts that are signed. If the contract is a verbal one, it is a good idea to make notes on the significant agreement points and then file these notes.

   Many hospitality operators find that it is best to keep a separate section in their files devoted specifically to contracts. Others place contracts in individual customer or vendor files, and some do both. Regardless of the filing approach, if the contract is easily available for review when clarification is needed, the likelihood of contract breach will be reduced.

4. *Use good faith when negotiating contracts.*

   Good faith is a term used to designate an individual's honest belief that what he or she is agreeing to do can, in fact, be done. In a hotel manager's case, this can be as simple a concept as deciding that the hotel will accept no contracts for room reservations unless it, in good faith, believes that guestrooms can be provided.

   It is always best to carefully weigh the commitments of any contract. Many times, contracts are breached because one of the contracting parties finds it impossible to perform the obligations. While circumstances can change and no one can be perfectly clear about the future, it is worth noting that a careful, realistic assessment of contract capability and capacity can go a long way in avoiding contract breach.

5. *Note and calendar time deadlines for performance.*

   When a contract requires specific actions to be taken by or on designated dates, it is a good idea to list those dates in calendar form so that there can be no mistaking precisely when performance is required. It is especially helpful to create these timelines prior to signing a contract. In this way, any potential conflicts or impossibilities can be detected before it is too late. Many lawsuits involving contracts are initiated because one party did not do what he or she agreed to do in a timely manner. Noting and calendaring time deadlines can help prevent this from occurring.

6. *Ensure the performance of third parties.*

Many times in the hospitality industry, a manager must rely on others to fulfill some portion of a contract. Consider, for example, the hotel that hosts a meeting for a nonprofit organization of health-care workers. In order to secure the contract for the sleeping rooms and meeting space required by the group, the hotel agrees to provide audiovisual services for the meetings. Like many hotels, this hotel uses a third-party vendor to provide the audiovisual equipment. Obviously, a failure on the part of this third-party vendor can result in a failure on the part of the hotel to keep its promises. While it is not possible to prevent such an occurrence, it is important to recognize that when the use of third parties will be required, contract language addressing the third party's possible failure to perform should be included.

7. *Share contract information with those who need to know, and educate staff on the consequences of contract breach.*

Often, managers negotiate contracts that their employees must fulfill. However, an employee's ability to honor contract terms is directly related to his or her knowledge of those terms. Consider, for example, the hotel sales department that works very hard to prepare a bid to house the flight crews of a major airline that must layover in the hotel's city. The contract is won, and the crews begin to stay in the hotel. A portion of the contract relates to the cashing of personal checks. While the hotel's normal policy prohibits cashing personal checks over $25, the airline contract calls for the hotel to cash the personal checks of airline crew members for up to $100. These checks are guaranteed by the airline itself. Unless every desk agent and night auditor, as well as the management team at the front desk and the accounting department, are aware of this variation in policy, problems can occur. All it would take is the refusal by one uninformed or newly hired desk agent to cash a check, and the hard work of the sales department could be severely compromised.

8. *Resolve ambiguities as quickly and fairly as possible.*

Despite the best of intentions of both parties, contractual problems can arise. When they do, it is important that they be dealt with promptly and in an ethical manner. By doing so, a potentially damaging situation may be resolved quickly and amicably.

Consider the case of a tour bus company that contracts to stop at a midpriced downtown hotel on its way to Florida. The tour operator has a contract for rooms and meals; it is in writing, and the conditions are clearly spelled out. Upon checkout, however, the tour operator is surprised to find that the hotel has added a parking charge for the bus to the operator's bill. The tour operator protests that no such charge was part of the contract, and thus they should not have to pay it. The hotel points out that nothing in the contract states that parking would be provided free of charge, and thus the bill is owed. In a case like this, honest people can agree to disagree about the intent of the original contracting parties. Had the issue come up prior to signing the contract, the matter might have been quickly resolved. At this point in the process, resolution is important because the reputation of the hotel and its integrity may well be more important than the small amount involved in the parking charge. It is the responsibility of management to weigh the costs of litigation in both time and money before making a decision to fairly resolve a contract dispute.

By attempting to put himself or herself in the position of the other party and trying to understand that party's concerns, the manager may be able to find a compromise that is fair to all concerned and that will help reduce the possibility of litigation.

disputes. These laws are normally referred to as **statute of limitations**. Generally, the statute of limitations for written contracts is four years from the date of the breach; however, this is an area where exceptions apply and where state laws sometimes vary. As a hospitality manager, you should become familiar with your state's statute of limitations on contracts.

Preventing Breach of Contract

It is generally best to do all that is possible to avoid breaching an enforceable contract. As with any litigation, prevention is typically better than attempting to manage the negative consequences that may result from a contract breach. Preventing breach of contract may not always be possible. In most cases, however, the hospitality manager can avoid breaching contracts by following specific steps before and after entering into a contractual agreement. The steps listed below can help minimize the chance of litigation in the future.

Forecasting Contract Capacity

You have learned that contracts, whether verbal or written, commit the parties to the contract to very specific legal obligations. As a result, managers must carefully consider the implications before they agree to enter into contracts. One of the most difficult tasks facing the hospitality manager is that of forecasting contract capacity—in other words, knowing exactly how many contracts for products and services to accept on any given day or night. It is important to remember that a guestroom or dinner reservation, even if made orally, could be a valid contract. While some legal experts would argue that a contract does not exist until a deposit or form of payment has been supplied, the majority of legal scholars would agree that a contract is established when the guest makes a reservation and the restaurant or

LEGALESE

Statute of limitations: Various laws that set maximum time periods in which lawsuits must be initiated. If this suit is not initiated (or filed) before the expiration of the maximum period allowed, then the law prohibits the use of the courts for recovery.

hotel accepts that reservation in a manner consistent with its own policies. Therefore, if a hotel or restaurant accepts only reservations that are guaranteed with either a deposit or a credit card number at that facility, the contract will not be said to exist until that deposit is received or the credit card number is supplied. If, on the other hand, the hospitality facility regularly accepts reservations on an exchange of promise basis (i.e., the guest agrees to show up and the facility agrees to provide space), a contract does indeed exist at the time the reservation is made, and the hospitality facility can be held accountable if it does not honor its part of the contract.

To illustrate the difficulty encountered by hospitality professionals, consider the situation facing the food and beverage director of a large public golf course and country club. At that club, Mother's Day brunch is the busiest meal of the year. The club dining room seats 300. The average party stays 90 minutes while eating. The club will serve its traditional Mother's Day buffet from 11:00 A.M. to 2:00 P.M. Reservations are required, and historical records indicate that, on average, 15 percent of those making reservations will not show up (are no-shows), for a variety of reasons. The club does not require either a deposit or a credit card number to hold a reservation. The challenge for the food and beverage director is to know just how many reservation contracts to accept. If the director accepts too few contracts, other potential guests will be told the facility has sold out, yet the club's revenue will not have been maximized because more guests could have been served. If too many contracts are accepted, guests may not be able to be served at the time they have reserved or, possibly, may not be served at all, because there is no place to seat them. In the former situation, the club has not maximized its profit potential; in the latter, it may not be able to fulfill its contractual promises.

Some segments of the hospitality industry are very different from many other businesses because of the highly perishable nature of their products. For example, a hotel room that goes unsold on a given night can never be sold on that night again. An unoccupied cruise ship's berth on the day the ship is set to sail could also never be sold in the future. The same is true of unoccupied airline seats at the time a plane takes off.

In a like manner, in the restaurant segment of the hospitality industry, a table for five at a Mother's Day brunch can likely be sold only once or twice on that day. If the table goes unsold, the revenue lost cannot be easily recouped. This is different from most retail environments, where excess inventory can be discounted if management so desires. Obviously, the cost of no-shows at the hotel, cruise ship company, airline, or country club would be passed on to other guests in the form of higher room rates, travel costs, or menu prices. Clearly, this is a difficult situation for both the hospitality operators and their guests.

Years ago, the airline industry tried to address the problem of no-shows by overforecasting its contract capacity. Air carriers would accept far more reservations for seats on its flights than actually existed. In a precedent-setting piece of litigation, Ralph Nader sued Allegheny Airlines (which became US Airways and merged into American Airlines) in 1973 for intentionally over-booking a flight on which he had reserved a seat.[1] Nader won the lawsuit, and due in part to his litigation, in 1997, the Civil Aeronautics Board required the airline industry to inform consumers of their rights whenever an airline must "bump," or deny seating to, a passenger on its reserved and ticketed flights. The lesson for the hospitality industry is quite clear: If widespread overforecasting of contract capacity takes place and consumers suffer, the federal or state government may step in with mandated remedies for guests and regulated operational procedures for the hospitality industry.

Establishing an Effective Reservation Policy

The solution to the problem of forecasting contract capacity in the hospitality industry is to make a clear distinction among reservations that are confirmed, guaranteed, and nonguaranteed and to take reasonable steps to reduce no-show reservations. In some facilities, the no-show rate for reservations made is as high as 50 percent. In an effort to address this issue in a legally responsible and morally ethical way, future hospitality managers and the entire industry should begin adopting and educating consumers about the precise definition of a **confirmed reservation**.

A confirmed reservation can be made orally or in writing. In the restaurant business, it is common to hold a reservation for 15 to 20 minutes past the originally agreed-on time. Thus, if a dinner reservation is made for 8:00 P.M., the manager will hold space for the dinner party until 8:15 P.M. or 8:30 P.M., depending on the restaurant's policy. If the guests do not arrive by that time, they will have breached the reservation contract and be considered a no-show. In the hotel business, confirmed rooms are generally held until 4:00 P.M. or 6:00 P.M., after which the guest, if he or she has not arrived, is considered a no-show.

The difficulty involved in collecting monies due when a guest no-shows a confirmed but **nonguaranteed reservation** is significant. As a practical matter, collections on nonguaranteed reservations are almost never undertaken. On the one hand, there is no doubt that the guest who verbally reserves a table for dinner on a Friday night and then no-shows the reservation has broken a contract promise. The problem,

[1] *Nader v. Allegheny Airlines, Inc.* 365 F. Supp. 128 (1973); reversed 512 F.2d 527; cert. Granted 96 S.C. 355.

LEGALESE

Confirmed reservation: A contract to provide a reservation in which the provider guarantees the guest's reservation will be honored until a mutually agreeable time. A confirmed reservation may be either guaranteed or nonguaranteed.

Nonguaranteed reservation: A contract to provide a confirmed reservation where no prepayment or authorization is required.

however, is that initiating a lawsuit for a sum as small as a party of five's dinner bill is truly prohibitive in both time and money. On the other hand, guests also find that they have little recourse when a restaurant denies their confirmed but nonguaranteed reservations. The courts have been hesitant to force restaurants to pay heavy penalties if they refuse to honor a nonguaranteed reservation even when there is clear evidence that the reservation was the result of a legitimate contract.

To prevent these types of problems, hotels and restaurants should strive to accept all or nearly all of their reservations as **guaranteed reservations** and to accept nonguaranteed reservations only on an as-needed basis. For example, a popular restaurant may accept dinner reservations on a busy weekend only if the reservations are accompanied by a credit card number that will be billed if a guest should no-show. Similarly, while it is easy to understand that a hotel in Indianapolis could likely require payment in full to reserve a room during the busy Indianapolis 500 race weekend, all hotels have the legitimate option of insisting that all guestroom reservations include billing information (i.e., valid credit or debit card numbers) that would allow for the guest's billing in the event the guest no-shows his or her reservation.

What is called for is a reasoned response on the part of both parties. Guests must understand that a reservation requires the setting aside of space that could be sold to another. Hospitality managers should train their reservation agents to explain that guests will be given a confirmed reservation only if they agree, in advance, to guarantee that reservation.

Three major points should be clearly explained to the guest before agreeing to the guaranteed reservation contract:

LEGALESE

Guaranteed reservation: A contract to provide a confirmed reservation in which the provider guarantees the guest's reservation will be honored regardless of time of arrival but stating that the guest will be charged if he or she no-shows the reservation. Prepayment or payment authorization is required.

1. The hotel or restaurant will honor the reservation and will never knowingly offer to rent space for which it already has valid, guaranteed reservations.
2. The cancellation policy of the hospitality facility will be explained at the time of the confirmed reservation so that it is clearly understood by the guest.
3. Payment in accordance with the reservation contract will be made by the guests in the event that they no-show the reservation.

It is interesting to note that the state of Florida passed a law that says hotels will be fined if they deny space to any guest who has guaranteed a reservation by paying a deposit (as set by the hotel). Because most people would agree that knowingly accepting more guaranteed reservations than can be accommodated is ethically questionable, it is important that those in the hospitality industry work hard to ensure that a reservation, once confirmed, is honored.

Even when reservations are guaranteed with a deposit, no-shows can present a legal challenge in the hospitality industry. For customer relations purposes, few hospitality managers are willing to take a no-show guest to court to recover the money lost from holding a reservation. The time and legal expense, as well as the possible loss of goodwill, is simply too great. Naturally, guests do not like to be billed for services they did not use, even if they have contracted for them. Differences of opinion and possible litigation can arise, especially when a hospitality manager takes an aggressive stance in billing no-show guests for their confirmed reservations.

It might appear that the billing of guaranteed no-show reservations would be fairly straightforward. It is not. Even when policies on billing no-shows are clearly explained, difficulties will arise and judgment calls will have to be made.

It may be difficult or even impossible to eliminate all no-shows. They are an inevitable part of the hospitality industry. However, it is in the best interest of any hospitality facility that must forecast contract capacity to do so as effectively as possible.

Legally Managing at Work

Reducing No-Show Reservations

The following steps can help improve managerial accuracy in the forecasting process. In addition, they will help reduce the chance of litigation when contractual obligations related to reservations cannot be fulfilled.

1. *Become known as a facility that honors its confirmed reservations. If you choose to overbook, advise your guests of the practice and the potential consequences to them.* Establish a consistent policy for placing guests in other comparable properties in the event it is not possible to honor a confirmed reservation.
2. *Whenever possible, document all reservations in writing.*
3. *Put all policies related to making guaranteed reservations and the billing of no-shows in writing.* Follow these written policies.

International Snapshot

International Contracts

With the increasing number of hotels and restaurants expanding outside the United States and the number of non-U.S. vendors that are transacting with those hotels and restaurants, there is an increasing need for managers to be aware of issues that arise in trans-border transactions.

In addition to the "normal" contractual provisions otherwise identified in this section of this chapter, a manager should keep certain issues in mind when contracting with a non-U.S. party or for performance of work or services outside of the United States. Although each jurisdiction is different and has its own requirements, the following checklist can be used to identify potential areas that require additional thought:

1. *Clarity:* Take care to fully and accurately describe the performance required under the agreement. Carefully record any discussion in writing. Keep all prior correspondences to ensure that there is a record of what was discussed. Also, do not take anything for granted, and remember that there may be cultural and language variances that contribute to the need for more specificity. Make sure that both parties have a clear expectation of performance, and specify the language to be used for the agreement.
2. *Currency risk issues:* Specify in the agreement the type of currency used to pay for the transaction in question. Give preference to the currencies that are stable. And in long-term contracts (or contracts that are performed over time), it is advisable to agree on a specific exchange rate if the agreement contemplates the use of local currency as part of the business activity (e.g., guests at a hotel in a non-U.S. country pay in the currency of that country).
3. *Repatriation of funds:* Look into foreign exchange restrictions to see if there are any prohibitions of funds out of a country or any currency conversion restrictions. These will likely impact how and when a party will be paid. If being paid in U.S. dollars is difficult due to the cost of exchange, alternative currencies may need to be considered. Also, look into withholding taxes or fees imposed on foreign-based entities for payment of fees or reimbursements (along with any U.S. tax ramifications). It may be necessary to include "gross up" provisions (to increase the actual amount paid to account for any taxes) to ensure that a party is made whole on any fees or reimbursements to be paid under any contract.
4. *Local law issues:* Consult a local lawyer on issues of local law. This is particularly important when business activities are being performed in countries other than the United States. There may be a number of issues that need to be considered, for example foreign exchange (as mentioned above), tax regulations, employment laws and practices, entity set-up, local operational permits and any specific registrations that may be required for foreign enterprises to engage in commerce, registration of contracts, intellectual property registrations and usage. A good starting point for "issue-spotting purposes" would be to consult with the local chapter of the American Chamber of Commerce or U.S. consulate—but be sure to consult with local lawyers.
5. *Dispute resolution:* Litigation is costly and may not be the most efficient way to resolve a dispute. Therefore, the agreement should contain provisions that provide for a mechanism to resolve matters in case of a dispute. This avoids confusion in the event of a dispute. Parties often rely on the resolution by senior executives of the contracting parties as a first step. If no resolution can be reached at that step, then the dispute resolution provision may call for arbitration by the International Chamber of Commerce or mediation by an expert familiar with the industry of the contracting parties. Experts are routinely used to resolve disputes regarding budgets and other operational matters in the United States—and our view is that this is also becoming routine in trans-border transactions as the economies become more globalized. In defining who would qualify as an "expert," it is critical to set out the expertise required and any other conditions that would establish the neutrality of the expert. The key is to spell out the terms and of any dispute resolution mechanism so that the parties will not be fighting about them when they are trying to resolve a dispute—which makes reaching a resolution more difficult and can potentially delay the resolution of the dispute at issue. To ensure the clarity of such terms, a lawyer familiar with international dispute resolution should be consulted.
6. *Choice of law/venue:* Make sure that that the agreement clearly states which laws govern the transaction. Will it be the laws of one of the parties or of a neutral location? Note that on certain issues, such as real estate, labor, or foreign exchange control issues, you may need to rely on local law. The laws of another jurisdiction, however, can still be elected to govern the other parts of the transaction or the agreement reached between the parties. Also, in case arbitration fails (if parties determine the arbitration is non-binding or if the arbitration award needs to be enforced), it is important to agree on the venue of the lawsuit. Because of the trans-border nature of transactions, parties often agree in the agreement to a location (often neutral) where the litigation can be initiated and carried out. One word of caution: Make sure that the courts of the venue chosen have the capability to apply the laws specified in the agreement.
7. *U.S. regulations and laws:* Also be sure to check and include any prohibition against the violation of any applicable U.S. laws and regulations which apply to U.S. companies engaging in businesses abroad, including the Foreign Corrupt Practices Act and the regulations of the Office of Foreign Asset Control, and any other applicable regulations. U.S. companies are legally required to ensure that any potential business partner is not on the "Specially Designated Nationals" list of the Office of Foreign Asset Control, and it is routine practice for U.S. companies and banks to conduct this initial "know your customer" research as a starting point of a business relationship. This issue should not be overlooked by any U.S. companies entering into a contract with any potential non-U.S. business partner. Provisions will need to be built into the agreement to provide for covenants to comply with applicable U.S. laws or not to engage in activities that would cause the business enterprise (and the U.S. party involved in the enterprise) to violate U.S. laws. For all applicable issues to consider, a good place to start would be the "Doing Business Abroad" page of the U.S. Department of State website for a general overview. Additionally, be sure to consult with knowledgeable counsel.

Provided by San San Lee of the Law Offices of San San Lee, Los Angeles, California. www.sansanlaw.com.

The foregoing is only a representative list of issues to consider in the context of an international contract. As always, local laws and customs should be reviewed and consulted along with the fundamental contract principles otherwise discussed in this chapter and other parts of the book.

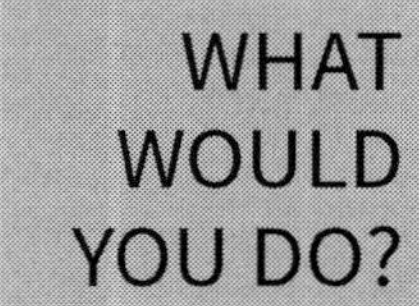

Assume that you manage a 300-room hotel. Your local university football team is playing a home game on Saturday, and the demand for rooms far exceeds supply. Your no-show rate on reservations for the past three football games has been 8, 12, and 9 percent, respectively. Currently, you have 100 nonreserved rooms.

Prepare a brief (half-page) report describing how you would answer the following questions.

1. How many room reservation contracts are you willing to accept?

2. Should you require that all reservations be confirmed?

3. What factors will you consider as you make your decision? What strategies will you employ to reduce no-shows? Write a short (half-page) essay answering questions 4 and 5 that follow, drawing from your personal perspective.

4. You and your family are traveling out of state to attend one of your school team's away football games. Upon arrival, the hotel where you have a confirmed reservation denies you a room because it has none available. What do you think the hotel should do for you?

5. What if no other rooms were available within a 50-mile radius of the hotel you originally booked?

WHAT DID YOU LEARN IN THIS CHAPTER?

Contracts are used in the hospitality industry to govern the many different promises and business transactions entered into on a daily basis. Contracts can take one of two forms, verbal or written. To be enforceable in a court of law, a contract must legally be entered into by competent parties and include an offer, consideration, and acceptance.

The Uniform Commercial Code (UCC) is the law regulating contracts related to buying and selling. This code gives protection to buyers, sellers, and financial lenders when goods are purchased under contract. Because reservations are considered to be a type of contract, it is important that hospitality managers develop reservation policies that will allow them to fulfill the promises made to their guests while maximizing their own revenue in the event that guests do not honor their reservations.

A breach of contract occurs when one of the parties is unable to fulfill the obligations set forth in a contract. When this occurs, the injured party may go to court and receive damages or some other type of remedy. The best way for managers to prevent a breach of contract is by thoroughly understanding their rights and obligations under the contracts they agree to and by taking the necessary steps to fulfill those requirements.

CHAPTER **5**

Significant Hospitality Contracts

5.1 Specific Contract Clauses

In the previous chapter, you learned about basic business contracts. Many of the contracts used in the hospitality and tourism industries are very similar to those used in other industries; these include contracts regarding employment, routine facilities and grounds maintenance, equipment purchases, employee insurance, and accounting services, to name but a few areas. There are, however, some unique and very specialized hospitality- and tourism-related contracts and contract terminology you will likely encounter during your hospitality career. In this chapter, you will learn about this industry-specific terminology, as well as some types of specialized contracts.

Types of Specialized Contracts

Although it is not possible to list all of the potential types of specialized contracts hospitality managers may confront, the following four types deserve special explanation because of their widespread use in the hospitality industry. Each of these contract/agreement types is examined in detail later in this chapter.

Franchise-Related Contracts As you learned in Chapter 3, in a franchise arrangement, the owner of a hospitality facility (the franchisee) agrees, in exchange for a franchise, to operate the business in a specific manner approved by the franchisor. The actual franchise contracts utilized in the selection, purchase, and implementation of franchise operating agreements are highly regulated and very detailed. Unless very carefully created and thoroughly read, these intricate agreements can often be misconstrued or misinterpreted by the contracting parties. Therefore, it is important to fully understand their intent and complexity.

Management Operating Agreements A management contract, or as it is very commonly known, a management **operating agreement**, is created when the owner of a hospitality facility allows another party to assume the day-to-day operation of that facility.

Hospitals, school foodservices, campus dining operations, and business dining facilities are commonly operated under management contracts. Hotels, from the smallest to the largest, can also be operated in this

LEGALESE

Operating agreement: A contract that details the areas of responsibilities of the owner of a business and the entity selected by the owner to operate the business. Also referred to as a "management contract."

CHAPTER OUTLINE

5.1. Specific Contract Clauses
5.2. Franchise Contracts
5.3. Management Contracts
5.4. Conference Services Contracts

IN THIS CHAPTER, YOU WILL LEARN

1. Contract clauses commonly utilized in hospitality contracts.
2. The purpose of a franchise contract (franchise agreement).
3. The purpose of a management contract (management operating agreement).
4. Important forms of meeting space contracts used in lodging operations.
5. Important forms of group rooms contracts used in lodging operations.

manner. In an operating agreement (management contract), the facility owner allows the management company to make the operational decisions that are necessary for the facility to effectively serve its clientele. Typically, a management contract will set forth, in great detail, the period that the agreement will be in effect, the payment terms, the responsibilities of each party, and the stipulations by which the arrangement can be ended, as well as a variety of legal and operational issues. These agreements are typically very detailed and, as a result, understanding their basic components as well as areas of possible contention is very important.

Meeting Space Contracts Although guestroom contracts of many limited-service hotels consist only of individual or group rooms sales agreements, full-service hotels will enter into many meeting space contracts in addition to their individual and group room contracts. Especially in larger hotels with significant amounts of meeting, event, and convention space, not only are meeting space contracts common, but also their proper management is essential to the profitability of their respective properties.

Hotels are not the only segment within the hospitality industry that utilizes meeting and space contracts. Convention centers, country clubs, restaurants, and catering halls are just a few of the many hospitality industry facilities that routinely rent space and may provide meetings related services to their guests. Such facilities must carefully detail, via a contract, the services they will provide their guests, as well as the terms under which they will provide them.

In many cases, the contract terms for meetings are negotiated between a hotel and one or more professional **meeting planners**.

Meeting planners annually buy large numbers of sleeping rooms, as well as reserve significant amounts of meeting and catering space. Meeting planners may negotiate group room contracts, meeting space contracts, or both combined into one contract.

These individuals may represent a variety of corporations, groups, and organizations. They are sophisticated buyers of hotel products who often use comparison-shopping techniques, and who can heavily influence a hotel's reputation based on their experience with it. It is not unusual for hotels to designate one (or more) very experienced staff members to deal exclusively with this group of professionals. As a result, understanding how these contracts are actually negotiated and developed is essential to hospitality managers in a variety of industry segments.

Search the Web 5.1

Meeting Professionals International (MPI) is the world's largest association of meeting planning professionals with over 20,000 members. You can learn more about this group by visiting its website at **www.mpiweb.org**.

Note the large number of educational services it offers. Many of these are designed to help the members better negotiate and administer the meetings contracts they execute with the hotels they select for their meetings.

Group Lodging Contracts A group room contract is developed when an individual or organization requires a large number of hotel rooms. Nearly all hotels rely, to some degree, on group business to help maximize their room sales revenue. The situations in which group rooms are sold can be as varied as an agreement with an airline to provide overnight accommodations for flight crews, to group meetings and conventions, and family weddings. In Chapter 4, "Business Contracts," you learned that hotels are required to honor individual guestroom reservations because when such reservations are made, they constitute valid business contracts. As well, when group reservations are made, a unique type of contract is created, and hotels must also honor these.

Group room contracts are different, in many ways, from individual room contracts, and they frequently contain distinctive features that must be well understood by hoteliers. Group room contracts are common because many hotels require that any room request exceeding a total of 10 sleeping rooms per night be confirmed by a written contract. The reason is simple: When a guest requests a large number of rooms, he or she may expect a discount for each room purchased. This is often agreeable to the hotel, but the precise conditions under which the discount is to be offered are best confirmed with a written contract. Furthermore, a group rooms contract may be drawn up months or years before the rooms will actually be used. This is often the case for large convention hotels that may contract for rooms and space several years ahead of time. A written contract guarantees that the sponsoring group will have the amount of rooms they need and the hotel can expect to receive revenue for the use of its rooms for a certain period of time. In this chapter, you will learn how group lodging contracts should be structured.

In addition to the unique types of contracts that are found in the hospitality industry, there are also industry-specific words and phrases that must be understood if contracts of these special types are to be properly created and their terms accurately followed. These special types of contract wording are known as essential **clauses**.

In the next portion of this chapter, you will examine essential contract clauses that hospitality managers should carefully examine in all of the contracts they execute. This also applies to those provisions utilized in the contracts hospitality

LEGALESE

Meeting planners: A group of professionals that plan and organize meetings and events for their employers and clients.

Clause (contract): A distinct contract provision or stipulation.

managers negotiate when they sell products and services to their customers and guests and to the essential clauses they utilize when they contract to purchase their own business-related products and services. When you understand all of these, you will be ready to learn more about specialized hospitality and tourism contracts.

Since business contracts can cover a variety of offer and acceptance situations, their form and structure can vary considerably. That said, all hospitality contracts should contain certain essential clauses, or stipulations, that a manager should identify and review carefully before entering into the contract relationship. These essential clauses are actually not specific wordings; rather, they are areas or terms of the agreement that should be clearly spelled out to ensure that both parties to the contract understand them completely. The reason for including these clauses in contracts, and for reviewing them carefully, is to prevent ambiguity and misunderstanding.

Essential Clauses for Providing Products and Services to Guests

It is always better to settle potential difficulties before agreeing to a contract than to be forced to resolve them later and perhaps create ill will or significant legal problems. Reviewing the following essential clause areas in contracts before agreeing to their terms can help you do just that.

Length of Time the Contract Price Terms Exist

When an offer is made, it generally will include the price proposed by the seller. It is just as important to clearly establish exactly how long that price is to be in effect. When issuing coupons, for example, the manager of a quick-service restaurant (QSR) will want to clearly inform consumers of the coupon's expiration date. If a hotel's director of sales grants a particular corporation a special discounted room rate based on anticipated rooms sales, it is important to note the length of time that the reduced rate will be in effect. When any offer for products or services includes a price, the wise and prudent hospitality manager will specify the time frame for holding, or honoring, that price.

Identification of Who Is Authorized to Modify the Contract

Unanticipated circumstances can cause guests to change their plans at the last minute. This is especially true in lodging, where group rooms or meeting contracts may be modified during the group's stay. A typical situation would be one in which an organization signs a contract for meeting space. In one of the meeting rooms, an invited speaker requests that a liquid crystal display (LCD) projector and projection screen (items not included in the original contract) be provided for his use. If, acting on the request of the speaker, the hotel provides the equipment, the contracting organization may later refuse to pay for it. Although the equipment was in fact provided, the invited speaker was not authorized to modify the original contract.

It is always important to identify, prior to agreeing to contract terms, exactly who will be given authority to modify the contract should the need arise. It is also best to require that any modifications to the contract be in writing wherever practical. Handwritten notes and email messages may be helpful in determining the intent of the parties when modifying contract terms.

Deposit and Cancellation Policies

Hotels often require deposits before they will reserve sleeping rooms for guests. It is important to remember that a hotel room is an extremely perishable commodity. Room nights cannot be "saved up" by hotel managers in anticipation of heavy demand, nor can their numbers be quickly increased in the face of heightened actual demand. Consequently, hotel managers must be very careful to ensure that rooms reserved by a guest will in fact be purchased by the guest. The portion of a contract that details an operation's deposit and cancellation policies is critical both to the hotel and to the guest, and thus must be made very clear.

Deposits guarantee reservations. Typically, unless approved direct billing is established with a group in advance, a deposit equal to the first night's room and tax bill will be required on group lodging contracts and some individual room reservations. This deposit may be required at the time of the contract's signing or 30 days prior to the group's arrival. For most individual room reservations, a credit or debit card number from a valid payment card is the method used to guarantee the reservation. In other cases, personal checks or certified checks may be required.

Cancellations of reservations can occur for a variety of reasons. If the hotel is to have a fair cancellation policy, it must consider the best interests of both the hotel and the guest, and the policy must be clearly stated in the contract. This is true whether the contract is oral or written. Generally, failure to cancel a guaranteed reservation by the agreed-on time will result in forfeiture of an advanced deposit or one night's room and tax, billed to the payment card number that was given to guarantee the reservation.

When groups are very large and the revenue expected from the group's stay at the hotel is substantial, cancellation penalties can be more tightly defined. Figure 5.1 shown on the next page illustrates the type of clause used in a convention hotel to protect it from last-minute cancellations of an entire group.

Allowable Attrition

Allowable **attrition** refers to the amount of downward variance that may be permitted in a contract before some type of penalty is incurred on the part of the guest. Attrition in the hotel industry is also known as slippage.

Attrition, then, is simply the loss of previously estimated guest counts. Consider, for example, the individual guest

---

LEGALESE

Attrition: Reduction in the number of projected participants or attendees.

Cancellation Clause

If arrangements for the event are canceled in full, a fee consisting of a percentage of the total anticipated revenue outlined in this contract will be charged. The fee is determined by the length of time between written notification of the cancellation and the scheduled arrival date as follows:

0–31 days prior to arrival	100% of anticipated revenue
32–90 days prior to arrival	75% of anticipated revenue
91–180 days prior to arrival	50% of anticipated revenue
181–365 days prior to arrival	25% of anticipated revenue

Anticipated revenue may include room, meal, gratuities, telephone, and hotel-provided services, as well as taxes due on recovered sums.

FIGURE 5.1 **Cancellation clause.**

responsible for hosting a large family reunion in his or her city. When the guest first approaches the hotel to reserve sleeping rooms and space for meals, the family reunion might be months away. The guest will want to know the specifics of room rates to be charged, as well as prices for meals. Both of these charges, however, might depend on the "pick-up," or actual number of served guests. This is true because, in most cases, the more sleeping rooms sold or meals provided, the lower the price. At the time of the contract signing, however, the actual number of guests to be served is likely unknown. The guest responsible for planning the reunion may estimate 200 attendees when planning the event, but at the reunion, only 100 individuals attend. Allowable attrition clauses inform both parties of the impact, on price, of a reduced number of actual guests served.

Figure 5.2 is an example of an allowable attrition clause in a group lodging contract. Notice that both parties to the contract are clearly informed about the consequences of reduced pick-up on the part of the guests. In addition, the clause has a statement clearly indicating that if the size of the group is reduced by too much, the hotel may relocate the meal or meeting space of the group. This is particularly important in a facility with restricted meeting space, where there might be only one large ballroom. If guests reserve this room based on a large estimate of attendees, which then fails to materialize, the hospitality manager might have no choice but to move the group to a smaller room, thus freeing the larger room for potential resale.

It is important to remember that guests often overestimate the projected attendance at their functions. If hospitality managers do not consider the impact of attrition, their operations may be hurt by this common guest tendency. As attrition disputes are becoming more common, meeting planners are insisting that contracts also include clauses that hold the hotel accountable for using reasonable diligence to resell any rooms unused by the meeting to reduce the damages caused by exceeding the allowable attrition.

Allowable Attrition Clause

The Hotel agrees to hold ample inventory to accommodate the rooms reserved in this Group Rooms Contract. In doing so, the Hotel may be put in a position to turn away other groups that may request rooms for the same dates. Therefore, the Hotel limits the amount of attrition or reductions in the contracted room block. Additional reductions will be billed at 100% of the contracted room and tax.

91 days or more prior to arrival	50% of room block
61–90 days or more prior to arrival	20% of room block
31–60 days or more prior to arrival	10% of room block
Less than 31 days prior to arrival	2% of room block

For all meal and meeting functions, the Hotel reserves the right to move groups to a room with capacity equal to the actual number of guests to be served.

FIGURE 5.2 **Allowable attrition clause.**

Indemnification for Damages

The phrase "to indemnify" means to secure against loss or damage. Indemnity language is important when a hotel contracts with an organization whose individual members will occupy rooms designated under a group contract. In one situation, an organization of law enforcement officers contracted with a hotel to hold its annual convention. During the course of the convention, a few members of the organization became intoxicated and caused some damage to the physical property of the hotel. The question then arose: Who should be held responsible for the damages? The law enforcement organization, the individual officers, and the cities that employed them were all considered possible sources of damage reimbursement.

It is important to make clear exactly who will be responsible if damages to rooms or space should occur. Although significant damage during a guest's stay is certainly the exception rather than the rule, the possibility of consequential damage does exist and should be addressed. A general clause covering this area in a group rooms' contract might read as follows:

> *The group shall be liable for any damage to the hotel caused by any of its officers, agents, contractors, or guests.*

Payment Terms

Although payments and terms for payment might seem relatively straightforward, in the hospitality industry, contract payment terms can sometimes become quite complex. Consider the case of a visiting college basketball team. The head coach reserves sleeping rooms and agrees to pay for the rooms with a college-issued credit card. One of the players, however, makes several hundred dollars' worth of long-distance telephone calls from his hotel room. Who is responsible for this payment? Further, how can the hotel hope to collect the monies due to it? The best way to address problems such as these is to clearly and precisely state the terms of payment and the responsibility for all expenses incurred.

Dining establishments generally require a cash, check, or credit/debit card payment at the time of meal service. In the lodging industry, payment can take a variety of forms:

- Individual guest pays all charges.
- Company or group pays all charges.
- Payment in full is required prior to arrival.
- Hotel directly bills the company or group for room and tax only.
- Hotel directly bills the company or group for all charges.
- Individual guest pays incidentals (e.g., telephone, meals, movies, laundry, and parking).
- Multiple guests are all billed to one common master bill.

Note that in the preceding example, if the coach's contract called for the group to pay all charges, then the college would indeed be responsible for the long-distance telephone charges. If the contract included a clause in which individuals pay for incidentals, then the individual player would be held responsible for the charges. The importance of using precise language to prevent ambiguity should be apparent.

Performance Standards Related to Quantity

Previously, we discussed ways for hospitality managers to address the problem of attrition and no-shows. But what of the guest whose actual numbers exceed the original estimate? If, for example, a catering hall anticipates serving 200 guests, but 225 people arrive to attend the event, the operation may face space and production shortages. Because this type of situation is also common, many operators will prepare food and create place settings in the dining room for a number of guests larger than the contracted guest count. This approach prevents frantic, last-minute attempts to meet an unanticipated demand.

While there is no industry standard established, many operators find that agreeing to prepare for 5 percent more guests than the contracted number is a good way to balance the potential needs of the guest with the actual needs of the operation. When the operation agrees to a performance standard related to quantity, this standard should be clearly stated in the contract.

When providing for products and services in the vastly diverse hospitality industry, additional essential clauses may be required based on the type and style of the hospitality facility. When that is the case, management should identify these potential problem areas and address them each and every time a contract is executed.

Essential Clauses for Purchasing Products and Services

Just as there are essential and important components of a contract that state when the hospitality manager is responsible for providing products and services, it is equally critical to ensure that essential clauses are in place when hospitality managers contract to purchase or receive products and services. Here, too, it is in the best interest of both parties to get all contractual arrangements in writing. Listed next are some of the important contractual elements to be considered before executing a purchasing contract.

Payment Terms Some of the most significant components of a contract for buying products and services are the payment terms. Consider the case of the restaurateur who wants to purchase a new roof for her restaurant. She gets three bids from contractors, each of whom quotes her a similar price. In one case, however, the builder wants full payment prior to beginning work. In the second case, the builder wants half the purchase price prior to beginning the job and the balance upon a "substantial completion" of the work. In the third case, payment in full is required within 30 days after completion of the job. Obviously, in this case, the payment terms could make a considerable difference in which contractor gets the bid.

Required down payments, interest rates on remaining balances, payment due dates, and penalties for late payments are points that should be specified in the contract and reviewed carefully.

Delivery or Start Date In the case of some delivery dates, a range of times may be acceptable. Thus, when purchasing sofas, a hotel could insert contract language, such as "within 60 days of contract signing" as an acceptable delivery date clause. In a like manner, food deliveries might be accepted by a kitchen "between the hours of 8:00 A.M. and 4:00 P.M."

In some cases, the delivery or start date may be unknown. Consider, for example, the following contract clause written when a hotel agreed to lease part of its lobby space to a flower shop. The time it would take to get the shop stocked and operational was unknown, and thus the start date of the lease could not easily be determined. The delivery/start clause here is part of that longer contract document. In the section titled "Start Date," it reads:

> The initial Operating Term of this agreement shall commence at 12:01 A.M. on the first day the Flower Shop is open for business and terminate at 11:59 P.M. on the day preceding the tenth (10th) anniversary thereof; provided, however, that the parties hereto may extend this agreement by mutual consent for up to two (2) terms of five (5) years each.

Note that, although the actual start date was uncertain, the language identifying precisely when the start date was to occur was unmistakable. In all cases, it is important that a start date be stated in the contract and that it be clear.

Completion Date Completion dates let the contracting parties know when the contract terms end. In the case of a painter hired to paint a room, this date simply identifies when the painter's work will be finished. If the contract is written to guarantee a price for a product purchased by a restaurant, the completion date is the last day that price will be honored by the vendor.

It is often difficult to estimate completion dates. This is especially true for construction contracts when weather, labor difficulties, or material delays can affect timetables. Despite these difficulties, completion dates should be included whenever products or services are secured.

As for ongoing contracts with vendors or suppliers, a hospitality manager may want the flexibility of terminating the contract early (prior to expiration) by providing a set number of days within which to terminate the contract (i.e., a 30-, 60-, or 90-day notice for termination). This type of clause is particularly helpful to a hospitality operator who may decide for various reasons to end the legal relationship with the vendor or supplier but without the added burden of proving a default under the contract or waiting for the time period for the contract to expire on its terms. Perhaps an ownership or management change, or the request to use a different vendor may be the reason for the termination. Many vendors and suppliers that are confident in their products and services will agree to allow such early termination without cause or penalty, so long as enough time has occurred for them to recoup any initial investment they may have made in the relationship.

Some contracts are written in such a manner that the completion or stop date of the contract is extended indefinitely unless specifically discontinued. The following clause is taken from an agreement to cooperatively market hotel rooms with a discount hotel broker. Note the language related to the contract's extension:

> Unless otherwise noted in the contract, this participation agreement between the hotel and Tandy Discount Brokerage automatically renews on an annual basis unless cancellation is received in accordance with established publication period deadlines.

Self-renewing contracts are very common in hospitality contracts and must be reviewed very carefully by management prior to acceptance of their terms. The fine print of some vendor contracts may say that the contract will automatically renew for another term unless notice is given 30 days prior to the renewal date. Many times, this provision is misinterpreted by management. Management needs to understand that the window of time "30 days prior to the renewal date" does not mean the hospitality company can terminate on 30 days' notice anytime during the contract. It is important to calendar (identify for future attention) any action required by management to discontinue a self-renewing contract so that critical dates will not be missed.

Performance Standards

Performance standards refer to the quality of products or services received. This can be an exceptionally complex area because some services are difficult to quantify. The thickness of concrete, the quality of carpeting, and the brand or model of a piece of equipment can, for example, be specified. The quality of an advertising campaign, a training program, or interior design work can be more difficult to evaluate.

The effective hospitality manager should quantify performance standards in a contract to the greatest degree possible and avoid making assumptions that their intent should be clearly known. With some thought and help from experts in the topic the contract is about, great specificity may be determined. Consider the foodservice manager who wishes to purchase canned peach halves. A purchase specification, such as the following, could be included as part of the purchase contract:

> U.S. Grade 3 (Choice), packed 6, number 10 cans per case, with 30 to 35 halves per can. Packed in heavy syrup, with 19 to 24 Brix; minimum drained weight, 66 ounces per number 10 can, with certificate of grade required.

Recall that under the Uniform Commercial Code (UCC), a vendor is contractually obligated to provide goods that are fit for use and free of defects. Clauses that specify performance standards in a purchasing contract give both buyers and sellers an added level of protection because the extra details will clearly spell out the expectations of both parties with regard to the nature and quality of the goods transferred.

Licenses and Permits

Obtaining licenses and permits, which are normally required for contracted work, should be the specific responsibility of the outside contracting party. Tradespeople, such as plumbers, security guards, air conditioning specialists, and the like, who must be licensed or certified by state or local governments, should be prepared to prove they indeed have the appropriate credentials. However, it is the responsibility of the hospitality manager to verify the existence of these licenses and their current status if they are required to perform the terms of a contract. A hospitality manager needs to know whom they are doing business with, especially new vendors and suppliers. In addition, a photocopy of these documents should always be attached to the contract itself. Figure 5.3 is an example of a general clause related to the issue of licenses and permits.

Indemnification/Insurance

Accidents can happen while an agreement is being fulfilled. In order to protect themselves and their organizations, hospitality managers should

Licenses and Permits Clause

The contractor represents and warrants that it has in effect all licenses, permits, and other authorizations or approvals necessary to provide the services from all applicable governmental entities, and that such licenses and permits shall be maintained and in full force and effect for the length of this contract. The revocation, suspension, or withdrawal of any license, permit, authorization, or approval shall be immediately reported in writing by the contractor, and in such an event, the contract will be suspended. The contractor shall provide evidence that all such licenses, permits, and other authorizations are in effect at the signing of this contract and at any time during its length at the request of the owner.

FIGURE 5.3 **Licenses and permits clause.**

insist that the contracts they execute contain **indemnification** language similar to this example:

> Contractor hereby agrees to indemnify, defend, and hold harmless the restaurant and its officers, directors, partners, agents, employees, and guests from and against any losses, liabilities, claims, damages, and expenses, including, without limitation, attorneys' fees and expenses that arise as a result of the negligence, intentional misconduct, or any omissions of contractor or any of its agents, officers, employees, or subcontractors.

To better understand indemnification, consider the case of Melissa Norin, the manager of a restaurant located near an interstate highway. Ms. Norin hired Twin Cities Signs Company to change the lights in a 60-foot-high road sign advertising the restaurant. While completing this work, a Twin Cities truck collided with a car parked in the restaurant's parking lot. The car owner approached Ms. Norin, demanding that the restaurant pay for the car's damages. Without an indemnification clause in the contract for services with Twin Cities, the restaurant might incur expenses related to the accident and/or a subsequent lawsuit.

An indemnification from a supplier or vendor is only as good as her or his ability to stand by the agreement. If the company providing the indemnification has few assets to make good on any claim, it is essential to have a third party to look to for relief. At a minimum, the vendor or supplier should list the hospitality company and the property as an additional insured on the vendor's or supplier's general liability insurance policy. Copies of the insurance coverage should be provided to the hospitality manager upon execution of the agreement. In Chapter 15, "Managing Insurance" we will look closely at insurance matters when we discuss the legal aspects of insurance in hospitality operations.

Certainly, it is a good idea to have all contracts reviewed by legal counsel, but because of the significance of indemnification and insurance, these clauses in a contract should be written only by a competent attorney.

Nonperformance Clauses

Often, it is a good idea to decide beforehand what two parties will do if the contract terms are not fulfilled or if the terms are performed but not up to acceptable standards. In the case of purchasing products and services, the simple solution may be for the hospitality manager to buy from a different vendor. If, for example, a fresh-produce vendor who has contracted with a group of family-owned restaurants frequently misses delivery deadlines or delivers poor-quality products, the nonperformance solution might simply be to terminate the contract. Language would need to be written into the contract that would address the rights of the restaurant group to terminate the agreement if the vendor consistently performed unsatisfactorily.

In some cases, nonperformance on the part of the vendor can have an extremely negative effect on the hotel or restaurant. If, for example, a hotel books a well-known entertainer as a major component in a weekend package, the failure of that entertainer to perform as scheduled would have a significant negative impact on the hotel.

It is very likely that the reputation of the hotel would suffer because it promised its guests something it did not deliver. The guests are likely to demand refunds in such a situation, and the potential that one or more of them could bring litigation against the hotel is very real.

In addition to the costs incurred due to unhappy guests, the cost of replacement entertainment might be quite high if the original entertainer canceled on short notice. Figure 5.4 is an example of nonperformance contract language that might be used to protect the hotel in such a case.

When nonperformance by a vendor would cause a negative effect on the hospitality operation, it is critical that language be included in the contract to protect the operation. The protection may be in general terms, such as the clause in Figure 5.4, or it may be quite specific. A common way to quantify nonperformance costs is to use a "dollars-per-day" penalty. In this situation, the vendor is assessed a penalty of agreed-on "dollars per day" if it is late in delivering the product or service.

Dispute Resolution Terms

In some cases, it is a good idea for contracting parties to agree on how to settle any disputes that may arise before they actually occur. To do so, several issues may need to be addressed. The first is the location of any litigation undertaken. This is not a complex issue when both parties to the contract and their businesses are located in the same state. When the contract is between two parties that are not located in the same state, contract language such as the following could be inserted into the contract:

> This agreement shall be governed by and interpreted under the laws of the State of __________ [location of business].

Additional terms may include the use of agreed-on, independent third parties to assist in problem resolutions. Litigation costs are another area of potential disagreement

Entertainer Nonperformance Clause

The "Entertainer" recognizes that failure to perform hereunder may require Hotel to acquire replacement entertainment on short notice. Therefore, any failure to provide the agreed-upon services at the times, in the areas, and for the duration required hereunder shall constitute a default, which shall allow the Hotel to cancel this contract immediately on oral notice. The "Entertainer" and or his or her agent shall be liable for any damages incurred by the Hotel, including without limitation, any costs incurred by the Hotel to secure such replacement entertainment.

FIGURE 5.4 **Entertainer nonperformance clause.**

LEGALESE

Indemnification: To make one whole; to reimburse for a loss already incurred.

Analyze the Situation 5.1

Laureen Statte was a guest at the Vacation Inn Express, a mid-priced, limited service hotel in an urban area. When she arrived at the hotel, she inquired about the availability of a workout room. Upon receiving assurances that the hotel did indeed have such an area, Ms. Statte checked into the hotel, put away her luggage, changed into workout attire, and proceeded to the workout area.

Upon entering the workout room, she noticed a sign prominently posted near the entrance to the workout room stating: "Hotel Not Liable for Any Injuries Incurred During Workouts."

According to her attorney, Ms. Statte lifted deadweights for approximately 10 minutes and then mounted a treadmill. As an experienced treadmill user, she started slowly, gradually increasing the treadmill's speed. Shortly after beginning the treadmill workout, Ms. Statte fell backward into a plate-glass window that was approximately 2 feet behind the treadmill. The glass shattered, and shards from the glass severely injured Ms. Statte.

Ms. Statte's attorney claimed the accident was the fault of the hotel because the treadmill was too close to the window and the hotel neglected to outfit the windows with safety glass. As its defense, the hotel pointed out the presence of the exculpatory clause sign, clearly posted, that Ms. Statte agreed she had read prior to beginning her workout.

1. Do you believe a guest who has agreed to be responsible for her own injuries during a workout has also agreed to be responsible for them in the presence of significant negligence on the part of the hotel?
2. As the hotel manager, how might you resolve this dispute?
3. Could a lawsuit have been prevented?

that can be addressed before any contract problems arise. Language such as the following makes clear who is responsible for the costs associated with contract litigation:

> Should any legal proceedings be required to enforce any provisions of this Agreement, the prevailing party shall be entitled to recover all of its costs and expenses related thereto, including expert witnesses' and consultants' fees and attorneys' fees.

Exculpatory Clauses

In addition to the essential elements related to providing and receiving products and services just listed, some hospitality managers would add an **exculpatory clause**, especially when providing products and services to guests. These clauses seek to exculpate, or excuse, the hospitality operator from blame in certain situations.

An example of an exculpatory clause is a sign in a pool area that states "Swim at Your Own Risk" or a clause in a meeting space contract that states "Operator not responsible for materials left in meeting rooms overnight." Although these clauses may help reduce litigation, it is important to understand why this is so. Exculpatory clauses generally alert and/or cause guests to exercise greater caution. Warning signs or contract language that cause guests to be more careful truly will work in the favor of both guests and the hospitality organization. In addition, some parties to a contract may accept the exculpatory statement as legal truth. That is, they will assume that they have somehow given up their right to a claim against the hospitality organization because of the exculpatory clause's language.

It is very important to note, however, that many courts have not generally accepted the complete validity of exculpatory clauses. In some cases, they do in fact exculpate; in others, for example situations adverse to sound public policy, they do not. Consequently, exculpatory clauses have the disadvantage of sometimes providing a false sense of security to the operator. In summary, these clauses can be useful, but they should not be relied upon to absolve the operator of his or her reasonable responsibilities to care for the safety and security of guests.

5.2 Franchise Contracts

In Chapter 3, you learned that franchising is a business strategy that allows one business entity to use the logo, trademarks, and operating systems of another business entity for the benefit of both. Because of the potential for abuse, the laws and contract language that govern the advertising for sale and purchase of franchises are closely regulated and complex. As well, the language of the franchise agreements that control the actions of franchisor and franchisee are typically very detailed and, as a result, must be well understood by both of these parties.

Purchasing a Franchise

Evaluating and purchasing a franchise is a very complex undertaking. This can be made even more difficult if the companies selling franchises are not open and honest in the description of their offerings. In the past, some franchisors in some industries were fraudulent or deceptive in their claims. Because of this, detailed regulations and laws have been enacted that specify **disclosure** requirements that franchisors must follow when, as shown in the example in Figure 5.5, they advertise their franchise for sale.

LEGALESE

Exculpatory clause (or contract): A contract, or a clause in a contract, that releases one of the parties from liability for his or her wrongdoings.

Disclosure: To reveal fully and honestly.

Crystal's Coneys and Chips

The International Franchise Leader in Coney Dogs and Fries

Crystal's Coneys and Chips is the worldwide segment leader in take-out Coney dogs and freshly made French fries (chips). There's a good reason why. Our franchisees realize that the support, training, and marketing assistance available through Crystal's Coneys and Chips (CC&C) ensure them the highest possible return on investment. It's true in Frankfort, Kentucky as well as Frankfurt, Germany!

America and the world love Coney dogs and chips. At CC&C we have developed the very best recipes for both of these popular items. This means strong customer counts and strong revenues. Strong revenues mean a strong bottom line, and that's why our franchisee retention rate is second to none in the industry.

Ninety percent of our 500-plus stores are franchisee-owned and -operated. CC&C operates only 10 percent of them. That's why we know that listening to you, not competing with you, makes us both successful.

We can assist in site selection, financing, and start-up. Our franchise fees and start-up costs are low. If you are serious about your future in the Coney dog and chips market, e-mail Maureen Pennycuff, international director of franchise sales at *mpennycuff@cc&c.com*, or visit our Web site at

www.cc&c.com

This is the one franchise opportunity that you can't afford to miss!

FIGURE 5.5 Fictional representation of the type and style of information typically placed in an advertisement for a franchise that would be found in the hospitality trade press.

The Franchise Rule The Federal Trade Commission (FTC), through its mandate to regulate unfair or deceptive trade practices, is the government agency assigned the task of regulating the offering of franchises. To do so, the FTC requires all franchisors to supply information that it believes is necessary for a potential franchisee to make an informed buying decision. (The types of information that franchisors must disclose will be discussed later in this section.) It is important to note that while the FTC requires that certain information be disclosed, it does not verify the accuracy of that information. Figure 5.6 is a statement from the FTC that must be prominently displayed on the cover or first page of a disclosure document, which the franchisor is required to supply to anyone considering purchasing a franchise.

In the mid-1970s, the FTC developed a document titled "Disclosure Requirements and Prohibitions Concerning Franchising and Business Opportunity Ventures," which took effect on October 21, 1979. Commonly known as the Franchise Rule, it established detailed disclosure requirements for franchisors.

Federal Trade Commission Warning Statement

To protect you, we've required your franchisor to give you this information. *We haven't checked it and don't know if it's correct.* It should help you to make up your mind. Study it carefully. While it includes some information about your contract, don't rely on it alone to understand your contract. Read all of your contract carefully. Buying a franchise is a complicated investment. Take your time to decide. If possible, show your contract and this information to an advisor like a lawyer or an accountant. If you find anything you think may be wrong or anything important that's been left out, you should let us know about it. It may be against the law.

There may also be laws on franchising in your state. Ask your state agencies about them.

FIGURE 5.6 Franchise warning statement.

Revised Franchise Rule In January 2007, the Federal Trade Commission approved amendments to the Franchising Trade Regulation Rule. The changes were optional from July 1, 2007, until July 1, 2008. After July 1, 2008, the changes became mandatory for all franchisors. The major changes in the new Franchise Rules occur in the areas of disclosures and exemptions.

The rules governing the content of the disclosures, as well as the substance of the disclosures, have been changed. Franchisors must now disclose all franchise-initiated litigation. Additionally, franchisors no longer have to disclose franchise brokers. Also, if current or former franchisees have signed confidentiality clauses in franchisor agreements in the last three years, the disclosure document must contain language about the existence of such clauses. However, the most significant change is the requirement of a fully reconciled summary of the inflow and outflow of franchised and company-owned outlets over the course of each year.

Search the Web 5.2

Visit **https://www.ftc.gov/enforcement/rules/rulemaking-regulatory-reform-proceedings/franchise-rule**.

Read the entire FTC Franchise Rule (16 CFR Part 436) to familiarize yourself with its requirements, and then write a one-page bulleted summary of the rule.

Procedures for disclosures have changed, as well. Franchisors can now deliver the disclosure document not only in hard copy or CD-ROM format but also through email or through the franchisor's website. The disclosure document must be delivered no later than 14 calendar days before the franchisee signs any agreement or pays any money. Last, the final franchise agreement must be disclosed to the franchisee at least seven calendar days before the franchisee executes it.

The amended rules have exempted certain franchise relationships. Purchases by owners, officers, or managers of franchisors are not covered by the new rules. If the franchisee has been in business for five years and has a net worth of $5 million, then the new Franchise Rules do not apply. If the franchisee's initial investment is larger than $1 million (excluding the value of the real estate and any amounts provided by franchisor), then the new rules do not apply. Last, the amended rules do not apply if the franchise location is outside the United States.

For more information, please visit www.ftc.gov/opa/2007/01/franchiserule.shtm.

The Franchise Rule imposes six different requirements in connection with the "advertising, offering, licensing, contracting, sale, or other promotion" of a franchise:

1. *Basic disclosures:* Franchisors are required to give potential investors a basic disclosure document at the earlier of the first face-to-face meeting or 10 business days before any money is paid or an agreement is signed in connection with the investment (Part 436.1(a)).
2. *Earnings claims:* If franchisors make earnings claims, whether historical or forecasted, they must have a reasonable basis for those claims, and evidence supporting the claims must be given to potential investors in writing at the same time as the basic disclosures (Parts 436.1(b)–(d)).
3. *Advertised claims:* The rule affects only promotional ads that include an earnings claim. Such ads must disclose the number and percentage of existing franchisees that have achieved the claimed results, along with cautionary language. The use of earnings claims in promotional ads also triggers required compliance with the rule's earnings claim disclosure requirements (Part 436.1(e)).
4. *Franchise agreements:* The franchisor must give investors a copy of its standard-form franchise agreement and related agreements at the same time as the basic disclosures and final copies intended to be executed at least five business days before signing (Part 436.1(g)).
5. *Refunds:* Franchisors are required to make refunds of deposits and initial payments to potential investors subject to any conditions on refundability stated in the disclosure document (Part 436.1(h)).
6. *Contradictory claims:* Although franchisors are permitted to supply investors with any promotional or other materials they wish, no written or oral claims may contradict information provided in the required disclosure document (Part 436.1(f)).

The Franchise Offering Circular Some states have franchise investment laws that require franchisors to provide presale disclosures, known as franchise offering circulars (FOCs), to potential franchisees. These states treat the sale of a franchise like the sale of a security. They typically prohibit the offer or sale of a franchise within their governance until a company's FOC has been filed as a public record with, and registered by, a designated state agency.

Those states with disclosure laws give franchise purchasers important legal rights, including the right to bring private lawsuits for violation of the state disclosure requirements. The FTC keeps a record of those states that require franchisors to provide FOCs. Potential franchise purchasers who reside in states that have these requirements should contact their state franchise law administrators for additional information about the protection these laws provide.

The FOC is a document designed to encourage the purchase of a franchise. These circulars generally will follow a format patterned after the FTC's Franchise Rule. It is important to remember, however, that the FTC does not verify the information contained in a circular. Because this is true, the documents making up the FOC should, like all contracts, be read very carefully.

The following information must be included in an FOC. This information is demanded by states that require FOCs in accordance with guidelines established by the FTC. After reading these items, you may realize that these state requirements are almost identical to the FTC's own disclosure requirements in the Franchise Rule:

- A description of the franchisor and the type of license it is offering.
- The business experience of the franchise company's owners and/or managers.
- Initial fees, continuing fees, and royalties if required.
- Initial investment estimates.
- The licensee's obligations.
- The licensor's obligations.
- Policies about the geographic territory protected by the license agreement.
- Restrictions on what the licensee may sell and how it may be sold.
- Renewal and termination policies.
- Transfer of ownership policies.
- Claims regarding average earnings or profitability of current franchisees.
- Locations of current franchisees.
- A sample franchise (license) agreement.
- Any information required by a specific state (e.g., California, Utah, Maine).
- The name and address of the legal representative of the franchisor.

Additional items may be included based on state law, FTC requirements, and the specific nature of the franchise. Again, it is important to remember that one of the goals of the FOC is to facilitate the selling of franchises. As with any disclosure, those who prepare it should be honest, or they face possible litigation for deception. Similarly, those who read the document for purposes of purchasing a franchise should be prepared to verify, to the greatest degree possible, the information it contains.

Franchise Agreements

If, after reviewing the FOC, an owner elects to execute a contract with a franchisor, then the two parties will sign a special form of hospitality contract called a **franchise agreement**.

The franchise agreement is the document that actually regulates the relationship between franchisee and franchisor. It is important for the franchisee to ensure that the information in the FOC is consistent with that found in the franchise agreement. Because the franchise agreement details the rights and responsibilities of both the franchisor and franchisee, the document will directly address the following topics:

License granted
Franchisee responsibilities
Franchisor responsibilities
Proprietary rights
Audit requirements
Indemnification and insurance requirements
Transfer of ownership policies
Termination policies
Renewal options
Relationship of the parties to the contract
Areas of protection
Terms of the agreement (start and stop dates)

As such, the franchise agreement should be carefully read and examined by an attorney. For a hospitality manager whose responsibilities include operating a franchise, either as a franchisee or as an employee hired by the franchisee, it is imperative that the contract terms be followed. If they are not, the franchisor may have the right to terminate the contract.

It is important to understand that, in most cases, franchisor companies do not actually own the hotels operating under their brand names. Instead, such companies own the right to sell the brand name and determine the standards that will be followed by those hotel franchisees who elect to affiliate with the franchise brands. With the ownership of a hotel vested in one business entity and the responsibility for brand standards resting with another business entity, it is not surprising that conflict can arise between the hotel's owners and the brand managers. For example, assume that the managers of a given brand decide that the bedding for their brand, and thus the mattresses, bedspreads, sheet quality standards, and pillow sizes, are not in keeping with the quality of that provided by competing brands. The brand managers may have the authority, under the franchise agreement, to require affiliated hotel owners to update their bedding. The owners, however, facing significant purchase and replacement costs for bedding that is in perfectly good condition but that has been declared "substandard" by the brand managers might attempt to resist the purchase of the new items. In fact, franchisee may disagree with their brand owners about numerous operating issues.

Because franchisors are generally in a stronger bargaining position than the franchisee, the franchise agreement is often heavily weighted in favor of the franchisor. However, like any contract, the franchise agreement is a negotiable document. Up-front or application fees, monthly royalties, areas of protection, required purchases, or renovations to facilities are all contract areas that can be negotiated prior to signing the franchise agreement. Difficulties and misunderstandings can arise between franchisors and franchisees, even when details seem to be clearly spelled out in the contract. Some of the most glaring areas of tension center on specific ways of operating the business and balancing the needs of the franchisee with those of the franchisor.

The franchise agreement is, in the final analysis, simply a contract between the brand owner and the franchisee. As such, it is negotiable. The stronger the position of each side, the more power each will bring to the negotiating process. It is always in the best interest of the business's owners to be represented by an attorney during the franchise agreement finalization period because these agreements are detailed and complex. In the opinion of many attorneys, franchise agreements, which are drafted by the franchisor, tend to be written in the favor of the franchisor. Because this is true, franchisees should carefully read every line of the franchise agreement to determine exactly what they must do to stay in compliance with the agreement as well as the penalties that will be incurred if they do not stay in compliance.

To become familiar with some of the many areas of potential conflict between the manner in which franchisors and franchisees interpret management agreement terms and clauses, follow the instructions in Search the Web 5.3.

Search the Web 5.3

Go to **www.hospitalitylawyer.com**

1. Select: Solutions.
2. Select: Find Academic Resources.
3. Select: Hospitality Law Textbook Support.
4. Select: Referenced Articles.
5. Select "Joint Franchisor-Franchise Relations by Robert Zarco, Richard Barrett-Cuetara, and Andrew Loewinger Presented at the Third Annual Hospitality Law Conference."
6. Review this article, and be prepared to discuss it in class.

LEGALESE

Franchise agreement: A special hospitality contract that details the responsibilities of both parties (franchisor and franchisee) involved in the operation of a franchise.

Selling a Franchise

Selling a nonfranchised business is sometimes complex. However, selling a franchise can be even more difficult because, in most franchise contracts, the sale of a franchise will generally require approval from the franchisor. The franchisor's rationale is clear: It is in its best interest to ensure that any owner who takes over a franchise indeed meets the requirements the franchisor has set out for its franchisees. This is, of course, a legitimate interest. It results, however, in a situation that places restrictions on the seller.

In some cases, the franchisor retains the **right of first refusal** in a franchise sale. In other cases, such as that in Figure 5.7, the franchisor will insert a clause in the franchise agreement that requires notification in the event of a pending sale. Should the new buyer elect not to renew the franchise, the franchisee may have to pay a termination fee to the franchisor.

An independent restaurant or lodging facility owner who elects to sell his or her business is free to determine a suggested selling price, advertise that the business is for sale, and sell the business as he or she sees fit. When a franchisee wants to sell his or her business, however, the franchisor often requires that the prospective buyer sign the current franchise agreement, which most often contains materially different financial terms from those in the selling franchisee's agreement. What the buyer is buying is often different from what the seller is selling.

Owning a franchise is an effective way for many entrepreneurs to improve their odds of success when starting a business. Investigating the many different alternatives available from various franchisors is an important part of this process. From a legal standpoint, the manager of a franchise operation has the dual burden of operating in such a way as to satisfy both franchisees of the operation and the franchisor. When conflicts occur between the best interests of the franchisee and those of the franchisor, it is important to remember where the agency relationship lies. In fact, language inserted by the franchisor in a franchise agreement is typically very clear about that issue, as can be seen in Figure 5.8.

Notification/Nonassumption Clause

In no event shall owner offer the hotel through public auction or through the media of advertising, either in newspapers or otherwise, without first obtaining the written consent of franchisor, which shall not be unreasonably withheld.

If in the event of the sale of the hotel the purchaser fails to assume owner's obligations hereunder, or in the event franchisor shall have elected to terminate this agreement, then owner agrees to pay to franchisor as liquidated damages and not as a penalty, no later than the closing, or 10 days following the effective date of such termination, a termination fee in an amount equal to the greater of 12 times the average monthly fees earned by the franchisor during the preceding 12 months or 12 times the basic fees projected in the current year's operating budget.

FIGURE 5.7 **Right of first refusal clause.**

Agency Relationship Clause

The franchisee is an independent contractor. Neither the franchisee nor franchisor is the legal representative or agent of the other. No partnership, affiliate, agency, fiduciary responsibility, or employment relationship is created by this agreement.

FIGURE 5.8 **Agency relationship clause.**

5.3 Management Contracts

In Chapter 3, you learned that some hospitality business owners choose to allow another entity to operate their businesses. When they do so, the terms and conditions of the operating arrangement are documented in a management contract or operating agreement, or, as it is also known, a **management agreement**.

Management companies are common in all segments of the hospitality industry. As a result, a great number of hospitality managers will, during their careers, work directly or indirectly with a management company. Because that is true, it is important that you understand how management companies are structured, the manner in which the management contracts (agreements) under which they operate are developed, and the unique relationship that results when an owner selects a management company to operate a franchised business.

Management Companies

A management company is an organization formed for the express purpose of managing one or more businesses. Management companies may be classified in a variety of ways, such as the industry segment in which they operate, their geographic location, and their size. From a legal perspective, however, one important way to classify management companies is by the ownership interest they have in the businesses they operate. This relationship can take a variety of forms, including these four:

1. *The management company is neither a partner nor an owner of the business it manages.* In this situation, the business's

LEGALESE

Right of first refusal: A clause in a contractual agreement between two parties in a business relationship in which one party, upon termination of the business relationship, can exercise the right to buy the interest of the other party before those rights can be offered for sale to another.

Management agreement: The legal agreement that defines the responsibilities of a business owner and the management company chosen to operate the owner's business. Also known as a "management contract."

owners simply hire the management company. This is common, for example, when lenders involuntarily take possession of a business. In other cases, the management company may, for its own philosophical reasons, elect to concentrate only on managing properties and will not participate in business investing (ownership).

2. *The management company is a partner (with others) in the ownership of the businesses they manage.* Although this common arrangement exists in many segments of hospitality, it is especially popular within the hotel industry. Frequently, in this situation, the management company either buys or is given a portion of business ownership (usually 1 to 20 percent) and then assumes the management of the property. Those business owners who prefer this arrangement feel that the partial ownership enjoyed by the management company will result in its better performance. However, if the business experiences losses, the management company will share in these losses, and this fact can help serve as a motivator for the management company.
3. *The management company manages only businesses it owns.* Some management companies form simply to manage the businesses they themselves own. These companies want to participate in business as both investors and managers. Clearly, an advantage of this situation is that the management company will benefit from its own success if the businesses it manages are profitable. If the company is not successful, however, it will be responsible for any losses incurred in its operations.
4. *The management company owns, by itself, some of the businesses it manages, and owns a part, or none at all, of others it manages.* To understand better the complexities of the various scenarios under which a management company can function, consider a very successful hotel management company operating in a large city. The company decides to vary its ownership participation in the businesses it manages, depending on the individual hotel it manages. Thus, in this example, the hotel management company might:
   - Own 100 percent of one or more hotels it manages.
   - Manage and be a partial owner of other hotels.
   - Manage, but not own any part of, yet another hotel property.

In each of the situations just described, it is important, as you learned previously, for hospitality managers actually employed by the management company to clearly understand the fiduciary responsibilities that accompany their employment (see Chapter 3).

Types of Management Contracts

Not surprisingly, there are as many different contracts between those who own businesses and the management companies they employ as there are businesses under management contract. Each business owner might, depending on the management company selected, have a unique management contract or operating agreement for each business owned. In some cases, these contracts may include preopening services provided before the business is officially open and may even include activities related to the sale of the business.

Management contracts can be complex and their terms subject to diverse interpretation. In his 1980 book *Negotiation and Administration of Hotel and Restaurant Management Contracts,* James J. Eyster detailed many of the components typically included in hospitality management agreements. Considered a classic work in the field of management contracts, it is an excellent examination of the complexities of hospitality contracts and issues. This is so because, while times have changed since 1980, and, certainly, each specific management contract is different, many of the negotiable issues identified in Eyster's book must still be addressed by owners and prospective management companies when they are discussing a potential management agreement:

- The length of time the agreement is to be in effect.
- Base fees to be charged.
- Incentives fees earned or penalties assessed related to operating performance.
- Contract terms in the event of the business's sale.
- Management company's investment required or ownership required.
- Procedures for early termination by either party.
- Procedures for extending the contract.
- Exclusivity (Is the management contract company allowed to operate competing businesses?).
- Reporting relationships and requirements (how much reporting detail is required and how frequently reports will be produced).
- Insurance requirements (who must carry the insurance—the owners or the management company—and how much).
- Employee status (Are the employees if the business employed by the owner of the business or the management company?).
- The control, if any, that the owner has in the selection or removal of the business's management personnel.

The interests of hotel owners and the management companies they employ frequently conflict, and these conflicts can sometimes become highly publicized. On the surface, it would seem that the interests of a business owner and the management company selected to operate its business would always coincide. Both the owner and management company, it would seem, are interested in operating a profitable business. In fact, however, disputes arise because business owners will typically seek to minimize the fees they pay to management companies (because reduced fees yield greater owner profits), while management companies, of course, seek to maximize their fees.

Owners who hire management companies often have serious disagreements with those companies over whether the businesses they manage are indeed operated in the best interest of the owners. There are various reasons for these disagreements. For example, in a typical management contract, the owner absorbs the costs of management company errors. Unlike a lease arrangement, in a management contract, it is generally the owner, not the management company, that is responsible for all costs associated with operating the business. As a result, the unnecessary costs incurred as a result of any errors in marketing or operating the business are borne not by the management company making the errors but by the business owner.

For another example of potential owner/management company conflict, consider that recent lawsuits filed by owners against management companies focus on the issue of how management companies purchase goods and services for the businesses they manage. Management companies in the hospitality industry are responsible for purchasing billions of dollars' worth of products, including, for example, food, furniture, fixtures, in-room amenity items, computers, and software, as well as services such as insurance, long-distance telephone, credit card processing, and payroll preparation services. Difficulties can arise when management companies, who are authorized by their management contracts to make purchases on behalf of owners, reap the benefits that accrue to large-volume buyers. In some cases, large management companies have negotiated contracts with literally hundreds of manufacturers and suppliers. These contracts often produce millions of dollars of rebates directly from the vendors back to the management company. The management company could retain these rebates and, in fact, may even operate their purchasing departments as separate profit centers. In other cases, the management company could have an equity investment in some of the vendors companies, or in the most egregious of cases, even own the vendor company outright. Although these types of arrangements are not automatically illegal, they must be disclosed to the owners of the businesses for whom the management company is under contract and to whom is owed a fiduciary duty.

It is important to remember that agency law requires agents to place their principals' interest over their own, precludes agents from competing with their principals, and precludes self-dealing. That is, agents should not operate on their own behalf without disclosure to and approval of their principals. If rebates received by a management company, as in this example, are not disclosed to the business owner, they might cease being rebates and simply become vendor **kickbacks**.

Ethical issues arise when a management company directly receives a benefit (discounts, commissions, or rebates) based on purchases made on an owner's behalf. Should those benefits accrue to the owner or the management company? The answer should be clearly spelled out in the management contract.

Search the Web 5.4

Go to **www.hospitalitylawyer.com**

1. Select: Resources.
2. Select: Solutions.
3. Select: Find Academic Resources.
4. Select: Hospitality Law Textbook Support.
5. Select: Referenced Articles.
6. Select "Management Contracts Litigation Update by David Moseley Presented at the Third Annual Hospitality Law Conference."
7. Review this article, and be prepared to discuss it in class.

Management Contracts for Franchised Properties

As you have learned, a hospitality business, especially hotels, may:

- Operate as a franchise
- Operate under a management contract

As well, a business may operate as a franchise under a management contract. Just as special legal issues arise when operating a business as a franchise and when operating under a management contract, issues also arise when operating a franchise business under a management contract. To better understand the legal issues that may occur in an operating arrangement that includes both a franchise and management company, it is instructive to examine, as an example, the hotel segment of the hospitality industry.

Hotel owners often find themselves in some level of conflict with or, at the very least, in disagreement with franchisors about how to best manage the franchised brand as well as how to operate the individual hotels making up the brand. For example, assume that the franchisor of a hotel brand has, as a brand standard, established breakfast hours for the hotel's complimentary continental breakfast to be from 6:00 A.M. to 9:00 A.M. Assume also that the hotel is operated for its owners under a management contract.

The hotel's owners have instructed the management company to begin the breakfast at 7:00 A.M., rather than 6:00 A.M. on the weekends to reduce labor costs. If the management company follows the directive of the brand owners, it has violated the owner's wishes (but fulfilled the terms of the franchise agreement); however, if it follows the clear instructions of the hotel's owner, it will be in violation of a brand standard and thus the owner's franchise agreement.

When owners instruct management companies to violate or ignore brand standards, the resulting influence on the hotel's relationship with the brand can be negative. Alternatively, when brand owners seek a management company's compliance with acts that may be in the best interest of the brand

LEGALESE

Kickback: A secret rebate of part of a purchase price given by the seller to the buyer in exchange for the buyer's influence in the purchasing decision.

managers, but not necessarily the hotel's owners, difficulties may also arise. This will, in most cases, be true despite the claims of franchisors that all of their actions are undertaken in the best interest of the brand's franchisees.

Even when a hotel's owners do not intentionally initiate brand-related conflict with their management companies, it can still occur. For example, assume that those brand managers responsible for selling franchises to owners were successful in convincing a hotel's owners to reflag (choose a new brand) their property. Assume also that this owner employs a management company to operate the hotel.

After one year of operation, the owner complains to the franchise company that the number of reservations received through the franchisor's national reservation center is not consistent with the amounts verbally promised by the brand's sales representatives. In fact, the owners complain, the volume of reservations received is only about one-half of that promised. In cases such as these, it is not at all unusual (and in fact is most likely), that the brand managers will claim that it is the management company operating the hotel, not the brand, that is the cause of the shortfall.

Not surprisingly, the management company is highly unlikely to agree with this assessment. The potential for resulting conflict is clear. This is simply one example of possible brand versus management company conflict.

As you learned, sometimes a management company owns all or part of the hotel it operates. In most arrangements, however, the management company does not own the hotel it operates. The result is that, in some cases, conflicts arise between the management company and the brand owner (but not the hotel owner). Many management companies have excellent relations with the brands they manage for owners, while others do not. This results because, at times, some of the wishes or even the directives of the brand managers are in conflict with the perceived best interest of the management company.

For example, a franchise company might, in an effort to promote business, send to a management company managed hotel several large, exterior banners, that advertise a special rate or hotel feature. Obviously, the franchisor (brand owner) wants these signs displayed on the property. The management company's sales philosophy, however, might not include hanging large exterior banners around the hotel because it believes such banners cheapen the image of the hotel. Because of this belief, the banners are not displayed. The resulting conflict is actually easy to understand from the perspective of both entities. The conflict should not, however, be allowed to escalate and significantly damage the relationship between the franchisor and management company because that could easily result in real harm to the long-term best interest of the business and its actual owners.

In addition, the franchisor (brand owner) may want to have some say or direction in connection with the management company's employees and how they are managed. In the past, franchisors were responsible only if they had direct control over working conditions of franchisee's employees. This standard may be changing as a result of The National Labor Board's general counsel who announced in 2014 that McDonald's Corporation is responsible for labor violations concerning its franchisee's employees under the joint employer rule.[1] Results of future litigation will provide additional direction for franchisors and will be watched carefully by all.

5.4 Conference Services Contracts

For many hospitality businesses, especially for hotels, well-executed contracts related to conference services are vital to the operation's profitability. Conference services contracts are unique in that they are typically executed between a hospitality business and a group. Group business is critical to the success of many hospitality businesses, but it is especially important to hotels and conference centers. Interestingly, however, there is no universally accepted definition of *group* business. Groups may, for example, consist of tour groups, sports teams, conventions, trade shows, corporate training meetings, wedding parties, and special travel packages marketed by the hotel's sales department and other multiroom night users. Despite the specific characteristics of a group or its reason for meeting, **conference services contracts** detail the terms and conditions of the group's meeting arrangements.

One of the most important components of conference services contracts is the language used to establish and assign responsibility for the group's **master bill**.

Master bills are helpful when one member of the group is responsible for paying all hotel charges. If, for example, a company sponsors a training session for its employees, it is likely to be most convenient for that company's accountant to pay one invoice for meeting space, meals, and hotel rooms rather than to reimburse individuals for their individual costs. Similarly, a coach traveling with a sports team will likely find a master bill to be the best way to pay for the team's rooms. Master bills, however, and their management are frequently one of the areas of greatest conflict in conference services contracts.

For most hospitality businesses, conference services contracts will take one of two basic forms: meeting and space contracts and group lodging or sleeping rooms contracts. In many cases, a group may utilize both a hotel's meeting space and its lodging facilities. In such cases, the contract between the group

[1] https://www.nlrb.gov/news-outreach/news-story/nlrb-office-general-counsel-authorizes-complaints-against-mcdonalds

LEGALESE

Conference services contract: An agreement that details the space, products, and services to be provided to a group before, during, and after its meeting.

Master bill: A single folio (bill) established for a group that includes specifically agreed-on group charges. Sometimes called a "master folio," "group folio," or "group bill."

and the hotel will, by necessity, include components found in each of the two basic types of conference services contracts.

Meeting Space Contracts

Although limited-service hotels primarily contract for the sale of sleeping rooms, full-service hotels, as well as conference centers and some other hospitality organizations, also offer guests the ability to reserve meeting space, meeting rooms, exhibition halls, and food and beverage services. For example, a large, full-service hotel might contract with a nonprofit organization to provide sleeping rooms, meeting space, and an exhibit hall for the use during the association's annual convention. When this occurs, the rental rate for the space may be tied to the number of sleeping rooms used by the group during its meeting; in other cases, however, the price of the meeting space is not related to the use of sleeping rooms. Since most hotels have limited meeting space and that space is used primarily as an enticement to sell sleeping rooms, experienced hotel managers must carefully contract for the sale of this space. The meeting space contract utilized by a hotel or conference center allows the manager to set precisely the terms and conditions on the sale of its valuable meeting space and services. Figure 5.9 provides an example of the level of detail typically found in such contracts.

Group Lodging Contracts

Although the meeting and space contracts developed by full-service hotels sometimes include provisions for sleeping rooms as well, contracts for "sleeping rooms only" are very

MEETING CONFIRMATION

DATE:

ORGANIZATION:

CONFERENCE:

GROUP CONTACT:

TITLE:

PHONE: **FAX:**

ADDRESS:

KEY DUE DATES: For your convenience, we have listed key dates mentioned within this Meeting Confirmation for your reference. Please review the corresponding sections for further information.

Acceptance/Signed Meeting Confirmation

Credit Arrangements/Completed Credit Application

Reservation Cutoff

Program Details/Menu Selections

Three Days Prior to Scheduled Events

Food and Beverage Guarantees

PROGRAM SPECIFICS:

DATES:

DAY:

DATE:

SINGLES:

DOUBLES:

CONCIERGE:

FIGURE 5.9 **Group meeting contract.**

Check-in time is 4:00 P.M.; check-out time is 12:00 P.M.; late checkout is $15.00 per hour until 4:00 P.M., after which time a full day's charge will apply. Complimentary luggage storage is available.

GUESTROOM RATES

Singles:

Doubles:

Conclerge Level: $40 additional

Early Arrival:

Late Departure:

The above room rates are subject to prevailing taxes, which are currently at 17%.

DAY MEETING PACKAGE RATES (for all meeting attendees):

Subject to 8.25% sales tax and 20% service charge

This DAY GUEST PACKAGE RATE Includes:

Lunch (A spen Dining Room): Lunch is available for seating at 11:30 A.M. or 12:30 P.M.

Meeting Room Supplies: Room setup, pads, pencils, Ice water pitchers, and hard candles.

Continuous Beverage Service (7:30 A.M.–5:00 P.M.): Coffee, decaf, tea, assorted sodas, and bottled water.

Community Refreshment Breaks

Morning Break (7:30 A.M.–10:30 A.M.): Assorted baked goods (varies dally), sliced fresh fruit, assorted mini-yogurts and orange juice.

Afternoon Break (2:00 P.M.–4:00 P.M.): Assorted afternoon snacks, fresh baked cookies or brownies of the day, candy, whole fresh fruit, and lemonade.

Standard Audio Visual

10–25 people: 2 flipcharts (including markers and masking tape), data projector, screen, podium and easel.

26–50 people: 2 flipcharts (including markers and masking tape), 2 data projectors, 2 screens, standard microphone, VCR/DVD player, easel, and message board.

51–75 people: 3 flipcharts, 2 data projectors, 2 screens, standard microphone, VCR/DVD player, easel, and message board.

76+ people: 4 flipcharts, 2 data projectors, 2 screens, standard microphone, lavaliere microphone, VCR/DVD player, easel, and message board.

RESERVATIONS

Procedure

We understand that reservations will be made with a rooming list. A copy of our rooming list is enclosed. The rooming list is to be returned to our office before the cutoff date.

Cutoff Date

All reservations must be received no later than_____. At that time, any uncommitted rooms in your guest room block will be released for general sale, and future reservations will be subject to space and rate availability. A payment guarantee will be required to continue holding guest rooms.

Billing

Arrangements have been made for all individuals to pay for their room, taxes; and incidental charges, and for all group charges be placed on a master account to be paid by the booking organization.

FUNCTION ARRANGEMENTS

We have reserved meeting spate as outlined below. Meeting rooms are not held on a 24-hour basis unless otherwise noted. A conference services manager personally assigned to your account will be contacting you to discuss and finalize your exact room setup requirements, menu selections, and audiovisual equipment needs.

FIGURE 5.9 *(continued)*

Please advise us of all changes to your agenda so that we may best serve your specific program requirements. Should there be a significant reduction in attendees, we serve the right to adjust function space accordingly.

Day	Date	Time	Function	Setup	Attendance

MEETING ROOM RENTAL

The charge for meeting space will be_____per break-out per day.

FUNCTION GUARANTEES

A final guarantee of the number of meeting attendees and/or catered food functions is due no later than three (3) business days prior to each scheduled event. This guarantee represents the minimum guest count for billing purposes and may not be reduced after this time.

CREDIT ARRANGEMENTS

Upon our accounting department's approval of your credit application, your master account will be direct-billed. Our credit terms are "Net due upon receipt of Invoice" with interest charged at 1.5% on all balances over 30 days of billing date.

CREDIT APPLICATION

Credit application due:_____

RECEIVING/HANDLING OF PACKAGES

Incoming materials for your meeting should arrive at the hotel no more than three (3) days prior to your meeting date. Packages for your meeting should be addressed to the attention of your hotel service manager, and list the name and date of your meeting. If more than one package is sent, please indicate the number of packages sent by listing, for example, "package 1 of 3" or "package 2 of 3." Five (5) or fewer boxes will be delivered complimentary to your meeting room. There is a $1.50 handling and delivery charge for six (6) or more boxes.

CANCELLATION

Acknowledgement of a definite commitment by the Hotel will in good faith, continue to protect the facilities and dates agreed, to the exclusion of other business opportunities. Therefore, the commitment of space and dates is of specified value to the Hotel. Due to the great difficulty in reselling guest rooms and conference space on short notice, cancellation of the entire program will be subject to an assessment according to the following schedule:

0 to 30 days prior to arrival. Full payment on total number of guest rooms, meeting charges, package plans, and any estimated banquet revenues as booked for the duration of the dates agreed upon.

31 to 60 days prior to arrival	75% of the above
61 to 90 days prior to arrival	50% of the above
91 to 180 days prior to arrival	30% of the above
181 days to 1 year prior to arrival	15% of the above
Signing date to one year prior to arrival	10% of above

ATTRITION

The rates and the availability for this program are based on the contracted guest-room block. Therefore, reduction in the guestroom block will be subject to an assessment according to the following schedule:

Up to 60 days prior to arrival: 10% can be reduced without any fee. Additional rooms over the 10% will be charged for one-night guestroom revenue.

60 to 31 days: 10% of the existing block can be reduced without any fee. Additional rooms over the 10% will be charged two nights guestroom revenue.

0 to 30 days prior to arrival: 5% of the existing guestroom block can be reduced without any fees. Rooms reduced over 5% will be charged for the full number of nights they were contracted for.

FIGURE 5.9 *(continued)*

PROGRAM ALTERATION CONTINGENCY

This agreement has been based on the sequence of days, number of agreed-upon guestrooms, and function requirements specified. If these requirements are significantly changed, we reserve the right to alter the terms and conditions of this contract, including assessment of cancellation fees and availability of specified rooms and rates.

ACCEPTANCE

If the above details meet with your approval, please sign this letter agreement and return to us by_____. If an approved agreement is not received by the above option date, the Hotel will release the tentative space reserved.

We sincerely appreciate the opportunity to serve_____. You can be assured of the effort of our entire staff and my personalized attention to help make your meeting and stay most enjoyable and successful.

ACCEPTANCE BY CLIENT	**ACCEPTANCE BY HOTEL**
Name:__________	**Name:**__________
Title:__________	**Title:**__________
Date:__________	**Date:**__________

FIGURE 5.9 *(continued)*

common in hotels that do not offer meeting space. Moreover, even full-service hotels frequently have clients who want to rent only sleeping rooms and require few, if any, of the services offered by the hotel. In cases such as these, a group lodging contract will be created to describe the very specific conditions under which the group will hold and pay for the rooms it desires.

A well-developed group lodging (rooms) contract will include detailed language about a variety of items including:

- The total number of rooms and room nights to be held for the group.
- The group's arrival and departure dates.
- Negotiated group rates by specific room type or run of house (any room type).
- The **cut-off date** or reservations rooming list due date.
- Reservation procedures.
- Complimentary rooms (if any) to be credited to the master bill.
- Disclosure of all fees (including any early departure fees, no-show fees, resort fees, housekeeping fees, and the like).
- All room taxes, surcharges, and, if applicable, extra person charges.
- Rates applicable to rooms booked after the cut-off or reservations due date.
- Rates honored for attendees arriving early or departing later than the scheduled event.
- Whether reservations booked by the groups' members for dates just before or just after the group's stay will be counted in the total, cumulative room block.
- If there is an early departure fee, who will advise each guest of the policy and whether fees count toward attrition fees, if any.
- How room rates will be calculated if the contract is signed prior to the establishment of the group's final room rates.

The existence of group lodging contracts is certainly not new, but the Internet has made this contract type increasingly more complex to develop and, for hoteliers, more difficult to negotiate properly. To better understand why this is so, consider the situation in which a group contracts with a hotel to provide the group's members with sleeping rooms for a date one year in the future. The hotel establishes the rate the group members will pay, and the individual members are to call into the hotel to make their own reservations from the block (group of rooms) reserved for the members.

Assume that, one month prior to the group's arrival, all of the rooms reserved for them have been picked up (reserved) by the group's members. Assume also, however, that the hotel is not full, and its revenue managers elect to offer, online and through the hotel's franchise-affiliated website, a room rate lower than the one offered to the group. Despite the overwhelming tendency of travelers to equate the online rate with the rate at which they have reserved their own room, such rates are not easily comparable. This is because the estimated cost of group giveaways and allowances must be factored into the room rate quoted to the group. As well, when the requests of a group room buyer involve a large amount of meeting space

LEGALESE

cut-off date: The date on which any rooms contracted, and thus held for sale, but not yet picked up (reserved) by the group are returned to the hotel's general rooms' inventory.

and/or significant numbers of complimentary rooms or services, the hotel may quote a room rate for the block that is equal to or even higher than the hotel's normal transient room rate.

As illustrated in this example, as a myriad of travel websites offer more choices and become easier to use, individuals attending meetings are discovering they can often obtain lower room rates for their stays than the rate that had been quoted to their group. In addition, independent travel companies have begun to aggressively target meetings and convention attendees with e-mails and faxes offering cheaper rooms at nonheadquarters (group host) hotels. As a result, as in this example, a hotel's own revenue managers may lower room rates when a group is meeting in the hotel (e.g., by posting discounted rates on Internet travel sites such as Expedia or Travelocity) to the detriment of the hotel. Inevitably, group members book these lower-priced rooms rather than the ones originally blocked for the group. The result is that the group may not get credit for booking the number of rooms it had originally reserved, thus triggering potential rate increases or penalties. In response, savvy meeting planners have begun to demand the insertion of clauses into their group lodging contracts that exert increased control over room rates that hotels may charge during the period of the group's stay in the hotel. The reason they seek to do so is easy to understand.

Of course, hotel revenue managers seek to maximize the revenue generated by each of their available rooms (RevPAR). Meeting planners, however, will respond negatively when, for example, a group's negotiated rate of $200.00 per night is listed in the group lodging contract but, for the same time period, the hotel's revenue managers list $125.00 per night rooms on an Internet travel site simply because they believe that "any room sale is better than no sale." In a case such as this one, heavily discounting rooms during a time of a group's meeting will likely:

- Upset the group's leadership because it will appear to the group's members that its leaders were poor negotiators who were "outsmarted" by the hotel.
- Upset the hotel's sales representative responsible for servicing the group because rather than appearing to have given the group a "good rate," the hotel's sales representative will now appear to have taken advantage of the group. The result is a loss of credibility on the part of the sales representative and the hotel.
- Create hard feelings and accounting difficulties as meeting planners attempt to receive the concession or "comp" terms promised in their group lodging contracts. These difficulties arise because, in many cases, a group's members will in fact have purchased the total number of room nights the group contracted to buy. However, because the hotel's yield management decisions drove attendees away from the group block (but not away from the hotel), the attendees' room night purchases were not counted as part of the group block pick-up.

The language utilized in developing conference services contracts is among some of the most complex and rapidly changing in the hospitality industry. This is so because meeting planners representing group space and sleeping room buyers are sophisticated professionals as are their hotel counterparts. As a hospitality manager, it is important to be aware of, and fully understand, the essential contract clauses currently used in conference services contracts. To learn more about these critically important clauses, follow the instructions found in Search the Web 5.5.

Search the Web 5.5

Visit **www.hospitalitylawyer.com**

1. Select: Solutions.
2. Select: Academic Resources.
3. Select: Hospitality Law Textbook Support.
4. Select: Referenced Articles.
5. Select "APEX Meeting Contracts Accepted Practices" provided by the Convention Industry Council.
6. Review this article, and be prepared to discuss it in class.

Analyze the Situation 5.2

Melissa Lange is the convention services director at her city's civic (convention) center. The center has been contracted to host a large press conference to announce the intention of the Republican senator representing her state to run for re-election. Despite Ms. Lange's best efforts, the senator's office is very unhappy with the physical condition of the civic center.

"This is awful," says the senator's chief of staff. "The carpet is worn and the interiors need painting. This isn't how the center looked six years ago when we booked our re-election announcement speech. It's too late to move the press conference now, but there is no way the senator is paying the contracted amount for this space. It's just six years after we selected you, and now the conditions are terrible!"

Despite the fact that the civic center is, indeed, six years older than it was at the time of the contract signing, it is not materially different, and Ms. Lange suspects that the complaint about the condition of the facilities is merely a ploy initiated by the senator's chief of staff to receive a reduction on the senator's conference services bill.

Assume that you are Ms. Lange.

1. What would be your response to the senator's aide?
2. Assume that you are responsible for drafting the contracts for all of the civic center's space requests that are to take place five or more years in the future. What would you do to ensure that guests such as these were not, in the future, able to make the claim that the facilities they contracted for previously were not the same as those they actually received on the date of their meeting?

International Snapshot

A Comparison of Franchise Disclosure Requirements under U.S. Law and International Law

Introduction

Due to the widespread increase in franchising as a method of doing business, there has been a tremendous increase in franchise legislation both in the United States and internationally. Specifically, in addition to the United States, the following 22 countries have enacted franchise disclosure laws: (1) Australia, (2) Belgium, (3) Brazil, (4) Canada, (5) China, (6) France, (7) Indonesia, (8) Italy, (9) Japan, (10) Korea, (11) Malaysia, (12) Macau, (13) Malaysia, (14) Mexico, (15) Romania, (16) Russia, (17) South Africa, (18) Spain, (19) Sweden, (20) Taiwan, (21) Tunisia, and (22) Vietnam. Both the United States and these foreign jurisdictions regulate franchising and offer protections to prospective franchisees through presale disclosures, which take the form of a Franchise Disclosure Document (FDD) in the United States.

Items to Be Disclosed

The FTC Franchise Rule requires disclosure of information in 23 specific categories that are set forth in the FDD. See 16 C.F.R. § 436-37 for Disclosure Requirements and Prohibitions Concerning Franchising and Disclosure Requirements and Prohibitions Concerning Business Opportunities. Of the items required, the only ones that are either required or recommended to be disclosed in all of the foreign jurisdictions are the basic franchisor information, ongoing fees, and investment costs. The other items of disclosure (i.e., franchisor management, bankruptcy, franchisor and franchisee obligations, exclusive territory, franchisor financing, franchisee outlets, and trademark information) are required in only some of the jurisdictions.

Another main difference between the United States and the foreign jurisdictions deals with public figures (persons whose names or physical appearance are generally known to the public in the geographic area where the franchise will be located). In the United States, information pertaining to public figures must be disclosed whereas the foreign jurisdictions do not require such disclosure.

The third distinction involves the disclosure of the franchise agreement in the FDD. In the United States, the franchise agreement must be included in the FDD whereas only a minority of the foreign countries requires the franchise agreement to be disclosed.

The fourth distinction between the United States and the foreign jurisdictions deals with the issue of exemptions from the disclosure requirements. Only Australia, Canada, South Korea, and the United States provide for any kind of exemption from the franchise disclosure laws. Furthermore, the exemptions in Australia, Canada, and South Korea are much narrower than those in the United States.

There are, however, also some similarities between the United States and the foreign jurisdictions. One similarity deals with the disclosure of financial performance representations in Item 19 of the FDD. A franchisor that does not make an Item 19 statement cannot offer the franchisee such guidance. While financial performance representations are not a mandatory disclosure in the United States, Item 19 does, in fact, permit franchisors to make financial performance representations as long as there is a reasonable basis for this information and such information is included in the FDD. Countries such as Australia, Malaysia, Indonesia, and Vietnam require the disclosure of financial performance representations in a manner similar to that required in the United States. In most of the other countries, there is no obligation to make financial performance representations with the exception of Malaysia, which requires a financial forecast for 5 years.

Another similarity between the United States and foreign jurisdictions centers on the franchisor's financial situation. In the United States, the franchisor's financial statements must be included in the FDD. Most foreign jurisdictions also require disclosure of financial statements. Only Mexico, Spain, Sweden, and Taiwan do not have an explicit requirement pertaining to the disclosure of financial statements.

Disclosure Requirements in China

Prompted by its commitment to the World Trade Organization (WTO) to lift restrictions on franchising by the end of 2004, the Chinese Government passed temporary Franchise Measures, which became effective on February 1, 2005. After two years of internal discussions, the Chinese State Council promulgated the current permanent rules, called the Regulations on Administration of Commercial Franchise (Regulations). The Regulations were effective May 1, 2007, in an attempt to safeguard the market order due to rampant fraud in domestic franchising activities in China. The Regulations are still effective today but were updated in 2012.

The Regulations require that a franchisor establish a comprehensive disclosure system, along with a copy of the Franchise Agreement. Article 22 of the Regulations lists the items that must be disclosed. They include (1) Franchisor information, (2) Initial fees, (3) Ongoing fees, (4) Investment information, (5) Costs and conditions for the products, (6) Supplier information, (7) Information on services provided for the franchisee, (8) Method and contents of guidance to the franchisee, (9) Franchisor duties, (10) Current and past franchises within the boundaries of China, (11) Financial statements, (12) Franchise-Related lawsuits and arbitrated matters in last 5 years, and (13) Contents of the franchise agreement.

Other Differences

These examples demonstrate just a few of the differences between United States and foreign jurisdictions with respect to presale disclosures. Other differences center on who is required to provide disclosures, who is required to receive disclosures, and when the disclosures are required. Further, as mentioned, there are differences between the United States and foreign laws as to the exemptions and exclusions under the franchise laws. In sum, before investing in a franchise, a potential franchisee should seek the advice of an experienced franchise attorney to review the franchisor's business and to prevent any overreaching by the franchisor.

Some of the factual information contained in this article was obtained from the following publications: Michael J. Katz, "The Revised FTC Franchise Rule: An Overview," Colo. Law, *September 2009; Jones & Wulff, "Franchise Regulation in China: Law, Regulation and Guidelines," 27* Franchise L.J. *57 (Summer 2007); Mark Forseth, Stephen Giles, & Tao Xu, "The Devil's in The Details: International Disclosure Laws," American Bar Association Forum on Franchising, October 2015.*

Provided by Robert Zarco and Himanshu M. Patel of the law firm of Zarco, Einhorn, Salkowski & Brito, P.A., Miami, Florida. www.zarcolaw.com.

WHAT WOULD YOU DO?

Assume that you are the group sales manager at the Claremont Hotel. John Pingston is one of your clients. Mr. Pingston, a professional meeting planner, works for a meeting planning company that was selected by the American Society of Hospitality Teachers (ASHT) to choose a hotel for that society's annual meeting.

At your hotel, like many others, the purchase of all hotel room nights is accompanied by the awarding to the buyer of major airline frequent flier credits (points). Mr. Pingston agrees to select the Claremont for the ASHT meeting but then states that, as the person responsible for "buying" the rooms, the airline award miles that accompany the room sales should be granted to him personally rather than to the ASHT, and, in fact, he strongly implies that if he is not granted the frequent traveler airline miles, he will move the contract for the group's 700 total room nights to one of the Claremont's competitors.

1. Would you grant the mileage award points to Mr. Pingston? Why or why not?
2. Assume that you granted the bonus miles to Mr. Pingston.
   a. Who do you feel would be more embarrassed by the disclosure that you did so, the planner or your hotel?
   b. If you decided to do so, to whom should you disclose Mr. Pingston's "booking bonuses"?
      i. The CEO of the planner's company?
      ii. The ASHT board of directors?
      iii. The membership of the ASHT?

WHAT DID YOU LEARN IN THIS CHAPTER?

Although the content of any contract signed by a manager is important, in the hospitality industry, the wording found in some forms of hospitality-specific contracts is especially important. As a result, hospitality managers know that there are essential phrases (clauses) that their contracts should contain. This is true for contracts relating to both the goods and services hospitality managers provide to their guests and to the products and services they themselves purchase. Individuals who undertake responsibility for signing contracts of these types must know and understand these clauses well.

Just as the wording found in some hospitality contracts is especially significant, some hospitality contract types are especially important to managers. The franchise-related contract is one type of agreement that is of special importance to hospitality managers. Critical components of these varied contracts can include very specific terms related to purchasing a franchise, operating a franchised business, and selling a franchise.

Management contracts, or management agreements, comprise another contractual area of special significance to hospitality managers. This is so because a great number of management companies operate hospitality businesses for these business owners. As a result, the contracts between the owners of a business and those who manage it can take many forms. Often, these contracts are complex and very detailed. Because this is so, hospitality managers must pay very close attention to the conditions and terms of management agreements. This is especially the case when the management contract describes an agreement for operating an owner's franchised business.

Finally, in the segment of the hospitality industry that routinely rents meeting space or sleeping rooms to guests, there are additional contract features that are unique. Meeting and space contracts, as well as group lodging contracts, are especially significant contract types encountered by many hospitality managers.

CHAPTER 6

Legally Managing Property

6.1 Introduction to Property

In the hospitality industry, when a hotel manager is away from the hotel, it is common to say that he or she is "off property." "Property," in this sense, refers to the grounds and building of the hotel. At the same time, when a guest enters the pool area, he or she may see a sign that states, "Towels are provided for your convenience but are the property of the hotel." In this case, "property" refers to a physical asset owned by the hotel. With so many different meanings and uses of the word "property" and its legal characteristics, it is an extremely important concept for a hospitality manager to understand.

In the hospitality industry, there are two types of property the future manager must learn to administer:

- Real property
- Personal property

Within the category of personal property, the two subtypes are tangible and intangible property, as shown in Figure 6.1 on the next page. A tangible item is one that can be held or touched. Thus, furniture is a tangible form of property, as are land, equipment, food inventories, and a variety of other materials needed to effectively operate a hospitality facility. Intangible items are those that cannot be held or touched but have real value, although that value can sometimes be difficult to establish, such as the goodwill of a business.

Understanding the way the law views property is important because it affects how property ownership disputes and claims are settled, the rights of an individual to use the property as they see fit, and even how ownership of the property is allowed to be transferred.

The law treats **real property** differently from **personal property**, and these distinctions are critical for managers to understand.

Real Property

Real property refers to land and all things that are permanently attached to land. **Real estate** is a related term that is frequently used when referring to real property.

LEGALESE

Real property: Land and all the things that are permanently attached to it.

Personal property: Tangible and intangible items that are not real property.

Real estate: Land, including soil and water, buildings, trees, crops, improvements, and the rights to the air above, and the minerals below, the land.

CHAPTER OUTLINE

6.1. Introduction to Property
6.2. Purchasing Property
6.3. Financing the Purchase of Property
6.4. Leasing Property
6.5. Respecting Intellectual Property Rights

IN THIS CHAPTER, YOU WILL LEARN

1. The difference between real property and personal property.
2. The function of the Uniform Commercial Code for buyers of property.
3. The role of liens and financing statements in protecting rights of buyers and sellers in purchasing property.
4. How to evaluate the purchase-versus-lease decision from a legal perspective.
5. How to avoid infringement of trademark, patent, copyright, and concept rights.

REAL	PERSONAL
	Tangible
	Intangible

FIGURE 6.1 **Property types.**

Certainly, the trees on a country club's land are part of its real estate. So, too, are the ponds, streams, and grassy areas that make up the golf course. **Improvements** are features such as fences, sewer lines, and the like, which are changes or additions to land that make it more valuable.

Fixtures

Although at first observation it appears simple to determine what is real property and what is personal property, at times it is quite complex. This difficulty comes from trying to distinguish between items that were intended to be improvements that are "permanently attached" to the land as opposed to simply being placed on the land.

Clearly, a chimney built into the golf course clubhouse would be considered permanently attached to the clubhouse building. But would a fan placed on the floor of the dining room be considered permanent? Would a fan affixed to the chimney to improve heat circulation be considered real property? Would it matter exactly how the fan was attached? The answer to these more complex questions comes with an understanding of the legal terms **chattel** and **fixture**.

A fan set on the floor of a dining room would not be considered real property because it is clearly movable. Thus, it would instead be classified as chattel. In contrast, a fan that has been permanently installed in the fireplace itself would be considered a fixture. Fixtures include all the things that are permanently attached to property, such as ceiling lights, awnings, window shades, doors, and doorknobs. It is important to note that it is possible to remove an item that has been permanently attached to real property. Thus, a ceiling fan that has been permanently installed in a dining room could, of course, be removed. However, from a legal standpoint, an item that is to remain with the property would ordinarily be identified as a fixture.

Questions often arise as to whether certain fixtures and/or improvements are to be considered real property or treated as personal property. The general rule is this: If an item can be removed without substantially damaging any real property, the item is generally considered to be personal property. When the issue is not clear, it is best to consult with an attorney skilled in this area of the law.

Personal Property

Anything that is not real property is personal property, and personal property is anything that isn't nailed down, dug into, or built into the land. A restaurant on an acre of ground is real property, but the tables and chairs in the dining room are not. A restaurant building permanently attached to a plot of land is real property. A van used for catering that is parked in the restaurant's parking lot is not.

As previously stated, personal property can be considered either **tangible** or **intangible**. Tangible property is the type that we most often think of when referring to goods owned by a company or individual. Tangible property can be thought of as all of those items that can easily be moved from one location to

Analyze the Situation 6.1

Jay Geier purchased a cinnamon roll franchise from a franchisor. To house the operation, he purchased a small, but ideally located, building from David Stein. The two individuals agreed on a fair price, and then both Mr. Geier and Mr. Stein signed the sales contract. Mr. Geier was to take possession of the property on March 1.

On the morning of February 28, Mr. Geier arrived at the property to take some exterior measurements he would need in order to get a contractor's bid on resurfacing the parking lot. He observed Mr. Stein removing a window air conditioning unit from the small manager's office at the rear of the building.

Mr. Geier protested that the air conditioner should not be removed as it was part of the sale. Mr. Stein replied that the air conditioner was his personal property and was never intended to be sold with the building, nor was it specifically mentioned in the sales contract.

1. Can Mr. Stein be permitted to take the air conditioner?
2. Would the air conditioner be considered real or personal property?
3. Should the air conditioner have been mentioned in the sales contract?

LEGALESE

Improvements: An addition to real estate that ordinarily enhances its value.

Chattel: Personal property, movable or immovable, that is not considered real property.

Fixture: An article that was once a chattel but that has become a part of the real property because the article is permanently attached to the soil or to something attached to the soil.

Tangible property: Personal property that has physical substance and can be held or touched. Examples include furniture, equipment, and inventories of goods.

Intangible property: Personal property that cannot be held or touched. Examples include patent rights, copyrights, and concept rights.

another. Automobiles, furniture, artwork, and food inventories are all examples of personal property.

Intangible property can be just as valuable as any real estate or tangible personal property. Intangible property includes items such as franchise rights, trademarks, money, stocks, bonds, and interests in securities. A share of Hilton Corporation stock is a tangible piece of paper, but its real value emanates from the fact that it represents an intangible shareholder interest in the Hilton Corporation. Money is also a form of intangible property. A five-dollar bill is a tangible piece of paper, but it represents an intangible interest in the monetary system used in the United States. The concept of money is intangible.

To appreciate the importance of intangible property, consider the case of Stanley Richards. He has invented a seasoning salt for beef, which chefs around the world agree is spectacular. His wife, Ruth, creates a small, stylized cartoon drawing of a cow for the label of his seasoning. Mr. Richards consults an attorney, who helps the Richards apply for and receive the exclusive right to use Mrs. Richards's drawing in their business. Mr. Richards's product is a huge success. Soon, the stylized cow is associated worldwide with creativity, good taste, and uncompromising quality. Millions of people immediately recognize the cow drawing and what it represents. Mr. Richards is approached by a multinational seasoning company that produces seasonings for poultry, pork, and fish. The company would like to use Mrs. Richards's drawing on its own products. The company feels that having the drawing prominently displayed on its own products would improve market awareness of its nonbeef seasonings.

The right to use the stylized drawing of the cow, so valuable in this case, is an example of an intangible property right. Although the drawing of the cow itself is easily duplicated and worth only a few cents, what the stylized cow drawing represents is extremely valuable and may not simply be taken from the Richards without their agreement; they, and they alone, have the right to determine how this property can be legally used.

It is important to note that a partnership or company as well as an individual can own personal property. Thus, the word "personal" designates that the property is not "real" property. Essentially, personal property could be considered all property that is not "real" or real estate.

6.2 Purchasing Property

For the hospitality manager, the buying, leasing, or selling of property occupies a great deal of time. The foodservice director at an extended-care facility will buy property from vendors, such as food, supplies, and equipment and then turn around and sell some of that property—in this case, the food—to the residents of the facility. At the same time, other equipment for the operation may be leased, such as a dishwasher or a soda-dispensing machine. On a much larger scale, the director of operations for a large hamburger chain may be responsible for buying or leasing land on which to put new stores, buying or leasing the equipment that will go into the new stores, and selling off real and personal property that the company no longer needs.

Purchasing Real Property

In order to sell property legally, the seller must have a legal **title** to that property. It is the responsibility of the buyer to verify this right, however; otherwise, the buyer may find after the purchase that he or she does not legally own the property at all!

Whether the hospitality manager is purchasing real or personal property, the establishment of title to the property being purchased is the responsibility of the manager. And although it might appear that title to lands and real estate would be very simple to verify, the process can, in fact, be quite complex.

Deeds Title to real property can be transferred from an owner in a variety of ways, such as through marriage, divorce, death, an act of the courts, bankruptcy, gift giving, or sale. A **deed** is the formal legal document used to transfer ownership of real property from one person or entity to another. A deed will consist of the date, the names and descriptions of the parties involved in the transfer, the consideration, a full description of the property, and any exceptions to the transfer.

Deeds may be either **warranty deeds** or **quitclaim deeds**. Warranty deeds can be further described as general or limited depending on the exact language in the deed and just how far the seller will defend the ownership title. Generally, residential sales will use general warranty deeds, and commercial property transactions will sometimes use limited warranty deeds. The laws governing deeds vary from state to state; thus, it is important to make sure that legal title to the real property is provided in the deed. A prudent hospitality manager will seek competent legal counsel who knows the appropriate state's laws.

When there is any doubt as to the legitimacy of the title to a property, it is sometimes necessary to conduct a **title search**.

LEGALESE

Title: The sum total of all legally recognized rights to the possession and ownership of property.

Deed: A written legal document for the transfer of land or other real property from one person to another.

Warranty deed: A deed that provides that the person granting the deed agrees to defend the title from claims of others. In general, the seller is representing that he or she fully owns the property and will legally stand behind this promise.

Quitclaim deed: A deed that conveys only the rights that the grantor has, if any. This type of deed transfers the owner's interest to a buyer but does not guarantee that there are no other claims against the property or that the property is indeed legally owned by the seller.

Title search: A review of land records to determine the ownership and description of a piece of real property.

Title Insurance Even when the ownership of a piece of real property is well established through a title search, it is advisable for a buyer to purchase title insurance. Some buyers are not aware that they can obtain title insurance that protects their equity in the real property.

Title insurance is a critical part of any commercial or private purchase of real estate. This insurance, usually obtained at the sale or closing of the property for a one-time premium payment for the duration of the buyer's interest in the property, helps protect the interests of the buyer should another individual claim ownership to the same piece of property after the buyer has completed the sale. Title insurance will cover losses as the result of these claims.

Some common instances where title insurance has protected a buyer include:

Forgery

Improper court proceedings

Survey mistakes

Missing heirs

Unfiled liens

Lenders, as part of the sale process or closing, will most likely require a buyer to obtain title insurance that protects the lender's interest in the property, which is the loan to the buyer for the purchase. Two policies, one for the lender and one for the buyer, can be obtained at the same time, usually for a reasonable expense.

To illustrate the importance of title insurance, consider the case of William Clark. Mr. Clark has a daughter named Kimberly. When her father dies, Ms. Clark inherits a piece of land outside a major city. Mr. Clark did not leave a will, but the house he lived in, and the land it rested on, was passed on to Ms. Clark, his only living heir, by state law. Thirty years later, Ms. Clark sells the land to Brian Lee, who builds a restaurant on the site. Five years later, Joshua Davidson produces a lien and a will that, he claims, was signed by Mr. Clark. The will clearly states that Mr. Clark wished to leave the land not to his daughter but to Mr. Davidson to settle an old debt. In this case, Mr. Lee's claim to the land may be questionable. Title insurance would protect Mr. Lee if the newly produced will were in fact proved to be valid.

Purchasing Personal Property

For the future hospitality manager, the number of purchases of personal property will, in most cases, vastly exceed that of purchases of real estate. Because this is true, it is very important to have a thorough understanding of the law and practices surrounding the transfer of ownership of personal property.

Bill of Sale A **bill of sale** is the formal legal document used to transfer ownership of personal property from one individual or entity to another. As shown in Figure 6.2, the following items are included in a bill of sale:

- Name of seller
- Name of buyer
- Consideration
- Description of property
- Statement of ownership by seller
- Date of sale
- Signature of seller

Because a bill of sale is a contract, it can take many forms. In the hospitality industry, it is common for a buyer to agree to purchase a certain type of good from a vendor on a regular basis. Consider the case of Renee Miller, the director of housing

---

LEGALESE

Bill of sale: A document noting that personal property is transferred from a seller to a buyer.

BILL OF SALE

I, __________, of [name of firm, if appropriate], in the County of __________, State of __________, in consideration of __________ dollars ($__________), to be paid by __________, of [name of firm if appropriate], the receipt of which is hereby acknowledged, do hereby grant, sell, transfer, and deliver to __________ and his [or her] heirs, executors, administrators, successors, and assigns, forever, the following:

(Description of Property)

I hereby warrant that I __________ [or name of firm, if appropriate] am the lawful owner of the Property, that it is free from all encumbrances; that I have the right to sell the property; and that I will warrant and defend my right to legally convey it against any lawful claims or demands by anyone.

In witness, whereof, I__________, hereunto set my hand, this __________ day of__________ 20__________.

Seller ______________________________

[Signature of individual or authorized representative of firm]

FIGURE 6.2 **A bill of sale.**

and foodservices at a state-supported university. Ms. Miller knows she will need a large amount of ground beef throughout the school year, but because she has limited freezer space, she must take delivery of the beef on a monthly basis. To negotiate the best possible price, she places all of her ground beef business with the same meat wholesaler. Ms. Miller executes a special contract for sale of goods with the seller to ensure that the quality, price, and terms she has agreed upon are maintained throughout the year (see Figure 6.3).

A contract developed to transfer ownership of personal property is common when the property cannot be viewed at the time of sale, as in Ms. Miller's case, or when the property has not yet been manufactured. For example, if a hotel orders custom-made drapes and bedspreads, they may not be manufactured by the seller until a contract for their sale has been signed by both parties. As is the case with all contracts, the contract for sale of goods should be carefully examined by both the buyer and seller.

It is important to determine exactly when the transfer of ownership occurs in a sale of personal property. Generally, goods are shipped FOB, which means, "free on board." When used, the term refers to the fact that shippers are responsible for the care and safety of goods until they are delivered to the buyer's designated location. Transfer of ownership occurs not at the time of sale in this case but upon delivery.

Notice that in both the bill of sale and the more formal contract for the sale of goods, the seller is not required to provide a title when transferring ownership. This is different from the sale of real property when a title (deed) is a required part of the transaction. It is important to note that unlike real property, ownership of personal property is generally assumed by its possession, and it is not customary for the seller to prove his or her ownership rights by a title. An exception to this rule is the sale of motor vehicles.

Ownership of Stolen Property Even though possession implies ownership, it does not equate to the lawful right to sell stolen property. There is no criminal penalty imposed by law if a buyer innocently purchases stolen goods from a seller who purports to own those goods. However, in the event the rightful owner takes steps to reclaim his or her goods, the innocent buyer would have no recourse except to go back to the thief; that is, the buyer could file a lawsuit against the thief for the return of any money paid. In reality, the ability of the buyer to identify and help prosecute the thief is often minimal. Obviously, it is in the hospitality manager's best interest to buy only from reputable sellers.

A restaurant or hotel manager may be punished if it can be shown that he or she knowingly purchased stolen goods. Although it might be easy to trace stolen goods, it is more

CONTRACT FOR SALE OF GOODS

Agreement made and entered into this [date] __________, by and between __________ [name of seller], of [address] __________ [city] __________, [state] __________, herein referred to as "Seller," and [name of buyer] __________, of [address] __________ [city] __________, [state] __________, herein referred to as "Buyer."

Seller hereby agrees to transfer and deliver to Buyer, on or before [date] __________, the following goods:

DESCRIPTION OF GOODS

CONSIDERATION TERMS

Buyer agrees to accept the goods and pay for them in accordance with the terms of this contract. Buyer agrees to pay for the goods at the time they are delivered and at the place where he [or she] receives the goods. Goods shall be deemed received by Buyer when delivered to address of Buyer as described in this contract. Until such time as goods have been received by Buyer, all risk of loss from any casualty to said goods shall be on Seller.

Seller warrants that the goods are now free from any security interest or other lien or encumbrance, that they shall be free from same at the time of delivery, and that he [or she] neither knows nor has reason to know of any outstanding title or claim of title hostile to his [or her] rights in the goods.

Buyer has the right to examine the goods on arrival and has [number] of days to notify Seller of any claim for damages on account of the condition, grade, or quality of the goods. The notice must specifically set forth the basis of his [or her] claim, and that his [or her] failure to either notify Seller within the stipulated period of time or to set forth specifically the basis of his [or her] claim will constitute irrevocable acceptance of the goods.

This agreement has been executed in duplicate, whereby both Buyer and Seller have retained one copy each, on [date] __________.

______________________________ ______________________________

Buyer Seller

[Signatures]

FIGURE 6.3 **Contract for sale of goods.**

Analyze the Situation 6.2

As the owner operator of a popular Italian restaurant, controlling costs is an important part of your day-to-day activities. Costs of labor, food, and equipment are your direct responsibility. Profit margins are good, but controlling costs is a constant challenge.

At a meeting of the local chapter of the state restaurant association, you see your friend Wayne, who excitedly tells you about a purchase he has just made. He owns and operates an upscale steakhouse in your town. He purchased 50 full-sized stainless-steel line pans for $2 each from a passing "liquidator." Wayne tells you that he jumped at the chance to buy them because when new, the line pans cost $75 each.

When you inquire about the seller, Wayne says that two men simply arrived at his restaurant in a small pick-up truck with a variety of equipment and small wares in the uncovered back.

"Best of all," Wayne says with a wink, "as soon as I washed them and put them in with my regular stock, there was no way anyone could tell the difference between the ones I just purchased from the ones I already had!"

Talk at the restaurant association meeting centers on rising food costs and the likelihood of having to raise menu prices. Several operators state that they are seriously looking at price increases. You, too, have been considering such a move. Wayne tells the group that at his place, "We are going to hold the line on price increases this year."

1. If you had needed them, would you have purchased the pans?
2. What are the legal issues at play here? What ethical issues are at play?
3. If the "sellers" in this scenario are caught and confess to selling stolen merchandise, do you think that Wayne will get to keep his pans?

difficult to determine if a buyer, in fact, knew the goods were stolen. However, it frequently can and will be inferred from circumstances surrounding the purchase.

A buyer is violating federal law if he or she knowingly purchases stolen goods, and those goods have (1) a value of over $5,000 and (2) been a part of interstate commerce.

The term "interstate commerce" merely refers to the movement of property from one state into another state. In order to commit a federal offense, a person must know that the property had been stolen but he or she need not know that it was moving through interstate commerce.

Because of the severe penalties involved, the prudent hospitality manager will avoid purchasing any property that is sold at far below its real value, is sold at odd times or by questionable salespersons, or is sold when there is doubt as to its origin. If something appears too good to be true, it generally is, and thus should be avoided.

Warranty

Those who sell property often find that any promises they make about that property can help to better sell it. For example, if the human resources manager at the corporate office of a franchise company decides to purchase a copy machine, the promises, or **warranties**, made by the copy machine's manufacturer may play a significant role in the machine selected. If two copy machines cost approximately the same amount, but the manufacturer of one warrants that it will provide free repairs if the machine breaks down in the first two years while the other manufacturer does not, the warranty of the first manufacturer would probably be a deciding factor in the selection of the copy machine, being the better value.

LEGALESE

Warranty: A promise about a product made by either a manufacturer or a seller that is a part of the sales contract.

When evaluating the final warranty offer, the following questions should be considered: Before signing any contract for the purchase of goods, it is a good idea to determine what warranties, if any, are included in the purchase. When purchasing real property, a deed helps explain exactly what is included with the purchase. In a similar manner, a warranty helps explain exactly what rights are included in a purchase of personal property. It is important to remember that a warranty is part of the sales contract. That is, the intangible rights a warranty offers the buyer are just as real as the property itself.

Because they are part of the contract, it is always important to make sure that any warranties offered verbally are documented in the sales contract. It is important to get them in writing. Warranties can be considered to be either expressed or implied. An expressed warranty is created when a manufacturer makes a statement of fact, either verbally or in writing, about the capabilities and qualities of a product or service. These statements can be made either by a salesperson or in promotional literature. Examples include statements such as "This copier will make 35 copies per minute" and "This dishwasher uses six gallons of water for each rinse cycle."

When a seller makes claims about the capabilities of a product or service being offered, that seller is obligated under the law to deliver a product that meets all of the capabilities described. Because express warranties are considered to be part of the sales contract, the law enforcing the truthfulness of warranties is the Uniform Commercial Code, which you read about in Chapter 4, "Contract Basics" When a buyer relies on factual representations to purchase a product or service and those statements later prove to be false, then a breach of the sales contract has occurred. Under Article 2 of the UCC, the buyer may be entitled to recover damages from the seller.

The UCC further protects the interests of buyers by requiring that any products sold be fit for use and free of defects. Thus, even if a seller does not specifically claim that his or her products are free of defects, a buyer would expect that any product purchased would be in good working order. This type of unwritten expectation is called an **implied warranty**.

Under Article 2 of the UCC, personal property that is sold must conform to two implied warranties. One implied warranty is that the item is fit to be used for a particular purpose. This is known as an implied warranty of fitness. The second implied warranty is that the item will be in good working order and will adequately meet the purposes for which it was purchased. This is called an implied warranty of merchantability.

In many states, consumers can enforce their rights with respect to implied warranties for up to four years after a purchase. This means that, for the first four years of a product's life, the seller is liable for any defects or breakdowns of his or her product, including the implied warranties established by the UCC.

The seller has the right to disclaim, or negate, any express or implied warranties by inserting language into the sales contract. The UCC has drafted standard contract clauses that can be used for those situations. As with any sales contract, the disclaimer must be in writing and must be agreed to by both parties.

Just as price is a negotiable part of any contract, so, too, are warranties. It is a good idea to try to negotiate additional warranties before making a purchase. Before buying personal property, it is imperative to understand the warranty offer and to compare warranties from competing brands before making a purchase. Effective hospitality managers seek to negotiate the longest, strongest, most comprehensive warranty possible and insist that the warranty be in writing.

Managers should try to include as much of the following information as possible in the warranty in order to ensure maximum protection:

1. How long is the warranty?
2. When does the warranty begin?
3. Will it include the charges for the parts and/or labor to make the repairs?
4. What parts of the purchase are covered by the warranty?
5. Can the buyer lose the warranty by not following manufacturer guidelines for routine service and maintenance, and who can perform these tasks?
6. Where is authorized service performed?
7. Who pays to deliver the defective product to the repair area?
8. Can the warranty be extended, and if so, for how long and at what cost?
9. What are the costs associated with maintenance agreements on the property once the warranty expires?

LEGALESE

Implied warranty: An unwritten expectation that a product purchased is free of defects.

Figure 6.4 is an example of a warranty a hotel manager might encounter when buying dishwashers for a new extended-stay facility. Notice the promises that are made by the dishwasher's manufacturer.

DISHWASHER WARRANTY

FULL ONE-YEAR WARRANTY

For one year from date of original purchase, we will provide, free of charge, parts and service labor in your place of business to repair or replace any part of the dishwasher that fails because of a manufacturing defect.

FULL TEN-YEAR WARRANTY

For ten years from date of original purchase, we will provide, free of charge, parts and service labor in your place of business to repair or replace the tub or door liner if it fails to contain water because of a manufacturing defect such as cracking, chipping, peeling, or rusting.

LIMITED SECOND-YEAR WARRANTY

For second year from date of original purchase, we will provide free of charge, replacement parts for any part of the water distribution system that fails because of a manufacturing defect. Associated inlet and drain plumbing parts are not covered by this warranty. You must pay for the service trip to your place of business and service labor charges.

This warranty is extended to the original purchaser and any succeeding owner for products purchased for in the 48 mainland states, Hawaii and Washington, DC. In Alaska, the warranty is the same except that it is LIMITED because you must pay to ship the product to the service shop or for the service technician's travel costs to your place of business.

All warranty service will be provided by our Factory Service Centers or by our franchised Customer Care servicers during normal working hours. Check the White Pages for XXXX COMPANY OR XXXX COMPANY FACTORY SERVICE.

FIGURE 6.4 **Manufacturer's warranty.**

What is Not Covered

Service trips to your place of business to teach you how to use the product.

Read your Use and Care material. If you then have any questions about operating the product, please contact your dealer or our Consumer Affairs office at the address below, or call, toll-free: 1-800-xxx-xxxx.

Improper Installation. If you have an installation problem, contact your dealer or installer. You are responsible for providing adequate electrical, plumbing, and other connecting facilities.

Replacement of fuses or resetting of circuit breakers.

Cleaning or servicing of air gap device in drain.

Failure of the product if it is used for other than its intended purpose.

Damage to product caused by accident, fire, floods, or acts of God.

WARRANTOR IS NOT RESPONSIBLE FOR CONSEQUENTIAL DAMAGES.

Some states do not allow the exclusion or limitation of incidental or consequential damages, so the above limitation or exclusion may not apply to you. This warranty gives you specific legal rights, and you may also have other rights, which vary from state to state. To know what your legal rights arc in your state, consult your local or state consumer affairs office or your state's attorney general.

FIGURE 6.4 *(continued)*

6.3 Financing the Purchase of Property

The buying and selling of property is fairly straightforward when the buyer pays the seller the entire purchase price all at once. It is more complicated, however, when the buyer decides to pay for property over time. Consider the case of Bill Humphrey. Mr. Humphrey operates a 400-room hotel in the downtown area of an extremely large city. He determines that the ice machines in his hotel must be replaced. The cost will be in excess of $100,000. His controller advises him that the hotel cannot afford to purchase the ice machines for cash at this time but could afford to make monthly payments toward the purchase price. Mr. Humphrey approaches the hotel's bank, explains the problem, and secures a loan to purchase the ice machines.

In this scenario, a number of problems could arise. What if the hotel cannot make its loan payments? What rights would the bank then have? Could it retake possession of the ice machines? These and other complications can arise any time personal property is financed.

Debtor and Creditor Relationship

A **lien** is the right of a person to retain a lawful interest in the property of another until the owner fulfills a legal duty. If, for example, a restaurateur purchases new tables and chairs from a seller but elects to pay one-half of the purchase price at the time the tables are delivered and the other half over a period of six months, the seller would retain a lien on the tables and chairs. That is, the seller would maintain a lawful ownership interest in the chairs until they were paid for in full. Of course, since the tables and chairs are housed in the restaurant, the restaurateur would also have partial ownership and rights to the property. In this scenario, two parties have legitimate and legal claims to the ownership of the tables and chairs. This complex relationship of dual ownership can be made easier to grasp with a better understanding of collateral and liens.

Collateral and Liens **Collateral** is an asset a person agrees to give up if he or she does not repay a loan. As noted, a lien is a claim against the property (the collateral) used to ensure payment of a debt. Liens can be recognized by contract, from general trade practices, or implied by law.

The process of legally recording a contractual lien is known as "making the lien **perfect**," or **perfecting the lien**. The possessor of a lien who files the appropriate records with the proper public office is known as a secured creditor. This type of creditor has a right that is superior over others claiming an interest in the property to possession of the collateral or any proceeds if the collateral is sold.

Implied by law, perfecting a lien is done by taking possession of the property. If, for example, an in-room air conditioning unit is taken to a repair facility, the repaired unit will normally

---

LEGALESE

Lien: A claim against property that gives the creditor (lien holder) the right to repossess and/or sell that property if the debtor does not repay his or her debt in a timely manner.

Collateral: Property that is pledged to secure the repayment of a debt.

Perfect a lien: To make a public record of a lien, or to take possession of the collateral.

stay in the possession of the service facility until payment for the repairs has been made.

Other liens include judgment liens, which are those ordered by the courts, and landlord liens, whereby a landlord can secure payment of rent by taking a tenant's property if necessary. In most states, mechanics or persons who furnish materials for buildings (suppliers) are entitled to a lien. In some states, these claims must be filed timely in the office of the clerk of the court or established by a suit brought within a limited time. Upon the subsequent sale of a building, these liens, if properly filed, are paid at the time of the closing.

Mortgages and Deeds of Trust

When financing the sale of real property, the creditor or lender will generally insist on securing the debt with a lien backed by collateral. In most cases, the lien will be filed on the real property being purchased. For example, if Marion Pennycuff wishes to purchase land and a building in which to house a café, he could secure funding for this purpose from a bank, providing his financial position is good. Mr. Pennycuff would actually buy the real property with money loaned by the bank, and the bank would file for a **mortgage** lien on the property. In this instance, the land and building would serve as collateral for the loan. In some states, a **deed of trust** (or a trust deed or deed to secure debt) is a substitute for a mortgage lien, but it serves an identical purpose.

If Mr. Pennycuff should decide to sell the property before he has completely repaid his mortgage, a buyer would not be able to obtain a clear title to the property until the original mortgage was completely repaid.

Assume, however, that Mr. Pennycuff wished to borrow the $100,000 to begin a consulting company instead of purchasing the land and building. It is most likely that the bank would still require him to provide collateral to secure the loan. This collateral could be in the form of real or personal property that Mr. Pennycuff owned, including intangible personal property such as stocks or bonds.

Security Agreements

When creditors retain some legal rights of ownership in a piece of personal property, they are said to have a **security interest** in that property.

When personal, rather than real, property, is involved, creditors protect and establish their interest by means of a security agreement. The **security agreement** is an arrangement similar to the mortgage or deed of trust. It certifies that the creditor makes a loan, and the debtor agrees to pay back the loan in a timely fashion. If the debtor does not, then the creditor has the right to seize the personal property, sell it, and apply the money generated by the sale to the debt. The debtor is still responsible for any remaining balance.

Article 9 of the Uniform Commercial Code is the law that regulates purchases made using security agreements and that gives a creditor the right to take back property that the debtor either cannot or will not pay for. As with other areas, the UCC requires debtors and lenders to follow specific procedures in order to finance the purchase of property in a way that is legally binding and that will be upheld by the courts. For example, because it is a contract, the security agreement must include a written description of the property that is being purchased and must be signed by both parties.

Financing Statements

Under UCC rules, in order for a security agreement to fully protect the creditor, it must be perfected. This is generally done by preparing and filing a financing statement. A **financing statement** is the tool used in most states to record (perfect), a lien on personal property. These statements are typically filed with either the secretary of state's office and/or the local county recorder of records. To perfect their lien, creditors file a financing statement, or UCC-1 form, with the appropriate official. The filing of the UCC-1 form publicly states that a lien exists on a particular piece of personal property.

Unless otherwise indicated, the financing statement remains in effect for five years. When the loan has been paid off, the debtor can request a termination statement that clears the financing statement from the public records.

Figure 6.5 shown on the next page is a copy of the UCC-1 form currently in use. Note that it lists the debtor, the creditor (secured party), and a description of the property that serves as the collateral. Be careful of blanket-type descriptions of personal property on the UCC-1 form. If the form covers all personal property located on or in the premises, it may in fact put a lien on all the intangible property associated with the tangible property, such as trademarks, service marks, and the good will of the company. A prudent hospitality manager will make sure any description of all personal property on the premises

---

LEGALESE

Mortgage: The pledging of real property by a debtor to a creditor to secure payment of a debt incurred to purchase the property.

Deed of trust: Used in some states instead of a mortgage. A deed of trust places legal title to a real property in the hands of a trustee until the debtor has completed paying for the property. Some states use names such as trust deed or deed to secure debt for securing a loan.

Security interest: A legal ownership right to property.

Security agreement: A contract between a lender and borrower that states that the lender can repossess the personal property the borrower has offered as collateral if the loan is not paid as agreed.

Financing statement: A formal notice of a lien being held on personal property required under the Uniform Commercial Code in most cases. Also called a UCC-1 because of its form number in the UCC.

UCC FINANCING STATEMENT

FOLLOW INSTRUCTIONS (front and back) CAREFULLY

A. NAME & PHONE OF CONTACT AT FILER [optional]

B. SEND ACKNOWLEDGMENT TO: (Name and Address)

THE ABOVE SPACE IS FOR FILING OFFICE USE ONLY

1. DEBTOR'S EXACT FULL LEGAL NAME - insert only one debtor name (1a or 1b) - do not abbreviate or combine names

1a. ORGANIZATION'S NAME			
OR 1b. INDIVIDUAL'S LAST NAME	FIRST NAME	MIDDLE NAME	SUFFIX

1c. MAILING ADDRESS	CITY	STATE	POSTAL CODE	COUNTRY

1d. TAX ID #: SSN OR EIN	ADD'L INFO RE ORGANIZATION DEBTOR	1e. TYPE OF ORGANIZATION	1f. JURISDICTION OF ORGANIZATION	1g. ORGANIZATIONAL ID #, if any ☐ NONE

2. ADDITIONAL DEBTOR'S EXACT FULL LEGAL NAME - insert only one debtor name (2a or 2b) - do not abbreviate or combine names

2a. ORGANIZATION'S NAME			
OR 2b. INDIVIDUAL'S LAST NAME	FIRST NAME	MIDDLE NAME	SUFFIX

2c. MAILING ADDRESS	CITY	STATE	POSTAL CODE	COUNTRY

2d. TAX ID #: SSN OR EIN	ADD'L INFO RE ORGANIZATION DEBTOR	2e. TYPE OF ORGANIZATION	2f. JURISDICTION OF ORGANIZATION	2g. ORGANIZATIONAL ID #, if any ☐ NONE

3. SECURED PARTY'S NAME (or NAME of TOTAL ASSIGNEE of ASSIGNOR S/P) - insert only one secured party name (3a or 3b)

3a. ORGANIZATION'S NAME			
OR 3b. INDIVIDUAL'S LAST NAME	FIRST NAME	MIDDLE NAME	SUFFIX

3c. MAILING ADDRESS	CITY	STATE	POSTAL CODE	COUNTRY

4. This FINANCING STATEMENT covers the following collateral:

5. ALTERNATIVE DESIGNATION [if applicable]: ☐ LESSEE/LESSOR ☐ CONSIGNEE/CONSIGNOR ☐ BAILEE/BAILOR ☐ SELLER/BUYER ☐ AG. LIEN ☐ NON-UCC FILING

6. ☐ This FINANCING STATEMENT is to be filed [for record] (or recorded) in the REAL ESTATE RECORDS. Attach Addendum [if applicable]

7. Check to REQUEST SEARCH REPORT(S) on Debtor(s) [ADDITIONAL FEE] [optional] ☐ All Debtors ☐ Debtor 1 ☐ Debtor 2

8. OPTIONAL FILER REFERENCE DATA

FILING OFFICE COPY — NATIONAL UCC FINANCING STATEMENT (FORM UCC1) (REV. 07/29/98)

FIGURE 6.5 **Financing statement excerpt from Uniform Commercial Code.**

will exclude any related intangible personal property, such as intellectual property.

If a creditor has been asked to use a piece of personal property as collateral for a loan, he or she can review the financing statements on file at the office of the governmental agency retaining these records. A creditor who finds that no previous liens have been recorded against the property can be assured that he or she will have perfected his or her interest in the property when properly filing a UCC-1 on that property.

It is common in the hospitality industry to buy personal property with a loan from a third-party creditor, such as a bank, or to have the purchase price financed over time by the seller. If, for example, you, as a manager, wish to purchase $30,000 worth of cash registers for a new restaurant, you have three options:

1. *Pay seller purchase price in full.* No UCC-1 required.
2. *Borrow purchase price from a third-party lender (such as a bank) and pay seller in full.* The third-party lender (bank) files UCC-1 on the cash registers, evidencing its lien on the registers.
3. *Convince the seller to finance purchase price over time.* The seller files UCC-1 on the cash registers, evidencing its lien on them.

6.4 Leasing Property

Just as it is common to buy personal property in the hospitality industry, it is equally common to **lease** it. Both real and personal property can be leased.

Because a lease is a type of contract, it must clearly indicate the item to be leased, the price or rent to be paid, and the consent of the two parties to the lease—the **lessor** and **lessee**. A lease is different from a purchase of property in that leases transfer possession rather than ownership. It is critical that hospitality managers fully understand the essential terms of any leases they enter into and the differences inherent in leasing, rather than owning, a piece of property.

Essential Lease Terms as a Lessor

Hospitality managers take on the role of a **landlord** when they designate specific space in their hotel or restaurant to be operated by a **tenant**. Historically, hotels would lease lobby space to businesses that would interest their guests. Thus, tailors, dressmakers, jewelers, florists, furriers, and the like would occupy hotel space and provide additional revenue for the property. Additionally, parking lot operators might lease the hotel's parking spaces.

More recently, in an effort to satisfy guest demands for regional or nationally known restaurants, some hotels have begun leasing their entire foodservice operations. In addition, airports and shopping malls have become landlords for well-known, or "branded," foodservice entities that appeal to a variety of guests.

When hospitality managers take on the role of landlord, it is critical that the lease contracts they enter into be drafted, negotiated, and reviewed by legal counsel prior to signing them. An attorney can help ensure that the duties of both landlord and tenant are clearly spelled out in the lease and that in the event of a breach of the agreement, appropriate remedies are available to the landlord. Consider the case of Michael Singh. Mr. Singh serves as the general manager of a 400-room hotel. He elects to lease his gift shop to an elderly couple with excellent references, and they operate the gift shop successfully for several years. Through no fault of their own, illness causes the couple to become less prompt in opening the gift shop. In fact, on a few days within the past two months, the shop has not opened at all. Mr. Singh knows that the couple's continued inability to open the store could severely damage the hotel's business. The rights of the hotel and the tenant in a situation like this must be clearly documented, so that the hotel manager can take appropriate steps to remedy the problem.

The hospitality lease, especially for real property, is generally different from that of an ordinary landlord and tenant relationship. When a landlord leases a home or apartment, the day-to-day use of that property is normally not subject to the inspection by the landlord. For the hotel operator, however, a lease is drawn up with the expectation that the space will be used for an activity that enhances the financial well-being of the hotel and provide needed amenities for the guests under terms contained in the lease. Thus, operating hours, products sold, and even pricing strategies may be contained in a hospitality manager's lease when he or she serves as landlord. While a residential landlord may not impose him or herself unduly on a tenant, the hospitality manager has a responsibility to make sure the tenant operates in compliance with the lease, since the tenant's actions can be helpful or harmful to the success of the entire hotel.

The following areas of a lease agreement deserve special attention when a hospitality manager assumes the role of the lessor (or landlord).

Length of Lease The lease length is important in that it directly affects rent amounts. Landlords prefer leases that are long because they minimize vacancies and guarantee a steady source of revenue for the use of the space. Increasingly, tenants also prefer long leases to avoid the rent increases that often occur when leases are re-executed. However, a lease that is too long may prevent a landlord from raising the rent

---

LEGALESE

Lease: A contract that establishes the rights and obligations of each party with respect to property owned by one entity but occupied or used by another.

Lessor: The entity that owns the property covered in a lease.

Lessee: The entity that occupies or uses the property covered in a lease.

Landlord: The lessor in a real property lease.

Tenant: Anyone, including a corporation, who rents real property for an extended period of time with the intent of establishing a permanent occupation or residency.

when necessary. In a like manner, the tenant may find that his or her business grows beyond the ability of the leased space to contain it, and a move to a larger space is required. In all cases, the lease length should be established to meet both the short-term and long-term interests of both parties.

Lease start dates, or occupation dates, should be clearly established in the lease agreement. Often, lessees will want early access to the space in order to install fixtures and make improvements. The number of days required to complete this work can be significant, and the party responsible for rent during that time period, or whether rent is to be paid at all, should be clearly spelled out.

Although it is less common that hospitality managers find themselves as lessors of personal property, sometimes it does occur. An example is the resort hotel that rents bicycles to its guests. This rental arrangement provides an excellent service to guests but creates special liability issues for the hotel. These issues will be discussed in Chapter 10, "Your Responsibilities as a Hospitality Operator to Guests."

Rent Amount Lease payments on real property are typically of four distinct types, based on the payment responsibilities of the lessee:

- A "net" lease is one in which the lessee pays some or even all of the taxes due on real property in addition to the base rent amount.
- In a "net net" lease, the lessee pays for both taxes and insurance as required by the lessor in addition to the base rent amount.
- In a "net net net," or triple-net, lease—the most common type in the hospitality industry—the lessee pays for all of the costs associated with occupying the property, including building repairs and maintenance, in addition to the base rent amount.
- In a "percentage" lease, tenants pay a fixed percentage of their gross revenue as part of their lease payment, sometimes in addition to the base rent amount. Although some fixed charges might also apply, the unique feature of this lease is its variability. Thus, a hotelier might charge the gift shop lessee monthly rent based on the sales achieved by the gift shop. In this way, rent payments are lower when business is slow for the shop but increase as the business and the lessee succeeds.

It is important that both landlord and tenant understand the costs for which they will be responsible. When leasing personal property, the hourly, daily, monthly, or quarterly payments required should be clearly identified in the lease agreement.

Subleasing Rights of Tenant Most lessees realize that conditions can change, and they may not be able to or want to fulfill all of the lease terms specified in the lease agreement. Consider for example, the shopkeeper who leases space for a flower shop in an urban hotel. The shopkeeper is very successful and elects to sell her rights to the flower shop space to open a larger shop in a different part of the city. In this situation, the shopkeeper will want to **sublet**—that is, to transfer or assign to another—her interest in the hotel lease to a new shopkeeper.

The concern of the hotel, as the lessor, is that the new shopkeeper must be able to meet the requirements set forth in the lease, including the standards of the hotel. For this reason, it is a good idea for the lessor (hotel manager) to insist that any sublessee demonstrate his or her financial strength and integrity before the lessor approves the sublease arrangement.

While it would not be reasonable for the lessor to have complete say over who the sublessee may be, it is also not reasonable for the choice of sublessee to be left solely in the hands of the original tenant. Accordingly, leases should address this issue with a clause acknowledging the right of the lessee to sublease, but only with the landlord's prior written consent. The clause should also state that the landlord's consent cannot be unreasonably withheld, delayed, or conditioned.

Insurance Landlords are favorite targets for litigation. If a tenant is negligent and the result is injury to an individual, the lessor must be protected. The size and types of policies that the lessor should require the lessee to purchase vary, but in all cases the lessor should insist that:

- The lessee's insurance carriers must be reasonably acceptable to the lessor.
- Copies of the insurance policies should be delivered to the lessor at the time of the lease signing and upon any renewals.
- Lessees and their insurance companies should be required to give at least 30-days' prior notice to the lessor if the policies are canceled, withdrawn, or not renewed.

In addition, landlords, when preparing leases, may insert exculpatory type clauses that seek to limit their liability. As seen previously, these clauses may not provide complete protection, but they can sometimes be helpful. It is best to have a commercial insurance agent or attorney who is experienced in insurance to review lease provisions and insurance policies to ensure that both lessor and lessee have adequate insurance coverage for the responsibilities allocated to each by the lease agreement.

Termination Rights Leases may be terminated for a variety of reasons, but these reasons must be clearly spelled out as part of the lease. If, for example, a tenant is delinquent in paying rent, the lessor can require that the premises be vacated. Most landlords will allow the payment to be made a few days late without penalty. This grace period should be clearly identified in the lease, as well as any penalties that will be assessed if the payment is tendered beyond the grace period.

LEGALESE

Sublet: To rent property one possesses by a lease to another. Also called subleasing.

Disturbances, violation of operating hours, significant damage to the property, and failure to abide by lease terms may all be justification for termination. However, while the reasons might be valid, they will not justify an **eviction** unless those reasons are distinctly identified in the lease.

When you, as a hospitality manager, serve as a landlord, the quality of the tenants who supply services to your guests can reflect well or poorly on the overall lessor's operation. If the tenant is experienced and provides superior services to hotel guests, most guests may not even be aware that the service is leased to a tenant and the services will appear seamless. This can prove troublesome from a liability standpoint if a guest is injured by the actions or omissions of a tenant. The injured guest will assume that the cause of the injury was a direct result of the hotel's actions, not an independent, unrelated lessee. A prudent hotel manager will provide written notice to guests that the service is provided by a business not owned or controlled by the hotel. This notification can be located in the guestroom within the information supplied in the book of hotel services, sometimes referred to as a compendium. Capable tenants who operate their businesses in a professional manner can be a real asset to a hospitality property; inexperienced or less-qualified tenants can cause great difficulty. When serving as a lessor, it is imperative that the hospitality manager examine the essential lease terms discussed in this section to ensure the best possible chance of the lessee's and the lessor's success.

Essential Lease Terms as a Lessee

When a hospitality manager takes on the tenant role in a lease arrangement, the lease may be for either real or personal property. When Mike Keefer decided to open a steakhouse, he discovered that his own favorite steakhouse was, in fact, for sale. Rather than sell Mr. Keefer the restaurant, the owner agreed to lease the land, building, and equipment to him in exchange for a percentage of the restaurant's gross sales. This arrangement provided Mr. Keefer with a lower-cost entry into the restaurant business and provided the landlord with continued ownership of the restaurant property.

Whether the hospitality manager leases land, buildings, or equipment, such as dishwashers, ice makers, and beverage machines, it is important that an attorney review the provisions of the lease prior to signing. The following items deserve the hospitality manager's special attention when leasing real or personal property.

LEGALESE

Eviction: The procedure that a lessor uses to remove a lessee from physical possession of leased real property, usually for violation of a significant lease provision, such as nonpayment of rent.

Landlord Representation and Default When a tenant leases real property, or an individual leases personal property, it is generally assumed that the lessor has the legal right to lease the property for its intended purpose. The issue of landlord representation and truthfulness, however, can become complex. Consider the case of the restaurateur who examined a property for use as a restaurant. The landlord stated in the lease that the space could lawfully be operated as a "restaurant." After the lease was executed, the restaurateur found that the restaurant's proximity to a school prevented him from obtaining a liquor license. The community zoning laws prohibited selling alcohol near a school. Thus, the landlord's representation that the space could be used as a restaurant was true, but only if that restaurant elected not to serve alcohol. The lesson here is that, as a tenant, any representation made by the landlord about the fitness of property for its intended purpose should be independently verified and put in writing if possible.

A related concern for lessees is the rights they have if the landlord should lose possession of the property through default. If, for example, a tenant pays his or her rent on time, but the landlord defaults on loans in which the property served as collateral, the rights of the lessee should be addressed in the lease. A clause can be inserted in the lease that guarantees that

Analyze the Situation 6.3

Sandy Aznovario leased a corner space in a shopping center to operate Olde Style Buffet, an all-you-can-eat buffet geared toward senior citizens and families. The buffet was especially popular on weekends, and its best business was done on Sundays before and after people in the community normally attended church.

Kathy Miley was the landlord for the shopping center. She and Mr. Aznovario signed a net net lease, clearly stating that maintenance and repair of the HVAC system would be the responsibility of the shopping center's commercial real estate company.

On Easter Sunday, the buffet's busiest day of the year, the head cook reported to Mr. Aznovario that the overhead exhaust system in the kitchen was not working, and the kitchen was becoming unbearably hot, smoky, and humid. Mr. Aznovario called the landlord's leasing office and heard a recorded message stating the office was closed because of the Easter holiday. He then contacted Beatty's 24-hour Emergency HVAC Repair Service, which sent a representative, who examined the HVAC system and then replaced a broken fan belt on the rooftop exhaust fan.

Mr. Aznovario submitted the bill from Beatty's, including a triple-time labor charge for holiday service, to Ms. Miley's company for payment. She refused to pay the bill, stating that Beatty's was not the authorized HVAC service company that she used nor did the lease specifically state that HVAC service would be provided on holidays.

1. Who is responsible for this bill?
2. What could have been done beforehand to keep this conflict from occurring?

the tenant's lease will be undisturbed by the lender. This is an area of the lease that is best carefully reviewed by legal counsel.

Expenses Paid by Landlord Whether the lease negotiated is a net, a net net, a triple net, a percentage lease, or some combination thereof, disputes over covered expenses are common sources of landlord/tenant disagreement. Because the landlord has limited ability to reduce expenses during periods of financial difficulty, there are few options available to the landlord when costs must be reduced. If electricity is to be paid by the landlord, it represents a significant expense and should be addressed directly by the hospitality operator (the landlord). A restaurant consumes a large amount of electricity through cooking equipment, dishwashing, and air conditioning. The lease should clearly identify whether any limits are set on the quantity of electricity that can be used as well as the types and capacities available. Similarly, when leasing space for a hair salon within a hotel, the lease should address the amount of supplied water allowed for the salon's services provided to customers and the rights and duties of the landlord and the tenant.

HVAC is the acronym for heating, ventilation, and air conditioning. In both a net and a net net lease, the repair and maintenance of these items are part of the lease arrangement and are ordinarily paid for by the landlord. The services provided for HVAC maintenance and repair can be critical and should be included in the lease along with a schedule of times when the services are available.

Like HVAC service and repair, cleaning services, if provided as part of the lease payment, should be clearly identified, and a schedule of cleaning times should be attached to the lease itself. The number of times the restroom is cleaned daily, as well as a definition of "cleaning," should be provided. Does it include floor mopping and the cleaning of toilets and mirrors each time? Or does the cleaning involve only removing large paper debris from the floors? Obviously, a guest will have a different experience under these two alternatives.

It is the responsibility of the hospitality manager who leases space or services to determine precisely what he or she will get in the way of services provided, and expenses paid for, by the landlord.

Terms of Renewal The terms under which a tenant may renew his or her lease should be of utmost importance to the hospitality manager who finds himself or herself in the role of lessee.

Consider the situation of David Berger. He is the district real estate manager for a chain of muffin shops. As part of his job, Mr. Berger negotiates the leases for the company's 800-square-foot operations. One of his prime concerns when negotiating a lease is the provision for renewal. If Mr. Berger selects a successful site, he will seek to renew his lease with as little upward change in rent as possible. If the site is less successful, he may elect not to renew the lease or to do so only with a significant reduction in lease payments.

It is important to note that a landlord has no legal obligation to continue a lease that has expired. Because of that, Mr. Berger often encounters landlords who wish to dramatically increase the rent payments for spaces where the muffin shops have shown great success. To prevent this, Mr. Berger insists that renewal formulas limiting rent increases to an acceptable amount be written into each lease when it is originally signed.

Normally, a lease can be extended only upon written notice from the lessee. Leases can, however, be written in such a way so as to renew automatically, unless terminated in writing by one of the parties to the lease.

Rights of the Landlord

Most tenants understand that a landlord will have the right to periodically inspect their property. This should be allowed, however, only at reasonable hours, and with reasonable notice except in the event of emergency situations when prior notice is not available to prevent harm or damage. Of even more importance to most tenants is the right of a landlord to lease other space to a competing business.

Leasing to Competing Tenants Consider the case of a landlord with a large, 30-store shopping center. It is in the best interest of the landlord to fill all the space with high-quality tenants. The space might even be large enough to house more than one hospitality operation—for example, a bagel shop and a pizzeria.

If, however, the landlord rents space in the shopping center to an upscale bakery, would it be fair for that same landlord to rent space in the same shopping center to a second upscale bakery? Unless the lease of the first bakery expressly prohibits it, the landlord would have the right to lease space to a direct competitor. Although few landlords will give a tenant veto power over any new tenants, it is reasonable to expect that a landlord will allow a tightly drawn definition of any future competitor in order to help ensure the success of a tenant considering the leasing of space.

Deposits, Damages, and Normal Wear and Tear Normally, a landlord will require a security deposit payment for the lease of real property. Landlords who lease personal property may also require deposits to ensure the return of the leased item in good condition. The amount of the deposit should be clearly spelled out in the lease.

Certainly, tenants must be held responsible for damages they incur on leased property. Tenants should not, however, be responsible for the normal wear and tear associated with the use of a piece of property. Difficulties can arise when the definition of normal wear and tear varies for landlord and tenant. Because it can be a source of conflict, the more detail that can be added to this section of the lease, the less likely it is for litigation to result. Dates by which a landlord must return a deposit upon lease termination and the appropriate method of resolving disputes about owed amounts should also be included.

Legally Managing at Work

Legal Considerations of Buying versus Leasing

1. Right to use

Purchase	**Lease**
Use is unlimited in any legal manner seen fit by the owner.	Use is strictly limited to the terms of the lease.

2. Treatment of cost

Purchase	**Lease**
Property is depreciable in accordance with federal and state income tax laws.	Lease payments are deductible by the lessor as a business expense, according to federal and state tax laws.

3. Ability to finance

Purchase	**Lease**
The property may be used as collateral.	The property may not generally be used for collateral.

4. Liability

Purchase	**Lease**
Owner is liable.	Lessee and/or lessor may be liable.

5. Improvements

Purchase	**Lease**
Improvements are made as desired by owner.	Improvements are limited to those allowed by lease terms.

6. Termination

Purchase	**Lease**
Ownership passes to estate holders.	Right to possess concludes with termination of lease contract.

7. Default

Purchase	**Lease**
Lender retains down payment and/or may foreclose on the property.	Lessor retains deposit and/or lender may evict and pursue balance of lease. With personal property, the lessor may reclaim the leased item.

Unfortunately, legal clashes between landlord and tenant are common occurrences. They can be reduced if both parties to the lease carefully consider the essential lease terms that most directly affect the success of the lessor and lessee relationship. When vacancies are high, landlords may be willing to negotiate on terms they otherwise would reject. Likewise, if space is in short supply, tenants may be in a weaker negotiating position. In our economy, these circumstances are constantly changing. Carefully reviewing lease terms is always a good idea and one that the hospitality manager would be well advised to undertake only with the aid of a qualified attorney and a real estate broker who is familiar with market conditions.

The Buy-versus-Lease Decision

The decision to purchase or lease a piece of property is an important one. Managerial philosophy can play a large part in this decision. Regardless of whether one elects to own or merely utilize property, the decision has wide-ranging effects on a number of business issues. The most important effects are addressed in the Legally Managing at Work.

Often, the decision to lease rather than purchase property is an economic one. A new passenger van for a hotel may cost over $50,000. If the van is purchased, the hotel has made a **capital improvement**. Payments for the van are not deductible as a business expense on the monthly profit and loss (P&L) statement. The value of the van, however, may be **depreciated** over a period of time fixed by law.

If a hotel operator wants to replace the air filters located in the ceiling of an atrium-style lobby four times a year, it makes little sense to purchase the mechanical lifts necessary to do the job. These pieces of equipment can be leased for a day and the task can be completed.

By contrast, if a restaurateur wants to operate a restaurant in a prime location in a mall food court, he or she may have no option other than leasing, because the mall owner is not likely to sell the restaurateur the space needed to operate, but rather, will lease the space under a **commercial lease**.

The owner of a piece of property has rights that a lessee does not enjoy. In some cases, however, the effective hospitality manager, for a variety of reasons including the financial considerations, may find it desirable to lease a piece of property instead of purchasing it. In either case, it is important to know and protect the rights associated with each type of property's possession.

6.5 Respecting Intellectual Property Rights

Some of the most important and personal property rights protected by law are those that relate to **intellectual property**—personal property that is both intangible and conceptual.

In the hospitality industry, some managers violate intellectual property rights by using, but not paying for, the intellectual property of others. Good managers both avoid infringing on the property rights of others and pay for those intellectual items they legitimately use to assist their business.

When an individual creates something that is unique and valuable, his or her right to enjoy the financial proceeds of that creation is protected by laws related to trademarks, service marks, patents, copyrights, and trade dress. It is important to note that intellectual property maintains its status even after the death of the person who created the property.

Trademark/Service Marks

Trademarks are used to identify the producer, manufacturer, or source of a product. They are frequently used in the hospitality industry. The reason is clear: Guests like to see name-brand products in use by the establishments they frequent. Well-established trademarks, or marks, as they are sometimes called, let consumers know precisely whose product they are buying or being served. For example, many restaurants find it convenient to serve ketchup directly from the bottle. As a consumer, a bottle manufactured and labeled by Heinz will elicit a much different response from one manufactured by Bob. When consumers see the Heinz name on the label, they associate the ketchup with the quality represented by the Heinz Company. An unscrupulous foodservice manager who buys Bob's ketchup and then puts it in a Heinz bottle violates not only food safety laws, discussed later in this text, but trademark property rights laws as well.

Service marks are similar to trademarks but instead of using them to identify a product, the marks are used to identify services. For example, a brand created by a hotel chain, such as Fairfield Inn by Marriott, creates a service mark instead of a trademark because they are not creating products but providing services under the service mark Fairfield Inn. Prior to a federal registration of a service mark, the mark is shown with small capital letters SM over the last word in the mark. Using the small capital letters SM is designed to provide notice to those who see the mark that the term is a service mark and is used while waiting to file and/or obtain a federal service mark registration. Examples of service marks are shown in Figure 6.6

Prior to a federal registration, use the small capital letters "SM" to indicate a service mark.

After obtaining a federal registration, change the "SM" to an "R" with a circle around it to designate a federally registered service mark.

FIGURE 6.6 **Examples of service marks.**

LEGALESE

Capital improvement: The purchase or upgrade of real or personal property that results in an increased depreciable asset base.

Depreciation: The decrease in value of a piece of property due to age and/or normal wear and tear.

Commercial lease: A lease that applies to business property.

Intellectual property: Personal property that has been created through the intellectual efforts of its original owner.

Trademark: A word, name, symbol, or combination of these that indicates the source or producer of an item. Sometimes called a mark.

Service mark(s): Similar to a trademark, a legally registered word, name, symbol, or combination of these used to indicate the source or producer of an organization's services.

for two e-commerce websites that provide education and legal services for the hospitality industry. Once a service mark obtains federal registration, then the small circle containing a capital letter, ®, replaces the use of SM above the last word in the service mark. Federal registration is not necessary to create proprietary rights in service marks but does provide additional protections.

The owner of a trademark and/or service mark has the right to prevent others from using that mark if the owner has legally registered or established that it was the first to use it in the respective marketplace. When a trademark has been properly applied for and received, no other person may manufacture or sell any article using the same or similar signs, marks, wrappers, or labels.

Trademark and service mark laws protect the public by making consumers confident that they can identify brands they prefer and can purchase those brands without being confused or misled. Trademark laws also protect hospitality managers by ensuring that they are getting the quality they are paying for.

Patent

When an inventor creates something new, he or she may apply for a **patent** on the invention. If, for example, a restaurateur invents a piece of kitchen equipment that can easily peel and remove the center from a large Spanish onion, that restaurateur would be able to quickly produce one of today's most popular appetizer items. It would not be fair or legal for another restaurateur to see that piece of equipment and proceed to manufacture it for sale him- or herself if the first restaurateur had applied for and received a patent on that piece of equipment.

The U.S. Patent and Trademark Office (www.uspto.gov) is the federal entity responsible for the granting of patents. An inventor, as the owner of the patent, has the right to exclude any other person from making or selling the invention covered by the patent anywhere in the United States for 20 years from the date the patent is issued for utility and plant patents and 15 years from the date the patent is issued on design patents. Anyone using a patented invention must obtain the owner's permission and pay him or her for using it. An inventor who has applied for but not yet received a patent may use the term "patent pending" or "patent applied for."

Copyright

A **copyright** is the set of rights given to reproduce and use intellectual property. For example, the writer of a song has the right to compensation any time that song is performed. If a singer takes the song, records it, and then sells the recording, the copyright laws would require the singer to fairly compensate the writer of the song's music and lyrics.

Copyright protection was considered so important that the founding fathers of the United States specifically granted the new Congress the responsibility of regulating copyrights. Figure 6.7 is an excerpt from the U.S. Constitution that addresses the issue of copyrights.

The owner of a copyright has the right to prevent any other person from reproducing, distributing, performing, or displaying his or her work for a specific period of time. The Copyright Act of 1976 states that copyrighted work can be a literary work, musical work, dramatic work, pantomime, choreographic work, pictorial work, graphic work, sculptural work, motion picture, audiovisual work, sound recording, or computer program. Most of the items found on the Internet are copyrighted also, including the text of websites, contents of email, and sound and graphic files.

In 1998, President Clinton signed the Digital Millennium Copyright Act (DMCA) into law. It amends the Copyright Act of 1976 and incorporates two major international treaties: the World Intellectual Property Organization (WIPO) Copyright Treaty and the WIPO Performances and Phonograms Treaty. The DMCA's main effect is to heighten the penalties for copyright infringement over the Internet and to criminalize the production and distribution against circumvention technology, and the act of circumvention, whether or not copyright infringement is involved.

When an individual has been granted a copyright, he or she is said to be the **copyright owner**. Copyright laws exist in foreign countries as well as the United States.

In some cases, under the doctrine of fair use, it is legal to use a copyrighted work without permission from the owner, but the purpose of such utilization is very important. A copyrighted work used for commentary, news reporting, teaching, scholarship, or research is normally not an infringement of a copyright because it is an educational, rather than a commercial, use of the work.

The Constitution of the United States of America

Article 1, Section 8

The Congress shall have the power:

to promote the progress of science, and the useful arts, by securing, for limited times, to authors and inventors, the exclusive right to their respective writings and discoveries.

FIGURE 6.7 Excerpt from the U.S. Constitution regarding the use of writings and discoveries.

LEGALESE

Patent: A grant issued by a governmental entity ensuring an inventor the right to exclusive production and sale of his or her invention for a fixed period of time.

Copyright: The legal and exclusive right to copy or reproduce intellectual property.

Copyright owner: A person or entity that legally holds a right to intellectual property under the copyright laws.

Search the Web 6.1

Enter **www.caselaw.findlaw.com**

1. Select: Cases and Codes.
2. Select: US Supreme Court.
3. Select: Party Name Search.
4. In the Search field type: "Two Pesos."
5. Select: "Two Pesos, Inc. v. Taco Cabana, Inc., 505 U.S. 763 (1992)."

Review the intangible property rights Supreme Court case involving Two Pesos, Inc. and Taco Cabana, Inc. Be prepared to describe in class the items of similarity between the two businesses on which the court based its decision.

In the hospitality industry, it is critical that copyrighted works be used only when appropriate authorization has been received, particularly when the use of a copyrighted work—such as the broadcasting of a boxing match—will provide a direct economic benefit to the hospitality establishment. Generally speaking, the courts are aggressive enforcers of copyright laws; thus, it is a good idea to be very clear about the origin and ownership of potentially copyrighted works before they are used in a manner to produce income and profit.

Trade Dress

Although the rights related to **trade dress** are actually a part of those rights related to trademarks, in the hospitality industry, they merit separate discussion. A trade dress is a very special and unique visual image.

Trade dress includes color schemes, textures, sizes, designs, shapes, and placements of words, graphics, and decorations on a product or its packaging. In the hospitality industry, an entire restaurant may be created in such a way as to be protected under the laws related to trade dress. The laws in this area can be murky. Certainly, no one restaurant chain has an exclusive right to operate a restaurant with a "down home" theme. A trade dress question arises, however, when one restaurant chain uses the same items to create that feel as does its competitor. A good visual example of a trade dress is the iconic contour fluted lines of the bottle introduced in 1916 and used by the Coca-Cola Company. Due to the company's trade dress protected rights, no other commercial seller of caramel colored cola beverages may use the distinctive lines, shape, and size of the bottle.

Italian, Mexican, French, and American restaurants, to name a few, all have unique characteristics associated not with the product served but with the feel and visual image of the establishment. Trade dress protection allows the creative restaurateur to protect his or her aesthetic ideas in an industry that highly rewards innovation and creativity. For an excellent examination of the trade dress issue, complete the Web exercise in Search the Web 6.1. It involves the case of two Mexican-style restaurants, one of which was accused of a trade dress violation.

Preventing Intellectual Property Rights Infringement

In order to prevent infringing on the rights of intellectual property owners, the U.S. Patent and Trademark Office maintains a database of registered patents and trademarks. Consult that database if there is any question regarding whether a mark or an invention is in the **public domain**.

If a company does not take care, its trademarks can become part of the public domain. "Aspirin" is often mentioned as a word that began as a trademarked term but later passed into such common usage that the courts would no longer enforce the property rights of the word's creator. Thus, a common word used frequently by society cannot become the subject of trademark protection.

Companies with registered marks need to be aggressive in defending infringement claims in order to protect their marks. A good example is the *Coca-Cola Company v. Overland, Inc.*[1] case where the defendant's restaurant was substituting another cola beverage in response to customer orders for a Coke without first giving the customer notice of the substitution. The defendant argued that the word "coke" is a generic term for all cola beverages and is no longer entitled to protection under the law. The court and the appellate court disagreed. Coca-Cola prevailed in the 1981 case, and that is why when a customer asks for a Coke in a restaurant that doesn't serve Coca-Cola products, the restaurant must tell the customer if it intends to substitute another cola product and get the customer's approval to do so.

The Lanham Act enacted in July 1946 (15 U.S.C.A. Section 1051) is the major comprehensive federal trademark statute in the United States that regulates the use of trademarks in commercial activity and prohibits trademark infringement, dilution, and false advertising.

Although most hospitality managers can, through thoughtful planning, avoid infringing on patent and trademark rights, copyright issues are more complex. Consider the case of the corporation that owns a theme park with a variety of thrill rides. One of the most popular is a seated ride where four passengers share a padded car that progressively goes faster and faster, traveling up and down on a circular track. The ride is fast, loud, and popular with teenagers. Hundreds of flashing lights and loud music, played by 25 broadcast-quality speakers, are an important ingredient in this ride. The corporation is free

[1] https://law.resource.org/pub/us/case/reporter/F2/692/692.F2d.1250.80-4376.html

LEGALESE

Trade dress: A distinct visual image created for and identified with a specific product.

Public domain: Property that is owned by all citizens, not an individual.

to put any type of lighting around the ride that it feels would be appropriate. However, the company is not free to broadcast any music it wishes over the speakers in conjunction with the ride unless the music is used in compliance with U.S. copyright laws. Figure 6.8 shows the section of the United States legal code that deals with the infringement of copyright.

Copyright laws in the United States give songwriters and publishers the right to collect royalties on their intellectual property whenever their songs are played in public. Note that the law allows the owner of the copyright to recover the profits made by any group that unlawfully uses copyrighted material.

Whether a hospitality manager plays songs in an establishment on CDs, television, tape, or in a live performance, the owners of the song have a right to royalties. This is because federal copyright laws state that playing copyrighted music in a public place constitutes a performance. When copyrighted music is performed in public, hospitality managers are in violation of the law if they do not pay the royalties due the owners of the music that has been played.

Of course, it would be extremely difficult for the practicing hospitality manager to know exactly who owns the rights to a particular piece of music. Most of the songs played in the United States are licensed by either Broadcast Music, Inc. (BMI); the American Society of Composers, Authors, and Publishers (ASCAP); or SESAC, which originally stood for the Society of European Stage Actors and Composers, but now is referred to solely by its acronym, pronounced SEE-sack. In order to play a given piece of music, a fee must be paid to the licensor that holds the right to license the music in question. Fee structures are based on a variety of factors, but the average restaurant, playing background music seven days a week, would be expected to pay only a few hundred dollars per year which gives the restaurant a blanket license for the right to broadcast most of the music available for play. The hospitality manager who refuses or neglects to pay the fees rightfully due a licensing group can be subject to fines or prosecution.

Congress has determined that any facility that plays its background music on a piece of equipment that could normally be found in a home will not be held to the normal copyright infringement rules if the facility does not charge admission to hear the music. Certainly, it is not the intent of the copyright laws to prohibit turning on a radio or television in a public

U.S. Code, Title 17, Section 504

Sec. 504. Remedies for infringement: Damages and profits

(a) In General. - Except as otherwise provided by this title, an infringer of copyright is liable for either:

(1) The copyright owner's actual damages and any additional profits of the infringer, as provided by subsection (b); or

(2) Statutory damages, as provided by subsection (c).

(b) Actual Damages and Profits. - The copyright owner is entitled to recover the actual damages suffered by him or her as a result of the infringement, and any profits of the infringer that are attributable to the infringement and are not taken into account in computing the actual damages. In establishing the infringer's profits, the copyright owner is required to present proof only of the infringer's gross revenue, and the infringer is required to prove his or her deductible expenses and the elements of profit attributable to factors other than the copyrighted work.

(c) Statutory Damages. -

(1) Except as provided by clause (2) of this subsection, the copyright owner may elect, at any time before final judgment is rendered, to recover, instead of actual damages and profits, an award of statutory damages for all infringements involved in the action, with respect to any one work, for which any one infringer is liable individually, or for which any two or more infringers are liable jointly and severally, in a sum of not less than $750 or more than $30,000 as the court considers just. For the purposes of this subsection, all the parts of a compilation or derivative work constitute one work.

(2) In a case where the copyright owner sustains the burden of proving, and the court finds, that infringement was committed willfully, the court in its discretion may increase the award of statutory damages to a sum of not more than $150,000. In a case where the infringer sustains the burden of proving, and the court finds, that such infringer was not aware and had no reason to believe that his or her acts constituted an infringement of copyright, the court in its discretion may reduce the award of statutory damages to a sum of not less than $200, The court shall remit statutory damages in any case where an infringer believed and had reasonable grounds for believing that his or her use of the copyrighted work was a fair use under section 107, if the infringer was:

(i) an employee or agent of a nonprofit educational institution, library, or archives acting within the scope of his or her employment who, or such institution, library, or archives itself, which infringed by reproducing the work in copies or phonorecords; or

(i) a public broadcasting entity which or a person who, as a regular part of the nonprofit activities of a public broadcasting entity (as defined in subsection [g] of section 118) infringed by performing a published nondramatic literary work or by reproducing a transmission program embodying a performance of such a work.

FIGURE 6.8 **U.S. Code Title 17, Section 504.**

place. In 1998, President Bill Clinton signed the Fairness in Music Licensing Amendment, a law that allowed small restaurants an exemption from some licensing fees. The law took effect in January 1999.

The specific provisions of the amendment providing for the free broadcast of music and video are quite clear. Restaurants under 3,750 square feet can play as many televisions and radios as they desire without paying royalty fees. There is no restriction on the size of the television that may be installed in a restaurant of this size. For specific information, visit www.copyright.gov. For restaurants larger than 3,750 square feet, if the owner applies for and receives an exemption, the restaurant may play up to four televisions (no more than one per room), and use up to six speakers (no more than four per room). The television sets cannot be larger than 55 inches.

Many hospitality venues utilize jukeboxes for their patrons' entertainment. It is ordinarily the provider of the jukebox who has the burden of paying the royalties for the music included in the jukebox, but this should be spelled out in the agreement between the venue and the provider prior to the installation of the jukebox.

Just as music is covered by copyright laws, so too are the broadcasts of such groups as the National Football League (NFL), Major League Baseball (MLB), the National Basketball Association (NBA), and others. The right to air these broadcasts is reserved by the group creating the programming, and the hospitality manager who violates their copyrights does so at great risk. If you have any doubt about the legality of your intended broadcasts, contact the broadcast company (i.e., cable operator) or the owner of the broadcasted product (NFL, Time Warner, etc.) to clarify the circumstances under which you may broadcast and to get written permission to do so.

For hotels, the broadcasting of in-room videos or movies on demand is treated in a similar way to jukeboxes in restaurants. The providers of the service to the hotel operator are ordinarily responsible for paying the royalties from showing the product. Again, this needs to be clarified in the agreement between the provider of the service and the hotel operator.

It is important for resort hotels that would like to show popular motion pictures, television shows, or videos to children while attending a kid's program on rainy days to obtain legal authorization to avoid claims of copyright infringement. See the Motion Picture Licensing Corporation (www.mplc.org) for more information and seek guidance from an intellectual property attorney before using these audiovisual works in such programs.

International Snapshot

U.S. Hotel Companies' Options for Seeking Trademark Protection Abroad

Most well-known hotel companies earn their profits primarily by managing hotels and franchising others that are allowed to operate under the hotel company's "flags." These flags (such as those of Marriott and Hilton) are trademarks. They represent a way of doing business ("branding"), the hotel company's valuable relationships with its customers ("goodwill"), and, in essence, the company's power to deliver economic performance to a hotel. Hotel companies, therefore, consider their trademarks to be among their most valuable assets.

Valuable assets must be protected, and trademarks are no exception. Trademarks are usually protected by registering them in the jurisdictions where they are used. These registrations must then be renewed at intervals prescribed by the laws of the applicable jurisdiction. Although not legally required in order to have, use, and enforce a trademark, registration nevertheless provides important benefits. The most important of these is that the owner of a registered trademark is in a far stronger position to enforce it and to prevent others from confusing the public by using similar marks.

Hotel companies often operate hotels internationally. This means that, to protect their marks, they should, at a minimum, register and renew their registrations in each country where the hotels are located. They should also consider "registering defensively" in countries where there is a high "knock-off" risk.

It was once necessary to engage in a country-by-country registration process to obtain foreign trademark protection. However, one shortcut registration process has existed for some time: Companies may apply for and obtain a European Union Trade Mark (EUTM) registration, which provides protection in all countries of the European Union for the cost of a single application. In addition, small groups of countries in Africa and Latin America have also joined together to offer similar "community" trademark registrations.

Since 2003, U.S. companies have had an additional shortcut alternative to country-by-country registration in the form of the Madrid Protocol. The Madrid Protocol is a treaty that allows trademark holders to file a single application covering all 60 protocol member countries and obtain an international registration. The process can greatly reduce costs associated with multiple international trademark applications.

Like any trademark protection regime, the Madrid Protocol has disadvantages as well as advantages:

- One-stop Madrid filings through the U.S. Trademark Office are more convenient and initially less costly than filing multiple international applications.
- International registrations offer the same scope of protection as a registration in the applicant's home country. Because U.S. trademark law requires applicants to describe the goods covered by their marks less specifically than that of other countries, an international registration based on a U.S. application might give a U.S. trademark holder less protection in some countries than non-U.S. trademark owners would receive.
- Because an international application must be based on an original "home country" application, if a U.S. applicant's original U.S. application is refused by the Patent and Trademark Office or fails for any other reason within five years, the entire international application based on it will also fail. An applicant may refile applications in each individual country while retaining the original filing date, but the fees and costs associated with the original pro-

(continued)

tocol application will be lost. This is equivalent to reverting to the old "country-by-country" filing system.

- If a member country's trademark office raises substantive objections to an international registration application, then local counsel will be necessary to resolve the objection. These kinds of objections rarely come from more than a handful of member countries. As a result, responding to them is still far less costly than having to engage counsel in each of the countries to secure registration one-at-a-time.
- Madrid filings do not cover countries that are not members of the Madrid Protocol. Some important countries that are not members include most Central and South American countries and Canada. As part of Canada's ongoing revisions of its trademark protection system, however, it is on track to join the Madrid Protocol and will likely do so in 2017 or 2018.
- Whether a company should seek international registration under the Madrid Protocol depends heavily on the countries where the company needs protection. If, for example, it expects to use its mark solely in Europe and the United States, a European Union Trade Mark will provide protection in all countries of the European Union for the cost of a single application, and the costs and benefits of prosecuting a EUTM application will be generally more favorable than those associated with a Madrid filing. If, however, the company requires broad, worldwide protection, an international application may be the best overall approach.

Provided by Robert C. Cumbow, Esq., of Miller Nash Graham & Dunn LLP (www.millernash.com) and Irvin W. Sandman, Esq., of Sandman Savrann PLLC (www.sandmansavrann.com).

WHAT WOULD YOU DO?

Assume that you are the food and beverage (F&B) director at a full-service hotel in a large East Coast college town. Your general manager, Mr. Peterson, is planning to have a large event centered on this year's Super Bowl. As the F&B director, you are an integral part of the event planning committee. One of the teams in the NFL final is from the state in which your hotel is located, so fan interest is very high.

Mr. Peterson proposes an event that will be held in the hotel's Grand Ballroom, which can hold 700 people. The festivities will begin at 3:00 P.M. on Super Bowl Sunday with the televised pregame show, a darts tournament, and a Mexican food buffet. At 6:30 P.M., the game is to be shown on five 60-inch TV screens that will be placed around the ballroom. The chief maintenance engineer has assured Mr. Peterson that the sets can be mounted on the ballroom's walls. The evening will conclude with a postgame "victory" party, which will end around midnight.

During one of the planning meetings, the discussion centers on the admission price that will be charged. The issue of reserved seating is raised by Scott Haner, director of sales and marketing. He believes that corporate clients of the hotel will be more inclined to attend if they can be assured good seats near the large-screen televisions.

1. As a hospitality professional, what issues must you consider prior to finalizing this Super Bowl party event?
2. If Mr. Peterson elects to charge a $20 fee for seats close to the large screens but only $5 for seats farther away from the screens, would your opinion be different? Why or why not?
3. What are the responsibilities of the management team in this scenario?

WHAT DID YOU LEARN IN THIS CHAPTER?

Property can be classified into several different categories. Real property refers to land and all the things attached to the land. Fixtures are personal items that were once separate but are now considered to be real property. Most items other than land and all the things attached to it are classified as personal property, which includes both tangible and intangible property. It is important to understand the difference among the categories of property because different methods of financing the purchase of property exist for each category.

When property is transferred from one owner to another, specific types of documents and sales contracts are used to ensure the legality of the purchase and to protect the buyer and seller. Warranties, or advertised claims about the performance or quality of a product, are often treated as part of the sales contract. Thus, a seller is obligated by law to back up any warranties made. The Uniform Commercial Code offers protection under the law to both buyers and sellers of personal property, as well as to financial lenders.

A lease is a contract that transfers possession, but not ownership, of a piece of property. Leasing real and personal property is a common occurrence in the hospitality industry today. Whether a hospitality manager assumes the role of a lessor (landlord) or lessee, it is important to make sure that the lease agreement contains essential terms that will spell out the details of the agreement and offers adequate protection to both parties.

Trademarks, service marks, trade dress, patents, copyrights, and concept rights are all protected under the law. Hospitality operators must make sure that they are in compliance with laws governing the serving of brand-name products; the use or creation of concepts, logos, or images; and the public broadcasting of music and video.

CHAPTER 7

Legally Selecting Employees

7.1 Employee Selection

Legally selecting and managing a staff can be a very challenging task in today's complex world of laws and regulations. Some managers, especially those with many years of experience, believe that finding, maintaining, and retaining a qualified, service-oriented staff is every manager's most difficult task. It is true that the challenges of managing people are generally greater than those involved in managing technologies or products. People are complex and are affected by so many nonwork-related issues that you will find it both difficult and rewarding to be a leader to your staff.

The law is very specific regarding what you, as an employer, can and cannot do as you secure your workforce. Both you and your workers have rights that affect the employment relationship. In this chapter and the next, we'll look at how to select and manage employees in accordance with the law.

As an employer, you will have wide latitude in selecting those individuals whom you feel would best benefit your business. However, it is critical that you develop an employee selection procedure that ensures fairness and compliance with the law (to avoid the risk of a discrimination lawsuit) while allowing you to hire the best possible candidate for the job. It is important to note that we are referring to selecting the right candidate for the job opening, not simply hiring an employee. Anyone can "hire" employees; just accept the next one who walks in the door. That is not a good idea for a number of reasons. A prudent hospitality manager will take the time and use all the tools at his or her disposal to make a selection for employment rather than hiring someone who meets the bare minimum to fill a position. Finding the right candidate for a position is essential. Selecting a candidate takes time and effort. Some benefits of using selection tools for the job position include reduced turnover rate, which will save the hospitality business excessive training expenses; provide better employee morale within the workplace—a happier employee who is well suited for the position; and, as a result, a generally better workplace for all. Putting a very shy person in a hotel's front desk position or as a hostess at the front of a restaurant will prove to be challenging for the employee, the management, and customers. In this chapter, we will explore the tools to use for making an informed selection for positions.

One tool that managers use to make good hiring decisions is the job description, which they use as a basis for establishing a list of job qualifications that each candidate should possess.

CHAPTER OUTLINE

7.1. Employee Selection
7.2. Discrimination in the Selection Process
7.3. Verification of Eligibility to Work
7.4. The Employment Relationship

IN THIS CHAPTER, YOU WILL LEARN

1. To utilize job descriptions, qualifications, and other tools for legally selecting employees.
2. To avoid charges of discrimination by knowing the classes of workers that are protected under the law.
3. To understand the procedure for verifying the work eligibility of potential employees before offering them employment.
4. To distinguish the rights of both employers and employees under the at-will employment doctrine.
5. To understand the concept of collective bargaining and the legal obligations when interacting with labor unions.

Job Descriptions

Before an employee can be selected to fill a vacant position, management must have a thorough understanding of the essential functions that the employee will need to perform. These are contained in the **job description**. Legally, only those tasks that are necessary to effectively carry out the responsibilities and perform the tasks required in the job should be used in the description.

Job descriptions need not be long. In most cases, a single typewritten page or two will be sufficient to detail the information that makes up the body of a job description. Figure 7.1 is a sample of a job description used in the hospitality industry. The description includes the job title, reporting relationship, tasks, and competencies required for the job.

The job description serves a dual role. It is important from an operational perspective in that it helps supervisors and the human resource (HR) department to keep track of the changing responsibilities of workers. However, it is also important from a legal perspective in that it is considered a legal document and may need to be produced in court to demonstrate that an employer fairly established the requirements of a job prior to selecting the candidates to fill that job.

If you review Figure 7.1 carefully, you will see that the job description does not mention the physical or mental abilities required to perform the job. The role of the job description is to define the job itself while the role of the **job qualification** is to define the personal attributes required to satisfactorily perform the job.

Job Qualifications

Once you know exactly what tasks employees must perform in a given job, it is possible to create a list of the skills or knowledge they must possess in order to successfully perform those tasks. These skills should be written down and attached to the job description. If a potential job candidate is not selected for employment and later elects to bring legal action against you, it will be critical that you can show how each component of your job qualification list is driven by, or logically flows from, the job description and which component the candidate did not possess.

Job qualifications can consist of both physical and mental requirements. It is important to remember that the job qualifications list must not violate the law or include any characteristics that would unfairly prevent a class of workers from successfully competing for the position. If, for example, a hotel groundskeeper job qualification lists a height of 6 feet, that qualification would be considered inappropriate because there are minority groups that would have difficulty meeting it.

Position Title: Executive Chef

Reports To: Food and Beverage Director

Position Summary: The department head responsible for any and all kitchens in a foodservice establishment. Ensures that all kitchens provide nutritious, safe, eye-appealing, and properly flavored food. Maintains a safe and sanitary preparation environment.

Tasks:

1. Interviews, hires, evaluates, rewards, and disciplines kitchen personnel as appropriate.
2. Orients and trains kitchen personnel in property and department rules, policies, and procedures.
3. Trains kitchen personnel in food production principles and practices. Establishes quality standards for all menu items and for food production practices.
4. Plans and prices menus. Establishes portion sizes and standards of service for all menu items.
5. Schedules kitchen employees in conjunction with business forecasts and predetermined budget. Maintains payroll records for submission to payroll department.
6. Controls food costs by establishing purchasing specifications, storeroom requisition systems, product storage requirements, standardization recipes, and waste control procedures.
7. Trains kitchen personnel in sale operating procedures of all equipment, utensils, and machinery. Establishes maintenance schedules in conjunction with manufacturer instructions for all equipment. Provides safety training in lifting, carrying, hazardous material control, chemical control first aid, and CPR.
8. Trains kitchen personnel in sanitation practices and establishes cleaning schedules, stock rotation schedules, refrigeration temperature control points, and other sanitary controls.
9. Trains kitchen personnel to prepare all food while retaining the maximum amount of desirable nutrients. Trains kitchen personnel to meet special dietary requests, including low-fat, low-sodium, low-calorie, and vegetarian meals.

Source: Antonymous

FIGURE 7.1 **Sample job description.**

The courts might interpret this job qualification as one that unfairly limits the potential for a minority candidate to secure the job. Even though the groundskeeper might be able to show that the tools normally used by the groundskeeping employees were located on shelves most easily reached by those who were 6 feet tall or taller, it is highly unlikely that this occupational qualification could stand up under the scrutiny of the courts unless the groundskeeper could prove that a height of 6 feet was a **bona fide occupational qualification (BFOQ)**.

To establish that a qualification is, in fact, a BFOQ, you must prove that a class of employees would be unable to perform the job safely or adequately and that the BFOQ is reasonably necessary to the operation of the business. In the case

LEGALESE

Job description: A written listing of a specific job's basic responsibilities and reporting relationships.

Job qualification: The knowledge or skill(s) required to perform the responsibilities and tasks listed in a job description.

Bona fide occupational qualification (BFOQ): A job qualification established in good faith and fairness that is necessary to safely or adequately perform the job.

of the groundskeeper, simply moving the tools or making the reasonable accommodation of providing a short ladder would open the job to candidates of any height and probably would prevent a discrimination lawsuit. The following types of qualifications are examples that are appropriate in jobs where knowledge or skill is a necessary requirement of the job.

Physical attributes necessary to complete the duties of the job include these:

Ability to lift a specific amount of weight

Education

Certifications

Registrations

Licensing

Language skills

Knowledge of equipment operation

Previous experience

Minimum age requirements (for serving alcohol or working certain hours)

Applicant Screening

When choosing potential applicants for employment, hospitality managers generally utilize some or all of the five major selection devices:

1. Applications
2. Interviews
3. Pre-employment testing
4. Background checks
5. References

Applications The employment application is a document completed by the candidate for employment. It will generally list the name, address, work experience, and related information of the candidate. The requirements for a legitimate, legally sound application are many; however, in general, the questions should focus exclusively on job qualifications and nothing else. Most hospitality companies will have their employment application reviewed by an attorney who specializes in employment law from time to time to make sure the application is current under the ever-changing laws. If, as a manager, you are responsible for developing your own application, it is a good idea to have the document reviewed by a legal specialist prior to its utilization.

It is important that each employment candidate for a given position be required to fill out an identical application and that an application be on file for each candidate who is ultimately selected for the position. The candidate should complete the application in its entirety without any omitted or blank items. Figure 7.2 shown on the next page is a sample of a legally sound employment application used by the Four Seasons Hotel, Houston. Note specifically that the questions are related to previous work history and job qualifications. Many hospitality companies today require potential employees to apply online without using paper applications.

Analyze the Situation 7.1

Cruz Villaraigosa owns and manages The Cruz Cantina, a lively bar and dance club that serves Cuban and other Caribbean-style cuisine. The club has a dance floor, has small tables, and serves outstanding food.

Cruz's clientele consists mainly of 20- to 40-year-old males who frequent the Cantina for its good food as well as the extremely low-cut, Spanish-style blouses worn by the young female servers who bring the food and drinks to the tables. The Cruz Cantina advertises to women and families as well as to young men, but the reputation of the facility is predicated upon the physical attractiveness of the women whom Cruz has hired to serve the guests and the uniforms these servers wear.

Ms. Villaraigosa employs women and men of all races and nationalities, but all food and drink servers are female. When she elects not to hire a young man for a job as a server, Ms. Villaraigosa is contacted by the young man's attorney. The attorney alleges the young man has been illegally denied a server's job at the Cantina because of his gender and that cannot be a bona fide occupational qualification for a food and beverage server position.

Ms. Villaraigosa replies that her operation employs both men and women, but that one necessary job qualification for all servers is that they be "attractive to men" and that the qualification of "attractiveness to men" is a legitimate one, given the importance of maintaining the successful image, atmosphere, and resulting business the Cantina enjoys. She maintains that the servers not only serve food and beverages but also play a role in advertising and marketing the unique features of the Cantina. Ms. Villaraigosa also maintains that attractiveness is indeed an occupational characteristic that she can use to promote her facility, citing modeling agencies and TV casting agents as examples of employers who routinely use attractiveness as a means of selecting employees. She states that her right to choose employees she feels will best benefit her business is unconditional as long as she does not unfairly discriminate against a protected class of workers.

1. Do you think that the requirement that servers be "attractive to males" is a bona fide occupational requirement, and "necessary" for the continued successful operation of The Cruz Cantina?
2. If you were on a jury, would you allow Ms. Villaraigosa to hire female servers exclusively if she so desired? Why or why not?
3. What damages, if any, do you feel the male job applicant not selected for employment at the Cantina would be entitled to?

www.fourseasons.com

We are an Equal Opportunity Employer
Complying with all applicable Federal and State Laws

Please Type or Print

DATE TODAY ________________

LAST NAME	FIRST	MIDDLE
SREET ADDRESS		
CITY	STATE	ZIP
PHONE-HOME	PHONE-WORK	
TO VERIFY PREVIOUS EMPLOYMENT, PLEASE INDICATE IF YOU HAVE WORKED UNDER A DIFFERENT NAME.		

POSITION(S) DESIRED	☐ FULL TIME ☐ PART TIME ☐ ON-CALL/CASUAL
SALARY DESIRED	DATE AVAILABLE FOR WORK
SOCIAL SECURITY NUMBER	
ARE YOU PRESENTLY EMPLOYED? ☐ YES ☐ NO IF YES, MAY WE CONTACT YOUR CURRENT EMPLOYER? ☐ YES ☐ NO	
DO YOU HAVE A LEGAL RIGHT TO WORK IN THE U.S.? ☐ YES ☐ NO	
IF YOU HAVE WORKED FOR FOUR SEASONS HOTELS BEFORE, PLEASE STATE WHEN AND WHERE:	

EMPLOYMENT RECORD

List your previous experience beginning with your most recent position.

(Include military experience as a job.)

PLEASE FILL-IN COMPLETELY, DO NOT USE "SEE RESUME"

#1 EMPLOYER	
ADDRESS	PHONE
STARTING POSITION	STARTING SALARY
LAST POSITION	FINAL SALARY
DATES EMPLOYED From: To:	SUPERVISOR
DUTIES	
REASON FOR LEAVING	

#2 EMPLOYER	
ADDRESS	PHONE
STARTING POSITION	STARTING SALARY
LAST POSITION	FINAL SALARY
DATES EMPLOYED From: To:	SUPERVISOR
DUTIES	
REASON FOR LEAVING	

#3 EMPLOYER	
ADDRESS	PHONE
STARTING POSITION	STARTING SALARY
LAST POSITION	FINAL SALARY
DATES EMPLOYED From: To:	SUPERVISOR
DUTIES	
REASON FOR LEAVING	

#4 EMPLOYER	
ADDRESS	PHONE
STARTING POSITION	STARTING SALARY
LAST POSITION	FINAL SALARY
DATES EMPLOYED From: To:	SUPERVISOR
DUTIES	
REASON FOR LEAVING	

FIGURE 7.2 Employment application from the Four Seasons Hotel, Houston.
(Reprinted with permission).

EDUCATION AND SKILLS (answer only if job related)

	DIPLOMA / GED
HIGH SCHOOL DEGREE OR GED EQUIVALENCY	☐ YES ☐ NO

	NAME	GRADUATED	MAJOR
COLLEGE		☐ YES ☐ NO	
OTHER EDUCATION / TRAINING: (List any special skill(s) related to the job you are applying for)			

AVAILABILITY

ARE THERE ANY HOURS, SHIFTS, OR DAYS OF THE WEEK THAT YOU WILL NOT BE ABLE TO WORK? YES NO

IF YES, PLEASE STATE DAYS AND REASON:

I AM WILLING AND ABLE TO WORK:

☐ FULL TIME ☐ PART TIME ☐ TEMPORARY/SEASONAL

☐ ON-CALL/CASUAL ☐ DAYS ☐ EVENINGS ☐ OVERNIGHT

☐ WEEKENDS ☐ HOLIDAYS ☐ OVERTIME

ARE YOU CAPABALE OF PERFORMING THE ESSENTIAL FUNCTIONS OF THE JOB YOU ARE APPLYING FOR WITH OR WITHOUT REASONABLE ACCOMODATION?

☐ YES ☐ NO

HOW WERE YOU REFERRED TO FOUR SEASONS? PLEASE BE SPECIFIC. ☐ ADVERTISEMENT ☐ INTERNET ☐ ON YOUR OWN

NAME OF SCHOOL: NAME OF COMPANY EMPLOYEE: NAME OF AGENCY:

OTHER:

DO YOU HAVE RELATIVES OR ACQUAINTANCES WORKING IN THE HOTEL? ☐ YES ☐ NO
IF YES, PLEASE LIST THEIR NAMES & RELATIONSHIP:

IF UNDER AGE 18, INDICATE DATE OF BIRTH:

IF APPLYING FOR A JOB INVOLVING ALCOHOLIC BEVERAGE SERVICE, ARE YOU AT LEAST AGE 21? ☐ YES ☐ NO

HAVE YOU EVER BEEN CONVICTED OF A FELONY? ☐ YES* ☐ NO DO YOU HAVE FELONY CHARGES PENDING AGAINST YOU? ☐ YES ☐ NO

IF YES, PLEASE GIVE DATES AND DETAILS:

*CONVICTION OF A FELONY WILL NOT NECESSARILY DISQUALIFY YOU FROM EMPLOYMENT.

CERTIFICATION AND SIGNATURE – Please read carefully.

I declare that my answers to the questions on this application are true, and I give Four Seasons Hotels the right to investigate all references and information given. I agree that any false statement or misrepresentation on this application will be cause for refusal to hire or immediate dismissal. I affirm that I have a genuine intent and for no other purposes in applying for a job with Four Seasons Hotels. I agree that my employment will be considered "at will" and may be terminated by this company at any time without liability for wages or salary except for such as may have been earned at the date of such termination unless or until superseded by specific written employment contract. If requested by management at any time, I agree to submit to a search of my person or of any locker that may be assigned to me and I hereby waive all claims for damages on account of such examination.
I understand that Four Seasons Hotels is a Drug Free Workplace and has a policy against drug and alcohol abuse and reserves the right to screen applicants and test for cause.
I acknowledge that if I need reasonable accommodation in either the application process or employment I should bring the request to the attention of the Human Resources department.

I authorize you to make such legal investigations and inquiries of my personal employment, criminal history, driving record, and other job related matters as may be necessary in determining an employment decision. I hereby release employers, schools or persons from all liability in responding to inquiries in connection with my application.

I understand that an offer employment and my continued employment are contingent upon satisfactory proof of my authorization to work in the United States of America.

CONFIDENTIAL MATERIAL AND THE PROPERTY OF
FOUR SEASONS HOTELS LIMITED

SIGN HERE:______________________________ DATE:________________
(APPLICANT'S SIGNATURE) MONTH/DAY/YEAR

FIGURE 7.2 *(continued)*

Interviews From the employment applications or resumes submitted, some candidates will be selected for the interview process. It is important to realize that the types of questions that can be asked in the interview are highly restricted because if improper questions are asked, job interviews can subject an employer to legal liability. If a candidate is not hired based on his or her answer to—or refusal to answer—an inappropriate question, that candidate has the right to file a lawsuit.

The Equal Employment Opportunity Commission (EEOC) suggests that an employer consider the following questions in deciding whether to include a particular question on an employment application or in a job interview:

- Does this question tend to screen out minorities or females?
- Is the answer needed in order to judge this individual's competence for performance of the job?
- Are there alternative, nondiscriminatory ways to judge the person's qualifications?

As a manager, you must be very careful in your selection of questions to ask in an interview. In all cases, it is important to remember that the job itself dictates what is an allowable question. Questions should be written down and asked. In addition, supervisors, coworkers, and others who may participate in the interview process should be trained to avoid questions that could increase the liability of the facility. Simply relying on a book of interview questions or obtaining a list from the Internet is not a prudent idea because the law changes, and reliance on material may be outdated by the time it is used in an interview. A specialist in employment law can provide guidance as to the appropriate questions to ask a candidate.

Generally, age is considered to be irrelevant in most hiring decisions; therefore, date-of-birth questions are improper. Age is a sensitive pre-employment question because the Age Discrimination in Employment Act protects employees 40 years old and older. It is permissible to ask an applicant to state his or her age if he or she is younger than 18 years old because that age group is permitted to work only a limited number of hours each week. It is also important when hiring bartenders and other servers of alcohol who must be above a state's minimum age for serving alcohol.

Race, religion, and national origin questions are also inappropriate as is the practice of requiring that photographs of the candidate be submitted prior to or after an interview.

Questions about physical traits such as height and weight requirements have been found to violate the law because they eliminated disproportionate numbers of female as well as Asian-American- and Spanish-surnamed applicants.

If a job does not require a particular level of education, it is improper to ask questions about an applicant's educational background. Applicants can be asked about their education and credentials if these are indeed bona fide occupational qualifications. Certainly, it is allowable to ask a potential hotel controller if he or she has a degree in accounting and which school granted that degree. Asking a potential table busser for the same information would be inappropriate.

It is permissible to ask an applicant if he or she uses drugs or smokes. It is also allowable to ask a candidate if he or she is willing to submit to a voluntary drug test as a condition of employment.

Questions concerning whether an applicant owns a home potentially discriminate against those individuals who do not own their own homes. Questions concerning the type of discharge received by an ex-military applicant are improper because a high proportion of other than honorable discharges are given to minorities.

Safe questions can be asked about a candidate's current employment, former employment, and job references. In most cases, questions asked on both the application and in the interview should focus on the applicant's job skills, and nothing else. Figure 7.3 contains some guidelines developed by the EEOC for asking appropriate interview questions.

Pre-Employment Testing Pre-employment testing is a common way to improve the employee screening process. Test results can be used, for example, to measure the relative strength of two candidates.

In the hospitality industry, pre-employment testing will generally fall into one of the following categories:

- Skills tests
- Psychological tests
- Drug screening tests

Skills tests were among the first tools used by managers to screen applicants in the employment process. In the hospitality industry, skills tests can include activities such as typing for office workers, computer application for those who use word processing or spreadsheet tools, or food production for culinary artists.

Psychological testing can include personality tests, tests designed to predict performance, or tests of mental ability. For both skills tests and psychological tests, the important rule to remember is this:

> *If the test does not have documented validity and reliability, the results of the tests should not be used for hiring* decisions.

Pre-employment drug testing is allowable in most states and can be a very effective tool for reducing insurance rates and potential worker liability issues. A drug-free environment tends to attract better-quality employment candidates with the resulting impact of a higher-quality workforce. There are, however, strict guidelines in some states as to when and how people can be tested. A document with language similar to that found in Figure 7.4 on page 124 should be completed by each candidate prior to drug testing, and the signed document should be kept on file with the employee's application form.

Subject	Inappropriate Questions (May Not Ask or Require)	Appropriate Questions (May Ask or Require)
Gender or marital status	• Gender (on application form) • Mr., Miss, Mrs., Ms.? • Married, divorced, single, separated? • Number and ages of children • Pregnancy, actual or intended • Maiden name, former name	• In checking your work record, do we need another name for identification?
Race	• Race? • Color of skin, eyes, hair, etc. • Request for photograph	
National Origin	• Questions about place of birth, ancestry, mother tongue, national origin of parents or spouse. • What is your native language? • How did you learn to speak [language] fluently?	• If job-related, what foreign languages do you speak?
Citizenship, immigration status	• Of what country are you a citizen? • Are you a native-born U.S. citizen? • Questions about naturalization of applicant, spouse, or parents.	• If selected are you able to start work with us on a specific date? If not, when would you be able to start? • If hired, can you show proof that you are eligible to work in the United States?
Religion	• Religious affiliation or preference • Religious holidays observed • Membership in religious organizations	• Can you observe regularly required days and hours of work? • Are there any days or hours of the week that you are not able to work? • Are there any holidays that you are not able to work?
Age	• How old are you? • Date of birth	• Are you 21 or older? (for positions serving alcohol)
Disability	• Do you have any disabilities? • Have you ever been treated for (certain) diseases? • Are you healthy?	
Questions that may discriminate against minorities	• Have you ever been arrested? • List all clubs, societies, and lodges to which you belong. • Do you own a car? (unless required for the job) • Type of military discharge • Questions regarding credit ratings, financial status, wage garnishment, home ownership.	• Have you ever been convicted of a crime? If yes, give details (if crime is job-related, as embezzlement is to handling money, you may refuse to hire). • List membership in professional organizations relevant to job performance. • Military service: dates, branch of service, education, and experience (if job-related).

FIGURE 7.3 Guidelines for conducting a job interview.

Source: Jack E. Miller, John R. Walker, and Karen Eich Drummond, *Supervision in the Hospitality Industry, Fifth Edition.* Hoboken, NJ: John Wiley & Sons, 2007.

If pre-employment drug testing is to be used, care must be taken to ensure the accuracy of the testing. In some cases, applicants whose erroneous test results have cost them a job have successfully sued the employer. The laws surrounding mandatory drug testing are complex. If you elect to implement either a pre-employment or postemployment drug-testing program, it is best to first seek advice from an attorney who specializes in labor employment law in your state.

Background Checks Increasingly, hospitality employers are utilizing background checks prior to hiring workers in selected positions. It has been estimated that as many as 30 percent of all resumes and employment applications include

Employee Consent Form for Drug Testing

I agree, fully and voluntarily to submit to a urinalysis or blood test conducted by ______________________ for a drug screen as a condition of my consideration for employment. I understand that failing to meet the standards established for this test may result in the disqualification of further consideration of my application. Lastly, I understand that these results will be used only as the basis for an employment decision and will not be shared with any individual or organization outside the company.

The undersigned represents that he or she has read this information in its entirety and understands it.

Employee Signature ______________________ Date ______________

Employer Witness Signature ______________________ Date ______________

FIGURE 7.4 Employee consent form for drug testing.

Adapted from *Foodservice Safety and Security Managers Handbook,* by the National Restaurant Association Educational Foundation. Reprinted with permission.

some level of falsification. Because this is true, employers are spending more time and financial resources to validate information supplied by a potential employee. Common verification points include the following:

Name

Social Security number

Address history

Education/training

Criminal background

Credit reports

Background checks, like pre-employment testing, can leave an employer subject to litigation if the information secured during a check is false or is used in a way that violates state and federal employment law. In addition, if the information is improperly disclosed to third parties, it could violate the employee's right to privacy. Not conducting background checks on some positions can, however, subject the employer to potential litigation under the doctrines of **negligent hiring** and **negligent retention**.

Consider the case of Holly Rosecrans. Ms. Rosecrans is the assistant general manager of a country club in Florida. One of her responsibilities is the selection and training of pool lifeguards, which are required in her facility by local statute. Each lifeguard must be certified in cardiopulmonary resuscitation (CPR). Ms. Rosecrans interviews a candidate who lists the successful completion of a CPR course as part of his educational background. If Ms. Rosecrans does not verify the accuracy of the candidate's statement and a death results because the lifeguard did not have CPR training, the club might well be held liable for the death of the swimmer.

Using background checks as a screening tool does involve some risk, as well as some responsibility. Employers should search only for information that has a direct bearing on the position a candidate is applying for. In addition, if a candidate is denied employment on the basis of information found in a background check, the employer should provide a candidate with a copy of that report. Sometimes, candidates can help verify or explain the content of their own background checks. Reporting agencies can make mistakes, and if you rely on obviously false information to make a hiring decision, it may put your organization at risk.

In all cases, a candidate for employment should be required to sign a consent form authorizing an employer to conduct a background check. Figure 7.5 is a sample consent form that could be used to document this authorization.

References In the past, employment references were a very popular tool for managers to use in the screening process. But in today's litigious society, they are much more difficult to obtain. Although many organizations still seek information from past employers about an employee's previous work performance, few sophisticated companies will divulge such information. It is important to note that some employers have been held liable for inaccurate comments that have been made about past employees. In addition, there are companies that specialize in providing job searchers with a confidential, comprehensive verification of employment references from former employers. Thus, employers are becoming more cautious about supplying information on employees who have left their organization.

To help minimize the risk of litigation related to reference checks, it is best to secure the applicant's permission in writing

LEGALESE

Negligent hiring: Failure on the part of an employer to exercise reasonable care in the selection of employees.

Negligent retention: Failure to terminate an employee after the employer becomes aware that an employee is a danger or threat to others and is unsuitable for the job.

Employee Consent Form for Background Checks and Application Verification

I agree, fully and voluntarily to checks related to:

1. (e.g., Criminal History)
2. (e.g., School Attendance Record)

as well as checks on information I have supplied in my employment application.

I understand that failing to meet the standards established for these checks as well as falsification of information on my application may result in the disqualification of further consideration of my application. Lastly, I understand that the results of these background checks and the accuracy of my application will be used only as the basis for an employment decision and will not be shared with any individual or organization outside the company.

The undersigned represents that he or she has read this information in its entirety and understands it.

Employee Signature ______________________ Date ______________

Employer Signature ______________________ Date ______________

FIGURE 7.5 Employee consent form for background checks.
Adapted from *Foodservice Safety and Security Managers Handbook* by the National Restaurant Association Educational Foundation. Reprinted with permission.

before contacting an ex-employer. Employers must be extremely cautious in both giving and receiving reference information. Employers are usually protected if they give a truthful reference; however, that does not mean these employers will be spared the expense of defending a **defamation** case brought by an ex-employee.

If, for example, an employer giving a reference states that an ex-employee was terminated because he or she "didn't get along" with his or her coworkers, the employer might have to be able to prove the truthfulness of the statement, as well as show proof that all of the blame for the difficulties were the responsibility of the ex-employee.

To minimize the risk of a lawsuit, you should never reply to a request for information about one of your ex-employees without a copy of that employee's signed release authorizing the reference check. How much you choose to disclose about an ex-employee is your decision; however, your answers should be honest and defendable. Also, it is best never to disclose personal information such as marital difficulties, financial problems, or serious illness because you could be sued for invasion of privacy. Many employers today give only the following information about past employees:

Employer's name

Ex-employer's name

Date(s) of employment

Job title

Name and title of person supplying the information

LEGALESE

Defamation: False statements that cause someone to be held in contempt, lowered in the estimation of the community, or to lose employment status or earnings or otherwise suffer a damaged reputation.

If a prospective employee provides letters of reference, always call the authors of reference letters to ensure that they did in fact write them. When possible, it is best to put any request for reference information in writing, and ask that the response be in written form. If a verbal response is all you can get, document the conversation; write down as much of the dialogue as possible, including the name of the party you spoke to and the date and time the contact occurred.

Even with authorization, many employers are reluctant to give out information about former employees. If this happens, simply ask if the company would rehire that worker. The response to that question combined with the information received from other employers should help to determine the accuracy of the information given by the applicant.

The selection of the right employee for the right job is a specialized area of human resources, and the hospitality manager will often be able to rely on a human resources department or personnel director for assistance when undertaking this important task. For the independent entrepreneur, it is critical that the entire employee selection process be reviewed by an expert in employment law and continually monitored for compliance with established and updated procedures.

Wording of Classified Advertisements

One final aspect of employee selection that you must be aware of involves the wording of classified ads that you might place in newspapers, Internet sites (such as LinkedIn), and journals when announcing a job opening. As with job descriptions and qualifications, it is important that the terms you use in a classified ad do not exclude or discriminate against individuals. Federal law prohibits the use of words or phrases that might prevent certain types of people from applying for an advertised position. Phrases to avoid include references to age ("ages 20 to 30"), sex ("men" or "women"), national origin, and religion. There are a limited number of cases where

Civil Rights Act of 1964

UNLAWFUL EMPLOYMENT PRACTICES

SEC. 2000e-2. [Section 703]

(a) It shall be an unlawful employment practice for an employer

(1) to fail or refuse to hire or to discharge any individual, or otherwise to discriminate against any individual with respect to his compensation, terms, conditions, or privileges of employment, because of such individual's race, color, religion, sex, or national origin; or

(2) to limit, segregate, or classify his employees or applicants for employment in any way which would deprive or tend to deprive any individual of employment opportunities or otherwise adversely affect his status as an employee, because of such individual's race, color, religion, sex, or national origin.

(b) It shall be an unlawful employment practice for an employment agency to fail or refuse to refer for employment, or otherwise to discriminate against, any individual because of his race, color, religion, sex, or national origin, or to classify or refer for employment any individual on the basis of his race, color, religion, sex, or national origin.

(c) It shall be an unlawful employment practice for a labor organization

(1) to exclude or to expel from its membership, or otherwise to discriminate against, any individual because of his race, color, religion, sex, or national origin;

(2) to limit, segregate, or classify its membership or applicants for membership, or to classify or fail or refuse to refer for employment any individual, in any way which would deprive or tend to deprive any individual of employment opportunities, or would limit such employment opportunities or otherwise adversely affect his status as an employee or as an applicant for employment, because of such individual's race, color, religion, sex, or national origin; or

(3) to cause or attempt to cause an employer to discriminate against an individual in violation of this section.

FIGURE 7.6 **Excerpt from the Civil Rights Act of 1964.**

a bona fide job qualification might limit the type of person who could apply and that can be mentioned; however, the manager should be prepared to document and defend the chosen language if challenged. In general, however, employers should focus their classified ads on a description of the job and any applicable educational, licensing, or background requirements needed.

7.2 Discrimination in the Selection Process

Although employers are free to hire employees as they see fit, they are not free to unlawfully discriminate against people in their employment selection. Employment discrimination laws have been established to protect certain classes of people from unfair or exclusionary hiring practices.

The Fifth and Fourteenth Amendments of the U.S. Constitution limit the ability of the power of the federal and state governments to discriminate. The Fifth Amendment has an explicit requirement that the federal government not deprive any individual of "life, liberty, or property" without the due process of the law. Although discrimination by employers in the private sector is not directly addressed in the Constitution, it has become subject to a growing body of federal and state laws, which were passed in recognition of the personal freedoms guaranteed by the Constitution. Although many antidiscrimination statutes affect employee selection, the most significant are:

Civil Rights Act of 1964; Title VII

Americans with Disabilities Act; Title I of 1990

Age Discrimination in Employment Act of 1967

Pregnancy Discrimination Act of 1978

Genetic Information Nondiscrimination Act of 2008 (GINA)

Civil Rights Act of 1964, Title VII

Title VII of the Civil Rights Act of 1964 and its resulting amendments applies to employers with 15 or more employees who are engaged in **interstate commerce**.

Figure 7.6 presents the original language of the bill that relates to employee selection.

The act prohibits discrimination based on race, color, religion, sex, or national origin. Sex includes pregnancy, childbirth, or related medical conditions. The act makes it illegal for employers to discriminate in hiring and in setting the terms and conditions of employment. Labor organizations are also prohibited from basing membership or union classifications on race, color, religion, sex, or national origin. The law also

---

LEGALESE

Interstate commerce: Commercial trading or the transportation of persons or property between or among states.

Analyze the Situation 7.2

Jetta Wong is the owner and manager of the Golden Dragon oriental restaurant. The restaurant is large, inexpensive, and enjoys an excellent reputation. Business is good, and the restaurant serves a diverse clientele.

Ms. Wong places a classified ad for a table busser in the employment section of her local newspaper. The response is good, and Ms. Wong narrows the field of potential candidates to two. One is the same ethnic background as Ms. Wong and the rest of the staff. The second candidate is Danielle Hidalgo, the daughter of a Mexican citizen and an American citizen. Ms. Hidalgo was born and raised in the United States.

While both candidates are pleasant, Ms. Wong offers the position to the candidate who matches the background of the restaurant and Ms. Wong. Her rationale is that, since both candidates are equal in ability, she has a right to select the candidate she feels will best suit her business. Because it is an oriental restaurant, Ms. Wong feels diners will expect to see oriental servers and bussers. No one was discriminated against, she maintains, because Ms. Hidalgo was not denied a job on the basis of race but rather on the basis of what was best for business. Ms. Wong simply selected her preference from among two equal candidates. Ms. Wong relates her decision to Ms. Hidalgo.

Ms. Hidalgo maintains that she was not selected because of her Hispanic ethnic background. She threatens to file a charge with the EEOC unless she is offered employment.

1. Do you think Ms. Hidalgo was denied the position because of her ethnicity?
2. In the situation described here, does Ms. Wong have the right to consider race as a bona fide occupational qualification?
3. How should Ms. Wong advertise jobs in the future to avoid charges of discrimination?

prohibits employers from retaliating against employees or candidates who file charges of discrimination against them, who refuse to comply with a discriminatory policy, and who participate in an investigation of discrimination charges against the employer.

One outcome of the Civil Rights Act was the formation of the Equal Employment Opportunity Commission, which oversees and enforces federal laws regulating employer/employee relationships. The EEOC investigates complaints by employees who think they have been discriminated against. Businesses that are found to have discriminated can be ordered to compensate the employee(s) for items such as lost wages, attorney fees, and punitive damages.

In later amendments, the Civil Rights Act was expanded to include **affirmative action** requirements. Affirmative action constitutes a good-faith effort by employees to address past and/or present discrimination through a variety of specific, results-oriented procedures. This is a step beyond equal opportunity laws like Title VII, which simply ban discriminatory practices. State and local governments, agencies of the federal government, and federal contractors and subcontractors with contracts of $50,000 or more—including colleges and universities—are required by federal law to implement affirmative action programs.

Employers have used a variety of techniques for implementing affirmative action plans. These include:

- Active recruiting to expand the pool of candidates for job openings.
- Revising the selection tools and criteria to ensure their relevance to job performance.
- Establishing goals and timetables for hiring underrepresented groups.

Originally, affirmative action activities were intended to correct discrimination in the hiring and promotion of African Americans and other people of color. Now, affirmative action protections are being applied to women, and some government jurisdictions have extended affirmative action provisions to older people, the disabled, and Vietnam-era veterans. The goal of affirmative action is to broaden the pool of candidates and encourage hiring based on sound, job-related, criteria. The result is a workforce with greater diversity and potential for all.

In addition to the Civil Rights Act, many states also have their own civil rights laws, which prohibit discrimination. Sometimes, the state laws are more inclusive than the Civil Rights Act in that they expand protection to workers or employment candidates in categories not covered under the federal Civil Rights Act, such as age, marital status, sexual orientation, and certain types of physical or mental disabilities. State civil rights laws may also have stricter penalties for violations, including fines and/or jail time. As a hospitality manager, you should know the provisions of your state's civil rights law in addition to the federal laws.

LEGALESE

Affirmative action: A federally mandated requirement that employers who meet certain criteria must actively seek to fairly employ recognized classes of workers. (Some state and local legislatures have also enacted affirmative action requirements.)

Americans with Disabilities Act of 1990

On July 26, 1990, the Americans with Disabilities Act (ADA) was enacted. The ADA prohibits discrimination against people with disabilities in the areas of public accommodations, transportation, telecommunications, and employment. The ADA is a five-part piece of legislation; Title I focuses primarily on employment.

There are three different groups of individuals who are protected under the ADA:

1. An individual with a physical or mental impairment that substantially limits a major life activity. Some examples of what constitutes a "major life activity" under the act are seeing, hearing, talking, walking, reading, learning, breathing, taking care of oneself, lifting, sitting, and standing.
2. A person who has a record of a disability.
3. A person who is "regarded as" having a disability.

Employers cannot reduce an employee's pay simply because he or she is disabled, nor can they refuse to hire a disabled candidate if, with reasonable accommodation, it is possible for the candidate to perform the job. Employers are also required to post notices of the Americans with Disabilities Act and its provisions in a location where they can be seen by all employees.

Even with the passage of the ADA, an employer does not have to hire a disabled applicant who is not qualified to do a job. The employer can still select the most qualified candidate provided that no applicant was eliminated from consideration because of his or her qualified disability.

Although the law in this area is changing rapidly, the following conditions, among others, currently meet the criteria for a qualified disability and are protected under the ADA:

- AIDS/HIV
- Alzheimer's
- Anxiety disorders
- Cancer
- Cerebral palsy
- Diabetes
- Tuberculosis
- Heart disease
- Hearing or visual impairments
- Alcoholism
- Epilepsy
- Paralysis
- Dwarfism
- Depression

Conditions that are not currently covered under ADA include:

- Kleptomania
- Disorders caused by the use of illegal drugs
- Compulsive gambling
- Sexual behavior disorders
- Nonchronic conditions of short duration such as a sprain, broken limb, or the flu

The ADA has changed the way employers select employees. Questions on job applications and during interviews that cannot be asked include the following:

- Have you ever been hospitalized or seen by a specialist?
- Are you taking prescription drugs?
- Have you ever been treated for substance abuse?
- Have you ever filed a workers' compensation insurance claim?
- Do you have any physical defects, disabilities, or impairments that may affect your performance in the position for which you are applying/interviewing?

In situations where a disabled person could perform the duties of a particular job but some aspect of the job or work facility would prevent the applicant from doing so, the employer may be required to make a reasonable accommodation for the worker.

Legally Managing at Work

Accommodating Disabled Employees

To reduce the risk of an ADA noncompliance charge related to reasonable accommodation, you can ask these questions:

1. Can the applicant perform the essential functions of the job with or without reasonable accommodation? (You can ask the applicant this question.)

   If no, then he or she is not qualified and is therefore not protected by the ADA. If yes, go to question 2.
2. Is the necessary accommodation reasonable? To answer this question, ask yourself the following: Will this accommodation create an undue financial or administrative hardship on the business?

   If yes, you do not have to provide unreasonable accommodations. If no, go to question 3.
3. Will this accommodation or the hiring of the person with the disability create a direct threat to the health or safety of other employees or guests in the workplace?

   If yes, you are not required to make the accommodation and have fulfilled your obligation under the ADA.

Search the Web 7.1

Go to **www.eeoc.gov**

1. Under About EEOC, select: Laws, Regulations, Guidance, & MOUs.
2. Select: Discrimination by Type.
3. Select: Disability.
4. From the document displayed, determine:

 a. What must an employer do after receiving a request for a reasonable accommodation?

 b. Is the restructuring of a job to meet the needs of a disabled person considered a reasonable accommodation?

For additional information on job accommodation under the ADA, log on to the Job Accommodation Network for the ADA at **janweb.icdi.wvu.edu.**

An employer has provided reasonable accommodation when it has made existing facilities readily accessible to individuals with mobility impairments or other disabilities and has restructured a job in the most accommodating manner possible to allow a disabled individual to perform it. The employer is not obligated to provide a reasonable accommodation when such accommodation would result in undue hardship to the employer. Generally speaking, an undue hardship occurs when the expense of accommodating the worker is excessive or would disrupt the natural work environment. The law in this area is vague; thus, any employer who maintains that accommodating a worker with a disability would impose an undue hardship should be prepared to document such an assertion. After investigation, the EEOC issues a "right to sue" letter to an employee if it concludes that an employer is in violation of the ADA.

One ADA provision that foodservice employers should be aware of concerns employees and job applicants who have infectious and communicable diseases. Each year, the U.S. Department of Health and Human Services publishes a list of communicable diseases that, if passed on through the handling of food, could put a foodservice operation at risk. Employers have the right not to assign to or hire an individual who has one of the identified diseases for a position that involves the handling of food, but only if there is no reasonable accommodation that could be made to eliminate such a risk.

Age Discrimination in Employment Act of 1967

The Age Discrimination in Employment Act of 1967 (ADEA) protects individuals who are 40 years of age or older from employment discrimination based on age.

The ADEA's protections apply to both employees and job applicants. Under the ADEA, it is unlawful to discriminate against a person because of his or her age with respect to any term, condition, or privilege of employment—including hiring, firing, promotion, layoff, compensation, benefits, job assignments, and training.

The ADEA applies to employers with 20 or more employees, as well as to labor unions and governmental agencies. The ADEA makes it unlawful to include age preferences, limitations, or specifications in job notices or advertisements. As a narrow exception to that general rule, a job notice or advertisement may specify an age limit in the rare circumstances where age is shown to be a bona fide occupational qualification (BFOQ) reasonably necessary to the essence of the business, or a minimum age qualification to legally perform the job.

Pregnancy Discrimination Act of 1978

The Pregnancy Discrimination Act of 1978 basically amends the Civil Rights Act of 1964 and creates a claim of discrimination by a prospective employee if denied employment on the basis of pregnancy, childbirth, and/or related medical conditions.

Genetic Information Nondiscrimination Act of 2008 (GINA)

This act protects prospective employees from discrimination because it is illegal to deny employment based on genetic information of the candidate and the candidate's family. In addition, it protects candidates and employees from being harassed because of genetic information.

7.3 Verification of Eligibility to Work

Even after an employer has legally selected an applicant for employment, the law requires the employer to take at least one more action before an employee can begin work. The employer must determine that the worker is, in fact, legally entitled to hold the job. Verification of employment status takes two major forms. The first is verification of eligibility to work; the second is verification of compliance with the child labor laws.

Immigration Reform and Control Act of 1986

The Immigration Reform and Control Act (IRCA) was passed in 1986. The act prohibits employers from knowingly hiring persons for work in the United States either because the individual is in the country illegally or because his or her immigration and residency status does not allow employment. The law also applies to employers who, after the date of hire, determine that an employee is not legally authorized to work but continue to employ that individual.

Under provisions of the IRCA, employers are required to verify that all employees hired after November 6, 1986, are legally authorized to work in the United States. Unlike many other federal laws, IRCA applies to organizations of any size and to both full- and part-time employees. The act requires that when an applicant is hired, a Form I-9 must be completed (see Figure 7.7).

Form I-9 is often misunderstood. Its purpose is to verify both an employee's identity and his or her eligibility to work; thus, it serves a dual role. The Department of Homeland Security via the United States Citizenship and Immigration Services (USCIS) imposes severe penalties on employers who do not have properly completed I-9s for all employees. USCIS has been very meticulous in its audits, issuing large fines for even minor errors such as incorrect dates and boxes or lines left blank on the form.

Every employee hired is required to complete an I-9 when beginning work; specifically, the employee is required to fill out Section 1 of the form. The employer is then responsible for reviewing and ensuring that Section 1 is fully and properly completed. At that time, the employer will complete Section 2 of the I-9 form.

Figure 7.8 on page 134 details the documents that can be used in completing an I-9. It is important to note that the documents used to verify eligibility and identity must be originals. To ensure compliance, employers will often remind individuals to bring necessary identification documents with them on their first day of employment

The employer's part of the Form I-9 must be completed within three business days or at the time of hire if the employment is for less than three days. Each completed I-9 should be kept for three years after the date of employment or one year after the employee's termination, whichever is longer. Keep all I-9s readily available, preferably in one file for all employees because they must be presented to the USCIS within 72 hours upon request. In a large hospitality organization, if managers must search through hundreds of personnel files to locate each completed I-9 form, the 72-hour mandate will most likely not be met.

An employer's good-faith effort in complying with the verification and recordkeeping requirements will ensure his or her defense if any charges surface that the organization knowingly and willingly hired a person who was not legally authorized to work. It is prudent practice to follow the letter of the law in this area because fines as high as $10,000 per illegal employee can be levied against the business by the government. To ensure compliance, more and more hospitality employers are using the E-Verify system found at https://www.uscis.gov/e-verify.

Fair Labor Standards Act of 1938

The Fair Labor Standards Act of 1938 (FLSA) protects young workers from employment that might interfere with their educational opportunities or be detrimental to their health or well-being. It covers all workers who are engaged in or producing goods for interstate commerce or who are employed in certain enterprises. Essentially, the law establishes that youths 18 years and older may perform any job, hazardous or not, for unlimited hours, subject to minimum wage and overtime requirements.

Children aged 16 and 17 may work at any time for unlimited hours in all jobs not declared hazardous by the U.S. Department of Labor. Hazardous occupations include working with explosives and radioactive materials; operating certain power-driven woodworking, metalworking, bakery, and paper-products machinery; operating various types of power-driven saws and guillotine shears; operating most power-driven hoisting apparatuses including nonautomatic elevators, forklifts, or cranes; working in most jobs in slaughtering, meat packing, and rendering plants; operating power-driven meat-processing machines when performed in wholesale, retail, or service establishments; working in most jobs in excavation, logging, sawmilling, roofing, wrecking, demolition, and shipbreaking; operating motor vehicles or working as outside helpers on motor vehicles; and working in most jobs in the manufacturing of bricks, tiles, and similar products.

Youths aged 14 and 15 may work in various jobs outside school hours under the following conditions:

- No more than three hours on a school day with a limit of 18 hours in a school week.
- No more than eight hours on a nonschool day with a limit of 40 hours in a nonschool week.
- Before 7:00 A.M. or after 7:00 P.M. except from June 1 through Labor Day, when the evening hour is extended to 9:00 P.M.
- A break provided after five contiguous hours of work.

Workers 14 and 15 years of age may be employed in a variety of hospitality jobs, including cashiering, waiting on tables, washing dishes, and preparing salads and other food (although cooking is permitted only at snack bars, soda fountains, lunch counters, and cafeteria-style counters) but not in positions deemed hazardous by the U.S. Department of Labor. As with other types of employment law, there are stiff penalties for employers who violate provisions of the Fair Labor Standards Act. Employers can be fined between $1,000 for first violations and $3,000 for third violations. Repeat offenders can be subject to fines of $10,000 and even jail terms.

All states have child labor laws as well. Employers in most states are required to keep on file documents and/or permits verifying the age of minor employees. Some states may require proof of school attendance. When both state and federal child labor laws apply, the law setting the more stringent standard must be observed. Federal child labor laws are enforced by the Wage and Hour Division of the U.S. Labor Department's Employment Standards Administration. State and local child labor laws can vary, so it is best to confirm the specifics of the child labor laws in your own state by contacting your local state employment agency or employment attorney.

Department of Homeland Security
U.S. Citizenship and Immigration Services

OMB No. 1615-0047; Expires 03/31/07

Employment Eligibility Verification

INSTRUCTIONS

PLEASE READ ALL INSTRUCTIONS CAREFULLY BEFORE COMPLETING THIS FORM.

Anti-Discrimination Notice. It is illegal to discriminate against any individual (other than an alien not authorized to work in the U.S.) in hiring, discharging, or recruiting or referring for a fee because of that individual's national origin or citizenship status. It is illegal to discriminate against work eligible individuals. Employers **CANNOT** specify which document(s) they will accept from an employee. The refusal to hire an individual because of a future expiration date may also constitute illegal discrimination.

Section 1- Employee. All employees, citizens and noncitizens, hired after November 6, 1986, must complete Section 1 of this form at the time of hire, which is the actual beginning of employment. **The employer is responsible for ensuring that Section 1 is timely and properly completed.**

Preparer/Translator Certification. The Preparer/Translator Certification must be completed if Section 1 is prepared by a person other than the employee. A preparer/translator may be used only when the employee is unable to complete Section 1 on his/her own. However, the employee must still sign Section 1 personally.

Section 2 - Employer. For the purpose of completing this form, the term "employer" includes those recruiters and referrers for a fee who are agricultural associations, agricultural employers or farm labor contractors.

Employers must complete Section 2 by examining evidence of identity and employment eligibility within three (3) business days of the date employment begins. If employees are authorized to work, but are unable to present the required document(s) within three business days, they must present a receipt for the application of the document(s) within three business days and the actual document(s) within ninety (90) days. However, if employers hire individuals for a duration of less than three business days, Section 2 must be completed at the time employment begins. **Employers must record: 1)** document title; **2)** issuing authority; **3)** document number, **4)** expiration date, if any; and **5)** the date employment begins. Employers must sign and date the certification. Employees must present original documents. Employers may, but are not required to, photocopy the document(s) presented. These photocopies may only be used for the verification process and must be retained with the I-9. **However, employers are still responsible for completing the I-9.**

Section 3 - Updating and Reverification. Employers must complete Section 3 when updating and/or reverifying the I-9. Employers must reverify employment eligibility of their employees on or before the expiration date recorded in Section 1. Employers **CANNOT** specify which document(s) they will accept from an employee.

- If an employee's name has changed at the time this form is being updated/reverified, complete Block A.
- If an employee is rehired within three (3) years of the date this form was originally completed and the employee is still eligible to be employed on the same basis as previously indicated on this form (updating), complete Block B and the signature block.
- If an employee is rehired within three (3) years of the date this form was originally completed and the employee's work authorization has expired **or** if a current employee's work authorization is about to expire (reverification), complete Block B and:
  - examine any document that reflects that the employee is authorized to work in the U.S. (see List A **or** C),
  - record the document title, document number and expiration date (if any) in Block C, and
  - complete the signature block.

Photocopying and Retaining Form I-9. A blank I-9 may be reproduced, provided both sides are copied. The Instructions must be available to all employees completing this form. Employers must retain completed I-9s for three (3) years after the date of hire or one (1) year after the date employment ends, whichever is later.

For more detailed information, you may refer to the Department of Homeland Security (DHS) Handbook for Employers, (Form M-274). You may obtain the handbook at your local U.S. Citizenship and Immigration Services (USCIS) office.

Privacy Act Notice. The authority for collecting this information is the Immigration Reform and Control Act of 1986, Pub. L. 99-603 (8 USC 1324a).

This information is for employers to verify the eligibility of individuals for employment to preclude the unlawful hiring, or recruiting or referring for a fee, of aliens who are not authorized to work in the United States.

This information will be used by employers as a record of their basis for determining eligibility of an employee to work in the United States. The form will be kept by the employer and made available for inspection by officials of the U.S. Immigration and Customs Enforcement, Department of Labor and Office of Special Counsel for Immigration Related Unfair Employment Practices.

Submission of the information required in this form is voluntary. However, an individual may not begin employment unless this form is completed, since employers are subject to civil or criminal penalties if they do not comply with the Immigration Reform and Control Act of 1986.

Reporting Burden. We try to create forms and instructions that are accurate, can be easily understood and which impose the least possible burden on you to provide us with information. Often this is difficult because some immigration laws are very complex. Accordingly, the reporting burden for this collection of information is computed as follows: **1)** learning about this form, 5 minutes; **2)** completing the form, 5 minutes; and **3)** assembling and filing (recordkeeping) the form, 5 minutes, for an average of 15 minutes per response. If you have comments regarding the accuracy of this burden estimate, or suggestions for making this form simpler, you can write to U.S. Citizenship and Immigration Services, Regulatory Management Division, 111 Massachuetts Avenue, N.W., Washington, DC 20529. OMB No. 1615-0047.

NOTE: This is the 1991 edition of the Form I-9 that has been rebranded with a current printing date to reflect the recent transition from the INS to DHS and its components.

EMPLOYERS MUST RETAIN COMPLETED FORM I-9

PLEASE DO NOT MAIL COMPLETED FORM I-9 TO ICE OR USCIS

Form I-9 (Rev. 05/31/05)Y

FIGURE 7.7 Form I-9.

Department of Homeland Security
U.S. Citizenship and Immigration Services

OMB No. 1615-0047; Expires 03/31/07

Employment Eligibility Verification

Please read instructions carefully before completing this form. The instructions must be available during completion of this form. ANTI-DISCRIMINATION NOTICE: It is illegal to discriminate against work eligible individuals. Employers CANNOT specify which document(s) they will accept from an employee. The refusal to hire an individual because of a future expiration date may also constitute illegal discrimination.

Section 1. Employee Information and Verification. To be completed and signed by employee at the time employment begins.

Print Name: Last | First | Middle Initial | Maiden Name

Address *(Street Name and Number)* | Apt. # | Date of Birth *(month/day/year)*

City | State | Zip Code | Social Security #

I am aware that federal law provides for imprisonment and/or fines for false statements or use of false documents in connection with the completion of this form.

I attest, under penalty of perjury, that I am (check one of the following):

- ☐ A citizen or national of the United States
- ☐ A Lawful Permanent Resident (Alien #) A ____________
- ☐ An alien authorized to work until ____________
  (Alien # or Admission #) ____________

Employee's Signature | Date *(month/day/year)*

Preparer and/or Translator Certification. *(To be completed and signed if Section 1 is prepared by a person other than the employee.) I attest, under penalty of perjury, that I have assisted in the completion of this form and that to the best of my knowledge the information is true and correct.*

Preparer's/Translator's Signature | Print Name

Address *(Street Name and Number, City, State, Zip Code)* | Date *(month/day/year)*

Section 2. Employer Review and Verification. To be completed and signed by employer. Examine one document from List A OR examine one document from List B and one from List C, as listed on the reverse of this form, and record the title, number and expiration date, if any, of the document(s).

	List A	OR	List B	AND	List C
Document title:	____________		____________		____________
Issuing authority:	____________		____________		____________
Document #:	____________		____________		____________
Expiration Date *(if any)*:	____________		____________		____________
Document #:	____________				
Expiration Date *(if any)*:	____________				

CERTIFICATION - Iattest, under penalty of perjury, that I have examined the document(s) presented by the above-named employee, that the above-listed document(s) appear to be genuine and to relate to the employee named, that the employee began employment on *(month/day/year)* ____________ **and that to the best of my knowledge the employee is eligible to work in the United States. (State employment agencies may omit the date the employee began employment.)**

Signature of Employer or Authorized Representative | Print Name | Title

Business or Organization Name | Address *(Street Name and Number, City, State, Zip Code)* | Date *(month/day/year)*

Section 3. Updating and Reverification. To be completed and signed by employer.

A. New Name *(if applicable)* | B. Date of Rehire *(month/day/year) (if applicable)*

C. If employee's previous grant of work authorization has expired, provide the information below for the document that establishes current employment eligibility. Document Title: ____________ Document #: ____________ Expiration Date (if any): ____________

I attest, under penalty of perjury, that to the best of my knowledge, this employee is eligible to work in the United States, and if the employee presented document(s), the document(s) I have examined appear to be genuine and to relate to the individual.

Signature of Employer or Authorized Representative | Date *(month/day/year)*

NOTE: This is the 1991 edition of the Form I-9 that has been rebranded with a current printing date to reflect the recent transition from the INS to DHS and its components.

Form I-9 (Rev. 05/31/05)Y Page 2

FIGURE 7.7 *(continued)*

LISTS OF ACCEPTABLE DOCUMENTS

LIST A

Documents that Establish Both Identity and Employment Eligibility

1. U.S. Passport (unexpired or expired)
2. Certificate of U.S. Citizenship *(Form N-560 or N-561)*
3. Certificate of Naturalization *(Form N-550 or N-570)*
4. Unexpired foreign passport, with *I-551 stamp or* attached *Form I-94* indicating unexpired employment authorization
5. Permanent Resident Card or Alien Registration Receipt Card with photograph *(Form I-151 or I-551)*
6. Unexpired Temporary Resident Card *(Form I-688)*
7. Unexpired Employment Authorization Card *(Form I-688A)*
8. Unexpired Reentry Permit *(Form I-327)*
9. Unexpired Refugee Travel Document *(Form 1-571)*
10. Unexpired Employment Authorization Document issued by DHS that contains a photograph *(Form I-688B)*

OR

LIST B

Documents that Establish Identity

1. Driver's license or ID card issued by a state or outlying possession of the United States provided it contains a photograph or information such as name, date of birth, gender, height, eye color and address
2. ID card issued by federal, state or local government agencies or entities, provided it contains a photograph or information such as name, date of birth, gender, height, eye color and address
3. School ID card with a photograph
4. Voter's registration card
5. U.S. Military card or draft record
6. Military dependent's ID card
7. U.S. Coast Guard Merchant Mariner Card
8. Native American tribal document
9. Driver's license issued by a Canadian government authority

For persons under age 18 who are unable to present a document listed above:

10. School record or report card
11. Clinic, doctor or hospital record
12. Day-care or nursery school record

AND

LIST C

Documents that Establish Employment Eligibility

1. U.S. social security card issued by the Social Security Administration *(other than a card stating it is not valid for employment)*
2. Certification of Birth Abroad issued by the Department of State *(Form FS-545 or Form DS-1350)*
3. Original or certified copy of a birth certificate issued by a state, county, municipal authority or outlying possession of the United States bearing an official seal
4. Native American tribal document
5. U.S. Citizen ID Card *(Form I-197)*
6. ID Card for use of Resident Citizen in the United States *(Form I-179)*
7. Unexpired employment authorization document issued by DHS *(other than those listed under List A)*

Illustrations of many of these documents appear in Part 8 of the Handbook for Employers (M-274)

Form I-9 (Rev. 05/31/05)Y Page 3

FIGURE 7.7 *(continued)*

DOCUMENTS THAT ESTABLISH EMPLOYMENT ELIGIBILITY

Social Security card
An original or certified copy of a birth certificate issued by a state, county, or municipal authority
Unexpired INS employment authorization
Unexpired reentry permit (INS Form I-327)
Unexpired Refugee Travel Document (INS Form I-571)
Certificate of Birth issued by the Department of State (Form FS-545)
Certificate of Birth Abroad issued by the Department of State (Form DS-1350)
United States Citizen identification (INS Form I-197)
Native American tribal document
Identification used by Resident Citizen in the United States

DOCUMENTS THAT ESTABLISH IDENTITY ONLY

State driver's license or identification card containing a photograph
School or university identification card with photograph
Voter's registration card
United States military identification card or draft record
Identification card issued by federal, state, or local governmental agencies
Military dependent's identification card
Native American tribal documents
United States Coast Guard Merchant Mariner card
Driver's license issued by a Canadian government authority

DOCUMENTS THAT ESTABLISH IDENTITY AND EMPLOYMENT ELIGIBILITY

Current United States passport
Alien Registration Receipt Card (INS Form I-151.)
Resident Alien Card (INS Form I-551), which must contain a photograph of the bearer
Temporary Resident Card (INS Form I-688)
Employment Authorization Card (INS Form I-68SA)

FIGURE 7.8 **Form I-9 qualifying documents.**

7.4 The Employment Relationship

The laws related to employment, like those in other areas, are fluid, and they change to reflect society's view of what is "fair" and "just" for both the **employer** and the **employee**. For example, in 1945, an employer in the United States could refuse to hire an individual on the basis of his or her race or religion. The employer would have had no fear of liability for such a decision, either from the government or the potential employee. Today, a decision to refuse employment on the basis of race or religion would subject the employer to legal liability both from the government and the spurned job candidate.

At-Will Employment

The right of employers to hire and terminate employees as they see fit is still a fundamental right of doing business in the United States. In most states, the relationship you create when you hire a worker is one of **at-will employment**.

Simply put, the doctrine of at-will employment allows an employer to hire or dismiss an employee at any time if the employer believes it is in the best interest of the business. However, employers are still subject to the antidiscrimination laws reviewed earlier in this chapter (and addressed further in Chapter 8, "Legally Managing Employees"). Assume, for example, that you have legally hired four full-time bartenders for a club you manage. Business becomes slow, and you elect to terminate one of the bartenders. The doctrine of at-will

---

LEGALESE

Employer: An individual or entity that pays wages or a salary in exchange for a worker's services.

Employee: An individual who is hired to provide services to an employer in exchange for wages or a salary.

At-will employment: An employment relationship whereby employers have a right to hire any employee, whenever they choose, and to dismiss an employee for or without cause, at any time, so long as the employee's civil rights are not violated; the employee also has the right to work for the employer or not, or to terminate the relationship at any time.

employment allows you to do so. Further, the doctrine allows you to reduce your bartender staff even if you have not experienced a downturn in business. You might elect to do so if you felt that you could secure the services of a better bartender should you need one. Generally speaking, any worker can be fired for cause (i.e., misconduct associated with the job). The at-will employment doctrine allows employers to dismiss a worker without cause.

As an employer, your actions can affect the at-will employment status of your workers (e.g., by explicitly entering into an employment contract or making promises to keep an employee on for a year). In order to preserve the maximum flexibility for your business, it is important that you maintain your at-will employment status to cover all staff members that you select and manage. The scope of the at-will employment doctrine varies among different states, so you should familiarize yourself with the requirements placed on employers in the state in which you operate. These requirements are available from the state agency responsible for monitoring employer/employee relationships and from employment lawyers who specialize in this area.

Labor Unions and Collective Bargaining

In some hotels and businesses, certain categories of employees may belong to an organized labor union. Unions were formed to protect the rights of workers and to establish specific job conditions that would be agreed to and carried out by employers and employees. In this type of arrangement, a group of employees will elect to make one collective employment agreement with an employer that will outline specific characteristics of their job position, such as the wage, hourly rate of pay, or limits on the hours per day or week that can be worked. The agreement would cover anyone employed in that position. This type of employment agreement is called a **collective bargaining agreement (CBA)** and can also be referred to as a "union contract."

The terms and conditions set forth in a CBA are developed using a process of collective bargaining between the employer and employees, and their attorneys. Generally, the members of a labor union working for a specific company (or industry) will elect a representative, who will negotiate the terms and conditions of a collective bargaining agreement for the entire group. The bargaining process is carried out according to rules established by the National Labor Relations Act of 1935, which guarantees the right of employees to organize and bargain collectively, or to refrain from collective bargaining. To enforce this act and oversee the relationship between employers and organized labor, Congress created an independent federal agency known as the National Labor Relations Board (NLRB) (www.nlrb.gov). The NLRB has five principal functions:

1. *Conduct elections*. The NLRB allows private-sector employees to organize bargaining units in their workplace or to dissolve their labor unions through a decertification election.
2. *Investigate charges*. Employees, union representatives, and employers who believe that their rights under the National Labor Relations Act have been violated may file charges alleging unfair labor practices at their nearest NLRB regional office.
3. *Facilitate settlements*. When a charge is determined to have merit, the NLRB will explain the decision and offer the charged party an opportunity to settle before a formal complaint is issued.
4. *Decide cases*. On the adjudicative side of the NLRB are 40 administrative law judges and a board whose five members are appointed by the president and confirmed by the U.S. Senate.
5. *Enforce orders*. The majority of parties voluntarily comply with orders of the board. When they do not, the agency's general counsel must seek enforcement in the U.S. Courts of Appeals. Parties to cases also may seek review of unfavorable decisions in the federal courts.

The NLRA identifies the activities and practices that would be considered "unfair." Employers are forbidden to:

- Threaten employees with loss of jobs or benefits if they join or vote for a union or engage in protected concerted activity.
- Threaten to close the plant if employees select a union to represent them.
- Question employees about their union sympathies or activities in circumstances that tend to interfere with, restrain, or coerce employees in the exercise of their rights under the act.
- Promise benefits to employees to discourage their union support.
- Transfer, lay off, terminate, assign employees more difficult work tasks, or otherwise punish employees because they engaged in union or protected concerted activity.
- Transfer, lay off, terminate, assign employees more difficult work tasks, or otherwise punish employees because they filed unfair labor practice charges or participated in an investigation conducted by NLRB.

Under the law, employers are also protected from unfair labor practices that might be undertaken by a union. Examples of prohibited activities by union representatives include:

- Threats to employees that they will lose their jobs unless they support the union.

LEGALESE

Collective bargaining agreement (CBA): A formal contract between an employer and a group of employees that establishes the rights and responsibilities of both parties in their employment relationship.

- Seeking the suspension, discharge, or other punishment of an employee for not being a union member even if the employee has paid or offered to pay a lawful initiation fee and periodic fees thereafter.
- Refusing to process a grievance because an employee has criticized union officials or because an employee is not a member of the union in states where union security clauses are not permitted.
- Fining employees who have validly resigned from the union for engaging in protected concerted activities following their resignation or for crossing an unlawful picket line.
- Engaging in picket line misconduct, such as threatening, assaulting, or barring nonstrikers from the employer's premises.
- Striking over issues unrelated to employment terms and conditions or coercively involving neutrals in a labor dispute.

It is up to the individual employer, union, or employee to request assistance from the NLRB in cases of unfair labor practices and to hold an election that may unionize a job position. Complaints must be filed with the NLRB within six months of the alleged unfair activity. A representative from the NLRB will investigate the complaint. If the complaint is justified and the parties have not taken steps to settle or withdraw the complaint, then the NLRB will hold a hearing. If an unfair labor practice is found to have occurred, then the NLRB will issue an order demanding that the unfair labor practice stop and may also require the guilty party to take steps to compensate the injured party through job reinstatement, by payment of back wages, or by re-establishing conditions that were in place before the unfair activity took place. Either party may appeal the order in federal court.

Under the NLRA, employees have the right to form unions and bargain collectively. Once a union is established, new employees hired for a specific position may be required to join the union that represents that job position. However, many states have passed "right-to-work" laws that stipulate that an employee is not required to join a union if hired for a given position, even if other employees holding that position are unionized. As a manager, you should learn if your state has a right-to-work law.

For managers, a collective bargaining agreement should be treated in the same manner as any other formal contract. Its provisions should be read, understood, and followed. Membership in a union may give employees certain freedoms or conditions as part of their jobs, but employees still must be accountable for their work, and managers are still responsible for ensuring that employees perform their jobs properly, safely, and in accordance with the company's established policies and procedures. If problems do surface, a hospitality manager should consult with his or her company's designated union representative. Most CBAs have specific conditions for hiring new employees for a given position. As a manager, you should review and know this segment of the CBA especially well.

Analyze the Situation 7.3

Walter Horvath is the executive housekeeper at the Landmark Hotel. This 450-room historic property caters to leisure travelers. Occupancy at the hotel is highest on the weekends.

Like many hotels in large cities, the housekeeping staff is difficult to retain. Turnover tends to be high and the labor market tight. Mr. Horvath works very hard to provide a work atmosphere that enhances harmony and encourages employees to stay. Although he has little control over wage scales, his general manager does allow him wide latitude in setting departmental policies and procedures as long as these do not conflict with those of the management company that operates the Landmark.

Housekeepers in Mr. Horvath's department highly prize weekends off, yet these are the busiest times for the hotel. In a staff meeting, Mr. Horvath and the housekeepers agreed to implement a policy that would give each housekeeper alternating weekends off with the stipulation that those housekeepers who are working on weekends might be required to work overtime to finish cleaning all the rooms necessary to service the hotel's guests. The housekeepers agreed to this compromise, and the policy was written into the department's procedures section of the employee handbook, which all new housekeeping employees must read and sign prior to beginning work.

When the holiday season approaches, Mr. Horvath finds that his department is seriously understaffed. The hotel is filling to capacity nearly every weekend as guests flock to the city to do their holiday shopping. During a job interview with Andreanna White, Mr. Horvath mentions the alternating weekend policy for housekeepers. Ms. White states that the she is the choir director for her church. "I could," she says, "miss alternating Sunday mornings, because I could arrange a substitute. Working overtime on Sundays, however, would cause me to miss both the morning and evening services, and I would not be willing to do that. I could, however, work an eight-hour day of Sundays with no problem because then I could go to either the morning or evening service."

1. Should Mr. Horvath hire Ms. White despite her inability to comply with the departmental policy in place at the hotel?
2. If Mr. Horvath hires Ms. White, can he still enforce the alternating weekend policy with currently employed housekeepers who also might prefer not to work overtime on Sundays?
3. Do you believe Ms. White's choir director position warrants an exception to the departmental policy?
4. How should Mr. Horvath advertise position vacancies in the future?

International Snapshot

Canadian Employment Laws

In Canada, the employment relationship is governed by legislation that sets out minimum standards as well as implied obligations from the common law. Further, each province or territory has its own employment legislation and regulations. Therefore, if you operate a hotel anywhere in Canada, you will need to consider the applicable employment law in each province or territory where the hotel is located. While there are similarities with U.S. policies, the following is a brief summary of some key differences between United States and Canadian employment law.

No "Employment at Will"

The concept of "employment at will" does not exist in Canada. Rather, in Canada, both employment standards legislation and the common law combine to require an employer who terminates an employee's employment without just cause to provide working notice or certain entitlements in lieu of notice to the employee.

Applicable employment standards legislation will provide that the employee is entitled to statutory notice of termination or pay in lieu of notice (unless the employee's employment is terminated for willful misconduct or other prescribed reasons). In general, statutory notice is approximately one week per year of service to a maximum of eight weeks. However, more notice is required if there is a group termination. In addition, some provinces require employers to pay severance pay in addition to providing notice of termination. For example, in Ontario, an employee with at least five years of service working for an employer that has an annual payroll of at least $2.5 million is entitled to statutory severance pay equal to one week's pay per year of service, up to a maximum of 26 weeks' pay. Therefore, a 10-year employee in Ontario would be entitled to 8 weeks' notice of termination (or pay in lieu), plus 10 weeks of statutory severance pay.

In addition to the legislative requirements, under the common law, employees are entitled to "reasonable notice of termination" or pay in lieu unless (1) the employee is represented by a union, (2) there is just cause for termination, or (3) there is an enforceable written agreement between the parties that provides otherwise. In view of the latter exception, many employers include termination clauses in their employment agreements that "contract out" of the obligation to provide reasonable notice of termination at common law. However, because employees often challenge the enforceability of such clauses, their careful drafting is required.

Common law reasonable notice is determined on a case-by-case basis and depends on a number of factors, such as the employee's position, age, length of service, and the availability of similar employment elsewhere. The courts are particularly generous when prescribing the length of notice of termination an employer must give managerial, professional, or long-term employees. Although courts approach each case on an individual basis, a very rough "ball park" approach that is sometimes a useful starting point for reasonable notice is one month's notice, or pay in lieu of notice for each year of service with a minimum of 3 months and a maximum of 24 months.

Pregnancy and Parental Leave

Whereas the U.S. Family and Medical Leave Act (FMLA) requires an employer to provide an employee up to 12 weeks of unpaid leave, employment standards legislation in all Canadian jurisdictions requires employers to permit employees to take job-protected, unpaid pregnancy and parental leave totaling up to 52 weeks in most jurisdictions and 70 weeks in Québec. Unlike in the United States, all employees are entitled to this leave, regardless of the size of their employer.

Discrimination, Harassment and Violence

Various U.S. statutes, such as Title VII of the Civil Rights Act of 1964, the Americans with Disabilities Act, and the Age Discrimination in Employment Act of 1967 provide prohibitions against discrimination and harassment in employment. Similar protections exist in Canada under provincial and territorial human rights legislation, such as the Ontario *Human Rights Code*. Human rights legislation in Canada prohibits discrimination and harassment at all stages of employment on the basis of grounds including, but not limited to, sex, disability, age, race, national or ethnic origin, color, religion or creed, marital status, and sexual orientation.

Unlike in the United States, there are generally no civil actions for discrimination in Canada. Instead, employees can make a complaint to the applicable provincial or territorial human rights tribunal. The tribunals have broad powers, including the ability to award monetary penalties, reinstate employees, and require the employer to take certain steps to prevent discrimination or harassment. Except in extreme cases, monetary awards are generally much lower than those of U.S. jury awards.

In addition to human rights legislation, occupational health and safety legislation in certain provinces includes protections against workplace violence and harassment regardless whether such violence or harassment relates to a prohibited ground of discrimination. For example, under the Ontario *Occupational Health and Safety Act*, harassment is defined quite broadly and can include conduct such as bullying, isolation, gossip, and other offensive behavior. Employers are required to implement workplace violence and harassment policies, train their employees on such policies, and investigate all incidents or complaints of workplace violence or harassment.

There are other significant differences between Canadian and U.S. employment laws. Local legal counsel can help to ensure that you are in compliance with all applicable laws. Other Canadian employment-related laws with which employers must comply include are:

- Employment standards legislation, which sets out the general framework of employer and employee rights and responsibilities (such as minimum wage, hours of work, breaks, overtime pay, vacation and holidays with pay, entitlements on termination, and leaves of absence).
- Labor relations legislation, which governs the relationship between workers, employers, and trade unions and sets out the procedures for certification/decertification of unions and collective bargaining.
- Occupation health and safety legislation, which governs an employer's obligation to provide a safe workplace.
- Workers' compensation/workplace safety and insurance legislation, which provides a form of insurance to employees injured in the course of employment and governs employer obligations respecting workplace injuries and accidents.

(continued)

- Pay equity and employment equity legislation, which require equal pay for equal work and equal employment opportunities for employees.
- Accessibility legislation, which governs employer obligations to improve accessibility for people with disabilities.

For more information on any Canadian employment law issues, contact Allan Wells or Allison Di Cesare of the Employment and Labour Law Department of Osler, Hoskin & Harcourt LLP Barristers & Solicitors, P.O. Box 50, 1 First Canadian Place, Suite 6200, Toronto, Ontario, M5X 1B8, (416) 362-2111. Or log on to www.osler.com, Osler, Hoskin & Harcourt's website, which contains numerous articles on Canadian labor and employment law; canadaonline.about.com/od/labourstandards/Canada_Employment_and_Labour_Standards.htm, which provides links to each provincial Ministry of Labour website for information on employment standards, health, and safety, and labor relations; and to www.ohrc.on.ca, for Ontario's Human Rights Commission, and links to other human rights agencies across Canada.

Provided by Allan Wells and Allison Di Cesare of Osler, Hoskin & Harcourt LLP, Toronto, Ontario. www.osler.com.

WHAT WOULD YOU DO?

Alex Bustamante is applying for the position of executive chef at the hospital where you serve as director of human resources. The hospital has more than 800 beds, and the meal service offered to patients and visitors alike is extensive. Patients in this facility are extremely ill, and because of their weakened condition, dietary concerns are an important consideration.

While reviewing Mr. Bustamante's work history with him during an interview, he states that he was let go from his two previous positions for "excessive absence." When you inquire as to the cause of his excessive absence, Mr. Bustamante offers that it was due to the effects of alcoholism, a condition with which he has struggled for over 10 years but for which he is currently undergoing weekend treatment and attending meetings of Alcoholics Anonymous (AA). He states that he never drank while at work but sometimes missed work because he overslept or was too hung over to go in. His past employers will neither confirm nor deny Mr. Bustamante's problem. Both simply state that he had worked for them as an executive chef and that he was no longer employed by their organizations.

Based on his education and experience, Mr. Bustamante is clearly the best-qualified candidate for the vacant executive chef's position. However, based on his life history, including his ability to overcome his dependence on alcohol is, in your opinion, clearly questionable. Your recommendation on Mr. Bustamante's hiring will likely be accepted by the manager of dietary services.

1. Have you broken the law by inquiring into Mr. Bustamante's excessive absences in his prior positions?
2. Is Mr. Bustamante protected under the ADA?
3. If Mr. Bustamante were hired but needed three days off per week to undergo treatment, would you grant that accommodation? Under what circumstances?
4. How do the rights of Mr. Bustamante and the concept of negligent hiring mesh in this instance?

WHAT DID YOU LEARN IN THIS CHAPTER?

Today, you cannot just hire anyone you wish to, and many different laws have been passed that affect the way in which you can legally hire and manage employees. Tools, such as written job descriptions, job qualifications, employment applications, and an established employee selection process that contains written guidelines for conducting interviews, pre-employment tests, background checks, and reference checks are all used by the companies to ensure—and document—that they are selecting employees in compliance with the law.

It is illegal to discriminate against protected classes of workers in the job selection process. The Civil Rights Act of 1964 outlaws discrimination on the basis of race, color, religion, sex, or national origin. The Age Discrimination in Employment Act protects of 1967 individuals 40 years old and older from discrimination based on age. The American with Disabilities Act of 1990 not only protects those with disabilities from discrimination in the selection process but also requires companies to make reasonable accommodations to facilities or job responsibilities that will permit disabled individuals to work in a given job.

A last step before assigning someone to your workforce is to ensure that he or she is eligible to be employed in the United States by complying with the requirements of the Immigrations Reform and Control Act of 1986.

The at-will employment doctrine defines the rights of employers and employees in most states unless an employment contract modifies that relationship. Labor unions are associations of workers that join together to bargain as a unit with management or business ownership. Collective bargaining agreements establish the regulations and the terms that must be followed by both unionized employees and nonunion managers during the employment relationship.

CHAPTER 8

Legally Managing Employees

8.1 Employment Relationships

After you have legally selected an employee for your organization, it is a good practice to clarify the conditions of the employment agreement with that employee.

All employers and employees have employment agreements with each other. The agreement can be as simple as an hourly wage rate for an hour's work and at-will employment for both parties. An agreement is in place even if there is nothing in writing or if work conditions have not been discussed in detail. **Employment agreements** may be individual, covering only one employee or, as discussed in the last chapter, they may involve groups of employees. Generally, employment agreements in the hospitality industry are established verbally, or with an offer letter.

Offer Letter

Offer letters, when properly composed, can help prevent legal difficulties caused by employee and/or employer misunderstandings. As their name implies, offer letters detail the offer made by the employer to the employee. Some employers believe offer letters should be used only for managerial positions, but to avoid difficulties, all employees should have signed offer letters in their personnel files. Components of a sound offer letter include:

- Position offered, including one's new title, if any
- Compensation
- Benefits
- Evaluation period and compensation review schedule
- Start date
- Location of employment
- Orientation information
- Special conditions of the offer (e.g., at-will relationship, pre-employment testing)

LEGALESE

Employment agreement: The terms of the employment relationship between an employer and employee that specifies the rights and obligations of each party to the agreement.

CHAPTER OUTLINE

8.1. Employment Relationships
8.2. Workplace Discrimination and Sexual Harassment
8.3. Family and Medical Leave Act
8.4. Uniform Services Employment and Reemployment Rights Act
8.5. Compensation
8.6. The Patient Protection and Affordable Care Act of 2010
8.7. Managing Employee Performance
8.8. Unemployment Claims
8.9. Employment Records and Retention
8.10. Employment Posters
8.11. Workplace Surveillance

IN THIS CHAPTER, YOU WILL LEARN

1. To differentiate between an employment agreement and an employee manual.
2. To establish a nondiscriminatory work environment.
3. To implement a procedure designed to eliminate sexual harassment and minimize the risk of penalties resulting from charges of unlawful harassment.
4. To legally manage the complex areas of employee leave, compensation, and performance.
5. To respond appropriately to unemployment claims.
6. To summarize and list the employment records that must be maintained to meet legal requirements.

- Reference to the **employee manual** as an additional source of information regarding employer policies that govern the workplace
- Signature lines for both employer and employee, along with a date the signatures were added

Consider the case of Antonio Molina. He applies for the position of maintenance foreman at a country club. Mr. Molina is selected for the job and is given an offer letter by the club's general manager. In the letter, a special condition of employment is that Mr. Molina must submit to, and pass, a mandatory drug test. Although he can sign the letter when it is received, his employment is not finalized until he passes the drug test.

Additional rules that Mr. Molina will be expected to follow, or benefits that he may enjoy while on the job, will be contained in the employee manual.

Employee Manual

In most cases, the offer letter will not detail all of the policies and procedures to which the employer and employee agree. These are typically contained in the employee manual. The manual may be as simple as a few pages or as extensive as several hundred pages. In either case, an important point to remember is that employee manuals are often referenced by the courts to help define the terms of the employment agreement if a dispute arises. The topics covered by an employee manual will vary from one organization to another. However, some common topic areas include:

General Policies

- Probationary periods
- Performance reviews
- Disciplinary process
- Termination
- Attendance
- Drug and alcohol testing
- Uniforms
- Lockers
- Personal telephone calls
- Appearance and grooming
- Smartphone and Internet usage

Compensation

- Pay periods
- Payroll deductions
- Tip-reporting requirements
- Timekeeping procedures
- Overtime pay policies
- Meal periods
- Schedule posting
- Call-in pay
- Sick pay
- Vacation pay

Benefits

- Health insurance
- Dental insurance
- Disability insurance
- Vacation accrual
- Paid holidays
- Jury duty
- Funeral or bereavement leave
- Retirement programs
- Duty meals
- Leaves of absence
- Transfers
- Educational reimbursement plans

Special Areas

- Antiharassment and antidiscrimination policies
- Grievance and complaint procedures
- Family medical leave information
- Dispute resolution
- Safety rules
- Security rules
- Emergency preparedness

Employee manuals should be kept up to date, and it should be clearly established in writing that it is the employer, not the employee, who retains the right to revise the employee manual.

Many companies issue employee manuals with a signature page, where employees must verify that they have indeed read the manual. This is a good idea, as it gives proof that employees were given the opportunity to familiarize themselves with the employers' policies and procedures. It is also a good idea to use wording similar to the following on a signature page. The wording should be emphasized in a type size larger than the type surrounding it.

> *The employer reserves the right to modify, alter, or eliminate any and all of the policies and procedures contained in this manual at any time and from time to time.*

An additional precaution taken by many employers is the practice of giving a written test covering the content of the employee manual before the employee begins work. The employee's test results are kept on file.

LEGALESE

Employee manual: A document written to detail the policies, benefits, and employment practices of an employer.

A hotel or restaurant's success can be jeopardized if its trade secrets and confidential information (such as recipes, marketing plans, sales data, and confidential pricing information) falls into the hands of its competitors. It is critical, therefore, that operators take adequate measures to protect against the unauthorized use and/or disclosure of their sensitive information. These measures may include:

- Labeling proprietary documents as confidential;
- Restricting access to certain sensitive information, and
- Issuing policies that limit the use and disclosure of confidential information.

In addition, there are contractual provisions, commonly referred to as restrictive covenants, that hospitality managers can require their employees to sign, as well as third parties (e.g., vendors, suppliers, potential business partners), to protect their:

- Trade secrets,
- Confidential information and
- Business relationships.

A non-disclosure covenant, for example, places restrictions on an employee's use and disclosure of the hospitality businesses' trade secrets and/or confidential information. Another type of restrictive covenant called a non-compete covenant, prohibits an employee from performing the same or similar job duties for a competitor within a designated geographic territory both during and after the employee's period of employment. To maintain a stable workforce, a hospitality manager may require its employees to sign a non-solicitation covenant, which prohibits the employees from:

- Recruiting,
- Soliciting or
- Hiring away the hospitality operator's employees.

In addition to contractual remedies, in the event an employee misappropriates information, a hospitality manager may be able to pursue relief under state and federal trade secret statutes. When information is misappropriated electronically using a computer, state and federal computer misconduct statutes may also provide a hospitality manager with relief.

Provided by Kenneth N. Winkler, Esq. of Berman Fink Van Horn P.C. of Atlanta, Georgia. www.bfvlaw.com

FIGURE 8.1 **Protecting trade secrets and confidential information.**

To clarify for employees that their status is "at-will," each page of the employee manual should contain the following wording at the bottom center of each page: "This is not an employment contract." A more formal statement should be placed at the beginning of the manual, such as:

> *This manual is not a contract, expressed or implied, guaranteeing employment for any specific duration. Although our company hopes that your employment relationship with us will be long term, either you or the company may terminate this relationship at any time, with or without cause or notice.*

The employee manual must be very carefully drafted to avoid altering the at-will employment doctrine. The document should be carefully reviewed by an employment attorney each and every time it is revised.

Protection of Trade Secrets

A prudent hospitality manager must anticipate that some unscrupulous employees may want to unlawfully use information they learned or obtained while working for the hospitality company to further their own interests. Such information can be found in the form of **trade secrets** or confidential information. Figure 8.1 highlights some of the concerns a hospitality manager faces about trade secrets and how to reduce liability.

8.2 Workplace Discrimination and Sexual Harassment

As noted in Chapter 7, various laws prohibit discrimination on the basis of an individual's race, religion, gender, national origin, disability, age (over 40), and in some states and communities, sexual orientation, and marital status.

LEGALESE

Trade Secrets: Business information that is generally not known or reasonably ascertainable by others that may provide another business organization or individual with an economic competitive business advantage over other businesses.

Although the federal government has taken the lead in outlawing discrimination in employment practices, many states, and even some towns and cities, also have antidiscrimination laws, which must be followed. In general, the state laws duplicate practices that are outlawed under federal law, such as discrimination based on race, color, national origin, and so on. It is important for a hospitality manager to know the provisions of a state civil rights law for several reasons.

Many state discrimination laws add categories to the list of prohibited behavior that are not covered under federal law, such as discrimination on the basis of marital status, arrest record, or sexual orientation. Also, while federal civil rights laws apply to businesses engaged in interstate commerce (which includes most restaurants and hotels), many state laws extend to other types of businesses, such as bars, taverns, stores, and "places of public accommodation." State discrimination laws are enforced by state civil rights agencies, which can assess severe penalties to businesses found in violation of the law. These penalties could include fines, prison terms, or both.

Some companies may also expand the protections that their workers receive under the law. As you saw in Chapter 1, "Prevention Philosophy," Hyatt's policy on conduct and ethics clearly states that its employees will not be discriminated against on the basis of their sexual preference. Since Hyatt Hotels are operated in many states and communities where the law does not prohibit Hyatt from discriminating on the basis of one's sexual preference, Hyatt has voluntarily broadened the protections for its workforce.

These prohibitions of discrimination in the employment area apply when selecting employees for a given job, as well as after they have been hired. With such a wide diversity of employees in the hospitality industry, it is not surprising that a variety of attitudes about work, family, and fellow employees will also exist. Managers cannot dictate conformity in all areas of their employees' value systems. However, as a manager, you are required to prevent discrimination by your staff, coworkers, and even third parties, such as guests and suppliers.

Preventing Discrimination

Workplace discrimination is enforced by the Equal Employment Opportunity Commission (EEOC) (eeoc.gov). Applicants and employees can bring claims concerning discrimination to the EEOC and/or their state's counterpart to the EEOC (e.g., the Texas Commission on Human Rights), which will investigate the charges and issue a determination of whether they believe discrimination has occurred. It is important to keep in mind that if a charge of discrimination is filed, the EEOC has the authority to examine all policies and practices in a business for violations, not just the circumstances surrounding a particular incident. If there is sufficient evidence of discrimination, the EEOC will first work with employers to correct any problems and try to voluntarily settle a case before it reaches the courts.

If a settlement cannot be worked out, the EEOC may file a lawsuit on behalf of the claimant or issue the claimant a right-to-sue letter. If the EEOC does not determine that unlawful discrimination occurred, then the claimant may accept that finding or privately pursue a lawsuit against the employer.

Penalties for violating Title VII of the Civil Rights Act can be severe. Plaintiffs have the right to recover back wages, future wages, the value of lost fringe benefits, other compensatory damages, attorneys' fees, and injunctive relief such as reinstatement of their job and the restoration of their seniority. In addition, federal fines for violating Title VII can be up to $50,000 (for businesses with fewer than 100 employees) to $300,000 (for corporations with 500 employees or more).

As we have stressed repeatedly, the best way to avoid litigation is by preventing incidents before they occur. Where discrimination is concerned, this involves making sure that your company's policies and your own actions as a manager do not adversely impact members of a protected class.

Some of the more common areas of potential conflict in the hospitality industry concern matters of appearance and language. For example, employers are permitted to require their employees to wear uniforms or adhere to certain common grooming standards (such as restrictions on hair length or wearing jewelry) provided that all employees are subject to these requirements and that the policies are established for a necessary business reason. Although the courts have not outlawed the establishment of "English-only" rules in business, lawsuits have occurred when companies discriminate against people who have pronounced accents or who do not speak English fluently, especially in job positions where speaking English would not be considered a bona fide occupational qualification.

Managing Diversity

Beyond preventing acts of overt discrimination, managers have a legal obligation to establish a work environment that is accepting of all people. The failure to establish such an environment is recognized by the courts to be a form of discrimination. Racial slurs, ethnic jokes, and other practices that might be offensive to an employee should not be tolerated.

As a manager, your ability to effectively work with people from diverse backgrounds will significantly affect your success. According to Gene M. Monteagudo, former manager of diversity for Hyatt Hotels International, "It is no longer possible to achieve success in the hospitality industry, either in the United States or abroad, unless you can effectively manage people in a cultural environment vastly different from your own." Recognition of the differences among individuals is the first step toward effectively managing these differences. This can be confusing in a society that increasingly equates equality with correctness. The truth is that people are different in many cultural aspects; however, it is also true that "we do not have to be twins to be brothers." In other words, just because we are equal under the law does not mean that we are the same.

One of the great myths of management today is that, because workers are equal under the law, all workers must be treated in exactly the same way. This is simply wrong. The effective manager treats people equitably, not uniformly.

If one worker enjoys showing pictures of her grandchildren to a unit manager, it is okay for that manager to show an interest in them. If another worker prefers privacy, it is equally acceptable for the manager not to ask that employee about his or her grandchildren. Is this more complicated than treating both workers exactly the same? Of course it is and it may be considered confusing by some. The key to remember here, however, is that the unit manager, by recognizing the real differences between the two employees and acting on those differences accordingly, is treating them both equitably. That is, they are both being treated with respect for their own system of cultural values.

As you consider the diversity issue in greater detail, you will realize that the recognition of cultural differences is not a form of racism at all, but, rather, the first step toward harmony. The true racist is not the person who notices real cultural differences but the person who ignores them. The culturally unaware foodservice manager, who does not recognize, for example, the uniqueness and importance of the Asian worker's culture, denigrates that culture in much the same way as the individual who is openly critical of it. In the hospitality industry, the management of cultural diversity and the inclusion of all people in all aspects of the business will remain an important fact of operational success.

Sexual Harassment

By their very nature, hospitality organizations are vulnerable to allegations of sexual harassment. Because of this fact, it has become increasingly important that managers be informed about the attitudes and conduct that fall under the classification of sexual harassment. Currently, federal and state law recognizes two types of sexual harassment:

- **Quid pro quo** sexual harassment in which the perpetrator asks for sexual favors in exchange for workplace benefits from a subordinate or punishes the subordinate for rejecting the offer.
- Hostile environment harassment, in which the perpetrator, through language or conduct, creates an intimidating or hostile working environment for individuals of a particular gender. In a subtler way, this also occurs when "freezing out" tactics are used against employees or when employees are shunned or relegated to an outer office or desk with little or nothing to do thus inhibiting all communication.

Title VII of the federal Civil Rights Act, as amended in 1972, prohibits sexual harassment in the workplace. The penalties for violating sexual harassment laws are the same as those for other types of civil rights violations. Claimants can recover lost wages, benefits, and attorneys' fees, and can be reinstated in their jobs. Many states have also adopted laws to protect employees from sexual harassment, which may carry additional fines or penalties.

Employer Liability

Some behavior that once may have been tolerated in the workplace is no longer acceptable. The result has been an explosion of sexual harassment claims, pitting employee against supervisor, employee against another employee, women against men, men against women, and even same-sex complaints.

In an important decision for employers, on June 26, 1998, the United States Supreme Court, in the case of *Faragher v. City of Boca Raton*, ruled on the circumstances under which an employer may be held liable under Title VII of the Civil Rights Act of 1964, 42 U.S.C., Section 2000e, for the acts of a supervisory employee whose sexual harassment of subordinates created a hostile work environment amounting to employment discrimination.

The Court held that an "employer is subject to **vicarious liability** to a victimized employee for an actionable hostile environment created by a supervisor with immediate (or successively higher) authority over the employee." In this case, the court found that "uninvited and offensive touching," "lewd remarks," or "speaking of women in offensive terms" was enough to create a hostile employment environment.

The Court then determined that if this type of harassment is by a supervisor, the employer may avoid liability by raising an affirmative defense if the following is met:

- The employer exercised reasonable care to prevent and promptly correct any sexually harassing behavior.
- The plaintiff employee unreasonably failed to take advantage of any preventive or corrective opportunities provided by the employer.

The Court also held that if a supervisor's harassment ultimately results in a tangible employment action, such as an employee's termination, demotion, or reassignment, the employer is not entitled to claim the affirmative defense just described, and the employer will be held strictly liable for any acts of sexual harassment by its supervisors.

The result of this ruling is that the main, and often only, legal defense for supervisors to allegations of sexual harassment is to demonstrate a history of preventive and corrective measures. Therefore, it is crucial that every hospitality employer have, at a minimum, an employee manual that outlines the company's antisexual harassment policy. This policy should be reviewed by an attorney to determine if it is legally sufficient.

LEGALESE

Quid pro quo: Latin term for "giving one thing in return or exchange for another."

Vicarious liability: A party's responsibility for the acts of another that result in an injury, harm, or damage. (See also *respondeat superior.*)

Zero Tolerance

In order to guard against the liability that results from charges of discrimination or harassment and to ensure a high-quality workplace for all employees, hospitality organizations should institute a policy of zero (no) tolerance of objectionable behavior. Listed here are some of the measures that companies institute to create a zero tolerance environment:

- Have clear policies that prohibit sexual harassment in the workplace.
- Require workshops to train supervisors and staff how to recognize potentially volatile situations and how to minimize potentially unpleasant consequences.
- Create provisions and avenues for seeking and receiving relief from offensive and unwanted behavior.
- Provide written procedures for reporting incidents and for investigating and bringing grievances to closure.

Of course, employers should not develop a zero tolerance policy toward harassment merely to avoid lawsuits. However, by creating a clear policy statement that includes severe penalties for violation, companies can demonstrate a good-faith effort to promote a safe, fair, work environment. An effective antisexual harassment policy should include the following:

- A statement that the organization advocates and supports unequivocally a zero tolerance standard when it comes to sexual harassment.
- A definition of the terms and behaviors discussed in the statement.
- A description of acceptable and unacceptable behaviors; that is, no sexually suggestive photographs, jokes, vulgar language, touching, and the like.
- An explanation of the reasons for the existing policy.
- A discussion of the consequences for unacceptable behavior. You should probably list sexual harassment as a punishable offense in all company handbooks and manuals. Types of disciplinary action available to the company should be stated as consequences for sexual harassment or hostile environment offenses.
- Specific identification of the complaint procedures to be followed by an employee.
- Several avenues for relief or ways to bring a complaint or concern(s) to the attention of management. If all grievances must be cleared through the supervisor and he or she is the culprit, this does provide an avenue to relief.
- Identification, by name, of the employer representative to whom complaints should be reported. This should be to someone who is not in an employee's chain of command. With the current state of the law, it is preferable to direct complaints to the personnel or human resources manager.
- A clear statement that all complaints and investigations will be treated with confidence. All investigative materials should be maintained in separate files with very limited and restricted access.
- A clear statement that the employer prohibits all forms of harassment and that any complaints by employees of forms of harassment based on any protected category will be addressed under the antiharassment policy.

Although a policy statement is a good beginning, it will not be effective unless it is adopted by managers and communicated to all employees. Most companies reprint their policy on sexual harassment in their employee manual. Other companies have taken additional steps by posting the policy in common areas such as in lunchrooms and on bulletin boards and discussing the policy at new employee orientations and other personnel meetings.

It is important to point out that not all legal jurisdictions react the same way when it comes to zero tolerance concerning inappropriate behavior in the workplace; not all courts deem a one-time offense as actionable on the employee's part even though the employer is free to take internal action in furtherance of its own policies. In other words, with some exceptions, a one-time offense does not always create a claim of harassment in the workplace against the employer. For example, if a manager should ask a subordinate out on a date once and the employee says no without any further requests on the part of the supervisor and any reprisals for this, that one incident will not support a charge of discrimination by the subordinate. If the supervisor continues to ask the employee out on dates numerous times after the employee has continuously said no, creating a pervasive environment of harassment, then the employee may have a claim for sexual harassment. As an exception to this one-time offense rule, if the offense is unconscionable, such as rape or other violent behavior, then the employee would have grounds to submit a charge of discrimination, as well as criminal charges for the behavior against the supervisor.

A training program is one of the most effective ways an employer can foster a safe working environment and ensure compliance with the law. All employees should participate in a sexual harassment training program, initially during orientation and thereafter on a regular basis. Some of the most effective training techniques include role-playing exercises, group and panel discussions, videos, behavior modeling, and sensitivity training. It is also important that employees become fully familiar with the avenues for seeking relief should they ever feel uncomfortable because of someone else's behavior. Employees with any kind of supervisory responsibility should be trained to identify circumstances that could be perceived as harassment and understand both the company's policy and their role in preventing unwelcome behavior and responding seriously to any complaints.

While training is important, it is even more important to evaluate the effects of training. This can be done by administering tests to employees before and after they participate in a training program, keeping the results, and documenting the number of harassment complaints received as well as taking care to note whether the number of complaints has gone up or down. If the feedback shows that a training program is

Analyze the Situation 8.1

Joseph Harper was a cook at the HillsTop resort hotel. He was 61 years old and had been employed by the resort for over 25 years. Sandra Shana was the new human resource director for the facility. As part of her duties, Ms. Shana conducted the hotel's sexual harassment training program for all new employees, as well as management. The training sessions used up-to-date material provided by the resort's national trade association, and Ms. Shana worked hard to evaluate the effectiveness of the training for both employees and management.

Mr. Harper attended three training sessions in the space of five years. When he was approached by Ms. Shana to attend another training session, he stated, "I don't know why I have to go through this again. It's nonsense and a waste of time. I have gone three times, and it's dumber each time I attend!" Mr. Harper had been heard to make similar comments each time he attended the training sessions and once even challenged the trainers about the "political correctness" of the training. In addition, he had been heard making similar comments in the employee breakroom while other employees were in the room. No staff member of the resort had ever formally accused Mr. Harper of sexual harassment, however. The HillsTop resort stated in its employee manual that it is an "at-will" employer.

1. As the human resource director, would you recommend either the discipline or termination of Mr. Harper based on his comments?
2. If the resort and Mr. Harper specifically were named in a guest-initiated lawsuit alleging harassment and found liable, would you recommend disciplinary action against the human resource director or the resort's general manager for failing to act?
3. Does Mr. Harper have the right to openly express his opinion about the resort's harassment training while at work?

ineffective, change the program. If the feedback shows that an individual was unable to learn the demonstrated skills or follow company guidelines, then either retrain or terminate the employee; otherwise, you may risk a negligent retention claim because based on the feedback you received, you should have known that this employee would violate company standards or regulations. A jury might conclude that termination of the employee would have prevented the incident that prompted the lawsuit.

Opposing attorneys will not walk away from a case just because you have a policy in place and state that training has occurred. They will want to see that training did in fact occur, what kind of training it was, and whether or not the training was effective. In order to win a lawsuit that accuses you of ineffective training, you must be able to document a training "trail" and be able to show those materials to a jury. Keep records of every seminar and workshop that is conducted, and note the people who attended. If you used supporting materials such as videos or handouts, keep copies of them. If you solicited feedback after the workshop in the form of test results or employee evaluations, keep them on file. Why? Because, unfortunately, it is rarely the truth that wins lawsuits; it is usually the evidence that prevails.

Investigating a Complaint

Unfortunately, even the most thorough prevention effort will not preclude all offensive behaviors. You must, therefore, have a procedure in place to deal with these incidents. This procedure must be strictly followed. Employees must be confident that they can come forward with their concerns without fear of ridicule, retaliation, or job loss.

When a complaint is lodged or the inappropriate activity is brought to the attention of management, the employer should act immediately. At the time of the complaint, the employer should obtain the claimant's permission to start an investigation. Written consent forms, such as the one shown in Figure 8.2 on the next page, are recommended. Note that the form asks for permission to disclose the information to third parties, if necessary, so that a thorough investigation can be conducted.

Often, the circumstances surrounding a claim of sexual harassment are very personal. There are occasions when an employee launches a complaint and later changes his or her mind or asks if the investigation can be conducted under certain conditions. As a manager, you need to be sensitive to an employee's emotions, but you must not allow him or her to interfere with a company's established investigation policies. Employees have the right to withdraw a complaint, but if they do so, you should have them sign a form, such as the one shown in Figure 8.3 on the next page, stating that they no longer wish to pursue the matter and that they are comfortable having no further action taken.

In some situations, it may be necessary to pursue action in spite of the employee's refusal to continue. For example, the facts brought to management's attention might be so serious that a company would need to consider taking some sort of immediate remedial action, such as the suspension or termination of the alleged harasser. Failure to do so could subject the company to liability for keeping the individual if he or she acts inappropriately again and management could not intervene. It is important to remember that just because an employee does not agree to formally complain or to follow through on a complaint, the employer is not relieved from the responsibility of providing a safe working environment.

If the complainant takes the position that the mere presence of the alleged harasser causes anxiety and distress, do not transfer that employee to another job or position as an interim measure. Suggest the alleged harasser take a couple of days off with pay while you investigate the complaint. A transfer tends to undermine the confidence of the victim,

Investigation Consent Form

i. Name: ______________________________

ii. Position and Title: ______________________________

iii. Facts of Situation (attach as many pages as necessary):

____

____

____

____

____

____

iv. I hereby request that the company investigate the facts set forth above. I also authorize the company to disclose as much of the facts set forth above as necessary to pursue the investigation. I also understand and acknowledge that the company shall use due diligence in keeping this matter as confidential as possible. I recognize, however, that in the course of the investigation the information may need to become public to do a thorough investigation.

Signature ______________________ Date ______________________

Employee

FIGURE 8.2 Investigation consent form.

Request for No Further Action

i. Name: ______________________________

ii. Position and Title: ______________________________

On the _____ day of __________ 200____, I previously completed a consent form which, among other things, requested that the company investigate certain facts stated by me, a copy of which is attached to this document. I have now decided that it would not be in my best interest to pursue this matter, and am comfortable with my environment in the workplace, as it presently exists. I have been made aware that in the event that I become uncomfortable, I can seek the assistance and support of the company at any time, and have been encouraged to do so. At this time, however, I am requesting that at least for my benefit, no further action be taken in this regard, and I fully understand that an investigation for my benefit shall not take place. I do understand, however, that the company, after having been made aware of these circumstances, may elect to pursue an investigation on its own behalf and for the benefit of other employees.

Signature ______________________ Date ______________________

Employee

FIGURE 8.3 Request for no further action.

particularly after being told that there would be no retaliation for bringing the concern to the attention of management.

If you choose to undertake an investigation, be sure to do so thoroughly. An ineffective investigation could subject you to legal liability just as if no such investigation took place. When conducting an investigation, employers should exercise discretion in selecting the employees who will be interviewed. It is advisable to confine the investigation to the circle of the alleged victim's immediate coworkers who witnessed the incident or who were privy to the claimant's situation and confidence. The objective is to garner as much information as possible in order to conduct an even-handed and fair investigation. The questions in Figure 8.4 are a few that you might want to consider asking those who are not directly involved in an allegation. Interviewers should be tactful and alert to the interviewees' attitude and be cognizant of their relationship with the victim as well as the alleged harasser. Witnesses should be reminded of the sensitive nature of the investigation and of the importance of maintaining confidentiality. Always conduct the interviews in private. The results should be discussed with

1. Have you noticed any behavior that makes people uncomfortable in the workplace?
2. Did it involve sexual or ethnic matters? Would you mind sharing with me who was involved?
3. What is the general atmosphere of the work environment?
4. Do you consider any employees or supervisors to be chronic complainers?
5. Do you think some people are treated differently from others for reasons that are not job-related?
6. Do you feel as if any employees receive the benefit of favoritism for reasons other than job performance?
7. Have you noticed any personality conflicts?
8. Will you let me know if you think of anything else?

FIGURE 8.4 Possible questions for interviewees not directly involved in a complaint.
Adapted from Jossen Jared, "Investigating Sexual Harassment." *In Litigating the Sexual Harassment Case.* American Bar Association, 1994. Copyright © 1994 the American Bar Association.

the accused in a nonthreatening manner. To maintain the integrity of the process, individuals identified by the accused who might be able to disprove the allegations should be contacted and interviewed.

At all times, the investigation should be carefully and accurately documented. Conversations and interviews with witnesses should be recorded in writing, and whenever possible, signed statements should be obtained. A record of the decision made after the investigation should also be on file. References to the claim should not, however, appear in a personnel file unless the offender has been issued a disciplinary action after a thorough investigation. A separate investigation file should be kept, and that file should be retained for as long as the statute of limitations on sexual harassment claims specifies. (That period can be as long as two years from the date an incident has occurred.)

Resolving a Complaint

In order to avoid liability, an employer must offer evidence that a complaint of sexual harassment was investigated thoroughly and undertook prompt remedial action to end the harassing conduct. The Equal Employment Opportunity Commission (EEOC) recognizes effective remedial action to include the following steps:

1. Prompt and thorough investigation of complaints.
2. Immediate corrective action that effectively ends the harassment.
3. Provision of a remedy to complainants for such harassment (e.g., restoring lost wages and benefits).
4. Preventive measures against future recurrences.

Should the results of an investigation remain inconclusive, or if, after an investigation, no corrective or preventative actions are taken, then the victim has the right to file a lawsuit against the employer. However, if an employer punishes an accused harasser without having conclusive evidence to back up a claim, then the alleged harasser has the right to file a defamation lawsuit or an invasion of privacy action against the employer. If the results of an investigation prove inconclusive, then the best actions to take are to advise the alleged harasser that the investigation was inconclusive, inform all employees of the organization's zero tolerance policy of sexual harassment, spell out the consequences for failure to abide by that policy, and conduct sensitivity training programs. If there is a resolution to the investigation, have the complainant sign a resolution form, such as the one shown in Figure 8.5, if possible.

Resolution of Complaint

i. Name: ______________________________

ii. Position and Title: ______________________________

iii. On the _____ day of _____________, 20__, I previously completed a form, which alleged facts regarding the environment in the workplace, a copy of which is attached to this document. I have been made aware of the results of the investigation by the company, as well as its proposed resolution of this matter, which I understand to be as follows:

(i). The alleged harasser shall undergo sensitivity training.
(ii). The alleged harasser shall be suspended without pay for five (5) days beginning on the _____ day of ___________ and ending on the ____ day of ____, 20__.
(iii). It is agreed by both parties that the alleged harasser shall return to work at the time stated above, but only after having undergone the sensitivity training.

I am satisfied with the resolution as set forth above, and understand fully that in the event the matter is not completely resolved by the foregoing actions, I have been encouraged to bring my concerns to the company for immediate attention.

Signature ______________________ Date ______________________

Employee

FIGURE 8.5 Resolution of complaint form.

Third-Party Harassment

Third-party sexual harassment occurs when someone outside the workforce harasses an employee or is harassed by an employee. Some examples are a supplier or vendor harassing an employee, a guest harassing an employee, or an employee harassing a guest. In the case of *EEOC v. Sage Realty Corporation*, 521 F. Supp. 263 (S.D.N.Y. 1981), a federal court in New York held the real estate company responsible when one of its employees violated federal law by terminating a female lobby attendant who refused to wear a uniform that she considered too revealing. She felt that wearing the uniform had caused her to be the victim of lewd comments and sexual propositions from customers and the general public.

In the hospitality industry, where the interaction between guests and employees is a critical component of the business, the risks of third-party harassment are especially great. The adage "the customer is always right" does not extend to harassment. The law clearly states that employees do not have to tolerate, nor should they be subjected to, offensive behavior. This means that employers have a responsibility to protect their employees from third-party harassment.

This is especially troublesome when one considers that managers have limited control over guests and that it is a natural desire to want to hold on to the customers' business and goodwill. From a legal and practical perspective, however, employees should know that they have the right to speak up when they are subject to unwelcome behavior, and managers should act quickly and reasonably to resolve any situations that do occur.

Liability Insurance

It is important to remember that zero tolerance does not necessarily mean zero claims of harassment. Incidents will occur. Because this is true, employers, especially in the hospitality industry, should purchase liability insurance that includes coverage for illegal acts of discrimination, including internal and third-party sexual harassment. This coverage is not provided in ordinary liability insurance policies; it must be specifically requested. The insurance should cover the liability for acts of the employer, acts of the employees and third parties, and any damages that may not be covered by workers' compensation policies.

8.3 Family and Medical Leave Act

A highly significant piece of federal legislation that greatly impacts employee management in the hospitality industry is the Family and Medical Leave Act of 1993 (FMLA) and its amendments (www.dol.gov/whd/fmla). The U.S. Department of Labor's Employment Standards Administration, Wage and Hour Division, administers and enforces the FMLA. The FMLA entitles eligible employees to take up to 12 weeks of unpaid, job-protected leave each year for specified family and medical reasons. The FMLA applies to all government workers and private-sector employers that employ 50 or more employees within a 75-mile radius. It is important to note that the 50 employees need not all work at the same location. For example, a multiunit operator whose total workforce equals or exceeds 50 employees within a 75-mile radius is covered by the act.

To be eligible for FMLA benefits, an employee must have worked for the employer for a total of at least 12 months and have worked at least 1,250 hours over the previous 12 months. A covered employer must grant an eligible employee up to a total of 12 workweeks of unpaid leave for:

- The birth of a child and to care for the newborn child within one year from birth.
- The placement with the employee of a child for adoption or foster care and to care for the newly placed child within one year of placement.
- To care for the employee's spouse, child, or parent who has a serious health condition.
- A serious health condition that makes the employee unable to perform the essential functions of his or her job.
- Any qualifying exigency arising out of the fact that the employee's spouse, son, daughter, or parent is a covered military member on "covered active duty".

Spouses who work for the same employer are jointly entitled to a combined total of 12 workweeks of family leave for the birth or placement of a child for adoption or foster care and to care for a parent (not a parent-in-law) who has a serious health condition. In 2013, the U.S. Supreme Court decision in *United States v. Windsor* amended the definition of spouse to include legal same-sex marriages by finding section 3 of the Defense of Marriage Act (DOMA) to be unconstitutional.

Alternatively, the FMLA allows for military caregiver leave, which entitles the employee to 26 workweeks of leave within a single 12-month period for the purpose of caring for a covered service member with a serious injury if that covered service member is the spouse, son, daughter, parent, or next of kin to the employee.

Under some circumstances, employees may take FMLA leave intermittently—which means taking leaves in blocks of time or reducing their normal weekly or daily work schedule. FMLA leave may be taken intermittently whenever medically necessary to care for a seriously ill family member or because the employee is seriously ill and unable to work.

A covered employer is required to maintain group health insurance coverage for an employee on FMLA leave if the insurance was provided before the leave was taken and on the same terms as if the employee had continued to work. In most cases, the employee is required to pay his or her share of health insurance premiums while on leave.

Upon return from FMLA leave, an employee must be restored to his or her original job or an equivalent one. An equivalent job need not consist of exactly the same hours but must include the same pay and level of responsibility. Some exceptions are made under the law, especially for salaried or "key" staff personnel.

Employees seeking to use FMLA leave may be required to provide:

- Thirty-day advance notice of the need to take FMLA leave when the need is foreseeable.
- Medical certifications supporting the need for leave due to a serious health condition.
- Second or third medical opinions if requested by and paid for by the employer.
- Periodic reports during FMLA leave regarding the employee's status and intent to return to work.

Covered employers must post a notice approved by the secretary of labor explaining rights and responsibilities under the FMLA. An employer that willfully violates this posting requirement may be subject to a fine of up to $100 for each separate offense. Also, employers must inform employees of their rights under the FMLA. This information can be included in an employee manual when one exists. In some cases, provisions for leaves of absence are also part of a labor union's collective bargaining agreement, and managers should be aware of those provisions.

8.4 Uniform Services Employment and Reemployment Rights Act

The Uniformed Services Employment and Reemployment Rights Act of 1994 (USERRA) was signed into law by President Bill Clinton to protect the employment rights of those individuals who voluntarily or involuntarily leave their jobs to take part in military service or other certain types of service in the National Disaster Medical System, including the Reserves and the National Guard. USERRA prohibits employers from discriminating against those current or past members of the uniformed services as well as applicants.

Under USERRA, in addition to being free from discrimination and retaliation in the workplace, veterans and members of military service have the right to be reemployed in the civilian job if they leave that job to perform in the military and

- They ensured that the employer received advanced notice (whether written or verbal).
- Had five years or less of cumulative service in the military while in that particular workplace.
- Returned to work or applied for reemployment in a timely manner after separating from the military.
- Had not been separated from the service with a disqualifying discharge or under other dishonorable conditions.

In 2011, USERRA was amended to include protection of servicemen and women from harassment in the workplace and from hostile work environment conditions. The VOW to Hire Heroes Act of 2011 was a direct response to a federal case that clarified that hostile work environment claims can and should be recognized under USERRA.

8.5 Compensation

Generally, employers are free to establish wages and salaries as they see fit. In some cases, however, the law affects the wage relationship between employer and employee. For example, the Equal Pay Act, passed in 1963 by the federal government, provides that equal pay must be paid to men and women for equal work if the jobs they perform require "equal" skill, effort, responsibility and are performed under similar working conditions. An employee's gender, personal situation, or financial status cannot serve as a basis for making wage determinations. In addition to equal pay for equal work, there are a variety of other laws that regulate how much an employer must pay its employees. In the hospitality industry, these laws have a broad impact.

In an effort to support the Equal Pay Act, the first piece of legislation that President Barack Obama signed into law after he was sworn in as President of the United States was the Lily Ledbetter Fair Pay Act of 2009. Lily Ledbetter, a 19-year employee with the Goodyear Tire and Rubber Company alleged that her employer had discriminated against her in regard to her low pay on the basis of her gender. She prevailed at the trial level but lost on appeal when the appeals court said she was barred by the statute of limitations and could seek redress for only the 180-day period before filing her claim, not for her entire 19-year career. On appeal, the U.S. Supreme Court agreed with the previous court that her claim was barred by time. Immediately following this decision, Congress created a law that if an act of discrimination is ongoing, claims about it can be made beyond the 180-days statute of limitations that apply.

Minimum Wage and Overtime

As mentioned in Chapter 7, the Fair Labor Standards Act (FLSA) established child labor standards in the United States. In addition, it established the **minimum wage** that must be paid

---

LEGALESE

Minimum wage: The lowest amount of wages that an employee covered by the FLSA or state law may be paid by his or her employer.

to covered employees, as well as wage rates that must be paid for working overtime. The FLSA applies to all businesses that have employees who are engaged in producing, handling, selling, or working on goods that have been moved in or manufactured for interstate commerce. Some, but not many, hospitality operations may be too small to be covered under the FLSA. To be sure, a small business owner should check with the local offices of the Wage and Hour Division listed in most telephone directories under U.S. Government, Department of Labor, Wage and Hour Division (www.dol.gov/whd).

The minimum wage is established and periodically revised by Congress. Nearly all hospitality employees are covered by the minimum wage, but there are some exceptions. The FLSA allows an employer to pay an employee who is under 20 years of age a training wage, which is below the standard minimum, for the first 90 consecutive calendar days of employment. Also, tipped employees can be paid a rate below the minimum if the tips they report plus the wages received from the employer equal or exceed the minimum hourly rate.

Some states have also established their own minimum wages. In those states, employees are covered by the law most favorable to them (in other words, whichever wage is higher, state or federal). The differences in state laws can be significant. Compare the current federal minimum compensation provisions with those of several states in Figure 8.6. You can see that each state has a great deal of latitude in enacting its own wage and overtime laws.

The FLSA does not limit the number of hours in a day or days in a week an employee over the age of 16 may work. Employers may require an employee to work more than 40 hours per week. However, under the FLSA, covered employees must be paid at least one and one-half times their regular rates of pay for all hours worked in excess of 40 in a workweek.

Some employees are exempt from the overtime provision of the FLSA. These include salaried professional, administrative, and executive employees. In May 2016, the Department of Labor issued a final rule effective December 1, 2016, updating the overtime regulations. The rule primarily focuses on updating the salary and compensation levels needed for executive, administrative, and professional workers to be exempt. See Figure 8.7 and www.dol.gov/whd/overtime/final2016.

Search the Web 8.1

Go to the Internet and enter **www.dol.gov in your browser**

1. Select: Search.
2. Enter in the search box: State Minimum Wages.
3. Select from the search results: Minimum Wage Laws in the States.
4. Select: The state where you live or go to school.
5. Identify the minimum wage rate for workers in your state.
6. Identify the overtime provisions (referred to as premium pay) for workers in your state.
7. Identify any exemptions or exceptions that relate to the hospitality industry.

Because the minimum wage and the laws related to it change on a regular basis, it is a good idea to regularly contact your local office of the Wage and Hour Division, listed in most telephone directories under U.S. government, Department of Labor, Employment Standards Administration, for legal updates.

Wage and Hour Division investigators stationed throughout the country enforce the FLSA. When investigators encounter violations, they recommend changes in employment practices in order to bring the employer into compliance and may require the payment of any back wages due employees. Employers who willfully or repeatedly violate the minimum wage or overtime pay requirements are subject to civil penalties of up to $1,000 per violation. Employees may also sue their employer when the Department of Labor does not, for back pay, and other compensatory damages, including attorney's fees and court costs.

State	Minimum Wage	Overtime Hours	Maximum Tip Credit	Rest Breaks
Federal	$7.25/hour regular rate	1.5 times	$3.02/hour	None required
Oregon	$9.25/hour regular rate	1.5 times	None Allowed	10 minutes per 4 hours worked
South Carolina	No state law	No state law	No state law	No state law
Vermont	$9.60/hour	1.5 times, but hotels and restaurants are exempt	$4.20/hour	No state law

Remember that whenever a state law or regulation is different from the federal law or regulation, the law or regulation most favorable to the employee must be followed.

FIGURE 8.6 **Variances in federal and state compensation provisions.**

U.S. Department of Labor
Wage and Hour Division

(May 2016)

Fact Sheet: Final Rule to Update the Regulations Defining and Delimiting the Exemption for Executive, Administrative, and Professional Employees

In 2014, President Obama directed the Department of Labor to update and modernize the regulations governing the exemption of executive, administrative, and professional ("EAP") employees from the minimum wage and overtime pay protections of the Fair Labor Standards Act ("FLSA" or "Act"). The Department published a notice of proposed rulemaking on July 6, 2015, and received more than 270,000 comments. On May 18, 2016, the Department announced that it will publish a Final Rule to update the regulations. The full text of the Final Rule will be available at the Federal Register Site.

Although the FLSA ensures minimum wage and overtime pay protections for most employees covered by the Act, some workers, including bona fide EAP employees, are exempt from those protections. Since 1940, the Department's regulations have generally required each of three tests to be met for the FLSA's EAP exemption to apply: (1) the employee must be paid a predetermined and fixed salary that is not subject to reduction because of variations in the quality or quantity of work performed ("salary basis test"); (2) the amount of salary paid must meet a minimum specified amount ("salary level test"); and (3) the employee's job duties must primarily involve executive, administrative, or professional duties as defined by the regulations ("duties test"). The Department last updated these regulations in 2004, when it set the weekly salary level at $455 ($23,660 annually) and made other changes to the regulations, including collapsing the short and long duties tests into a single standard duties test and introducing a new exemption for highly compensated employees.

This Final Rule updates the salary level required for exemption to ensure that the FLSA's intended overtime protections are fully implemented, and to simplify the identification of overtime-protected employees, thus making the EAP exemption easier for employers and workers to understand and apply. Without intervening action by their employers, it extends the right to overtime pay to an estimated 4.2 million workers who are currently exempt. It also strengthens existing overtime protections for 5.7 million additional white collar salaried workers and 3.2 million salaried blue collar workers whose entitlement to overtime pay will no longer rely on the application of the duties test.

*** Key Provisions of the Final Rule ***

The Final Rule focuses primarily on updating the salary and compensation levels needed for EAP workers to be exempt. Specifically, the Final Rule:

1. Sets the standard salary level at the 40th percentile of earnings of full-time salaried workers in the lowest-wage Census Region, currently the South, which is $913 per week or $47,476 annually for a full-year worker;

2. Sets the total annual compensation requirement for highly compensated employees (HCE) subject to a minimal duties test to the annual equivalent of the 90th percentile of full-time salaried workers nationally, which is $134,004; and

1

WHFR29CFR541

FIGURE 8.7 **Final rule.**
https://www.dol.gov/whd/overtime/fs17a_overview.pdf

3. Establishes a mechanism for automatically updating the salary and compensation levels every three years to maintain the levels at the above percentiles and to ensure that they continue to provide useful and effective tests for exemption.

Additionally, the Final Rule amends the salary basis test to allow employers to use nondiscretionary bonuses and incentive payments (including commissions) to satisfy up to 10 percent of the new standard salary level. The Final Rule makes no changes to the duties tests.

Effective Date

The effective date of the Final Rule is December 1, 2016. The initial increases to the standard salary level (from $455 to $913 per week) and HCE total annual compensation requirement (from $100,000 to $134,004 per year) will be effective on that date. Future automatic updates to those thresholds will occur every three years, beginning on January 1, 2020.

Standard Salary Level

The Final Rule sets the standard salary level at the 40th percentile of weekly earnings of full-time salaried workers in the lowest-wage Census Region, currently the South ($913 per week, equivalent to $47,476 per year for a full-year worker).

The standard salary level set in this Final Rule addresses our conclusion that the salary level set in 2004 was too low given the Department's elimination of the more rigorous long duties test. For many decades the long duties test—which limited the amount of time an exempt employee could spend on nonexempt duties and was paired with a lower salary level—existed in tandem with a short duties test—which did not contain a specific limit on the amount of nonexempt work and was paired with a salary level that was approximately 130 to 180 percent of the long test salary level. In 2004, the long and short duties tests were eliminated and the new standard duties test was created based on the short duties test and was paired with a salary test based on the long test.

The effect of the 2004 Final Rule's pairing of a standard duties test based on the short duties test (for higher paid employees) with a salary test based on the long test (for lower paid employees) was to exempt from overtime many lower paid workers who performed few EAP duties and whose work was otherwise indistinguishable from their overtime-eligible colleagues. This has resulted in the inappropriate classification of employees as EAP exempt who pass the standard duties test but would have failed the long duties test.

The Final Rule's salary level represents the most appropriate line of demarcation between overtime-protected employees and employees who may be EAP exempt and works appropriately with the current duties test, which does not limit non-EAP work.

The Department also is updating the special salary level for employees in American Samoa (to $767 per week) and the special "base rate" for employees in the motion picture industry (to $1,397 per week).

HCE Total Annual Compensation Requirement

The Final Rule sets the HCE total annual compensation level equal to the 90th percentile of earnings of full-time salaried workers nationally ($134,004 annually). To be exempt as an HCE, an employee must also receive at least the new standard salary amount of $913 per week on a salary or fee basis and pass a minimal duties test. The HCE annual compensation level set in this Final Rule brings this threshold more in line with the level established in 2004 and will avoid the unintended exemption of large numbers of employees in high-wage areas who are clearly not performing EAP duties.

2

FIGURE 8.7 *(continued)*

Automatic Updating

The Final Rule includes a mechanism to automatically update the standard salary level requirement every three years to ensure that it remains a meaningful test for distinguishing between overtime-protected white collar workers and bona fide EAP workers who may not be entitled to overtime pay and to provide predictability and more graduated salary changes for employers. Specifically, the standard salary level will be updated to maintain a threshold equal to the 40th percentile of weekly earnings of full-time salaried workers in the lowest-wage Census Region. Similarly, the Final Rule includes a mechanism for automatically updating the HCE compensation level to maintain the threshold equal to the 90th percentile of annual earnings of full-time salaried workers nationally. The Final Rule will also automatically update the special salary level test for employees in American Samoa and the base rate test for motion picture industry employees. The Department will publish all updated rates in the Federal Register at least 150 days before their effective date, and also post them on the Wage and Hour Division's website.

Regularly updating the salary and compensation levels is the best method to ensure that these tests continue to provide an effective means of distinguishing between overtime-eligible white collar employees and those who may be bona fide EAP employees. Experience has shown that these earning thresholds are only effective measures of exempt status if they are kept up to date.

Inclusion of Nondiscretionary Bonuses and Incentive Payments

For the first time, employers will be able to use nondiscretionary bonuses and incentive payments (including commissions) to satisfy up to 10 percent of the standard salary level. Such payments may include, for example, nondiscretionary incentive bonuses tied to productivity and profitability. For employers to credit nondiscretionary bonuses and incentive payments toward a portion of the standard salary level test, the Final Rule requires such payments to be paid on a quarterly or more frequent basis and permits the employer to make a "catch-up" payment. The Department recognizes that some businesses pay significantly larger bonuses; where larger bonuses are paid, however, the amount attributable toward the standard salary level is capped at 10 percent of the required salary amount.

The Final Rule continues the requirement that HCEs must receive at least the full standard salary amount each pay period on a salary or fee basis without regard to the payment of nondiscretionary bonuses and incentive payments, and continues to permit nondiscretionary bonuses and incentive payments (including commissions) to count toward the total annual compensation requirement. The Department concludes that permitting employers to use nondiscretionary bonuses and incentive payments to satisfy the standard salary amount for HCEs is not appropriate because employers are already permitted to fulfill almost two-thirds of the total annual compensation requirement with commissions, nondiscretionary bonuses, and other forms of nondiscretionary deferred compensation.

Duties Tests

The Final Rule is not changing any of the existing job duty requirements to qualify for exemption. The Department expects that the standard salary level set in this Final Rule and automatic updating will work effectively with the duties test to distinguish between overtime-eligible workers and those who may be exempt. As a result of the change to the salary level, the number of workers for whom employers must apply the duties test to determine exempt status is reduced, thus simplifying the exemption. Both the standard duties test and the HCE duties test remain unchanged.

3

FIGURE 8.7 *(continued)*

For additional information, visit our Wage and Hour Division Website: www.wagehour.dol.gov and/or call our toll-free information and helpline, available 8 a.m. to 5 p.m. in your time zone, 1-866-4-USWAGE (1-866-487-9243).

This publication is for general information and is not to be considered in the same light as official statements of position contained in the regulations.

U.S. Department of Labor
Frances Perkins Building
200 Constitution Avenue, NW
Washington, DC 20210

1-866-4-USWAGE
TTY: 1-866-487-9243
Contact Us

4

FIGURE 8.7 *(continued)*

Tipped Employees

The hospitality industry employs a large number of individuals who customarily receive **tips** in conjunction with their work duties. On the one hand, some employees, such as hotel housekeepers, may receive tips only occasionally. Food servers, on the other hand, often receive more income in tips than their employer pays them in wages.

The FLSA defines tipped employees as individuals engaged in occupations in which they customarily and regularly receive more than $30 a month in tips. The employer may consider tips as part of wage, but must pay at least $2.13 an hour in direct wages. Employers who elect to use the tip credit provision must inform the employee in advance and must be able to show that the employee receives at least the applicable minimum wage when direct wages and the tip credit allowance are combined. If an employee's tips combined with the employer's direct wages of at least $2.13 an hour do not equal the minimum hourly wage, the employer must make up the difference. Also, employees must retain all of their tips except to the extent that they participate in a valid tip pooling or sharing arrangement.

Consider the case of Lawson Odde who is employed in a state that has adopted the federal minimum wage guidelines with a minimum wage of $7.25 per hour. Under the law, his employer is allowed to consider Mr. Odde's tips as part of his wages. Thus, the employer is required to pay Mr. Odde

LEGALESE

Tips: A gratuity given in exchange for a service performed. Literally an acronym for "to insure prompt service."

Legally Managing at Work

Calculating Overtime Pay for Tipped Employees

Tipped employees are generally subject to the overtime provisions of the FLSA. The computation of the overtime rate for tipped employees when the employer claims a tax credit can be confusing to some managers. Consider, for example, a state in which the minimum wage is $8.00 per hour and the applicable overtime provision dictates payment of one and one-half the normal hours rate for hours worked in excess of 40 hours per week. To determine the overtime rate of pay, use the following three-step method:

1. Multiply the prevailing minimum wage rate by 1.5.
2. Compute the allowable tip credit against the standard hourly rate.
3. Subtract the number in step 2 from the result in step 1.

Thus, if the minimum wage were $8.00 per hour and the allowable tip credit were 50 percent, the overtime rate to be paid would be computed as:

1. $8.00 x 1.5 = $9.00
2. $8.00 x 5.0 = $3.00
3. $9.00 – $3.00 = $6.00 overtime rate

at least $2.13 per hour and take a **tip credit** for the remainder of the wages needed to comply with the law. However, if Mr. Odde does not make enough money in tips to equal $5.12, the remainder of the minimum wage amount less the hourly wage already paid by the employer, the employer must pay Mr. Odde the remaining difference so that he is paid a minimum wage.

Like the minimum wage and the requirements for overtime pay, state laws regarding tipped employees and allowable tip credits can also vary. Refer to Figure 8.6 for some differences in how state and federal laws consider tip credits. It is important to remember that because tips are given to employees, not employers, the law carefully regulates the influence that you, as an employer, have over these funds. In fact, if an employer takes control of the tips an employee receives, that employer will not be allowed to utilize the tip credit provisions of the FLSA. For more information on tipped employees, read "Uncovering the Mysteries of the Tip Wage" by Terrence Robinson at http://hospitalitylawyer.com/solutions/find-academic-resources/hospitality-law-textbook-support/.

Tip Pooling

In some hospitality businesses, employees routinely share tips. Consider, for example, the table busser whose job includes refilling water glasses at a fine dining establishment. If a guest leaves a tip on the table, the size of that tip will certainly have been influenced by the attentiveness of the busser assigned to that table. The FLSA does not prohibit **tip pooling/sharing**, but it is an area that employers should approach with extreme caution. A tip, by its nature, is given to an employee, not the employer. In that way, a tip is different from a **service charge** that is collected from the guest by the employer and distributed in the manner deemed best by the employer.

Generally speaking, when a tip is given directly to an employee, management has no control over what that employee will ultimately do with the tip. An exception to this principle is the tip-pooling arrangement.

Tip pooling/sharing is a complex area because the logistics of providing hospitality services is sometimes complex. When a hostess seats a guest, a busser—who has previously set the table—provides water and bread, a bartender provides drinks, and a member of the wait staff delivers drinks and food to the table, the question of who deserves a portion of the tip can become perplexing.

Employers are free to assist employees in developing a tip-pooling/sharing arrangement that is fair based on the specific duties of each position in the service area. This participation should be documented in the employee's personnel file. The tip-pooling/sharing consent form should include the information presented in Figure 8.8.

Because it involves compensation, even well-constructed, voluntary tip-pooling arrangements can be a source of employee conflict. In addition, state laws in this field do vary, so it is a good idea to check with your state trade association or Wage and Hour Division regulator to determine the regulations that apply in your own area.

LEGALESE

Tip credit: The amount an employer is allowed to consider as a supplement to employer-paid wages in meeting the requirements of applicable minimum wage laws.

Tip-pooling/sharing: An arrangement whereby service providers share their tips with each other on a predetermined basis.

Service charge: An amount added to a guest's bill in exchange for services provided.

Taxes and Credits

Employers are required to pay taxes on the compensation they pay employees and to withhold taxes from the wages of employees. Federal and state statutes govern the types and amounts of compensation taxes that must be paid or withheld. In some cases, tax breaks, called "credits," are granted to employers or employees. While these taxes and credits can change, the most important employee taxes are the following:

Income tax: Employers are required to withhold state and federal income taxes from the paychecks of nearly all employees. These taxes are paid by the employee but collected by the employer and forwarded to the Internal Revenue Service (IRS) and state taxation agency. The amount that is to be withheld is based on the wage rate paid to the employee and the number of federal income tax dependents and deductions the employee has indicated he or she is entitled to. It is important to remember that tips are considered wages for income tax purposes if they are paid by cash, check, or credit card, and amount to more than $30.00 per calendar month.

FICA: Often called "Social Security taxes," the Federal Insurance Contributions Act (FICA) is a federal law requiring the collection of funds to the Social Security and Medicare programs. Both employers and employees are required to contribute to FICA. FICA taxes must be paid on the employee's wages, which include cash wages and the cash value of all remuneration paid in any medium other than cash. The size of the FICA tax and the amount of an employee's wages subject to it are adjusted on a regular basis by the federal government.

FUTA: The Federal Unemployment Tax Act (FUTA) requires employers, but not employees, to contribute a tax based on the size of the employer's total payroll. Again, it is important

Tip-Pooling Consent Form

1. Employee name
2. Date
3. A complete explanation of the facility's tip-pooling policy
4. The statement: "I understand the tip-pooling procedures and procedures stated above, and agree to participate in the tip-pooling and redistribution program."
5. Employee signature line below the preceding statement

FIGURE 8.8 **Tip-pooling consent form.**

Analyze the Situation 8.2

Stephen Rossenwasser was hired as a busser by the Sportsman's Fishing Club. This private club served its members lunch and dinner, as well as alcoholic beverages. Mr. Rossenwasser's duties were to clear tables, replenish water glasses, and reset tables for the wait staff when guests had finished their meals. His employer paid a wage rate below the minimum wage because the club utilized the tip credit portion of the FLSA minimum wage law.

When he was hired, Mr. Rossenwasser read the tip-pooling policy in place at the club and signed a document stating that he understood it and voluntarily agreed to participate in it. The policy stated that "all food and beverage tips are to be combined at the end of each meal period, and then distributed, with bussers receiving 20 percent of all tip income."

John Granberry, an attorney, was a club member who enjoyed dining in Mr. Rossenwasser's assigned section because he was attentive and quick to respond to any guest's needs. Mr. Granberry tipped well, and the dining room staff was aware that Mr. Granberry always requested to be seated in Mr. Rossenwasser's section.

One day after Mr. Granberry had finished his recent meal, had added his generous tip to his credit card charge slip, and had begun to depart, he stopped Mr. Rossenwasser in the lobby of the club and gave him a $20 bill with the words, "This is for you. Keep up the good work." A club bartender observed the exchange.

Mr. Rossenwasser did not place Mr. Granberry's tip into the tip pool, stating that the gratuity was clearly meant for him alone. His supervisor demanded that he contribute the tip to the pool. Mr. Rossenwasser refused.

1. Is Mr. Rossenwasser obligated to place Mr. Granberry's tip into the tip pool?
2. If he continues to refuse to relinquish the tip, what steps, if any, can management take to force Mr. Rossenwasser to do so?
3. Can Mr. Rossenwasser voluntarily withdraw from the tip-pool arrangement and still maintain his club employment?

to remember that payroll includes tip income and remuneration paid in forms other than cash. This tax is used to help fund state workforce agencies.

WOTC: The Work Opportunity Tax Credit was enacted in 1996 and amended in 2015 when the law Protecting Americans from Tax Hikes Act of 2015 (the PATH Act) was signed. This act gives employers a tax credit ranging from $1,200 to $9,600 (depending on the employee hired) for hiring individuals from certain groups who have often faced significant barriers to employment such as qualified long-term unemployment recipients, unemployed veterans, food stamp recipients, ex-felons, summer youth employees, and others (see https://www.doleta.gov/business/incentives/opptax/eligible.cfm).

As a hospitality manager, it is critical that you keep up to date with the compensation, taxes, and credit legislation enacted at both the federal and state levels. Certainly, all taxes that are due should be paid, but the hospitality industry often employs workers who are eligible for tax credits. In addition, employing certain individuals may make the employer eligible for tax credits. It is always advisable to seek the assistance of an employment lawyer or accountant to keep up with the changes in tax credits.

8.6 The Patient Protection and Affordable Care Act of 2010

The Patient Protection and Affordable Care Act of 2010, commonly called the "Affordable Care Act" or ACA and also known as "Obamacare," is a federal law that has significantly modified the U.S. health-care system by enacting a comprehensive health insurance reform intended to increase not only the quality of health care but also the affordability of health insurance in the United States. The ACA sought to address the condition of the millions of U.S. citizens who did not have health insurance coverage yet continued to use health-care services. The law was passed by the U.S. Congress and signed by President Barack Obama on March 23, 2010, and has been the subject of much political debate in the United States.

One of the key provisions of the ACA is the mandate that requires most Americans to maintain health insurance coverage containing minimum essential features for health care. If insurance coverage is not provided by an employer, then by the year 2014, all citizens must purchase insurance coverage protection or face a penalty.

The U.S. Supreme Court upheld the constitutionality of most of the law's provisions when challenged by the *National Federal of Independent Business* in 2011. The case primarily addressed the constitutionality of the individual mandate. The plaintiffs contended that the mandate exceeded the power given to Congress to pass the law, that the Medicaid expansions were coercive, and that the employer mandate interfered with the state's sovereign rights. The U.S. Supreme Court disagreed and stated that the individual mandate was constitutional.

According to the U.S. Department of Health & Human Services (www.hhs.gov/healthcare), some of the other key features of the ACA that take effect over a period of years include:

Coverage

- *Ends Pre-Existing Condition Exclusions for Children:* Health plans can no longer limit or deny benefits to children under 19 due to a pre-existing condition.
- *Keeps Young Adults Covered:* If you are under 26, you may be eligible to be covered under your parent's health plan.

- *Ends Arbitrary Withdrawals of Insurance Coverage:* Insurers can no longer cancel your coverage just because you made an honest mistake.
- *Guarantees Your Right to Appeal:* You now have the right to ask that your plan reconsider its denial of payment.

Costs

- *Ends Lifetime Limits on Coverage:* Lifetime limits on most benefits are banned for all new health insurance plans.
- *Reviews Premium Increases*: Insurance companies must now publicly justify any unreasonable rate hikes.
- **Helps You Get the Most from Your Premium Dollars**: Your premium dollars must be spent primarily on health care, not administrative costs.

Care

- *Covers Preventive Care at No Cost to You:* You may be eligible for recommended preventive health services with no copayment.
- *Protects Your Choice of Doctors:* Choose the primary care doctor you want from your plan's network.
- *Removes Insurance Company Barriers to Emergency Services:* You can seek emergency care at a hospital outside of your health plan's network.[1]

The opposition to the ACA continues, especially regarding the concerns of businesses and others about the overall cost of health care and issues related to religious freedom. For the hospitality manager, it is essential to stay abreast of the changes in this area, specifically to the mandates and the potential penalties that can be imposed on the business. Those who support the intent of the ACA claim that health-care costs continue to rise and it is important to provide better health-care insurance coverage for all U.S. citizens.

[1] http://www.hhs.gov/healthcare/about-the-law/index.html (Content last reviewed August 13, 2015).

8.7 Managing Employee Performance

Most employees come to a job with the expectation that they can complete or learn to complete the tasks assigned to them. In the hospitality industry, some of the workers hired are entering the workforce for the first time whereas others may have many years of experience. Regardless of ability or background, to effectively manage employee performance, employers must have a valid and defensible system of employee evaluation, discipline, and, if necessary, termination.

Evaluation

Employee evaluation is often used in the hospitality industry as a basis for granting pay increases, determining who is eligible for promotion or transfer, and modifying employee performance. Unfortunately, the subjective nature of many employee evaluation methods makes them susceptible to misuse and bias. When an employee can demonstrate that

LEGALESE

Employee evaluation: A review of an employee's performance, including strengths and shortcomings; typically completed by the employee's direct supervisor.

Analyze the Situation 8.3

Gerry Hernandez worked as a breakfast cook at a large day care facility. His attendance and punctuality were both good. Written into the facility's employee manual (which all employees sign when they begin their employment) was the following policy: "To be fair to the facility, your fellow employees, and our clients, you must be at your work station regularly and on time."

Mr. Hernandez had worked at the facility for 10 months when, one day, he was 15 minutes late for work. While Mr. Hernandez was aware of the facility work rule regarding punctuality, his supervisor, Pauline Cooper, rarely enforced the rule. Employees who were 5 to 20 minutes late might have been scolded, but no disciplinary action was usually taken, unless, according to Ms. Cooper, the employee was "excessively" tardy. In her words, she preferred to "cut some slack" to employees and thus was considered one of the more popular supervisors.

On the day Mr. Hernandez was late, a variety of problems had occurred in the kitchen. Frozen food deliveries arrived early and no cook was available to put them away, the sanitation inspector arrived for an unannounced inspection, and the rinse agent on the dish machine stopped functioning so dishes had to be washed by hand. Ms. Cooper was very angry, so when Mr. Hernandez arrived at work, she terminated him, stating, "If you can't get here on time, I don't need you here at all!"

The next day, Mr. Hernandez filed suit against the day care facility claiming that he was terminated because of his ethnic background. Ms. Cooper and the day care facility countered that he was an at-will employee, and thus the facility had the right to terminate employees as they see fit, especially when the employee was in violation of a communicated work rule.

1. Does Ms. Cooper have the right under at-will employment to terminate Mr. Hernandez?
2. If Ms. Cooper has no records documenting her actions in cases similar to that of Mr. Hernandez, is it likely she will be able to help defend her organization against a discrimination charge?
3. How would you advise Ms. Cooper to handle tardy employees in the future?

the evaluation system is biased against a class of workers specifically protected by the law, the liability to the employer can be great.

In most larger hospitality companies, the human resource department will have some type of form or procedure in place for use in employee evaluations. In smaller organizations, the process may be less formalized. In all cases, however, the hospitality manager must use great care to ensure that all employees are evaluated on the basis of their work performance and nothing else. Therefore, it is critical that you base evaluations only on previously established criteria and expectations, such as the job descriptions discussed in Chapter 7, "Legally Selecting Employees."

A false negative employee evaluation that results in the employee's loss of employment subjects the employer to even greater liability. **Wrongful termination** is the term used to describe the unlawful discharge of an employee. The at-will employment status that exists in most states does not mean that employers are free to unfairly evaluate employees and then use the results of the evaluation as the basis for a termination.

Discipline

Companies have the right to establish rules and policies for their workplaces as long as those rules do not violate the law. Even potentially controversial policies such as drug testing or surveillance have been upheld by the courts provided that those policies do not discriminate against or single out specific groups of employees.

Workplace rules should be properly communicated and consistently enforced. The communication process can include written policies and procedures (including an employee manual), one-on-one coaching, and formal training sessions. The enforcement process is just as important a part of the discipline process as is training. If, for example, a restaurant manager in violation of stated sanitation policies allows a cook to work without an effective hair restraint on Monday, it will be difficult for the employee to understand why the rule is enforced on Tuesday.

Many organizations implement a policy of **progressive discipline** for employees. This system is used for minor work rule infractions and some major ones. In a progressive disciplinary system, employees pass through a series of stages, each designed to help the employee comply with stated organizational workplace rules.

Progressive disciplinary systems usually follow five steps:

1. *Verbal warning:* In this first step, the employee is reminded/informed of the workplace rule and its importance. The employee is clearly told what constitutes a violation and how to avoid these violations in the future.
2. *Documented verbal warning:* In step 2, the supervisor makes a written record of the verbal reprimand, and the document is signed by both the supervisor and employee. One copy is given to the employee and one copy is retained in the employee's file.
3. *Written warning:* An official, written reprimand is the third step, generally accompanied by a plan for stopping the unwanted behavior and setting forth the consequences if the behavior does not stop. This document is placed in the employee's file.
4. *Suspension:* In this step, the employee is placed on paid or unpaid leave for a length of time designated by management. A record of the suspension, its length and conditions, is placed in the employee's file.
5. *Termination:* As a last option, the employee is terminated for continued and willful disregard of the workplace rule.

LEGALESE

Wrongful termination: An employer's violation of the employment relationship resulting in the unlawful firing of the employee.

Progressive discipline: An employee development process that provides increasingly severe consequences for continued violation of workplace rules.

In all of these steps, a written record of the action is required. Figure 8.9 is an example of a form that can be used to document the steps in the progressive discipline process.

Not all incidents of workplace rule violations are subject to progressive discipline. Destruction of property, carrying weapons, falsifying records, substance abuse while on the job, and some safety violations may be cause for immediate termination; in fact, failure to do so may place the employer in greater legal risk than not terminating the employee. Employers should make it clear that they reserve the right to immediately terminate an employee for a serious workplace violation as part of the progressive disciplinary procedure.

Termination

Although states and the federal government give employers wide latitude in the hiring and firing of workers, the at-will employment doctrine does not allow an employer unrestricted freedom to terminate employees. An employer may not legally terminate an employee if it is done:

1. *In violation of company employee manuals or handbooks:* Employers must follow their own manuals or handbooks. Failure to follow the procedures outlined in employee manuals and handbooks could result in legal action against the employer because of the implied contract that such documents may establish.
2. *To deny accrued benefits:* These benefits can include bonuses, insurance premiums, wages, stock or retirement options, and time off with pay. If, however, the employee is fired for cause, the firing could be legal and the accrued benefits may be forfeited.
3. *Because of legitimate illness or absence from work:* This is especially true if the employee was injured at work and has filed a workers' compensation claim. Should the absence become excessive, however, the employer may be able to force the employee to accept disability status.

Employee's Progressive Performance Review

Date ____________________

Employee's Name: ____________________

Employee's Position: ____________________

Type of Action for this Discussion:

_____ Oral Warning _____Written Warning _____Probation _____Suspension

Employer's view of the violation: ____________________

____

____

Employee's view of the violation: ____________________

____

____

Is the employee being placed on probation? ___No ___Yes, until what date: ___/___/___

Is the employee being suspended? ___No ___Yes, until what date: ___/___/___

What specific action steps have been agreed upon between the employee and supervisor to improve and/or resolve the violation? (action steps and date): ____________________

____

____

I have reviewed and discussed this performance violation with my supervisor and understand the terms listed above to correct my performance.

____________________ ____________________

Employee's signature Date

____________________ ____________________

Employer's representative signature Date

____________________ ____________________

Signature of Human Resources witness Date

FIGURE 8.9 **Progressive discipline form.**

4. *For attempting to unionize coworkers:* Some employers are reluctant to allow this type of activity to occur, but it is a right protected by federal law.
5. *For reporting violations of law:* In some states, private business **whistle-blowers protection acts** have been passed to ensure that employees who report violations of the law by their employers will not be terminated unjustly. These laws penalize employers that retaliate against workers who report suspected violations of health, safety, financial, or other regulations and laws.
6. *For belonging to a protected class of workers:* Employers may not fire an employee because he or she is over 40; is of a particular race, color, religion, gender, or national origin; or is disabled. In addition, employers may not treat these workers any differently than they would those workers who are not members of a protected class.
7. *Without notice:* This applies to some circumstances related to massive layoffs or facility closings. In general, larger employers are covered by the Worker Adjustment and Retraining Notification (WARN) Act of 1989. WARN provides protection to workers, their families, and their communities by requiring employers to provide notification 60 calendar days in advance of plant closings and mass layoffs. A covered plant closing occurs when a facility or operating unit is shut down for more than six months or when 50 or more employees lose their jobs during any 30-day period at the single site of employment.

Consider the case of the Mayflower Hotel, a large, independent facility employing 150 people. The hotel is purchased by new owners on June 1. On June 2, the new owners

LEGALESE

Whistle-blowers protection acts: Laws that protect employees who have reported illegal employer acts from retaliation by that employer.

announce that all employees hired by the previous owners will be terminated from employment and then rehired by the new ones. But employees will be subject to review before rehiring. In such a circumstance, the WARN Act would allow any employees who prefer not to work for the new company the time required to secure other employment.

8. *If the employee has been verbally promised continued employment:* The courts have ruled, in some cases, that a verbal employment contract is in effect if an employer publicly and continually assures an employee of the security of his or her employment.
9. *In violation of a written employment contract:* This is true whether the contract is written for an individual worker or the worker is a member of a labor union that has a collective bargaining agreement (CBA).

In some cases, an employer may be called on to produce evidence that an employee was terminated legitimately and legally. The seven guidelines in the Legally Managing at Work section can be used to ensure that terminations are defensible, should the need arise.

Employee termination reflects a failure on the part of both the employer and employee. The employee has performed in a substandard manner, but perhaps the employer has improperly selected or poorly trained and managed that person. The details of these failures need not be shared with those who do not have a need to know. Nothing is gained by confiding this information with others; in fact, greater employer liability is incurred when management shares details of an employee's termination with others.

In-House Dispute Resolution

The cost of a lawsuit is very high. In the case of employment litigation, many companies have found that the cost of defending themselves against the charges of an unfair employment

Legally Managing at Work

Guidelines for Conducting Defensible Employee Terminations

1. *Conduct and document regular employee evaluations.*

   It is the rare employee whose performance becomes extremely poor overnight. Generally, employee performance problems can be identified in regular employee evaluation sessions. These evaluations should be performed in a thoughtful, timely manner with an opportunity for employee to provide input. These written evaluations should be reviewed by upper management to ensure consistency between and among reviewers.

2. *Develop and enforce written policies and procedures.*

   As a manager, you may set yourself up for accusations that your discharge policies are unfair if you cannot show that employees were informed in writing of the organization's rules of employee conduct. All employees should be given a copy of any employment rules both because it is a good employment practice and to help avoid potential lawsuits. Employees should be given the chance to thoroughly review these rules and ask questions about them, and then they should be required to sign a document stating they have done so. This document should be placed in the employee's personnel file.

3. *Prohibit "on-the-spot" terminations.*

   The hospitality industry is fast paced, and tensions can sometimes run very high. Despite that, it is never a good idea to allow a supervisor or manager to terminate an employee without adequate consideration. This is not to say that a violent employee, for example, should not be required to leave the property immediately if his or her presence poses a danger to others. It does say, however, that terminations made in the heat of the moment can be very hard to defend when the emotion of the moment has subsided.

4. *Develop and utilize a progressive disciplinary system.*

   Make sure that each step of the disciplinary process is reviewed by at least one person other than the documenting manager and the employee. A representative from the human resources department or in small properties, the general manager of the facility is a good choice.

5. *Review all documentation prior to discharging an employee.*

   Because of the serious nature of employee termination, it is a good idea to thoroughly review all documentation prior to dismissing an employee. If the evidence supports termination, it should be undertaken. If it does not, the organization will be put at risk if the discharge is undertaken despite the lack of documentation. If a progressive disciplinary process is in place, each step in that process should be followed every time. In this way, you can defend yourself against charges of discriminatory or arbitrary actions.

6. *When possible, conduct a termination review and exit interview.*

   Employees are less likely to sue their former employers if they understand why they have been terminated. Some employers, however, make it a policy to refuse to tell employees why they have been let go, citing the at-will status of employment as their rationale. Each approach has its advantages and disadvantages. An employee who is shown documented evidence of his or her consistent, excessive absence, along with the results of a well-implemented progressive discipline program, is less likely to sue, claiming unfair treatment because of nonrelated demographic issues such as gender, race, ethnicity, and other protected class status.

7. *Treat information regarding terminations as confidential.*

   In the most common case, an employee's discharge will be initiated by the employee's supervisor or manager and should be reviewed prior to implementation by the immediate superior of that supervisor or manager. The actual exit interview may be witnessed by a representative from human resources or a second manager.

practice often exceeds the amount of the employee's claim of damages. For example, a simple dispute in which an employee asks for damages in the amount of $5,000 may cost the employer five times that amount to defend the charge.

The cost to employees for pursuing such an unfair employment claim is high also. Because the employee who charges an employer with an unfair practice is often no longer employed, the employee may face great legal expense at a time he or she can least afford to do so.

Cases involving unfair employment practices may drag on for years, which not only increases legal expenses but can also diminish the likelihood of an amicable settlement between employer and employee. By the time the litigation has been completed, several years may have passed, much expense may have been incurred on both sides, witnesses are gone or no longer available, the personal relationship between the employee and employer has been damaged, and both sides may well have come to realize that having one's day in court is often too long in coming and too expensive to undertake.

Because of the disadvantages just listed, a system of resolving disputes between employers and employees that is gaining widespread acceptance is the **in-house dispute resolution** process. It is a management tool that seeks to provide three benefits:

1. *Fairness to employees:* This is achieved by involving employees in the development and implementation of the program. At a corporate level, employers should realize that the purpose of an in-house dispute resolution program is the prevention of litigation, not the winning of every dispute.
2. *Cost savings to employers:* The in-house dispute resolution program should result in reduced costs for employers. It is also important to realize that costs can be measured in terms beyond legal fees.
3. *Timely resolution of complaints:* An in-house dispute resolution program grants, as its greatest advantage, the ability to deal quickly with a problem. Sometimes, this can save the employee/employer relationship and get the employee back to work feeling that his or her concern has been heard and that the employer really cares about him or her, something that rarely happens at the conclusion of a lawsuit.

A well-designed in-house dispute resolution program can have an extremely positive effect on an organization if it is established and operated in the proper manner. Here are four features of an effective in-house dispute resolution program:

1. *Development with employee input:* Employees and employers generally will work toward developing a program that is easy to access, is perceived as fair, provides a rapid response, and includes a legitimate appeal procedure.
2. *Training for mediators:* Those individuals who will hear and help resolve disputes should be specially trained in how to do so. In some companies, these individuals are called **ombudspersons**. Effectively trained mediators can resolve up to 75 percent of all worker complaints without litigation. The resolutions can range from a simple apology to reinstatement and substantial monetary damages.
3. *Legal assistance for employees:* The best programs take into account that employees may need advice from their own legal counsel, and thus payment for this advice is provided. While it might seem strange to fund the legal counsel of an employee in a work-related dispute, the reality is that costs savings will occur if an amicable solution to the problem can be developed.
4. *Distinct and unique chain of command for appeal:* Sometimes, the original finding of the review process will be perceived by the employee as unfair.

8.8 Unemployment Claims

Of the many costs related to maintaining a workforce, the cost of unemployment insurance is one of the largest and most difficult to administer. The **unemployment insurance** program is operated jointly by the federal and state governments. Each state imposes different costs on employers for maintaining the state's share of a pool of funds for assisting workers who have temporarily lost their jobs.

Figure 8.10 shown on the next page details the contribution rate charged to employers in the state of Ohio in 2014, 2015, and 2016. It is presented as an example of a method used by several states to charge higher taxes to those employers that cause more of the fund pool to be used and less to those with fewer claims. Thus, two restaurants with identical sales volume but very different experiences in maintaining staff, can pay widely different unemployment tax rates based on how well they manage their staffs and their **unemployment claims**.

A worker who submits an unemployment claim does not automatically qualify for payments. The employer has the right to challenge this claim. It is important to remember that each

LEGALESE

In-house dispute resolution: A program funded by employers that encourages the equitable settlement of an employee's claim of unfair employment prior to or without resorting to litigation.

Ombudsperson: A company official appointed to investigate and resolve worker complaints.

Unemployment insurance: A program, funded by employers, that provides temporary monetary benefits for employees who have lost their jobs.

Unemployment claim: A petition, submitted by an unemployed worker to his or her state unemployment agency, which asserts that the worker is eligible to receive unemployment benefits.

Contribution Rates

For 2015, 2016 and 2017 the ranges of Ohio unemployment tax rates (also known as contribution rates) are as follows:

	2015	2016	2017	
Lowest Experience Rate	0.3%	0.3%	0.3%	
Highest Experience Rate	8.6%	8.7%	8.8%	
Mutualized Rate	0.0%	0.0%	0.6%	
New Employer Rate	2.7%	2.7%	2.7%	
*Construction Industry	6.5%	6.4%	6.2%	*except construction
Delinquency Rate	10.8%	10.9%	11.8%	

Rate Notification

Contribution Rate Determinations are mailed for the coming calendar year on or before December 1. The tax rate is also printed on the employer's Quarterly Tax Return (JFS-20127), which is mailed to employers quarterly for reporting and payment of taxes due. To determine how much tax is due each quarter, multiply the rate by the total taxable wages you paid during the quarter.

Experience Rate

Once an employer's account has been chargeable with benefits for four consecutive calendar quarters ending June 30, the account becomes eligible for an experience rate beginning with the next calendar year. The experience includes taxable wages reported, contributions paid (including voluntary payments) and benefits charged. Unemployment taxes paid are credited to an employer's account. Unemployment benefits paid to eligible claimants are charged to the accounts of the claimant's employers during the base period of the claim. These factors are recorded on the employer's account and are used to compute the annual tax rate after the employer becomes eligible for an experience rate.

Due to economic conditions and unemployment claims filed, the Ohio Unemployment Compensation Trust Fund is more than sixty percent below the "minimum safe level" as of the computation date of the 2017 rates (The "minimum safe level" is, in essence, the balance required in the UC Trust Fund to fund a moderate recession). Therefore, the tax rate schedule in effect for 2017 includes an across the board minimum safe level increase to protect the financial integrity of the trust fund. This increase will help re-build the trust fund to the appropriate level. The additional taxes paid as a result of the minimum safe level increase are credited fifty percent (50%) to the mutualized account and fifty percent (50%) to the employer's account.

The experience rate shown on the Contribution Rate Determination is a combined total of the employer's individual experience rate and the minimum safe level increase.

Mutualized Rate

The primary purpose of the mutualized account is to maintain the unemployment trust fund at a safe level and recover the costs of unemployment benefits that are not chargeable to individual employers. These costs are recovered and the money restored to the fund through the mutualized tax levied on all contributory employers. The mutualized tax is used solely for the payment of benefits. For calendar year 2016, the mutualized rate is 0.0%.

In June 2016, Governor Kasich signed HB 390 giving ODJFS the authority to pay off the remaining balance of the Federal Unemployment loan using state funds. This early payoff means employers will see a reduction of $72 per employee in their overall Federal/State unemployment cost. Without the early payoff, Ohio employers would have been assessed an additional 1.8% per employee in FUTA taxes.

To replenish the state loan, experienced rated employers will pay an additional rate on their 2017 state unemployment quarterly reports. This additional rate (0.6%) will be listed in the Mutual Rate portion of the 2017 rate notice. Money collected from this additional rate will be used to repay the state loan. If you have any questions, please do not hesitate to contact the Contribution Section at 614-466-2319.

New Employer Rate

If an employer's account is not eligible for an experience rate, the account will be assigned a standard new employer rate of 2.7% unless the employer is engaged in the construction industry, in which case the 2015 rate is 6.5%, the 2016 rate is 6.4% and the 2017 rate is 6.2%.

Delinquency Rate

Employers who did not furnish the wage information necessary for the computation of their 2017 experience rate by the time the 2017 rates were calculated, are assigned a contribution rate equal to one hundred

FIGURE 8.10 Unemployment tax rates for Ohio.
Source: Ohio Job and Family Services, available at jfs.ohio.gov/ouc/uctax/rates.stm

twenty-five percent (125%) of the maximum experience rate possible for 2017. However, if the employer files the necessary wage information by December 31, 2016, the rate will be revised to the appropriate experience rate.

Penalty Rate

Employers who file the necessary wage information after December 31, 2016, but within 18 months after that date, will have their 2017 rate revised to one hundred twenty percent (120%) of the rate that would have applied if the employer had timely furnished the wage information.

FIGURE 8.10 *(continued)*

successful claim will have an impact on the employer's experience rate, which is the rate by which future contributions to the unemployment fund are determined. Thus, it is in your best interest, as an employer, to protest any unjust claim for unemployment benefits made by your ex-employees.

Criteria for Granting or Denying Benefits

Each state will set its own criteria for determining who is eligible for unemployment benefits. Variances can occur based on answers to any of the following questions:

- How soon can the unemployed worker petition for benefits?
- When will any allowable payments begin?
- What will the amount of the payments be?
- How long will the payments last?
- What must the unemployed worker do in order to qualify and continue receiving benefits?
- How long does the employee have to work for the former employer in order to qualify for assistance?

Generally speaking, an employee who quits his or her job for a nonwork-related reason is not eligible for benefits. Employees who are terminated, except for good cause associated with their work performance, generally are eligible. Again, the laws in this area are complex and vary widely; thus, it is a good idea to thoroughly understand who is eligible for unemployment benefits in the state where you work. This can be accomplished by visiting a branch of your state agency responsible for administering unemployment compensation benefits.

The following are common examples of acts that usually justify the denial of unemployment benefits based on employee misconduct:

- Insubordination or fighting on the job.
- Habitual lateness or excessive absence.
- Drug abuse on the job.
- Disobedience of legitimate company work rules or policies.
- Gross negligence or neglect of duty.
- Dishonesty.

Claims and Appeals

If the state agency responsible for granting unemployment benefits receives a request for unemployment assistance from an unemployed worker, the employer will be notified and given a chance to dispute the claim. It is important that you, as an employer, respond to any unemployment claims or requests for information in a timely manner.

An employer should not protest legitimate unemployment benefit payments. It is appropriate, however, to protest those that are not legitimate. Employers often have difficulty proving that workers should not qualify for unemployment benefits, even in situations that might seem relatively straightforward. In addition, the state unemployment agents who determine whether or not to grant benefits often initially decide in favor of the employee. An employer who does not agree with the state's decision has the right to appeal.

In an appeal of unemployment benefits, each party has the right to take these steps:

1. Speak on his or her own behalf.
2. Present documents and evidence.
3. Request that others (witnesses) speak on his or her behalf.
4. Question those witnesses and parties who oppose his or her position.
5. Examine and respond to the evidence of the other side.
6. Make a statement at the end of the appeals hearing.

An unemployment hearing is often no different from a trial. Witnesses must testify under oath. Documents, including personnel information, warnings, and performance appraisals, are submitted as exhibits. The atmosphere is usually not friendly. You must organize your case before the hearing to maximize your chances of success. If you have elected to have a lawyer help you, meet with him or her before the hearing to review your position.

Analyze the Situation 8.4

Carolyn Moreau was employed for nine years as a room attendant for the Windjammer Hotel. The hotel was moderately busy during the week and filled up with tourists on the weekends.

In accordance with hotel policy, Ms. Moreau submitted a request on May 1 for time off on Saturday, May 15, to attend the graduation ceremony of her only daughter. The hotel was extremely short handed on the weekend of the 15th due to some staff resignations and a forecasted sellout of rooms. Ms. Moreau's supervisor denied her request for the day off. She was visibly upset when the schedule was posted and she learned that her supervisor had denied her request. She confronted her supervisor and stated, "I am attending my daughter's graduation. No way am I going to miss it!" The supervisor replied that she was sorry, but all requests for that particular weekend off had been denied and Ms. Moreau was to report to work as scheduled.

On the Saturday of the graduation, Ms. Moreau called in sick four hours before her shift was to begin. The supervisor, recalling the conversation with her, recorded the call-in as "unacceptable excuse," and filled out a form stating that Ms. Moreau had quit her job voluntarily by refusing to work her assigned shift. The supervisor referred to the portion of the employee manual that Ms. Moreau signed when joining the hotel. The manual read, in part:

Employees shall be considered to have voluntarily quit or abandoned their employment upon any of the following occurrences:

1. Absence from work for one (1) or more consecutive days without excuse acceptable to the company;
2. Habitual tardiness;
3. Failure to report to work within 24 hours of a request to report.

Ms. Moreau returned to work the next day to find that she had been removed from the schedule. She was informed that she was no longer an employee of the hotel. She filed for unemployment compensation. In her state, workers who voluntarily quit their jobs were not eligible for unemployment compensation.

1. Do you believe Ms. Moreau was terminated or that she resigned from her position?
2. Do you believe she is eligible for unemployment compensation?
3. Whose position would you prefer to defend in the unemployment compensation hearing? Why?

Decisions are not typically obtained immediately after the hearing. You will probably be notified by mail of the judge's decision. If you lose the decision, read the notice carefully. Most judges and hearing examiners give specific reasons for their rulings, and this information may help you avoid claims in the future.

8.9 Employment Records and Retention

Several federal and state agencies require employers to keep employee records on file or to post information relative to employment rules and regulation. Although the number of requirements is large and can frequently change, the following examples will illustrate the type of responsibility employers have for maintaining accurate employment records.

Department of Labor (DOL) Records

Every employer subject to the Fair Labor Standards Act (FLSA) must maintain the following records for every employee:

- Employee's full name and social security number.
- Address, including zip code.
- Birthdate, if younger than 19.
- Sex and occupation.
- Time and day of week when employee's workweek begins.
- Hours worked each day.
- Total hours worked each workweek.
- Basis on which employee's wages are paid (e.g., "$9 per hour," "$440 a week," "piecework").
- Regular pay rate.
- Total daily or weekly straight-time earnings.
- Total overtime earnings for the workweek.
- All additions to or deductions from the employee's wages.
- Total wages paid each pay period.
- Date of payment and the pay period covered by the payment.

DOL Records on Employee Meals and Lodging

Every employer that makes deductions from wages for meals, uniforms, or lodging must keep records substantiating the cost of providing these items and cannot deduct expenses that would reduce the employee's wage below the minimum wage. For example, David Pung manages a cafeteria in the southwest. As part of his employees' compensation, they are allowed one meal per four-hour work shift. Employees who participate in this meal program are charged a rate of $0.25 per hour worked, or $1.00 per meal. Mr. Pung must document both the deductions he makes for the meal (according to the preceding list) and the cost of providing the meal. Since it is impossible to determine the cost of each employee's meal, Mr. Pung uses a method whereby the cost of the meal is determined by the following formula:

1. Total food sales less gross operating profit.
2. Equals cost of all meals provided.
3. Divided by total meals served (including all employee meals).
4. Equals cost per meal served.

Mr. Pung documents this cost on a monthly basis using his profit and loss statement as the source of his sales and gross operating profit figures and using a daily customer count as his total number of meals served. Generally, the DOL will provide a good deal of latitude as to how an employer computes the cost per employee meal or costs of providing other services. These costs must be computed and maintained in the employer's records.

DOL Records for Tipped Employees

All employers must keep the following records for tipped employees:

- A symbol, letter, or other notation placed on the pay records identifying each employee whose wage is determined in part by tips.
- Weekly or monthly amount reported by the employee to the employer of tips received.
- Amount by which the wages of each tipped employee have been deemed to be increased by tips as determined by the employer (not in excess of the difference between $2.13 and the applicable minimum wage). The amount per hour that the employer takes as a tip credit shall be reported to the employee in writing each time it is changed from the amount per hour taken in the preceding week.
- Hours worked each workday in any occupation in which the employee does not receive tips and total daily or weekly straight-time payment made by the employer for such hours.
- Hours worked each workday in occupations in which the employee receives tips and total daily or weekly straight-time earnings for such hours.[2]

In larger organizations, the payroll department will maintain the records required by the DOL. It is important to remember, however, that it is the facility manager who is responsible for producing these records if required to do so by the DOL. Under current DOL rules, employers must maintain their records for the following time periods.

For Three Years

- Payroll records.
- Certificates, agreements, plans, notices, etc., including without limitation collective bargaining agreements, plans, trusts, and employment contracts.
- Sale and purchase records, including the total dollar volume of sales or business and total volume of goods purchased or received during such periods (weekly, monthly, quarterly, etc.).

For Two Years

- Basic employment and earnings records, including from the date of last entry, all basic time and earning cards or sheets on which are entered the daily starting and ending times of individual employees.
- Wage rate tables used in computing straight-time earnings, wages, or salary or overtime pay computation.

DOL Records on Family and Medical Leave

The federal Family and Medical Leave Act (FMLA) requires employers to maintain the following records for at least three years:

- Basic payroll and identifying employee data.
- Dates FMLA leave is taken by FMLA-eligible employees (leave must be designated in records as FMLA leave), including the hours of the leave if FMLA leave is taken in increments of less than one full day.
- Copies of employee notices of leave provided to the employer under the FMLA, if in writing, and copies of all eligibility notices given to employees as required under the FMLA (copies may be maintained in employee personnel files).
- Any documents (including written and electronic records) describing employee benefits or employer policies and practices regarding the taking of paid and unpaid leave.
- Premium payments of employee benefits.
- Records of any dispute between the employer and an eligible employee regarding designation of leave as FMLA leave, including any written statement from the employer or employee of the reasons for designation and for the disagreement.

Immigration-Related Records

As discussed in Chapter 7, the Immigration Reform and Control Act (IRCA) requires employers to complete an employment eligibility verification form (Form I-9) for all employees hired after November 6, 1986. Employers must retain all I-9 forms for three years after the employee is hired or one year after the employee leaves, whichever is later.

Records Required by the ADEA

The federal Age Discrimination in Employment Act (ADEA) requires that employers retain employee records that contain

[2] https://www.dol.gov/whd/regs/compliance/WH1261.pdf

the employee's name, address, date of birth (established only after the hiring decision), occupation, rate of pay, and weekly compensation. In addition, records on all personnel matters, including terminations and benefit plans, must be kept for at least one year from the date of the action taken.

As can be seen from the list of recordkeeping requirements just given, these stipulations in the hospitality industry are varied, complex, and sometimes overlapping. As a manager, it is important for you to ensure that your facility's recordkeeping is current and complete. An employment attorney who specializes in hospitality employment law can be very helpful in ensuring compliance in this area.

8.10 Employment Posting

Often, regulatory agencies will require that certain employment-related information be posted in an area where all employees can see it. The following regulations are examples:

- DOL regulations require that every employer subject to the FLSA post, in a conspicuous place, a notice explaining the FLSA. Posters can be obtained by contacting a regional office of the DOL.
- EEOC regulations require that every employer subject to Title VII of the Civil Rights Act of 1964 and the Americans with Disabilities Act of 1990 post in a conspicuous place a notice relating to discrimination prohibited by such laws. These posters may be combined, and they can be obtained by contacting a regional office of the EEOC.
- OSHA regulations require that every employer post in a conspicuous place a notice informing employees of the protections and obligations under OSHA. Posters can be obtained by contacting a regional office of OSHA.
- DOL regulations require that every employer post in a prominent and conspicuous place a notice explaining the Employee Polygraph Protection Act of 1988. Posters can be obtained by contacting a regional DOL office.
- DOL regulations require that every employer subject to the Family and Medical Leave Act post in a conspicuous place in the establishment a notice (as shown in Figure 8.11) explaining this federal leave law. Posters can be obtained by contacting a regional DOL office.

8.11 Workplace Surveillance

According to www.business.com in 2014, 82 percent of managers use some type of electronic monitoring in the workplace. Some common procedures include listening in on phone calls, reviewing voice mails, monitoring email and computer files (such as sites visited on the Internet), or some form of video surveillance. That number is even higher if you add in the companies that monitor their employees in other ways such as by conducting locker, bag, and desk searches.

Unfortunately, there is no one national policy that you can look to for guidance regarding privacy in the workplace. Many companies believe that they are protecting their proprietary business interests by monitoring employees and their work product. Additionally, as companies establish work conduct guidelines (such as zero tolerance sexual harassment policies) to comply with the law, monitoring employees enables the employer to ensure compliance. Even though the law is difficult to pin down in this area, a few general principles can be established by reviewing a cross-section of federal and state laws and court cases.

Whether or not a particular monitoring technique is legal usually depends on four factors:

1. *Did the employee have a legitimate expectation of privacy as to the item searched or the information, conversation, or area monitored?* In an employee lounge, probably not; in a restroom, absolutely!
2. *Has the employer provided advance notice to the employees and/or obtained consent for the monitoring activity from the employees?* If so, it is difficult for employees to argue that they had an expectation of privacy.
3. *Was the monitoring performed for a work-related purpose, and was it reasonable given all of the circumstances?* Generally, the courts have allowed searches and monitoring that seem to be necessary for operating a business (e.g., protecting trade secrets, enforcing policies and procedures, and ensuring high-quality service levels).
4. *Was the search or monitoring done in a reasonable or appropriate manner?* Was it discriminatory? In other words, was it utilized only on a minority work subgroup?

If you do elect to monitor specific activities of employees, adopting the Employee Privacy Policy, shown in Figure 8.12 on page 168, is a good way to minimize any misunderstandings or legal difficulties. Let your employees know exactly what is expected of them, and give them a chance to question any part of your policy that are unclear to them. Because the laws in this area are complex and vary by location, it is a good idea to have your attorney review your company's monitoring/privacy policy before it is implemented.

Obviously, it is in the best interest of both employers and employees to work together to create a workplace that is productive for management and fair to all employees. As a hospitality manager, your legal liability will definitely be affected by your ability to achieve this goal. Following the guidelines presented in this chapter will help you manage your operation legally and reduce your risk of liability.

EMPLOYEE RIGHTS

UNDER THE FAMILY AND MEDICAL LEAVE ACT

THE UNITED STATES DEPARTMENT OF LABOR WAGE AND HOUR DIVISION

LEAVE ENTITLEMENTS

Eligible employees who work for a covered employer can take up to 12 weeks of unpaid, job-protected leave in a 12-month period for the following reasons:

- The birth of a child or placement of a child for adoption or foster care;
- To bond with a child (leave must be taken within 1 year of the child's birth or placement);
- To care for the employee's spouse, child, or parent who has a qualifying serious health condition;
- For the employee's own qualifying serious health condition that makes the employee unable to perform the employee's job;
- For qualifying exigencies related to the foreign deployment of a military member who is the employee's spouse, child, or parent.

An eligible employee who is a covered servicemember's spouse, child, parent, or next of kin may also take up to 26 weeks of FMLA leave in a single 12-month period to care for the servicemember with a serious injury or illness.

An employee does not need to use leave in one block. When it is medically necessary or otherwise permitted, employees may take leave intermittently or on a reduced schedule.

Employees may choose, or an employer may require, use of accrued paid leave while taking FMLA leave. If an employee substitutes accrued paid leave for FMLA leave, the employee must comply with the employer's normal paid leave policies.

BENEFITS & PROTECTIONS

While employees are on FMLA leave, employers must continue health insurance coverage as if the employees were not on leave.

Upon return from FMLA leave, most employees must be restored to the same job or one nearly identical to it with equivalent pay, benefits, and other employment terms and conditions.

An employer may not interfere with an individual's FMLA rights or retaliate against someone for using or trying to use FMLA leave, opposing any practice made unlawful by the FMLA, or being involved in any proceeding under or related to the FMLA.

ELIGIBILITY REQUIREMENTS

An employee who works for a covered employer must meet three criteria in order to be eligible for FMLA leave. The employee must:

- Have worked for the employer for at least 12 months;
- Have at least 1,250 hours of service in the 12 months before taking leave;* and
- Work at a location where the employer has at least 50 employees within 75 miles of the employee's worksite.

*Special "hours of service" requirements apply to airline flight crew employees.

REQUESTING LEAVE

Generally, employees must give 30-days' advance notice of the need for FMLA leave. If it is not possible to give 30-days' notice, an employee must notify the employer as soon as possible and, generally, follow the employer's usual procedures.

Employees do not have to share a medical diagnosis, but must provide enough information to the employer so it can determine if the leave qualifies for FMLA protection. Sufficient information could include informing an employer that the employee is or will be unable to perform his or her job functions, that a family member cannot perform daily activities, or that hospitalization or continuing medical treatment is necessary. Employees must inform the employer if the need for leave is for a reason for which FMLA leave was previously taken or certified.

Employers can require a certification or periodic recertification supporting the need for leave. If the employer determines that the certification is incomplete, it must provide a written notice indicating what additional information is required.

EMPLOYER RESPONSIBILITIES

Once an employer becomes aware that an employee's need for leave is for a reason that may qualify under the FMLA, the employer must notify the employee if he or she is eligible for FMLA leave and, if eligible, must also provide a notice of rights and responsibilities under the FMLA. If the employee is not eligible, the employer must provide a reason for ineligibility.

Employers must notify its employees if leave will be designated as FMLA leave, and if so, how much leave will be designated as FMLA leave.

ENFORCEMENT

Employees may file a complaint with the U.S. Department of Labor, Wage and Hour Division, or may bring a private lawsuit against an employer.

The FMLA does not affect any federal or state law prohibiting discrimination or supersede any state or local law or collective bargaining agreement that provides greater family or medical leave rights.

For additional information or to file a complaint:

1-866-4-USWAGE

(1-866-487-9243) TTY: 1-877-889-5627

www.dol.gov/whd

U.S. Department of Labor | Wage and Hour Division

WH1420 REV 04/16

FIGURE 8.11 **Employee rights under the Family and Medical Leave Act of 1993.**
https://www.dol.gov/whd/regs/compliance/posters/fmlaen.pdf

Policy Regarding Employee Privacy

The Company respects the individual privacy of its employees. However, an employee may not expect privacy rights to be extended to work-related conduct or the use of company-owned equipment supplies, systems, or property. The purpose of this policy is to notify you that no reasonable expectation of privacy exists in connection with your use of such equipment, supplies, systems, or property, including computer files, computer databases, office cabinets, or lockers. It is for that reason the following policy should be read; if you do not understand it, ask for clarification before you sign it.

I, __________________, understand that all electronic communications systems and all information transmitted by, received from, or stored in these systems are the property of the Company. I also understand that these systems are to be used solely for job-related purposes and not for personal purposes, and that I do nut have any personal privacy right in connection with the use of this equipment or with the transmission, receipt, or storage of information in this equipment.

I consent to the Company monitoring my use of company equipment at any time at its discretion. Such monitoring may include printing and reading all electronic mail entering, leaving, or stored in these systems.

I agree to abide by this Company policy and I understand that the policy prohibits me from using electronic communication systems to transmit lewd, offensive, or racially related messages.

______________________________ ______________

Signature of employee Date

FIGURE 8.12 **Employee privacy policy.**

International Snapshot

Managing Employees Abroad

Today's hoteliers may be called on to travel to different countries to manage hospitality facilities. The laws and regulations governing employment vary from country to country, sometimes in ways that are subtle but just as often in ways that are fundamental. Some of the most common and most obvious examples are described here.

The Nature of the Employment Relationship

In most places in the United States, an employer or employee may terminate the employment relationship at any time for any lawful reason or no reason at all; this is often referred to as "employment at will." Although this notion seems natural in the United States, it often does not apply overseas.

To the contrary, many countries have laws that are much more protective of employees' rights to retain their employment. Such laws may explicitly define the permissible reasons for terminating the employment relationship, or they may more broadly prohibit termination except in the most egregious of circumstances. There may be more intensive regulation of layoffs for economic or operational reasons (sometimes called "retrenchment" or "redundancy").

Many countries require employment contracts, and where they are not in place, contract terms are implied. It is common for minimum contract terms to include a notice period (under which both the employee and the employer must give advance notice of a number of months) before the employment relationship is terminated.

In some cases, an employer may simply be prohibited from terminating the employment relationship; if the law is violated, the government may require that the employee be reinstated. In other cases, the employer can end the relationship by the payment of a defined monetary amount, sometimes called "redundancy payments."

Unions and Works Councils

In the United States, individual hotel properties are sometimes organized by unions, and this is more prevalent in some markets than others. In most cases, collective bargaining agreements are negotiated by each property, although sometimes a group of hotels in a market area will engage in multiunit bargaining.

By contrast, unions in many European countries are organized on a national level and agreements are in place with the entire industry for all employers nationwide. Local or company matters are often addressed through work councils. Unions and work councils may be required under law. If management wants to implement changes, even some that do not appear to affect the workforce, it may be required to inform or consult with the appropriate work council.

Work Permits

Some countries protect their citizens' right to work by prohibiting the employment of foreigners except with special permission of the government. Employers may be required to look first to the local population for all employment needs at every level. Sometimes permits are easily obtainable for executive-level management or for persons who have scarce skill sets. Often, though, the employer will be required to demonstrate its efforts to hire employees within the jurisdiction before permits are issued. As a result, it may be more difficult, and it may take more time to fill key vacancies.

Application of U.S. Laws in Foreign Countries

Employers based in the United States (or controlled by U.S. companies) that employ U.S. citizens in locations outside of the country are subject to most of the antidiscrimination laws discussed earlier in this chapter

(continued)

with respect to those U.S. citizens. This can create significant challenges where the cultural norms and even government regulations conflict with rights protected under U.S. law (consider Title VII's prohibition of sex discrimination in the context of legal regimes in some Middle Eastern countries). The U.S. discrimination laws do not apply to non-citizens of the United States in operations outside the United States.

Conversely, multinational companies that operate in the United States are subject to the laws of the United States to the same extent as are U.S. employers. Just as managers familiar with U.S. employment laws must be aware of potentially drastic differences in employment laws (and the respective effect on operations) when they move abroad, companies entering the United States must adjust to employment laws and regulations that differ in the places from which they came.

Other Differences

These examples demonstrate just a few of the more common and obvious differences between U.S. employment laws and those that may be typical in other countries. There are likely to be other significant differences in such areas as minimum wages and methods of compensation, required compliance with government welfare benefits programs, workplace safety standards, and taxation schemes. Upon beginning work in any foreign country, every manager should quickly become familiar not just with local customs and practices but with the laws that must be observed with respect to the hotel's employees.

Provided by David Comeaux, an in-house employment lawyer at a global company.

WHAT WOULD YOU DO?

Naomi Yip is the sous chef at one of the city clubs managed by Clubs International, a company that specializes in the operation of golf, city, and other private clubs. The company manages over 50 clubs nationally. Ms. Yip has been with the organization for five years and is considered one of the company's best and brightest culinary artists.

Thomas Hayhoe is the executive chef at the club where Ms. Yip works and is her immediate supervisor. Her annual evaluations have been very good, and she has been designated as "ready for promotion" in her past two evaluations. In January, Ms. Yip announces she is pregnant and her due date is in July. In March, Chef Hayhoe completes his annual evaluation of Ms. Yip. He does not recommend her for promotion to executive chef, her next step up, citing, "the extraordinary demands on time placed on an executive chef within the Clubs International organization," which he claims Ms. Yip will be unable to meet. Chef Hayhoe also cites conversations he has overheard with Ms. Yip in which she declared, "I'm looking forward to spending as much time as possible with my baby."

Clubs International has just been awarded the contract to operate a new and lucrative account, the Hawk Hollow Golf Club. Assume that you were the human resource director advising the company's vice president of operations.

1. Do you feel Chef Hayhoe's evaluation of Ms. Yip is valid?
2. Based on Chef Hayhoe's recommendation, would you advocate that Ms. Yip be named the executive chef's position at the new account?
3. How would you respond if the new client objected to the appointment of Ms. Yip based on her pregnancy?

WHAT DID YOU LEARN IN THIS CHAPTER?

It is a good practice to define the employment relationship between employers and employees. The agreement can be spelled out in an offer letter. An employee manual can help employees understand what is expected from them and set out policies and procedures for the workplace.

Just as you cannot discriminate illegally in the selection process, you cannot discriminate after someone has been hired. Both federal and state civil rights laws exist to protect employees against discrimination in the workplace. You must invoke a zero tolerance policy for sexual harassment and other forms of illegal discrimination. Educate your employees about appropriate and inappropriate behavior. You must also be prepared to do a thorough investigation if inappropriate behavior is brought to your attention.

The Family and Medical Leave Act (FMLA) allows most employees of larger companies to take time off to address personal issues such as the birth of a child or to take care of an injured service member.

Compensation for employees is a complex area, particularly in the hospitality industry as it is labor intensive and the primary beneficiary of the tip credit toward the minimum wage. Utilizing an objective method to evaluate employees can help to reduce potential litigation for discrimination and wrongful termination. Establishing an in-house dispute resolution program can also reduce potential liability from employee conflict or disputes. Unemployment insurance is available for employees who are discharged without cause related to the workplace (i.e., layoffs).

Certain records and documents (e.g., applications and payroll information) must be retained for a certain length of time. Also, posting information (several posters are available) that outlines employee rights in several areas must be displayed prominently in the workplace.

CHAPTER 9

Your Responsibilities as a Hospitality Operator

CHAPTER OUTLINE

9.1. Duties and Obligations of a Hospitality Operator
9.2. Theories of Liability
9.3. Legal Damages
9.4. Anatomy of a Personal Injury Lawsuit
9.5. Responding to an Incident

IN THIS CHAPTER, YOU WILL LEARN

1. To differentiate between the types of legal duties required of a hospitality operator from the consequences of the failure to exercise reasonable care in fulfilling these duties.
2. To evaluate operational activities in light of their impact on guest safety and potential legal damages.
3. To understand how a lawsuit is initiated and moves through the U.S. court system.
4. To create a checklist of the steps that should be initiated immediately following an accident.

9.1 Duties and Obligations of a Hospitality Operator

Duties of Care

Hospitality operators owe a **duty of care** to those individuals who enter their establishments. Some duties of care are rather straightforward. For example, a restaurateur has a duty of care to provide food that is safe and wholesome for guests. While hospitality operators are not required to be insurers of their guests' safety and are generally not held liable for events they could not reasonably foresee, they are required to act prudently and use reasonable care, as defined later in this chapter, to fulfill their duties of care.

Because of the wide variety of facilities they operate, hospitality managers can encounter a variety of duties of care. These include the duties:

1. *Provide a reasonably safe premise.* This would include all public space, the interior of guestrooms, dining rooms, and the exterior space that make up the operator's total physical facility.
2. *Serve food and beverages fit for consumption.* This duty of care is shared with those who supply products to a foodservice operator and include the techniques used by an operator to prepare and serve food or beverages.
3. *Serve alcoholic beverages responsibly.* Because of its extreme importance, this duty of care will be examined separately in Chapter 12, "Your Responsibilities When Serving Food and Beverages."
4. *Hire qualified employees.* This duty must be satisfied to protect yourself against charges of negligent hiring and other potential liabilities.
5. *Properly train employees.* This duty must be satisfied to protect yourself against charges of negligent staff training.
6. *Terminate employees who pose a danger to other employees or guests.* This duty must be satisfied to protect yourself against charges of negligent employee retention.

LEGALESE

Duty of care: A legal obligation that requires a particular standard of conduct.

Analyze the Situation 9.1

Alan Brandis arrived at the Golden Fox restaurant for a Friday-night fish fry. During his meal, a severe thunderstorm began, which caused the ceiling of the men's restroom to leak. After finishing his meal, Mr. Brandis entered the men's room to wash his hands. He slipped on some wet tile, which was caused by the leak in the roof. He struck his head during the fall and was severely injured.

One week later, Mr. Brandis' attorney contacted the owners of the Golden Fox with a claim for damages. The restaurant owners maintained the fall was not their responsibility, claiming they were not the insurers of guest safety. Although the owners knew of the condition of the roof, they said it leaked only during extremely heavy thunderstorms and was too old to fix without undue economic hardship. Most important, because the storm was not within their control, the owners maintained that it was not reasonable to assume they could have foreseen the severity of the storm, and thus they could not be held liable for the accident.

1. Was the severity of the storm a foreseeable event?
2. What duty of care is in question here?
3. Did the restaurant act prudently?
4. Are the restaurant's defenses valid? Why or why not?

7. *Warn about unsafe conditions.* When an operator is aware (or, in some cases, should be aware) of conditions that pose a threat to safety (such as a wet floor or broken sidewalk), those conditions must be made obvious to the guest.
8. *Safeguard guest property, especially when voluntarily accepting possession of it.* In the hospitality industry, guests may retain control of their own property (such as when they take an item into their hotel room), or the operator may take possession of it (such as when a guest's car is parked by a valet, a coat is checked, or valuables are deposited in a hotel's safety deposit box). In each case, the law will detail the duty of care you must exercise to protect guests' property.

Standards of Care

In fulfilling the duties of care just detailed, you must exercise a **standard of care** appropriate to the given situation. An appropriate standard of care is determined, in part, on the level of services a guest would reasonably expect to find in a hospitality facility. For example, a guest departing on a seven-day cruise of the Pacific would reasonably expect that the ship's staff would include a full-time doctor. The same guest visiting a quick-service restaurant at 11:00 P.M. would not expect to find a doctor on hand. In both cases, it is possible that a guest could suffer a heart attack and require medical care. The ship's standard of care, however, would include medical treatment, while the restaurant's standard of care would not.

Many disputes involving liability and negligence in the hospitality industry revolve around the question of what an appropriate standard of care should be. Like the law itself, these standards are constantly evolving. Generally speaking, you as a hospitality manager are required to apply the same diligence to achieve your standards of care as any other reasonable hospitality manager in a similar situation. Because standards are constantly changing and because the standard of care you apply may be assessed during litigation by people who are not familiar with you or your operation, you must strive to stay abreast of changing procedures and technology. To help you do that, refer back to the continuing education components of the STEM principles discussed in Chapter 1, "Prevention Philosophy."

9.2 Theories of Liability

Despite the best efforts of management, accidents involving people can and do happen in hospitality facilities. Employees and guests are subject to many of the same risks in a hospitality facility that they are subject to outside the facility. For example, it is just as possible to trip and fall in a restaurant parking lot as it is to fall in a grocery store parking lot. It is not your responsibility as a hospitality manager to ensure that accidents never happen in your facility; that would be impossible and an unreasonable expectation. It is your responsibility to operate in a manner that is as safe as possible and to react responsibly when an accident does occur. If you do not, the legal system is designed to hold you and your operation accountable.

Reasonable Care

Hospitality managers must strive to provide an environment that is safe and secure. For example, a hotel manager who rents a room with a lock on the door should be responsible for ensuring that the lock is in proper working order, which a guest would reasonably expect the hotel to provide. In fact, the concept of reasonability is so pervasive in law that it literally sets the standard of care that hospitality organizations must provide for their employees and guests. That standard is embodied in the concept of **reasonable care**.

LEGALESE

Standard of care: The industry-recognized, reasonably accepted level of performance used in fulfilling a duty of care.

Reasonable care: The degree of care that a reasonably prudent person would use in a similar situation.

Essentially, reasonable care requires you to correct potentially harmful situations that you know exist or that you could have reasonably foreseen. The level of reasonable care that must be exercised in a given situation can sometimes be difficult to establish. In the case of the manager supplying a guestroom with a working lock, the standard is quite clear. It becomes complex, however, when the guest actually uses the lock. What if the guest does not use the lock properly or forgets to use it at all? What if the guest abuses the lock to the point where it does not function and then has a theft from his or her room? Clearly, in these cases, the guest bears some or all of the responsibility for his or her own acts.

The doctrine of reasonable care places a significant burden on you as a hospitality manager. It requires that you use all of your skill and experience to operate your facility in a manner that would be consistent with that of a reasonable person (or manager) in a similar set of circumstances. The key is to anticipate issues before they arise and to take necessary preventative action to minimize the risk of damage to people and property.

Torts

A **tort** is a civil wrongful act against an individual in the same way that a crime is a wrongful act against the state. For example, a patron who drinks too much in a bar and then drives a motor vehicle is guilty of driving under the influence (DUI) of alcohol, a crime against the state. If that same driver causes an accident that injures another motorist, the intoxicated driver would be liable for commission of a tort, that is, an act that results in injury to another.

There are two types of torts: intentional and unintentional.

Intentional Torts

- Assault
- Battery
- Defamation
- Intentional infliction of emotional distress
- Intentional interference with contractual relations

Unintentional Torts

- Negligence
- Gross negligence

Negligence is the most common unintentional tort.

Many legal actions a hospitality manager will experience are those that involve torts. The following sections explain the main types of torts affecting patrons and that a hospitality manager will most likely face.

Negligence

A person or organization that has not used reasonable care in a situation is deemed to have been **negligent**. Assume, for example, that a guest dives into a resort swimming pool and injures her neck. She thought the pool was deep enough for diving, but the point where she jumped was only 4 feet deep. The pool was not marked in any way to indicate the water's depth. If a lawsuit follows and a judge decides that the resort knew, or could have foreseen, that its guests might dive into the pool, the resort could be found negligent; that is, it did not do what reasonable facility operators would do to protect their guests, such as posting signs prohibiting diving or installing visible depth markers.

Negligence is said to legally exist when all of the following four conditions have been met:

1. A legal duty of care is present.
2. The defendant has failed to provide the standard of care needed to fulfill that duty of care.
3. The defendant's failure to meet the legal duty was the **proximate cause** of the harm (i.e., the defendant had or should have had the **foreseeability** that harm would occur).
4. The plaintiff was injured or suffered damages.

If a defendant's lawyer is able to prove that one or more of the above elements for a negligence claim does not exist, then the claim for negligence will fail.

In the hospitality industry, managers not only are responsible for their own actions but, under the doctrine of *respondeat superior,* also for the work-related acts of their employees. In some cases, managers are even held responsible for the acts of their guests or guests of their guests. The degree of responsibility that a hospitality manager might have for the acts of others ordinarily depends on the foreseeability of the act. If a dangerous act or condition was foreseeable and no action was taken to warn patrons or prevent the accident, then liability will usually attach.

It is important to note that negligence can result from either the failure to do something or because something was done that probably should not have been. In the swimming pool example, the resort's negligence was the result of a failure to act. But what if the pool's depth was 4 feet and the resort incorrectly marked it as 8 feet? In this situation, if a guest dives into the pool and is injured, the resort's negligence would be the result of a specific inappropriate action it took, not inaction.

LEGALESE

Tort: An act or failure to act (not involving a breach of contract) that results in injury, loss, or damage to another (e.g., negligence is an unintentional tort, whereas battery, physically touching someone, is usually an intentional tort).

Negligent (negligence): The failure to use reasonable care.

Proximate cause: The event or activity that directly contributes to (causes) an injury or harm.

Foreseeability: The ability of a reasonable, prudent person to know or reasonably anticipate that harm, damage, or injury would occur or was likely to occur as a result of an action or omission.

Analyze the Situation 9.2

Paul and Beatrice Metz took their 11-year-old daughter Christine on a weekend skiing trip; they stayed at the St. Stratton ski resort. The St. Stratton owned and maintained four ski trails and a ski lift on its property.

One morning, Mr. and Mrs. Metz were having coffee in the ski lodge while their daughter was riding the ski lift to the top of the mountain. On the way up, the car containing Christine Metz and one other skier jumped off its cable guide and plunged 300 feet down the mountain. As a result of the fall, Christine was permanently paralyzed from the neck down.

The Metzs filed a lawsuit against the resort. Their attorney discovered that the car's connections to the cable were checked once a year by a maintenance staff person unfamiliar with the intricacies of ski cable cars. The manufacturer of the cable car recommended weekly inspections performed by a specially trained service technician.

The ski resort's corporate owners maintained that all skiers assumed risk when skiing that the manufacturer's recommendation was simply a recommendation, and that their own inspection program demonstrated they had indeed exercised reasonable care. In addition, they maintained that Christine's paralysis was the result of an unfortunate accident for which the cable car's manufacturer, not the resort, should be held responsible.

1. Did the resort exercise reasonable care?
2. What level of negligence, if any, was present? Ordinary negligence? Gross negligence?
3. What amount of money do you think a jury would recommend the resort be required to pay to compensate Christine Metz for her loss if it is found to have committed a tort against her?
4. Are the resort's defenses valid ones? Why or why not?

An operator can be considered negligent even when he or she is only partially responsible for the harm caused to another. Consider the case of a man who slips on an icy sidewalk in front of a restaurant and falls into a street with heavy traffic where he is subsequently hit by a car. The fall by itself may have caused only minor injuries, but an even greater injury occurred because he was struck by the car. It is likely that the owner of the sidewalk will face potential charges of negligence even if the majority of the damages suffered by the injured man were caused by the car, not the fall itself.

Gross Negligence

When an individual or organization behaves in a manner that demonstrates a total disregard for the welfare of others, the act is deemed to be **gross negligence**. The distinction between negligence and gross negligence is an important one for a simple reason: The penalty is usually more severe in a situation involving gross negligence than one involving ordinary negligence. That is because an operator found to have been grossly negligent may be assessed punitive damages (discussed later in the chapter) to serve as an example and to deter others from committing the same act. Often it is difficult to determine the difference between negligence and gross negligence. The difference in the eyes of a jury, however, can be millions of dollars in an award to a party that can prove it was harmed as a result of the total disregard in action or inaction of the operator.

Contributory and Comparative Negligence

Sometimes guests, through their own carelessness, can be the cause or partial cause of their own injury or harm. In legal parlance, this is called **contributory negligence**.

Consider the case of the wedding guest who attends an evening reception at a local country club. In the course of the evening, the guest leaves the clubhouse and wanders onto the golf course. Because the course is not lit at night, the guest trips over a railroad tie used to define the tee box on the third hole. The guest may claim that the club should have marked the railway tie as a hazard and that it should have reasonably foreseen that guests would leave the clubhouse and walk on the golf course. The club's attorney, however, is likely to maintain, and rightly so, that walking at night on an unlighted golf course is dangerous and the guest did not exercise reasonable care. Although many variables may determine the final outcome of this situation, the courts have held that the contributory negligence of the injured party can reduce an operator's liability for the damages suffered. Judges and juries will be able to compare the negligence of the plaintiff and the defendant when assessing responsibility for the injuries.

The doctrine of **comparative negligence** has become an acceptable way in which to recognize that reasonable care is a responsibility shared by both hospitality operators and those who claim to have been injured by them. If the court determines, for example, that a plaintiff was 25 percent responsible for his or

LEGALESE

Gross negligence: The reckless or willful failure of an individual or an organization to use even the slightest amount of reasonable care.

Contributory negligence: Negligent conduct by the complaining party (plaintiff) that contributes to the cause of his or her injuries.

Comparative negligence: Shared responsibility for the harm that results from negligence comparing the degree of negligence by the defendant with that of the plaintiff. Also known as *comparative fault.*

her injuries and the defendant was 75 percent responsible, the amount of damages awarded to the plaintiff would be reduced by 25 percent. The laws that determine comparative negligence vary widely across the 50 states. What is important for you, as a hospitality manager, to remember is not to overlook evidence of negligence on the part of the injured party during your investigation of an incident. Check with local attorneys to find out how the law works in the state in which you are operating.

Search the Web 9.1

Go to **www.findlaw.com**

1. Select: "Learn About the Law."
2. Select: "Accidents and Injuries."
3. Type: Your state and city in the Location field.
4. Select: Find Lawyers.
5. Select the name of an attorney practicing in your city.
6. Contact the attorney's office by telephone or letter and ask if he or she can help you understand how your state and/or local courts view comparative negligence in his or her practice area.

Strict Liability

In some cases, a hospitality organization can be found liable for damages to others even if it has not acted negligently or intentionally. This is because some activities are considered to be so dangerous that their very existence imposes a greater degree of responsibility on the part of the person conducting the activity. For example, if an amusement park elected to train a wild tiger as part of its promotional activities, it would be held responsible for the tiger's actions even if the park could not be proved to be negligent in the tiger's handling. This is true because keeping dangerous animals in close proximity to people is, in itself, a dangerous activity, and one that was voluntarily undertaken by the amusement park. In these types of circumstances, those who engage in the activity are judged not by their actions but by the nature of the activity itself, which creates absolute or **strict liability**.

In the hospitality industry, the greatest operational threat imposed by strict liability is that involved with the serving of food and beverages. Recently, the courts have more often begun using the doctrine of strict liability to penalize those who sell defective food and beverages. The position of the courts is that the selling of unwholesome food and beverages is, in itself, so dangerous that those who do so, even unwittingly, will be held to a limited form of strict liability.

Intentional Acts

Although the law makes a distinction between negligence and gross negligence, it reserves the greatest sanctions for those who not only do not exercise reasonable care but also commit **intentional acts** that cause harm to others. If the employees of an innkeeper intentionally invade the privacy of a guest (e.g., viewing guest behavior in a guestroom via a hidden video camera), the innkeeper is subject to severe liability, including punitive damages.

To illustrate this concept, consider this situation: It is late Friday night, about 11 P.M., and your bar is packed—210 people at last count. Your fire occupancy limit is 125, but nobody pays attention to those signs. So far, the night has been fairly peaceful. You finally have a chance to sit down for a moment, so you take a seat at the end of the bar where you can see what's going on, and you ask your bartender to pour you a long, tall, cold ginger ale.

The drink arrives, and as it touches your lips—flash!—out of the corner of your eye, you see a flurry of activity. Two guys are fighting and really going at it. You grab one guy and the bouncer grabs the other. There is blood all over the face of the guy you grabbed, and he is wailing. You notice a broken beer mug on the table. Three girls are screaming hysterically and wiping blood off their clothes and skin.

You finally get things calmed down, transport the injured patron to the hospital, and start collecting information. You find out:

- The fight started when a guy asked one of the girls to dance; she declined, and everyone at the table, including the subsequently injured patron, began laughing.
- The guy who asked the girl to dance took offense, picked up an empty beer mug, and smashed it into the face of "Mr. Laughter."
- The two guys had never seen each other before.
- The girls had never seen the "dancer" before the incident occurred.

Are you financially responsible for the injuries? Historically, the courts have decided that a hospitality operator is not responsible for damages suffered by a patron that were caused by the intentional actions of a third party who is a customer or guest. The courts' rationale is that the intentional or criminal act of a third party could not be foreseen by the operator; therefore, it would be impossible for the operator to take any precautions or preventative measures to keep it from happening.

Crimes against Guests

Recently, however, the courts in many jurisdictions have concluded that if violent acts previously occurred on a property or even if the property is in a "high-crime zone," an incident and

LEGALESE

Strict liability: Responsibility arising from the nature of a dangerous activity rather than negligence or an intentional act. Also known as *absolute liability* or *liability without fault*.

Intentional act: A willful action undertaken with or without full understanding of its consequences.

resulting injury could be considered foreseeable. Hence, the operator might be held responsible if it failed to use reasonable care in managing the establishment. Additionally, courts have concluded that even though no crime has previously occurred a property in some instances has the duty to provide additional security and can be found negligent if it does not. Some courts have awarded high-dollar judgments against hospitality facilities for negligent security. Consider the *Van Blargen* case. An assault victim sued and recovered $500,000 from the hotel property he patronized. Mr. Van Blargen was assaulted in a private outdoor area while he was walking back to his room. Since the court likened the pool area to a private passageway because of the surrounding foliage and landscape enclosures, it determined that the hotel had a duty to provide heightened security in such a private area.

Negligence per se

The barroom brawl just described does not provide enough facts to discern whether the incident and resulting injury were foreseeable by the operator. But what is readily apparent from the facts is the concept of **negligence per se**.

You may recall that the bar had more than the allowed number of patrons. Is this negligence per se? Quite possibly. The injured patron's attorney will certainly argue that the occupancy restrictions should have been maintained, not just for fire regulations but also for physical safety as well. The occupancy restrictions would have helped to maintain order. More than likely, an expert in building safety or club management would concur.

It could also be argued that the excessive occupancy contributed to the likelihood of a fight breaking out on the premises, and that likelihood should have been foreseeable by the operator. In other words, fights, altercations, and injuries are more likely to occur when there is not enough space between patrons (another reason for restrictive occupancy rules).

The moral of this story is to follow the law. It is tempting to pack the house, but there can be dire consequences if an injury occurs and you have violated an ordinance, such as excessive occupancy or serving an underage customer. Always obey local, state, and federal laws.

9.3 Legal Damages

If an injured party suffers a demonstrable loss as a result of a tort, the law requires that the entity responsible for the loss be held accountable. The process for doing so is by awarding damages to the injured party. There are two types of damages for personal injuries most likely to be encountered by a hospitality manager: compensatory damages and punitive (or exemplary) damages.

Compensatory damages are actual, identifiable damages that result from wrongful acts. Examples of actual damages include doctor, hospital, and other medical bills, pain and suffering, lost income as a result of an injury, or the actual cost of repairing damage to a piece of real or personal property. The recovery of these damages is said to "compensate" the injured party for any out-of-pocket costs incurred as a result of the accident, as well as for pain and suffering. If, for example, a maintenance worker for a hotel accidentally leaves some tools in the hallway of a hotel and a guest falls and breaks her watch, the cost of replacing the watch can be easily identified, and the hotel would likely be expected to reimburse the guest. The same could well be true of any medical bills the guest might incur due to the fall.

Punitive damages seek to serve as a deterrent not only to the one who committed the tort but also to others not involved in the wrongful act. The principle here is that an individual who was grossly negligent or acted maliciously or intentionally to cause harm should be required to pay damages beyond those actually incurred by the injured party. In this way, society sends a message that such behavior will not be tolerated and that those who commit the act will pay dearly for having done so.

Generally, punitive damages will be awarded only when a defendant's conduct was grossly negligent (the reckless disregard or indifference to the plaintiff's rights and safety) or intentional. In the hospitality industry, a manager could be found to have reckless disregard for the safety of a guest if, for example, the manager knew that a guestroom's lock was defective yet sold that room to a guest who was subsequently assaulted and seriously injured or if the front desk agent rented a guestroom to a guest knowing that bed bugs are known to exist in that room.

9.4 Anatomy of a Personal Injury Lawsuit

Hospitality managers do not want to operate their business in a way that will result in legal action being taken against them. In today's litigious society, even for a prudent operator, the threat of loss to the business because of lawsuits is very real. Some

---

LEGALESE

Negligence per se: Violation of a rule of law by the operator; such violation of a rule of law is considered to be so far outside the scope of reasonable behavior that the violator is assumed to be negligent.

Compensatory damages: Monetary amount awarded to restore an injured party to the position he or she was in prior to the injury (e.g., medical expenses, lost wages); also referred to as *actual damages*.

Punitive damages: A monetary amount used as punishment and to deter the same wrongful act in the future by the defendant and others.

of the lawsuits that are filed are frivolous, while others raise serious issues. In either case, the effective hospitality manager must be aware of how lawsuits are filed, how they progress through the court system, and, most importantly, the role the hospitality manager plays in the process.

Personal Injury

Much of your concern as a hospitality manager will focus on the potential for damages that result from **personal injury**. The reason for this is fairly straightforward: Hospitality managers provide guests with food and beverages, lodging accommodations, and entertainment, yet the process of providing these goods and services can place a business in potential jeopardy. The adage "accidents can happen" can be extended today to "accidents can happen, and if they do, the affected parties may sue!"

Certainly, it is best to manage your business in such a way as to avoid accidents. Nevertheless, accidents and injuries will occur, and many times determining where to place the responsibility for the accident is unclear. Consider the case of Norman and Betty Tungett. The Tungetts check into a motel and at about midnight, Mrs. Tungett goes out to her car to get a piece of luggage. While she is in the parking lot, she is assaulted. In addition to being badly frightened, she suffers physical harm, as well as lingering apprehension about being out after dark by herself. Listed here are just a few of the questions that could be raised in a case such as this:

1. Were the lights in the parking lot working well enough to minimize the chance that a guest would be assaulted?
2. Was management vigilant in eliminating potential hiding places for would-be assailants?
3. Were the Tungetts warned on check-in that the parking lot might not be safe late at night?
4. Were there any access doors allowing Mrs. Tungett to easily get to her room after visiting the lot?
5. Had the motel experienced similar incidents in the past, and if so, what precautions had been taken to prevent them?

Notice that, in this example, there is no clear-cut reason for believing the motel is in any way responsible for the Tungetts problem. It is important to remember, however, that the court system gives the Tungetts and their attorney the right to file a personal injury lawsuit in an effort to determine if, in fact, the motel was totally or partially responsible for the assault. In doing so, the Tungetts will seek damages resulting from the assault. Such a lawsuit will, without doubt, be time consuming for management and expensive to defend against. Nevertheless, such lawsuits are filed on a daily basis, and it is rare that hospitality managers do not find themselves involved to some degree whether defending a claim, being a witness to the action related to a claim, or filing a claim in such a suit at some time in their career. For this reason, we will examine the anatomy of a personal injury lawsuit from its inception to conclusion.

Demand Letter

Typically, a manager will learn that he, she, and/or the business is being sued when a **demand letter** is received. The demand letter comes from an attorney who has been contacted and retained by the injured plaintiff and has agreed to take up the plaintiff's cause. As shown in Figure 9.1 on the next page, the typical demand letter sets forth the plaintiff's version of the facts surrounding an alleged personal injury and might include the monetary amount of damages being sought and usually a deadline for the manager to respond to the charges.

Attorneys generally will accept a personal injury case with one of three payment plans. The first is the hourly fee, whereby the attorney bills his or her client (the plaintiff) at an hourly rate for each hour or partial hour the attorney works on the personal injury claim. Some attorneys will bill in six-minute intervals and will charge one-tenth of an hour for work done even if the full six minutes are not utilized, such as only two minutes of work. In this case, it is clearly in the best interest of the plaintiff to seek a conclusion to the case as quickly as possible to minimize attorney fees. In a second type of plan, the attorney agrees to take the case for one flat fee. In this situation, it is clearly in the best interest of the attorney to seek a quick resolution of the case. The third payment form is the **contingency fee**. In most states, contingency fee agreements must be put in writing. Lawyers representing defendants charged with crimes may not charge contingency fees. Clearly, in a case where the attorney is representing the client on a contingency basis, it is in the best interest of the plaintiff and the attorney to seek the most favorable, rather than the fastest, settlement possible.

Regardless of the form of payment agreed on between the plaintiff and his or her attorney, the demand letter is the first step in the litigation process. After receiving the demand letter, the defendant is given the opportunity to respond. If the response to the demand letter does not satisfy the plaintiff, he or she will likely instruct the attorney to file suit against the defendant.

LEGALESE

Personal injury: Damage or harm inflicted upon the body, mind, or emotions.

Demand letter: Official notification, typically delivered to a defendant via registered or certified mail usually in advance of litigation that details the plaintiff's cause for impending litigation to seek a settlement between the parties.

Contingency fee: A method of paying for a civil attorney's services as a percentage of any money awarded as a settlement in the case. Typically, these fees range from 20 to 40 percent of the total amount awarded.

January 15, 2000
Via Certified Mail: Z 123 456 789

Nina Phillips, General Manager
XYZ Hotel
Re: My client: Ginny Mayes
Date of Accident: January 1, 2000

Dear Ms. Phillips:

Please be advised that I represent Ginny Mayes. Ms. Mayes has retained my firm to represent her in her claim for damages against the XYZ Hotel and others that might be responsible for causing the incident that led to her injuries.

As you are aware, my client attended the New Year's Eve Gala that was hosted by the XYZ Hotel on December 31, 1999. At midnight, and until a few minutes thereafter, employees of the XYZ Hotel began opening champagne bottles by "popping the corks" (releasing the corks and allowing them to fly into the air).

My client was dancing on the dance floor when she was suddenly struck in her left eye by one of the corks. The cork was traveling at a high rate of speed, and when it struck her eye, she lost her balance and fell, striking her head on the wooden dance floor.

As a result of the negligent ads of the employees/agents of the XYZ Hotel, my client suffered severe injuries including a subdural hematoma, a concussion, facial lacerations, and a permanent partial loss of sight in her left eye.

You are further advised that my client's occupation for the past fifteen (15) years has been as a pilot for a major airline. Airlines require high vision standards to be met their pilots. Ms. Mayes's physicians have advised her that she will no longer meet the minimum vision standards required to be a pilot (report enclosed), as a direct result of the injuries she sustained while attending the New Year's Eve Gala.

Accordingly, demand is hereby made for the sum of $25,000,000 (twenty-five million dollars) to compensate my client for the injuries she suffered due to the negligence and gross negligence of the employees of XYZ Hotel Company; including past, present, and future pain and suffering; past, present, and future medical expenses for both treatment and rehabilitation; and past, present, and future lost wages.

If you have liability insurance, you are strongly urged to advise the carrier of this claim, as most policies require prompt notification when a claim is made.

Please be advised that in the event this matter is not resolved to my client's satisfaction within ten (10) days of your receipt of this correspondence, that she has authorized me to pursue any and all legal remedies available to her in this regard, including filing suit seeking the recovery of compensatory damages, punitive damages, costs of court, and reasonable attorney fees.

Finally, you are advised that time is of the essence in this regard and that your silence will be deemed an admission. Please contact me or have your attorney contact me as soon as possible if you have any questions.

Thank you for your courtesy and cooperation.

Very Truly Yours,

Ms. Alixandre Caroline, Attorney at Law

FIGURE 9.1 Demand letter.

Filing a Petition

Filing a petition (also called a "pleading" or "complaint") is the term used to describe the process of initiating a lawsuit. A petition is a document that officially requests a court's assistance in resolving a dispute. The petition will identify specifically the plaintiff and the defendant. In addition, it will describe the matter it wishes the court to decide. Included in the complaint against the defendant will be the plaintiff's suggestion for settlement of the issue. The plaintiff may, for example, ask for monetary damages. After the petition has been filed with the administrative clerk of the court, the lawsuit officially begins.

Once the complaint is filed with the court, the court will notify the defendant of the plaintiff's charge and will include a copy of the complaint in the notification. This is known as "service of process" in which a private process server or the local law enforcement officer will hand deliver a copy of the complaint to the plaintiff notifying him or her that the lawsuit has begun. Receiving a complaint and deciding what to do next are very time sensitive. The clock begins to tick upon serving the defendant, and it is extremely important for the defendant not to ignore the lawsuit or put it aside to deal with at a later date. Upon receipt of the complaint, the defendant needs to respond in writing, known as an "answer," within the time specified in the notice from the court, usually 30 days from when the defendant received the complaint. Failure to file an answer within such time period may result in a default judgment against the defendant (in favor of the plaintiff) and could result in a judgment and damages against the defendant without having a chance to have his or her day in court to propose and argue a defense.

Discovery

In the discovery phase of a civil lawsuit, both parties seek to learn the facts necessary to best support their position. This can include answering questions via **interrogatories** or **depositions**, requests for records or other evidence, and sometimes visiting the scene of the incident that caused the complaint.

The discovery process can be short or very lengthy. Either side may ask for information from the other using a procedure known as "motions," and if necessary, a judge will rule on whether the parties to the suit must comply with these requests. In some instances, one party in a lawsuit may obtain a court order demanding that the other party turn over specific documents or that specific individuals be called to testify in court. This order is called a **subpoena**. A subpoena may also be used to obtain further evidence or cause a witnesses to testify while a trial is ongoing.

The plaintiff in the lawsuit has the burden of proving the allegations set forth in the petition. This is the responsibility of proving to the finder of fact (judge or jury) that a particular view of the facts is true. In a civil case, the plaintiff must convince the court "by a preponderance of the evidence," that is, over 50 percent of the believable evidence or "more likely than not." In a criminal case, because one's freedom is at stake, the government has a higher standard and must convince the court "beyond a reasonable doubt" that a defendant is guilty. An example of the different standards used in a civil versus a criminal proceeding is the OJ Simpson trials for the 1994 deaths of Nicole Brown Simpson and Ronald L. Goldman. In the criminal trial, Mr. Simpson was acquitted and was found not guilty of the double slayings. In the civil trials, on the same set of facts as shown in the criminal trial, Mr. Simpson was found negligent of wrongful death and subject to paying damages. In civil action, the jury looked again at the same incident and the same set of facts, but because the burden of proof was not as high as in the criminal matter, Mr. Simpson was found liable in each case and ordered to pay $25 million in punitive damages to the family of Nicole Brown Simpson and $8.5 million in compensatory damages to the Goldman family.

Trial and Appeal

The trial is the portion of the injury suit process during which the plaintiff seeks to persuade the judge or jury that his or her version of the facts and points of law that should prevail. In a like manner, the defendant also has an opportunity to persuade for his or her side. Most personal injury cases are tried in front of a jury. After a jury is selected to hear the trial, the process, while it may vary somewhat from state to state, is as follows:

1. Presentation by plaintiff.
2. Presentation by defendant.
3. Plaintiff's rebuttal.
4. Summation by both parties.
5. Judge's instructions about the applicable law and procedures to the jury.
6. Jury deliberation.
7. Verdict.
8. Judgment or award.
9. Appeal of verdict and/or award.

Either side has the right to appeal a verdict or award. In the personal injury area, it is common for a losing defendant to **appeal** the size of the award if it is considered by the defendant's counsel to be excessive. Most appeals deal with procedural errors that may have occurred at the trial level, not an opportunity for the parties to relitigate the facts of a case.

Alternative Dispute Resolution

There are alternatives to resolving personal injury claims in court. The parties at any time during the litigation process can agree on a settlement. Two other common methods used in the hospitality industry are mediation and arbitration. Both can be highly effective alternatives to the time, cost, and stress involved in going through a trial.

In mediation, a trained and neutral individual (the mediator) facilitates negotiation between the parties in order to achieve a voluntary resolution of the dispute. In most cases, one full day of mediation can result in a compromise acceptable to both the plaintiff and defendant. Mediation can involve sessions jointly held with both parties and their attorneys or separate meetings with each party, their attorneys, and the mediator. The cost of mediation will

---

LEGALESE

Interrogatories: Questions that require written answers, given under oath, asked during the discovery phase of a lawsuit.

Depositions: Oral answers, given under oath, to questions asked during the discovery phase of a lawsuit. Depositions are recorded by a certified court reporter and/or by videotape.

Subpoena: A court-authorized order to appear in person at a designated time and place, or to produce evidence demanded by the court.

Appeal: A written request to a higher court to modify or reverse the decision of a lower-level court.

Legally Managing at Work

The Manager's Role in Litigation

Demand Letter

Upon receipt of a demand letter, turn it over to your insurance company and your attorney for advice. Follow the recommendations of the insurance company and your attorney. Be as cooperative as possible with any investigations that your insurance company or attorney may instigate.

Notification of Filing a Lawsuit

Ordinarily, a representative of the court (e.g., constable, sheriff, or a private person authorized by the court) will personally hand you the pleading to ensure that the court knows you received it. If you are served with a pleading, you must recognize that these pleadings, and your company's obligations to respond, are time-sensitive. You need to deliver the pleading to your attorney as prescribed; make sure your insurance company gets a copy and that you keep one for future reference.

Discovery

As stated previously, the discovery process enables each party to obtain information from the other party, which will be used as documentary evidence to help prove the facts of a case. Managers will often be asked to turn over records of their business, repair invoices, reports, email transmissions, and information stored electronically. Plaintiffs often must turn over medical records and reports, doctor bills, receipts for damages, and other types of personal information. Often, a manager or staff member may be asked to prepare a personal statement during the discovery process, or even go to court and testify as a witness during the trial.

The cost of responding to discovery requests, either by testifying or preparing documents, can be a very expensive proposition for your operation, not only from a financial perspective but also because of the time involved and the disruption it causes to your staff. Accordingly, the better organized you are at the outset of the incident, the less of a burden the discovery process will be. Work closely with your attorney during this phase, be cooperative, and be sure to meet all time limits imposed for responses, as missing a deadline can be fatal to your side of the case.

Trial and Appeal

Request that your attorney update you frequently about trial settings (the date the trial will commence). Reciprocally, you need to let your attorney know about any times that you or your employees will be unavailable to testify (such as vacations, scheduled surgeries, etc.).

If your case is appealed, your involvement in the appellate process will be very minimal, if at all. This process rarely requires anything new from you that was not provided before the trial. Nevertheless, you should continue to maintain your records of the case and keep track of any witnesses.

vary based on the complexity of the case, but is generally far less than that involved in going to a trial. If the mediation is unsuccessful, the parties may still pursue a trial. If a settlement is made, the parties sign a settlement agreement approved by their attorneys. This agreement, if drafted properly, is an enforceable contract and is therefore binding on both parties.

In arbitration, a neutral third party (usually chosen by mutual agreement of both parties) makes a binding or nonbinding decision (depending on what the parties agree) after reviewing the evidence and hearing the arguments of all sides. The parties may agree to nonbinding arbitration in order to get a perspective on how the trial might play out and how a jury may decide the case. Many times the nonbinding arbitration decision will lead to a settlement.

Make sure that you and your attorney have established guidelines about what you can say, if anything, and when you can say it. Be patient. To be effective, the negotiation process can sometimes appear tedious, but the art of compromise usually takes time. Be flexible and willing to compromise. Many times, an apology at this point in the process will help pave the way for compromises on other significant issues, including the amount of money to be paid.

9.5 Responding to an Incident

Despite all of your careful planning, preparation, and prevention techniques, guests can still be seriously injured on your property. Because of the explosion of litigation in this country and the large jury awards that can result, owners and operators of hospitality facilities have spent great amounts of time, energy, and money to implement training programs and procedures that will reduce accidents. But, when accidents do occur, you must be prepared to act in a way that serves the best interest of both your operation and the injured party.

In his book *Accident Prevention for Hotels, Motels, and Restaurants* (Van Nostrand Reinhold, 1991), author Robert L. Kohr states that the first 15 minutes following an accident are "critical" in eliminating or greatly limiting your legal liability. He is correct. It is your job to know what to do—and, just as important, what not to do—during this critical time period.

The moments following an accident are often confusing and tense. For a manager, they will demand excellent decision-making skills. The steps given in the next Legally Managing at

Work box describe how control people (such as people in positions including owners, managers, and supervisors) should react during this crucial time period. Remember, the objective is to act in such a way as to protect both the business and the accident victim. The steps described in Legally Managing at Work will help you accomplish both.

As you can see, it is imperative that control people take charge of the scene immediately after an accident occurs. They should be the only ones talking to the injured party, and they need to be prepared to react and think quickly under pressure. Role-playing is a great way to train people to know how to respond appropriately when an accident or emergency situation arises, and training should be an ongoing process.

Hospitality operations must continue to undertake serious prevention efforts, but they should also be prepared for reality: Accidents do happen, and the steps taken the first few minutes after an accident can be crucial in minimizing the negative impact of a potential claim.

Legally Managing at Work

Responding to an Accident

Step 1. Call 911.

First and foremost, get qualified, professional help. Do not leave it to the discretion of an untrained person to determine whether an injury requires professional medical treatment. Do not allow the delay of a decision-making process to increase your chance of liability. Your written hotel procedures should state that 911 will be called, and failure to follow your own policies may be crucial. Call 911.

Step 2. Attend to the Injured Party.

Let the injured party know that you have requested emergency assistance. Try to make him or her as comfortable as possible. If you have certified care providers on your staff, allow them to administer appropriate first aid. Restrict the movement of the injured party as much as possible unless the injury makes immediate movement necessary.

Step 3. Be Sensitive and Sincere.

Do not treat the injured person as a potential liability claim. If you do, you will probably end up with one. In discussions with many injured patrons who later filed lawsuits, it was found that a significant reason for making their claim was the insensitive treatment exhibited by the establishment after the accident occurred. Treat the injured party with sensitivity, sincerity, and concern.

Step 4. Do not Apologize for the Accident.

Being sensitive, sincere, and concerned does not equate to taking responsibility for the accident. Besides, until the investigation is completed, you do not truly know if an apology by you for the accident is appropriate.

Step 5. Do not Admit That You or Your Employees Were at Fault. Do Not Take Responsibility for the Accident.

Statements such as these made immediately following an accident are often based on first impressions without knowing all of the facts. Unfortunately, making such statements may have a profound impact on the injured party, as well as a judge or jury, who may perceive them to be a credible admission of guilt or liability. Even when the circumstances surrounding an incident seem glaringly obvious, refrain from admitting fault or responsibility. There is no reason to discuss liability, negligence, or responsibility at this time. The focus should be on the guest's injuries, not on the cause of the accident.

Step 6. Do not Offer to Pay for the Medical Expenses of the Injured Party.

By offering or promising to pay for medical expenses, the person in control is possibly entering into a contractual arrangement with the injured party or the medical provider to pay for the cost of treatment. This contract might be enforceable even if the outcome of the accident investigation shows that the hospitality operation was not at fault. In minor injury situations, you can offer to call a particular doctor or treatment center for the injured party, but allow him or her to choose the provider. In very limited circumstances, you might want to agree to pay for the initial treatment only, but specify your position in writing with the medical provider.

Step 7. Do not Mention Insurance Coverage.

Fortunately, most hospitality operations have insurance for many types of accidents and injuries that occur on their premises. Unfortunately, the fact that an operator has insurance will sometimes be reflected as dollar signs in the eyes of the injured party. Psychologically, it is much easier to pursue a big, cold, indifferent, and unfamiliar insurance company than it is to pursue a very warm, concerned, and well-meaning hospitality manager.

Step 8. Do not Discuss the Cause of the Accident.

Discussing the cause of the accident with the injured party is a no-win situation. If the injured party argues or implies that the hospitality operation is at fault for the accident, and the person in control agrees, fault has been admitted. If the person in control disagrees, it will only create ill feelings and exacerbate the situation. Remaining silent is not an admission of liability and is preferable to arguing with the injured party. Another alternative is for the person in control to reassure the injured party that he or she will conduct a complete investigation and will be happy to discuss the circumstances upon its completion.

Step 9. Do not Correct Employees at the Scene.

This immediate reaction can have a very serious negative impact in the future. On-the-scene reprimanding of employees is sometimes interpreted by the injured party that a mistake was made or that the operation caused the accident. People in control need to remember that they cannot change what has already occurred. They can only hope to positively influence the future decision-making process of the injured party. This can best be accomplished by focusing on the injured party, not on the operation. There will be plenty of time to assess each employee's performance and to take appropriate corrective action if it is warranted after the investigation has been completed.

Step 10. Conduct a Complete and Thorough Investigation.

Although it will take a great deal longer than 15 minutes, a significant amount of the information for a thorough investigation needs to be gathered immediately after the accident. If other guests saw the accident, request that they write down what they saw. Ask them to sign and date their statements and to leave their address and phone number in case you need to contact them in the future. It may take years for a claim to be resolved. Attorneys and investigators will need to be able to locate the people who gave statements. An incident report, such as the one shown in Figure 9.2, can be used to help gather such information. Only facts, not conclusions, should be recorded in the incident report because this form is a legal document that will be critical in a personal injury case. Remember that evidence wins lawsuits, and the more evidence and documentation you have, the better your chances for a favorable ruling or one that minimizes the amount of damages you will have to pay.

It is also important to have your employees fill out and sign a written report. Employees may change jobs, voluntarily leave, or be terminated from an operation before an accident claim is resolved. Depending on why they left, employees' perceptions of an accident or the events leading up to it may change over time along with their overall perception of the operation and its owners and supervisors. It is not unusual for an employee to first recount a positive rendition of the events from the employer's perspective and then upon being terminated to later report information that would make the employer look negligent in the eyes of an attorney or judge.

Step 11. Complete a Claim Report and Submit It to Your Insurance Company Immediately.

Most insurance policies require prompt notification of any and all potential claims if they are to provide coverage under the policy. The reason is that insurance companies want their experts to become involved in the investigation as early as possible. Your failure to report the claim could cause the claim to be excluded from coverage.

Step 12. Do not Discuss the Circumstances Surrounding the Accident or the Investigation with Anyone Except Those Who Absolutely Need to Know.

Conversations with and opinions given to employees or even people not associated with the business can come back to haunt you. Restrict your conversations to the hospitality operation's attorneys or authorized representatives of the insurance company.

Step 13. Do not Throw Away Records, Statements, or Other Evidence Until the Case Is Finalized.

Cases can be resolved in several different ways: The claim could be settled prior to trial; the case could be tried in court and decided or perhaps appealed until all avenues for appeal are exhausted. Sometimes a potential injury claim may not be filed as a lawsuit right away. Whatever the circumstance, the case will not be considered closed until the statute of limitations runs out (ordinarily two years from the date of the injury in a personal injury claim). If you are not absolutely certain whether a claim has been finalized, check with your operation's attorney or the insurance company and request a letter of consent to destroy the evidence.

INCIDENT REPORT

Business ______________________ Date ______________________

Address ______________________ City ____________ State ____________

Complainant

____

Last Name   First Name   Initial

____

Address   City   State   Zip

____

Home Telephone   Business Telephone

Type of Incident

____

Theft   Accident   Property Damage   Other

Injury

First aid given? Yes________ No________

First aid refused Yes________ No________

EMS called? Yes________ No________

Taken to emergency? Yes________ No________

Nature of injury ____

____

____

FIGURE 9.2 **Incident report form.**

Detail of Incident

____
____
____
____
____
____
____
____
____
____
____

Property and Value

Damaged/Missing Property Description ______ Estimated Value ______

Room Entry **Room Number** ______

Room entered? ______ Time ______

Door locked? ______ Door chained? ______

Entered by ______ Witnessed by ______

Police Report

Police Officer Name ______

Shield # ______ Report # ______

Arrest made? ______ Citation issued? ______

Witnesses:

Name ______ Tel: ______

Address ______ City ______ State ______

Name ______ Tel: ______

Address ______ City ______ State ______

Name ______ Tel: ______

Address ______ City ______ State ______

Comments: ______

____
____
____
____
____
____

Prepared by ______ Reviewed by ______

Date ______ Date ______

FIGURE 9.2 *(continued)*

International Snapshot

Negligence

Negligence overseas can spell liability at home. The standards used in the United States to determine whether the employees of a hospitality facility exercised reasonable care also may apply to the foreign operations of U.S. hospitality companies. Consider the following:

- Many Americans desire to travel overseas.
- Many of those Americans are more comfortable staying at a facility that has a familiar name and appearance.
- The U.S. hospitality industry purposefully seeks to attract the business of those people through its marketing.
- Those marketing efforts often succeed because the industry is able to combine the allure of exotic places with the peace of mind that accompanies known corporate brands.

Americans who travel overseas expect to be treated consistently by facilities with which they have had experiences in the United States. U.S. travelers eventually come home, and when they have suffered losses overseas at facilities operated by U.S. companies, any suit they file is likely to be filed at home. When that happens, U.S. courts usually impose U.S. legal standards. The following factors, either alone or in combination, will be considered:

- *Whether the parties to the litigation, namely the dissatisfied guest and the U.S. operator of the overseas facility, are United States citizens.* U.S. courts are not comfortable imposing foreign legal standards on U.S. citizens.
- *The nature of the foreign jurisdiction's legal principles.* Some of these are repugnant to the policy of the U.S. jurisdiction. Similarly, U.S. courts are unaccustomed to analyzing and applying foreign legal standards.
- *Whether the foreign hospitality facility is under the control of a U.S. company.* For example, U.S. hospitality companies typically impose their corporate practices and procedures on their foreign operations. The managers of the foreign operations may have been trained in the United States by the U.S. operator.
- *Whether the guest who suffered harm sought and received relevant assurances from the U.S. operator of the overseas facility before traveling.* Reasonable reliance on such assurances warrants the application of U.S. standards.

Managers of overseas hospitality facilities operated by U.S. companies should strive to meet U.S. standards of care in all aspects of the hospitality operation. U.S. courts evaluating these managers' performance after a U.S. tourist has an unfortunate experience abroad will most likely expect them to do nothing less.

U.S. companies with hospitality facilities overseas are not guarantors of happy vacations, and liability depends on more than a breach of the standard of care (whether through careless hiring, insufficient training, lax supervision, or a performance lapse). Causation is an element of every negligence claim. If injury or death would have occurred even with the exercise of due care, liability will not be imposed.

Provided by Perrin Rynders, of the Varnum LLP Law Firm, in Grand Rapids, Michigan. www.varnumlaw.com.

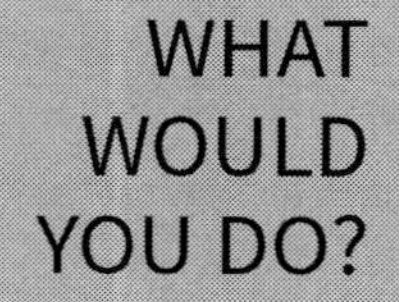

Assume you are a mediator whose job is to help opposing parties limit the expense and time of going to trial in matters of personal injury. In your current case, Jeremy and Anne Hunter have filed a personal injury suit against the Fairview Mayton Hotel's ownership group and its franchisor, Mayton Hotels and Resorts Inc.

According to the Hunters, they checked into their suite at the Fairview Mayton, one of 150 independently owned, franchise-affiliated properties on a Friday night. Their daughter Susan, who was eight years old at the time, opened a sliding patio door, and upon seeing the outdoor hot tub that was part of suite, asked her parents if she could get in. They told her yes. Upon entering the tub (it is agreed by both parties that Susan "jumped" into the hot tub), she suffered third-degree burns over 80 percent of her body, and her facial features were permanently disfigured because the water in the hot tub was 160 degrees Fahrenheit, not 102, the maximum recommended by the tub's manufacturer, and well above the 105-degree maximum dictated by local health codes. An investigation determined that the hot tub safety switch, designed to prevent accidental overheating, had been bypassed when some wiring repair had been performed by the hotel's maintenance staff. (The Hunters are also suing the franchise company because a mandatory inspection of property safety, which, as part of the franchise agreement, was to have been performed annually, had not been done in the three years prior to the accident.)

The hotel's insurance company takes the position that Susan's parents gave her permission to use the tub despite a written warning on the side of the tub saying it was not to be used by persons under age 14, and thus they bear a majority of the responsibility for the accident. The Mayton franchise company's insurance company states it is not responsible for the acts of its franchisees, and thus cannot be held accountable. The hotel's manager has been terminated. The Hunters, whose lawyer has accepted the case on a contingency basis, is suing for a total of $5 million.

1. What would you recommend the Fairview Mayton's insurance company do?
2. What would you recommend the franchise company's insurance company do?
3. What would you recommend the Hunters do?

WHAT DID YOU LEARN IN THIS CHAPTER?

All hospitality businesses must operate in a reasonably safe manner or face potential liability for accidents and injuries that occur to their guests. Specific areas (or duties) have been identified in the law that help to define the scope of the responsibility of a business to visitors. These include the duty (or obligation) to provide a reasonably safe facility and grounds, to serve food and beverages fit for consumption, and to hire qualified employees. The term "reasonably," however, is sometimes a difficult standard to define because it is based on current and customary practices in the industry.

If you failed to operate in a reasonably safe manner and damages occur as a result, you might be found to have been negligent and be held liable for damages. If you ignored the safety and well-being of visitors, then you may be found to have been grossly negligent and face greater liability than for ordinary negligence. The visitor also has a responsibility to act reasonably, or he or she may be found to have contributed to the cause of damages.

Types of damages include property loss, medical expenses, lost wages, pain and suffering, punitive fines, and legal fees. Not all types of damages are recoverable in every type of claim.

A personal injury claim is usually initiated with a demand letter. If the situation cannot be resolved amicably, a lawsuit may commence. The steps in a lawsuit include the filing of a petition, the discovery period, and a trial before a judge or jury. You, as a manager, have a crucial role in the litigation and/or resolution process. Claims do not always have to end up in trial; they are sometimes resolved through mediation or arbitration techniques.

If an accident should occur on your property (and one probably will despite your best prevention practices), the way your staff responds can have a significant impact on the consequences that arise from the accident.

CHAPTER 10

Your Responsibilities as a Hospitality Operator to Guests

10.1 Accommodating Guests

Guests are the lifeblood of any hospitality organization. Guests are so important that management's role could be defined simply as the ability to develop and retain a viable customer base. Without a sufficient number of guests, success and profitability in the hospitality industry is impossible. The reality, however, is that with guests come guest-related challenges, particularly when the legal implications are considered. In this chapter, we will examine guests and their rights, as well as your rights as a manager or proprietor.

Definition of a Guest

The law views a hospitality manager's responsibility to those who come onto a property differently according to the characteristics of the visitor. Consider the case of Eva Barrix. She is a motel owner who maintains a pool for the convenience of her guests. Late one night, a robber scales a fence around the property and, because the thief is not familiar with the grounds, accidentally trips, falls, and stumbles into the pool. Clearly, the law does not require that Ms. Barrix inform would-be criminals about the layout of her facility. In addition, despite the occasional well-publicized personal injury case, thieves would have a difficult time proving to the court that the owner of a business owes a duty of care to them as discussed in Chapter 9, "Your Responsibilities as a Hospitality Operator." Contrast this example with a guest who may experience a similar fall near the pool area, and you will see why it is important to understand the distinctions involved in determining precisely who is a **guest** and who is not.

Certainly, duties of care apply to guests, and in most cases, to guests of guests. In the restaurant area, a guest is not limited merely to the individual who pays the bill. In fact, all diners are considered to be guests of the facility.

LEGALESE

Guest: A customer who lawfully utilizes a facility's food, beverage, lodging, or entertainment services.

CHAPTER OUTLINE

10.1. Accommodating Guests

10.2. Guest Privacy

10.3. Facility Maintenance

10.4. Responsibilities to Nonguests

10.5. Removal of Guests

IN THIS CHAPTER, YOU WILL LEARN

1. To understand your legal responsibility to admit guests and the circumstances when such admission can be denied.
2. To protect guests' right to privacy.
3. To operate and maintain a facility in a way that maximizes the safety of guests and compliance with the law, including Title III of the Americans with Disabilities Act (ADA).
4. To differentiate among various types of nonguests and understand your obligations toward them.
5. To generate the procedures required to safely and legally remove guests from a property.

Analyze the Situation 10.1

Nicole Frost and Steve Merchand were brother and sister. When their grandfather, Wayne Merchand, was hospitalized for care after a heart attack, the two began to visit him regularly at Laurel Memorial Hospital.

One Sunday afternoon, after visiting with their grandfather, Nicole and Steve went to the hospital's cafeteria for a light lunch. A professional foodservice management company operated the cafeteria under contract to the hospital. Nicole and Steve selected their lunches from an assortment of beverages and prewrapped sandwiches that were displayed unrefrigerated on a tray in the middle of the cafeteria serving line. The sandwiches were made of ham and cheese with a salad dressing spread, lettuce, and tomato. Steve paid for the sandwiches, beverages, and some chips, and then he and Nicole took a seat in the cafeteria dining room.

Approximately four hours after eating lunch, both Steve and Nicole became ill. They determined that they both had suffered from foodborne illness. The two filed suit against the hospital and its contract foodservice management company. When the facts of the case came out, the hospital maintained that, as visitors, not patients, the hospital had no liability toward Nicole and Steve. The foodservice management company operating the hospital cafeteria maintained that its liability extended only to Steve since he was the only guest who in fact purchased food from its service. Management maintained it should not be held responsible for the illness suffered by an individual that it did not actually serve.

1. Was Nicole a guest of the foodservice facility?
2. Should Steve bear partial responsibility for the damage he and Nicole suffered because he purchased the sandwiches?
3. What type of liability (from Chapter 9, "Your Responsibilities as a Hospitality Operator") applies in this case? Why?

In the lodging area, guests can be considered to be either a **transient guest** or a **tenant**, and the differences are significant. As can be seen by the definitions, the precise demarcation between transient guests and tenants is not easily established. It is important to do so, however, because the courts make a distinction between the two even when hospitality managers do not. For example, a transient guest who checks into a hotel for a one-night stay but does not pay for the room by the posted checkout time the next morning may be "locked out." That means that in a hotel with an electronic locking system, the front desk manager could deactivate the guest's key, thus preventing his or her readmittance to the room until such time as the guest settles the account with the front desk. A tenant with a lease, however, could not be locked out so easily and thus enjoys greater protection under the law.

Whether an individual is a transient guest or tenant is sometimes a matter for the courts to decide, but the following characteristics can help you determine which category an individual might fall into:

- *Billing format:* Transient guests tend to be charged a daily rate for their stay while tenants are more likely to be billed on a weekly or monthly basis.
- *Tax payment:* Transient guests must pay local occupancy taxes while tenants are ordinarily exempt from such payment.
- *Address use:* Tenants generally use the facility's address as their permanent address for such things as mail, driver's license, voter registration, and the like. Transient guests generally list another location as their permanent address.
- *Contract format:* Transient guests generally enter into a rooming agreement via a registration card while tenants would normally have a lease agreement or specific contract separate from, or in addition to, their registration card.
- *Existence of deposit:* Tenants are almost always required to give their landlord a deposit. Often this deposit is equal to a specified number of months of rent. Transient guests, by contrast, do not generally put up a deposit. This is true even if the hotel requires a transient guest to present a credit card upon checking into the hotel.
- *Length of stay:* While it is widely believed that any guest who occupies a room for more than 30 days becomes a tenant, the fact is, the length of stay is usually not the sole criterion on which the transient guest/tenant determination is made. In fact, most guests who occupy the same hotel room for over 30 days may do so without affecting their transient status. It is true, however, that the length of stay for a tenant does tend to be longer than that of a transient guest.

Because the line between a transient guest and tenant is unclear and because the states have addressed this situation differently, if you are a hotel manager and are unsure about the status of a guest/tenant, it is best to seek the advice of a qualified attorney before taking steps to remove the individual from his or her room.

LEGALESE

Transient guest: A customer who rents real property for a relatively short period of time (e.g., few number of days with no intent of establishing a permanent residency).

Tenant: Anyone, including a corporation, who rents real property for an extended period of time with the intent of establishing a permanent occupation or residency.

Analyze the Situation 10.2

Ketan Patel operated the Heartworth Suites, an extended-stay, limited-service hotel of 85 rooms. Approximately 40 percent of his guests were extended-stay, which Mr. Patel's company defined as a stay longer than five consecutive days. The remaining rooms were sold to traditional transient guests whose average stay was approximately 1.8 days.

Bob Thimming was an extended-stay guest at the Heartworth, and an employee of Katy Highway Contractors. Mr. Thimming held the position of construction foreman for a stretch of interstate highway being repaired in the vicinity of the Heartworth Suites. His company signed a contract with the Heartworth confirming that Mr. Thimming would be given a special monthly rather than daily rate because he was staying in the hotel for six consecutive months as part of his work assignment.

In the third month of his stay, Mr. Thimming arrived at the hotel from his job site at approximately 5:30 P.M. to find the door to his room ajar. He entered the room and discovered that his $4,000 watch, which he had left on the nightstand, was missing. Mr. Thimming contacted Mr. Patel to complain about the theft. Because the hotel was equipped with electronic locks, Mr. Patel was able to perform a lock audit and retrieved the following information for the day in question.

Time	Key Used	Key Issued To	Results
6:30 A.M.	7J 105–60	Guest	Entry
6:32 A.M.	7J 105–60	Guest	Entry
1:30 P.M.	1M 002–3	Maintenance	Entry

Mr. Thimming maintained that someone had negligently left the door open and, as a result, his watch was stolen. He contacted his company, whose in-house attorney called Mr. Patel. The attorney stated that Mr. Thimming was a tenant of the hotel, and as a landlord, Mr. Patel was responsible for the negligent acts of his employee and should reimburse Mr. Thimming for his loss. Mr. Patel replied that Mr. Thimming was not a tenant but a transient guest, and thus was subject to a state law that limits an innkeeper's liability in such cases to $350. The attorney disagreed, based on the six-month "lease" signed by Katy Highway Contractors for Mr. Thimming. He demanded that the watch be replaced and threatened to file suit if it was not. Mr. Patel contacted his attorney, who offered, based on his view of the complexity of the case, to defend the Heartworth Suites for $3,000, with a required retainer (down payment) of $2,000.

1. Was Mr. Thimming a transient guest or a tenant?
2. Why is the distinction important in this situation?
3. What should Mr. Patel do in the future to avoid the expense of litigation such as this?

Admitting Guests

As facilities of **public accommodation**, hotels and restaurants historically were required to admit everyone who sought to come in. More recently, as a result of evolving laws and the changing social environment in which hotels and restaurants operate and as the protection of guests and employees becomes more complex, the right of the hospitality business to refuse to serve a guest has broadened in scope, with the caveat that legislation has been enacted at the federal, state, and local levels that prohibits discrimination in public accommodations. Violations of these laws can result in either civil or criminal penalties. Beyond the legal expenses, negative publicity from this type of discrimination against guests can also cost a business significant amounts of lost revenue and can damage its reputation for years to come. Consequently, it is important for you to know when you have to admit guests as well as the circumstances in which you have the right to deny admission.

It is a violation of Title II of the Federal Civil Rights Act of 1964 to deny any person admission to a facility of public accommodation on the basis of race, color, religion, or national origin. In addition, it is a violation to admit such guests but then **segregate** them to a specific section(s) of the facility or discriminate against them in the manner of service they receive or the types of products and services they are provided.

State or local civil rights laws are usually more inclusive in that they expand the "protected classes" to categories not covered under federal law, such as age, marital status, and sexual orientation and may also have stricter penalties for violations.

Historically, it has been argued that "private" clubs were exempt from the Civil Rights Act and could discriminate in their admission policies because they were not in fact public facilities. However, courts across the United States have slowly dismantled this argument by continuing to broaden the definition of public facilities, and, concomitantly, to narrow the definition of a private club. (For instance, if a country club is very selective about its membership, but nonmembers can rent its facilities for meetings, wedding receptions, and the like, is it really private?) In addition, many cities and towns have passed local

LEGALESE

Public accommodation: A facility that provides entertainment, rooms, space, or seating for the use and benefit of the general public.

Segregate: To separate a group or individual on any basis, but especially by race, color, religion, or national origin.

ordinances that outlaw discrimination in private clubs, even if those clubs meet the "private" club definition under federal law. Accordingly, most clubs today have opted to comply with the Civil Rights Act and other antidiscriminatory laws.

It is legal and in some cases, mandatory, for a facility of public accommodation to separate guests based on some stated or observed characteristic. Some communities, for example, require that restaurants provide distinctly separate spaces for their smoking and nonsmoking guests. It is important to note that such a practice is not illegal because it does not discriminate against a protected class of individuals as defined by the Civil Rights Act.

Search the Web 10.1

Log on to **www.usconstitution.net**

1. Select: The Constitution twice.
2. Scroll until you reach the Fourteenth Amendment, and read it carefully.
3. Are women specifically mentioned in the Fourteenth Amendment?
4. How does the wording of this amendment impact admission policies in the hospitality industry?
5. Do you believe the amendment prohibits "ladies only" or "men only" nights?

Denying Admission to Guests

Although it is illegal to unlawfully discriminate against a potential guest, you do have the right to refuse to admit or serve guests in some situations. A public accommodation may legally deny service to a potential guest when:

1. *The individual cannot show the ability to pay for the services provided.* In this situation, it is important that management be able to clearly show that all potential customers are subjected to the same "ability to pay" test. In a restaurant, for example, if only youths of a specific ethnic background are required to demonstrate ability to pay prior to ordering, the manager of that facility is discriminating on the basis of ethnicity and is in violation of the law.
2. *The individual has a readily communicable disease.* An operator is not required to put the safety of other guests and employees aside to accommodate a guest who could spread a disease to others.
3. *The individual wishes to enter the facility with an item that is prohibited.* It is permissible to refuse service to individuals attempting to bring into the premises animals with the exception of guide animals for the physically or emotionally impaired and to those carrying guns, knives, or other weapons. Some operators actually post a policy specifically referring to firearms. Figure 10.1 is an example of such a policy.

It is strictly prohibited for any person to carry a weapon, including but not limited to a handgun, or a concealed weapon anywhere on this property including parking lots.

We reserve the right to search each person, his or her personal effects, and vehicle as a condition of entry onto or presence on this property.

This policy supersedes any right an employee or guest may believe he or she has to carry a weapon, concealed or otherwise, pursuant to state law.

Violators will be prosecuted.

FIGURE 10.1 **Weapons policy.**

4. *The individual is intoxicated.* It is not only illegal to deny service to a guest who is visibly under the influence of drugs or alcohol but also admitting or serving such an individual could put you at great risk. (The duty of care required for an intoxicated person will be discussed more fully in Chapter 12, "Your Responsibilities When Serving Food and Beverages.") It is clear that an individual whose reasoning is impaired by drugs or alcohol poses a significant threat to the safety of others and thus loses his or her right to be served. Care must be taken in these circumstances not to put the guest or the general public at risk.
5. *The individual presents a threat to employees or other guests.* Obviously, alcohol and drugs need not be present for a guest to pose a threat to other guests or employees. If the guest behaves in any manner that is threatening or intimidating to either employees or other guests, then that individual need not be served as long as this policy is applied uniformly to all guests. Should such a situation arise and service is indeed denied, it is best to document the situation using the Incident Report Form from Chapter 9, "Your Responsibilities as a Hospitality Operator" in case your actions are ever called into question. Some operators require guests to sign a "house rules" document that clearly states behaviors that the operator will not permit. Figure 10.2 is an example of such a statement.
6. *The individual does not seek to become a guest.* Although hotels and restaurants are considered places of public accommodation, they are also businesses. For example, a guest could enter a coffee shop in a downtown city hotel, order a cup of coffee, and occupy a seat for a reasonable amount of time. However, that same guest would not be permitted to enter the hotel's most exclusive dining room on a busy Friday night and order the same cup of coffee rather than a full meal. A reasonable person would assume that dining tables in a restaurant are reserved for those wishing to eat full meals, and thus denying service to a guest who does not want to do so is allowable.
7. *The individual is too young.* Those businesses that serve alcoholic beverages may be required by law to prohibit

The following rules regulate the renting of rooms, suites, and cottages on this property. Occupants will be bound, by these rules and policies, and failure to comply will result in termination of agreement and removal from property.

1. Renter is 21 years of age or older.
2. Renter will remain in room and not sublease or turn over room to other parties.
3. Renter will not utilize room for parties or unauthorized social gatherings.
4. Renter will not create noise or other disturbance.
5. Renter will not exceed maximum limit for number of occupants per room (five, or local code).
6. Renter will declare to hotel and pay for all occupants.
7. Renter will be responsible for all damage and excess wear and tear to room and property.

Guest Signature	Date
Property Witness	Date

FIGURE 10.2 House rules statement.

individuals under a predetermined age from entering their facilities. It is important to note that laws in this regard tend to be state or local ordinances. In some communities, young people are allowed to eat in a bar as long as a person of legal age accompanies them. In others, that same young person may not be allowed to sit in a dining area that would permit them even to view the bar area. Because the line between a bar or lounge that serves alcohol as its primary product and a restaurant that serves alcohol as an accompaniment to its food can be very unclear, managers should always check with the local or state agency granting liquor permits to ensure that they are up to date on the regulations regarding minors.

In most states, a hotel may refuse to rent a room to those under a specific age; however, it is important that this not be used as a method for unfairly discriminating against a protected class. To do so would be a violation of federal and state law. Even though a state's laws and regulations may not expressly address minors checking into hotels, some local ordinances may require that a minor be present with an adult or guardian in order to rent a room. Always check with local sources to learn more about admitting minors into the hotel.

8. *The facility is full.* Obviously, the hotel that is full can deny space to a potential guest. The same is true of a restaurant, bar, or club that has reached its capacity. A hotel or restaurant that is full, however, faces a somewhat different situation when it denies space to a guest with a confirmed reservation. This would be a breach of contract and would, as described in Chapter 4, subject the hotel to possible litigation on the part of the injured party. That said, in the case of a guest who arrives unreasonably late for a dinner reservation, the restaurant is not obligated to seat the guest because the late arrival would be considered a breach of contract by the guest.

10.2 Guest Privacy

When a guest rents a hotel room, the courts have held that the guest should enjoy many of the same constitutional rights as he or she would in his or her own home. The hotel is, however, allowed to enter the room for routine maintenance, cleaning, and emergency services such as might be required in a fire or other disaster.

Guestroom Privacy

The guest's expectation of privacy should always be respected even when routine intrusions become necessary. In general, you and your staff must be sensitive to guests' needs and expectations at all times. But when the guest is no longer classified as a guest, that is, if a guest unlawfully possesses a room, the courts will allow a hotel manager to remove the guest and his or her belongings in order to make the room rentable to another guest. (The process for legally doing so will be explored later in this chapter.) Additionally, a guest has the right to expect that no unauthorized third party will be allowed to enter his or her guestroom.

Privacy of Guest Records

Just as a guest's room is private, so too are the records created by the hotel that document the guest's stay. Consider the case of Russell Hernandez, the manager of a resort about 50 miles away from a major university. Mr. Hernandez receives a letter from representatives of the National Collegiate Athletic Association (NCAA) stating that they are undertaking an investigation of the local university's football recruiting efforts. They wish to know if a particular person was a registered guest on a date two years earlier and, if so, who paid the bill for the

Analyze the Situation 10.3

Jessica Bristol and her two young children checked into room 104 of the Travel-In motel at 9:00 P.M. on Friday night. She produced a credit card issued in her name as a form of payment and requested that she be given the room for two nights.

On Saturday afternoon, a man identifying himself as Preston Bristol, Mrs. Bristol's husband presented himself at the front desk and asked for the key that she was supposed to have left for him at the front desk. He stated that he was joining his wife and children at the motel; they were visiting relatives, but he had had to work the day before.

The desk clerk replied that no key had been left and proceeded to call the room to inform Mrs. Bristol that her husband was at the front desk. There was no answer in the room.

Mr. Bristol then produced his driver's license for the desk clerk, which had the same address that Mrs. Bristol had used on her registration card. Mr. Bristol also produced a credit card issued in his name with the same account number as that used by Mrs. Bristol at check-in. As the clerk perused the license and credit card, Mr. Bristol offhandedly referred to a picture in his wallet of Mrs. Bristol and his two children. Based on the positive identification, the clerk issued Mr. Bristol a key to Mrs. Bristol's room.

At approximately 6:00 P.M. on Saturday, a guest in room 105 called the front desk to complain about a loud argument in room 104, Mrs. Bristol's room. The desk clerk called room 104 but got no answer.

The clerk then called the local police. When they arrived, they found Mrs. Bristol badly beaten and her children missing. A description of Mr. Bristol's car quickly led to his arrest and the recovery of the children by the police.

Mrs. Bristol recovered from her injuries and completed the divorce proceedings she had begun against her husband. In addition, she filed assault and battery charges against him. She also sued the motel's manager, owner, and franchise company for $8 million, stating that the motel was negligent and had violated her right to privacy. The motel's position was that it acted reasonably to ensure Mr. Bristol's identity and that it was not an insurer of guest safety and could not have foreseen Mr. Bristol's actions.

1. Did the desk clerk act in a reasonable manner?
2. Did Mr. Bristol have a right to enter the room?
3. What should management do in the future to prevent such an occurrence?

Legally Managing at Work

Law Enforcement and Guest Privacy

There are occasions when local law enforcement officers, for reasons they believe are valid, demand entrance to a guestroom. Should such an event occur, it is imperative that hotel management:

1. Attempt to cooperate with a legitimate law enforcement official. You must, however, balance that cooperation with your guests' right to privacy. See the International Snapshot at the end of this chapter for additional consideration under the 2001 Uniting and Strengthening America by Providing Appropriate Tools Required to Intercept and Obstruct Terrorism (USA PATRIOT) Act.
2. Ask to see a search warrant. The U.S. Supreme Court has ruled that hotel guests have a constitutional right to privacy in their rooms and cannot be subject to illegal search or seizure. Hotel managers should not allow a guest's room to be searched by police without a proper search warrant.
3. Document the event for the hotel's protection. This would include securing identification information on the law enforcement officer, his or her official police unit, the specifics of the demand, and any witnesses to the demand.

room. If Mr. Hernandez provides that information, he does so at the resort's peril because guests have an expectation of privacy with regard to such records. However, if a court order or subpoena is issued for the records, then the hotel must either provide the records in question or else seek legal counsel to inform the court why it is unable to comply or should not have to comply with the court order.

If a law enforcement agent is requesting the information, the USA PATRIOT Act may now control the best practice for a hospitality manager. See the International Snapshot at the end of this chapter for more details.

Guest privacy is a matter not to be taken lightly in the hospitality industry. Guests have a valid reason to expect that their rights will be protected by management. Ensuring these rights is the morally and legally correct course of action for hospitality managers.

Data Privacy

Another important area of guest privacy is the requirement to keep guest financial data information safe by implementing and monitoring data security practices so hackers are not able to access such information. The Federal Trade Commission (FTC) works on behalf of consumers in order to limit fraud and deceptive business practices. Under Section 5 of the Federal Trade Commission Act, the FTC has the general authority to investigate unfair and deceptive acts affecting commerce. In 2012, the FTC filed a legal action against Wyndham Hotels, alleging that they had failed to implement appropriate data security measures in 2008 and 2009 to protect their information technology systems, This failure had resulted in three data breaches disclosing more than 619,000 guests' personal financial information. Wyndham responded by arguing that the FTC had exceeded its authority. The U.S. Court of Appeals unanimously disagreed with Wyndham and held that the FTC does have the authority to regulate deceptive practices related to cybersecurity. In 2015, the parties reached a settlement, and Wyndham agreed, as part of the settlement, to create a comprehensive information security program to protect guests' credit card data and to undergo future audits to ensure compliance with the Payment Card Industries Data Security Standard (PCI DSS). Wyndham was not required to pay any monetary damages under the settlement.

As a hospitality manager, you are required to safeguard guest financial information by creating a security program that is designed to protect the security, confidentiality, and integrity of guest financial data pursuant to the PCI DSS. In Chapter 14, additional information on the PCI DSS will be discussed.

10.3 Facility Maintenance

Just as you have a responsibility to protect a guest's privacy, you also have a responsibility to operate your facility properly and safely. Recall that in Chapter 9, we discussed the duty of care that hospitality operators have to provide safe premises. Failure to do so will place your operation at risk for a personal injury lawsuit.

Safe Environment

As a manager, you are responsible for providing at a minimum a facility that meets the building codes of your local area. In most cases, this involves maintaining a facility in compliance with local, state, and federal laws as well as the Americans with Disabilities Act. In addition, you are required to operate your facility in a manner that is reasonable and responsive to the safety concerns of guests. You can do this if you remember that a safe facility is a combination of:

- A well-maintained physical facility.
- Effective operating policies and procedures.

Each year, too many lawsuits are filed against hospitality operations resulting from accidents that have occurred inside or on the grounds of an operation's physical facility. Consider the case of William Oliver from Wisconsin. One January night, Mr. Oliver arrived at a restaurant at 7:30 P.M., well after sundown. On his way from the restaurant parking lot to the front door, he slipped on some ice and hurt himself very badly. If Mr. Oliver decides to sue, the restaurant, in order to defend itself in the lawsuit, will need to demonstrate that it had the proper procedures in place to maintain the safety of its parking lot during the winter. If the restaurant cannot demonstrate and provide documentation of such efforts, it will likely lose the case.

A large number of slip and fall accidents, both inside and outside hospitality facilities, are litigated annually. (Next to motor vehicle accidents, slips and falls are the second leading source of personal injury incidents. They are also a major cause of accidental death and injury in the United States.) The resulting judgments against hospitality companies can be costly. You can help protect your operation against slip and fall and other accident claims if you take the necessary steps to maintain your physical facility, implement effective operating policies and procedures, and document your efforts.

Although it is not the goal of this book to detail all of the preventative maintenance techniques and operating policies used by competent hospitality operations, recall from Chapter 9 that the courts will measure a hospitality operation's negligence based on the standard of care applied by the operation and the level of reasonable care expected by guests and provided by other facilities.

Establishing the appropriate standard of care might not always be easy. By way of example, let's examine the safety requirements and operating policies for one area of hotel operation that is potentially dangerous and can subject operators to significant liability: the maintenance of recreational facilities such as pools, spas, and workout areas.

Swimming Pools Swimming pools, including spas and hot tubs, can be the source of significant legal liability. The dangers of accidental drowning, diving injuries, or even slipping on a wet surface can pose a significant liability threat to the operators of hotels, amusement parks, and other facilities. While this list is not exhaustive, following these 20 recommendations will go a long way toward reducing the liability related to pools.

1. Pass all local inspections.
2. Train the individual who is maintaining the pool to make sure that pH levels in the water are acceptable and chlorine is added as required.
3. Supply a trained lifeguard whenever the pool is open. If no lifeguard is supplied, post a sign stating this.
4. Mark the depths of pools accurately; if you have many international visitors in your hotel, you may want to consider posting the depths in meters as well as feet.
5. Do not allow guests to dive into the pool. Remove diving boards, post warning signs, and write "No Diving" on the floor area surrounding the pool.
6. Clearly identify the "deep" end of the pool. Use ropes to separate it, and keep them in place.
7. Fence off the pool area, even if it is inside the building. Install self-closing and self-latching and/or locking gate doors.
8. Make sure that the pool area and the pool itself is well lit and that all electrical components are regularly inspected and maintained to meet local electrical codes.
9. Provide a pool telephone with emergency access.

10. Prohibit glass in the pool area.
11. If the pool is outdoors, monitor the weather, and close the pool during inclement weather.
12. Prohibit pool use by nonguests.
13. Strictly prohibit all roughhousing.
14. Restrict the use of the pool by young children, by people who are intoxicated, and by those who would put the pool over its occupancy limits. Require swim diapers for all very young children.
15. Have lifesaving equipment on hand and easily accessible.
16. Install slip-resistant material on the floor areas around the pool.
17. Post warning signs in the languages of your customers.
18. Do not allow the pool area to be opened unless at least one property employee who has been trained in first aid is on duty.
19. Document all of your pool-care efforts.
20. Make sure your insurance policy specifically includes coverage for your pool.

Spas/Hot Tubs

Like pools, spa/hot tubs are also potential sources of liability. As a manager, it is your job to see that your staff implements the type of signage, physical care, and policies required to safely maintain these areas. The following list can help you maintain your spa in a manner consistent with current best practices:

1. Pass all local inspections.
2. Train the individual who is maintaining the spa, make sure pH levels in the water are acceptable and chlorine is added as required.
3. Install a thermometer and check the spa temperature frequently (102 degrees Fahrenheit is the maximum recommended temperature); record your efforts.
4. Mark the depth of the hot tub in feet and in meters for international guests.
5. Do not allow children under 14 to use the spa at all, and post signs to that effect.
6. Do not allow older children (under 18 years) to use the spa alone.
7. Display a sign recommending that the following individuals not use the spa:
    - Pregnant women
    - People who are elderly
    - Individuals with diabetes
    - People who have a heart condition, are on medication, or are under the influence of drugs or alcohol
    - Children under 14 years of age
8. Install a spa-area telephone with emergency access.
9. Prohibit glass in the spa area.
10. Prohibit alcohol in the spa area.
11. Prohibit spa use by nonguests and solo use by guests.
12. Install nonslip flooring surfaces around the spa.
13. Display signage indicating maximum spa occupancy.
14. Make sure your insurance policy specifically includes coverage for your spa.
15. Have lifesaving equipment on hand and easily accessible.
16. Check the hot tub's water quality frequently, and document your efforts.
17. Post warning signs in the language of your customers.
18. Do not allow the spa area to be opened unless at least one property employee who has been trained in first aid is on duty.
19. Restrict guest access to spa chemicals and heating elements.
20. Document all of your spa care efforts.

Workout and Fitness Areas

Workout rooms can also be a source of potential liability. Many operators of facilities with workout and fitness areas post a general "rules" notice as well as signs governing the use of specific equipment in the workout area. Figure 10.3 is an example of a set of general rules. As you can see, maintaining a pool, spa/hot tub, or workout/fitness area requires great care and attention. Accidents can occur, so the effective manager must take special care to prevent potential liability.

As a hospitality manager, safety should be one of your major concerns. All of your policies, procedures, and maintenance programs should be geared toward providing an environment that maximizes guest safety and security. To stay current in this field and to locate other forms, checklists, and procedures, log on to www.HospitalityLawyer.com.

Bedbugs

Recently, there has been a surge in pest and bedbug-related lawsuits instituted against hotels and apartment complexes. These suits are often quite costly with some judgments against hotels totaling hundreds of thousands of dollars in

1. Equipment in this room is for the use of reasonable adults only. Improper use may result in serious injury.
2. Children under 16 could be seriously injured by improper equipment use or nonsupervision.
3. Please limit workouts to 30 minutes on cardiovascular machines.
4. Only water is allowed in workout area. No other food or beverage is permitted.
5. Please wipe off all equipment after use.
6. Lower and raise all equipment carefully.
7. Because of high risk of injury, you must use a spotter when using free weights.
8. Please replace all weights, dumbbells, bars, and plates when finished.
9. Children not allowed unless accompanied by an adult.

FIGURE 10.3 Workout area rules.

compensatory and punitive damages. The most costly aspects of these suits are that punitive damages rarely are covered by insurance policies and the removal of a bedbug infestation. Thus, hospitality facilities must institute a quick, effective, and cost manageable procedure in the event an infestation occurs.

It is paramount to remove the infestation quickly because bed bugs reproduce quickly and the farther it spreads, the more the costs of eradication increase. Consistent inspection and treatment programs are important because it is difficult to ever totally remove the possibility of a bedbug situation. This is because guests sometimes bring the bedbugs in with them via their clothing and luggage. No lodging facility is ever safe from an infestation. It can happen in high-end hotels as well as low-budget facilities.

Preventative measures should be taken to eliminate any threat of an infestation. Employees should be trained in detecting the signs of an infestation, and a reporting procedure should be in place.

Defibrillators

On November 13, 2000, President Bill Clinton signed the Cardiac Arrest Survival Act (CASA) into law. The purpose of the act is to improve the survival rates of people who have sudden cardiac arrest in two major ways: (1) by the placement of automated external defibrillators (AEDs) in federal buildings and (2) in an effort to spur the use of AED devices in the private sector, by establishing protections from civil liability for persons (good Samaritans) who use AEDs in an emergency situation except in cases of gross negligence or willful misconduct. The AED device can be utilized by trained, nonmedical personnel in order to increase the survival rate from a cardiac episode. Since enacting CASA, many states have also implemented regulations in order to broaden the use of AEDs. Check with your state to see if providing AED devices is required in your particular establishment.

Americans with Disabilities Act (ADA), Title III

Facilities must not only be safe but also accessible. Title III of the Americans with Disabilities Act addresses the requirements involved with removing barriers to access public accommodations. (Recall that Title I of the ADA addresses making employment accessible to Americans with disabilities.) Title III requirements for existing facilities became effective on January 26, 1992, and were amended on September 15, 2010.

Title III affects businesses that are considered to be places of public accommodation as defined by the Department of Justice, which is responsible for enforcement of the act. These businesses are facilities operated by a private entity whose operations affect commerce and fall within at least one of the following dozen categories:

1. Place of lodging except for an establishment located within a facility that contains not more than five rooms for rent or hire and that actually is occupied by the proprietor of the establishment as the residence of the proprietor. A "place of lodging" includes:
   - An inn, hotel, or motel
   - A facility that provides guest rooms for sleeping for stays that primarily are short-term in nature (generally 30 days or less) where the occupant does not have the right to return to a specific room or unit after the conclusion of his or her stay and that provides guest rooms under conditions and with amenities similar to a hotel, motel, or inn, including the following:
   - On- or off-site management and reservations service
   - Rooms available on a walk-up or call-in basis
   - Availability of housekeeping or linen service
   - Acceptance of reservations for a guest room type without guaranteeing a particular unit or room until check-in and without a prior lease or security deposit.[1]
2. Establishment serving food or drink: restaurant, bar.
3. Place of exhibition or entertainment: theater, cinema, concert hall, stadium.
4. Place of public gathering: auditorium, convention center, lecture hall.
5. Sales or rental establishment: bakery; grocery, hardware, clothing, athletic equipment, and video rental stores; shopping malls; carpet showrooms.
6. Service establishment: bank, lawyer's office, gas station, funeral parlor, laundromat, dry cleaner, barber shop, beauty shop, insurance office, hospital, travel service, pharmacy, health-care office.
7. Public transportation: terminals, depots, stations (not including facilities relating to air transportation).
8. Place for public display or collection: museum, library, or gallery.
9. Place of recreation: park, zoo, amusement park.
10. Place of education: preschool, nursery, elementary, secondary, undergraduate, or postgraduate private school.
11. Social service center establishment: homeless shelter, day care center, independent living center, food bank, senior citizen center, adoption agency.
12. Place of exercise and/or recreation: gymnasium, health spa, bowling alley, golf course.

As per the definition of place of lodging outlined above, many Airbnb host properties may not be subject to the requirements of the ADA as they pertain to accessibility requirements. See https://www.airbnb.com/help/article/898/ada-and-fha-compliance-policy.

Title III requires places of public accommodation to provide goods and services to people with disabilities on an equal basis with the rest of the general public. The goal is to give

[1] https://www.ada.gov/regs2010/titleIII_2010/titleIII_2010_regulations.htm#a104

everyone the opportunity to benefit from our country's businesses and services and to allow all businesses the opportunity to benefit from the patronage of all Americans. Under Title III of the ADA, any private entity that owns, leases, leases to, or operates an existing public accommodation has four specific requirements:

1. *Getting guests and employees into the facility.* This involves removing barriers to make facilities available to and usable by people with mobility impairments to the extent that it is readily achievable. Examples could include parking spaces for the disabled, wheelchair ramps or lifts, and accessible restroom facilities.
2. *Providing auxiliary aids and services so that people with disabilities have access to effective means of communication.* This involves providing aids and services to individuals with vision or hearing impairments. Auxiliary aids include such services or devices as qualified interpreters, assistive listening headsets, television captioning and decoders, telecommunications devices for deaf persons (TDDs), videotext displays, readers, taped texts, Braille materials, and large-print materials. The auxiliary aid requirement is flexible. For example, a Braille menu is not required if waiters are instructed to read the menu to customers with sight impairments.
3. *Modifying any policies, practices, or procedures that may be discriminatory or have a discriminatory effect.* An example is a front desk policy advising people with disabilities that there is "no room at the inn" rather than attempting to accommodate them or inappropriately assessing additional charges for people who require guide animals.
4. *Ensuring that there are no unnecessary eligibility criteria that tend to screen out or segregate individuals with disabilities or limit their full and equal enjoyment of the place of public accommodation.* These include, for example, requirements that guests provide a driver's license. Many people with disabilities do not have a driver's license. So the best practice is to request photo identification rather than a driver's license specifically.

As you can see, Title III compliance involves the removal of physical barriers as well as discriminatory policies. Physical barrier requirements are generally achievable if you consider the following four priorities recommended for Title III compliance:

Priority 1: Accessible approach and entrance

Priority 2: Access to goods and services

Priority 3: Access to restrooms

Priority 4: Any other measures necessary

The Amendments to Title III address changes in technology regarding specific requirements to accommodate persons with mobility devices, such as motorized wheelchairs and video remote interpreting (VRI) communication technology. The 2010 amendments also clarified the term "service animals" to include only dogs and miniature horses. As always, it is important to check that your facility complies with the new Title III requirements, and if there are any questions that arise from the new legislation, you should consult an attorney.

To evaluate a facility for its compliance with these four priorities, you must carefully compare your property with the requirements of Title III. A thorough checklist dealing with Title III can be found online at https://www.ada.gov/racheck.pdf.

It is important to note that changes in your facility must be made where it is "reasonable" to do so. Because reasonability is determined on a case-by-case basis, it is important to plan and document your compliance efforts. To do so, the steps given in the Legally Managing at Work feature can be of great value.

Legally Managing at Work

Five Steps to Facility Evaluation

1. Plan the evaluation.
   a. Set an evaluation completion date.
   b. Decide who will conduct the survey.
   c. Obtain floor plans.
2. Conduct the survey.
   a. Use a checklist to evaluate the facility.
   b. Use a tape measure.
   c. Record results.
3. Summarize recommendations.
   a. List barriers found, along with ideas for removal.
   b. Consult with building contractors if necessary.
   c. Estimate costs of barrier removal.
4. Plan for improvements.
   a. Prioritize needs.
   b. Make barrier removal decisions.
   c. Establish timetables for completion.
5. Document efforts.
   a. Record what has been done.
   b. Plan for an annual review.
   c. Monitor changes in the law.

Search the Web 10.2

Log on to **www.usdoj.gov/crt/ada/adahom1.htm**

1. Select: 2010 ADA Standards for Accessible Design.
2. Select: 2010 ADA Standards for Accessible Design, either in HTML or PDF format.
3. Browse through the standards established for accessible design and answer the following questions:
   a. How many rooms with a roll-in shower are required for a hotel with 800 rooms?
   b. How many rooms in the same size hotel must be designed to accommodate the visually impaired?
   c. Explain the term equivalent facilitation as it pertains to room charges for disabled guests.

Laws regarding ADA compliance are complex, so it is a good idea to familiarize yourself with Title III requirements, especially if you are a facility manager. Before building a new facility or renovating an existing one, it is important to select an architect or contractor who is familiar with Title III requirements. And as you learned in Chapter 4, "Contract Basics," it is important to have your construction and/or renovation contract specify who is responsible for ensuring ADA compliance.

10.4 Responsibilities to Nonguests

Guests are not the only individuals who may lawfully enter a hospitality property, of course. Owners, managers, employees, vendors, and a guest's own invited guests will all utilize a hospitality company's facilities or services. Because restaurants, clubs, and hotels are open to the public, people can come in for a variety of reasons, not all of which are for the purpose of becoming a guest. An individual could enter a hospitality facility to visit a friend, ask for directions, use the restroom, use the telephone, shop, or commit a crime. As a manager, you have responsibilities for the safety and well-being of those who are not guests although that level of responsibility will vary based on the type of nonguest in question. In this section, we will examine three distinct types of nonguests and your responsibilities to each.

Guests of Guests

Most hotels allow guests great freedom in permitting invited friends and family members to visit them in the hotel. Most guests expect, and most hotels allow, guests of guests to enjoy many of the privileges enjoyed by the guest. It is important to note that it is the hotel that allows this practice; it is not a guest's right that is inherent in renting a room. Obviously, it is unlawful for a hotel manager to refuse to allow guests of guests on a discriminatory basis. In addition, hoteliers may impose the same type of reasonable conduct standards on a guest's guest as they do on the guests themselves.

From a personal injury liability point of view, the guests of a guest, if they are on the premises in accordance with hotel policy, should be treated in the same manner as a guest. That is, they should be provided with a safe and secure facility. A question arises, however, as to a hotel's liability for the acts of those not associated with the hotel. Under many state laws, a hotel has no legal responsibility to protect others from the criminal acts of third parties. But a legal responsibility may come into existence if the danger or harm was foreseeable. For example, if dangerous incidents of a similar nature had occurred on or near the premises previously, a jury might find that the hotel could have anticipated such an occurrence and should have taken reasonable steps to attempt to prevent it.

Because it is not possible to know whether someone is a guest or a guest of a guest, reasonable precautions should be taken to protect everyone who uses your facility. These precautions will be discussed more fully in Chapter 14, "Safety and Security Issues."

Invitees

A guest is an **invitee** of a hotel. By the same token, many individuals who are not guests can be considered invitees as well. An invitee enters a property because he or she has been expressly invited by the owner or because his or her intent is to utilize the property in some manner permitted by law and the property's ownership, usually, but not always, for the commercial gain of the property. In either case, the hotel is required to take reasonable care in maintaining its facility and to notify or warn the invitee of any potential danger; also in some cases, the hotel also has the duty to fix and eliminate these potential dangers.

Invitees include employees, managers, contractors, vendors, and individuals such as those entering to ask directions, use a telephone, or make a purchase. Because hotels and restaurants are open to the public, the number of situations in which an invitee enters the premises can be large indeed.

Consider the case of Jeremy Cavendar. He is the manager of a hotel facility attached to a large shopping mall in a major southwestern city. Because of its location, many shoppers pass through the hotel's lobby as they enter or exit the

---

LEGALESE

Invitee: An individual who is on a property at the expressed or implied consent of the owner.

Analyze the Situation 10.4

Walter Thomas was visiting Jeff Placer, who had registered as a guest at a newly opened Lodger-Inn hotel. The hotel was located off an interstate highway exit; it had been open for only three days. When Mr. Thomas left Mr. Placer's room in the evening, he was assaulted in the hotel's parking lot.

Mr. Thomas contacted an attorney, who threatened to sue the hotel for the injuries. Lashondra Tyson, the attorney for the hotel, replied to Mr. Thomas's attorney that the hotel was not responsible for the acts of third parties and that the hotel had no history of criminal activity taking place on its grounds. Thus, the hotel could not have foreseen any potential problem. In addition, Mr. Thomas was not a registered guest in the hotel.

Mr. Thomas's attorney replied that many hotels experience problems in their parking lots, so the hotel should, in fact, have anticipated potential problems. He also stated that Mr. Thomas was an invitee of the hotel and thus the hotel was required to guard his interest in the same manner as that of a guest.

1. What was the legal status of Mr. Thomas?
2. Why is the distinction important in this situation?
3. What records would Ms. Tyson need from the hotel's manager to give her the best chance of winning any potential lawsuit?

shopping mall. If an individual were hurt while passing through the lobby, Mr. Cavendar would likely be responsible for demonstrating that he and his staff had demonstrated reasonable care in maintaining the hotel lobby. This would be true even though the invitee in this case may have had no intention of utilizing any of the services offered by Mr. Cavendar's hotel. The mere fact that the hotel decided to locate within the shopping mall would demonstrate to most juries and personal injury attorneys that the hotel could have reasonably foreseen that a large number of shoppers would be passing through the area; hence, it should take reasonable care in protecting their safety.

Trespassers

Legally, hospitality managers do not owe the same duty of care to an individual who is unauthorized to be on a property as they do to one who is authorized. For example, a restaurant that has its floors mopped nightly has a duty to place "wet floor" signs around any area that is wet and that is likely to have foot traffic passing through it. However, the operator does not have a duty of care to illuminate those signs when the restaurant is closed. So, assuming that access is restricted, a burglar who enters the restaurant after hours has no legal right to expect that the operator will warn him or her of slippery floor conditions.

Some cases of trespass can be more complex, and operators should be very careful to make a distinction between a trespasser and a wandering guest. Consider the example of Deitra Reeves. Ms. Reeves was a guest of the Red Door Lounge, a very quiet and dimly lit club in a large city. One night, while seeking the ladies room, Ms. Reeves accidentally opened the door to a storage room, ran into a storage rack, and was injured in a fall. The lounge's attorney argued that Ms. Reeves was a trespasser since guests are not allowed in storage areas. Ms. Reeves's attorney argued that Ms. Reeves was a guest, and the lounge was negligent because it should have had the storeroom locked. A facility can expect that guests, if allowed, may wander into restricted areas. When they do, they will, in most cases, still be considered guests, and the reasonable standard of duty of care would be imposed on the hotel.

10.5 Removal of Guests

Just as guests must be admitted in accordance with the law, you must also treat those guests who are to be removed from your business in a way that is legally sound. Generally, guests can be removed from the premises for lack of payment, for inappropriate conduct, or for certain conditions of health.

Lack of Payment

When guests check into a hotel or order food in a restaurant, it is reasonable to assume that they will pay their bill. On occasion, a guest, for a variety of reasons, will not pay. Sometimes the reason may be that it is a scam, known as "dine and dash" where the patron will say he or she is stepping outside to smoke a cigarette and will be right back to pay the bill but never comes back to do so.

In a restaurant setting, the manager has few options for collecting. Clearly, the manager can refuse to serve the guest anymore during that visit and can rightfully refuse service in the future as long as the bill remains outstanding. However, if the guest leaves the premises, there is often little that can be done to recover losses.

It is legal for a hotel to require payment in advance for the use of a room as long as that requirement is applied uniformly in a manner that does not unlawfully discriminate among guests. If a guest does not present himself or herself at the front desk for payment by the posted check-out time or authorize a charge to an established credit card or account, that guest can be removed from the hotel for nonpayment. The hotel has a right, subject to local laws, to remove a transient guest from a room for nonpayment of charges due. A tenant with a lease, however, could not be removed or locked out of his or her apartment by a landlord without following state and local laws regarding eviction.

When a guest in a hotel does not pay, or cannot pay, the rightfully due bill, the term **eviction** is often used to denote the guest's removal. Legally, however, a hotel rarely will file a suit of unlawful retainer, which is required in an official tenant eviction. The term "eviction" continues to be used, however, to refer to a guest who is removed by a variety of means from a hospitality property.

Whether it is in the best interest of the hotel to evict a guest is a judgment call made by the manager. Clearly, lost credit cards or travelers checks and a variety of other circumstances might cause a guest to be temporarily unable to pay his or her account. In this situation, it is up to you to protect the financial interest of the hotel while accommodating the guest to the greatest degree possible. When it is clear, however, that the guest either will not or cannot pay and refuses to vacate the room, it is best to contact the local law enforcement agency to assist in the guest's removal. This protects the hotel in the event that the nonpaying guest claims the hotel used excessive force in the removal of the guest.

Often, the arrival of a law enforcement official at a restaurant or hotel is sufficient to encourage the guest to pay the bill. It is important to note, however, that the police will rarely, if ever, arrest a guest for failure to pay a bill that is owed. Efforts to collect on money owed to a hospitality operation should be pursued according to applicable state and local laws. This would entail filing a suit in **small claims court** or another appropriate court to get a judgment against the debtor (nonpaying guest). The cost of doing so is high in both time and money. Thus, it is best to avoid the situation whenever possible. In Chapter 14, we will discuss several ways that you can protect your operation from guests who have no intention of paying their bill.

Inappropriate Conduct

Guests who pose a threat to the safety and comfort of other guests or employees may be removed from a hotel or restaurant. Indeed, you have a duty of care as a manager to provide a facility that is safe for all guests and your employees. Thus, a guest who is extraordinarily loud, abusive, or threatening to others should be removed. Also note that inappropriate conduct may be considered a violation of a hotel's or restaurant's house rules (as discussed earlier in the chapter). Thus, a guest's disruptive behavior could be considered a breach of contract, which would give the hospitality establishment the authority to lawfully remove the guest. Again, this is a situation best handled jointly by management and local law enforcement officials.

Whether such a guest should be refunded any prepaid money or charged for any damages that may occur varies with the situation. In general, it may be said that a guest who has utilized a room and is removed for inappropriate behavior must still pay for the use of that room. Whether management in fact levies such a charge is subject to the principles of sound business judgment.

Overstays

Because a hotel rents rooms on a transient basis, it can also decide not to allow a guest to **overstay** his or her reservation contract. For this reason, guests may be removed from their rooms if they in fact have breached their contractual reservation agreement with the hotel. Although it might appear odd that a hotel would refuse to extend a guest's stay, it does happen. Consider the case of Giovanni Migaldi. Mr. Migaldi operates a hotel in Indianapolis, Indiana. The weekend of the Indianapolis 500 race is always a sellout for his hotel, and he is careful to require that all guests reserving rooms for that weekend pay in advance. On the morning before the race, a tour group that was scheduled to leave requests to stay an extra night when the tour bus experiences mechanical difficulty. Mr. Migaldi is expecting the arrival of another tour bus filled with racing fans coming to town for a three-night stay. If Mr. Migaldi allows the current tour bus passengers to stay, he will have no room for the prepaid racing fans due to arrive. All local hotel rooms are sold out, so Mr. Migaldi has no opportunity to move the race fans, nor does he want to violate his contract with them. Clearly, in this case, Mr. Migaldi will have to use all of his management skills to tactfully achieve the removal of the first group in order to make room for the second, confirmed group. This situation also illustrates the difficulty managers can face in maintaining their legal obligations while attempting to serve guests who encounter unexpected travel delays and difficulties.

Registration cards that are completely filled out, including a space for the guest to initial to verify arrival and departure dates, can be of great assistance in dealing with the overstay guest. Additionally, the registration card can state that additional nights, if approved by the hotel, will be at the "rack rate" (which is usually significantly higher than the rate a guest is actually paying).

In anticipation of a sold-out event in the area, the hotel that has prepaid rooms already under contract could take steps to prevent any overstays. The hotel might have the guests checking in a day or two prior to the arrival of the prepaid guests acknowledge in writing that they will vacate the

---

LEGALESE

Eviction: The procedure that a lessor uses to remove a lessee from physical possession of leased real property, usually for violation of a significant lease provision, such as nonpayment of rent.

Small claims court: A court designed especially to hear lawsuits entailing relatively small sums of money. They can provide a speedy method of making a claim without the necessity of hiring a lawyer and engaging in a formal trial.

Overstay: A guest who refuses to vacate his or her room when he or she has exceeded the number of nights originally agreed to at check-in; also known as a "hangover."

guest rooms as specified and that if they do not, their personal belongings will be taken from the rooms and held in storage at the guest's expense. Please note that if a hotel does in fact set aside guests' personal belongings, it is recommended that two managers collect all of them and make a written inventory of them and place them in a secured storage area. These steps should prevent any controversy over alleged missing items from the guest room.

Accident, Illness, or Death

A guest stricken with a severe illness and a guest's death create a traumatic experience for any hospitality facility. Just as people have accidents, get sick, die, attempt suicide, or overdose on drugs in their home, similar situations can also occur in hotels and restaurants. When they do, it is important that everyone in the facility know exactly how to respond. The priority should be to maintain the dignity and privacy of the guest while providing the medical attention appropriate for the situation. Comforting the family may be subject to ongoing police investigations. There may be a time when a guest decides to end his or her life in a hotel guest room. Some people may do this to prevent the family and loved ones from finding their bodies after the act. Room service order takers can be trained to be observant for what is known in the industry as the "last supper" when a guest who has checked in alone orders a large number of the most expensive dishes with wine and/or other alcohol. The food and beverage department should contact the hospitality manager on duty who may want to visit the guest to see if he or she is okay and if there is anything the hotel can do to help.

If an emergency calls for the removal of a guest, extreme care should be taken. The checklist in the next Legally Managing at Work feature can be helpful in the removal in a discreet but effective manner.

Legally Managing at Work

Responding to Guest Health Emergencies

1. Train and frequently retrain employees on their role in responding to a medical emergency.
2. Instruct employees to contact the manager on duty (MOD) and/or security personnel immediately if it appears that a guest is seriously ill, unconscious, or nonresponsive.
3. Designate someone to call 911 or other emergency care provider(s). If the circumstances surrounding the incident seem suspicious, also notify the police.
4. Provide basic first aid; however, do not touch the guest unless you are trained to provide aid.
5. Instruct the MOD to survey the situation to determine whether other guests or employees are at risk or the area needs to be secured against entry by others.
6. Designate a specific individual to keep unauthorized persons away from the area until the emergency medical team arrives.
7. When the emergency medical team arrives, provide them with any information you have that can help to establish the identity of the guest.
8. If the guest is removed from the property, secure and hold any personal property belonging to her or him. The length of time you must retain personal property and the method of disposing of the property at the end of that time will vary from state to state.
9. Document the incident using an incident documentation form.
10. Report the incident to local law enforcement authorities if required to do so by law.

International Snapshot

Should Foreign Governments Adopt Provisions from the USA PATRIOT Act to Combat Terrorist Acts against the Hospitality Industry?

The scene is becoming all too familiar. Terrorists are attacking hotels and other hospitality venues in greater frequency. First, it was in Egypt. On April 18, 1996, terrorists attacked the Hotel Europa in Cairo, killing 18 Greek nationals. Next, it was the island of Bali on October 12, 2002. In the late evening, a terrorist attack struck a nightclub on the island, murdering over 180 people and injuring hundreds. More recently, in November 2015, hospitality venues in Paris were attacked, killing 130 people at a major stadium, a concert hall, and several local cafes and restaurants. Between January 2015 and January 2016, four hotels in Africa were targeted, killing nearly 100 people. In February 2016, a terrorist suicide bomber attacked and killed at least 15 people at a Somali hotel. Nor is the United States immune from terrorist attacks. In June 2016, a gay nightclub in Orlando, Florida, was attacked, killing 49 people and wounding 53 others.

International terrorists will continue to attack nonmilitary installations, known as "soft" targets. Unfortunately for the hospitality industry, today's soft targets include hotels, restaurants, and nightclubs. The central question for the international community, as well as hoteliers and others, is how to protect the hospitality industry from future terrorist attacks. The answer lies in the introduction of aggressive antiterrorism legislation abroad and increased vigilance by the hospitality industry.

In response to the terrorist attacks of September 11, 2001, sweeping legislation, know as the USA PATRIOT Act (Patriot Act) was passed.

(continued)

The full title for this law is Uniting and Strengthening America by Providing Appropriate Tools Required to Intercept and Obstruct Terrorism Act of 2001. On May 26, 2011, President Barack Obama signed legislation to extend the Patriot Act called the PATRIOT Sunsets Extension Act of 2011, which allowed for a four-year extension of three major provisions. These three major provisions include roving wiretaps, searches of business records, and conducting surveillance of "lone wolves" or individuals suspected of a connection with terrorist activities not linked specifically to terrorist groups. In addition, the USA Freedom Act was signed into law in 2015, renewing provisions of the Patriot Act through 2019. Parts of the Patriot Act were amended to prevent the National Security Agency from continuing the mass phone data collection program. The Patriot Act, not surprisingly, is applicable to hotels in the United States in several ways.

The Patriot Act provides for the use of emergency warrants to search hotel rooms and to obtain guest information. Under the Patriot Act, federal agents of the U.S. government may, with a search warrant, obtain "tangible records" from a hotel relating to guests or "groups of guests" that registered at the hotel. Even without a search warrant, registration records of a hotel guest may be obtained by a federal agent if proper law enforcement identification is produced and shown to hotel management. Furthermore, records of all electronic transactions relating to a guest at the hotel must be produced if requested by a governmental entity.

Those records include telephone records, email correspondence, and transactions involving more than $10,000 in cash.

The Patriot Act grants immunity to hotels that provide voluntary registration information to a governmental entity if the hotel "reasonably" believes that an emergency involving immediate danger of death or serious physical injury to any person justifies disclosure of the information. In addition, the Patriot Act provides criminal liabilities for individuals who "harbor" or "conceal" a person known, or with reasonable grounds, is believed to have committed or is about to commit an act of terrorism. If, however, a hotel reports in "good faith" a suspected terrorist directly to the federal government or federal agency (such as the FBI), the hotel will not be subject to liability under the Patriot Act.

The Patriot Act is not the only antiterrorism legislation in the world. Such legislation exists in the United Kingdom, the European Union, and other foreign countries. But many countries have limited antiterrorism legislation or have failed to implement any at all. For instance, it was not until after the J. W. Marriott Hotel in Jakarta was attacked by terrorists that Prime Minister Thaksin Shinawatra rushed into law new antiterrorist legislation before world leaders attended the APEC meeting in Bangkok in October 2003. If the actions of the Thai government represent a barometer of sorts, then the worldwide community has a long way to go in confronting terrorism. However, the international community should consider adopting relevant provisions from the Patriot Act so that foreign law enforcement agencies may investigate, apprehend, and prosecute terrorists before further hotels and other hospitality venues are attacked.

Provided by Richard Barrett-Cuetara, Esq., of Barrett-Cuetara, PLLC Law Firm, Dallas, Texas. www.BarrettCuetara.com. (214) 556-3876 and Diana S. Barber, JD, Assistant Professor of Hospitality Law and Liability at Kennesaw State University.

WHAT WOULD YOU DO?

You are the area vice president of franchising for a quick-service restaurant (QSR) company that serves a unique grilled chicken product that has become extremely popular. Because of a strong marketing effort and solid operating results, your company's growth has been very rapid. In your five-state area, the company is considering purchasing a small chain of 15 units that sells a comparable chicken product. Those units, consisting of older buildings in excellent locations, are to be converted to units owned and operated by your company. Your immediate supervisor, the company president, has asked you to respond to the following:

1. How will you determine which units are not in compliance with Title III of the American with Disabilities Act requirements?
2. What criteria will you use for prioritizing needed improvements?
3. How will you document a good-faith effort to meet Title III of the ADA requirements?

Draft answers to your president's questions.

WHAT DID YOU LEARN IN THIS CHAPTER?

Guest is a term used to describe a transient customer, as opposed to a tenant who may utilize a facility for a longer, or more permanent, time period.

Because most hospitality establishments are considered places of public accommodation, they must observe all applicable federal, state, and local civil rights laws that prohibit discrimination in the admission of guests into a facility as well as the types of services provided.

Guests in hospitality establishments have expectations of privacy, both personally and for any information about their stay. Hospitality establishments are legally obligated to honor those expectations.

A hospitality operator has a legal obligation to provide a reasonably safe physical facility for its guests. This requires significant attention to potential dangers and preventative maintenance procedures. In addition, Title III of the American with Disabilities Act requires hospitality operators to remove barriers from their facilities to allow access to people with disabilities. Managers also may have a duty of care to provide a reasonably safe premise for individuals, actual guests or not, on their property.

The process of removing guests from an establishment should be undertaken as a last resort and with caution.

CHAPTER 11

Your Responsibilities for Guests' Property

11.1 Liability for Guests' Property

Most hotels and restaurants are safe places to visit and work. As explained in Chapter 10, "Your Responsibilities as a Hospitality Operator to Guests," you, as a hospitality manager, have a responsibility to make your facility as safe as possible. This responsibility pertains to the well-being of the guests themselves, and to the security of their property.

Common Law Liability

Historically, under common law, innkeepers were held responsible for the safety of a guest's property. In fact, the inns would often advertise that travelers could rely on their personal protection during their stay. For example, if a traveler stayed at the Heidelberg Arms Inn, he or she was under the protection of the Heidelberg family, including the "arms" (weapons) that the family would muster against any intruders who would dare attack. This was important because, in the past, travel was risky, and those travelers who arrived for a night's lodging needed to know that the innkeeper could provide them with a secure haven during their stopover. Because of the importance of providing protection when traveling, an innkeeper became, under common law, an insurer of the safety of a guest's property. If the common law had not required innkeepers to maintain a protected environment, robbers and bandits would have made the inns unsafe places indeed, and travel would have been greatly restricted.

In today's world, hotel and restaurant guests still face the threat of robbery and burglary. The number of crimes reported annually by hotels and restaurants is large and growing. Jewelry, credit cards, and cash, as well as personal property such as cameras and furs, entice those who are not honest. Vacationers, business travelers, or simply those dining out are under the threat of an increasingly sophisticated type of thief. Unfortunately, even hospitality employees can also be a threat to guest property.

Hospitality managers must remain vigilant to various threats from sophisticated con artists to "grab and go" thieves because today's law may still hold those in the hospitality industry liable for the safety of their guests' property. Consider the case of Evan Gainer. Mr. Gainer checks into a hotel carrying a bag of diamonds valued at $100,000. The bag is stolen from his room. Under common law, the innkeeper could be liable to reimburse Mr. Gainer for the full value of his stolen diamonds, even if he or she was unaware that the luggage contained such valuable items.

CHAPTER OUTLINE

11.1. Liability for Guests' Property

11.2. Bailments

11.3. Property with Unknown Ownership

IN THIS CHAPTER, YOU WILL LEARN

1. To understand fully the responsibility hospitality managers have to safeguard the personal property of their guests.
2. To carry out the procedures needed to limit potential liability for the loss of guest property.
3. To assess the theories of bailment so as to be able to implement policies that limit potential legal liability.
4. To create the procedures required to legally dispose of personal property whose ownership status is in question.

Of course, property liability extends beyond the threat of theft. Consider the case of Tony Mustafa. Mr. Mustafa allowed a hotel's valet parking staff to park his new Mercedes-Benz convertible in its elevated parking garage. While retrieving the car, a valet driver scraped the side of the car against a concrete pillar, damaging it extensively. As could be expected, Mr. Mustafa was quite upset, and would, in all likelihood, hold the hotel responsible for the damage done to his vehicle. In this case, the guest's property, while not stolen, was clearly damaged while in the possession of the hotel.

In summary, theft, negligent handling, fire, flooding, and a variety of other factors can threaten a guest's property. The general rule of common law is that the innkeeper will be liable for damage to, or loss of, a guest's property; unless an act of nature, civil unrest, or the guest's own negligence caused the damage or loss. Consequently, hospitality managers have an extraordinarily difficult task. Fortunately, in every state, the legislatures have moved to modify, under very specific circumstances, the common law liability requirements placed on innkeepers.

Limits on Common Law Liability

When innkeepers face great liability exposure, they should also have a great deal of control over a guest's possessions. It was this recognition of the great risk taken by innkeepers that moved state legislatures to modify the centuries-old common law liability for innkeepers. Beginning in the mid-1800s and continuing today, each state has developed its own view of the extent of innkeeper liability for the possessions of their guests. The laws in each state vary considerably, however, so it is extremely important that hotel managers familiarize themselves with the law in their own state.

Figure 11.1 is a copy of the Innkeepers Liability statute for the state of Ohio. It is an excellent example of the type of law that state legislatures have passed for the benefit of innkeepers. Let's look carefully at several characteristics of the Ohio statute, which are common to most state liability laws.

Posting Notice

When a state legislature modifies the common law liability of innkeepers, it is only right that guests be notified of the limitation. This is a critical point, and one that must be fully understood by the hospitality manager. Simply put, if a hotel wishes to take advantage of a state's laws limiting its liability for a guest's possessions, the guest must be made aware of the existence and content of that law. Notice that in the Ohio statute, guests must be made aware of the statute by requiring that the innkeeper keep "a copy of this section printed in distinct type conspicuously suspended in the office, ladies parlor or sitting room, bar room, washroom, and five other conspicuous places in such inn, or not less than 10 conspicuous places in all."

A Secure Safe

If a hotel is to limit its liability for a guest's possessions, the hotel must provide a safe where guests can keep their valuables during their stay. Note that the Ohio statute states an

Section 4721.01 Liability for Loss of Property (GC Section 5981)

An innkeeper, whether a person, partnership, or corporation, having in his [or her] inn a metal safe or vault in good order suitable for the custody of money, bank notes, jewelry, articles of gold and silver manufacture, precious stones, personal ornaments, railroad mileage books or tickets, negotiable or valuable papers, and bullion, arid keeping on the doors of the sleeping rooms used by his [or her] guests suitable locks or bolts, and on the transoms and windows of such rooms, suitable fastenings, and keeping a copy of this section primed in distinct type conspicuously suspended in the office, ladies parlor or sitting room, bar room, washroom, and five other conspicuous places in such inn, or not less than 10 conspicuous places in all, shall not be liable for loss or injury suffered by a guest, unless such guest has offered to deliver such property to such innkeeper for custody in such metal safe or vault and the innkeeper has omitted or refused to take and deposit it in the safe or vault for custody and give the guest a receipt therefore.

Section 4721.02 Extent of Liability Agreement (GC Section 5982)

An innkeeper should not be obliged to receive from a guest for deposit in the safe or vault property described In section 4721.01 of the Revised Code exceeding a total value of five hundred dollars, and shall not be liable for such property exceeding such value whether received or not. Such innkeeper, by special arrangement with a guest may receive for deposit in such safe or vault property upon such written terms as may be agreed upon. An innkeeper shall be liable for a loss of any of such property of a guest in his [or her] inn caused by the theft or negligence of the innkeeper or his [or her] servant.

Section 4721.03 Limit of Liability for as to Certain Property (GC Section 5983)

The liability of an innkeeper whether person, partnership, or corporation, for loss of or injury to personal property placed in his [or her] care by his [or her] guests other than that described in section 4721.01 and 4721.02 of the Revised Code shall be that of a depositary for hire. Liability shall not exceed one hundred and fifty dollars for each trunk and it's contents, fifty dollars for each valise and it's contents, and ten dollars for each box, bundle or package and contents, so placed in his [or her] care, unless he [or she] has consented in writing with such guests to assume a greater liability [sic].

FIGURE 11.1 **State of Ohio limitations on innkeeper liability.**

Analyze the situation 11.1

Traci Kennear checked into the Pullman House Hotel. During her stay, jewelry with an estimated value of $5,000 was stolen from her hotel room. Ms. Kennear maintained that the hotel should be responsible for the jewelry's replacement and sued the hotel for the amount of the stolen jewelry. The hotel stated that its liability was limited to $300 under state law because Ms. Kennear failed to deposit the jewelry in the safe deposit boxes provided by the hotel.

Ms. Kennear's attorney countered that the notice of the law, which the legislature stated must be "conspicuously posted" in order to be applied, was in fact posted on the inside of a dresser drawer filled with extra blankets for the guestroom, and that, further, the type size was so small that an average person would not be able to read the notice from a distance of 2 feet. The hotel replied that the notice was, in its view, conspicuously posted, and that Ms. Kennear should have asked for help from the hotel if she could not find or read the notice.

1. Did the hotel comply with the state legislature's requirement that the notice be conspicuously posted?
2. How could the hotel manager in this case ensure compliance with the "conspicuous posting" requirement of the state legislature?

innkeeper must provide access to a "metal safe or vault." Hotels in most states are required to provide a safe for guest valuables and to operate the safe in a reasonable manner. That is, the safe should be in good working order, and access to the safe should be restricted and closely monitored.

Suitable Locks on Doors and Windows

Obviously, the hotel that intends to limit its liability must provide a reasonably safe room for its guests. This would include providing functioning locks for doors and windows, or as stated in the Ohio statute, "suitable locks or bolts, and on the transoms and windows of such rooms, suitable fastenings."

Limits on Required Possession

In most states, an innkeeper is not required to accept for safekeeping an unlimited amount of personal property or items high in value. A hotel is not a bank, and it is not reasonable to assume that it would be as secure as a bank. Note the limitation allowed the innkeeper in the Ohio statute, which states, "An innkeeper should not be obliged to receive from a guest for deposit in the safe or vault property described in . . . the Revised Code exceeding a total value of five hundred dollars, and shall not be liable for such property exceeding such value whether received or not."

Limits on Replacement Values of Luggage

Because it is impossible to know for certain exactly what may have been contained in a lost piece of luggage, most states place a dollar limit on the replacement value of such items. Thus, if a piece of luggage placed in the care of the innkeeper is lost, the hotel's liability will be limited to the dollar value specified in the statute. Note the wording in the Ohio statute: "Liability shall not exceed one hundred and fifty dollars for each trunk and it's [*sic*] contents, fifty dollars for each valise and it's [*sic*] contents, and ten dollars for each box, bundle or package and contents."

This limitation provision is very similar to that provided to airlines by federal law for lost or damaged luggage. Also, be aware that some limited liability laws also protect the innkeeper (and their insurance companies) in the event of a fire or natural disaster.

Penalty for Negligence

In nearly all states, if an innkeeper is negligent, the statute limiting liability becomes ineffective. As the Ohio statute states, "An innkeeper shall be liable for a loss of any of such property of a guest in his [or her] inn caused by the theft or negligence of the innkeeper or his [or her] servant." Note that the Ohio statute makes an innkeeper responsible for theft if an employee (servant) commits it. Even more important, the innkeeper becomes liable for the full amount of any property loss resulting from the negligence of the hotel or its staff (subject to the contributory negligence of the guest).

Ensuring the Limitation of Liability

Although it is implied, rather than explicitly stated, in the Ohio statute, failure on the part of the innkeeper to fulfill the statute's requirements will cause the innkeeper to lose the protection of the statute. Simply put, it is the responsibility of the innkeeper to prove that the hotel fully complied with all requirements set forth in the state law (i.e., appropriate notice with the right language, posted in the right number of conspicuous places, in an easy-to-read format, etc.). If the innkeeper does not meet the statutory requirements, the innkeeper cannot avail him- or herself of the limitation of liability provided by the statute.

11.2 Bailments

There are situations when a hotel or restaurant manager may be entrusted with a guest's property in circumstances not covered directly under a state's liability statute. For example, suppose that a guest arrives at a hotel and is greeted by a bellman who immediately takes the guest's bags and gives the guest a receipt before checking in. Who is responsible for the luggage? In this case, the guest has not had an opportunity to read the posted liability statutes and has not even technically become a guest yet. However, because the bellman has taken voluntary possession of the bags, the hotel bears some responsibility for the safety and return of the guest's luggage.

Restaurants are not generally covered under the state laws that limit the liability of innkeepers. Nevertheless, restaurants too have responsibilities for the safety of their guests' property, especially in situations in which the restaurant takes temporary possession of that property.

These responsibilities have been established by the courts through the application of a legal concept known as a **bailment** In the hospitality industry, bailments are quite common. Coat checks, valet parking, safety deposit boxes, laundry services, luggage storage, and luggage delivery services are all examples of bailments. Restaurant and hotel managers must understand that they are responsible for the safety of a guest's property when a bailment is established.

Bailment Relationship

In a bailment relationship, a person gives property to someone else for safekeeping. For example, a restaurant guest may check his or her coat in a coatroom. The diner assumes that the restaurateur will safely hold the coat until he or she comes back for it. While there may or may not be a charge for the service, the restaurateur assumes responsibility for the safety of the coat when it is received from the guest. In this situation, a bailment has been created.

The word "bailment" is derived from a Latin verb, *bajulare*, meaning "to bear a burden" and then from an old French word *bailler*, which means "to deliver." In a bailment relationship, the person who gives his or her property to another is known as the **bailor**. The person who takes responsibility for the property after receiving it is known as the **bailee**.

To create a bailment, the property must be delivered to the bailee. The bailee has a duty to return the property to the bailor when the bailment relationship ends. Thus, if a guest delivers a suit of clothes to an in-house hotel tailor, the bailment relationship begins when the tailor accepts the clothing and ends when the clothing has been returned to the guest.

It is important to note that a bailment may be for hire; that is, the bailor may have to pay the bailee to hold the property (as in paying for valet parking), the bailee may pay for the privilege of using the property (as is the case when renting a car), or the relationship may take the form of a **gratuitous bailment**.

LEGALESE

Bailment: The delivery of an item of property for some purpose with the expressed or implied understanding that the person receiving it shall return it in the same or similar condition in which it was received, when the purpose has been completed. The property involved relates to coat checks, valet parking, safety deposit boxes, laundry, luggage storage, and delivery.

Bailor: A person or entity that gives property to another in a bailment arrangement.

Bailee: A person or entity that receives and holds property in a bailment arrangement.

Gratuitous bailment: One in which there is no payment (consideration) in exchange for the promise to hold the property.

Types of Bailments

The law surrounding bailments is vast and varied. Essentially, however, bailments are in three categories:

1. *Bailments for the benefit of the bailor:* In this arrangement, only the bailor gains from the agreement. This arrangement exists, for example, when a refrigeration repairman asks if he can leave his tools in a restaurant's storeroom for the night so they do not have to be reloaded into the repair truck. The tools will be used the next day to finish a repair job covered by the refrigerator's warranty. The restaurant that accepts the tools for safekeeping also accepts the responsibility of a bailment relationship and so must exercise a high degree of care for the safety of the property (tools). If the restaurant is unwilling to do so, it can, of course, simply refuse to accept possession of the property.
2. *Bailments for the benefit of the bailee:* In some cases, the person holding the property gains from the bailment relationship. When the foodservice director of the local country club borrows chafing dishes from the food and beverage director of the local athletic club in order to service an extremely large wedding, the bailment is for the benefit of the bailee only. Again, it is important to note that this bailment relationship could be a gratuitous one, or the dishes could be rented to the country club. In either case, the bailee who benefits from the relationship is responsible for the safety of the property while it is in his or her possession.
3. *Bailments for the benefit of both parties:* In many cases, a bailment, either for payment or gratuitous, is for the benefit of both parties. This would be the case, for example, when a restaurant agrees to park its guests' cars for them while they dine. The guests (bailors) gain the convenience of having their cars parked for them, and the restaurant (bailee) gains because of the increase in business that comes from providing the parking service.

Although the rule of law varies somewhat in each of these three types, as a manager, you need to realize that guest property, when in your possession, subjects you to the duty of reasonably caring for that property. A simple way to consider your responsibility is to assume that you should exercise as much care for the property of a guest as you would for your own property. If you cannot exercise that degree of care, it is best not to enter into a bailment relationship.

Liability under a Bailment Relationship

A hospitality facility is liable only if a bailment relationship is established. For example, many restaurants and hotels provide coat racks or unattended coatrooms for their guests. Generally, a restaurant would not be responsible for any theft or damage to a patron's property on an unattended coat rack because the restaurant did not legally take possession of the property. Thus, a bailment was never created.

Analyze the Situation 11.2

The Fox Mountain Country Club was a popular location for weddings in a midsized town. The country club offers a free coat check service to its members and guests. A staff member employed by the country club operates the coat check service. The coat checkroom is located just outside the entrance to the club's Crystal Ballroom.

At a wedding held on June 15, Mrs. Kathy Weldo presented her full-length sable coat to the uniformed coat check attendant at the country club. Mrs. Weldo was given a small plastic tag with a number, which she observed corresponded to the number on a coat hanger where her coat was hung. Standing outside the coatroom, Mrs. Weldo had a clear view of her fur as it hung on the coat rack. Mrs. Weldo remarked to the attendant that the coat was "very valuable" and that she hoped the attendant would watch over it carefully.

Upon leaving the club at 1:00 A.M., Mrs. Weldo went to the coat check area to retrieve her coat only to find that it was missing. When she inquired about the coat's location, the coat check attendant apologized profusely but could not explain the coat's disappearance. The attendant stated that he had left the coatroom unattended only twice that evening, one time for a 15-minute dinner break and the other for a 5-minute cigarette break. The door to the coatroom was left open and unlocked during those periods so that guests who left early could retrieve their own coats.

Mrs. Weldo returned to the club the next day to speak to Ms. Miles, the club manager. Ms. Miles pointed to a sign prominently displayed near the coatroom door stating, "The club is not responsible for lost or stolen property." She recommended that Mrs. Weldo refer the matter to her insurance company.

1. What was the nature of the bailment relationship in this situation?
2. Did the club exercise reasonable care in the handling of Mrs. Weldo's coat?
3. What should the club manager do in the future to avoid situations such as this?

This concept also applies to items inside bailed property. For example, a restaurant that offers valet parking would be liable for damage to a guest's automobile. When the guest presents the car keys to the valet, possession of the car is transferred from the guest to the restaurant, and a bailment is established. However, the restaurant would probably not be liable for the loss of an expensive camera that was left inside the car. The restaurant knowingly accepted ownership only of the automobile. No bailment relationship was established for the camera left inside the automobile.

It is important to remember that, in cases where a bailment relationship does not exist and a hospitality operation does not assume liability, managers should still exercise a degree of care over their guests' property to avoid the risk of a negligence lawsuit.

When a bailment relationship has been established, a hospitality operation will be liable for any loss or damage to a guest's property. In many states, a hotel or restaurant's liability for damage will be limited if the operation (bailee) can prove that it exercised the standard of care required under the law.

A bailee can also reduce its liability by establishing a set liability limit in an express agreement with the bailor provided the limitation is not in violation of law or public policy. For example, a country club may post a sign stating it will reimburse guests for lost property up to a set amount. Although some states may recognize this type of sign as a reasonable agreement between bailor and bailee to limit liability, other states do not recognize the validity of such a posting because it against public policy. Thus, a hospitality manager should read his or her state law carefully or consult an attorney before posting such a sign.

A hotel may also be liable for any bailed property of nonguests using its facilities, such as a hotel guest who has already checked out or an individual using a hotel's restaurant or meeting room. However, the hotel's liability for such property may be limited under the terms of the state's liability law.

In all cases, if the loss or damage to a guest's property is the result of the hospitality operation's own negligence or fraud, the hospitality operation will be liable for the full amount of that property. By the same token, if a guest's own negligence contributes in some way to the property's loss, the hospitality operation's liability may be reduced or even eliminated altogether.

Note that, historically, the common law held a hotel liable for the loss of a guest's property if the property and the guest were within the premises of the hotel. This concept was known as **infra hospitium**. Today, most states determine responsibility for lost or stolen items by applying bailment and/or negligence theories.

Consider the case of Alexis Lee who operates a tailor shop in the city. As part of her business, she makes the rounds of local hotels, seeking alteration and mending jobs. One day, Alexis takes an expensive man's suit from a guest staying at a luxury hotel. The guest had delivered the suit to the bellstand for pickup by the alteration company. Unfortunately, in her hurry to finish her collection rounds, Alexis leaves her truck unlocked, and the suit is stolen from the back of it before she returns.

In this situation, it is likely that the guest would expect the hotel to replace the suit. The hotel, of course, may be able to press a case against Ms. Lee if it can be shown that her actions were negligent. However, a bailment was created between the bellman and the hotel guest. Under the law, an outside agent acting as a bailee on behalf of a restaurant or hotel may subject the operation to liability. Even though the suit was outside the physical confines of the hotel, the bailment between the hotel guest and the bellman and the subsequent bailment established between the bellman and Ms. Lee, served, in effect,

LEGALESE

Infra hospitium: A Latin term meaning "within the hotel."

to extend the confines of the hotel to include her truck. Thus, the hotel could be liable for the loss of the suit.

Perhaps the most difficult application of bailment and liability concerns the safekeeping of guests' automobiles. Under common law, innkeepers were responsible for the protection of their guests' means of transportation (which, up until the twentieth century, typically meant the care and feeding of horses). Today, however, the use of automobiles presents a unique challenge because they generally exceed the state's liability amounts yet cannot be placed in a safe.

In cases where a restaurant or hotel offers valet parking, the situation is clear. The guest turns over his or her key to the valet, creating a bailment relationship, thereby placing liability for the automobile with the restaurant or hotel. In situations where a hotel has an agreement with an independent parking garage, the hotel may still be liable for a guest's automobile, since the garage could be considered to be an agent of the hotel.

Many motels have free parking lots on their premises but accept no liability for their guests' automobiles. Guests are permitted to park on the lot if they so desire but must keep their car keys with them. Thus, no bailment relationship is established between the guest and the motel that would cover any loss or damage to the automobile; that is, the motel would not be liable. That said, some states consider the availability of a parking lot to be a gratuitous bailment, which would hold the hospitality operation liable for any damage. In cases where guests keep their car keys but a fee is charged for use of the parking lot, the courts may decide that charging a fee creates a bailment relationship, which could hold the parking lot owner liable. The laws covering liability for automobiles vary widely from state to state. As a hospitality manager, you should have a thorough knowledge of all the liability provisions included in your state's laws.

Detained Property

Bailees have significant responsibilities when a bailment is created, but so too do bailors. The bailee has the right to charge a fee to cover any costs that may be associated with holding or protecting property, such as a parking fee or charges for the services of a dry cleaner or tailor. However, the bailor may be required to pay reasonable charges for property requiring special handling or maintenance. If the bailor is unwilling or unable to pay the agreed-on charges, the bailee may detain or keep the goods of the bailment as a lien until full payment is made.

Consider the case of the hotel that operates a parking garage and charges a nightly parking fee for guests. A guest arrives at the front desk to check out one morning and claims to be dissatisfied with the hotel and its services. The guest refuses to pay for either the room charges or the parking fees incurred. The hotel may choose to withhold the automobile from the guest until payment is made. In this situation, the automobile would be considered **detained property**. Of course, during the time the property was being withheld, the hotel, as the bailee, would have an obligation to protect the detained property from harm with the same measure of care it would normally exercise.

The situation just described illustrates not only the concept of detained property but also why you must use your legal knowledge, as well as good judgment, when operating a hospitality facility. The hotel manager may well be within his or her legal rights to detain the automobile and demand payment, but that action may not be in the hotel's best interest. To maintain good customer relations and to avoid a lawsuit, the manager may decide that a better approach would be to release the automobile. The procedure of detaining property can subject you to a possible lawsuit if not done properly. It is a course of action that should be pursued only after careful consideration of the legal consequences.

LEGALESE

Detained property: Personal property held by a bailee until lawful payment is made by the bailor.

Innkeeper's Lien

The innkeeper's lien is a concept that helps to protect innkeepers from nonpaying guests. Essentially, it enables a hotel to detain certain property that guests may bring with them into the inn if they refuse, or are unable, to pay their bill. Most states allow the innkeeper to hold a guest's property until the appropriate charges have been paid. In the event the guest chooses not to pay the bill, the innkeeper is usually authorized to sell the items and apply the proceeds from the sale to the bill. The innkeeper can also use the proceeds to pay any costs that may have been associated with selling the property. Any surplus left over must be returned to the guest. Certain personal items, such as necessary clothing and wedding rings, have been held to be outside the scope of the innkeeper's lien.

Ordinarily, the lien can be used only to pay charges incurred by the guest directly with the hotel. So, a charge incurred by the guest at an independent business center, for example, even though located within the hotel, would not qualify for a lien. Due to customer relationships and the ultimate goal of keeping guests happy, it may not be in the hotel's best interest to withhold such property even though this legal avenue is available. State laws vary, so be sure to consult with the state hotel association for the proper methods to be used. Remember, though, that if at any time a guest pays the bill, the lien is extinguished and the property must be returned immediately.

Search the Web 11.1

Go online to **www.HospitalityLawyer.com** to see a review of the history of innkeeper statutes and a proposed uniform statute for all states.

1. Hover over: Solutions in top menu.
2. Select: Academic Resources in the drop-down menu.
3. Select: Hospitality Law Textbook Support.
4. Select: Referenced Articles button.
5. Select: Model Innkeeper Statute link.

11.3 Property with Unknown Ownership

As a manager, you may experience occasions when you and your staff will discover personal property whose ownership is uncertain. Under common law, there are three classifications of property whose ownership is in doubt, each of which carries with it unique responsibilities for the hospitality manager:

1. Mislaid property
2. Lost property
3. Abandoned property

Mislaid Property

Mislaid property comes into existence when the property owner forgets where he or she has placed it. For example, in a restaurant, a guest may enter with an umbrella, place the umbrella in a stand near the door, but upon leaving the restaurant, forget to retrieve it. In this case, the umbrella is considered to be mislaid property, and the restaurant's manager or owner is responsible for the safekeeping of the umbrella until the rightful owner returns. In fact, if the umbrella is given by the manager to someone who claims to be the owner but who in fact is not, common law would find the manager liable to the true owner for the value of the umbrella.

Search the Web 11.2

Go online to **www.law.cornell.edu/ucc/ucc.table.html**. You will arrive at the Uniform Commercial Code.

1. Select: Article Seven from the list of articles available.
2. Scroll to: Part 2, Warehouse Receipts: Special Provisions.
3. Select and read: §7-209. Lien of Warehouseman and §7-210. Enforcement of Warehouseman's Lien.
4. What does it mean if a bailee has a lien on a bailor's property?
5. Does a lien permit the possessor of property to sell it to satisfy the lien?
6. What are the implications of section 4 of 7-209 for the hospitality manager who proceeds without an attorney?

A manager is required to use reasonable care to protect mislaid property until the rightful owner returns to claim it. If the rightful owner does not return in a reasonable amount of time, ownership of the property would be transferred to the property finder. Most hotels and restaurants require their employees to turn in any mislaid property they find in the normal course of their work. Thus, ownership of the mislaid property would be transferred to the employer, not the employee.

Lost Property

Lost property comes into being when the rightful owner accidentally or inadvertently forgets where he or she has placed the belonging. Under common law, the individual who finds lost property in a public place is allowed to keep it unless the rightful owner returns to claim it. In many states, the finder has a legal obligation to make a reasonable effort to locate the rightful owner of both lost and mislaid property.

Like mislaid property, employees who find lost property in the course of their work must turn the property over to their employer. This is true even if the property was found in a public place. Thus, a hotel lobby cleaning attendant who finds a portable computer on the floor near a chair would be required to turn the property over to the hotel because the employer could be responsible for the value of the property if the rightful owner were to return to claim it.

A question can arise over the length of time a finder of lost property must retain that property. One would expect the length of time that the property should be held would increase with the value of the property. Thus, a pair of diamond earrings found in a hotel guestroom would likely require a longer holding time than a pair of gym shoes. Many hotel operators solve this problem by requiring that all property be held a minimum length of time before it is given to the employee who found it (as a reward for honesty) or given to charity. Figure 11.2 shown on the next page is a sample form that a hotel or restaurant can use to properly track these lost and found items.

Abandoned Property

When an owner abandons property, he or she has no intention of returning to reclaim it. Obviously, it can be difficult for a manager to know when property has been abandoned, not just misplaced or lost.

Under common law, a finder has no obligation to take care of, or protect, **abandoned property**. In addition, the finder of abandoned property is not required to seek its true owner. Broken umbrellas, magazines, worn clothing, and inexpensive toilet articles such as razors and toothbrushes are examples of

---

LEGALESE

Mislaid property: Personal property that has been put aside on purpose but then has been forgotten by the rightful owner.

Lost property: Personal property that has been inadvertently put aside and then forgotten by the rightful owner.

Abandoned property: Personal property that has been deliberately put aside by the rightful owner with no intention of ever returning for it.

Lost-and-Found Ticket

Facility Name ______________________ Today's Date ______________________

Item Description ____

____

____

____

Location found: ______________________ Room Number ______________________

Name of finder ____

Supervisor who received item(s) ____

____

DISPOSITION OF PROPERTY

Date item returned to owner ______________________

Owner Name ______________________ Owner Address ______________________

Owner Telephone ______________________ ______________________

Returned to owner by ______________________

Date item:

Returned to finder ______________________ Disposed of ______________________

FIGURE 11.2 Form used to track lost and found items.

abandoned property commonly found in hotels. The statement that "one man's trash is another man's treasure" certainly holds true in regard to abandoned property. Still, it is a good idea to make sure that any property that the hotel discards is, in fact, abandoned. When in doubt, it is always best to treat property of doubtful ownership as mislaid or lost rather than abandoned.

Disposing of Unclaimed Property

When items of value are found in a hotel or restaurant, your first goal as a manager or owner should be to return the property to its rightful owner. When that is not possible or hotel policy prohibits contacting the guest who most recently checked out of the guestroom to determine the ownership of the item, your next goal should be to safely protect the property until the rightful owner returns for it. Only after it is abundantly clear that the original owner will not be returning should the property be liquidated.

As a guardian of guest property, it is your responsibility as a manager to protect and, when appropriate, properly dispose of property with unknown ownership. If you do so correctly, your guests and your employees will benefit.

Analyze the Situation 11.3

Kari Renfroe was employed as a room attendant at the Lodge Inn motel. One day, as she came to work, she discovered an expensive leather jacket stuffed inside a plastic shopping bag in the employee section of the parking lot. The jacket had no ownership marks on it, and neither did the plastic bag. Ms. Renfroe turned the jacket over to the manager of the motel despite the fact that there was no policy in place regarding items found outside the motel.

The jacket was still unclaimed 120 days later, at which time Ms. Renfroe approached the manager and asked if she could have the jacket since she had found it. The manager refused to give her the jacket, stating that all unclaimed property found on the motel's premises belonged to the motel.

1. Would the jacket be considered mislaid, lost, or abandoned property?
2. Who is the current, rightful owner of the jacket?
3. How could the motel manager avoid future confusion about handling "found" property?

Legally Managing at Work

Disposing of Found Property

The following six guidelines can help you as you devise a policy to protect the rights of original property owners and to reward the honesty of your employees:

1. Review your state's lost and found laws to determine any unique requirements that apply to the property in question.
2. Require all employees and management staff to turn in to the property manager or to his or her designee all personal property found in public places (lobbies, foyers, restrooms, etc.) as well as in rented areas such as guestrooms, suites, cabins, and campgrounds.
3. Keep a lost and found log book in which you record the name of the finder, the individual who received the found goods, the location where the property was found, and the date found.
4. If the value of the found item is significant, make all reasonable efforts to locate the rightful owner and document these efforts.
5. Hold found property for a period of time recommended by your company or a local attorney familiar with the laws in your state regarding found property. Sixty days should be a minimum length for most found property.
6. Permit only the property manager or his or her designee to return found property to purported owners but only after taking extra care to return the item only to its rightful owner.

If the original owner does not come forward, dispose of the property in accordance with written procedures that have been shared with all employees and reviewed by your attorney. Many managers give found property to those who found it as a reward for employee honesty. They theorize that it is in the best interest of the facility and its guests to have all property returned promptly, and rewarding employees for doing so is one way to achieve this goal. Other facilities donate all valuable lost property to a local charity, and still others sell lost property once or twice a year to liquidation companies.

International Snapshot

Limited Liability of Innkeepers in Canada

In Canada, innkeepers' liability is governed by legislation in each province and territory, not at the federal level, so the limitations of liability vary depending on the jurisdiction.

With the exception of Quebec, all provinces and territories limit or exclude liability for damage to, or loss of, a guest's property subject to two exceptions: Innkeepers are liable if (1) goods are stolen or lost through the willful act, default, or neglect of the innkeeper or his or her employees or (2) goods are stolen or lost after being deposited for safe custody with the innkeeper (some exemptions exist). The legislation in most of these provinces and territories provides that, except for these two exceptions, innkeepers have no liability at all. In three provinces, innkeepers are liable for damage or loss except for these two exceptions, but that liability is capped. The cap is $200 in Newfoundland and Labrador, $100 in New Brunswick, and $40 in Ontario.

In Quebec, innkeepers can be liable for up to 10 times the nightly rate for the loss of a guest's property and up to 50 times the nightly rate if the innkeeper accepted the property for deposit. Where the loss is caused intentionally, the liability can be unlimited.

Additional limitations and exceptions exist in some provinces. Examples follow:

In 12 jurisdictions,* an exception is that innkeepers can be liable for refusing to receive goods for safe custody or when guests are unable to deposit the goods for safe custody through the fault of the innkeeper. In most of these jurisdictions,† however, this liability is limited when the establishment does not have a proper safe and the guest is informed of this when the innkeeper refuses to receive the goods.

Saskatchewan, the Yukon, Nunavut, and the Northwest Territories provide that the innkeeper will not be liable for goods lost in a part of the hotel other than the guestroom of the owner of the goods unless the goods were deposited with the innkeeper for safekeeping. The innkeeper is also not liable for trunks or their contents or personal effects left by a guest in his or her room if there is a proper lock and key for the door of the room unless the room is locked during the absence of the guest and the key is left at the inn's office. In Alberta, innkeepers may be liable for property belonging to persons who are not registered guests.

Given the variations among jurisdictions, it is critical to consult the legislation of the relevant province.

**British Columbia, Alberta, Ontario, Quebec, Manitoba, Saskatchewan, New Brunswick, Nova Scotia, Newfoundland and Labrador, the Yukon, Nunavut, and the Northwest Territories.*

†British Columbia, Alberta, Manitoba, Saskatchewan, Newfoundland and Labrador, the Yukon, Nunavut, and the Northwest Territories.

Provided by Dominic Mochrie, partner, Andraya Frith, partner, and Jasmyn Lee, student-at-law, with Osler, Hoskin & Harcourt LLP, Barristers and Solicitors, in the firm's Toronto, Ontario, Canada office. www.osler.com.

WHAT WOULD YOU DO?

You are the manager of a restaurant in the downtown area of a large city. Because of your location, no parking is available directly adjacent to your facility. For the past five years, you have made valet parking service available to your customers through A-1 Parking. Essentially, A-1 provided valet drivers who would stand outside your restaurant doors, approach cars as they arrived, give guests a claim check for their cars, and deliver the car to a parking garage owned by A-1. The parking garage is located one-fourth of a mile from your restaurant. When guests finish dining, the valet outside your restaurant radios the parking lot with the claim check number, and a driver from A-1 delivers the car to your front door where guests pay a parking fee before they regain possession of their car. A-1 currently provides this service to several restaurants.

The arrangement has been a good one for both you and A-1. No trouble of any kind has ever been reported. Today, however, the owner of A-1 has announced he is retiring; he approaches you to inquire whether the restaurant would be interested in buying his business.

Draft a letter to the owner of A-1 Parking stating whether or not you wish to buy the parking garage business. In your letter, be sure to address the following points:

1. How operating the valet parking service yourself would change the relationship you have with your restaurant customers.
2. The need for insurance to cover potential damages to automobiles and other areas of liability you might need to insure against.
3. The potential pros and cons of assuming the responsibility for parking your guests' automobiles as compared to the current situation.
4. The agency, liability, and bailment issues that would arise if the purchase were made.

WHAT DID YOU LEARN IN THIS CHAPTER?

As a hospitality operator, you have a responsibility to take reasonable steps to safeguard the personal property that guests bring with them onto your premises. Fortunately, laws have been passed in all states that limit the liability of the operator. There are several requirements that must be met by the operator for the limits to apply. Because the laws vary widely, it is crucial that you become familiar with the requirements of the statute in your state.

From time to time, operators will voluntarily accept possession of guest property (e.g., valet parking, luggage storage). These are called "bailment relationships." Your responsibilities vary, depending on the type of bailment that is created. An innkeeper's lien gives a lodging establishment the right to detain a guest's belongings in the event the guest refuses to pay his or her bill.

Property can also be mislaid, lost, or abandoned, and a manager must understand the distinctions between those three classifications in order to dispose of the property responsibly.

CHAPTER 12

Your Responsibilities When Serving Food and Beverages

CHAPTER OUTLINE

12.1. Serving Food

12.2. Truth-In-Menu Laws

12.3. Serving Alcohol

IN THIS CHAPTER, YOU WILL LEARN

1. A foodservice establishment's responsibilities under the Uniform Commercial Code (UCC) and other laws to serve wholesome food and beverages.
2. To apply "truth-in-menu" concepts to the service of food and beverage products.
3. To assess the current legal risks associated with serving alcohol.
4. To implement training programs that result in the responsible service of alcohol.

12.1 Serving Food

People all over the world love to dine out. And when they are not dining out, Americans have increasingly begun to patronize foodservice operations that offer preprepared food they can take home to eat. In fact, 1996 was the first year that takeout occasions exceeded on-premise occasions in the U.S. foodservice industry. Whether the food is eaten in a restaurant or taken home, the National Restaurant Association (www.restaurant.org) states that restaurant industry sales are projected to total $782.7 billion in 2016 and restaurants are on track to employ over 14.4 million employees. American diners are now much more interested in food sourcing, production, and sustainability than they ever have been in history. Many diners now have special dietary needs, and a restaurant manager must stay on top of the legal implications regarding those needs.

Uniform Commercial Code Warranty

As a hospitality manager involved with the service of food, you have a legal obligation to sell only food that is wholesome and to deliver that food in a manner that is safe. This responsibility is mandated by the Uniform Commercial Code (UCC), as well as other state and local laws. Figure 12.1 shown on the next page details one section of the UCC that relates to selling safe food. When a foodservice operation sells food, there is an implied warranty that the food is **merchantable**. Simply put, a foodservice manager is required to operate his or her facility in a manner that protects guests from the possibility of contracting **foodborne illness** or experiencing any other injury that could be caused by consuming unwholesome food or beverages. Unfortunately, sometimes, food is served that contains something that the guest normally would not expect to find in the dish (e.g., a small stone in a serving of refried beans). The question that must be answered in these cases is whether or not the food or beverage served was "fit" for consumption.

The courts usually apply one of two different tests to determine whether a foodservice establishment is liable to a guest for any damages

---

LEGALESE

Merchantable: Suitable for buying and selling.

Foodborne illness: Sickness or harm caused by the consumption of unsafe foods or beverages.

Uniform Commercial Code: IMPLIED WARRANTY

§ 2-314.: Merchantability; Usage of Trade.

1) Unless excluded or modified (Section 2-316), a warranty that the goods shall be merchantable is implied in a contract for their sale if the seller is a merchant with respect to goods of that kind. Under this section the serving for value of food or drink to be consumed either on the premises or elsewhere is a sale.

FIGURE 12.1 Uniform Commercial Code: Implied Warranty.

suffered from eating the food. (In the case of the stone found in the refried beans, the damage may consist of a broken tooth from biting down on the small stone.) One test, the "foreign/natural test," seeks to determine whether the object is foreign to the dish or a natural component of it. If the object is foreign, then the implied warranty of merchantability (fitness) under the UCC is breached, and the foodservice operator would be held liable. If it is a natural component, the warranty would not be breached. For example, the stone in the refried beans, though commonly found in large bags of raw beans, would be considered foreign, and thus the foodservice operator would probably be held responsible for serving it. If instead the guest had broken a tooth on a piece of clamshell while enjoying a steaming bowl of New England clam chowder, the guest would probably not recover any damages under this test. The clamshell, as a natural component of clams, the court reasons, is also a natural component of clam chowder.

The foreign/natural test is slowly being replaced by states with the "reasonable expectation" test. This test seeks to determine whether an item could be reasonably expected by a guest to be found in the food. The clamshell situation is a perfect example of why the law (and assessing liability) can be difficult at times. Clamshells are natural parts of clams, but are they really natural components of clam chowder? Put another way, would you, as a guest, reasonably expect to find pieces of clamshell in a bowl of clam chowder that was served to you? If a judge or jury decided that it was not reasonable to expect to find a clamshell in the chowder, then the foodservice operator would be held liable. A tricky situation arises if someone orders a fish filet sandwich. Because the word "filet" means boneless, a guest would not expect to find bones in the sandwich. Accordingly, if a bone were present and the guest choked on that bone, the consequences could be substantial for the foodservice operator.

Guest Safety

To help foodservice operators prevent foodborne illness, local health departments conduct routine inspections of restaurants and other food production facilities and may hold training or certification classes for those who handle food. It is important to know the local health department requirements that relate to food handling in your area and to work diligently to ensure that only safe food is served in your operation. If you do not, the results can be catastrophic.

Consider the case of Kelly Kleitsch. She worked long hours to establish her own successful restaurant. With much hard work and a considerable investment of capital, Ms. Kleitsch built the reputation of her restaurant by serving high-quality food at fair prices. When a careless member of the food preparation team forgot to refrigerate a chicken stock one night and then used the stock the next day to flavor an uncooked sauce, which was later served, several individuals became very ill. The good reputation of Ms. Kleitsch's restaurant disappeared overnight as social media as well as local newspapers and television stations reported that one elderly lady had been hospitalized after eating at the restaurant. Customer counts plummeted, and Ms. Kleitsch lost her business. And that was before the lawsuit was filed on behalf of the elderly diner.

The law in this area is very clear. Restaurants will be held responsible for the illnesses suffered by their guests if those illnesses are the direct result of consuming unwholesome food. Thus, managers must make every effort to comply with local ordinances, train staff in effective food-handling

Analyze the Situation 12.1

Harry Dolinski was the executive chef at the Regal House Hotel. One of his specialties was a hearty vegetable soup that was featured on the lunch buffet every Thursday. Pauline Guilliard and her friends decided to have lunch at the Regal House one Thursday before attending an art exhibit. Ms. Guilliard read the lighted menu at the front of the buffet line. The chef's specials, including the vegetable soup, were written on the menu with a felt-tip pen.

Ms. Guilliard selected the vegetable soup and a few other items and consumed one full bowl of the soup. Three hours later, at the art exhibit, she suffered seizures and had difficulty breathing. It turned out that the soup contained MSG—a food additive to which she had severe reactions. Ms. Guilliard recovered, but her attorney contacted the hotel with a demand letter seeking compensation for her suffering.

The hotel's attorney replied that the soup served by the hotel was wholesome and that Ms. Guilliard's reaction to the MSG could not have been reasonably foreseen. In addition, the hotel maintained that MSG is a common seasoning in use worldwide for many years. Thus, it would have been the diner's responsibility to inform the foodservice operation of any allergies or allergic reactions. As a result, the liability for Ms. Guilliard's illness was hers alone.

1. Did the hotel have an obligation (or duty as outlined in Chapter 9, "Your Responsibilities as a Hospitality Operator") to notify guests that the soup contained MSG?
2. How do you think a jury would respond to this situation? What level of damages, if any, do you think a jury would be inclined to award in this case?
3. What should the chef do to avoid similar problems in the future?

Legally Managing at Work

Steps to Take When a Guest Complains of Foodborne Illness

1. Document the name, address, email address, and telephone number of the guest who complains of an illness as well as the date and time the guest patronized your facility.
2. Document all items eaten in your facility by the guest during the visit in question.
3. If provided by the guest, obtain the name and address of the physician treating him or her. If he or she has not contacted a physician, encourage him or her to do so.
4. Contact the physician to determine if in fact a case of foodborne illness has been diagnosed. Because of patient privacy laws, however, the doctor may not provide any information.
5. Notify the local health department immediately if a foodborne illness outbreak is confirmed so its staff can assist you in determining the source of the outbreak and identifying affected guests and employees.
6. Evaluate and, if necessary, modify your training and certification efforts that relate to the areas involved in the incident.
7. Document your efforts, and notify your attorney, your public relations specialist, and/or company risk manager.

and production techniques, and document their efforts. The National Restaurant Association and its ServSafe program can be a great asset in managers' efforts to ensure the safety of the food they serve. ServSafe is a national educational program designed to help foodservice operators ensure food safety.

Of course, you should take all reasonable measures to ensure that the food you serve is safe and consumable by your guests. Disclosing ingredients and warning guests of potential concerns is the best practice. If a potential incident does occur, however, the steps itemized in the following Legally Managing at Work feature should be taken to ensure the safety of all guests and to prevent further potential liability.

The quality of the food a restaurant serves is important, as you have seen, but how that restaurant serves its food can be just as important from a legal standpoint. Again, the UCC addresses the issue of a restaurant's responsibility to serve food properly. As the code in Figure 12.2 specifies, a restaurateur is considered an expert—that is, an individual with skill and judgment—when it comes to the proper delivery of prepared food and beverages.

Restaurants can not only be found guilty (in a criminal proceeding) of serving unwholesome food but also can be found liable (in a civil proceeding) if they serve wholesome food in an unsafe or negligent manner. Consider Terry Settles. He and his wife were guests at Remington Restaurant. He ordered cherries jubilee for dessert. When the server prepared the dish, a small amount of alcohol splashed out of the flambé pan and landed on the arm of Mrs. Settles. As she jumped back in her chair to try and avoid the burning liquid, she fell and severely injured her back. There is little question in this case that the restaurant will face severe penalties for the carelessness of its server.

Uniform Commercial Code: GENERAL OBLIGATION AND CONSTRUCTION OF CONTRACT

§ 2-315. Implied Warranty: Fitness for Particular Purpose.

Where the seller at the time of contracting has reason to know any particular purpose for which the goods are required and that the buyer is relying on the seller's skill or judgment to select or furnish suitable goods, there is unless excluded or modified under the next section an implied warranty that the goods shall be fit for such purpose.

FIGURE 12.2 Uniform Commercial Code: General Obligation and Construction of Contract.

Management should frequently review all food temperatures, serving containers, food production techniques, and delivery methods. Chipped plates and glasses or poorly washed utensils can present just as much of a legal risk as serving spoiled or unwholesome food. Some states even require restaurants to post signs disclosing the use of microwave ovens when applicable to notify restaurant patrons who have pacemakers.

In addition, restaurants should strive to accommodate guests who ask that dishes be prepared without a specific ingredient to which they are allergic and to provide close supervision of the preparation of that dish. In fact, the issue of food allergies has become a topic of increasing importance in recent years. Both federal and state governments have begun to initiate regulations for foodservice providers on preventing allergic reactions. For example, the Food Allergen Labeling and Consumer Protection Act of 2004, which became effective in 2006, requires the labeling of foods that contain major allergens (that account for over 90 percent of all documented food allergies in the United States and those that are most likely to result in life-threatening or severe reactions), for example, milk, eggs, fish (such as bass, flounder, and cod), shellfish (such as crab, lobster, and shrimp), peanuts, tree nuts (such as almonds, walnuts, and pecans), wheat, and soy. These ingredients must be disclosed, even if they are used in minimal amounts, such as a spice blend, or if used as a processing aid in the preparation of a food product, such as peanut oil and soy lectin.

States have also crafted legislation related to food allergies. Massachusetts, for example, requires restaurants to educate their staff on the issue of food allergies and managers to earn certification in a food allergy training course. With the

Analyze the Situation 12.2

Penny Mance was a single mother of three children living in an urban apartment complex. She worked as a paralegal in a downtown attorney's office. One morning, Ms. Mance was asked to come into work an hour later than her usual time. She used the opportunity to treat her three children to breakfast at a fast-food restaurant near their home. The Mance family arrived at the restaurant at 8:00 A.M. and ordered breakfast. For their beverage selections, Ms. Mance ordered hot chocolate and the children selected orange juice.

After the family sat down, Tina, Ms. Mance's six-year-old daughter told her mother that she wanted to try the hot chocolate. The beverage had been served in a Styrofoam cup with a plastic lid. Penny replied that the chocolate was "probably too hot for her to try." This comment was overheard by several guests sitting near the Mance family. Tina reached for the chocolate anyway; her mother, while trying to pull the chocolate away, spilled it on her own hands. Ms. Mance suffered second- and third-degree burns from the hot chocolate and was forced to miss work for three weeks. Upon returning, her typing speed was severely reduced as a result of tissue scarring on her left hand.

Ms. Mance retained one of the attorneys where she worked to sue the fast-food restaurant. In court depositions taken later on, it was estimated that the chocolate was served at a temperature of 190 degrees Fahrenheit. The restaurant's attorney claimed the chocolate was not unsafe when it was served. He pointed to the fact that Ms. Mance knew the beverage was probably too hot for the child as an indication that she was willing to accept the risk of drinking a hot beverage. In addition, the restaurant's attorney maintained that it was the child's action, not the restaurant's, which was the direct cause of the accident. Undeterred, Ms. Mance's attorney sued for damages, including medical expenses, lost wages, and a large amount for punitive damages.

1. Did the restaurant act negligently in the serving of the hot chocolate?
2. Do you think that Penny Mance was negligent? If so, how much difference, if any, do you believe that her negligence would make in the size of the jury's award?
3. Whom should the restaurant manager and company look to for guidance on property serving temperatures and techniques? Could you defend this source in court?

growing notoriety of food allergies, it is likely that more and more regulations will be passed in the future. As a manager, be sure to check your state laws to make sure that you are in compliance with any regulations that have been or are expected to be adopted. Additionally, it is the best practice to disclose ingredients that are known to cause allergic reactions so that guests can make informed choices. Be sure to train your employees about allergies and to be sensitive to guests with allergies and be patient with their inquiries about menu ingredients. Perhaps food and beverage establishments suggest to the guest that he or she have a small preprinted card listing any food allergies or special requests so that the guest can simply hand the card to any server in order to minimize any miscommunication of special dietary requests.

If an incident occurs that involves how a food was served rather than what was served, the manager should complete an incident report at the earliest opportunity. (Refer to the Incident Report Form in Figure 9.2.)

12.2 Truth-in-Menu Laws

As a hospitality manager, you have a right to advertise your food and beverage products in a way that casts them in their best light. If your hamburgers contain eight ounces of ground beef, you are free to promote that attribute in your advertising, your menu, and your server's verbal descriptions. You are not free, however, to misrepresent your products. To do so is a violation of what has come to be commonly known as **truth-in-menu laws**. These laws, which could perhaps better be described as "accuracy in menus," are designed to protect consumers from fraudulent food and beverage claims. Many foodservice operators believe that truth-in-menu laws are recent legislation. They are not. In fact, the federal government, as well as many local communities, has a long history of regulating food advertisement and sales (see Figure 12.3).

The various truth-in-menu laws currently in effect run to thousands of pages and are overseen by dozens of agencies and administrative entities, thereby taking the labeling of food to higher degrees of accuracy. Although these laws are constantly being revised, it is possible for a foodservice operator to stay up to date and in compliance with them. The method is relatively straightforward, and the key is honesty in menu claims in regard to both the price that is charged and the food that is served.

Certainly, menus should accurately reflect the price to be charged to the customer. If one dozen oysters are to be sold for a given price, one dozen oysters should be delivered on the plate, and the price charged on the bill should match that on the menu. Likewise, if the menu price is to include a mandatory service charge or cover charge, these must be brought to the attention of the guest. If a restaurant advertises a prix fixe dinner with four courses and a choice of entrees, the guest should be told the price of the dinner, which courses are included, and the types of entrees he or she may choose from.

LEGALESE

Truth-in-menu laws: The collective name given to various laws and regulations that have been implemented to ensure accuracy in the wording on menus.

1906

The Federal Food and Drugs Act and the Federal Meat Inspection Act authorize the federal government to regulate the safety and quality of food. The responsibility falls to the U.S. Department of Agriculture (USDA) and the Bureau of Chemistry, the Food and Drug Administration's predecessor.

1913

The GOULD Amendment requires food packages to state the quantity of contents.

1924

In *U.S. v. 95 Barrels Alleged Apple Cider Vinegar*, the Supreme Court rules that the Food and Drug Act condemns every statement, design, or device that may mislead, misdirect, or deceive, even if technically true.

1938

The Federal Food, Drug, and Cosmetic Act replaces the 1906 Food and Drugs Act. Among other things, it requires the label of every processed packaged food to contain the name and address of the manufacturer or distributor. A list of ingredients also is required on certain products. The law also prohibits statements in food labeling that are false or misleading.

1957

The Poultry Products Inspection Act authorizes the USDA to regulate, among other things, the labeling of poultry products.

1966

The Fair Packaging and Labeling Act requires all consumer products in the interstate commerce to contain accurate information and to facilitate value comparisons.

1974

The Safe Drinking Water Act authorizes the Environmental Protection Association (EPA) to establish standards for drinking water safety and water quality. (Mineral water, seltzer, and club soda are exempt from these provisions, because the FDA classifies them as soft drinks.) In addition, the FDA has established strict criteria and labeling requirements for all types of bottled water, mineral water, and sparkling water.

1990

Congress passes the Nutrition Labeling and Education Act (NLEA), which makes nutrition information mandatory for most foods. Among the few foods exempted were restaurant items, unless they carried a nutrient or health claim.

1993

The FDA issues regulations under NLEA that require restaurants to comply with regulations for nutrient and health claims that appear on signs and placards. Menu claims are exempt.

1996

The U.S. District Court in Washington, DC, rules that Congress had intended restaurant menus to be covered by NLEA, and orders the FDA to amend its nutrition labeling and claims regulations to include menu items about which claims are made.

1997

The FDA's regulations for nutrition labeling of restaurant menu items that bear a nutrition or health benefit claim take effect.

2002

The Organic Foods Production Act and the National Organic Program (NOP) are intended to assure consumers that the organic foods they purchase are produced, processed, and certified to consistent national organic standards. The labeling requirements of the new program apply to raw, fresh products, and processed foods that contain organic ingredients. Foods that are sold, labeled, or represented as organic will have to be produced and processed in accordance with the NOP standards.

2003

To help consumers choose heart-healthy foods, the Department of Health and Human Services announces that FDA will require food labels to include trans fat content, the first substantive change to the nutrition facts panel on foods since the label was changed in 1993.

FIGURE 12.3 **Laws regulating food labeling and advertising.**
http://www.fda.gov/AboutFDA/WhatWeDo/History/Milestones/ucm128305.htm

2004

Passage of the Food Allergy Labeling and Consumer Protection Act requires the labeling of any food that contains a protein derived from any one of the following foods that, as a group, account for the vast majority of food allergies: peanuts, soybeans, cow's milk, eggs, fish, crustacean shellfish, tree nuts, and wheat.

2007

Food Protection Plan of 2007

Addresses changes in food sources, production, and consumption to protect our food supply from both intentional and unintentional contamination.

2011

Food Safety Modernization Act (FSMA)

Signed by President Barack Obama in January 2011 to ensure the safety of the U.S. food supply by shifting the focus from responding to contamination to preventing contamination.

FIGURE 12.3 *(continued)*

Analyze the Situation 12.3

Jeffery and Latisha Williams arranged a fiftieth anniversary party for her parents. They reserved a private room at the Tannery, an upscale steak and seafood house located two miles from their suburban home. The Williams hosted a total of 10 people. Unfortunately, the service they received from the restaurant staff was not very good. When the check arrived, Mr. Williams noticed that a 15 percent charge had been added to the total price of the bill. When he inquired about the charge, his server informed him that it was the restaurant's policy to assess a 15 percent "tip" to the bill of all parties of more than eight persons. The policy, explained the server, was not printed on the menu but was to be verbally relayed anytime a guest made a reservation for more than eight people. Mr. Williams replied that the reservation was made by his secretary, and she mentioned no such policy when she informed Mr. Williams of the restaurant's availability.

Mr. Williams refused to pay the extra charge, claiming that it should be he, not the restaurant, who determined the amount of the gratuity, if any. When the restaurant manager arrived on the scene, he informed Mr. Williams that the server had misspoken and that the extra charge was in fact a "service charge," not a tip. Mr. Williams still refused to pay the added charge.

1. Does Mr. Williams owe the extra 15 percent to the restaurant?
2. Does it matter whether the surcharge is called a gratuity or a service charge? How would that be determined?
3. What should the restaurant do to avoid similar problems in the future?

"Accuracy in menu" involves a great deal more than honestly and precisely stating a price. It also entails being careful when describing many food attributes, including the preparation style, ingredients, origin, portion sizes, calories, and any health benefits. A menu-labeling requirement is part of the Patient Protection and Affordable Care Act of 2010 (ACA) that requires restaurants and similar retail food establishments with 20 or more locations operating under the same name and serving substantially the same menu items to post calorie information for standard menu items and provide guests a list of nutritional information upon request. The Food and Drug Administration (FDA) delayed its final menu-labeling regulations until December 1, 2016, to give businesses more time and guidance to comply with them. The new rules go into effect May 5, 2017.

Because this area is so complex under the ACA and because consumers increasingly demand more accurate information from restaurants, the National Restaurant Association (NRA) and many state associations have produced educational material designed to assist foodservice operators as they write and prepare menus. In addition, the federal government issues food description standards that can be of great assistance. You should pay particular attention to the following areas when you begin writing the menu for your own foodservice establishment.

Preparation Style

Under federal law, certain food items and preparation techniques must be carried out in a very precise way if that item or technique is to be included on a menu. In many cases, the federal government, through either the Food and Drug Administration or the Department of Agriculture, has produced guidelines for accurately describing menu items. Consider the following common items and the specificity with which their preparation style is determined by federal guidelines:

Grilled: Items must be grilled, not just mechanically produced with "grill marks" and then steamed before service.

Homemade: The product must be prepared on premises, not commercially baked.

Fresh: The product cannot be frozen, canned, dried, or processed.

Breaded shrimp: This includes only the commercial species, Pineaus. The tail portion of the shrimp of the commercial species must comprise 50 percent of the total weight of a finished product labeled "breaded shrimp." To be labeled "lightly breaded shrimp," the shrimp content must be 65 percent by weight of the finished product.

Kosher-style: A product flavored or seasoned in a particular manner; this description has no religious significance.

Kosher: Products that have been prepared or processed to meet the requirements of the orthodox Jewish religion.

Baked ham: A ham that has been heated in an oven for a specified period of time. Many brands of smoked ham are not oven baked.

It is important that your menu accurately reflect the preparation techniques used in your kitchen, not only because the law requires you to but also to help ensure your operation's credibility with the public.

Ingredients

Perhaps no area of menu accuracy is more important than the listing of ingredients that actually go into making a food item. Before the passage of the ACA, restaurants were not required to divulge their ingredient lists to their guests. In accordance with FDA regulations and guidelines, restaurants must disclose the number of calories in each item as they are usually prepared and offered for sale beginning May 5, 2017, Restaurants must also provide customers a list of nutritional information upon request, which many restaurants are already providing. If, for example, an operator offers Kahlua and cream as a drink on a bar menu, the drink must be made with both the liqueur and the dairy product stated. Kahlua is a specific brand of Mexican coffee liqueur, and cream is defined by the federal government as a product made from milk with a minimum fat content of 18 percent. Of course, a bar manager is free to offer a different, less expensive coffee liqueur to guests and use half-and-half (which contains 12 percent fat) instead of cream, but the drink could not be called a Kahlua and cream. To do so is unethical at best and illegal in most areas.

Whenever a specific ingredient is listed on a menu, that item and that item alone, should be served. For example, if the menu says maple syrup, then colored table syrup or maple-flavored syrup should not be served. This is especially important when listing brand-name products on a menu. (Recall the discussion of trademarks and brand-name items in Chapter 6, "Legally Managing Property.")

If substitutions of the menu items must be made, the guest should be informed of that before ordering. As consumers' interest in their own health continues to rise, foodservice operators can expect more involvement and consumer activism in the area of accurate ingredient listings.

Recently, in response to the growing number of obesity-related health issues in the United States, municipalities, state legislatures, and the federal government have begun to take a stance on what ingredients should not be included in dishes served to the public. For example, trans fat is a type of unsaturated fat that is mostly used to increase the longevity of food products. However, trans fat intake has been related to several dire health issues, such as coronary artery disease, Alzheimer's, breast cancer, diabetes, and infertility. In 2006, the FDA required trans fats to be listed on nutrition labels, an action that by some accounts has reduced their consumption by about 78 percent. In 2015, the FDA informed food manufacturers to stop using partially hydrogenated oils, the source of trans fats, in their products within three years because they are no longer generally recognized as safe (GRAS).

Some states have their own laws relating to food ingredients. In 2013, New York passed a law intending to prohibit the sale of many sweetened sugary drinks of more than 16 ounces. This ban was very controversial and after litigation, the New York State Court of Appeals—the state's highest court—refused to reinstate the limitation on such drinks. This was a major victory for the soft-drink industry. Proponents of the ban are not giving up, however, and legislation continues to be introduced in local communities and states that would ban single-serving sales of sugary sodas 16 ounces or more for children under the age of 18.

Hospitality managers need to be aware that such laws exist, and while there are many opponents that argue the unconstitutionality of the bans on multiple grounds, if your state or local government entity has enacted a law or ordinance that bans certain ingredients, you should be mindful of compliance unless you wish to pay a fine and high legal fees.

Origin

The origin of many menu items or their ingredients is very important. Many consumers prefer Colorado trout to generic trout, Washington apples to those from other states, and Bluepoint (Long Island) oysters to those from other areas. It can be tempting to use these terms to describe similar menu items from other places, which may cost less to purchase. But to do so is fraudulent. Moreover, it sends the wrong message to employees who know of the substitutions as well as the guests who ultimately are deprived of the items they thought they were purchasing. It is also illegal.

Size

Product size is, in many cases, the most important factor in determining how much a guest is willing to pay for a menu item. For example, a steakhouse could offer different cuts of beef and price them appropriately according to size. An 8-ounce steak might sell for $17.95, the 12 ounce might sell for $23.95, and the 16 ounce for $25.95.

Other types of food products may be harder to associate with precise quantities and sizes. For example, legally, "large" East Coast oysters must contain no more than 160 to 210 oysters per gallon, and "large" Pacific Coast oysters may contain no more than 64 oysters per gallon. Nevertheless, whether it is the size of eggs sold in a breakfast special or the use of the term "jumbo" to refer to shrimp, specifying size on a menu is an area that must be approached with the understanding that the law will expect you to deliver what you promise. A simple rule of thumb for avoiding difficulties in this area is: If you say it, serve it.

Health Benefits

For many years, the only menu item most restaurants offered as a healthy one was the "diet" plate, generally consisting of cottage cheese, fruit, perhaps some grilled poultry, and a lettuce leaf. It is no surprise that today's health-conscious consumer demands more. In response, restaurants generally have begun to provide more detail about the nutritional value of their menu items. The federal government, however, issues very strict guidelines on what you can and cannot say about your menu offerings. Thus, truth-in-menu laws relate not just to what is charged and what is served but also to the nutritional claims made by foodservice operators.

According to FDA estimates, well over half of all printed menus in the United States contain some type of nutritional or health benefit claim. There are two types of claims generally found on menus: nutrient and health benefit. Nutrient claims contain specific information about a menu item's nutritional content. When a dish is described on a menu as being "low fat" or "high fiber," the restaurateur is making a nutrient claim. Health benefit claims do not describe the content of specific menu items but instead show a relationship between a type of food or menu item and a particular health condition. For example, some restaurants include a note on their menu stating that eating foods low in saturated fat and cholesterol can reduce the risk of heart disease. Other restaurants identify nutritionally modified dishes on their menu using terms such as "heart healthy" or "light," or use symbols such as a red heart to signify that a dish meets general dietary recommendations.

The Food and Drug Administration (FDA) has issued regulations to ensure that foodservice operators who make nutritional and/or health benefit claims on their menus can indeed back them up. These regulations, published in the August 2, 1996, Federal Register, apply the Nutrition Labeling and Education Act (NLEA) of 1990 to restaurant items that carry a claim about a food's nutritional content or health benefits. All eating establishments must comply with these regulations. The following are two examples of FDA regulations surrounding the use of common menu terms.

Nutrient Claim A low-sodium, low-fat, low-cholesterol item must not contain amounts more than FDA guidelines for the term "low." Light or "lite" items must have fewer calories and less fat than the food to which it is being compared (e.g., "light" Italian" dressing). Some restaurants have used the term "lighter fare" to identify dishes containing smaller portions. However, that use of the term must be specified on the menu.

Health Benefit Claim To be considered "heart healthy," for example, a menu item must meet one of the following conditions:

- The item is low in saturated fat, cholesterol, and fat and provides without fortification significant amounts of one or more of six key nutrients. This claim indicates that a diet low in saturated fat and cholesterol may reduce the risk of heart disease.
- The item is low in saturated fat, cholesterol, and fat; provides without fortification significant amounts of one or more of six key nutrients; and is a significant source of soluble fiber (found in fruits, vegetables, and grain products). This claim indicates that a diet low in saturated fat and cholesterol and rich in fruits, vegetables, and grain products that contain some types of fiber (particularly soluble fiber) may reduce the risk of heart disease.

When printing health benefit claims on a menu, further information about the claim should be available somewhere on the menu or be available on request. The FDA permits restaurants to back up their menu claims with a "reasonable" base, such as cookbooks, databases, or other secondhand sources that provide nutrition information. (By contrast, the FDA requires food manufacturers to adhere to a much more stringent set of standards. Many food manufacturers perform chemical analyses to determine the nutritional value of their products to ensure that the information about their product printed on the food label is true.)

The enforcement of truth-in-menu regulations is undertaken by state and local public health departments, which have direct jurisdiction over restaurants by monitoring their food safety and sanitation practices. The general public can also act as a regulator in this area. In today's litigious society, a restaurant manager should have any menu containing nutritional or health claims reviewed by both an attorney and a dietician.

In addition to carefully developing menus, truth-in-menu laws require that restaurants truthfully and accurately specify what their servers say about menu items as well as how their food products are promoted or shown in advertisements, photographs, and promotions.

General Nutrition and Obesity

There is no denying the rising numbers of obesity, morbid obesity, and obesity-related diseases in the United States. Although much debate exists as to what the cause(s) of this increase is, the fact remains that more and more people are dying from obesity-related illness each year. Recently, many states began to tackle the obesity problem with regulations that are meant to encourage healthy eating habits and discourage unhealthy ones. You have already learned about one of the ways governments are regulating foods to promote healthy lifestyles—ingredient bans. However, there are many other ideas circulating throughout legislatures that a hospitality manager needs to be aware of. For example, the so-called Happy Meal laws seek to prevent including toys with food that does not meet certain nutritional standards, restrict the use of food stamps to pay for drinks with high sugar content, and require fast-food restaurants to post the caloric content of food items on the menu.

Regulation enacted to tackle obesity is a quickly moving, controversial, and murky area of the law. Often these laws are newly created, and there is not much, if any, precedent on which they are based; thus, it is difficult to say which laws will be long lasting and which ones will be deemed unconstitutional. However, it is certain that these issues will not go away soon, so it would be wise for a hospitality manager to stay current on any obesity-related movements and legislation.

Search the Web 12.1

Visit **www.bk.com**

1. Select: *BK* Cares at the bottom of the page.
2. Select: Nutrition Information. Answer the following:
   a. What are the 12 nutritional categories about which this company supplies information?
   b. Do you think restaurateurs have a duty of care to provide this level of nutritional information? Why or why not?
   c. What do you think the future holds for the level of nutritional information that foodservice operators will be required to supply?

12.3 Serving Alcohol

Throughout history, alcoholic beverages have played many roles. In some societies, they were thought to possess magical or holy powers. They were also an important part of medical treatment well into the 1800s. In various cultures, alcoholic beverages were considered a basic and essential food. Because beer, ale, and wine did not carry the diseases associated with drinking contaminated water, they became an accepted part of everyday meals. They were particularly valued by travelers, who had to be especially cautious about contracting strange diseases. In fact, most early taverns, as well as hotels, considered the service of alcohol to be a basic traveler's amenity. By the time the first settlers left for the New World, taverns were essential social centers, providing drink, food, and sometimes lodging. The early settlers brought this tradition with them to the New World. In the vast wilderness of the new continent, taverns took on new importance. By the mid-1800s, the largest taverns became the first hotels.

In 1920, Congress passed the Eighteenth Amendment to the Constitution, which prohibited the manufacture, sale, transportation, and importation of alcoholic beverages. The amendment was effective only in stopping the legal manufacture, sale, and transportation of liquor. Many people still drank, but they drank poor-tasting, illegally produced (and in some cases unmerchantable) alcoholic beverages. In 1933, Congress recognized the failure of prohibition and repealed the act with the passage of the Twenty-First Amendment. However, even after the appeal, the consumption of alcohol was not quickly reaccepted into U.S. society.

The Twenty-First Amendment gave individual states, counties, towns, and precincts the authority to control the sale and use of alcoholic beverages within their jurisdiction. As a result, a variety of alcohol-related laws exist throughout the United States today. As a hospitality manager, it is your responsibility to know and carefully follow the laws that apply to you. If you manage a facility that serves alcohol, you should have copies of the state and local laws regulating the service of alcohol in your community.

Privilege of Alcohol Service

Alcohol is a drug. Historically, one of its uses was, like that of other drugs, to treat disease. And like other drugs, it is also a substance to which people can become addicted. Despite the fact that alcohol often creates a euphoric state in the user, it is a **depressant**.

Other depressants include barbiturates and tranquilizers. Interestingly, society very tightly regulates the dispensing of most depressants. To become a pharmacist, people must go to school in order to earn the right to legally dispense many types of depressants. In most cases, a depressant can be requested from a pharmacist only after presenting a prescription from a licensed medical doctor. Alcohol, by contrast, can be served by any individual over a state-specified age who may have had little, if any, mandatory training prior to being employed as a bartender.

All that said, it is important to remember that no hospitality manager has a "right" to serve alcohol; rather, it is a privilege that is carefully regulated by law and one that cannot be taken lightly.

There is no alcoholic beverage that is safer or more moderate than another. According to the federal government's dietary guidelines, the alcohol content in standard servings (drinks) of beer (12 ounces), table wine (5 ounces), and distilled spirits (1½ ounces in a mixed drink) is equal. Thus, the service of all types of alcoholic beverages must be treated in the same serious manner. Put another way, the major factor in controlling the risks associated with serving alcohol is to realize that it is not what you serve but how much you serve that is most important.

LEGALESE

Depressant: A substance that lowers the rate of vital body activities.

The amount of alcohol consumed by an individual in a specific time period is measured by the individual's **blood alcohol concentration (BAC)**. Many factors, in addition to the number of drinks consumed, influence the BAC of an individual. Because the liver digests alcohol at the slow, constant rate of about one drink per hour, a 160-pound man may typically reach a BAC of .08 (or 8 percent) by drinking two to four drinks in one hour, which is legally drunk in all 50 states. Ten drinks would produce a BAC of approximately .25 or higher. Figure 12.4 details some of the effects felt by individuals with increasing BACs.

Alcohol affects different individuals in a variety of ways. Lawmakers commonly use specific BACs to define legal **intoxication**. In October 2000, the federal government passed legislation to establish a .08 blood alcohol level (BAL) as the standard determination of intoxication in all states. Although the federal government cannot directly force the states to enact the standard, the threat of withholding federal highway construction funds from any state that did not utilize the .08 standard pretty much guaranteed that all states would comply. Unfortunately, hospitality managers do not have the ability at this point in time to easily measure the BAC of their guests. Still, the law prohibits serving alcohol to an intoxicated guest. Thus, a hospitality manager must rely on his or her own knowledge of the law, operational procedures, and staff training programs to avoid doing so.

Alcohol is sold in an amazing variety of hospitality locations. Bars, amusement parks, golf courses, sporting events, and restaurants are just a few of the venues where a guest may legally buy alcohol. Each state regulates the sale of alcohol in the manner it sees fit. Regional differences do exist, but in all cases, those who sell alcohol are required to apply for and obtain a **liquor license** or liquor permit to do so.

Effects of Increasing BALs

BAL Level	*Effect*
0.06–0.10	Significant decrease in reaction time and visual abilities
0.11–0.15	Slurred speech and volatile emotions
0.22–0.25	Staggering, difficulty talking, blurred vision
0.40	Induced coma
0.50	Cessation of breathing and heart failure

FIGURE 12.4 Effects of increasing blood alcohol concentrations (BACs).

Recall our discussion of alcohol regulation from Chapter 2, "Government Agencies That Impact the Hospitality Industry." Every state has an alcoholic beverage commission (ABC) that grants licenses and regulates the sale of alcohol. At the local level, some cities or counties also have a local alcohol control board that works with the state agency to grant licenses and enforce the law. As a hospitality manager, you should request a copy of your state and local area's regulations.

Although different types of liquor licenses exist to meet the needs of various types of businesses, they can be divided into two general categories:

1. Licenses for on-premises consumption (required for restaurants, taverns, clubs, etc.)
2. Licenses for off-premises consumption (required for liquor stores and other markets that sell alcohol)

Various types of on-premises licenses also exist, such as a beer-only license, a wine license (which may or may not include beer but does not include mixed drinks), and a liquor license (which includes, beer, wine, and mixed drinks). In most states, liquor licenses are issued for a period of one year at the end of which the establishment must apply for a license renewal.

Once an establishment has been granted a liquor license, it is required to operate in accordance with all rules and regulations established by state and local ABCs and alcohol control boards. Some common areas of operation that are regulated by these agencies include:

- *Permitted hours of sale:* Local communities may prohibit the sale of alcohol after a specified time of day. Some communities have "blue laws," which restrict or prohibit the sale of alcohol on Sundays.
- *Approved changes for expansion or equipment purchases:* Before a liquor license is issued, the state or local agency may inspect the applicant's establishment prior to granting approval. Once a premise has been inspected, any further changes to the size of the establishment or the equipment used must first be approved by the state ABC or local alcohol control board. In some states, establishments that serve alcohol are prohibited from operating in close proximity to a school or a church.
- *Maintaining records:* Establishments that sell alcohol must keep detailed records of the amount of alcohol purchased

LEGALESE

Blood alcohol concentration (BAC): A measurement, expressed in a percentage, of the concentration level of alcohol in the bloodstream. Also known as "blood alcohol content" or "blood alcohol level" (BAL).

Intoxication: A condition in which an individual's BAC reaches legally established levels. These levels are not uniform across the United States. An intoxicated person may not sell or purchase alcohol, nor operate a motor vehicle.

Liquor license: A permit issued by a state that allows for the sale and/or service of alcoholic beverages. The entity holding the license is known as the licensee.

each day, on the vendors from which alcohol is purchased (including the vendor's license and other business information), and the establishment's daily sales of alcoholic beverages. A state ABC will perform random audits to determine the accuracy of the information received.

- *Methods of operation:* As discussed previously, employees working as waiters, servers, or in any other capacity who may be required to handle alcoholic beverages must be above the state's specified minimum age for serving alcohol. Some states have regulations restricting the types of promotions and advertising that a bar can undertake.

In addition to licensing, special rules may apply to specific situations in which alcohol is sold. In each case, however, its service is tightly regulated. Figure 12.5 is an example of one such regulation. Note how precisely the state of Connecticut regulates the sale of alcohol from minibars located in guest hotel rooms.

In order to combat increasing alcohol-related injuries and deaths, many states have enacted happy-hour laws, which are meant to decrease the excessive consumption of alcohol. These statutes vary from state to state, but they all contain some, if not all, of the following prohibitions:

- Distribution of free alcoholic beverages
- Providing additional servings of alcohol until the previous serving has been consumed
- The sale of alcoholic beverages at a reduced price during specified days or times
- Unlimited beverages—an unrestricted amount of alcoholic beverages at a fixed price for a fixed period of time
- Increasing the volume of alcohol in a beverage without increasing the price
- Giving alcoholic beverages as prizes

States and local agencies are very careful when granting licenses to sell liquor, and they are generally very aggressive in revoking the licenses of operations that fail to adhere to required procedures for selling alcohol. In most states, a liquor license can be revoked as a result of:

- Experiencing frequent incidents of fighting, disorderly conduct, or generally creating a public nuisance
- Allowing prostitution or solicitation on the premises
- Allowing the sale or use of drugs and narcotics
- Offering illegal adult entertainment, such as outlawed forms of nude dancing
- Failing to maintain required records
- Selling alcohol to minors

In some states, representatives from the ABC conduct unannounced inspections of the premises where alcohol is served and/or intentionally send minors into an establishment to see if the operator will serve them.

Liability Associated with Alcohol Service

Because alcohol can so significantly change the behavior of those who overindulge it, society is left to grapple with the question of who should be responsible for the sometimes negative effects of alcohol consumption. In cases when intoxicated individuals have caused damage, injury, or death either to themselves or others, society has responded with laws that can place some portion of responsibility on those who sell or serve alcohol, primarily because those in the business of selling and serving alcohol are making revenue as a result of such sales.

Every state has enacted laws to prevent the sale of alcohol to minors, to those who are intoxicated, and to individuals known to be alcoholics. Figure 12.6 shown on the next page is an example of how one state, Texas, has developed laws to discourage minors from drinking and to penalize those who would serve them. It is presented here as an example of how seriously society takes the sale of alcohol to minors.

Connecticut permit law

Sec. 30-37i. Hotel guest bar permit

a) A hotel guest bar permit, available to a hotel permittee, shall allow the retail sale of alcoholic liquor located in registered hotel guest rooms. The annual fee for a hotel guest bar permit shall be fifty dollars for each hotel room equipped for the retail sale of alcoholic liquor, (b) A hotel guest bar shall: (1) be accessible only by key, magnetic card, or similar device provided by the hotel to a registered guest twenty-one years of age or older; and (2) restocked no earlier than nine o'clock A.M. and no later than one o'clock A.M. (c) The Department of Consumer Protection shall adopt regulations, in accordance with the provisions of Chapter 54, for the operation of hotel guest bars.

History: P.A. 95-195 amended Subsect. (c) by substituting Department of Consumer Protection for Department of Liquor Control, effective July 1, 1995; June 30 Sp. Sess. P.A. 03-6 and P.A. 04-169 replaced Department of Consumer Protection with Department of Agriculture and Consumer Protection, effective July 1, 2004; P.A. 04-189 repealed Sec. 146 of June 30 Sp. Sess. P.A. 03-6, thereby reversing the merger of the Departments of Agriculture and Consumer Protection, effective June 1, 2004; June Sp. Sess. P.A. 09-3 increased fee in Subsect. (a) from $50 to $100.

FIGURE 12.5 **Connecticut permit law.**

Minor in Possession: If caught with alcohol, a minor will be charged with a Class C misdemeanor. Maximum fine of $500, mandatory attendance at an alcohol awareness class, 8-40 hours community service and 30-180 days loss of driving, privilege.

Minor Driving While Intoxicated (DWI): Zero BAL allowed for minor drivers. If caught, a minor will be charged with, a Class C misdemeanor, Maximum fine of $500, mandatory attendance at an alcohol awareness class, 20–40 hours community service, and 60 days loss of driving privilege.

Possession of Fake Identification: If caught, a minor will be charged with a Class C misdemeanor. Maximum fine of $500, mandatory attendance at an alcohol awareness class, 8–12 hours community service, and 30 days loss of driver's license for first offense.

Adult Purchase of Alcohol to a Minor: A Class A misdemeanor. Maximum fine of $4,000, confinement in jail for up to 1 year, or both.

Bar That Sells Alcohol to a Minor: Bar owner to receive administrative penalties of 7–20 day liquor license suspension, and a fine not to exceed $25,000 for each day of the suspension. The bartender or employee who sold the alcohol to the minor faces a Class A misdemeanor charge with a maximum punishment of one year in jail and a $4,000 fine.

FIGURE 12.6 **Summary of selected Texas laws that address minors and alcohol.**

To understand the complex laws that regulate liability for illegally serving alcohol, it is important to understand that there can be at least three parties involved in an incident resulting from the illegal sale of alcohol.

- *First party:* The individual buying and/or consuming the alcohol.
- *Second party:* The establishment selling or dispensing the alcohol.
- *Third party:* An individual not directly involved in a specific situation having to do with the sale or consumption of alcohol.

There is a misconception by some that the common law does not hold an organization that serves alcohol liable for serving an intoxicated person. That is not the case. Under common law, a facility that negligently serves alcohol to an obviously intoxicated guest can be sued for negligence if harm came to the guest. What is relatively new in many jurisdictions is that **third-party liability** can also be imposed on those that serve alcohol.

Social Host

Historically, courts in the United States have not found that those who host parties where alcohol is served liable for the subsequent actions of their adult intoxicated guests. While this position, like all areas of social law, may change someday, the current finding of most courts is that a social host has no common law duty to generally avoid making alcohol available to an adult guest. There are several reasons why a social host is not held to the same standard of care responsibilities as a licensed provider of alcohol. Consider the case of Brad Seeley. He is a real estate agent who hosts a party in his home for past customers and potential clients. If you analyze the situation that Mr. Seeley has created by hosting this party, you will see that:

1. Mr. Seeley's guests will likely make their own decisions on how much to drink.
2. It is unlikely Mr. Seeley has acquired the knowledge and training to detect those who have become intoxicated.
3. He has no effective means of controlling the number of drinks consumed by his guests.
4. If large numbers of guests attend his party, it will be extremely difficult for Mr. Seeley to know who, if anyone, is becoming intoxicated.

Despite the court's position on social host liability for adults, the slogan "Friends don't let friends drive drunk" is a good rule to live by. As a responsible party host, Mr. Seeley should be cautious about allowing his guests unlimited alcohol consumption.

A social host does have a responsibility not to serve alcohol to minors. Because doing so is illegal, even a social host can be accused of negligence should he or she allow it. Social host liability is the law in most states where a guest under the legal age of drinking becomes intoxicated and ends up causing an injury to a third party. The host would then be liable for any injuries or damage due to serving alcohol to a minor.

The most important thing for you, as a hospitality manager, to remember about social host liability is that the courts will not view your operation as that of a social host. As a license holder, you and your operation will be held responsible for the service of alcohol in a very different way.

LEGALESE

Third-party liability: The two areas of liability theory that a hospitality manager should be aware of focus on the duties of a host who holds a party where alcohol is served, and that of an establishment licensed to sell alcohol.

Dram Shop

Prior to the 1990s, most courts did not hold those who were licensed to serve liquor responsible for the damages sustained by a third party that resulted from a customer's intoxication. Today, nearly every state has established

Sec. 30-102. Dram Shop Act; liquor seller liable for damage by intoxicated person. No negligence cause of action for sale to person twenty-one years of age or older. If any person, by such person or such person's agent, sells any alcoholic liquor to an intoxicated person, and such purchaser, in consequence of such intoxication, thereafter injures the person or property of another, such seller shall pay just damages to the person injured, up to the amount of two hundred fifty thousand dollars, or to persons injured in consequence of such intoxication up to an aggregate amount of two hundred fifty thousand dollars, to be recovered in an action under this section, provided the aggrieved person or persons shall give written notice to such seller of such person's or persons' intention to bring an action under this section. Such notice shall be given (1) within one hundred twenty days of the occurrence of such injury to person or property, or (2) in the case of the death or incapacity of any aggrieved person, within one hundred eighty days of the occurrence of such injury to person or property. Such notice shall specify the time, the date and the person to whom such sale was made, the name and address of the person injured or whose property was damaged, and the time, date and place where the injury to person or property occurred. No action under the provisions of this section shall be brought but within one year from the date of the act or omission complained of. Such injured person shall have no cause of action against such seller for negligence in the sale of alcoholic liquor to a person twenty-one years of age or older.

FIGURE 12.7 **Connecticut dram shop law.**

dram shop laws that impose third-party liability on those who sell or serve alcohol.

Under the dram shop legislation instituted in most states, liquor licensees are responsible for harm and damages to both first and third parties subject to any contributory negligence offsets by these parties if three circumstances exist:

1. The individual served was intoxicated.
2. The individual was a clear danger to him- or herself and others.
3. Intoxication was the cause of the subsequent harm.

It is important to understand that there can be criminal liability as well as civil liability when alcohol is sold irresponsibly. Civil liability, under state dram shop laws, could require an alcohol establishment to pay for various expenses to injured or deceased parties, such as medical bills, property damage, lost wages, monetary awards to surviving family members, awards for pain and suffering, and punitive damages. Criminal liability could subject a hospitality operator to a revocation of the liquor license, severe fines, and/or jail time.

Figure 12.7 is an example of the dram shop law for the state of Connecticut. Note the wording that holds alcohol servers responsible for injuries to third parties, the amount of damages they could be liable to pay, and the time limits placed on filing a lawsuit. Connecticut is one of several states that places a monetary limit on the amount of damages a hospitality operator would have to pay if found liable. Figure 12.8 shown on the next page summarizes the civil liability for a licensee and a social host with respect to first and third parties who have been harmed by the irresponsible and illegal service of alcohol.

LEGALESE

Dram shop: A name given to a variety of state laws establishing a liquor licensee's third-party liability.

Analyze the Situation 12.4

Mark Hadley entered the Squirrel Cage Tavern at 4:00 P.M. on a Thursday afternoon. He sat down at the bar and, according to eyewitnesses, uttered just a single word when approached by the bartender. The one word was "draft."

The bartender had only one brand of beer on draft, so she silently pulled the beer, handed it to Mr. Hadley, and accepted the $5 bill he offered in payment. Mr. Hadley left the bar some 15 minutes later having never said another word to anyone, leaving the change from his $5 on the bar counter.

Subsequently, Mr. Hadley was involved in an auto accident in which a 10-year-old boy was rendered sightless. The boy's parents sued the Squirrel Cage Tavern and another operation, the Dulcimer Bar. The Dulcimer Bar was sued because Mr. Hadley had consumed 10 beers in three hours at that establishment prior to leaving it and driving to the Squirrel Cage.

Attorneys for the Squirrel Cage argued that their client could not have known of Mr. Hadley's condition when he entered their establishment, and that they were indeed acting responsibly in that they served him only one beer. Attorneys for the injured boy countered that the Squirrel Cage had served alcohol to an intoxicated person, a violation of state law, and, thus, under the state's dram shop legislation, was responsible for Mr. Hadley's subsequent actions.

1. Did the Squirrel Cage violate the liquor laws of its state?
2. Did the Squirrel Cage bartender act responsibly in the service of alcohol to Mr. Hadley? Did she act differently from bartenders in similar situations?
3. What should the owner of the Squirrel Cage do in the future, if anything, to minimize the chances of recurrence?

	Alcohol Liability		
	Licensee Common Law	Licensee Dram Shop	Social Host Common Law
First-Party Liability	Yes	Yes	No
Third-Party Liability	No	Yes	No
Liable If Minors Served	Yes	Yes	Yes, in most cases

FIGURE 12.8 **Alcohol liability.**

Training for Responsible Alcohol Service

In many states, legislatures have sought to limit the liability of those who serve alcohol by enacting regulations that insulate, to some degree, those establishments that commit to thoroughly training their employees who are involved in the sale of alcohol. In most jurisdictions, responsible alcohol server training will be either mandated or strongly encouraged. The absence of such training would, without doubt, be a significant hindrance should you ever face a lawsuit that accuses your operation of irresponsible alcohol service. The National Restaurant Association (NRA), the American Hotel & Lodging Association (AH&LA), and many private organizations provide excellent training materials that can help make your training task easier. A popular training tool endorsed by the NRA is ServSafe Alcohol Training & Certification (see www.suresellnow.com). The AH&LA endorses the training program Controlling Alcohol Risks Effectively (CARE). Training for Intervention Procedures (TIPS) is another well-recognized program to train responsible servers.

Regardless of whether you choose to create your own responsible server program or to purchase and implement one of the many available on the market, you should carefully review your program to ensure that it meets five criteria:

1. *It is an approved training course:* The training program you use should be approved by the agency that monitors alcohol service and licensing in your area. If you create your own training program, it too must be submitted for approval. The best of the nationally available training programs will be preapproved for use in your area, but it is your responsibility to make sure that the one you use is preapproved. Never purchase or use a training program that has not been approved. A jury could perceive the use of such a program as an indication that management was not serious about responsible alcohol server training.
2. *It explains the nature of alcohol's absorption into the bloodstream:* A basic understanding of how alcohol is absorbed in the body is crucial for serving responsibly. A variety of factors affect an individual's BAL. These include:
   - *Body weight:* The larger the body, the more the alcohol is diluted. Because of this, given the same amount of alcohol, a large person will be less affected by alcohol than a smaller person.
   - *Food consumption:* The consumption of food slows the rate at which alcohol is absorbed into the system. In addition, different foods affect absorption rates in different ways.
   - *Amount of sleep:* Tired people feel the effects of alcohol more than those who are well rested.
   - *Age:* Younger people feel the effects of alcohol more quickly than older people. But the eyesight of older customers is more affected by drinking alcohol.
   - *Health:* The liver plays an important part in removing alcohol from the system. Customers with liver problems are more apt to become intoxicated.
   - *Medication:* Many medications do not mix well with alcohol, and in some instances mixtures can be very dangerous.
   - *General metabolism:* Some people's bodies convert alcohol faster than others do.
3. *It extensively instructs servers in the methods of checking for legal identification, as well as for spotting false IDs:* Minors who wish to drink often secure false identification documents in order to gain access to establishments where they can buy alcoholic beverages. This puts the beverage server in a difficult legal position. Although not expected to know whether a minor is presenting false identification, the beverage server is required to use reasonable care in spotting those who attempt to use a false ID. Because false IDs are in such widespread use, a major component of any responsible alcohol server program should be instruction in how to identify them. Make sure that your training materials address the following areas:
   - Alteration of type style, including font and point size
   - Cut-and-paste techniques
   - Physical identification/picture match
   - Relamination detection (take the card out of the wallet and feel it)
   - Random information verification (address, Social Security number, etc.)
   - A list of qualifying ID documents

   Helpful guidebooks such as the I.D. Checking Guide can help your hospitality business in checking to determine whether the ID presented is an up-to-date valid driver's license, ID card, and/or other government-issued identification document.[1]
4. *It emphasizes early intervention when confronted with possible overconsumption by guests:* It is clearly against the law to serve an intoxicated person. The difficulty, of course, lies in identifying when a person is intoxicated. The number of drinks (and/or the amount of alcohol in multishot drinks, carbonated drinks, and high energy drinks) served in a given

[1] https://www.driverslicenseguide.com/

time period gives an indication of possible BAC, but as we have seen, many factors affect it. A good, responsible, server training program will teach your servers to note the observable behavioral changes that occur with advancing stages of intoxication. When these are noted, there are specific techniques that can be employed to limit the quantity of alcohol served to such guests and, if necessary, to refuse service completely.

5. *It provides for documentation of training effectiveness.* It is not enough for employees to attend responsible service training sessions. They must demonstrate a mastery of the material as well. The best of the training materials on the market have examination components to test trainee competence. The tests should be both reliable and valid. The examinations should be scored by an independent source, and the results should be reported to management in a timely fashion. If you must defend your use of a particular program in court, you almost certainly will be defending its effectiveness as well. The inability to demonstrate that your responsible server training results might damage your

Analyze the Situation 12.5

Michele Rodgers entered the Golden Spike Bar and Grill on a Friday night at approximately 10:30 P.M. At the door, she was stopped briefly by the bar's security guard, Luis Sargota. He inspected Ms. Rodgers' photo ID as he had been trained to do during the one-hour orientation class he attended on his first day of work.

The photo ID presented by Ms. Rodgers showed her age to be 21 years and three months. The photo on the picture was clearly her own. She was not asked to remove the ID from her wallet. Ms. Rodgers entered the bar and, over a period of three hours, consumed five fuzzy navel drinks, each containing approximately 1.5 ounces of 80-proof alcohol served with fruit juice.

Upon leaving the bar at 1:30 A.M., Ms. Rodgers was involved in a traffic accident that seriously injured a man who was driving home after working the late shift at a local factory. The family of the injured man sued Michele and the Golden Spike when it was discovered that Michele was, in fact, only 20 years old, and thus was not of legal age to drink alcohol.

The attorney for the Golden Spike maintained that the bar acted responsibly in that it trained its security guards to check for identification prior to allowing admission to the bar and that Ms. Rodgers had presented a falsified identification card that the bar could not reasonably have known was false. In addition, the security guard stated that Ms. Rodgers "looked" at least 21 when she entered the bar. Thus, the bar was not guilty of knowingly serving minors.

1. Is the bar responsible for illegally serving Ms. Rodgers? Was she served excessively?
2. Do you think a jury would find one hour of orientation sufficient in the guard's training?
3. What could the owners of the Golden Spike do in the future to prevent a reoccurrence such as this?

Analyze the Situation 12.6

Samuel Vosovic attended a reception in the ballroom of the Altoona Pike Country Club. He was a salesman for a photography studio, and he attended a reception at the invitation of Ronald Thespia, one of the club's well-known members. Mr. Thespia's company sponsored the reception, which consisted of light hors d'oeuvres and an open bar.

Over the course of two and one-half hours, it was determined that Mr. Vosovic consumed approximately nine drinks. The reception was large enough to require three bartender stations in the room. No single bartender served Mr. Vosovic more than three drinks in the course of the evening. Lea Tobson, one of the club's bartenders, did finally detect a significant change in Mr. Vosovic's behavior and, when Mr. Vosovic requested another drink, refused to serve him and summoned a manager.

The club's food and beverage director determined that Mr. Vosovic was in all likelihood intoxicated. The director asked him to turn over his car keys, and then instructed one of the club's wait staff to drive Mr. Vosovic home, give the car keys to his wife, and take a cab back to the club. One hour after being taken home, Mr. Vosovic got back behind the wheel of his car and, still intoxicated, lost control of the vehicle and crashed into a tree, and he died instantly. His wife brought suit against the country club under dram shop legislation in her state.

The club responded that it had acted responsibly in both refusing to service Mr. Vosovic and in ensuring that he got home safely. Mrs. Vosovic replied that her husband was upset at his treatment by the club when he arrived home and that she "couldn't stop him" when he took the car keys from her, intent on returning to the club. She held the club responsible because, as she stated, "They got him drunk." As additional evidence of the club's irresponsibility, she pointed to the tipping policy in place during open bars; essentially, in an open bar situation, the bartenders at the club were paid a percentage of the sales price of the alcohol consumed. Mrs. Vosovic's attorney claimed that the club's tipping policy encouraged its bartenders to overpour the drinks they served to build the sales value of the event and thus their own income.

1. Did the country club act responsibly in this situation?
2. What steps could a responsible beverage manager take to reduce the possibility of such an incident recurring?
3. Would the club's tipping policy influence a jury's view of responsible alcohol service by the club if the case went to trial? Why?
4. Was it foreseeable by the club that Mr. Vosovic, once home, would leave the house in his intoxicated condition?

ability to prove that you have conducted your training in a responsible manner. Responsible alcohol service training should be conducted frequently and documented in employment files. Some hospitality businesses require all their employees to attend a training course whether or not their primary duties are serving alcohol. Imagine how helpful it would be to have a front desk agent notice the staggering behavior of a guest as he or she is walking across the lobby of the hotel to retrieve his or her car. Safety of guests is paramount, and having all employees in alignment on what to look for in behavior can be a very valuable step in preventing injury and damage.

International Snapshot

Understanding Barriers to Entry and Regulatory Requirements for Foreign Producers of Alcohol Seeking to Import to the United States

The United States has a three tiered system for the distribution and sale of alcohol beverage products which is unique in the world. Although those of us working in this space here in the United states are familiar with this system and sometimes take it for granted, it is important to remember how unusual our structure is to foreigners. Therefore, anytime we provide legal or business advice to individuals from overseas desiring to ship alcohol products here or wanting to be in the hotel or restaurant business, we need to prepare them up front. Depending on the business, U.S. law may require licensing and compliance measures which take time. Lack of information about the required steps can be costly if the result is a delayed opening or a lost shipment or sale.

As a result of mandates imposed by federal and state laws, alcohol beverages in the United States are sold by manufacturer/supplier entities to "middlemen" (distributors/wholesalers), and then those distributors/wholesalers sell to retail customers. Retail customers in the U.S. range from hotels to restaurants, to package stores and grocery stores, and beyond, and, unlike in other countries, for the most part only these concerns sell directly to end user individuals.

Imagine the following real life situation. I am at a wine conference in Verona, Italy. I meet a small wine producer from a remote area in Campania, Italy. He has had some success selling his wine in Italy and other parts of Europe, and now he feels ready to enter the coveted U.S. market. He excitedly relays that his second cousin is working in a package store in New York City. He would love to ship bottles to the cousin for resale in the package store to see how it goes, and split the profits with the package store.

Although I hate to dash the hopes of the Italian producer, I gently explain to him that he simply cannot sell his wine this way under U.S. laws. We, in contrast to Europe, have a broad structure of licensing and regulation. He will need to find a U.S. importer (licensed by both the state and federal government) to bring his product into the country. That importer may or may not also be licensed as a distributor; in any case, the importer will need to sell the wine to the distributor, who will need to have New York distribution in order to sell to the New York City package store where the cousin is working. And, at the end of it all, the only sale the Italian producer will earn money on is the one he makes to the importer. More confounding still, if my new friend finds success in New York and wants to expand his business to other U.S. states, he will realize that he will be subject to different licensing requirements in every jurisdiction.

These details will be shocking to those who are not familiar with our three tier system, because this system does not exist anywhere else. There are of course additional wrinkles. In many parts of Europe, suppliers use brand representatives, brokers, or négociants to sell their products to retailers. They assign exclusivity to these individuals through contractual arrangements (sometimes even hand shake deals), and they rely upon them to get products sold for a share of the proceeds. Many expect to do the same thing here in the United states, only to discover that the regulation of brokers is a state law issue, and employment of these individuals does not circumvent the sales requirements of the three tier system.

The three tier system involves numerous other requirements not discussed here, including financial arrangements among different tier members, advertising restrictions, and more. Again, most of these legal restrictions do not exist in other countries, and those seeking to be involved in an alcohol based business here in the United states may not be aware of them. Education and information are key to the due diligence process. Salut!

Provided by Elizabeth A. DeConti, Esq., of Gray Robinson in Tampa, Florida.

WHAT WOULD YOU DO?

You are the General Manager of a resort hotel which is located in the relaxed atmosphere of the Caribbean islands. Your Director of Sales goes to an off-site event to network with potential group clients from 4-8 p.m. As you know, this is an important aspect of the Director of Sales activities in order to develop and continue relationships with future clients to further the business of the resort.

After the networking event has ended, your Director of Sales is joined by her sister and several girlfriends, while continuing to drink alcohol. After an hour or so, the manager of the establishment asks your Director of Sales and her friends to leave as they were being very loud and boisterous, causing other patrons to complain. The Director of Sales says to the manager, "Leave me alone. I'm off the clock and can have a few drinks." The manager of the establishment is an acquaintance of yours and knows that the Director of Sales works for you. One of your trusted employees witnesses the behavior of your Director of Sales and shares the information with you.

1. What action, if any, will you take against your Director of Sales?
2. When you learn of the location of the scene, what do you do?
3. What policies will you create to prevent this type of incident from happening again?
4. How do you handle the whistleblower employee who shared his/her knowledge of that evening?

WHAT DID YOU LEARN IN THIS CHAPTER?

You are the general manager of a casual restaurant that includes both a cocktail area and a dining room. Average sales per restaurant are $4 million per year with 30 percent of the sales attributed to alcohol. At the annual conference of managers sponsored by your company, your supervisor, who is the district manager, assigns you to a company task force charged with making recommendations about a new training program regarding liability for bartenders working in your operations.

Your specific task is to recommend the length of this portion of a bartender's training and to estimate the costs associated with it.

1. Assuming that bartenders earn $15 per hour, including benefits, and that trainers in your company average $40 per hour, develop a short outline of required training topics, estimate the time to cover each one, and assign a per bartender cost assuming that the bartenders must be trained in a one-on-one setting.
2. Prepare a 3- to 5-minute presentation for your district manager and the other conference attendees that justify your costs as developed.
3. Estimate the yearly cost of bartender liability training if your company of 400 restaurants hires 1,100 bartenders per year. Give your opinion on the cost likely to be incurred if no such training is implemented.

CHAPTER 13

Legal Characteristics of Travel and Tourism

13.1 Travel

The word "travel," which means "to make a journey," is an English variation of the old French word "travailler," which meant "to labor long and hard in dangerous conditions." In fact, in the earliest days of travel, transportation from place to place was expensive and difficult, dangers to life and limb were plentiful, and risks to personal health were significant. Despite this history, the travel and tourism industry is now, according to the World Travel and Tourism Council (WTTC), the world's largest industry with an estimated economic value of 7.2 trillion dollars in gross domestic product (GDP); moreover, it employs 1 out of every 11 workers worldwide.[1]

As the global economy continues to make the world smaller and as declining transportation costs (relative to income) make in-country and international travel available to larger and more diverse segments of society, it is not surprising that the legal issues raised by travel and travelers are significant. Recall that "law" was defined in Chapter 1 of this text, as "the rules of conduct and responsibility established and enforced by society." When members of two very different societies make contact through travel, the possibility that their "rules of conduct" will vary and even come into direct conflict can be very high indeed. As a professional hospitality manager, part of your job is to understand which rules of conduct (laws) should be followed. This is, of course, extremely difficult in a world with so many law-making countries, states, regions, regulatory agencies, and international governing bodies to consider.

The Travel Industry

In many parts of the world, the travel industry is referred to as the "travel and tourism industry" or simply the "travel industry." In the United States, few observers would identify businesspeople traveling across their home states to attend a company sales conference as tourists, yet such a journey certainly would expose those travelers to many features and conveniences used by tourists. For purposes of this text, the term "travel industry" will refer to those transportation services (airlines, trains, cruise ships, buses, and rental cars), lodging facilities (hotels, motels, resorts, etc.), eating and drinking places, sightseeing venues, amusement and recreation activities used by all travelers, and to those travel professionals who market these products and services to travelers.

CHAPTER OUTLINE

13.1. Travel

13.2. Travel Agents and Tour Operators

13.3. Transportation and Common Carriers

13.4. Tourism

13.5. Online Travel Sales

IN THIS CHAPTER, YOU WILL LEARN

1. To identify the components of the travel industry, how they interact, and the complex legal issues that surround this huge industry.
2. To understand fully the roles and potential liabilities of travel agents and tour operators as each group fulfills its unique role in marketing and providing travel services.
3. To identify those common carriers typically utilized by the travel industry as well as the recurrent areas of potential liability inherent in each of them.
4. To evaluate tourism as it relates to gaming, resorts, timeshares, and theme park operations based in part on the unique liability issues and managerial responsibilities inherent in each of these growing areas.
5. How, from a legal perspective, the unique characteristics of the Internet can impact restaurant and hotel managers' efforts to integrate the power of the Internet into their own operations.

[1] WTTC Research Report, March 2016.

1. Preplanning Services
2. Transportation
3. Lodging
4. Foodservices
5. Attractions and Activities

FIGURE 13.1 **Five key components of the travel industry.**

The number of laws, regulations, and standardized procedures used in all of the individual industries that collectively make up the travel industry is high indeed. **Travel law** refers to those laws that directly impact the travel industry. The field is so extensive that some attorneys specialize in this field of law. **International travel law** combines aspects of contract law, employment law, antitrust rules, regulatory and agency compliance, and knowledge of certain international agreements and treaties into a comprehensive set of guidelines for the travel industry.

Industry Components

The travel industry is composed of many segments. Consider the case of Benny and June, two U.S. college students who wish to spend their summer break traveling throughout Europe. To examine their entire travel experience, as well as to identify those travel-oriented industries that the students are likely to encounter during their trip, it is useful to view travel as consisting of five key components as listed in Figure 13.1.

Search the Web 13.1

Despite the popularity of the Internet as a way to plan your own travel, the services of professional travel agents continue to be in high demand. To view the website of the largest travel agent associations, go to **www.astanet.com**. This is the website of the American Society of Travel Agents (ASTA).

1. Click: ASTA.
2. Select: "Who We Are."
3. Explore: The subcategories to read about the goals of this effective organization.

Preplanning Services To plan their trip, Benny and June may enlist the assistance of a travel agent, a professional whose job is to plan and sell travel-related products and services and make part or all of the arrangements of the tour. Travel agents work directly and indirectly with travel service providers and tour operators. Tour operators actually operate the tours and purchase most, if not all, of the travel services, and then market these services directly to travelers or offer them to travel agents, who, in turn, sell them to travelers such as Benny and June.

Travel agents also work with transportation providers, those who sell lodging services, and those who market attractions and recreational activities.

Transportation If Benny and June indeed travel to Europe from the United States, the number of transportation services they will use is likely to be extensive. Starting in a bus, taxi, or ride-sharing car from a company such as Uber or Lyft to an airport, they will continue across the Atlantic on an international airline flight or cruise and arrive, perhaps, via rental car, bus, or rail at their destination of choice. Most journeys normally rely, in part, on the services of the very large segment of the travel industry related to transportation.

Uber was founded in 2009 in San Francisco, California, and has expanded to international cities. It allows consumers to book auto transportation on their smartphones. Lyft was founded in 2012 in San Francisco and facilitates peer-to-peer ride sharing booked through the use of smartphones. The legality of these types of popular **sharing economy** businesses has been challenged by local governments and the taxi industry. These types of services have been challenged as operating as unlicensed taxi services. Several issues such as licensing and insurance coverage for ride share companies are still to be determined. More to come as to the viability of these businesses is considered by local laws and regulations.

Lodging Although Benny and June may decide to stay at traditional hotels as they travel, they will have many choices as they plan their overnight accommodations. On one extreme, they may choose an extravagant destination resort in a desirable location that, in addition to their sleeping rooms, offers many recreational alternatives, gourmet food and beverage outlets, and numerous other amenities and activities. Alternatively, they may select more modestly priced lodging housed in a private home through Airbnb or VRBO (vacation rentals by owner) that provides them sleeping rooms and, perhaps, a limited breakfast in the morning.

Airbnb was founded in 2008 in San Francisco and is part of the sharing economy. It is a model that enables individual travelers to reserve assets owned by someone else for overnight accommodations. The laws on providing Airbnb stays are subject to state and local ordinances. Not all properties are allowed to be used as an Airbnb site. For example, a college student was prohibited from signing up his dorm room as an Airbnb site.

LEGALESE

Travel law: The laws regulating business and individual behavior in the travel industry.

International travel law: The ordinances, rules, treaties, and agreements used to regulate the international travel industry.

Sharing economy: An economic system in which assets or services are shared between private individuals for a fee, typically by means of a smartphone and the Internet.

Search the Web 13.2

For more information, see **www.airbnb**

1. Scroll to: Hosting.
2. Click: Responsible Hosting.
3. See: Legal restrictions local governments are currently placing on Airbnb.

The lodging segment of the travel industry is sizable and offers travelers a wide range of accommodation choices. In addition to traditional hotels, many private clubs, casinos, cruise ships, timeshare condominiums, and campground sites provide overnight alternatives to travelers. Most of these facilities are open to all of the traveling public. Some other types of facilities offer overnight accommodations for people away from their homes for other reasons. These include schools, colleges, and universities offering residential services; health-care (hospital and nursing homes) facilities; correctional institutions (prisons); and military bases.

Foodservices One of the greatest joys, as well as sometimes one of the most daunting aspects, of traveling is the ability to sample local foods prepared in ways and combinations that are different from those typically found "back home." From the leisurely meal to the hurried snacks also known internationally as "take-away" foods, the traveling public can choose from a wide variety of food venues. It is likely that Benny and June will find exploring the various cuisines and beverages of Europe one of the most talked-about features of their trip when they return.

Internationally, as well as in the United States, the foodservice industry consists of a plethora of food and beverage outlets that range from the exquisite and expensive to the very modestly priced "eat-on-the-street" meals offered by vendors in most large cities.

Attractions and Activities For many travelers, the food and lodging experiences they will encounter will be substantially less important than are the sites these travelers will see and the things they will do on their trips. For Benny and June, a walk through Heidelberg Castle in central Germany, a chance to see the masterpieces contained in the famous Louvre museum in Paris, or renting bikes to cycle through the mountains of Switzerland may be the actual reasons for traveling to their chosen destinations.

In well-developed countries, the number of things a traveler can see and do can be extensive. The traveler to New York City, for example, can spend days exploring the sights, sounds, and activities available. In less-developed countries and areas, the natural attractions of beaches, mountains, or forests may be enough to attract significant numbers of travelers. In all cases, however, the attractions and activities offered are likely managed and staffed by local employees and operated according to the prevailing culture and customs of the area hosting the traveler. This will likely be the case regardless of whether the activity selected involves attending a concert, a sporting event, or the theater; visiting a museum, art gallery, or historical site; gambling in a casino; visiting an amusement park; or simply enjoying the area's natural physical setting.

Each of the five major components of the travel industry has developed, over time, its own set of rules, regulations, customs, and laws related to how it does business. Most travelers will not be as aware of how these operational procedures affect their travel experience, as will the managers working in the industry. As a result, an important part of many travel industry managers' jobs is to communicate these specific procedures to the individual travelers they encounter.

Economic Breadth and Impact

The travel industry is big business. In 2016, the U.S. Travel Association reported that travel generates $2.1 trillion for the U.S. economy. Direct travel spending in the United States totaled $947.1 billion by domestic and international travelers in 2015. Accordingly, in 2015, direct spending by resident and international travelers in the United States averaged $2.6 billion a day, $108.1 million an hour, $1.8 million a minute, and $30,033 per second. These figures indicate that each U.S. household would have to pay $1,187 more in taxes without the tax revenue generated by the travel industry. In addition to revenue, the travel industry supports more than 15.1 million jobs in the United States; one in every nine American jobs depends on travel.[2]

Just as the travel professionals in the United States recognize the magnitude and impact of travel on the national economy, so do travel professionals worldwide. The World Travel and Tourism Council (WTTC) is the association created by global business leaders in the travel industry. Its members are chairs and chief executive officers from 100 of the industry's foremost companies, including airlines and other passenger transportation venues; hospitality, manufacturing, entertainment, and tour operators; car rentals; and other travel-related services. Founded in 1990, the WTTC is headquartered in London. Its mission is to raise awareness of the impact of travel and tourism and to persuade governments to make the

Search the Web 13.3

The U.S. Travel Association helps connect, promote, advocate, and research all aspects of travel, foreign and domestic. Go to **www.ustravel.org** to read about its mission and strategic priorities.

1. Click: Membership.
2. Select: Key Resources.
3. Click: Regular Membership Resource Guide.

---

[2] https://www.ustravel.org/sites/default/files/Media%20Root/Document/Talking_Points_NTTW16.pdf

industry an economic and job-creating priority. The travel industry helps local economies in many ways:

- *Export earnings:* Currency earned by tourism results in the addition of "new" money in a local economy. For many countries and geographic areas, especially those that are not rich in natural resources, tourism dollars may be the single largest source of new income.
- *Enhancement of rural areas:* Tourism jobs and businesses are usually created in the most underdeveloped regions of a country, helping to equalize economic opportunities throughout a nation and providing an incentive for residents to remain in rural areas rather than move to cities that may already be overcrowded and unable to easily support additions to the population.
- *Employment:* The travel and tourism industry is an important job creator. In addition, it is essential to understand that the vast majority of tourism jobs are in small or medium-sized, family-owned enterprises such as restaurants, shops, and the management/provision of tourism-related leisure activities.
- *Development of infrastructure:* The travel and tourism industry encourages enormous investments in new infrastructure, most of which helps to improve the living conditions of local residents, as well as the enjoyment of the tourists. Tourism development projects include airports, roads, sewage systems, water treatment plants, restoration of cultural monuments, and the creation or expansion of museums.
- *Tax collections:* The travel and tourism industry provides local governments with hundreds of millions of dollars in tax revenues each year through hotel occupancy and restaurant taxes, airport users' fees, sales taxes, park entrance fees, and employee income taxes.

Complexity of Legal Issues

The travel industry is large and complex; thus, its legal issues are as well. Travel law is unique in that it encompasses many countries, industries, regulatory agencies, cultures, and even traditions. Returning to the example of Benny and June, and given your understanding of sources of potential liability, imagine the complications that might arise if these two travelers bought a 21-day package tour of Europe (operated by a tour company based in Amsterdam) and that the tour company then subcontracted meals and accommodations for the tour with hotels and restaurants in a variety of European cities. Assume the following facts. Benny and June purchased the tour from a New York state travel agent and they took an Amtrak train to get to their departure city, where they stayed in a hotel that they reserved through an Internet booking site operated by a travel wholesaler located in Atlanta. The next day, they flew on a transatlantic airline (operated by a non-U.S. company) to reach their destination. Finally, their plane arrived late, and they missed the assigned departure time for their tour. No doubt you can begin to see the potential difficulties faced by consumers, as well as those who do business in a specific travel segment.

Travel law is complicated for a variety of reasons, including:

- *Interconnectivity:* When one travel-related business controls the sale and delivery of a complete travel product or service, the liability for poor or nonperformance may be easily assessed. When one business is dependent on the performance of another business, however, liability for poor performance is more difficult to determine. For example, assume that a travel services seller, relying on the promise made by a resort developer that a new resort would be ready to accept business on January 1 of a given year, sells a three-night stay at the resort. Upon the guests' arrival, however, the swimming pools, tennis courts, and golf course are not yet fully operational. Is fault to be assigned to the travel seller, the resort operator, or both? The interconnectivity of travel services makes it critical for hospitality managers to understand travel law.
- *Jurisdiction:* By its very nature, much of the activity in the travel industry occurs in a variety of legal settings. Suppose that a New Jersey traveler books a night's stay at a hotel in Dallas via an Internet site operating out of Florida. This person ultimately feels that the hotel did not deliver the services promised. Does he seek relief through the New Jersey, Texas, or Florida courts? Where many travel-related legal issues are concerned, the question of precisely which court has **jurisdiction** is crucial to understanding the applicable law.
- *Variation in terminology and resulting expectations:* In the United States, the term "first class" has a specific meaning to most travelers. But is it realistic for American travelers to assume that the rest of the world is bound by the same expectations when the term is used? Clearly, everyone in the world is not required to think exactly as Americans do. Alternatively, what if unscrupulous travel salespeople knowing the ambiguity of the term "first class" seek to defraud unwitting travelers? The question of honest differences in terminology and resulting expectation is complicated by multiple languages and multiple translations of travel-related words, phrases, and concepts.
- *Identity of the actual service provider:* Travel services are often packaged; that is, travelers will, in many cases, buy a complete travel experience that includes transportation, meals, lodging, and leisure activities. When a component part of that travel experience is defective, it may be very challenging to determine exactly who is responsible to the traveler. For example, if a company that puts tours together purchases, at a discount, 100 sleeping

---

LEGALESE

Jurisdiction: The authority given by law or treaty to a court to try cases and make decisions about legal matters within a particular geographic area and/or over certain types of cases.

rooms from a hotel and then uses those rooms to lodge a tour group, is the hotel's customer the tour company or the individual traveler? If the hotel does not operate in the manner the tour company promised the travelers purchasing the tour and if monetary compensation is due to the tour group for that poor hotel service, is the compensation more appropriately refunded to the tour operator that purchased the rooms, or the guests who stayed in the rooms? In complicated cases, it may well require a court to sort out a resolution.

- *Uncontrollable forces:* Travel is affected by many factors beyond the control of travel services providers. Severe weather, civil unrest, war, disease, and a variety of other variables can serve to make travel either unpleasant or impossible. Most observers would say that these forces should not generally be used to hold a travel services provider responsible for nonperformance of a contract. But what is the responsibility of the travel services provider that knowingly subjects travelers to these forces? For example, if a cruise ship captain knowingly sails his or her ship into waters that are in the direct path of a hurricane, that captain will likely, in most travelers' opinions, assume some level of liability for the potential outcome. A jury may be required to determine the actual degree of the cruise operator's responsibility.

In the remaining sections of this chapter, you will learn about some of the governmental and quasigovernmental groups that help regulate and set national and worldwide policy for the travel industry. You will also become familiar with the travel agents, wholesalers, and tour group operators that make up the distribution segment of the travel industry. In addition, we will examine those industries that provide the means of passenger transportation, (i.e., buses, trains, planes, etc.) for their unique regulation and liability issues. The intent is to demonstrate the interconnectivity of the travel industry and to direct you to sources of further information in those areas that entail specialized legal knowledge appropriate for hospitality managers.

13.2 Travel Agents and Tour Operators

Not all travelers need the help of travel professionals when they decide to take a trip. For many, however, the knowledge and skills of such professionals are extremely important to the success of their trip. As a result, travel agents, tour companies, and travel wholesalers are essential components of today's travel industry, making it critical to understand how each operates and how travel law relates to them individually and to the hospitality industry as a whole.

Search the Web 13.4

Important travel-related news affects travel agents throughout the world. Log on to the Internet and enter **www.travelagentcentral.com**

1. Select: News.
2. Review: Different current news articles on matters that affect the travel agent segment of the travel and tourism industry.

Travel Agents

Historically, and despite the increased popularity of the Internet, individual and corporate travel agents remain the primary distributors of travel services. They offer customers packages or services provided by tour companies, organize tailor-made travel on request, and sell services such as vacation packages, airline tickets, train tickets, cruises, hotel bookings, car rentals, and other services. Whether individual or corporate, as travel experts, their job is to inform and advise travelers. In the hospitality industry, hotel managers interact with travel agents on a daily basis because, in most hotels, a high percentage of the reservations made are booked by travel agents via the global distribution system (GDS) that electronically links travel agents worldwide to individual hotel reservation systems.

Constantly changing airfares and schedules, literally thousands of available vacation packages, and a vast amount of travel information on the Internet can make travel planning frustrating and time consuming for travelers. To sort out their options, tourists and businesspeople often turn to travel agents. These professionals are truly "agents" in the agent/principal relationship defined in Chapter 3. That is, they act on behalf of a principal. For example, when a travel agent acts on behalf of a tour company (the principal) when selling a tour to a client, the principal will be bound by the actions of the travel agent. In turn, the travel agent will be responsible for informing the client about the identity of the tour company.

Compensation Travel agents contract for travel services on behalf of their clients. Accordingly, they have a **fiduciary** responsibility to those clients. This is an important concept because travel agents are expected to act in the best interests of their clients, not those of the hotels, airlines, or other travel organizations that may actually compensate the travel agent.

Travel agents are expected to be knowledgeable about the products they sell and to exhibit reasonable care in their dealings with clients. When they do not, they risk assuming liability for their own actions, as well as for the service levels and behavior of the third-party travel services suppliers with which they affiliate. For example, assume that a travel agent books a room for a client at a hotel in a large city. The agent

---

LEGALESE

Fiduciary: A relationship based on trust and the responsibility to act in the best interest of another when performing tasks.

represents to the client that the hotel is of "four-star" quality in a "safe" part of the city. In fact, the agent knows that the hotel is a "two-star" hotel in a high-crime area of the city. In this case, the travel agent's client is likely to have cause for legal action against the travel agent because of misrepresentation, even if the travel agent was compensated for the booking by the hotel, not the travel agent's actual client.

Travel agents have historically worked on a commission basis for the hotels, airlines, and other travel suppliers with which they do business. Even when travel agents are paid their commission by a third party, a hotel, or airline, they still owe a fiduciary responsibility to their client, the traveler. More recently, as airlines have reduced travel agent commissions and as the Internet has made it increasingly popular to book travel without the assistance of a travel agent, some agents are directly charging their clients fees for services provided. When a travel agent charges a client a fee for booking a hotel or airline reservation, it is clear that the travel agent has a fiduciary responsibility to that client.

Responsibilities Travel agents routinely perform a variety of tasks. Essentially, however, a manager in the travel agent industry has a duty to train and inform his or her in-office and outside sales staff on all phases of travel offered to the public so that these individuals are in a position to provide professional travel advice and to secure the most appropriate travel services available for each client. To that end, travel agents should make every effort to provide accurate information so that their clients can make an informed choice as to travel services. In particular, travel agents who work with clients wishing to travel internationally have a responsibility to advise their clients of the necessary passport and visa requirements for the trip to be undertaken. In addition, travel agents are required, at the time of booking any travel service on behalf of a client, to inform that client about any cancellation fee, revision fee, supplier service charge, or other administration charges, and the amount of these fees. When possible, agents must also inform clients of the existence of cancellation protection and/or insurance.

Regulatory Structure Travel agents and their actions are, of course, subject to the same rules of law as any other business; at this time, there are no federal licensing requirements specifically for travel agents. State regulation does vary, however, and every license-issuing state requires registration, payment of fees, and compliance with the applicable regulation or statute. The laws are constantly changing as states amend and repeal sections of their laws from time to time. And because different departments and agencies are responsible for the oversight of travel agents in these states, regulations may vary widely indeed.

The individual state's office of attorney general or the department that deals with commerce is the most likely source of information regarding specialized state laws affecting travel agents.

Like professionals in many other businesses, travel agents have traditionally been primarily responsible for the regulation of their own industry and its members. The Travel Institute (www.thetravelinstitute.com) has various certifications to indicate that an individual is knowledgeable in the field of travel sales. The initial certification is the certified travel associate (CTA). The candidate must have 18 months of industry experience and complete various classes or workshops on essential elements of industry prior to receiving this designation. A CTA can earn an additional certification, the certified travel industry executive (CTIE), which focuses on leadership. Finally, individuals with these two certifications can earn the coveted designation of certified travel counselor (CTC), which focuses on project management, accounting fundamentals, team building, and conflict management.

Potential Liability Issues Travel agents routinely act as agents for airlines, hotels, car rental agencies, and others. Thus, they have a duty to both their clients and their principals. Common areas of potential travel agent liability, and, as a result, possible litigation, have revolved around five issues:

1. *Failure to provide promised services:* When a travel agent books a service for a client (the traveler) from a travel services provider, the agent should be confident about the ability of the provider to deliver as promised. That said, not all failures to provide services result in travel agent liability. For example, if a travel agent in good faith books a client at a Hilton Hotel that normally operates a swimming pool, but the pool is closed for repairs when the client checks in, the agent is unlikely to be held responsible for this because the client could reasonably foresee that such events happen at hotels. If, on the other hand, the travel agent booked a suite with a whirlpool at the hotel for the same client knowing that the hotel did not have whirlpool suites, the travel agent would likely be held liable for the inability of the hotel to provide the promised services. Travel agents have a duty to exercise reasonable care when promising specific travel services will be available from specific travel service providers.
2. *Failure to honor agreed-upon pricing:* The ability of a travel agent in one part of the world to control the pricing behavior of a travel service provider in another part of the world is often quite limited. As a result, the traveler who paid a travel agent $100 to secure a hotel room reservation in a foreign country could, upon arrival at the hotel, be forced to pay additional monies before the hotel will actually honor the reservation. In such a situation, the traveler might have no immediate option except to pay the additional amount. He or she would likely, however, have a claim against the travel agent for failure to secure the services purchased at the agreed-on price. To avoid such situations, travel agents should deal only with reputable hotels and any other providers of travel services.
3. *Misrepresentation:* Travel agents generally are paid only upon the sale of a travel service. Unfortunately, this can cause unscrupulous travel agents to intentionally misrepresent the services they market in order to make more sales, and thus more personal income. When they do so and are caught, they face potential liability. However, actual liability in this area is not always easy to determine. For example, Florida is known worldwide as the sunshine state, yet it rains there in some months more than in others. If a travel agent represents to a client living in Vermont that a vacation to Florida during one

of the rainy months would be a chance to "escape to the sunshine," it might be unclear as to whether this statement constituted actual misrepresentation on the agent's part or was in fact a legal marketing effort designed to generate vacation sales and, thus, the agent's commissions. It is highly unlikely that a jury would hold a travel agent responsible for the weather in Florida, but that same agent might be held responsible if it could be established that the agent willfully misrepresented the facts about Florida weather during a specific time period in order to sell more Florida tours.

4. *Failure to discover and disclose:* Travel agents generally are not held liable for the negligent acts of the hotels, restaurants, airlines, and other travel service providers they represent, but they are responsible for informing clients about known hazards and risks. Thus, the travel agent who sells an excursion package for a rafting trip down a river would be required to disclose, if it were known, that several couples typically drown on the same trip each rafting season. The failure to discover and disclose such information puts the travel agent (as well as the clients!) at risk. To avoid this risk, travel agents must become knowledgeable about the products they sell, and then they must be forthright with their clients about what they know. In addition, travel agents are liable for disclosing information that could be interpreted as creating a conflict of interest, which could be detrimental to the interests of their client. For example, a travel agent who is also acting as a tour operator selling his or her own packages to clients, he or she must disclose this fact. A travel agent's responsibility is to discover and disclose information to clients. For example, a travel agent who knew that a particular group of female clients wanted to go on a ski trip specifically to meet eligible bachelors should discover and disclose that their week of skiing would coincide with the resort's annual LGBT ski week. Damages in that event might be difficult to prove, but a successful travel agent needs to do his or her homework when special requests and needs arise.
5. *Negligence:* Faced with the difficulties involved with relying on other parties to provide the services they sell, travel agents have commonly sought to limit their liability exposure through the use of contracts that include exculpatory clauses or disclaimers. As noted in Chapter 2, however, the courts are not likely to limit a travel agent's liability via the use of exculpatory clauses or disclaimers when it can be proved that the agent exhibited negligence or gross negligence when interacting with his or her clients.

Of course, consumers who feel they have been treated unfairly by a travel agent have the ability to file a lawsuit against the agent. When large numbers of consumers experience the same alleged breach of law, it is often to their advantage to combine their complaints into a **class action lawsuit**. This is frequently the case when the same incident affects many potential plaintiffs in the same manner. If a class action lawsuit is successful, a period of time is generally established by the court to allow people who can prove they fit the class (suffered the same or similar damages due to the same or similar treatment) to file claims to share in any judgment amounts.

To illustrate, assume that a cruise ship returns to port after four days of what was to be a seven-day cruise. The ship does so because 300 of the 1,500 passengers became ill with a Norwalk-type virus. In this case, all 300 passengers, as well as the 1,200 who had their cruise cut short, may be able to file a successful class action lawsuit if it is determined that there was negligence on the part of the cruise ship's owners or operators that contributed to the viral outbreak.

Tour Operators

Tour operators are an important part of the travel industry, and while they often work closely with travel agencies, they are, from a legal perspective, distinctly different. Hospitality managers will generally encounter both travel agents and tour operators in their normal course of work.

Tour operator is the broad term used to identify those varied companies that purchase travel services in a large quantity and then market those same services to individual travelers. In many cases, tour operators, because they purchase travel services in bulk, are able to buy them at a significant discount, add a markup that represents the tour operator's profit margin, and still offer travelers lower prices for these travel services than the individual traveler could negotiate on his or her own.

Sometimes travel agencies serve a dual role, also functioning as tour operators. Legally, however, a tour operator is not an agent but rather is the principal in the provision of travel services. As a result, the tour operator is directly responsible for the delivery of the travel services it has marketed and sold. This distinction is an important one because principals are responsible for the failure to deliver services as promised, while agents are generally not held responsible unless they knew or should have known at the time of the booking that services could not be delivered as promised.

Another difference between travel agents and tour operators is the way they earn their income. Tour operators do not work on commission; travel agents do. The tour operator's profit must come from the sale of travel services he or she has previously purchased. For example, if a tour operator purchases 100 tickets to the Super Bowl with the intention of packaging those tickets with airfare and overnight accommodations to create a "Super Bowl Extravaganza" vacation package, the tour operator will have incurred the cost of the football tickets, whether the sale of the vacation packages is successful or not. Thus, while travel agents may lose an unearned commission

---

LEGALESE

Class action lawsuit: A lawsuit filed by one or more people on behalf of themselves and a larger group of people who were similarly affected by an event.

Tour operator: A company whose primary activity is the planning, packaging, and marketing of travel services, including transportation, meals, accommodations, and activities.

when a vacation package they offer for sale does not sell, the tour operator will likely face an out-of-pocket monetary loss.

Tour operating companies can offer either a limited or a large number of services. Thus, one tour operator may simply market self-guided trips, relying on selected transportation, hotels, and attractions to make up the trip's itinerary. An example of a trip not guided or managed by the tour operator, is a tour package from such an operator that might consist of airline tickets to a large city, hotel reservations, and tickets to the theater. Other tour operators elect to offer full-service tours that include transportation, accommodations, meals, attractions, and the actual tour guides or leaders who serve as escorts. Of course, from a legal perspective, the potential for misunderstandings and litigation increases as the number of services offered by the tour operator increases.

Regulatory Structure Just as travel agents are regulated primarily at the state level, so too are tour operators. In most cases, states are concerned about the financial stability of tour operators. Since tour operators must generally purchase travel services ahead of their actual use, the financial risk taken by tour operators can be great. Some tour operators overextend themselves and then face financial difficulties that result in nonperformance or nondelivery of promised services for which they have previously received client monies. State statutes that seek to protect consumers in these situations are varied, but all contain provisions designed to ensure that tour operators can provide the services promised or that consumers can recover money they have paid when the contracted-for services are not provided. Figure 13.2 is an example of this type of law in Hawaii. Note that Hawaiian travel agencies, as well as charter tour operators, are affected by this statute.

Generally, when a person agrees to buy from a tour operator services or products that include transportation, lodging, an interest or investment in a timeshare plan, travel investments, or other travel services, the travel operator must provide the buyer with written disclosure of all terms of the purchase within five business days. After receiving full written disclosure, typically the buyer may cancel such an agreement until midnight of the third business day after the disclosure is received.

Contracts made between tour operators and hospitality services suppliers such as hotels or restaurants will generally be governed by basic contract law. As a result, hospitality managers who do business with tour operators should become familiar with the laws and regulatory requirements that affect their own operations and those of tour operators. One such source of information is the National Tour Association (NTA), the leading global association for packaged travel. Its members are based in all 50 states, each of the 13 Canadian provinces, and more than 40 countries in the world. It specializes in sharing ideas, opening markets, and developing relationships with travel partners. The association membership includes tour operators, travel suppliers, and individuals representing destinations and attractions.

Potential Liability Issues Tour operators have specific responsibilities to those from whom they purchase travel services as well as to those persons actually using the services. Common areas of potential tour operator liability and, as a result, possible litigation, have revolved around five issues:

1. *Nonpayment for prearranged services:* As a hospitality manager, you are most likely to interact with tour operators when they contract with you for food or lodging services. In most cases, the terms of such agreements are subject to the traditional tenets of contract law. Nevertheless, disagreements can arise, so the best practice for restaurant and hotel managers is to seek payment from tour operators for the services they are to render before those services are supplied. Clearly, it is more difficult for a hotel or restaurant to collect payments due to them after services have been provided than it would be if payment were required in advance. Payment terms of contracts with tour operators should be clearly spelled out in any agreements made.

§468L-5

Client trust accounts; maintenance of and withdrawal from such accounts.

a) Within five business days of receipt, all travel agencies shall deposit all sums received from a consumer, for travel services offered by the travel agency in a trust account maintained in a of the consumers paying money to the travel agency.

b) The trust account required by this section shall be established and maintained for the benefit of the consumers paying money to the travel agency. The travel agency shall not in any manner encumber the amounts in trust and shall not withdraw money therefrom except: (1) In partial or full payment for travel services to the entity directly providing the travel services; or (2) To make refunds as required by this chapter. federally insured financial institution located in Hawaii.

§468L-23

Charter tour client trust account. Every travel agency engaged in the business of a charter tour operator shall establish and maintain a separate charter tour client trust account solely for the purpose of the travel agency's charter tour business. The charter tour client trust account shall be maintained in accordance with sections 468L-5 and 468L-24.

FIGURE 13.2 **Hawaii Revised Statutes, Chapter 468L.**

2. *Nondelivery of promised services:* Most travel supplier and consumer-oriented complaints about tour operators revolve around the question of whether the travel services supplied were, in fact, those promised. Honest differences of opinion can easily exist in this area. As noted, tour operators usually concentrate on selling travel services—they rarely provide them. Thus, these businesses rely on others to transport, feed, and house their travelers. Inevitably, disputes can arise when promised services are not delivered. For example, did a restaurant selected by a tour operator actually provide tour participants "delicious" meals, as promised in a travel advertisement? Was a rafting trip "exciting"? Was a tour guide "qualified"? Often, the courts are asked to decide these issues because the actual written contracts including such terms are difficult to interpret and quantify.
3. *Adhesion contracts.* An **adhesion contract** exists when one party to the contract dictates its non-negotiable terms to the other party. If the terms of the contract are so one-sided as to be deemed unconscionable by the courts, the offending portion—or, in some cases, all of the contract terms—will be set aside and the contract interpreted as the court sees appropriate. Because a tour operator's booking conditions often fit the profile of an adhesion contract—that is, tour buyers are often offered a "take it or leave it" form to sign when selecting a tour—it is important that tour operators offer contracts that will be deemed by the courts to be fair to both parties. Thus, excessive cancellation or change fees, broad liability disclaimers, and unreadable fine print (so small it can be assumed to have been used to put off buyers) should be avoided in tour operator contracts. In addition, the reputation of the tour operator is essential for success and if clauses are offensive or unconscionable, clients will soon learn not to trust the tour operator. This is an area where social media can truly harm or help a tour operator.
4. *Liability for injury or accident:* Despite all the advances made by the travel industry, travel can still be dangerous. This is especially true in this day of worldwide terrorist activities that are purportedly directed toward specific governments but inevitably strike individual travelers on a random basis. In addition, many tour activities such as rock or mountain climbing, skiing, motorized sports, and hunting are all inherently risky regardless of the safety precautions taken. In cases such as these and even on tours that involve no more strenuous or dangerous an activity than walking, accidents will happen, dangerous unforeseen as well as foreseen events will occur, and even the weather may cause injury or accident. All these raise the question of liability, especially for tour operators who, in most cases, contract for rather than directly provide the services they sell. Generally, the courts will not hold a tour operator liable for the negligent actions of travel services suppliers unless they are owned by the tour operator. Tour operators will be held liable, however, for their own negligence.
5. *Misrepresentation:* Most tour operators are honest, but some are not. Misrepresentation can occur whenever a tour operator knowingly misrepresents the fares and charges for their services, knowingly sells transportation when the tour operator has not made a binding commitment with the carrier designated in the agreement sold to the buyer, or knowingly misrepresents other travel services to be provided in an unscrupulous effort to entice buyers to buy. Unfortunately, misrepresentation can be difficult to prove. Therefore, as a hospitality manager doing business with a tour operator, you should strive to understand exactly what you have been contracted to supply, as well as how your company will be presented in the marketing efforts of the tour operator.

LEGALESE

Adhesion contract: A contract whose terms were not truly negotiated or bargained and, as a result, may be so one-sided in favor of the stronger party so that the contract is often deemed unenforceable by the courts.

Corporate and Government Travel

Many legal issues arise during the domestic and international travel of corporate and government employees. When employees who travel domestically or internationally are faced with a volatile situation, employers need to be aware of their responsibility to extract their employees from the volatile or unsafe situation. Specifically, corporations, governments, and nongovernment organizations (NGO) have a duty of care to their employees. These employers may end up being responsible for injuries, medical evacuation, medical treatment, et al. needed by their employees. This duty of care is similar to that of a negligence standard, and it is assessed by asking whether the actions taken by the corporation, government, NGO were reasonable—a sort of reasonable person standard for corporate managers.

Search the Web 13.5

The Global Congress on Travel Risk Management is an annual event where professionals from all aspects of the travel industry can come together to discuss their legal, safety, and security experiences and best practices. To learn more about the Global Congress's mission, and learn how to participate, visit its website at **www.globalcongressontravel.com**

To keep employees safe and secure and to reduce liability, as well as further injury to employees, corporate managers and government travel managers should enact internal protocols for mobile employees. These managers should specify the steps to be taken when an emergency affects an employee while traveling. There are many organizations that offer education and assistance to corporations, government, and NGO travel managers in the area of employee travel. A few of these are the Association of Corporate Travel Executives (www.acte.org), the Global Business Travel Association (www.gbta.org), and the Society of Government Travel Professionals (www.sgtp.org).

Analyze the Situation 13.1

As part of a three-day Mystery Tour, Joan Larson of Apex Travel, Inc., a Wisconsin-based tour operator, contacted the Ragin Cajun restaurant in Illinois, for the purpose of reserving 120 seats for dinner on a Friday night in September. The tour group arrived, and one male group member, after three drinks, began making rude and suggestive comments to one of the restaurant's female servers. When Mr. Stevens, the restaurant manager approached Ms. Genero, the Apex tour leader, about the situation, she maintained the comments were probably made in harmless fun and should be overlooked by the restaurant. "Besides," she stated, "Our bus is leaving to go back to our hotel in one hour and that particular tour group member lives several hundred miles away and is unlikely to ever see that server again." As the Ragin Cajun's restaurant manager:

1. What are your legal responsibilities to your server?
2. Who is responsible for controlling this guest's behavior?
3. How would you respond to Ms. Genero, the tour operator?
4. What potential liability does Apex face in this situation?

Corporations and businesses, governments, and NGOs need to consider various policies and procedures when authorizing business travel for employees. Ground rules need to be established because these employees are representing the company, usually traveling with proprietary data. Businesses have an obligation to exercise reasonable care to keep mobile employees safe and secure, so there are key factors to consider. An employee who travels globally needs sufficient training in cultural matters and travel safety to fulfill the purpose of and requirement for travel. Such issues as travel risk warnings, terrorist target areas, and introductions and taboos related to local cultural matters and language can impose unnecessary failures and risks for the business traveler.

Mandatory rules for air travel, ground transportation, hotels, and crisis management/travel disruption protocols should all be a part of the policies, procedures, and training that corporations, governments, NGOs and businesses require. Will your business allow employees to take personal excursions during the business trip? Will the company have copies of employees' passports and visas on hand? Are spouses allowed to accompany employees on business trips? Is it prudent to allow all the company's executives on the same airplane? Does the company have predetermined, carefully vetted vendors for ground transportation such as car rental companies and those businesses in a sharing economy? Are hotels and locations preapproved based on safety and security assessments? What happens when an employee is exposed to an illness or pandemic? Is there insurance coverage for these situations? These are some of the questions that should be addressed in the company procedures in order to minimize risk inherent with travel. For more information, see Global Congress on Travel Risk Management at www.globalcongressontravel.com.

13.3 Transportation and Common Carriers

The method of transportation that travelers select for their trip is typically one of the most important decisions they make. Speed, comfort and safety, and cost are all factors that determine which method of transportation they will choose. Of those, the reduction in the cost of transportation is a primary factor contributing to the total amount of world travel and, subsequently, to the increase in the number of **common carriers**.

Travel-related common carriers have a responsibility to service the transportation needs of almost any passenger who wishes to travel except those whose names appear on the No Fly List, created and maintained by the U.S. government's Terrorist Security Administration. It restricts air travel on commercial aircraft in or out of the United States for safety concerns (www.no-fly-list.com). Generally, these carriers have no more right to refuse a passenger, if they have sufficient room than an innkeeper has to refuse a guest (see Chapter 10). A common carrier has a special duty to its passengers to see that they arrive at their destination safely, which includes using the highest degree of care to protect them against physical harm. This is so important that the quality of common carriers taking passengers into a country or region determines, in large part, the amount of tourism activity in that area, as well as how much others in the travel industry want to invest in and develop the area's tourism infrastructure.

The Transportation Industry

The transportation industry includes both those businesses carrying people and those moving freight. This is true because manufacturers need to safely transport their goods from one place to another in the same way that passengers must be transported. Historically, stagecoaches, steamships, and railroads developed operating systems that accommodated mail, freight, and passengers. Today, some businesses in the transportation industry, such as United Parcel Service (UPS) and Federal Express (FedEx), specialize in the transportation of freight, others emphasize passenger transportation, and still others provide both. For the hospitality manager, knowledge of the laws related to the passenger transportation industries is

LEGALESE

Common carrier: A company or individual that is in the regular business of transporting people and/or freight for a fee. Examples include airlines, cruise lines, trains, and buses.

very important. These include the airlines, as well as rail, cruise ship, bus, and—although they are not technically common carriers—car rental companies.

International travel has become an important topic, particularly as it relates to common carriers. As technology advances and people are able to move around the world with much ease and relatively low cost, the United states and foreign governments have worked together in order to find ways to more safely and effectively regulate international travel. Specifically, there are numerous international travel treaties that have been executed between the United States and other governments; two of the major treaties are the Warsaw Convention and the Montreal Convention. The **Warsaw Convention**, or the Convention for the Unification of Certain Rules Relating to International Carriage by Air, seeks to create a uniform body of law pertaining the rights and responsibilities of international passengers, shippers, and air carriers. The main purpose of the Warsaw Convention is to limit the liability of air carriers by fixing their liability for harm to passengers, baggage, and goods as well as creating uniform documentation, procedures, and law for claims arising out of international air carriage.

The Warsaw Convention was subsequently amended in 1999 by the Convention for the Unification of Certain Rules for International Carriage by Air drafted in Montreal, called the "Montreal Convention." It has been described as favoring passengers rather than the air carriers. Specifically, the Montreal Convention provides that a carrier is liable for damages sustained in cases of death or bodily injury of a passenger if the injury occurred aboard the aircraft or at any time during embarking or disembarking.

Airlines U.S. airlines carry over 500 million passengers per year. In most cases, airplanes are the preferred method of long-distance travel for both leisure and business travelers—despite the tragic events of 9/11. Since 1954, the total number of passengers served by the airline industry has increased significantly each year because of the speed and relatively low cost. Of course, with high numbers of travelers comes the potential for high numbers of legal issues. This is especially due to the number of factors that can effect on-time arrivals and departures, along with the inconvenience and difficulty caused by missed connections, damaged luggage, or physical injury. While it is rare, airplanes can and do crash and lawsuits inevitably result. In all cases, the cause of the crash is investigated thoroughly, and the findings are used to assist in the assignment of liability for the accident, and to determine the law that applies to the particulars of the crash.

Precisely which laws apply to the relationship between a service provider and a consumer depends, in large measure, on what each party has promised and agreed to. The same is true of the relationship between airlines and their passengers. The details of the contract made between an airline and the passengers it carries is called the **tariff**, which, by law, must be made available, in its entirety, from the airline. To enforce the terms of its tariff, an airline must:

- Ensure that passengers can receive an explanation of key terms identified on the ticket from any location where the carrier's tickets are sold, including travel agencies.
- Make available for inspection the full text of its contract (tariff) at each of its own airport and city ticket offices.
- Mail a free copy of the full text of its tariff to the passenger upon request.

The terms of the tariffs affect how passengers are treated. For example, each airline has its own policies about what it will do for passengers whose flights are delayed. There are no federal laws or requirements in this area. Some airlines, especially those charging very low fares, do not provide any amenities to stranded passengers. Others may not offer amenities if the delay is caused by bad weather or something else beyond the airline's control. Contrary to popular belief, airlines are not required to compensate passengers whose flights are delayed or canceled. Compensation is required by law only when a passenger is "bumped" from a flight that has been overbooked.

U.S. airlines operate flights regionally, nationally, and internationally. When operating solely within the borders of the United States, federal law applies. This is because the U.S. Supreme Court has ruled that the Airline Deregulation Act of 1978 and the Federal Aviation Act 1958 preempt all state statutory and common law claims related to rates, routes, or services of air carriers.

In a similar manner, when airlines operate internationally, they are subject to the rules and liability limitations of the Warsaw Convention. The agreements made at the Warsaw Convention have been amended and updated several times. Today, as modified, it governs claims arising from international air transportation and preempts common law and those laws created by various countries in which airlines operate. The Warsaw Convention applies to all international transportation supplied to persons, baggage, or goods by any aircraft for hire. It sets forth a comprehensive scheme that defines the liability of international air carriers for personal injuries, damage, loss of baggage and goods, and damage caused by delay. The United States is a **signatory** of the Warsaw Convention, which means that, for international flights, U.S. consumer protection laws are preempted by its terms.

LEGALESE

Warsaw Convention: Short for the Convention for the Unification of Certain Rules Relating to International Carriage by Air signed at Warsaw on October 12, 1929, this agreement set limits on the liabilities of airlines that follow established guidelines for the safe operation of international airline flights.

Tariff: The agreement between an airline and its passengers. When purchasing a ticket, the passenger agrees to the terms of the tariff.

Signatory: An entity that signs and agrees to abide by the terms of a document.

Trains Train transportation was instrumental in the early development of the United States, but today its role is far smaller than that of airplanes and automobiles. Although rail companies can move freight efficiently and make money doing so, given the present structure of the rail system in this country, it is simply unprofitable in most cases to operate trains for the purpose of passenger transportation. This should come as no surprise. Public dollars are routinely used to build airports, and the airlines that utilize them profit from this. In a similar manner, the automobile industry has benefited from the immense investment in public roads and highways undertaken by federal, state, and local governments. The average U.S. citizen has been less enthusiastic, however, about using tax dollars to invest in the land, track, signals, and equipment needed to build and maintain a reliable passenger rail system. Consequently, with the exception of specific areas or routes, especially in highly populated regions, passenger rail service is not routinely available. There are, however, still nationwide passenger rail routes operated by Amtrak.

Despite a widely held belief to the contrary, Amtrak—whose name is a blend of the words "American" and "track"—is not a part of the federal government. Officially the National Railroad Passenger Corporation, Amtrak is, ostensibly, the nation's for-profit passenger rail service. However, since its inception in 1971, it has been dependent on the federal government (as well as some state governments) for grants that enable it to continue offering its services. In fiscal year 2015, more than 30.8 million passengers rode Amtrak, representing the fifth straight year in which ridership exceeded 30 million. Amtrak serves more than 500 destinations in 46 states, the District of Columbia, and three Canadian provinces with 21,300 miles of routes. Amtrak has more than 20,000 employees and in fiscal year 2015 earned approximately $3.2 billion in revenue.

Search the Web 13.6

Rail travel takes longer than air travel, but passenger fares, in some cases, make it more cost effective. Log on to the Internet and enter **www.amtrak.com**

1. At the site, price a passenger fare between New York City and Chicago.
2. Now price the same trip by airplane on **www.Travelocity.com**
3. Compare the travel time involved with the fare savings. To whom do you believe train travel would be most appealing?

Since its inception, New York City, Philadelphia, and Washington, D.C., have been the most popular boarding and disembarkment points for Amtrak rail travelers, reflecting actual use of the railroad for large-city commuting rather than long-distance travel.

Amtrak, like all other common carriers, is responsible for the safe delivery of its travelers and can be held liable for its negligence. And as on airplanes, train delays can occur and travelers can be inconvenienced, and as a common carrier, Amtrak may bear some responsibility for the resulting impact on travelers. As can be seen in Figure 13.3, Amtrak's liability disclaimer seeks to limit its liability for the effects of traveler inconvenience by carefully detailing its responsibility in the event of a travel disruption.

Cruise Ships Before the advent of airplanes, ships, and luxury liners were the only available method of traveling between continents separated by oceans and seas. While the use of ships for business and vacation travel has generally decreased from the early 1900s through today, the use of cruise ships specifically for vacation travel has increased steadily. According

> Amtrak's fares, time schedules, equipment, routing, services, and information (hereinafter "Amtrak services") are not guaranteed and are provided "as is" without any warranties of any kind, either express or implied, and Amtrak disclaims all warranties, express or implied. Applicable law may not allow the exclusion of implied warranties, so the above exclusions may not apply to you.
>
> Amtrak reserves the right to change its policies without notice.
>
> Amtrak further specifically disclaims liability for any inconvenience, expense, or damages, incidental, consequential, punitive, lost profits, loss business or otherwise, resulting from errors in its timetable, shortages of equipment, or due to delayed trains, except when such delay causes a passenger to miss an Amtrak train guaranteed connection. When a guaranteed Amtrak train connection is missed, Amtrak will provide passenger with alternate transportation on Amtrak, another carrier, or provide overnight hotel accommodations, at Amtrak's sole discretion, but only when such circumstances resulted from the actions of Amtrak and this shall constitute Amtrak's sole liability and passenger's sole and exclusive remedy. Some states may not allow the exclusion of incidental or consequential damages, so the above limitation or exclusion may not apply to you.
>
> Amtrak also disclaims any liability for the products and/or services of Amtrak's advertisers, business partners, sponsors, suppliers, licensors and agents to the extent permissible under the law and Amtrak shall only be responsible for the rail transportation services that it provides.*

FIGURE 13.3 Amtrak liability disclaimer.

**https://www.amtrak.com/servlet/ContentServer?c=Page&pagename=am%2FLayout&cid=1241337896158*

to the Cruise Lines International Association (CLIA) (www.cruising.org), about 22 million passengers took a cruise in 2014 and 24 million passengers are projected to do so in 2016.[3]

The U.S. government also keeps statistics on cruise lines. The Maritime Administration (MARAD, www.marad.dot.gov), which is part of the U.S. Department of Transportation, is responsible for the U.S. oceangoing transportation system of freight cargo and cruise travel. MARAD's statistics cover the major cruise lines that offer North American cruises with a U.S. port of call. They include AIDA, Azamara, Carnival, Celebrity, Costa, Crystal, Cunard, Disney, Fred Olsen, Holland America, MSC, Norwegian (NCL), Oceania, Princess, Regent, Royal Caribbean, Seabourn, Seadream, Silversea, and Windstar. For vacation cruises, Miami is the departure port for the highest number of travelers in the United States; Ft. Lauderdale is second. The western Caribbean was the most visited destination in 2011 with the Bahamas in second place and Alaska third. Cruises typically range in length from three days to three months with those cruises in the six- to eight-day category having the largest share of both number of cruises and passengers.

Perhaps part of the reason for the increase in cruise ship popularity is that cruise itineraries include some of the calmest waters in the world. In addition, stabilizers on modern ships, the availability of advance weather information, and the development of effective preventative medications have, for the most part, eliminated the incidence of motion (sea) sickness. In 2011, four organizations accounted for 98 percent of the cruise passenger nights: Disney, Carnival, Royal Caribbean, and Norwegian. The addition of the *Disney Dream* (2,500 passenger capacity) enabled Disney to double its share of the market from 2010 to 2011.[4]

Legal issues related to cruise travel also exist. In many respects, a cruise ship is very much like a floating full-service hotel. Thus, managers working in the cruise industry face many of the same guest safety, security, and liability issues as their land-based hospitality management counterparts. Like all common carriers, those who operate cruise ships are subject to many local, state, national, and international laws. Cruise ships and their passengers are also subject to **maritime laws**, many of which may preempt more localized laws.

Buses Buses are still an extremely important mode of transport for the travel and tourism industry. True, their use for long-distance travel is substantially less than that of either airplanes or automobiles, yet they play an important role in many areas, including shuttle services from train stations, bus depots, and parking lots. Bus companies such as Greyhound and Megabus provide relaxing, comfortable rides for passengers to certain destinations and are still very popular among travelers. Buses are also widely used for charters on routes between destinations within 200 or 300 miles of each other. On these routes, buses may actually be faster than air travel, especially considering new time-consuming airport security measures. Transporting groups to hotels, restaurants, and nightclubs; to historic sites and local attractions; to attend concerts, sporting events, and competitions; and to locations for shopping trips are additional popular ways groups make use of bus travel.

The federal government defines a bus as a passenger-carrying vehicle designed to seat at least 16 people, including the driver. The U.S. Department of Transportation's Motor Carrier Safety Administration (www.fmcsa.dot.gov) is the major regulatory agency responsible for bus safety. The agency develops rules and regulations in an effort to ensure the safety of bus passengers. Such rules pertain to the number of hours a bus driver may be required to drive, safety features of buses, and operator license requirements.

In the hospitality industry, the word "bus" is sometimes misunderstood, and that misunderstanding can lead to contract disputes. Consider, for example, the corporate executive who contracts with a bus operator for a bus to transport 30 high-level managers to and from a pro football game. Greytrails Bus Lines agrees to supply a bus for the trip; however, when the day of the trip arrives, the bus provided turns out to be a school bus. Clearly, it is unlikely that the desired bus and the bus provided are one and the same in the mind of the executive arranging the travel. Although no mandated definitions exist, those in the bus industry generally recognize the following bus types:

- *Economy:* School-type buses represent the basic, lowest-cost option for group travelers wishing to minimize their expense. These buses typically are arranged with bench (not individual) seating and contain no restroom facilities.
- *Deluxe motor coach:* This type of tour bus is most often selected for long trips or for those groups seeking greater comfort than is afforded by economy buses. The typical seating is 47 to 55 individual seats, and they have VCR/DVD capability, Wi-Fi, multiple monitors, advanced sound systems, and restroom facilities.
- *Executive motor coach:* This top-of-the-line bus is chosen by those who prefer extra-luxurious bus travel. Executive coaches are custom-made, so options vary, but typically they include full bedrooms, showers, social and meeting space, Wi-Fi, and state-of-the-art telecommunications. The maximum capacity for buses of this type ranges from 5 to 20 persons.
- *Specialty:* In some cases, trolley or double-decker buses are appropriate and are contracted for on a special-case basis.

For managers in the hospitality industry, bus travelers can be a significant source of income. Restaurant managers

[3] http://www.cruising.org/about-the-industry/research/2016-state-of-the-industry

[4] U.S. Department of Transportation, *Maritime Administration, Office of Policy and Plans, North American Cruise Statistical Snapshots, 201 1.* http://www.marad.dot.gov/wp-content/uploads/pdf/North_American_Cruise_Statistics_Quarterly_Snapshot.pdf

LEGALESE

Maritime law: Also called "admiralty law" or "the law of admiralty," the laws, regulations, international agreements, and treaties that govern activities in navigable waters.

encourage buses to stop at their restaurants for meals, and hotel managers seek to contract with bus operators for the overnight hotel stays required in long-distance bus travel.

Car Rentals

Car rental companies are not technically common carriers because they lease cars rather than transport passengers. The car rental business is, however, an important component of the transportation industry, and it comprises establishments primarily engaged in renting or leasing passenger cars, vans, trucks, and utility trailers. There are more than 10,000 such operations within the United States alone. These businesses generally operate from a retail facility. Some establishments offer only short-term rental, others only longer-term leases, and still others provide both types of services. Not surprisingly, the top five cities to rent a car in 2015 were Los Angeles, Boston, San Francisco, New York, and Denver.[5]

Rental car companies operate under laws within the states they do business. The terms of the rental agreements made must be clear to the person renting the vehicle, and rental companies are held responsible for renting safe vehicles to persons qualified to drive them. When they are not, the car rental company may, under a variety of statutes, be held liable for the accidents that ensue or the consumer rights violated.

Regulation in the Transportation Industry

The transportation industry is one of the most highly regulated industries in the world. In the United States, for example, local and state laws may govern the terms of transportation service that can be provided (e.g., at what speed a bus may drive when transporting passengers on a state-maintained highway), federal law may dictate how those in the transportation business must maintain their equipment (e.g., the Federal Aviation Administration's requirements for plane maintenance). Similarly, international maritime law may dictate the responsibilities of an internationally registered cruise ship docked in a U.S. port.

In addition to various state and local regulation enforcement agencies, at the federal level, the agencies that impose requirements on various businesses in the transportation industry include the Federal Trade Commission (FTC), Department of Transportation (DOT), National Transportation Safety Board (NTSB), U.S. Postal Service, Environmental Protection Agency (EPA), Internal Revenue Service (IRS), Interstate Commerce Commission, Department of Labor, Bureau of Citizenship and Immigration Services, Department of Agriculture, and other federal agencies. Nonfederal governmental agencies such as local airport authorities also enforce related regulations.

For those businesses in the transportation industry that operate across national borders, compliance with international law is critical. To facilitate the legal conformity of these businesses, each industry segment maintains its own voluntary compliance enforcement group. For example, in the airline industry, those companies that transport passengers internationally belong to the International Air Transport Association (IATA) (www.iata.org). The IATA was founded in Havana, Cuba, in April 1945. It is the prime vehicle for interairline cooperation in promoting safe, reliable, secure, and economical air services. At its founding, IATA had 57 members from 31 nations, mostly in Europe and North America. Today it has over 260 members from more than 117 nations. Since January 1, 2000, all airlines joining IATA have been required to demonstrate, as part of the membership eligibility process, that they operate according to an existing set of recognized international operational quality standards (OQS). These standards encompass not only flight safety but also engineering, maintenance, security, and flight operations.

Potential Liability Issues

A myriad of legal issues confront consumers and those who do business in the transportation industry. Those of most interest to hospitality managers are discussed in the following subsections.

Legal Jurisdiction

One of the most difficult issues to resolve in a legal dispute related to transportation is the identification of the appropriate court to hear the complaint. If, for example, a traveler residing in Texas purchased from a Texas-based travel agent an airline ticket for an intrastate (within the state) flight operated by an airline incorporated in Texas, and that traveler experienced difficulty, it is likely the traveler's complaint would be heard in a Texas court. But, if, instead, the traveler were an Israeli citizen who purchased via a London-based travel agent a vacation cruise operated by a Scandinavian cruise line that docked in the Bahamas, and, while docked there, the traveler was injured on the ship, the question of which court of law should hear this traveler's complaint would, of course, be much more complex. Often, the travel contracts themselves will specify which location will have jurisdiction should a dispute arise, but others may not, and the battles can be fierce because "home-field" jurisdictions often provide the same advantages in litigation as they do in sporting events.

The hospitality manager involved in international travel and venues must be certain to operate under the applicable laws at the appropriate times.

Overbooking

Just as hotels can sometimes miscalculate their occupancy forecasts and oversell their capacity, so too can airlines and rental car companies. Thus, hotel managers often find themselves housing guests who are affected by the overbooking of a transportation provider. In many such cases, guests are understandably upset and, consequently, may express much more dissatisfaction with their accommodations than would a guest whose travel plans had not been disrupted by overbooking. When this happens, it is important for the hotel manager to understand that the client paying for the hotel's services (generally, the transportation provider) is

[5] http://blog.vroomvroomvroom.com/2016/01/top-5-us-cities-rent-a-car.html

in an unfortunate situation as is the guest staying in the hotel, and that both parties should be accommodated in the best manner possible.

U.S. federal regulations do not require any compensation to be made for a delayed or canceled flight if the delay or cancellation is due to circumstances beyond the airline's control, such as inclement weather. For other kinds of delays and schedule interruptions, each airline has its own policies on offering compensation to a passenger. Those policies are either included with the paperwork associated with passenger tickets or are available from an airline's airport or ticket offices. Typical compensation offered for a delayed flight may range from free meals to hotel accommodations.

When faced with a delay, passengers should either review the airline's policy to see what compensation is available.

Federal law specifically allows airlines to overbook flights to allow for no-show passengers. But when passengers are involuntarily bumped, airlines are first required to request volunteers to give up their seats in exchange for compensation. Involuntarily bumped passengers are subject to minimum compensation as follows:

- No compensation if alternative transportation is available to get the passenger to his or her destination within one hour of the original scheduled arrival.
- The equivalent of an amount equal to 200 percent of the one-way fare to the final destination that day with a $675 maximum in the following circumstances: substitute domestic flights that arrive between one and two hours after the original scheduled arrival time or for substitute international flights that arrive between one and four hours after the original scheduled arrival time.
- If the substitute transportation is scheduled to get the passenger to his or her destination more than two hours later (four hours internationally), or if the airline does not make any substitute travel arrangements, the compensation doubles (400 percent of the one-way fare) to a maximum of $1,350.

The compensation schedule does not apply to charter flights or scheduled flights operated with planes that hold 30 or fewer passengers, or international flights inbound to the United States.[6]

Responsibility for Baggage With millions of people traveling each year, it is inevitable that some of those travelers get separated from their luggage. Also, despite their best efforts, common carriers may damage baggage that has been entrusted to them. Airlines, by far, handle the highest number of passenger luggage. Thus, airlines flying domestic routes may, as part of their tariffs, set limits on the amount they will pay for lost or damaged bags. For travel wholly between U.S. points, federal rules require any limit on an airline's total baggage liability to be at least $3,500 per passenger. This information must be communicated to the passenger. This liability limit is adjusted every two years for inflation. For international flights, provisions of the Montreal Convention limit liability for lost or damaged baggage and is adjusted for inflation every five years. The current limit is 1,131 Special Drawing Rights, which is a currency surrogate that floats daily.[7] At this time, 1,131 SDRs is worth about $1,675.

Baggage that has been lost is an inconvenience to both the traveler and the business responsible for the loss. Hospitality managers hosting travelers who have lost their luggage should, of course, ensure that their operations will do all they can to assist these travelers.

Unplanned Changes in Itinerary Travel plans can be disrupted by a variety of factors, some controllable, some not. Inclement weather, mechanical failures, traffic congestion, acts of terrorism, and human error can all disrupt travel plans, resulting in losses of both time and money. For example, if a couple's flight delay means that they miss a cruise ship departure, an entire vacation may be in jeopardy. Regardless of who is responsible, when travel plans are disrupted, those in the restaurant and hotel business may be affected. Meals may be delayed or canceled, hotel rooms may go unused, or, when travel departure plans are disrupted, a hotel may be overbooked.

Managers must be sensitive to the needs of the inconvenienced traveler as well as the needs of their own business. The best time to address the potential difficulties that could result from unanticipated itinerary changes is prior to signing a contract with a service provider. For example, assume that a restaurant agrees to serve dinner to a sports team traveling from one state to another. The 45-person team is scheduled to arrive at the restaurant at 6:00 P.M. The food for the group is prepared and the dining area reserved. But due to mechanical trouble with the bus used to transport the players, the team is stranded 100 miles away and elects to eat dinner in the town where the bus has broken down. The terms of the contract signed between the restaurant and the team's representative will dictate the level, if any, of charges that will be assessed by the restaurant.

Industry-Specific Issues Because the transportation industry is so diverse, certain laws apply only to specific segments of it. This is especially true with regard to catastrophic events. Catastrophic events involving common carriers include plane crashes, train derailments, bus accidents, and maritime accidents. Additionally, a common carrier might be liable for other noncatastrophic incidents such as a slip and fall on a cruise ship, a sexual assault by a cruise ship employee or passenger, and other occurrences. Generally, common carriers are held to a very high safety standard and, hence, may be liable for even the slightest amount of neglect. Moreover, laws

[6] https://www.transportation.gov/airconsumer/fly-rights

[7] www.imf.org

have been passed in direct response to specific incidents. For example, in 1996, after the TWA crash that killed 230 people off Long Island, New York, Congress passed the Aviation Disaster Family Assistance Act (revised in 2008) and the Foreign Air Carrier Family Support Act of 1997, which provide that, after a crash involving fatalities, the National Transportation Safety Board's Transportation Disaster Assistance Division will coordinate federal, state, and local resources with the American Red Cross to meet the needs of family members and survivors. Such assistance includes:

- Provision of time given to family members to notify other relatives before the names of passengers are made public.
- Daily briefings to update families, friends, and survivors on the progress of the investigation.
- Victim recovery, identification, and death certification including helping family members retrieve dental records and X-rays to identify the victims.
- Crisis counseling.
- Provision of hotel rooms and food available for relatives.
- Transportation of families to and from the crash site.

Hotel and restaurant managers are not, of course, expected to be experts in all areas of travel law; nevertheless, managers whose jobs bring them in regular contact with specific segments of the transportation industry are well advised to familiarize themselves with the industry-specific legislation that directly affects their hospitality operations.

13.4 Tourism

The terms "travel" and "tourism" are not synonymous. Travel, especially for business-related reasons, is conducted for a specific commercial purpose. These travelers typically have little or no time to take in the sights and attractions of the places to which they travel. Tourism, in contrast, consists of the activities directly related to pleasure travel. Tourists, in most cases, select their destinations based on what they want to see and do when they get there. There is, of course, some crossover between the two definitions. Business groups, for example, may choose their meeting locations based on what attendees can do after their scheduled daily activities have concluded. As noted earlier in this chapter, tourism can have a major impact on local economies and ecologies. As a result, circumstances, such as those related to zoning, taxation, environmental impact, and human resources management to name but a few, can often cause legal conflict.

For those hospitality managers working in areas that cater to large numbers of tourists, tourism may represent a substantial portion of the total income generated by their business. Many legal issues specifically related to tourism are important to hospitality managers, but four areas are of particular interest: the **gaming** industry, the resort industry (including **timeshare**), the **amusement park** industry, and the **medical tourism** industry.

Gaming Operations

Gaming is a form of recreational activity that is expanding both in the United States and internationally. Few segments of the tourism industry elicit a more passionate response from both its advocates and adversaries than the gaming industry. Not surprisingly, the litigation surrounding gaming is significant and continues to increase. The result for those working in the industry is a unique set of regulatory requirements, as well as potential liability issues.

History of the Gaming Industry Gambling is not a recent phenomenon. The Chinese, Japanese, Greeks, and Romans all were known to play games of chance as early as 2300 B.C. Gambling is not new to the United States, either. Both Native Americans and colonists brought a history of gambling from their own cultures that helped shape America's gaming views and practices. Native Americans even developed language to describe gambling, and in 1643, the minister Roger Williams wrote about the games of chance developed by the Narragansett Native Americans of Rhode Island.

Government-approved gambling and the idea of using gaming proceeds to pay for societal projects is also a concept with a long history in the United States. Lotteries, a popular form of voluntary taxation in England during the Georgian era (1720–1750), subsequently became popular in the colonies as European settlers arrived here. Lotteries sponsored by prominent individuals such as Ben Franklin, John Hancock, and George Washington operated in each of the 13 colonies to raise funds for building projects. Between 1765 and 1806, the state of Massachusetts authorized lotteries to help build dormitories and supply equipment for Harvard College (now Harvard University), as well as many other institutions of higher learning. Dartmouth, Yale, and Columbia are examples of educational institutions whose early development was

---

LEGALESE

Gaming: Legalized gambling.

Timeshare: A form of shared property ownership in which a buyer acquires the right to occupy a piece of real estate, such as a condominium in a resort area, for a specific period of time each year.

Amusement park: An entertainment facility featuring rides, games, food, and sometimes shows. Theme parks have rides, attractions, shows, and buildings that revolve around a central theme or group of themes. Examples include the Disney- and Universal Studios-owned amusement parks.

Medical tourism: The travel by patients who are residents of one country or region to another country or region for the purpose of obtaining health care benefits and general medical treatments.

financed, in large part, through lotteries. A lottery was even approved to provide funds for the American Revolution.

Today, the gaming industry in the United States is large and growing. Its exact size is difficult to establish; thus, estimates can vary widely. Although there are many ways to measure the size of an industry, conventional standards include the number of employees, the output of products, tax receipts, and customer count. The most common measure, however, is gross revenues, or sales. When this method is used, it is common to measure either how much consumers bet or how much the gaming operator wins on legal gambling games. This undertaking is more complex than it may first appear.

For example, assume that Bessie Hale, a retired schoolteacher, elects to visit a local casino with her friends. Ms. Hale intends to play some slot machines and attend a Doug Stone concert held in the casino's ballroom. While at the casino, Ms. Hale exchanges $100 in cash for 100 $1 tokens to use in the slot machines. One token at a time, she bets all of the original 100 tokens. Based on the machine's payout, Ms. Hale will win some of her $1 bets, and because the average slot machine pays out 90 cents for every dollar put in, she will end up with about 90 tokens. She continues to bet one token at a time until she has gone through her 90 remaining tokens. Again Ms. Hale wins about 90 percent of her bets, and thus, after betting each of her tokens, retains about 81 tokens (90 percent win rate times 90 tokens equals 81 tokens). By this time, the concert is about to begin, and so Ms. Hale cashes in her 81 tokens and goes to the concert. Of her original $100, she has $81 left. She will have, in the opinion of most observers, spent $19 on the slot machines. The slot machine records, however, $190 in total wagers (her original $100 plus $90 winnings). The casino's winnings are, of course, only Ms. Hale's actual "loss" of $19.

Confusion between the amount actually bet, which is sometimes referred to as the "handle," and the amount actually spent (lost) accounts for the widely varying estimates of the size of the legalized gaming industry. But most observers agree that the amount actually spent (lost) by customers, not the total amount they may have wagered repeatedly over the course of an evening, is the best way to measure the industry's size. Based on that approach, legalized gambling is an industry with revenue estimates exceeding $75 billion per year. The industry encompasses state-operated lotteries, casinos, horse and dog tracks, and other locations where gambling is legally allowed (such as off-track betting parlors—OTBs).

Gaming Regulation and Control All states that allow gaming regulate it. The federal government also regulates gaming through the U.S. Justice Department, the U.S. Treasury Department, and the Department of the Interior. Other agencies with oversight relationships to gaming include the FBI, the IRS, the U.S. Attorney General's Office, the U.S. Marshals, the Secret Service, and the Bureau of Indian Affairs. Gaming is also allowed, under strict control, in casinos operated by Native Americans (Indians). The Indian Gaming Regulatory Act of 1988 (IGRA), which provides for a thorough system of regulation of Native American gaming, divides gaming activity into three categories:

Class I: Social or traditional and cultural forms of Native American gaming conducted for minimal prizes or in connection with ceremonies or celebrations and solely regulated by the tribes.

Class II: Includes bingo and related games, as well as nonbanking card games if those games are otherwise lawful within the states where tribes conduct those activities. This gaming is regulated by the National Indian Gaming Commission and Tribes through the Tribal Gaming Commissions (TGC). TGCs are established and operated by Native American nations to regulate gaming activities on reservations. There are some 186 TGCs in full operation nationwide.

Class III: All other gaming, including casino gaming. Class III gaming is regulated according to the terms of compacts that tribes negotiate with the governments of the states where they are located. These compacts often give tribal gaming commissions the primary, on-site regulatory responsibility for gaming.

Gaming is one of the most highly regulated industries in the United States. The governmental agencies involved with gaming regulation have their own professional association, the North American Gaming Regulators Association (NAGRA) (www.nagra.org). Formed in 1984, NAGRA is composed of federal, state, local, tribal, and provincial government agencies that are responsible primarily for the regulation of legalized gaming activities. NAGRA's oversight responsibility includes Native American gaming, riverboat gaming, casino and video gaming, and pari-mutuel wagering. A recent conference was held to discuss the future of regulations concerning daily fantasy sports.

Potential Liability Issues Hospitality managers operating hotels or food and beverage outlets within casinos or near other gambling venues face a number of liability issues. Those managers should continually monitor the legal environment surrounding gaming. There are three current issues of significance in this area:

1. *Accountability for reckless gaming behavior:* If a society allows gaming, does it follow that an individual should have the right to wage (and lose) all of his or her family possessions? This question is one with both ethical and legal implications. It also raises the question: What responsibility does a gaming operator have to prevent excessive or reckless wagering by those who are compulsive gamblers, visibly intoxicated, or underage? These are difficult questions to answer. To avoid problems, well-managed casino operations train their employees to watch for telltale signs that indicate threats to responsible gaming and might result in litigation in which the gaming operator is accused of irresponsible behavior. Harrah's casinos have pioneered efforts in this area through their "Operation Bet Smart" program

designed to alert casino employees to gamblers who may have problems controlling their behavior. In 1995, Caesars Entertainment, the owner of the Harrah's brand, collaborated with the U.S. National Council on Problem Gambling to help launch a toll-free number helpline and train casino staff. Caesar's "Project 21" is designed to help employees enforce regulations related to the minimum legal age requirements of gamblers. These award-winning programs have helped casino employees recognize issues with guests, puts employees at ease, helps them to understand Caesar's position on these issues, and provides valuable information and direction to help others.

2. *Employee working conditions:* The operation of gaming facilities involves legal issues that affect employees as well as consumers. One such issue is smoking. Some casinos still allow smoking throughout their premises. Increasingly, employee rights groups and state and local communities are seeking to restrict smoking in casinos because of the dangers of second-hand smoke. There are currently more nonsmoking commercial casino states than casino states that allow smoking. Native American-run casinos are not bound by nonsmoking state laws. Those casino operators who continue to allow smoking where it is prohibited do so at some legal risk. Other current issues affecting casino employees are sexual harassment of workers by guests, the legality of extensive employee background checks, and employees' level of training and experience required to demonstrate that reasonable care standards in operations are met.
3. *Internet gambling:* Brick-and-mortar casinos in the United States are subject to federal corporate taxes; publicly traded companies must comply with Securities and Exchange Commission rules; and casinos must report large winnings with the IRS as well as withhold federal taxes on certain winnings. In addition, "land-based" casinos must adhere to antimoney-laundering statutes and regulations administered by the U.S. Treasury Department. In contrast, individual gaming operators currently engaged in the business of taking Internet wagers from U.S. citizens are not currently subject to such federal legal requirements. Banks and credit card companies are subject to the Unlawful Internet Gambling Enforcement Act (UIGEA) passed in 2006 that prohibits them from sending or receiving money for Internet gaming. Some people believe the UIGEA prohibits all online gaming, but it does not. It only makes it more difficult to send or receive money from a gaming site. And though it is unlikely that the U.S. government will ban all Internet gaming, Internet gaming operators probably will become subject to state and federal gaming oversight in the future. Legislation addressing the differences between currently "approved" gaming and Internet gaming is taking shape and is well worth monitoring by those managers working in the gaming industry.

Gaming remains an activity that is enjoyed by millions in this country, and it is an area within the travel and tourism industry that carries with it the potential for a great deal of enjoyment. But it also presents complex legal challenges for the businesspeople, lawmakers, and public at large.

Resort/Timeshare Operations

For many travelers, a resort is the ideal location for a vacation or holiday. There is no universally accepted definition for the term "resort," but in the hospitality industry, it generally refers to an operation offering food and beverages, lodging, and entertainment and/or recreation. Thus, resorts are found in many locations. Favorite resort types include:

- Summer resorts
- Winter resorts
- Beach resorts
- Ski resorts
- Spa and health-related resorts
- Fishing resorts
- Recreational resorts (e.g., golf, tennis, etc.)

Some travelers have become so enamored with a specific resort that they seek to reserve space at it year after year. This gave rise to the development of the timeshare concept whereby a buyer acquires the right to occupy a piece of real estate, such as an apartment or condominium in a resort area, for a specific period of time or a specific length of time each year. From this grew the practice of timeshare owners trading their occupancy rights with others.

Background of the Resort/Timeshare Industry

In most respects, the resort industry is not unlike the mainstream hotel industry but with two significant differences. One is that guests at resorts are likely to engage in activities that can, potentially, put them at some level of physical risk. Resorts typically offer their guests the chance to participate in optional recreational activities. Whereas offering a show or concert presents minimal physical risk, other activities are not so benign. For example, assume that a couple elects to visit a Western-style "working ranch," which features outdoor camping and the opportunity to herd cattle while on horseback. Obviously, these activities raise the risk for numerous kinds of accidents and injuries.

The other major difference is that the resort industry has embraced timesharing as a method of development and expansion. There are essentially two main types of timesharing plans: "deeded" and "undeeded." Under the deeded plan, buyers purchase an ownership interest in a piece of real estate. Under the undeeded plan, buyers purchase a lease, license, or club membership that lets them use the property for a specific amount of time each year for a specific number of years. Another twist on timesharing plans is the points system, typically tied to a deeded property, but not always. This plan gives owners points to use at other vacation sites operated by that particular company. Under both plans, the cost of the timeshare unit is related to the dates and length of time the property will be occupied.

Search the Web 13.7

The timeshare industry has been helped tremendously by the entrance of large and well-established hotel companies seeking to promote the resorts they own and operate.

Go to **www.hiltongrandvacations.com**

1. Click on: Learn and then read About Vacation Ownership.
2. Respond: Do you believe Hilton does a good job explaining the advantages and limitations of a timeshare purchase?

Potential Liability Issues Liability issues raised by the resort and timeshare industry revolve around the impact of resorts on their local communities and the sales techniques used to sell timeshare units. On the face of it, the process of selling timeshares appears to be fairly straightforward, but the tactics used in some real estate transactions have resulted in major legal difficulties in this segment of the resort market. Consider three possible liability issues:

1. *Economic and environmental impact of resorts and resort activities:* Resorts, especially those in countries with underdeveloped economies, can have a tremendously positive financial impact on the local area. Approximately 20 million households own timeshares with the total sales worldwide exceeding US$14 billion. Over 180 countries have time shares.[8] Jobs, improvements to utilities, construction of roads and other infrastructure components can all result when a resort is developed. But resort development can also drive up the cost of living for local residents, damage ecosystems, and consume a disproportionately large share of natural resources. In some local economies, other businesses cannot compete with resorts for available labor, and so these communities come to depend almost entirely on the resort(s) for their livelihood. The result is litigation between the entities operating the resorts and residents and governments seeking to control the impact of the resort on the local area.
2. *Deceptive sales tactics:* With over 7,400 resorts worldwide participating in timeshare sales, it is inevitable that some would employ unscrupulous means to sell their products. Most states regulate timesharing sales either under existing state real estate laws or under laws that were specifically enacted to address timeshare operations. The regulating authority is usually the real estate commission in the state where the timeshare is located. In the past, problems have arisen with regard to sales deception in the areas of total costs, exchange programs, and facility operations.

   The cost of buying a timeshare includes its purchase price as well as any required monthly or annual maintenance fees. Maintenance fees are related to the normal upkeep of common ownership property areas such as pools, tennis courts, and the like. These fees typically rise at rates that equal or exceed inflation although some timeshare operators have used increases in annual maintenance fees to generate exorbitant profits.

   For many vacationers, the chance to participate in exchange programs is a major factor in their buying decision. Exchange programs offer the opportunity to arrange trades with the owners of other resort units in different locations. Some timeshare operators require a reservation fee in addition to the use of points for timeshare owners to use other timeshare locations.

   But promises about the specifics of such exchange programs can be exaggerated and hence result in litigation alleging deceptive sales practices.

   In sum, a timeshare may be a good investment for a particular buyer if it is operated properly and within legal means. And buyers must consider the track record of the seller, developer, and management company before making a purchase. In short, they must do their homework.
3. *Rights in event of default:* Perhaps the worst-case scenario for timeshare purchasers (or managers!) is the closure or bankruptcy of the resort they partially "own." If a developer, builder, or management company defaults on its financial obligations for a resort, the impact on the individual timeshare owners of that resort can be significant. To help ensure against problems of this type, timeshare buyers should insist that their contracts include a **nondisturbance clause**. This provision ensures that individual timeshare owners will continue to have the use of their timeshare unit in the event of default by the developer, builder, or management company and subsequent third-party claims against the resort's developer or management firm.

Given the popularity of resorts and the perceived advantages of timeshare ownership, these two components of the travel and tourism industry will continue to grow. Those hospitality managers involved in these industry segments should, as appropriate, monitor the legal environment related to them.

Amusement Park Operations

Amusement parks are extremely popular with visitors of all ages. Founded more than 90 years ago, The International Association of Amusement Parks and Attractions (IAAPA) (www.iaapa.org) estimates that there are over 400 amusement parks and attractions in the United States and approximately 375 million guests annually. In 2011, these theme and amusements parks (including zoos, museums, water parks, and aquariums) produced $219 billion nationwide. Hospitality managers working within these parks typically provide food, beverage, and lodging services, and many hospitality

LEGALESE

Nondisturbance clause: A clause in a contract that stipulates that leases or other ownership investments in the property will be allowed to continue uninterrupted in the event of a default or insolvency by the landlord/seller.

[8] Timeshare Consumers Guide, "Timeshare Statistics." http://www.timeshareconsumerguide.org/timeshare-information/timeshare-statistics/ (Accessed June 2016.)

managers work in communities whose travel patterns and economies are heavily influenced by the amusement parks in their area. This industry employs more than 1.3 million workers and indirectly creates 1 million other jobs in the United States.

History of the Amusement Park Industry The amusement park industry began in medieval Europe when pleasure gardens were developed on the outskirts of major European cities. These gardens, forerunners of today's amusement parks, featured live entertainment, fireworks, dancing, games, and even some primitive amusement rides. Pleasure gardens remained extremely popular until the 1700s when the political environment caused most of them to close. But one such park, in Bakken, north of Copenhagen, Denmark, still exists. It opened in 1583 and now enjoys the status of being the world's oldest operating amusement park.

In the late 1800s, the growth of the amusement industry shifted to the United States and the amusement park entered what many say was its golden era, culminating with the 1893 World's Columbian Exposition in Chicago. This world's fair introduced the Ferris wheel and the midway to the world. The midway, with its wide array of rides and concessions, was a huge success. The following year, Captain Paul Boyton borrowed the midway concept and opened the world's first modern amusement park on the south side of Chicago. The success of his Chicago park inspired him to open a similar facility at the then-fledgling Coney Island resort in New York City in 1895. That, too, was a great success, and subsequently, many amusement parks were developed following the Coney Island model. In 1929, when America entered the Great Depression, spending declined, and by 1935, those amusement parks that still operated were struggling to survive.

The end of World War II brought a brief resurgence to amusement parks, but by the 1950s, television began replacing the amusement park as a major source of entertainment. Thus, when Walt Disney opened Disneyland in 1955, many were skeptical that an amusement park without any of the traditional attractions would succeed. But Disneyland, as everyone knows, proved the skeptics wrong. Instead of a midway, Disneyland offered five distinct themed areas, providing visitors with the fantasy of travel to different lands and times. It also offered many activities that could be enjoyed by the very young and the young at heart. An immediate success, Disneyland gave rise to the theme park era.

But by the 1980s, the theme park boom began spreading around the world, but the industry growth had slowed considerably in the United States, due to high operational costs and a lack of markets large enough to support a theme park. Today, those parks that remain are very large and thus have substantial impact on the economies of those communities in which they are located.

Potential Liability Issues In addition to issues related to food and beverage service, hospitality managers working at or near major amusement parks may face three specific amusement park legal challenges:

1. *Safety of activities:* Although they typically receive widespread publicity, accidents related to amusement park rides are actually quite rare. Injury figures are but a small fraction of those attributed to other recreational activities. There has been a marked decrease in the number of patron-related injuries since 2003. In 2014, in fact, 1,150 ride accidents were reported to the National Safety Council,[9] most of which were minor bruises, strains, and sprains. Nevertheless, amusement park operators implicated in the injury of a visitor will be expected to have exhibited an appropriate amount of care in the maintenance and operation of their rides. If they do not, they probably will be held liable to a certain extent for the damages.
2. *Performance expectations:* When guests are charged an admission fee to enter a park, there are expectations on the part of the park's operators that the guests will behave

[9] National Safety Council Research and Statistical Services Group, "Fixed-Site Amusement Ride Injury Survey, 2015 Update," Prepared for the International Association of Amusement Parks and Attractions, Alexandria, Virginia, November 2015. www.iaapa.org/safety/RideSafetyReports.asp (Accessed, June 2016.)

Analyze the Situation 13.2

Sandra Wilkens was a roller-coaster enthusiast who, along with others, attended the Harley Amusement park's "Roller Fest," a POP (pay-one-price) event featuring unlimited roller-coaster riding by all attendees. Ms. Wilkens, 25 years old, paid the $50 admission fee and was, at the time of her fatal accident, riding the Superman, a wooden double-loop coaster. On the final loop, Sandra was thrown from the coaster and killed. Witnesses say she was standing in the coaster car as it approached the final loop.

Ms. Wilkens' family filed suit against the park and its state ride inspectors, claiming negligence because Ms. Wilkens was placed in a car where she had the ability to stand up. Park officials countered that all riders were informed via a public address system not to stand during the ride's operation. In addition, they pointed to posted signs that warned riders not to stand up during the entire length of the ride. Further, they said, the ride was operating properly, and all rider restraints had been inspected and approved that morning. They also noted that by standing up, which was prohibited, Ms. Wilkens had taken action to defeat the restraining devices built into the ride.

1. What level of responsibility should the park operators be assigned for Ms. Wilkens' behavior?
2. List five specific actions the park management could take or institute to help eliminate such guest behavior in the future.
3. What similar situations might you face in your own area of hospitality for which responsibility for guest injury may be all or partially related to guest behavior?

appropriately. If guests do not, they can be removed from the park. In a similar manner, guests will have expectations, too, for example, that advertised rides will be available, that appropriate facilities such as restrooms and food and beverage outlets will be provided, and that these will be maintained in an appropriate manner. If they are not, guests may have a legitimate basis for legal action against the park.

3. *Litigation related to employee training:* Much of the work required to appropriately maintain amusement type rides can be dangerous if not performed properly. Thus, adequate staff training programs are critical if park employees are to safely perform their required tasks. If such training, as well as the proper tools and safety devices, are not provided by a park's management, potential lawsuits related to resulting accident or injury are very likely to occur.

Medical Tourism

Medical tourism, also referred to as "health-care tourism," has become a viable economic sector in several regions and countries. The number of regions that recognize the potential revenue-generating opportunities of offering diverse medical procedures and products to tourists is steadily growing. The global health-care market is expected to grow at approximately US$4.4 billion annually. Research indicates that tourists to the United States for medical care are projected to spend US$17 million by the year 2017.[10] In this viable tourism niche, it is important for providers and users to be mindful of potential unethical and unsustainable practices and to seek legal assistance if problems occur.

History of Medical Tourism Some of the earliest forms of travel and tourism can be traced back to health-care travel. Many seeking care in the Roman era of the 19th century traveled to European spas for medical treatments. The procedures performed and the related healing services and products can be divided into three main categories: (1) alternative therapies, including acupuncture, beauty care, homeopathy, massage, yoga, and other general treatments, (2) cosmetic surgeries, including facelifts, liposuction, dermabrasion, and (3) health screenings, cancer treatment, surgeries, and the like with after-care and healing therapies.

Potential Liability Issues The medical tourism industry should be considered as a risk for potential liability due to the nature of the services performed. There are numerous controversies regarding unethical treatment provided by facilities involved in medical tourism. One issue is that promoting and developing health-care tourism creates social inequalities within locations offering such services. Instead of promoting and supporting the development of medical infrastructure and services for the local citizens, a region may spend more on private health-care facilities for tourists that are cost prohibitive for local residents. Of course, local governments, whether in the United States or in other countries, can work to limit these issues by developing regulations regarding medical tourism and better local medical services.

The rising cost of health care in the United States and wait time for approval of procedures by one's insurance company may lure patients to seek medical care in other countries where laws regarding the practice of medicine are often less stringent than U.S. laws. One such issue is whether a procedure is illegal in the United States but is legal in the host country offering the service. Research needs to be conducted to fully understand the consequences of seeking health care treatments in foreign lands and the recourse one may have, if any, in the event that a procedure is botched. Issues of privacy are also a concern for the consumer.

To engage in medical tourism, it is crucial that a hospitality business located in the United States seek legal advice. Whether it wishes to offer medical procedures such as dermabrasion performed by a medical staff that it employs or in connection with a medical partner, the hospitality business must seek advice of lawyers to ensure that it is not providing medical care without the proper licensing and approvals from state and local regulatory agencies.

A potential liability that hospitality managers need to be aware of involves massage therapy treatments offered by their resorts. It is essential that all massage therapists, whether working as independent contractors or employees, are properly vetted before hiring and are professionals trained to perform such services. A resort's therapist should be taught to explain the services provided to guests new to the service and to use proper draping techniques. The therapist must be assessed on his or her knowledge of these areas. Documentation of the training can be very helpful if a legal issue should arise. Therapists should not perform any procedure for a guest who appears to be inebriated or who the therapist believes may take advantage of the private nature of the service performed behind closed doors and act inappropriately. Legal charges involving massages and other private treatments can be difficult to prove or deny because privacy issues prevent having security or surveillance cameras in the massage rooms, and there are usually only two witnesses, the therapist and the guest. It is critical for the therapist to educate the guest who is new to massage treatments and how they are performed before services are rendered to eliminate any misunderstandings.

13.5 Online Travel Sales

Online travel sales are completed via use of the Internet. They include the sale of hotel rooms, car rentals, and other transportation services such as airline tickets and cruise reservations. Travelers who use online services tend to be computer-savvy users of the Internet at a higher rate than the general public, according to a Travel Industry Association of America "Travelers' Use of the Internet" study. Currently, over 100 million

[10] Leonard A. Jackson and Diana S. Barber, "Ethical and Sustainable Healthcare Tourism Development: A Primer," *Tourism and Hospitality Research Journal*, no. 15 (2014): 19–26. http://thr.sagepub.com/content/15/1/19.full.pdf?ijkey=RmuC4rLQsupx3PH&keytype=finite

travelers use the Internet to seek travel information or to book travel. This number includes both business and leisure travelers.

The online travel agents (OTA) segment is also one of the Internet's largest components. According to the January 2015 issue of *Forbes* magazine, OTAs had gross bookings of more than $150 billion in 2013, representing 38 percent of the global online market and 13 percent of the global travel market.

Search the Web 13.8

E-commerce sites by definition must allow consumers to buy goods and services while at the sites. PayPal is one credit card–processing company required to allow such purchasing. Log on to the Internet, and enter **www.paypal.com**

1. Select: Business.
2. Review: The different payment options.
3. Describe: The differences between these options.
4. Respond: Which do you believe would be the best choice for a business in the hospitality industry?

Background of the Online Travel Sales Industry

In 1995, the total revenue generated by the online travel sales industry was close to zero. Online travel sales generated approximately US$533.52 billion in 2015.[11]

The enhanced accessibility of last-minute travel specials via the Internet coupled with everyday low prices has resulted in a tremendous increase in online travel sales. Whether true or not, the majority of travelers believe that the best travel "deals" can be found on the Internet, and for these travel buyers, price is a very important decision factor. As a result, the online travel sales industry will likely continue to play a larger and larger role in the overall travel industry.

Essentially, there are two basic types of websites used to sell online travel services. One type serves as electronic brochures (e-brochures) and in this capacity displays information about one or more travel products. An e-brochure might include, for example, pictures of a hotel room, departure and arrival schedules of a common carrier, or details of a travel package. These websites also act as catalogs, basically displaying information about a business and include, in most cases, a method (typically email) that enables the website visitor to ask for additional information about ordering products or services or about communicating directly with the entity identified on the site.

The other type of website enables consumers to make a purchase or reservation online. Thus, an airline ticket can be purchased, a hotel reservation made, or a rental car reserved directly at the website. These e-commerce sites allow the traveler to see the product offered as well as buy and pay for it online. In order to do so, however, the site must have Internet tools not required by an e-brochure site. Their application can raise legal issues regarding the use of e-commerce sites. These tools include:

- *A bank account that can process Internet purchases:* This means an Internet merchant must have an account that is different from a typical business bank account because it is designed specifically to handle Internet purchases. Funds from Internet purchases are deposited in such an account.
- *An agreement with a credit (bank) card processor:* A credit or bank card processing company is responsible for collecting funds from the buyer and depositing those funds into the Internet merchant's bank account. For this service, the processor will take, from the revenue generated by the merchant, an agreed-on fee for each purchase. This fee will vary, based on the type of bank card used by the purchaser.
- *A secure connection:* When a website takes private and sensitive information like a credit card number from a visitor, it must provide a level of security to protect that information from unscrupulous individuals. To do so, an e-commerce website must have a "secure" connection. Sites can purchase their own secure connection or share the use of one with others for a small percentage of the purchase price of the items sold on the site.

Because of the fees involved, the total cost of developing and maintaining an e-commerce site is higher than that of maintaining an e-brochure site. Thus, some travel providers elect to allow online purchases while others prefer the brochure approach. Each type is involved in a rapidly developing and specialized area of law associated with the online travel sales industry. The online industry is made up of not only e-commerce sites but also consumer review sites such as TripAdvisor, which can truly affect the consumer's buying decisions.

Legal Issues Related to Online Travel Sales

The advent of the online travel industry has raised some new legal issues and caused the modification of some existing issues. Here are five of the most important ones:

1. *Parties to the contract:* On websites, it is sometimes difficult to determine exactly who is party to a consumer transaction. For example, assume that a business traveler utilizing the Internet logs on to the Priceline.com travel site. While there, the traveler bids for a room and is successful in getting a reservation for the Chicago Hilton. Upon arrival, however, the Chicago Hilton has no record of the traveler's

[11] Statista, the Statistics Portal. http://www.statista.com/topics/2704/online-travel-market/ (Accessed, June 2016.)

reservation. If, indeed, the error was on the part of Priceline.com, the traveler's legal action would likely be, all or in part, with Priceline.com. In this scenario, a judge would likely rule that Priceline.com advertised the ability to secure for the traveler a reservation that, in this example, it did not. Alternatively, if the traveler had made the same reservation on Hilton's own website, the responsibility for providing the room and hence for failure to provide it would ultimately rest with the hotel. With multiple third-party websites and the ownership of websites frequently shared by members of the travel industry, the entity responsible for performing the terms of a web-initiated contract may not be readily apparent to any but the most sophisticated of users.

Search the Web 13.9

Hospitality managers and service providers seeking to offer consumers the ability to reserve accommodations online can choose from a variety of options. Log on to the Internet, and enter **www.webervations.com**

1. Scroll to: Online Reservations.
2. Describe: The differences between a "reservation request" and a "real-time reservation."
3. Answer: Why would a hotel manager elect to choose one or the other?

2. *Data interface issues:* When airlines, hotels, cruise lines, and others take reservations on the Internet, the potential for problems, and thus litigation, increases. The reason is that reservation systems on the Internet are often not directly connected to (interfaced with) the service provider. To clearly understand the problem, it is important to understand that an independent hotel in, say, Manhattan is not likely to directly connect its reservation systems with the thousands of websites offering hotel rooms for sale. Such direct connections are expensive and frequently technologically unwieldy. As a result, if a third-party–operated website advertising hotel reservations for a specific hotel is not interfaced with the hotel's reservation system through the **global distribution system (GDS)**, the website must communicate with the hotel via fax or email to confirm that the website has sold a room. The problem, of course, is that in the time between the sale of the room on the website and the hotel's notification (and acknowledgment) of the sale, the same room may have been sold by the hotel itself or even on another website. The result may be either an oversold situation or that the product reserved (and in many cases confirmed on the website making the sale) is not available upon the guest's arrival.

   Hospitality managers entering into sales agreements with websites that are not interfaced in real time with their own product inventories should have a very clear understanding with the website provider as to responsibility in the event guests arrive with reservations erroneously made due to the lack of real-time interfacing.

3. *Data security/ownership issues:* When a reservation for a hotel room, cruise, or airline flight is made, personal information is typically gathered from travelers. Other businesses in the travel industry are often interested in this information, especially as it relates to the latest economic data on travel to an area, where those travelers come from, and their spending patterns. Consumers, on the other hand, have a right to privacy, and when personal information is accessed by organizations unknown to them or unapproved by them, they may have cause for concern and complaint.

   Even within a single company, sharing personal guest information can be cause for litigation. For example, consider the case of Marques Johnson. He is a hotel franchisee who owns and operates a Best Sleep hotel. Best Sleep is one of five hotel brands franchised by United Hotels Inc., a large franchise company. United instructs all franchisees that they are to begin collecting email addresses from guests and then make the database of those email addresses available to United so that corporate advertising efforts can be better targeted. Mr. Johnson objects on three grounds: First, that it is his staff, not the franchisor who will collect the information and thus it rightfully belongs to Mr. Johnson's company, not United Hotels. Second, he is concerned that the addresses of his guests will be shared by United with other United franchisees operating different United brands in the same city. These hotels, in many cases, compete directly with Mr. Johnson's hotel. Therefore, sharing data on his guests would, in his opinion, unfairly assist these other hotels in competing with him. Finally, Mr. Johnson states that his guests have a right to know when he is sharing their email addresses with others; thus, ethically, unless he has these guests' preapproval, he does not believe he should share their email addresses. The franchisor maintains that to remain a franchise in good standing, he must collect and share the addresses.

   This disagreement, of course, is the issue of the guests' right to privacy. Although the law in this area in the United States is still developing, the best practice today is that personal data related to guests should not be shared with organizations that did not directly collect the data unless the guest has been explicitly informed about the sharing arrangement prior to the information's collection and has given permission to do so. In addition, those who collect personal data on guests have a responsibility to take reasonable care in securing that data from theft or misuse by others. For privacy restrictions on transferring guest and employee information from the United States or another

LEGALESE

Global distribution system (GDS): An interconnected computer system that connects travel professionals worldwide to those companies selling travel services.

country where the data has been collected, seek help from a knowledgeable attorney. Guest information, including medical history, religious preferences, and employment information may not be transferred outside the country where the information is collected without approval of the guest or employee as appropriate. See the Data Protection Act of 1998 enacted in the United Kingdom for more information.

4. *Forum (venue) selection issues:* **Forum (venue) selection issues clause** refers to the location in which a lawsuit or dispute related to a contract's terms may properly be filed. In many cases, where a legal dispute has taken place and thus should be settled is relatively straightforward. For example, assume that a restaurant manager working in Alabama hires a local electrician to install additional lighting in the restaurant's parking area. If the restaurateur does not believe the electrician has adequately performed the terms of his contract, the dispute would be resolved, in all likelihood, by a court in Alabama and in accordance with Alabama law.

   Now assume that the same restaurateur purchased, online, a cruise for herself and her husband. The cruise was advertised on a website managed by a New York state travel agency. It offered a 10-day Caribbean cruise departing from Miami. The cruise ship itself is operated by an Italian cruise line company. If, ultimately, the cruise supplied did not meet the expectations of the restaurateur, the proper venue for her potential legal action would be less clear. But there would be no question if the contract agreed to by the restaurant manager included information about the appropriate location for any needed legal action.

   Those travel companies doing business on the Internet will typically insert forum selection clauses into their contracts in an effort to preclude having to defend against lawsuits that might be filed anywhere in the world. The courts will generally enforce Internet forum selection clauses if they are clearly communicated to purchasers. Although forum selection clauses are commonly used by hotels and international cruise line operators, it is important to point out that the U.S. Department of Transportation (DOT) has prohibited the use of these clauses for the purchase of airline tickets.

   In addition to identifying the location of potential litigation, website travel providers may, for instance, insert contract clauses that require buyers to agree that any dispute arising would be resolved before an arbitration tribunal rather than a court.

LEGALESE

Forum (venue) selection clause: A statement in a contract identifying the agreed-on tribunal for resolving legal disputes related to the contract's terms.

5. *Lawful advertising:* Internet travel advertising, like all advertising, is subject to regulation through state consumer protection statutes, state and federal telemarketing statutes, FTC and DOT regulations, and the Sellers of Travel statutes enacted by some states. Many of these are intended to address the problem of deceptive advertising versus "puffing." As discussed in Legally Managing at Work, puffing is a common and allowable advertising technique used by both e-brochure and e-commerce sites. It is, essentially, the act of "accentuating the positive" when promoting a travel product. Thus, a hotel site may claim that its rooms are "beautiful," "modern," or "spacious," and the assumption by law is that consumers should recognize such terms as an attempt by the advertiser to encourage sales. But when such superlatives are considered sufficiently misleading and deceiving, they may fall under deceptive advertising or actionable misrepresentation statutes depending on the specific conditions of the accommodations or actual inferiority of the services purchased online. Certainly, puffing makes for interesting and effective advertising copy, but truth in advertising is as necessary a practice when describing products and services on a website as it is on a restaurant menu.

6. *Americans with Disabilities Act (ADA) and websites:* Since the Internet has evolved and continues to evolve into being the primary research and purchase tool for travel and tourism products, one thing a hospitality business must keep in mind is that according to federal law, places of public accommodation must ensure "full and equal enjoyment of the goods, services, facilities, privileges, advantages, or accommodations" by those travelers who have disabilities.[12] There is ongoing discussion about whether the term "place" used in the federal statute includes electronic places as well as physical spaces and to the duties associated with legal compliance. For example, what is the travel provider's responsibility to a consumer who is visually challenged and thus may have difficulty reading the text on a provider's website? The travel provider may be obligated to include a feature on the website that will read the contents to the potential purchaser who is disabled upon accessing the site. This area continues to be in the spotlight and will likely change in the future, so it is important for hospitality businesses to make sure their websites are in strict compliance with all applicable laws at all times.

For the most part, websites are just another form of advertisement, and thus the law related to advertising that has been developed applies to them as well. Some special managerial considerations about website advertising are given in the Legally Managing at Work section.

[12] 42 U.S.C. Section 12182(a).

Legally Managing at Work

Internet Advertising Checklist

The Federal Trade Commission (FTC) considers as deceptive any ad that is likely to mislead consumers acting reasonably and that is material (i.e., important) to a consumer's decision to buy the product or service. To avoid charges of deceptive or illegal advertising, hospitality managers should review with its website developers the following Internet advertising checklist. If the answer to any of the checklist items is no, the site content should be revised until the answer is yes.

1. *Are all statements and claims true?*

   A "claim" is a legal advertising term referring to any provable statement contained in an advertisement. It is the responsibility of the advertiser to be able to "prove" all claims made. Hospitality managers should ensure that they have the ability and proof required to substantiate all claims made before they are published on the website. If there is any doubt about the validity of the claim, it should not be posted on the Internet.

2. *Are prices accurate?*

   Prices, if given, must be stated accurately. If taxes or local assessments will be added, these too must be identified. In addition, any conditions that must be met to get the advertised price must also be disclosed.

3. *Are conditions spelled out clearly?*

   It is best to disclose all conditions necessary to enable the buyer to fully understand what is offered for sale. For example, a hotel offering "free breakfast" with the price of a room would be well advised to detail whether there are limits to the number of guests per room who are allowed to eat as well as when the breakfast is offered. In general, the use of the word "free" should be avoided when there are, in fact, conditions that must first be met unless those conditions are prominently disclosed. In addition, the words "sale" and "discount" should be avoided unless there have been substantial and recent real-life sales made at a higher price.

4. *Is inappropriate puffery avoided?*

   The development of an Internet site typically involves the use of sight, sound, and text on a webpage. Although puffery is allowed, the information that is presented must be carefully reviewed to ensure that it is within acceptable bounds. It is difficult, for example, to claim that a web ad contains allowable puffery when a hotel displays the picture of one very nice room and uses the phrase "great rooms," when, in fact, other rooms of the same quality do not exist within the hotel.

   The Web has spawned some new views toward puffery. In a recent lawsuit against a college textbook retailer stating on its site that its store was "the globe's largest college bookstore," the website owners claimed that the statement was puffery and thus allowable. The National Advertising Division of the Council of Better Business Bureaus Inc. disagreed, stating that claims like this might have been puffery in a non-Web context, but online, which is accessible worldwide, and where the product advertised on the website can appear large or small with few obvious clues to actual size, statements such as this one appear, on their face, to be believable, and thus are no longer puffery.

5. *Have web-specific advertising issues been considered?*

   The FTC has developed some web-specific standards for advertising. Some of those standards include:

   - Placing disclosures near, or on the same screen as, the related claims
   - Ensuring that, when using links or hyperlinks to disclosures, the links are obvious and easy to find
   - Ensuring that text, graphics, or sound is not used to distract attention from disclosure information
   - Ensuring that disclosures are repeated, as needed, on lengthy websites

6. *Are proper marks, logos, and business names used correctly?*

   Are proper symbols, such as the trademark symbol, used where appropriate? Are trademarks and logos accurate and used only when written, prior approval has been granted? Many website developers create a style manual that details the approval procedures to be used before including such marks, logos, or business names on their sites.

7. *Have photos and drawings used been cleared for intellectual property ights?*

   The Internet abounds with pictures and images that can be easily copied or downloaded. The best rule to follow when creating your own website is quite simple: If your organization did not directly create or pay for the creation of the image you wish to use, you should obtain written permission from the owner of that image prior to its use unless its reproduction and sharing has been authorized by the owner.

International Snapshot

Government Support of Tourism

The local economy of many communities depends on travelers and their cash. Without the tax revenue from visitors, many local coffers would run dry or not meet their needs.

Governments around the globe are recognizing that tourism is an effective way to earn needed income. Visitors come for a few days, stay at a hotel, eat at local restaurants, visit a museum or other entertainment venue, and then depart, leaving behind revenue some of which is used for taxes. In addition, tourists have minimal impact on infrastructure because they rarely use the services of police, firefighters, libraries, schools, hospitals, and other assets that governments must financially support.

(continued)

Experiences in several countries indicate government interest in developing travel and tourism. For example, the Eastern Black Sea Development Agency of Turkey understood the importance of attracting travelers and tourists. The eastern Black Sea region bordering the country of Georgia was virtually untouched by travelers. Turkey is rich with attractions: Istanbul, Ephesus, Mt. Ararat, sparkling beaches, and historic landmarks. With its natural beauty, historical heritage, bird-watching areas, and cultural attractions, Turkey was ripe for tourism development. The Eastern Black Sea Development Agency brought experts from around the world to the country for two purposes. One was to show tourism professionals the richness of its attractions, hotels, and food through a familiarization trip with the hope that these professionals would promote the area to other tourism specialists. The second purpose was to sponsor a local conference on the virtues of sustainable tourism. The Development Agency sought tourism, but it wanted the "right" kind. Having witnessed unfettered growth in Istanbul and experienced some of the negative aspects of mass tourism at local beaches, the agency wanted to ensure the natural splendor of the region would be preserved so that future generations would have the opportunity to enjoy it. At the conference, specialists presented information on all aspects of tourism: recycled and reclaimed materials, promotion, social media, price points, and green energy experienced by venues around the world. The government provided the resources to seek expert knowledge on growing the economy through tourism and then to develop and implement a long-range strategic plan with local hoteliers, merchants, and restaurateurs.

Another area with interest in developing travel and tourism is Cuba. After U.S. President Barack Obama formally opened a dialogue with Raul Castro, Cuba's highest governmental official, in December 2014, the Cuban government readied itself for the rush of U.S. visitors. It hoped that tourism would bring prosperity to the island nation that has lagged behind the rest of the Western hemisphere economically. Cuban tourism had relied on a steady stream of sojourners from Russia, Germany, Canada, and South America for the last 50 years. But with the end of the U.S. embargo of the country, Cuban tourism is expected to be markedly different. Amistur, the only tour operator allowed to operate in Cuba, is preparing for a new stream of visitors. Motor coaches from China are being bought, new collaborations with European hotel groups are being explored, and new consumer goods and technology are being pursued. Until 2007, Cuban citizens were not allowed to stay in a Cuban hotel, fearing it would upset the status of the classless, communist society; now Cubans are encouraged to explore their own country to understand what it has to offer and to increase government revenue.

The largest travel and trade show in the world, ITB Berlin, is held each March in Germany. Representatives from more than 180 countries have access to 11,000 exhibitors and 7,000 journalists. This show enables attendees to meet tour operators and others to conduct serious meetings with them in the hope of bringing the traveling public to their respective areas. The attendees from various locations can gain information on pricing, tour points of interest, and dates of scheduled events. Virtually every country displays its tourist attractions and facilities to tour operators and the public.

In an about-face from previous years, the Democratic People's Republic of Korea now sends a delegation to the show. While its booth and meeting space are modest in size, they represent the country's interest in attracting tourism and travelers. In dire need of hard currencies (U.S. dollar, British pound, and European euro), the government of North Korea recognizes that tourism can be a source of currency the country desires. With the worldwide average of US$5,000 spent per person on a global trip, North Korea can hardly afford not to look at travel and tourism as ways to sustain its economy.

With the encouragement and promotion of governments, international tourism can be an avenue to increase funding for local economies as well as to help visitors have a new understanding of the local culture.

Provided by Neville Bhada, Founder and CEO of Tourism Skills Group, www.tourismskillsgroup.com.

WHAT WOULD YOU DO?

You are the manager of a franchised, 90-room limited-service hotel property located across the highway from 7 Flags, a major amusement park that is extremely busy in the summer. One of the most popular family packages your hotel sells includes a two-night stay (in on Friday night, out on Sunday morning), complimentary breakfast, and tickets to 7 Flags. You purchase the tickets in a large quantity from the 7 Flags group sales department. Your packages are marketed directly by your hotel and sold through select travel agents to whom you pay a sales commission.

At 3:00 P.M. on a Saturday afternoon in July, lightning from a severe thunderstorm strikes a major electrical transformer in the area, causing a power outage that includes the amusement park and results in the its immediate closure. Your hotel is sold out. The power company is unsure how long it will take to fully restore power, but its estimate is hours, not minutes. Your hotel has a backup generator—thus, essential hotel services such as emergency lighting and power to the property management system (PMS) are maintained.

Your lobby, however, is filled with families seeking to check out (it is 4:30 P.M.) so they can leave the area and drive back to their homes (where most of them will have power.) Approximately 60 guests want to check out. None of these guests believe they should have to pay for their Saturday night stay because, due to the power outage, they will not use their reserved rooms. Some want a refund for Friday night as well, claiming the hotel did not provide the complete two-day "package" that was promised.

1. Would you bill these 60 guests for Saturday night's stay even if they elect to leave?
2. Would you give the guests any other compensation?
3. Would your course of action be affected if you learned the theme park had made the decision to refund the price of admission to all those who entered the park on that day?
4. If the theme park had made the refund mentioned, do you believe the amount of the refund belongs to the disappointed park attendee or to your hotel?
5. Describe briefly how the decision you make will affect:
   a. Your relationship with the theme park's management
   b. The relationship with your franchisor
   c. Your relationship with travel agents marketing your packages

WHAT DID YOU LEARN IN THIS CHAPTER?

The hospitality industry is one component of the larger travel (and tourism) industry, which is heavily regulated. Because it is so large and diverse, the number of groups and organizations responsible for the legal oversight of travel activities is large. Some of the most notable of these include governmental agencies, at both the federal and the state level, as well as nongovernmental groups that operate internationally to coordinate travel policies.

The travel industry has historically relied on travel experts (travel agents) to assist travelers in planning their trips. These agents, who have a fiduciary responsibility to travelers, are a highly professional group. Tour operators, whose role is to develop travel and vacation packages, typically use travel agents to market these packages, thus creating a special, mutually dependent relationship between travel agents and tour operators.

The transportation industry also plays a critical role in the travel industry. It consists primarily of common carriers, which include those entities providing transportation services to all travelers. These companies, providing airline, bus, cruise ship, and train services, are a large and highly regulated segment of the travel industry. The rental car portion of the transportation industry, including sharing economy players such as Uber and Lyft, while not technically common carriers, also plays a critical role in the U.S. travel market, as well as in those countries with well-developed road and highway systems.

Because so many people travel for enjoyment, the tourism business is, for many communities, a critical factor in the local economy. Gaming establishments, resorts, and amusement parks are all popular leisure-time venues, but they also have the potential for legal entanglements for those who operate them, as well as for those who visit them.

The Internet has emerged as a major force in the travel and tourism industries. It has affected how industry products are marketed and sold and has raised new legal questions relating to the uniqueness of the electronic product distribution systems now in widespread use on the Internet.

CHAPTER 14

Safety and Security Issues

14.1 The Importance of a Protected Environment

As you have seen in the previous chapters, you are responsible for taking reasonable care that people are not hurt when they enter or stay in your establishment and for ensuring that their possessions are safe during their stay. In Chapter 10, "Your Responsibilities as a Hospitality Operator to Guests," we used examples of recreational facilities, such as pools and fitness facilities, to show you one way that hospitality operations can demonstrate reasonable care for the safety of their guests. Of course, safety extends beyond guests to include management, staff, vendors, and the general public.

The courts will not expect you to protect everyone who comes into contact with your operation against all possible calamities. They will, however, expect you to use good judgment in carrying out the procedures necessary to show you care about the well-being of your guests, employees, and visitors, as well as the security of their property. In this chapter, we will examine some procedures used to protect people and assets in the hospitality environment; as well as the procedures used before, during, and after a period of potentially devastating circumstances, such as a fire, storm, criminal activity, or other threatening activity.

Safety and Security Management

As the manager of your facility, you will be responsible for a large number of activities designed to protect people and property. All of these activities can be grouped under the commonly used terms of **safety programs** and security programs. In order for a safety and security program to be effective, hospitality managers must make sure that the program covers every component of a guest's visit and every aspect of the facility's operation. Effective managers may implement several different policies, procedures, and training programs that together make up a comprehensive safety and security program.

Large restaurants and hotel companies generally employ directors of safety, directors of loss prevention, or directors of safety and security. It is the job of these individuals to design safety and security programs and then to encourage on-site managers to implement and maintain them.

LEGALESE

Safety programs: Those procedures and activities designed to ensure the physical protection and good health of guests and employees.

CHAPTER OUTLINE

14.1. The Importance of a Protected Environment

14.2. Safety and Security Programs: Four-Step Safety and Security Management Method

14.3. Crimes Against Hospitality Businesses

14.4. Human Trafficking

14.5. Crisis Management Programs

IN THIS CHAPTER, YOU WILL LEARN

1. To recognize the responsibility hospitality managers have to protect the safety and security of guests and employees in hospitality operations.
2. To carry out the procedures needed to limit the potential liability of safety and security risks.
3. To minimize the risk of crimes against your own business operation.
4. To recognize the need for and benefit of implementing an effective crisis management plan.

Analyze the Situation 14.1

Mr. and Mrs. Angelo were frequent diners at the Buffet World restaurant, a moderately priced operation that featured an all-you-can-eat lunch and dinner buffet. Jessie Carroll was the manager of the restaurant. On a busy Sunday, Mr. and Mrs. Angelo entered the restaurant, paid for their meal, and were directed to their table by the dining room greeter. As Mrs. Angelo sat down, the wooden dining room chair snapped under her weight. Her neck was injured as she fell on the restaurant's tile floor.

The Angelos sued Buffet World, charging negligence in the operation of the restaurant. Their attorney argued that the normal wear and tear of chairs was a foreseeable event, and thus an inspection program should have been in place. No such program could be shown by the restaurant to have existed.

The attorney for the restaurant countered that Mrs. Angelo was "larger" than the average guest, and therefore Buffet World could not have foreseen that she would be seated in a chair that was not capable of holding her weight. The restaurant's attorney also noted that Buffet World had never experienced a problem like this before.

1. Is Mrs. Angelo's weight a relevant issue in her case against the restaurant?
2. What evidence could the restaurant have provided to its attorney to demonstrate reasonable care in the inspection of its dining room furniture?
3. If it were independently owned, who would be responsible for designing and implementing an effective furniture inspection program for Buffet World?

In smaller or independent hospitality operations, you may be the individual responsible for developing and maintaining your own safety and security programs. In later portions of this chapter, we will show you how to implement and evaluate a safety program.

Crisis Management

Hospitality managers face a myriad of routine but generally minor challenges and problems in the day-to-day operation of their facilities. In some situations, however, the challenges are anything but minor. Many types of circumstances have the potential to cause devastating damage to a hospitality operation. These are called **crisis** situations. These include:

Active shooters
Human trafficking
Power outages
Vandalism
Arson/fire
Bomb threats
Robbery
Looting
Severe storms
- Hurricanes
- Tornadoes
- Earthquakes
- Floods

Snow and ice
Accident/injury
Drug overdose
Medical emergency
Need for rescue breathing/cardiopulmonary resuscitation (CPR)
Death/suicide of guest or employee
Intense media scrutiny
Adversarial governmental agency investigation
Civil disturbance

LEGALESE

Crisis: An occurrence that holds the potential to jeopardize the health of individuals and/or the business.

Although it is reasonable to assume that you might not have much control during a crisis such as a snowstorm, it is also reasonable to assume that, prior to the storm, you would have preplanned for the difficulties your operation might face during such a storm. Crisis management consists of (1) preplanning for a crisis, (2) responding properly during a crisis, and (3) assessing your operation's performance after the crisis to see how your response could be improved for the next time.

Advantages of Preplanning

By preplanning for certain types of accidents and events, you will be able to minimize the possibility of injury or loss, demonstrate reasonable care, and show a jury that you were able to foresee a potentially dangerous situation, as well as take appropriate steps to prevent the harm from occurring or to mitigate the consequences. (Recall the importance of "foreseeability" in personal injury lawsuits, as discussed in Chapter 9, "Your Responsibilities as a Hospitality Operator.") There are also at least 11 other advantages for considering ahead of time how your operation could be made safer and what types of actions you and your staff can take on a daily basis to keep it safe:

1. *Improved employee morale:* When employees see you implementing safety and security programs, they know that there is a direct benefit to them. In an age of increasing workplace violence, employees have a legitimate concern for their own security.

Analyze the Situation 14.2

Wayne Dobinion was the district manager of a franchised quick-service Mexican-style restaurant in a large city. On a Friday night at 11:30 P.M., just after the restaurant locked its front doors to the general public, three masked men entered the store through the unlocked back kitchen door. They demanded that the 19-year-old assistant manager on duty turn over all the restaurant's cash. Nervously, assistant manager explained that all the cash had been deposited in a safe in the manager's office and that he had no ability to open it.

Angry at their inability to rob the restaurant, the gunmen shot two of the restaurant workers, including the assistant manager, as they fled the restaurant. The assistant manager later died from his wounds. The attempted robbery and shooting made that night's local television news.

A lawsuit filed by the assistant manager's parents charged that the restaurant lacked proper alarms and locks on the back door. In addition, they charged that the restaurant owners and the franchise company failed to provide any training to its staff regarding the proper response to an armed robbery. The lawsuit was reported in a front-page article in the local paper.

An investigative reporter from another television station in the city called the restaurant's manager to request an on-air interview regarding the training the restaurant's employees receive related to robberies. The manager referred the call to Mr. Dobinion.

1. What issues will the courts and jury likely consider as they evaluate the legitimacy of the parents' lawsuit?
2. What legal position might the franchisor have taken if it had provided training materials to the local franchisee, but the franchisee had never utilized those materials?
3. What is the likely outcome if Mr. Dobinion refuses to meet with the investigative reporter? What if Mr. Dobinion has not been trained to do so?

2. *Improved management image:* Often, managers are accused, directly or indirectly, of putting the needs of the business ahead of those of the individual worker. Regardless of the legitimacy of such criticism, the implementation of safety and security programs demonstrates management's concern for staff and guests in a way that is both visible and undeniable.
3. *Improved employee recruiting effectiveness:* For prospective employees, the mention of effective safety and security programs can often mean the difference between accepting or rejecting a position. Consider the parents of a teenage worker helping to counsel their son or daughter to look for an after-school job. Having a safety-oriented workplace will clearly be important in the decision-making process of the potential employee and his or her parents.
4. *Reduced insurance rates:* In many cases, your insurance company will reward your safety and security efforts with reduced insurance premiums. It simply makes sense for them to do so. Just as auto insurance companies provide lower rates for safe drivers, business insurers look at the potential for loss when establishing rates for providing coverage.
5. *Reduced employee costs:* Employees who avoid injury by working in a safe business are more productive and reliable than those who do not. Because that is true, it is up to you as a manager to help employees avert accidents. Workers' compensation claims are lower in a safe work environment, and lost productivity due to injury-related absence is reduced. No one wins when workers are injured on the job.
6. *Improved operating ratios:* When theft by guests or employees is reduced, profitability increases. Restaurants and hotels particularly have inventory items that many employees and guests find desirable because they can be used or consumed in their own homes. Well-conceived programs that reduce theft or raise awareness about security measures result in lower operating costs and thus enhance gross operating profits.
7. *Reduced penalty costs for violations:* Hospitality establishments are visited by federal and state inspectors from a variety of agencies to ensure compliance with the different laws that regulate the industry. Often the inspections are unannounced, and the fines for violating the law, as we have shown you, can be severe. The best way to avoid expensive fines and penalties is by operating safely and legally at all times. An effective safety and security program can help ensure your compliance with the law.
8. *Support in the event of an accident:* When accidents happen, attorneys and upper management will look to the hospitality manager to provide documented evidence that safety and training programs were in place to reduce the chance of a mishap. This evidence is crucial because, as we have seen, juries will be interested in whether or not the manager exercised reasonable care in the operation of his or her facility. If the manager cannot do so, the chances of successfully defending the operation in court are greatly reduced.
9. *Increased guest satisfaction:* Today's traveling public is sophisticated. Guests have come to expect that their personal safety and the safety of their possessions will be protected to the greatest degree possible by hospitality managers who care about their repeat business. The hotel that does not provide adequate locks on its guestrooms, for example, neglects to do so at its own peril. Potential guests will simply find other, safer, lodging options. The restaurant that does not protect its inventory from employee theft and then runs out of a needed ingredient on a busy Saturday night faces the same probability of guest dissatisfaction. Dissatisfied customers seldom return and seem to recount their stories to others thereby further reducing potential sales.

10. *Marketing advantages:* All hospitality facilities, even those in the nonprofit sector, compete for customers or resources. When an operation can legitimately represent itself as one that takes a genuine and documented proactive stance in the area of safety and security, it becomes easier to market that facility to the general public. For example, the tour bus operator selecting a hotel for a tour group's overnight accommodations will, all other things being equal, select the hotel that provides the lowest risk to the group's safety and thus the least likelihood of adverse guest experiences. To do so is merely good business judgment on the part of the tour operator.
11. *Reduced likelihood of negative press:* Few events can have as adverse an impact on the success of a business as sustained negative press. Although such press is often undeserved, the reality is that today's media, including the impact of social media, will sensationalize some misfortunes in a way that casts the business owner in the least favorable light. As we will see later in this chapter, your ability to deal honestly with the media in a time of turmoil is very important, but it is always easier to avoid accidents than to defend yourself in the press. Many managers have the attitude, "It can't happen to me." It can, and the results can be crippling to your business.

14.2 Safety and Security Programs: Four-Step Safety and Security Management Method

Because the safety and security needs of hospitality organizations vary so widely, it is difficult to provide one all-purpose, step-by-step, list of activities that should be implemented to minimize the chances of accident, injury, or loss. That said, from a legal perspective, your basic obligation is to act responsibly in the face of threats to people and property. One way to analyze and respond to those responsibilities is illustrated by a four-step safety and security management method presented in Figure 14.1.

Four-Step Safety and Security Management Method

1. Recognition of threat
2. Program development (response to threat)
3. Program implementation
4. Monitoring of program results

FIGURE 14.1 Four-step safety and security management method.

Recognition of Threat

Safety and security programs generally start with the recognition of a need, that is, a realization that a threat to people or property could exist. Consider the case of Garth Rivers. Mr. Rivers is the manager of a popular pizza parlor that also serves beer and wine. Over the past six months, he has had four guests and two employees complain of vandalism to their cars. The damage ranged from scratched paint to broken windows, and in at least one case, it appeared that the vandals attempted to break into the car. Before these six incidents, Mr. Rivers never had a problem. Now, however, he realizes that he must act responsibly to serve the interests of his guests and employees and protect their property. A need for security has surfaced.

Figure 14.2 lists the most common areas of security concern in the hospitality industry. The list is not intended to be exhaustive, but it does give some indication of the vast number of areas within a facility that must be considered when developing an overall safety and security program. Note the five major areas into which this list is divided: guests, employees, property, facility assets, and crisis situations.

Program Development

Once a threat to safety or security has been identified, managers and security personnel can develop an appropriate response to address that threat. Figure 14.3 details the many different components of an effective hotel safety and security program, which would have to be addressed by management. Responses and programs can take a variety of forms, as follows.

Training for Threat Prevention In many cases, the proper response to a safety and security threat is proper training for employees. If, for example, employee safety is threatened by a large number of back injuries caused by the use of improper lifting techniques, training employees in proper lifting techniques could reduce or eliminate that threat.

Other examples include training room attendants in the proper manner for disposing of bloody items found in rooms, teaching cooks the proper way to use a meat slicer, and instructing employees and guests in what should be done in the event of a fire emergency.

Increased Surveillance and/or Patrol In some cases, the best response to a threat simply involves monitoring the activities in a particular area with greater frequency, and, as mentioned in Chapter 9, you can be found negligent for not doing so. In the parking lot problem just described, one of Mr. Rivers' best responses could be to increase surveillance of the parking lot of his pizza parlor. Routine patrols carried out by management, employees, an outside security firm, or the police may serve as a significant deterrent to vandals.

Other safety and security threats can be addressed by installing video cameras in public areas to record activity. Stairwells, halls, and storerooms are appropriate areas for the installation of these devices. In many cases, the presence of the

Areas of Safety and Security Concern

Guests	**Guest Property In**
Parking lots	Coatrooms
Guestrooms	Guestrooms
Public areas	In-room safes
Dining rooms	Parking lots
Bars and lounges	Safety deposit boxes
Employees	**Facility Assets**
Work site safety	Cash and cash equivalents
Workplace violence	Operating supplies
Worker accidents	Food inventories
Employee locker rooms	Beverage/mini-bar inventories
All People and Property	Vending income/equipment
Medical emergency	Telephone access
Criminal activity	
Natural disaster	
Utility outages	

FIGURE 14.2 **Areas of safety and security concern.**

Significant Elements of a Hotel Security Program

- Key controls
- Effective guestroom lock system
- Proper and adequate training of security staff
- Guestroom doors with one-way viewers and chain/latch bars
- Adequate lighting and ongoing maintenance
- Perimeter controls
- Employee background checks
- Employee education
- Guest safety education (safety videos on TV, safety literature in guest directory, recommended hiking/jogging paths, recommended vendors)
- Written security policies and procedures
- Established responses to incidents and corrective action
- Liaison with local authorities

FIGURE 14.3 **Significant elements of a hotel security program.**

camera itself can help deter crime. Video camera systems can either record action or simply display the activity of a specific area in real time with no recording of the events.

It is important to understand that an owner's right to unlimited monitoring and surveillance even on his or her own property is not absolute. A business operator needs to constantly balance the guest's expectation of privacy with safety and security approaches. In today's digital age, illegally monitoring the behavior of guests and of employees can dramatically increase an employer's potential liability.

Systematic Inspections In some cases, holding a routine and comprehensive inspection of facilities can help identify possible threats to safety and security. As a professional hospitality manager, you will be expected to carefully monitor your facility's compliance with accepted standards for a safe and secure operation. It is important that you not only regularly monitor your facility for compliance but also document your efforts.

Many sophisticated travel agency companies concerned about the safety of their clients and corporations concerned about the safety of their employees have developed their own safety and security checklists. As a manager, these can be very instructive because they let you know what travel agents think is important in a facility they would recommend to their clients.

Modification of Facilities When the facility itself contributes to a threatening situation, that facility may require modification. For example, worn carpets should be replaced before a guest falls; sidewalk curbs should be painted if they are not visible to pedestrians; and extra lighting might have to be added in specific areas to increase safety and security. It is important to remember that facility defects that have been recognized or should have been foreseen by management but not corrected can be very damaging in the event of a lawsuit.

Establishing Standard Procedures Routine policies and procedures can also serve as an effective response to threats to safety and security. Consider the case of the hotel that offers guests the use of a safety deposit box. Obviously, procedures should be in place to ensure the security of the items placed on deposit with the hotel. In a similar way, a restaurant must have appropriate procedures in place for counting and depositing the cash it takes in on a daily basis. Periodic product inventories, plate counts on buffet meals, and signing in and out of management keys are all examples of standard operating procedures that directly impact the safety and security of an operation.

Program Implementation

Once a hospitality firm has identified the threats to its operation and designed a safety and security program that addresses those threats, it must put the program into action. Large hospitality facilities may have individuals specifically designated for these tasks, and in smaller properties, every employee may have responsibilities for implementing those programs. Both large and small properties may find the need for temporary or longer-term security assistance, which may be provided by a security guard company. In all cases, local law enforcement officials should be a vital component of a property's safety and security programs.

Safety and Security Departments In a large hospitality facility, a safety and security department may exist. The department head would ordinarily report to the general manager of the facility. Staff members in the department would be responsible for routine duties such as patrolling the facility for unauthorized people or suspicious activity, performing inspections, assisting the police with crime reports, and serving as a liaison with insurance carriers. In addition, the department might advise the general manager on topics related to safety and security. The Educational Institute of the American Hotel &

Analyze the Situation 14.3

The Commodore Hotel was owned by the First Community Insurance Company and managed by Fieldstone Hospitality Management. After two separate guest assaults occurred on the hotel property, Fieldstone Management approached First Community Insurance with the idea of either installing a closed circuit video camera (CCVC) system in all hallways or increasing the lighting levels of the hotel's corridors. First Community Insurance authorized Fieldstone Management to purchase a video surveillance system consisting of six cameras and a central location to view them. The events shown by the cameras were not being recorded.

Late on the evening of February 6, Mrs. Cynthia Larson checked into the Commodore and was assigned a room at the end of one of the hotel's corridors. As she attempted to insert her electronic key into the door lock, she was assaulted.

Mrs. Larson sued both Fieldstone Management and First Community Insurance, claiming that both companies' failure to monitor their cameras was a direct cause of her assault. In addition, she claimed that the cameras' use was deceptive in that it gave her a false sense of security. As she stated, "The cameras showed me the hotel cared about my security, and I wanted to stay in a safe location." According to timesheets provided under subpoena by the hotel, an employee was assigned to view the cameras in the central location for an average of two hours per night between the hours of 8:00 P.M. and 6:00 A.M. The assault occurred at a time when no employee was monitoring the cameras.

The attorney for First Community Insurance stated that the company was merely the owner of the hotel and not responsible for day-to-day management; thus, is should not be held responsible for Mrs. Larson's injuries. Fieldstone Management maintained that it too should not be held responsible just because the cameras installed were not monitored at all times. The presence of the cameras themselves and electronic locks on their doors demonstrated that the company used reasonable care in the protection of its guests.

1. Will First Community Insurance be held partially responsible for the actions of Fieldstone Management?
2. Did Fieldstone Management use reasonable care in the installation and operation of the camera system? Would it matter if the cameras were recording?
3. What could the hotel owners do in the future to help avoid a similar situation with a guest?

Lodging Association (www.ahlei.org) offers member safety and security departments an excellent certification program, the Certified Lodging Security Director or CLSD, which is the most prestigious certification available for a security or loss prevention officer in the hotel industry.

Safety and Security Guards If yours is a small facility, you may decide that it makes sense to contract with a security guard company to hire a guard to implement all or a portion of your safety and security program. Consider the case of Teddy Ross. He manages a resort that includes lodging, foodservice, and entertainment facilities. Mr. Ross decides to renovate his 200 hotel rooms. All of the new furniture for the renovation is to be delivered to Mr. Ross's facility at the same time, but it will be stored in tractor-trailers in his parking lot until the building contractor finishes the room renovation. The process is expected to take 10 weeks with 20 rooms per week being furnished from the items in the trailers. Because Mr. Ross does not have the extra staff required to guard the trailers at night, it might make good economic sense for him to contract with a security company that could provide such a guard.

Generally, it is the role of a security guard to:

1. Monitor the facility as an onsite deterrent to would-be thieves.
2. Report observations to management or the police if needed.
3. Intervene only if it can be done safely or to protect the life of a guest or employee.
4. Record activities and findings.

Having security guards is an excellent choice when additional help is needed—for example, in the event of a large party or whenever management expects that additional safety or security protection is warranted. Security guards are not, however, a substitute for a comprehensive and ongoing safety and security program. If such guards are to be used, it is a good idea to insist that the security guard company:

- Provide an acceptable indemnity/hold-harmless agreement.
- Supply proof of liability insurance that names your operation as an additional insured.
- Demonstrate proof that it carries workers' compensation insurance.
- Supply the hospitality facility with a copy of its hiring standards/procedures and training procedure.
- Draw up a written agreement detailing the specific services it will provide.
- Provide references.

Safety Committees Many managers find that property safety committees can play a valuable role in the identification and correction of safety and security problem areas. Ideally, a safety committee should consist of members from each of a property's departments. For example, a large restaurant might have members from the preproduction, production, and cleanup areas in the back of the house and bartenders, servers, and hosts in the front of the house. A hotel's safety committee might have one or more members from housekeeping, laundry, maintenance, food and beverage services, front desk, guest services, and the administrative offices.

Once a committee is established, regular meetings should be scheduled on a weekly, biweekly, or monthly basis. The meetings need not be long; typically, one hour is sufficient. An agenda for a property-level safety and security committee meeting might include:

- *Safety or security instruction:* Training videos, new policies and procedures, and related instruction can be presented. It is critical that the committee members see their role as that of a teacher, not just a police officer, because a worker's peers can often best reinforce the dissemination of important safety and security information.
- *Review of safety concerns:* Members should be informed of the actions that were taken in response to safety and security concerns raised in prior meetings. If, for example, a member of the dishwashing crew expressed concern in a previous meeting that the chemical sanitizer in the automatic dispenser was not working properly, he or she should be informed of the actions that have been taken to correct the problem. In addition, any new concerns of the group should be discussed at this time with each department having an opportunity to contribute. Suggestions, corrections, and improvements to the property's safety and security programs should be encouraged.
- *Effectiveness report by manager:* If accidents have decreased, committee members should be made aware of that fact. If accidents have increased, that too should be shared. The safety and security committee meeting is also a good time to let committee members know how important you consider their contribution to the overall success of your facility.

The most significant resource you have for reducing safety and security liability is the commitment of your staff. Safety committees are an exemplary way to demonstrate your own safety and security commitment and an excellent way to utilize your staff's eyes, ears, and ideas for the betterment of your operation.

Law Enforcement Relationships In addition to your own staff, local law enforcement officials are an important part of any safety and security effort. Establishing and maintaining a good working relationship with them is an integral part of your job. Law enforcement organizations can interact with your business in five key ways:

1. *Have regularly scheduled meetings:* It is a good idea to meet on a regular basis with the chief law enforcement official in your area. This can be a time of sharing mutual concerns and ideas for support. If the time comes that you need the help of your local law enforcement officials, a personal working relationship with them is a tremendous asset in resolving any difficulties quickly and efficiently.

2. *Be active in neighborhood business watch programs:* These programs involve business owners who report any suspicious individuals or activities encountered within their place of business.
3. *Conduct property safety and security reviews:* Many law enforcement officials will conduct a courtesy "walk-through" of your property to help detect possible security threats or problems and offer suggestions for improvement. Because the police are familiar with the difficulties encountered by other businesses, they are in a unique position to point out problems you may have but might not easily recognize. In most cases, law enforcement officials are quite willing to identify areas for improvement.
4. *Participate in interdiction programs:* These special programs involve law enforcement officers who are assigned to a specific area of crime prevention, such as human trafficking or drug enforcement. In many communities, law enforcement and other officials create **interdiction programs** that allow hospitality managers and employees to inform members of the interdiction team in the event that they observe specific behaviors previously identified by the team. When you make a call to an interdiction program, you are calling as a concerned citizen, not as a police agent. By working together, hospitality organizations and police officials can help prevent crimes and look out for the safety interests of their customers and their business.

LEGALESE

Interdiction program: An arrangement whereby citizens contact police to report suspected criminal activity before a crime is committed.

Legally Managing at Work

Establishing an Effective Guestroom Lock Policy

The following steps outline an effective policy to protect the security of hotel guests by controlling the distribution of room keys and to ensure the effectiveness of guestroom locks. This also serves as a good example of how a safety program should be implemented. Notice the number of different components of a hotel's operation that contribute to the effectiveness of this policy from the use of technology (by installing electronic locking systems) to staff training (following procedures such as never announcing room numbers out loud) to management functions (performing a lock audit).

1. Install an electronic locking system:

   Essentially, an electronic locking system uses a computer to generate a specific number for a room key for each guest (and today many hotels are experimenting with personal mobile device access to guestrooms). At the conclusion of the guest's stay, the key "expires" or is made inoperable. In addition, the key system computer records the number of times a key is used to enter each room and to whom the key was issued. For example, if a room attendant is issued a submaster key to all rooms on the first floor of a hotel, each time the room attendant uses the key, the time of use and the identification number of the key will be recorded in the computer's memory, where it may be retrieved if needed.

   Traditional mechanical locking devices do not help ensure guest safety, nor do they allow you to monitor the use of the key. Guest safety is compromised because any guest could make a copy of his or her room key, and return after he or she has checked out of the hotel to gain access to the room he or she had used. Employees could also make duplicate keys. Management cannot monitor key usage in any way because a mechanical lock does not record the identification number of the key used to open the door.

2. Train all new employees on the procedures used to ensure key security:

   Every new hotel employee needs to understand the importance of guest safety and key control. Housekeepers, maintenance staff, front desk staff, and even food and beverage staff should all be trained prior to beginning work. Excellent key control and training materials about guest privacy can be secured from the Educational Institute of the American Hotel and Lodging Association at a very reasonable cost. And remember that it is important to document your training efforts.

3. Never announce guestroom numbers out loud:

   When guests check into a hotel, it is never appropriate to say their room number out loud. You never know who might be listening. The number should be written on the envelope or key cardholder containing the guest's room key. Also, it is important never to give a guest's room number to a caller or other guests in the hotel regardless of their relationship to the original guest. Some hotels located in a mall or a nearby shopping center arrange for retail stores to hold purchases of your guests until the hotel can retrieve them or the purchases can be delivered to the guests some other way (this may typically happen around holiday times). Remind the guest not to say his or her room number out loud in the retail store in order to protect his or her security at the hotel.

4. Never mark the room number directly on the key:

   Guestroom keys should never be imprinted with the guestroom number.

5. Do not identify the hotel with the key:

   Despite the widespread practice of customizing electronic key cards, it is never a good idea to "market" the hotel by printing property-specific information on the key card itself. This would prevent potential thieves from using a lost or stolen key to determine where the key originated. It may be good marketing to custom print key cards, but it makes for poor security. Avoid the practice.

6. Do not reissue keys to guests without a checking their IDs:

   When guests lock themselves out of a room or lose their keys, they must be required to positively identify themselves before they are issued a duplicate key. This rule simply cannot be broken. If a guest maintains that he or she has left his or her identification in the guestroom and thus cannot produce it, the guest should be escorted by management to the room where the proper identification can be secured. Employee violations of this rule should lead to immediate disciplinary action because requesting and receiving an unauthorized key to a room is the primary way a thief can foil an electronic locking system.

7. Do not issue duplicate keys to anyone except the registered guest:

   The registered guest, and only the guest, should be able to request and receive a duplicate or replacement room key. Keys should not be issued to either spouses or children. Remember that it is the guest, not the hotel, who has the right to determine who is to be allowed access to his or her room.

8. Minimize the number of master keys:

   Electronic locking systems preclude the making of master keys. In addition, master keys with restrictions can be created. That is, a housekeeping supervisor may be issued a submaster key that opens all guestroom doors on the first floor but not the electronic lock to the liquor storeroom, which is also on the first floor. A master key should be available to the manager on duty in case of emergency.

9. Keep a log of all existing masters and submasters:

   All master and submaster keys that are issued should be recorded. The key identification number, the individual receiving the key, and the key's expiration date should be noted. In all cases, the number of master and submaster keys should be limited and accounted for on a regular basis. In addition, all such keys should be voided and reissued on a regular basis. The regulation of these key types should be well documented. Some hotel companies immediately terminate an employee who fails to return a master key to its required location after his or her shift.

10. Train all managers on duty (MODs) on the procedures to conduct a lock audit. Record the results of any audits performed:

    When it is necessary to determine who has gained access to a room, an audit of all keys used to open a guestroom door should be performed. Possible instances that could necessitate an audit include a guest report of theft from a room, reports of poor service to a room, and so on. In all cases, a record should be kept of who performed the audit and its results, including any subsequent action taken by management. Every MOD should be trained to perform the lock audit and to record the results.

5. *Training programs:* Some police departments offer training programs for crime detection and deterrence. These classes are usually offered free of charge or at very little cost for management and staff employees alike. Many police departments have a variety of training programs that cover topics such as personal safety, preventing employee theft, credit card fraud, identifying counterfeit money, and detecting drug trafficking. Although it is important to alert law enforcement officers when a customer has left without paying for services rendered, which is a crime, law enforcement should not be contacted or used in your efforts to collect the debt of a vendor or customer.

Monitoring Program Results

If a safety program is not working—that is, if it is not reducing or eliminating the threats to people or property you have identified—then the program must be reviewed for modification. Consider the case of Dave Berger. He is a regional manager for a chain of 30 delicatessens. The restaurants serve sandwiches and homemade soups. While reviewing his stores' performance, Mr. Berger noticed that each store averaged three critical sanitation violations per health inspector visit. In response to this, Mr. Berger purchased a food safety video and required each store manager to view it. Six months later, the number of sanitation violations reported per store remained unchanged. From this information, Mr. Berger learns that he will have to do more than show a video to ensure food safety in his stores.

Legally, you are in a much stronger position if you can document not only that you have a safety and security program but also that the program has proven effective. There are a variety of ways to measure your program's effectiveness. Some tangible measurements include:

- Investigate the number of inspections performed.
- Review the inspection or quality scores.
- Review the number of incidents reported.
- Determine the dollar amount of losses sustained.
- Check the number of insurance claims filed.
- Investigate the number of lawsuits filed.
- Check the number of serious or minor accidents.
- Investigate the number of lost workdays by employees.
- Question the reason for insurance premium increases.
- Review the number of drills or training exercises correctly performed.

Less tangible measures include guest satisfaction scores, employee morale, and product marketability. The important point to remember is that a program has been successfully designed for implementation only after an appropriate evaluation component has been developed. Unless you know that a program has made a measurable difference, you may be lured into a false sense of security about the program's effectiveness.

Analyze the Situation 14.4

Peggi Shulkey managed the commissary for a large cafeteria company. Her facility prepared food products for 75 company restaurants. Although her operation did not have a tremendous number of work-related accidents, Ms. Shulkey believed the number of those that did occur could be reduced. To that end, she formed a safety committee made up of employees and management, and charged them with the task of developing a model program to reduce employee injuries. The committee proposed the six-step plan presented here along with their rationale for each step.

1. **Proper selection of employees:**

   An employee with a drug problem is dangerous; therefore, applicants should be required to take a drug test before being hired. The applicant must also execute a continuous authorization for drug testing, which permits the employer to administer a drug test in the event of an accident.

2. **Designation of a safety/injury coordinator:**

   The safety/injury coordinator will review past accident records and implement programs to reduce situations that can result in accidents. The safety coordinator will maintain a logbook of incidents, which each department supervisor can review for incident trends.

3. **Implementation of mandatory safety training:**

   Each employee will be trained in safety related to his or her job.

4. **Increased awareness of safety:**

   Through the implementation of programs, games, and posters, employees will be reminded to think intelligently and safely.

5. **Implementation of incentive programs for safety:**

   To further encourage safety, rewards and incentives will be given to employees who practice such behavior.

6. **Measurement of results:**

   To be determined by the general manager.

1. What specific measurements might Ms. Shulkey use to gauge the effectiveness of the group's plan?
2. How effective is training likely to be in reducing employee injuries?
3. Analyze the committee's plan for thoroughness. Are there potential liabilities that still need to be addressed?

Analyze the Situation 14.5

Karin Pelley was employed as a district manager by Ron's Roast Beef, a regional chain of 150 quick-service restaurants serving sandwiches, soups, and soft drinks. Most of the stores were located in shopping mall food courts or strip malls. Ms. Pelley worked out of her home office, traveling to visit her 12 assigned stores on a regular basis.

Ms. Pelley communicated with the corporate office via telephone and email through a wireless system in her home using a modem, both of which were installed in her home by Advance Technology, a telecommunications company selected by Ron's Roast Beef to supply telecommunications equipment and services to employees. As part of its contract with Ron's Roast Beef, Advance Technology serviced the machines used by Ms. Pelley in her daily work.

When Ms. Pelley's modem stopped working one day, she contacted her home office, which then called Advance Technology to request that a service technician be dispatched to Ms. Pelley's home. In the course of his visit, the technician assaulted Ms. Pelley. The technician was later apprehended by the police and convicted of felony assault, his third such conviction in three years.

Ms. Pelley sued Advanced Technology, claiming negligent hiring. In addition, her attorney submitted a demand letter to Ron's Roast Beef, requesting a $400,000 settlement from the company for negligence in contracting its telecommunications services from Advance Technology. The attorney for Ron's Roast Beef refused to pay the claim stating that:

- Ron's had no control over the hiring practices of Advance Technology.
- Ms. Pelley was prohibited by law from pursuing any injury claim against her employer other than workers' compensation because the assault occurred in Ms. Pelley's "office."

1. What responsibility did Ron's Roast Beef have for providing a safe home working environment for Ms. Pelley?
2. Will Ron's Roast Beef be held liable for the damages suffered by Ms. Pelley? Will Advance Technology be held liable?
3. What should Ron's do in the future to avoid potential liability in situations such as this?

14.3 Crimes Against Hospitality Businesses

Most of our discussion so far has centered on the protection of guests and employees from outside threats, but hospitality managers also need to be aware of threats and criminal activities aimed directly at their own operation. The three most common threats are as follows:

1. Consumer theft of services, which involves a guest who leaves without paying a bill or one who refuses to pay it.
2. Fraudulent payment of a bill with an unauthorized credit card (stolen, canceled, or revoked), a bad check, or counterfeit money.
3. Internal theft of assets, committed by your own staff.

Undoubtedly, your safety and security plan has provisions to protect your business from some types of property theft; often, however, additional measures for preventing theft of services, fraudulent payment, and internal theft will be required. These measures could involve a different set of procedures and extra vigilance on the part of you and your employees. It is also important to be aware of legislation that addresses these types of criminal behavior.

The federal government has passed a law prohibiting the fraudulent use of credit cards. Individuals who fraudulently use credit cards in interstate commerce to obtain goods or services of $1,000 or more in any given year could be subject to fines of up to $10,000 and prison terms of up to 15 years. Recently, technology in the prevention and detection of credit card fraud has advanced. New technologies, such as Payment Card Industry Data Security Standard (PCI DSS) are making it easier for merchants to proactively protect consumer account data. PCI DSS is a multifaceted security standard created in 2006 that includes requirements for security management, policies, procedures, network architecture, software design, and other critical protective measures. More specifically, PCI DSS helps protect guests' privacy by creating an additional level of protection for card issuers such as Visa, MasterCard, and Discover by ensuring that merchants meet minimum levels of security when they store, process, and transmit credit card data. For more information on PCI DSS, visit the Payment Card Industries Security Standard Council website (the organization that administers PCI DSS) at www.pcisecuritystandards.org.

In addition, every state has passed laws prohibiting individuals from taking advantage of hospitality services without paying for them. These laws are strict and often carry large fines or prison terms for those found guilty. As in many areas of the law, the specific provisions of these state statutes vary widely, so check with your attorney to learn their specifics. Interestingly, many of these laws favor the hospitality operation by requiring an accused defendant to prove that he or she did not intentionally try to avoid payment of a bill. The responsibility for security in these three important areas, however, still falls on you and your staff and thus is examined in detail next.

Consumer Theft of Services

When guests are legitimately unhappy with the level of service they have received for a meal or during an overnight stay, they may become angry and protest all or a portion of their bill. As a manager, you must help calm the customer and fashion a solution that is fair to both the customer and the business. But when unprincipled and devious individuals consume services with no intention of paying for them, the action you take will be entirely different. In the foodservice industry, these customers are said to have "skipped" or "dined and dashed," meaning that they have evaded the process of paying the cashier; in the lodging industry, a guest of this type is said to have "walked" his or her bill because he or she has left the hotel without paying.

In either case, the loss of revenue to your business can be substantial if you do not take the necessary steps to reduce this type of theft. Unfortunately, in a busy restaurant or hotel, it can sometimes be relatively easy for a guest or an entire party to leave without settling their bill unless everyone on the staff is extremely vigilant.

Legally Managing at Work

Procedures to Reduce the Incidence of Skipping

1. If the custom of the restaurant is to allow the ordering of food prior to receiving payment, present the bill for the food promptly when the guests have finished eating.
2. If the facility has a cashier in a central location in the dining area, make sure that person is available and visible at all times.
3. If the facility operates in such a manner that each server collects for his or her own guests' charges, instruct the servers to return to the table promptly after presenting each guest's bill to secure a form of payment.
4. Be observant of exit doors near restrooms or other areas of the facility that may give an unscrupulous guest an easy "out."
5. In a hotel dining situation, if it is the custom of the restaurant to allow food and beverage purchases to be charged to a room or master bill, verify the identity of the guest with both a printed and signed name. Guest identity verification may take a variety of forms, but in all cases should firmly establish that the guest requesting credit privileges is indeed authorized to do so.
6. If an employee sees a guest leave without paying the bill, he or she should notify management immediately.
7. Upon approaching a guest who has left without paying the bill, the manager should ask if the guest has inadvertently "forgotten" to pay. In most cases, the guest will then pay the bill.
8. Should a guest refuse to pay or flee the scene, the manager should provide an incident report including:
   a. Number of guests involved
   b. Amount of the bill
   c. Physical description of the guest(s)
   d. Vehicle description if the guests flee in a car as well as the license plate number if possible
   e. Time and date of the incident
   f. Name of the server(s) who waited on the guest
   g. Name of the server who notified management of the skip

If the guest is successful in fleeing the scene, the police should be notified. In no case should staff members or managers be instructed to attempt to physically detain the guest. The liability that could be involved should an employee or the guest be hurt in such an attempt is far greater than the value of a food and beverage bill.

The Legally Managing at Work feature on "page 269" details steps you should consider implementing to help reduce the instances of food and beverage skips.

Hotel room "walks" are best addressed at check-in because it is impossible to know when hotel guests are leaving their rooms for a legitimate reason as opposed to walking their bill. Because this is so, employee intervention techniques are less successful in hotels than in a food and beverage situation. The best way to limit the possibility of a guest walking the bill is to verify the guest's payment information and identity at check-in. If the guest intends to pay by credit card, the card should be authorized for an appropriate amount. If a cash payment will be used, it should be taken in advance. If the guest writes a check, the check should be authorized using the facility's established policy. Some facilities also require a verifiable form of positive identification when a guest pays with cash or check (usually a copy of a driver's license or some other generally accepted form of identification). When guests know that the hotel is aware of their true identity and can contact them after their stay, the likelihood of walking an entire folio (charge) is greatly reduced.

Fraudulent Payment

In the United States, credit cards, cash, and personal checks are the most common forms of payment for hospitality services. Unfortunately, all three can be used fraudulently by deceitful guests.

Credit Cards Credit card security has come a long way since the cards' introduction. Today, credit cards are being issued with the latest technology named after the original developers Europay, MasterCard, and Visa (EMV). This chip and pin/signature process (becoming the standard authorization process in the United States), reduces the chance of consumer fraud, including counterfeiting and cloning. Other names for this type of technology include chip card, smart card, chip-enabled smart card, or chip and choice card. Unlike magnetic stripe cards, each time the EMV card is used, the card chip creates a unique transaction code that cannot be used again. The EMV credit card rollout is slow, however, as of April 2016, more than 282 million Visa chip cards have been issued in the United States.[1] In addition, today's electronic credit card verification systems are fast, accurate, and designed to reduce the chances of loss by businesses.

Hospitality operations should use a credit card verification service even if credit cards are used infrequently for payment. These verification services charge a fee, but they guarantee that the business will receive its money for a legitimate credit card charge even if the cardholder does not pay the bank that issues the monthly statement. In many cases, businesses face challenges with credit card holders who pay the full bill using their card but later voice dissatisfaction and protest all or part of that bill. Unless the guest can be placated, the business may well face the prospect of defending its procedures.

Each major credit card issuer has its own procedures, and hospitality managers should become familiar with those of each card they accept. It is also important that managers realize that credit card companies have a responsibility to both the hospitality business and the cardholder. To be fair to both, the card issuer will require a business to follow its procedures for accepting cards and billing for services. This is to ensure both that when a guest has a legitimate complaint, he or she is treated fairly and that any fraudulent intent on a guest's part is resolved in a way that protects the business.

New forms of mobile payment through a smartphone or other device are becoming commonplace in the hospitality industry. These forms use credit cards, debit cards, and gift cards through consumer mobile apps such as Apple Pay, PayPal, and Samsung Pay. They can be used on selected devices to create alternative ways for the mobile payment of goods and services. Numerous businesses in the hospitality industry

[1] http://www.creditcards.com/credit-card-news/emv-faq-chip-cards-answers-1264.php

Legally Managing at Work

Guidelines for Handling Credit Cards

1. Confirm that the name on the card is the same as that of the individual presenting the card for payment. Use a driver's license or other acceptable form of identification for this purpose.
2. Examine the card for any obvious signs of alteration.
3. Confirm that the card is valid, that is, that the card has not expired and is in effect.
4. Compare the signature on the back of the card with the one produced by the guest paying with the card.
5. Initial the credit card receipt. This should be done by the employee processing the charge.
6. Keep credit card charges that have not yet been processed in a secure place to limit the possibility that they could be stolen.
7. Do not issue cash in exchange for credit card charges.
8. Do not write in tip amounts for the guest. These should be supplied by the guest only, unless the tip is mandatory and that fact has been communicated in advance to the guest.
9. Tally credit card charges on a daily basis, making sure to check that the preceding procedures have been followed. If they have not, take immediate corrective action to ensure compliance.

Legally Managing at Work

Personal Check Verification

1. Ask for a form of identity verification to ensure that the name on the check is the same as that of the individual presenting the check for payment.
2. Make a notation on the check of the identification source and identifier used to verify the individual presenting the check as payment (e.g., driver's license number, student identification number).
3. Establish a maximum on the amount for which the check can be written without preauthorization directly from the bank named on the check.
4. Ensure that the check has:

   Correct name of your business

   Correct date

   Correct dollar amount

   Same numerical dollar amount and written dollar amount

   Clearly ident fiable issuing bank address

   Signature that matches the name on the check
5. Examine the check carefully for any obvious signs of alteration.
6. Deposit all checks you receive promptly with your own bank.
7. Keep a list of individuals who have passed uncollectable checks to you previously, and require cashiers to refer to this list each time they accept a check.
8. Insist that all checks include a local telephone number and address.
9. Accept out-of-town checks with caution or not at all because these checks may be more difficult to collect.
10. Instruct all employees accepting checks for payment to initial and date them.

are now using these more secure methods for paying. Procedures and equipment for the use of such methods should be considered at the time usage becomes desired or expected by customers.

The Legally Managing at Work on "page 270" details nine general procedures that should be followed by employees when accepting any type of credit card.

Cash Guests who use cash to defraud a business usually fall into two categories. The first is the so-called quick-change artist, an individual who intentionally tries to confuse or distract the cashier when tendering payment for a bill. The best defense against such an attempt is to instruct cashiers to take their time and make change carefully. Handling cash is confusing only when cashiers do so too quickly or carelessly. It is this type of cashier that the quick-change artist seeks out.

The second type is one who attempts to use counterfeit money to pay his or her bills. Fortunately, as with credit cards, great strides have been made by the issuer—in this case the federal government—to reduce the likelihood of creating passable counterfeit U.S. currency. Redesigned bills printed by the federal government began to be circulated in the late 1990s, and they have made the counterfeiter's task much more difficult. Even so, managers and, if possible, staff members who routinely accept cash for payment should enroll in one of the counterfeit-detection training programs generally offered by local law enforcement officials.

Personal Checks Even today, in some hospitality businesses, customers may prefer to pay with a personal or business check, but such payment raises a number of risks. Guests may either deliberately or through an oversight write checks that the guest's account does not have sufficient funds to cover. Also, fraudulent customers may attempt to write checks on closed accounts, accounts at nonexistent banks, or legitimate checking accounts owned by other individuals.

Although there are services that can be used to preauthorize the validity of personal checks similar to credit card authorization, these services do not generally agree to reimburse the business for the value of the check should it be returned as unpayable by a bank. To minimize the number of such occurrences at your business, implement the procedures in the Legally Managing at Work feature shown above.

If a check is returned to you because the account either does not exist or has insufficient funds to cover the amount, contact your local law enforcement officials. Accepting partial payment of the check's original amount in exchange for not prosecuting the check writer is usually not a good idea. Doing so indicates your acceptance of treating the check amount as a "loan" that is to be paid back rather than as a debt that must be paid at once. Local laws vary in this area, so take the time to become famil ar with them.

Internal Theft of Assets

The internal theft of assets by employees generally is the theft of financial assets, a crime known as "embezzlement" or the theft of company property.

Embezzlement Guarding your business against embezzlement consists of implementing and maintaining financial controls that regarding the following:

Product sales receipts

Services sales receipts

Deposits

Accounts receivable

Accounts payable

For a detailed discussion of the procedures involved in income control, consult your accountant or one of the many cost control or income control books on the market today. One procedure many hospitality operators employ to protect themselves against embezzlement is to **bond** employees whose tasks include the handling of financial assets.

In addition to theft of a business's financial assets, the hospitality industry presents opportunities for employees to defraud guests as well. Some common techniques in this regard include the following:

- Charging guests for items not purchased and then keeping the charges for them.
- Changing the totals on credit card charges after the guest has left or imprinting additional credit card charges and pocketing the cash difference.
- Overcharging with the intent of keeping the excess.
- Purposely shortchanging guests when giving back change and then keeping the extra change.
- Charging higher-than-authorized prices for products or services, recording the proper price, and then keeping the overcharge.

Theft of Company Property

The potential for theft of company property in the hospitality industry is high for the simple reason that employees can easily use so many typical hospitality-related items in their own homes. Food, trash bags, and guestroom supplies are common targets of employee theft. It is impossible to prevent every instance of employee theft, but best-practice preventative measures will reduce the number. One employee was caught stealing steaks in a restaurant during his shift by triple bagging the fine steaks in trash bags and throwing them into the dumpster. Upon his return to retrieve the steaks later that night after his shift, he was caught and turned over to the police. These measures fall into three main categories:

1. Screening employees at the hiring stage.
2. Creating an environment that discourages theft.
3. Eliminating the opportunity to commit theft.

Figure 14.4 details some of the activities that can be undertaken in each of these areas.

Theft, whether by guests or employees, greatly impacts your ability to operate a profitable business. Although there are laws in place to help you protect your operation against theft and perhaps even to recover damages, it is important to understand that being the plaintiff in a lawsuit you initiate can be just as costly and disruptive as defending your business against one brought against it. Thus, the best way to protect your operation is by establishing safeguards and procedures that prevent these types of activities from happening in the first place. Some police departments offer training sessions that demonstrate how to recognize forgeries, bad checks, counterfeit money, and stolen credit cards and to identify threats to internal assets. Services such as these, along with your own vigilance and effective antitheft procedures, can be of tremendous assistance as you train employees in the proper procedures required to avoid and prevent problems of consumer theft of services, fraudulent payment, and internal theft problems.

LEGALESE

Bond(ing): An insurance agreement in which the insurer guarantees payment to an employer in the event of financial loss caused by the actions of a specific employee.

Employee Theft Prevention	Activities
Screen employees.	Do preemployment reference checks.
	Do criminal background checks.
	Consider psychological prescreeing tests.
Create an antitheft atmosphere.	Enforce all theft-related policies fairly and consistently.
	Let employees know the real cost of theft and how it relates to them personally.
	Reward employees for their efforts to reduce theft.
Eliminate the opportunities to steal.	Do not let "off-the-clock" employees loiter around the property.
	Allow employee purchases of products only by a manager.
	Consider a policy to eliminate the opportunity to enter with or leave with unexamined packages, bags, knapsacks and the like.
	Implement effective inventory controls.

FIGURE 14.4 **Activities to reduce employee theft.**

14.4 Human Trafficking

Polaris—Fighting Human Trafficking in the Hotel Industry

Polaris is a leader in the global fight to eradicate modern slavery. Named after the North Star that guided slaves to freedom in the United States, Polaris systemically disrupts the human trafficking networks that rob human beings of their lives and their freedom. Our comprehensive model puts victims at the center of what we do—helping survivors restore their freedom, preventing more victims, and leveraging data and technology to pursue traffickers wherever they operate. Through initiatives such as running the national anti-trafficking hotline in the United States, Polaris restores freedom to survivors everyday and has identified over 30,000 cases of human trafficking in the United States since 2007. Our work also focuses on equipping our corporate partners, including our robust hotel industry partners, to address and prevent human trafficking in their businesses and supply chains.

One of the most commonly reported venues for sex trafficking to the National Human Trafficking Hotline is hotels and motels. We know that pimps and traffickers use hotel and motel rooms when setting up the so-called "dates" between victims of sex trafficking and those individuals purchasing sex. We also know labor trafficking is present in both the hotel industry's work force and in the supply chain of its products. Since 2007, over 1,400 cases of human trafficking in hotels and motels have been reported to the National Human Trafficking Hotline and Polaris's BeFree Textline, and over 1,800 victims and survivors have been identified.[2]

Traffickers are capitalizing on the lack of awareness around this issue within the hotel industry. All too often, they continue to exploit their victims unchecked because staff, managers, and executives do not know what to look for on their premises.

Human Trafficking Indicators

Sex Trafficking:

- Pays for room in cash or with pre-paid card
- Extended stay with few possessions
- Requests room overlooking parking lot
- Presence of excessive drugs, alcohol, sex paraphernalia
- Excessive foot traffic in/out of hotel room
- Frequently requests new linens, towels, and restocking of fridge
- Exhibits fearful, anxious, or submissive behavior
- Dresses inappropriately given the climate

[2] As of 2015.

Sex and Labor Trafficking:

- No control of money, cell phone, or ID
- Restricted or controlled communications
- No knowledge of current or past whereabouts
- Signs of poor hygiene, malnourishment, or fatigue
- No freedom of movement, constantly monitored

Labor Trafficking:

- Prevented from taking adequate breaks
- Doing different work than was contracted
- Living and working on-site
- Forced to meet daily quotas
- Forced to turn over wages
- Exorbitant fees deducted from paychecks
- Not paid directly

> **"As an industry, we recognize that hotels can play an important role in fighting human trafficking networks which often rely on legitimate businesses, including hotels, to sustain their illegal operations and infrastructure."**
> **– Katherine Lugar, AH&LA president & CEO**

Polaris provides tools for businesses to identify all forms of human trafficking, raise awareness on the issue, and equip the National Human Trafficking Hotline to support potential victims who reach out for help. For instance, through our partnership with Wyndham Hotel Group, we have trained their hotel employees on signs of trafficking and ensure survivors receive critical short-term shelter services through a Points for Polaris program with Wyndham.

Based on our experience working with Wyndham and other leading hotels across the country, we are in a ripe position to help your hotel combat human trafficking and restore freedom to survivors. Please reach out to us to learn more about our services at corporateengagement@polarisproject.org.

If you believe you have identified a potential trafficking situation, it is important to assess the immediate safety and welfare of the potential victims, guests, and staff. If you have witnessed or been informed there were incidents or threats of violence, alert security and/or law enforcement. If you have the opportunity to speak with the victim alone, ask if they would like assistance and provide them the National Human Trafficking Hotline number (1-888-373-7888) or send a text to Polaris at BeFree (233733).

14.5 Crisis Management Programs

Just as the safety and security needs of hospitality organizations vary widely, so too do their crisis management needs. Hotels, for example, would more likely face challenges associated with evacuating guests during a weather-related crisis than would the manager of a take-out restaurant. A property's physical location is another factor in crisis preparations. Hospitality managers in the midwestern part of the United States, for example, might not have to worry about preparing for a hurricane, but they would have to be ready for snow and ice storms that can be just as disruptive and threatening. And there are certain circumstances that could cause a crisis situation no matter where your property is located, such as power failures, criminal acts, fires, and workplace violence. If any of these should occur, it is up to you, as the manager, to be ready.

Essentially, crisis management consists of these distinct activities:

- Precrisis planning
- Crisis response
- Postcrisis assessment

Precrisis Planning

Obviously, it is too late to prepare for a crisis when you are experiencing one. If you are unprepared, not only will you respond poorly but also you may be held legally responsible for your lack of planning. Consider the case of Roland Naimo. While eating dinner at a steakhouse, a piece of steak became lodged in his throat, and he began to choke. No one on the restaurant staff had been trained to deal with such an emergency, and had it not been for a fellow diner who administered the Heimlich maneuver, Mr. Naimo might have died. Had that been the case, no doubt the restaurant would have faced a lawsuit along with the associated expenses and negative publicity. Everyone involved would have asked: Why wasn't the restaurant prepared for such an occurrence? Why wasn't someone employed by the restaurant to help?

To prepare for a crisis effectively, a hospitality manager should develop and practice an **emergency plan**. It simply identifies likely crisis situations and then details how the operation should respond to them. Finally, that plan must be practiced so that everyone on the site will know what to do and when.

Emergency Plan Development

Needless to say, no one can prepare for every crisis that could occur in a hospitality facility. But it is possible to be ready for those you can foresee. Moreover, many crises will require the same response as other types of crises. For example, training employees in the proper procedures for handling general medical emergencies will prepare them for responding to slips and falls, employee accidents, guest injuries, and other threats that could require medical attention. Similarly, preparing a facility evacuation plan will be helpful not only in case of a fire but also during a weather-related disaster or power outage. The point is you will find that by developing responses to a relatively small number of circumstances, you and your staff will be well equipped to address a wide variety of potential crises because all crises have some characteristics in common:

- Urgency
- Halt in normal operations
- Human suffering and/or financial loss
- Potential scrutiny by the media
- Threat to the reputation or health of the business

You must commit your emergency plan to writing. This is important for two reasons: First, a written plan will clarify precisely what is expected of management and employees in times of crisis; second, if you are involved in a lawsuit, the written emergency plan can serve as evidence to support your defense. A judge or jury would readily acknowledge that a policy was in place, indicating reasonable care on the part of your operation.

That said, an emergency plan need not be complicated. In fact, it is best if it is not. A crisis is a stressful time, during which confusion itself is a real threat. Thus, any planned response to an emergency should be clear and simple, regardless of the number of steps required. In its simplest form, a written emergency plan should address:

- The nature of the crisis
- Who is to be informed when the crisis occurs
- What is to be done in response to the crisis
- When is it to be done
- Who is to do it
- Who will communicate to whom regarding the crisis

LEGALESE

Emergency plan: A procedure or series of procedures to be implemented in response to a crisis.

Although the specific threats that you may encounter will vary widely based on the type of facility you operate and where, the following should be covered in any effective emergency plan:

- Emergency telephone numbers
- Fire procedures
- Storm procedures
- Hurricanes
- Tornadoes
- Earthquakes
- Snow and ice storms
- Power failure
- Injury/accident
- Illness of guest or employee
- Death of guest or employee
- Evacuation of nonworking elevator
- Robbery
- Bomb threat
- Active shooters
- Human trafficking
- Media relations

After the emergency plan has been finalized, each manager and affected employee should be given a copy of it or have immediate access to it. Subsequently, it is important to review, revise, and practice the emergency plan on a regular basis. Figure 14.5 is an example of the type of information required in an emergency telephone list, one component of a comprehensive emergency plan.

Emergency Plan Practice

Once your emergency plan has been developed, the next step is to practice the procedures you have included in it. Obviously, it is not possible to create, for example, a snowstorm in order to practice your staff's response to it. But you can practice your response to such a storm. Practicing your emergency plan might include a verbal plan review or an actual run-through. Figure 14.6 on the next page shows a section of an emergency plan related to a fire crisis. The emergency plan itself becomes a blueprint for practice sessions.

EMERGENCY TELEPHONE NUMBERS

Property Manager ____________________

Emergency Services

Fire Department ____________________

Fire Alarm Service Provider ____________________

Police Department ____________________

Ambulance ____________________

Paramedics ____________________

Elevator Service Company ____________________

Insurance Company Representative ____________________

Telephone Repair Service ____________________

Utility Services

Gas ____________________

Electric ____________________

Water ____________________

Property-Specific Numbers

District Manager ____________________

Owner (with approval) ____________________

Other ____________________ ____________________

Other ____________________ ____________________

Other ____________________ ____________________

FIGURE 14.5 **Emergency telephone list.**

FIRE ALARM PROCEDURES

1. When an alarm sounds: All nonemergency committee personnel will go out the first available exit that is safe and then to the parking lot.
2. Room attendants will push their carts into the nearest vacant room before exiting to clear hallways.
3. Front office manager/supervisor will examine the fire panel to determine location of the smoke/fire.
4. Front desk will call fire department (after receiving signal from manager on duty) and notify them of alarm and approximate location of fire (if the fire department is not wired directly to the hotel).

FIRE RESPONSE INSTRUCTIONS

1. Without endangering yourself, notify any employees or guests in immediate danger of smoke, heat, or fire.
2. Close all doors to prevent the spread of the fire.
3. If possible, and trained to do so, help extinguish the fire by using one of the public/department fire extinguishers.
4. Never permit the fire and/or smoke to come between you and your route of escape.
5. Via telephone or direct council, advise all guests/employees of the nearest safe fire exit.
6. Immediately notify all disabled guests in rooms marked with a red marker on the bucket registration cards). If a guest does not answer by phone, direct someone to make an attempt to physically assist the guest out of the room, if it can be done safely. If unable to reach a guest, notify firefighters when they arrive.
7. Do not attempt to use the elevator under any circumstances.
8. If you or a guest are inside a room with smoke/fire, *do not open* the door. Stuff wet towels under the door and call for help. Place wet towels over your head and shoulders and stay low until help arrives.
9. If you encounter smoke in a hallway, stairwell, anywhere, *stop*; go back to a safe area and look for another means of escape.
10. Keep doors and windows in the area of the fire closed to minimize further fire spreading.

EVACUATION

Evacuation of the building should be done quickly and calmly. Safety of guests should be the primary concern. Each department will appoint one of its staff to oversee fellow staff members' evacuation from the building. This employee will be responsible for needed supplies and the general safety of the department's staff members.

Time permitting, the manager in the following departments will be responsible for:

Food and Beverage

1. Secure food, storage, and liquor rooms.
2. Place cash in a sealed envelope and drop into safe.
3. Take kitchen keys.

Accounting

1. Back up computer programs onto disks.
2. Take current payroll register.
3. Take all master keys.

Sales

1. Take banquet event book and group/function book binder.

Engineering

1. Take master key log.
2. Deactivate all gas-operated equipment.
3. Shut down elevators.

Front Office

1. Take bucket (guest registration files).
2. Take blankets from the supply cabinet.
3. Pull off current guest list by PBX.
4. Seal up cash in envelopes; drop in safe.

Housekeeping

1. Take all time cards for roll call.
2. Take all master keys and floor keys.
3. Fill laundry cart with blankets.

General Manager (GM)/Manager on Duty (MOD)

1. Meet the department outside and advise them of the current situation.
2. Assist police/fire personnel to secure exit and entrance to the hotel.

FIGURE 14.6 **Fire crisis emergency plan.**

Legally Managing at Work

The Manager's Responsibilities in a Crisis

1. Take the immediate action required to ensure the safety of guests and employees.
2. Contact the appropriate source of assistance; for example, the fire department, police, or a medical professional.
3. Implement the relevant portion of your emergency plan.
4. Contact those within the organization who need to be informed of the crisis. This might include your supervisor, the owners, insurance companies, and company safety and security professionals.
5. Assume the leadership role expected of management during a crisis. Demonstrate your competence and professionalism by showing a genuine concern for the well-being of those affected by the crisis.
6. Communicate with your employees about the crisis.
7. Inform those guests who need to know what is being done and what will be done to deal with the crisis.
8. Secure organizational property, but only if it can be done without risking injury to guests or employees.
9. Prepare for and make yourself available to the media.
10. Using an incident report form or a narrative style document in writing your efforts and activities during the crisis.

Of course, the question of which sections of the emergency plan to practice and how often can only be answered by management. The objective in developing a schedule for practicing your emergency plan should be to emphasize the most likely and serious threats and to allow each staff member with responsibilities during the crisis to fully understand his or her role. The aftermath of a crisis, especially one that results in injury or loss of life, will inevitably lead to finger-pointing and intense scrutiny of your and your staff's actions. As a manager concerned with the safety and security of your staff and guests and the potential liability resulting from poor execution of an emergency plan, you must always ensure that your operation knows how to perform in a crisis.

Crisis Response

No matter how well prepared you and your staff are, when a crisis does occur, you will nevertheless be faced with an overwhelming number of reactions and responses from your staff, your guests, and perhaps even the media. Your ability to properly manage and control these responses will, in great part, determine the ultimate impact of the crisis on the reputation, potential legal liability, and financial health of your business.

Management Response During a crisis, events unfold at an extremely rapid pace. Managers who have done their homework by preparing and practicing an emergency plan are more likely to behave professionally than those who have not. That said, a manager's particular response will depend, of course, on the nature and location of the crisis. The specific steps you would take to investigate a guest's claim of a coat stolen from your dining room would be very different from those you would take if the National Weather Service issued a warning that a hurricane was bearing down on the city in which your hospitality operation is located.

The checklist in the Legally Managing at Work feature shown above is a helpful guide for recalling the major duties of management during a crisis. These steps can be modified as needed to apply more specifically to your own hospitality operation, and they should become a part of the orientation training program for each manager and supervisor.

Staff Response Your staff's response to a crisis is just as important as yours. Essentially, the role of your staff in a crisis is to help you protect people and property without risking danger to themselves. In a fire, for example, staff can play a crucial role in notifying guests, helping to evacuate a building, securing assets if time permits, and helping to calm distraught and shaken guests. Remember that, you, as a manager, simply cannot be everywhere during a time of crisis. In the case of a robbery or suicide attempt in your facility, you may not even be aware of the crisis until it has essentially passed. The crisis preparedness of your employees in such a case, therefore, will determine how they respond.

It is also vital in a crisis that employees do nothing to further endanger guests or the business. Consider the case of the restaurant employee who refuses to immediately summon medical help for an injured guest because he or she fears that by doing so, the restaurant will be admitting responsibility for the guest's injury and might be held liable. But if the guest dies and it can be shown that the actions of the employee contributed directly to that death, the operation will face far greater exposure to liability and cost than if the employee had called an ambulance in the first place. Remember that the courts will hold you and your employees to the standard of reasonable care. Reasonable people do not value money above life. No piece of property or amount of money is worth risking personal harm to employees or other individuals on the property. An important concept to teach employees is this: Protect people before property.

Unfortunately, workers themselves can become victims in a crisis. The threat of harm from robbery, vandalism, and even other coworkers is very real. Good employees will not stay long with an organization that does not actively demonstrate concern for their safety. Effective managers take the training and security steps needed to help protect employees while on the job.

Legally Managing at Work

Guest Relations in a Crisis Situation

1. Recognize that the guest may be agitated and feel confused, scared, or angry. Accept these feelings as legitimate, and take them into consideration when speaking to the guest.
2. Introduce yourself, and state your position title. Immediately ask for the guest's name, and repeat it to make sure you say it correctly. Use the guest's name in your conversation with him or her.
3. Give the guest your undivided attention, maintain eye contact, and avoid interrupting the guest. Listen more than you talk.
4. Stay calm. Do not lose your temper regardless of the guest's comments.
5. Apologize for the inconvenience suffered by the guest. Be genuine. Put yourself in the guest's position, and treat the guest as you would want someone you care for very much to be treated.
6. If practicable, tell the guest what is currently being done or what will be done to alleviate the crisis.
7. Arrange for medical treatment if needed. This can be done without accepting blame for the accident because the responsibility for the problem may be unclear at the time of your conversation. What can be made clear, however, is your real concern for the safety of the guest.
8. Offer alternative solutions to the problem, if possible, and seek a solution that satisfies the needs of the guest to whom you are talking.
9. Let the guest know that you will follow up to ensure that all you have promised will be done.
10. Thank the guest for talking with you; afterward, make notes of the conversation if you feel they are needed.

If a crisis of any type does occur, it is important that you keep employees informed about the status of the situation. In a serious situation, daily briefings may be required. Employees will want to know how the crisis will affect them and their families. If the business will close for a time, will they continue to be paid? If not, what alternative assistance might be available? Will additional hours be required of staff? If so, of whom?

Realize that a crisis will affect your employees both in the short and long run. Experiencing a crisis, especially one that entails injury or loss of life, can be very stressful. Negative effects on employees can include anxiety, depression, nightmares, flashbacks, and even physical effects such as insomnia, loss of appetite, and headaches. Collectively, these and related symptoms are known as **post-traumatic stress disorder (PTSD)**. Increasingly, employers have been called on to recognize and respond to PTSD symptoms of employees following their exposure to a crisis.

Search the Web 14.1

Go online to **www.gozoe.org**

1. Click on: LEARN.
2. Click on: What Is Human Trafficking?
3. Describe: The nature of human trafficking is in today's world.
4. Identify: How big is this problem in the world? In the United States?
5. Answer: What are the U.S. government's efforts to end human trafficking?
6. Identify: What government agency oversees the efforts?
7. Answer: What can hotels do to help limit human trafficking in them?

LEGALESE

Post-traumatic stress disorder (PTSD): A severe reaction to an event that threatened an individual's physical or emotional health.

Guest Response When a crisis occurs, guests may be involved in a variety of ways. They might be witnesses to crimes or accidents, they themselves might be victims, or they might simply be innocent and concerned bystanders. You cannot control a guest's reaction to a crisis situation; what you can control is your response to the guest, and that can have a major impact on the ultimate reaction of the guest.

Never forget that a guest in a crisis situation will, in all probability, be upset, scared, angry, and sometimes all the three. Consider, for example, Mr. and Mrs. Rahshad, two elderly hotel guests who were awakened in the middle of the night when a fire alarm went off. Though it was a false alarm, understandably, they were agitated by the interruption of their sleep, concerned whether there was an actual fire, and somewhat angry at both the hotel and the travel agency that had arranged for their stay. Most likely, they would demand to speak with a manager and perhaps even threaten a lawsuit. And if the hotel is full of guests who feel just like Mr. and Mrs. Rahshad, it will be your job, as the manager, to calm them and diffuse a difficult situation. If you find yourself in this position, remember the points in the Legally Managing at Work feature shown above. Your objective is to show genuine concern, treat the guests fairly, and avoid any needless legal fallout.

Often, plaintiffs in lawsuits state that they would not have sued an establishment if they had received an expression of sincere concern from the establishment about their inconvenience. Even in a crisis caused by severe weather, which is completely beyond the control of management, it is likely that some guests will become upset, and they may, from fear or anger, blame management. Let those guests know that you are genuinely concerned about their plight and that you are doing everything possible to ease the difficulties of the situation.

Legally Managing at Work

Guidelines for Dealing with the Media during a Crisis

Do Not

- Allow any media inside your property during a crisis.
- Speculate on what happened or why it happened.
- Ever release the names of victims; respect their privacy.
- Ever speak **off the record.**

There is no such thing.

- Provide lurid or graphic descriptions of what happened.
- Ever reply to a question with "no comment." If you truly cannot comment, give the honest reason why you cannot. Legitimate reasons not to respond to a specific question include:
  - **a.** Pending legal investigation
  - **b.** Incomplete information
  - **c.** Responsibility to respond falls to another (give that person's name)
- Speak in hotel jargon (e.g., back of the house, 86).
- Be sarcastic or use humor.
- Speak to the media without first preparing a written statement.
- Lie about what happened.
- Allow members of the press to tour your property unescorted.
- Estimate the monetary value of the loss.
- Ask to review the reporter's notes.
- Allow reporters to bully you.
- Disparage the competition of your hotel.

Do

- Emphasize the company's concern for the safety of guests and employees.
- Remember that your primary responsibility to the media during a crisis is to provide factual information and to express genuine concern for any crisis victims. But you also have an opportunity to emphasize the positives of your organization even in the face of the crisis. Mention, for example, safety and security efforts in place, training programs implemented that relate to the crisis, and your commitment to cooperate fully with all investigating authorities.
- Respond promptly to every media call.
- Speak clearly and stick to your professional statement.
- Cooperate fully with all law enforcement and government agencies.
- Make sure the general manager or public relations director is the only spokesperson.
- Maintain a professional appearance and a positive attitude.
- Show sympathy and care for what happened.
- Introduce yourself and give your title.
- Speak calmly and professionally.
- Provide just the facts.
- Inform the corporate office, insurance company, and attorney.
- Temporarily suspend advertising for a period of time appropriate for the crisis endured.
- Refer to technical experts.
- Give all media access to the same information.
- Tell reporters you will update them with information as soon as possible.
- Update your website.
- Monitor press coverage.
- Keep a file on all newspaper articles and video clips.

The Educational Institute of the American Hotel & Lodging Association has a professional certification called Certified Guest Service Professionals (CGSP) that contains information on how to provide excellent guest service, a tool that provides training which can be very useful during a crisis situation.[3]

Media Relations

When a crisis occurs at your property, it, and your business, may become the news story of the day. When, for example, a restaurant is robbed at gunpoint, newspaper, radio, and television reporters may call or descend on the property to find out what happened. Although most reporters are fair and even handed in their coverage of a story, some are not. And, remember, a poorly prepared management statement or **press release** can magnify a crisis rather than help diffuse it.

Unfortunately, even the best preparation cannot turn bad news into good. During a crisis, you can, however, help ensure that you are allowed to tell your side of the story on behalf of the company and the property and in so doing preserve your image as an organization that is professional, caring, and concerned. If you do not achieve this goal, not only might your liability for the crisis increase but also you might also face litigation simply because you did not express an appropriate amount of concern for the victims of the crisis. The guidelines in the Legally Managing at Work feature shown above of dos

[3] https://www.ahlei.org/Certifications/AHLEI-Professional-Certification/

LEGALESE

Off the record: An oral agreement between a reporter and an interviewee wherein the reporter promises not to quote the interviewee's comments for publication.

Press release: An announcement made by an organization or individual distributed for use by the media.

and don't's can be helpful if you are called on to serve as the spokesperson for your organization during a crisis.

Some managers believe that they and their operations are treated unfairly by reporters during a crisis. Certainly, when a crisis occurs, the potential for negative publicity is great, and it is natural not to want to see yourself or your operation cast in a negative light. It is important, however, that you not do anything to make a difficult situation worse by attacking the media. You cannot control the actions of reporters; you can only conduct yourself in a positive, professional manner while expressing genuine concern for crisis victims. As a professional manager, it is your responsibility to do so.

Postcrisis Assessment

As stated previously, evaluating your emergency plan should be an ongoing process, and in the aftermath of a crisis, it is imperative to do so. At this time you will be able to review your performance and that of your staff and guest as well as your effectiveness in dealing with the media.

A variety of approaches may be used to do a postcrisis analysis of performance. The STEM model introduced in Chapter 1, "Prevention Philosophy," is a good place to start. Consider the case of Brenda Mendez who managed a 64-room limited-service hotel near the airport. Her largest customer, Northeast Airlines, housed its crew members in her hotel during their layovers. One night, as her van driver was returning from the airport with a crew, a serious accident occurred, severely injuring four crew members and the driver. Although the cause of the accident was not initially apparent, negative publicity ensued and threatened to damage the hotel's safety reputation and, of course, relations with Northeast Airlines were strained. Fortunately, Ms. Mendez had a plan in place to deal with the accident. Afterward, however, she felt that certain elements of the plan could be improved, so she decided to undertake a postcrisis assessment. Using the STEM approach, she reviewed:

- *Selecting:* Were procedures in place to ensure that the drivers were qualified for the job? Had background checks on licenses been performed? Were vision tests required as a part of the selection process, and corrective glasses mandated if needed? If an opposing attorney sued the hotel for negligence, the answers to these questions and others would be required. It might be too late to correct any deficiencies related to a current crisis, but it certainly is not too late to prepare for, and attempt to prevent, a second occurrence.
- *Teaching:* Part of the STEM approach involves teaching employees properly, which includes using feedback devices such as competency testing to ensure that the training was effective. In the van accident just described, the number of employees who would have required training in anticipation of such a crisis is large indeed. Certainly, the van drivers would need to be trained in administering first aid. Additionally, front desk and night audit staff would need to be trained in how to field possible calls from the media, the airline, and families of the victims. Those involved in sales would certainly be called on to reassure customers of the hotel's safety. When employees know what to expect and have been trained how to react, the chance of their making a mistake that would exacerbate the crisis is greatly reduced.
- *Educating:* Remember that managers too must continuously educate themselves. If a lawsuit results from a crisis, a plaintiff's attorney will want to know the competency level of management. Employee selection and employee training are ultimately a management responsibility. Therefore, an effective postcrisis assessment also includes an examination of management's competency. Proof of continuing education, certification, and expertise in the specific safety and security area involved in the crisis can be crucial in reducing legal liability. In addition, management's performance in handling the press should

Analyze the Situation 14.6

Irving Nash managed a 24-hour table-service restaurant that specialized in breakfast items. Lendal Ketchar, a customer, arrived at the restaurant at approximately 2:00 A.M. one morning. Before entering the restaurant, Mr. Ketchar tripped over the curb alongside the sidewalk and broke his hip. Because Mr. Ketchar was a city councilman, the incident was reported in the local paper.

Mr. Nash was interviewed extensively about the cause of the accident. He specifically mentioned to reporters that the curb had not been painted bright yellow as a warning to guests, nor were lighting levels very high at the entrance area where Mr. Ketchar fell. Mr. Nash later read the interviews and shared them with his two assistant managers. Both suggested that the restaurant paint the curb area, install additional lighting, and inform the media that these actions were taken. Mr. Nash's boss vetoed this idea, however, stating that any action such as painting the curb and installing better lighting could imply previous negligence on the part of the organization and thus could increase the organization's potential legal liability.

1. Which factors would influence the potential liability of Mr. Nash's restaurant for the accident?
2. Is the future liability of the restaurant greater under the proposed actions of Mr. Nash's assistant managers or those of his boss?
3. What effective safety and security programs could be undertaken to limit legal liability if Mr. Nash is required to follow the advice of his boss?
4. As a professional hospitality manager, is Mr. Nash ethically obligated to take action to prevent a further occurrence of this type?

be reviewed. Were employees told who would serve as the media spokesperson in the event of a crisis? Was the spokesperson/manager well studied and prepared? Was anything said by management or the staff that could increase the operation's potential liability?

- *Managing:* Management is a process. It includes the actions of the manager as well as the processes and procedures established and enforced by management. A postcrisis assessment necessarily involves reviewing those processes and procedures for improvement. For the van accident, a review would involve an examination of all hiring and training practices related to van drivers, training of employees affected by the crisis, and the processes and procedures related to management's emergency response. In addition, an analysis of diverse areas such as the availability of first-aid supplies, insurance coverage, and the property's relationships with law enforcement agencies would be undertaken. The goal, of course, is to use what is learned in one crisis to help prevent future crises and to utilize your knowledge of the law to respond in a more effective manner should a similar crisis arise in the future.

International Snapshot

Legal Claims and Recovery for Injury under Mexican Law

A family from California traveled to Cabo San Lucas, Mexico, for vacation. The family (mom, dad, and two young daughters) checked into a hotel that had magnificent ocean views. There was a bronze statue in the lobby that was situated in a square cut out in a wall. The girls climbed up into the cut out to pose for a photo. One girl sat in front of the statue, while the other got behind the statute and leaned on it. When she leaned on it, the statue rocked to the side and crushed two fingers on her sister's hand. This was not the first time that visitors had caused the statue to move, but it was the first time any injury had resulted. The family returned home and filed suit in California, seeking to hold the property liable under California premises liability (negligence) laws and seeking recovery not only for the injured girl but also for the parents and noninjured sister for the emotional distress caused by having witnessed the injury-producing event (i.e., a negligent infliction of emotional distress or a "By-Stander" claim). Collectively, the family was seeking under California law hundreds of thousands of dollars.

Under California law, the property arguably had liability because it was on notice of the potential dangerous condition caused by a heavy bronze statue that was not fully secured. However, under the controlling Mexican law, the family was not entitled to a jury trial and would not be able to prove liability or damages. In fact, even if the family were to prevail on the issue of liability under Mexican law, the recoverable damages would have been extremely restricted and the only person with standing to sue would have been the injured girl.

Negligence under California law is codified in California Civil Code section 1714(a), which provides, in part: "Everyone is responsible, not only for the result of his or her willful acts, but also for an injury occasioned to another by his or her want of ordinary care or skill in the management of his or her property or person, except so far as the latter has, willfully or by want of ordinary care, brought the injury upon himself or herself." The elements of a cause of action for negligence are well established under California case law: (1) a legal duty to use due care, (2) a breach of such legal duty, and (3) the breach as a proximate or legal cause of the resulting injury. See *Ladd v. County of San Mateo*, 12 Cal.4th 913, 917 (1996).

Negligent Infliction of Emotional Distress is a cause of action under California law that allows a bystander who witnesses the negligent infliction of death or injury of another to recover for resulting emotional trauma even though he or she did not fear imminent physical harm. See *Dillon v. Legg*, 68 Cal.2d 728, 746-747 (1968). With no exceptional circumstances, recovery under this theory is limited to relatives residing in the same household, or parents, siblings, children and grandparents of the victim. Refer to *Thing v. La Chusa*, 48 Cal.3d 644, 647 (1989).

Conversely, the law of Baja California Sur, Mexico (i.e., the Mexican state in which the hotel was located), does not recognize the causes of action of Negligence or Negligent Infliction of Emotional Distress. Under the law of Baja California Sur, there is no duty on possessors or owners of real property to exercise ordinary care in the management of such premises in order to avoid exposing persons to an unreasonable risk of harm.

The law of Baja California Sur does, however, impose liability and allows recovery for physical injuries when the injury is caused by an illicit (illegal) act or an act against "good customs" (*Civil Code of Baja California Sur, Article 1815*). Climbing on and/or tipping over the statue is not considered an illicit act, as there is no law prohibiting climbing on and/or tipping over a statue or object in the State of Baja California Sur. Therefore, there was no illicit act causing an injury.

Furthermore, under the law of Baja California Sur, the proper defendant in a cause of action for harm caused by an illicit act or an act against good customs is only the natural person who performed the injury-causing act. For example, liability would not attach to persons other than those specifically listed in the Civil Code of the state of Baja California Sur, including parents of minors who live with them and are under their control. In this case, the property is not a natural person, and it did not perform the injury-causing act. Significantly, if the court determines that although not illicit, causing the statue to move was "an act against good customs", then only the natural person(s) who performed the injury-causing act can be liable by virtue of vicarious liability. In this case, that would have been the sister who caused the statue to move, not the property.

As for Negligent Infliction of Emotional Distress claims, Article 1821 of the Civil Code for the State of Baja California Sur is the tort that most closely resembles such a cause of action. Mexican law imposes liability and allows recovery for "moral harm" caused by an illicit act. Under Mexican law, a plaintiff for this kind of tort is required to prove (1) a violation of the law by defendant and (2) direct causation of the harm

(continued)

by such conduct. Again, climbing on and/or tipping over the statue was not considered an illicit act under Mexican law.

Finally, even if the property could be found liable, Mexican law significantly restricts recoverable damages. Under the laws of the State of Baja California Sur, when a person suffers bodily harm that results in temporary or permanent disability or death, damages are calculated according to Mexico's Federal Labor Law. In this case, the statutory amount that the injured girl would have been entitled to under for compensatory damages would have been $10,480.46 Mexican pesos (approximately US$850.47 at that time). Additionally, she would have been entitled only to expenses paid from her estate to cover her medical expenses. Medical expenses incurred by third parties, including her parents, were not recoverable. See Article 2014 of the Civil Code of the State of Baja California Sur. An award of monetary damages for moral harm (noneconomic damages) under the laws of the State of Baja California Sur is between 33 percent to 80 percent of the monetary award for the ordinary damages awarded under any other cause of action (33 percent to 80 percent of US$850.47). See Article 1840 of Civil Code of the State of Baja California Sur. Accordingly, even if the property were held liable under Mexican law, the maximum potential recovery would have been less than US$1,500.

Provided by David M. Samuels, Esq., Michelman & Robinson, LLP (www.mrllp.com).

WHAT WOULD YOU DO?

You are the manager of a 150-room limited-service, all-suite hotel located off the interstate highway near a large metropolitan area. Kate Roessler is your executive housekeeper. Ms. Roessler asks you to go with her to inspect room 415, which is occupied by a guest, Mr. Barney.

Ms. Roessler explains that the guest has been checked in for 10 days and has had a "Do Not Disturb" sign on the door for all but two of those days. She asks you to view the room before it is cleaned because she says she is concerned for the safety of her housekeepers in their routine cleaning tasks.

Upon entering the room, you observe several ripped plastic baggies, money wrappers, large quantities of empty fast-food containers, a scale, and a pistol holster partially hidden under a mattress. You recall that this is the same man who arrived by cab to the hotel and paid cash up front for a two-week stay.

1. Write a memo to your executive housekeeper outlining the steps she is to take for servicing Mr. Barney's room.
2. Assuming a drug interdiction program is in place in your city, would you contact that program to report Mr. Barney?
3. Regardless of your decision in regard to question 2, if the police asked to use the room next to that of Mr. Barney for an undercover operation, would you allow them to do so?
4. Write a memo to the chief of police stating your position in question 3 along with your rationale for the decision.

WHAT DID YOU LEARN IN THIS CHAPTER?

This chapter emphasized the need to prevent liabilities from occurring and to be prepared for events that give rise to liabilities. A four-step safety and security management method was introduced:

1. Recognize the threat.
2. Develop a program to respond to particular threats.
3. Implement the program.
4. Monitor the program results.

It is crucial to develop emergency plans so that you and your staff are prepared in the event of a crisis and to practice those plans regularly. During a crisis, you have a responsibility to respond to the community at large via the media, to your staff, and to your guests. The way you respond can have a major impact on your future reputation once the crisis has subsided. It is always important to assess your performance in any situation, and an assessment following a crisis is vital.

CHAPTER 15

Managing Insurance

15.1 Introduction to Insurance

Every individual faces risk. Illness, accidents, the acts of others, and even death are all potential hazards each of us faces in life. Your business will face possible calamities also. Floods, fire, and the acts of guests, employees, and others can put your business at risk. To guard against the financial loss these risks can bring, both individuals and businesses need to **insure** themselves. In its simplest form, insurance involves the spreading of risk from one person or business to a larger group.

Hospitality businesses seek **insurance**, or protection from risk, for two basic reasons. First, because doing so makes good financial sense. Second, some types of insurance coverage are required either by law (such as workers' compensation) or by lenders to protect their collateral. Consider, for example, the restaurateur who owns a business that provides her with a salary of $100,000 per year. The restaurant is her sole source of income. If the restaurant were to burn down, she would lose this source of income. To protect her business and her income, she would want to buy a fire insurance policy that would pay to completely replace the restaurant in the event of a fire, provided that the cost of the insurance was reasonable. Not buying the insurance would put this restaurateur and her family at great financial risk. Buying the insurance would provide the restaurateur with both financial security in the event of an accidental fire and the peace of mind that such security brings.

To be protected from risk does not mean that hazardous events will not occur. Insurance does mean, however, that the person with insurance is provided some protection against the financial loss he or she may incur as a result of a hazardous event.

The insurance industry is built on four fundamental premises:

1. The type of hazard the insurance company is underwriting must be faced by a large enough number of individuals or businesses so that statisticians can use actuarial (**actuary**) methods to predict the average frequency of loss involved in the risk.
2. The monetary value of the loss must be calculable against an accepted standard. For example, if a hotel seeks coverage for broken windows

LEGALESE

Insure (insurance): To protect from risk.

Actuary: A mathematician or statistician who computes insurance risks and establishes premium rates.

CHAPTER OUTLINE

15.1. Introduction to Insurance

15.2. Types of Coverage

15.3. Selecting an Insurance Carrier

15.4. Selecting the Insurance Policy

15.5. Policy Analysis

IN THIS CHAPTER, YOU WILL LEARN

1. To understand the value of insurance in protecting a business from financial loss.
2. To become familiar with the different types of insurance required of hospitality operations.
3. To understand the role of workers' compensation and the requirements of an employer.
4. To critically evaluate the financial rating of an insurance company and other information to help you select an insurance carrier.
5. To distinguish between the terms "primary" and "umbrella" insurance coverage and determine appropriate amounts of coverage.
6. To analyze an insurance policy and determine what types of claims will be covered and what types of claims will not be covered.

caused by vandals, it must be possible for the **insurer** to fairly determine the cost of replacing such a window.

3. The **premiums** (fees) for the insurance must be low enough to attract those who seek to be **insured** but high enough to support the number of losses that will be incurred by the insurer.
4. The risk must not have the possibility of occurring so frequently during any given time period that the insurer cannot pay all legitimate claims. Insurance companies spend millions of dollars annually researching industries to determine the risk factor of providing insurance for a specific market, such as hospitality. Obviously, the fewer number of casualty losses, workers injured, lawsuits, and so on, the lower is the risk that the insurance company may have to pay out money on a claim. Logically, then, the safer the operation, and the safer the industry as a whole, the lower the cost of insurance.

The insurance contract between an insurer and an insured is called a **policy**. There are various policy types, but they can be conveniently grouped into three categories:

1. Life insurance
2. Health insurance
3. Property-casualty insurance (often referred to as "property-liability")

Life insurance policies generally are written to pay a certain amount of money at the time of the insured's death or to pay the insured an **annuity** when the insured reaches a specified age. Health insurance is generally created to pay for hospital and doctor bills, as well as annuity payments for those who are disabled. In the hospitality industry, it would be common for you, as a manager, to receive some level of both life and health insurance as part of your compensation package.

Property-liability insurance provides financial protection (**indemnification**) in the event of occurrences such as floods, fires, lawsuits, and automobile accidents. As a manager, it is important to know the types of insurance policies that make sense for your operation and how to evaluate the quality of the companies that offer insurance as well as the merits of the actual policies.

It is also important to remember that insurance companies, like hospitality companies, are in business to make a profit. Profits in the insurance industry are the result of increasing premium amounts, increased return from the investment of premiums, and the reduction of costs, including the payment of insurance **claims**. Because this is true, insurers are very careful to pay only those claims that are proven to be legitimate and within the terms of the insurance policy.

Because insurance protects against risk at an agreed-upon price, it is critical that you as a hospitality manager know:

- The risks you are insuring against
- The amount of coverage you will receive
- Any exceptions to your coverage that are written into your policy
- How much the insurance will cost
- The likelihood that the insurance company is financially sound enough to pay if it becomes necessary

To purchase insurance, a potential buyer must demonstrate that he or she has an insurable interest in the premises to be insured. That is, he or she must demonstrate that a loss would, in fact, affect him or her in a material way. This insurance concept is fundamental and helps protect against possible intentional acts of destruction or fraud. In addition, an insured must honestly divulge information needed by the insurer to enable it to establish appropriate premium rates.

As with any purchase, careful comparison shopping before selecting insurance is a very good idea. Because insurance is a contract between the insurer and the insured, it is also a good idea not only to read the contract carefully yourself but also to have an expert evaluate it for you. Insurance contracts can be complicated, and the review by a competent expert will certainly be valuable. As with any type of contract, it is critical that the insurance policies be kept in a safe, secure location.

Purchasing insurance is often complex and can be confusing. You may find it easier if you think of buying insurance as a three-step process:

1. Determine the type of insurance coverage you need. In this step, you are looking at various aspects of your operation and deciding which risks to protect against. This is where an industry expert, not necessarily someone who wants to sell you an insurance policy, is great to have on your team.
2. Determine the ideal monetary amount of insurance coverage and the type of policy you will require. Remember, as the dollar value of your coverage increases, so will the premiums you have to pay.

LEGALESE

Insurer: The entity that provides insurance.

Premium: The amount paid for insurance coverage; it can be paid in one lump sum or over time, such as monthly.

Insured: The individual or business that purchases insurance against a risk.

Policy (insurance): The contract for insurance agreed upon by the insurer and insured.

Annuity: Fixed payments, made on a regular basis, for an agreed-upon period of time or until the death of the recipient.

Indemnification: To make one whole; to reimburse for a loss already incurred.

Claim: Demand for money, property, or repairs to property.

Analyze the Situation 15.1

Samuel Renko, president of Senframe Hotel Management Company, authorized the purchase of a $2 million fidelity insurance policy, the purpose of which was to protect the company in the event of employee theft or fraud. In discussing the purchase with the insurance agent, Jana Foster, Mr. Renko assured Ms. Foster that all hotel controllers were subject to a thorough background check before they were hired. As a specific condition of the insurance policy, background checks on controller candidates were required prior to employment.

The insurance policy was purchased and went into effect on January 1, 2011. On June 1, 2011, the Senframe Hotel Management Company took over the management and operation of the Roosevelt Hotel, a 300-room property in a resort area. As part of the operating agreement with the Roosevelt Hotel's owners, the hotel's controller and its director of sales were retained by Senframe. On December 20, 2011, Senframe management discovered that the Roosevelt Hotel's controller had been creating and submitting false invoices. The invoice payments were deposited in a bank account he had established for himself five years earlier. Total losses for the five-year period that the falsification occurred were over $500,000.

The controller resigned, but the hotel owners sued Senframe for the portion of misappropriated fund ($70,000) taken during the period the hotel was under Senframe's management. Ms. Foster maintained that her insurance company was not liable to indemnify Senframe, because the controller had not been subjected to a background check as Mr. Renko had promised. Mr. Renko countered that the controller, although not background checked, had no criminal record of any kind, and thus a background check would not have prevented the hotel from hiring the controller.

1. Must Ms. Foster's company defend Senframe in the litigation brought by the hotel's ownership?
2. If you were on a jury, would you hold Senframe responsible for the employee theft?
3. Regardless of the outcome of this situation, what changes in operational procedure should be implemented by Mr. Renko and the Senframe Hotel Management Company?

3. Select a specific insurance company from which you will buy your policy.

The next three sections of this chapter examine each of these steps in detail and offer some guidelines for helping you determine the appropriate type of insurance coverage.

15.2 Types of Coverage

Because the hospitality industry is made up of a variety of operations in different locations, the insurance needs of restaurants and hotels will vary considerably. A hospitality establishment's insurance policies will reflect the unique characteristics of the type of business being operated and the location in which it does business. For example, a restaurant on the U.S. Gulf Coast may well feel that hurricane insurance makes sense whereas the same type of operation in South Dakota would not. Similarly, the resort that offers overnight camping excursions for families may desire insurance against animal attacks whereas the yogurt store in a shopping mall would be hard pressed to justify purchasing such a policy.

Insurance companies offer a wide variety of products designed to meet the needs of their customers. Because this is true, hospitality managers must be very careful to make sure that they select the proper insurance coverage for their specific situation. With too much coverage or with coverage that is not necessary, operational profits are reduced because premium payments are unnecessarily high. With no insurance, or too little insurance of the right type, however, the economic survival of the hospitality operation and its members may be at risk.

Many states have laws requiring businesses to carry certain types of insurance, at specified minimum amounts, in order to conduct business within the state. In addition, when hospitality firms lease space in buildings, the lease agreement may also require them to carry minimum amounts of insurance.

Although the specific types and amounts of insurance needed for any given hospitality operation will vary, the following types of insurance coverage are common.

Property-Casualty/Business Interruption

Just as its name indicates, property-casualty insurance is purchased to protect against the loss of property. These losses include damages incurred due to a fire, flood, or storm. Some insurance companies will classify threats to property in different ways, but in all cases, property-casualty insurance protects property and its contents. The determination of which risks to insure against must be made on the basis of each hospitality operation's special circumstances.

Consider the case of Ralph Escobar. He operates a seafood restaurant that is housed on a ship that is permanently docked on one of the Great Lakes. Mr. Escobar, unlike many other restaurateurs, must insure his operation against a variety of water-related events that could destroy his business. These include accidentally being hit by another boat, high- or low-water damage, and seasonal storms that could damage his floating restaurant. Mr. Escobar must select casualty insurance that will cover these incidents and reimburse him for the cost of repairs and any potential loss of business.

Property-casualty insurance, in its many forms, is the most common type of business insurance purchased. It may be purchased in policies covering losses as small as a few hundred dollars or as large as many millions of dollars.

Business interruption insurance coverage is as essential as property-casualty coverage. Many small businesses fail to consider just how extensive damages would affect their businesses. If your business must close down for a period of time due to renovation after a fire or other casualty, you must prepare for the down time the business is not fully opened. Business interruption coverage will compensate you for lost income due to the disaster-related damage. The coverage will provide financial support in an amount based on the financial records. Operating expenses such as electricity, security, debt service, and taxes will continue even though your business activities have stopped. You will also want to continue paying your managers and staff a salary so as to not lose them to a competitor during your down time. Insurance consultants recommend a period of 90 days coverage of business interruption insurance. Even though your business may be up and running in 30 or 60 days, you will need the financial help until such time as your business can ramp up to the predisaster revenues it enjoyed before the catastrophic event.

Liability

General liability insurance is selected when you wish to protect against injuries to other people resulting from the operation of your own hospitality facility. For example, Diane Sulayman operates a French fine-dining establishment that serves a variety of items, including flamed desserts. One evening, her server accidentally sloshes flaming alcohol out of a flambé pan and it splashes onto the suit of a diner. The diner is not injured seriously but suffers some minor burns and is quite upset. Should the diner elect to bring a lawsuit against Ms. Sulayman, her general liability insurance would help cover the expenses and potential damages that might be awarded in such a lawsuit.

There are a variety of liability insurance types on the market today. The following are some of the most popular:

- Property damage liability coverage protects against claims resulting from damage to the property of others.
- Personal injury liability coverage protects for such offenses as false arrest, libel, slander, invasion of privacy, and food poisoning.
- Advertising injury liability coverage protects your legal liability for offenses arising out of the advertising of your business's goods and services.

Insurance companies have the right and obligation to defend any lawsuit against their insured customers that seeks damages for bodily injury or property damage even if the allegations in the suit are groundless, false, or fraudulent. The insurance company can also enter into any settlement agreement it deems expedient. It is important to remember, however, that the company is not obligated to pay any claim or judgment or to defend any suit after the applicable limit of the company's liability has been reached or that falls outside the coverage of the policy.

Consider the case of Roger Kuhlman. He owns and operates a hotel in which a guest accidentally discharges a pistol in one of the guestrooms. The shot passes through the wall of the room and injures a guest in the next room. The injured guest sues both Mr. Kuhlman and the guest responsible for the accidental shooting. His insurance company defends his hotel in the lawsuit. In the resulting jury trial, Mr. Kuhlman's hotel is deemed to be partially responsible for the accident and is ordered to pay the victim $3 million. The hotel's insurance policy provides only $1 million of coverage. In this case, Mr. Kuhlman's hotel is responsible for paying the remaining $2 million.

With the increasing monetary value of awards resulting from litigation today, wise hospitality managers are attempting to confirm that they have sufficient liability coverage. This is not an easy task. You must weigh the cost of coverage (the premium payments) versus the risk (possible damages) and assess your ability to absorb or pass on these insurance costs to your customers.

Employee Liability

An employee liability policy is taken when as an owner or manager, you wish to supplement your general liability coverage with additional coverage for any harmful acts your employees may commit in the course of their employment. This type of policy is known as "employment practices liability insurance," or EPLI. Some areas of coverage to be considered include those related to:

Wrongful termination
Workplace harassment
Retaliation
Invasion of privacy
Sexual harassment
Breach of employment contract
Discrimination
Failure to employ or promote
Deprivation of a career opportunity
Negligent evaluation
Employment-related misrepresentation
Defamation
Theft
Mismanagement of employee benefit plans
Wrongful infliction of emotional distress

Dram Shop

Liquor liability, or dram shop, insurance provides coverage for bodily injury or property damage of establishments that sell alcohol that may result from any or all of the following acts:

- Causing or contributing to the intoxication of a person
- Serving alcoholic beverages to a person under the legal drinking age
- Serving alcohol to an intoxicated person
- Violating any statute, ordinance, or regulation relating to the sale, gift, distribution, or use of alcoholic beverages

Serving alcoholic beverages in today's society makes a hospitality manager subject to great risk. Dram shop insurance is truly a necessity in today's legal environment, and states may require it as a condition for granting a liquor license. Some owners or managers may think that coverage is included within the general liability policy; however, some such policies exclude liability coverage for alcohol-related events. All liquor liability policies exclude coverage if the business sells alcohol to an underage drinker who then hurts someone.

Health/Dental/Vision

One of a hospitality manager's greatest costs and one that continues to rise dramatically is that of employee medical insurance. As of 2016, employers with 50 or more full-time equivalent employees are required to provide health coverage to full-time employees or pay a tax penalty. This requirement is commonly referred to as the "employer mandate" under the Affordable Care and Patient Protection Act (ACA), also known as "Obamacare." Those employers with fewer than 50 full-time employees are not subject to the mandate, but if they do provide coverage, they may be eligible for tax credits. Although coverage such as dental and vision insurance is not a requirement under the ACA or other federal law, the degree to which that coverage is offered can have a significant effect on a manager's ability to retain and maintain a quality workforce.

Like all types of insurance, the varieties of coverage available for medical insurance are tremendous. In addition, this is one area of insurance where the cost is generally split, in some manner, between the employer and the employee. Employers can choose from contributing 100 percent of medical insurance premiums for their employees to simply making such coverage available to employees on a voluntary basis.

Employees often depend on such coverage for their families and can maintain that insurance even if they lose their jobs. The Consolidated Omnibus Budget Reconciliation Act (COBRA) passed by the federal government in 1986 requires employers to continue providing health, dental, and optical coverage benefits to employees who have resigned or been terminated and to family members of employees who have lost their health insurance due to death, divorce, or dropping out of school. Such employees are responsible for paying the entire cost of their premiums. COBRA participants may continue their benefits for up to 18 months with possible extensions to a maximum of 36 months following the loss of their insurance.

Workers' Compensation

The Workmen's Compensation Act of 1908 was the first effort to provide injury-related insurance to those workers who were hurt while on the job. This law passed by Congress that covers federal employees, spurred the states to enact similar legislation covering workers in their states. Today, all states require public- and private-sector employers to provide some form of mandatory workers' compensation insurance.

Workers' compensation policies provide payments to workers or their families in the event of an employee's injury or death. Coverage normally includes medical expenses and a significant portion of the wages lost by the injured employee. In more serious cases, lump-sum payments can be made to those workers who have been partially or permanently disabled. In addition, if a worker is killed while on the job, payments may be made to the worker's family. The injury must have happened in the **course and scope** of employment. The courts sometimes have broadly defined course and scope to include commuting to and from the place of employment, during mealtimes, and on or off the work site.

Injured employees are generally prohibited from suing their employer for damages beyond those awarded by workers' compensation. Only in the case of gross negligence or an intentional act will an employer potentially be subject to paying higher damages than those normally imposed by workers' compensation.

It is important to know that some states will designate specific doctors who will examine those employees who appear to have been injured. This is an effort on the part of the state to hold down premium costs and reduce incidents of fraud. It is also important to remember that employers cannot claim the negligence of the worker as a defense for a work-related injury. Usually, only in cases where the worker has been proven to be under the influence of drugs or alcohol at the time of the injury or the injury was fraudulent will an employer be able to mount a legally valid defense against a workers' compensation claim.

In cases when another employee or third party has caused a worker injury or when the employer challenges the legality of a worker's claim for compensation, a hearing is held before the state workers' compensation board. A judge will determine whether the claim has merit and how much compensation the worker is entitled to receive, if any. Both parties have the right to appeal the judge's decision if they choose.

Because some form of workers' compensation is mandatory in every state, the failure on the part of management to provide it is punishable by fines and/or imprisonment. Employers are also required by law to accurately report on-the-job accidents to the state agency overseeing the workers' compensation program. This information is significant because the cost of providing workers' compensation insurance varies based on a

---

LEGALESE

Course and scope: The sum total of all common, job-related employee activities dictated or allowed by the employer.

Analyze the Situation 15.2

Christina Fleischer was 16 years old when she was hired to work as a busser for a private country club. On Sundays, the club operated a popular brunch that served 500 to 1,000 people between the hours of 9:00 A.M. and 3:00 P.M. On Ms. Fleischer's first day of work, her supervisor quickly detailed the job requirements. As part of her job, Ms. Fleischer was to remove the guests' used dishes from the table, take the dishes to a bussing station, and scrape any leftover food from the dishes into a garbage receptacle lined with a plastic trash bag. Periodically, she was to bring the dishes to the kitchen to be washed and take the garbage receptacle to a designated area where she would then remove the plastic trash bag and replace it with an empty one. The filled bags were left in the designated area until they could be taken out to a dumpster by a member of the dish room staff. The garbage receptacles would often be very heavy, and all bussers were instructed to replace the plastic bags in them when they were half-full. Ms. Fleischer's supervisor made a point of mentioning that during her 15-minute training session.

The club was very busy with Sunday morning brunch patrons on Ms. Fleischer's first day of work. Halfway through her shift, she forgot to replace one of the garbage bags until it was nearly full. She placed the garbage bag with the others in the designated location. Later that afternoon, a dish room attendant, while taking out the 20 plastic garbage bags filled from the brunch, attempted to lift the bag that Ms. Fleischer had accidentally overfilled. The dish room attendant seriously injured his back.

The injury was deemed within the scope of his work, so the dish room attendant was awarded a monetary settlement by the workers' compensation board in his state. However, he then threatened to sue the country club, claiming negligence in Ms. Fleischer's training, and stated that this negligence was the direct cause of his accident. He also stated that management had provided workers with garbage receptacles that were too large and thus directly contributed to the accident.

1. Was management negligent?
2. Does the dish room attendant have a viable claim against the club?
3. Do you believe the workers' compensation premiums for the club should be increased because of this incident?
4. What steps might the country club take to avoid paying higher premiums?

specific employer's safety history and the potential risk of injury to employees. For example, a restaurant manager who does not encourage the immediate clean-up of spills in the kitchen and thus experiences a higher than average number of employee injuries due to slips and falls will pay a higher premium than an employer in an identical situation whose internal policies help prevent such accidents. Many state workers' compensation boards use experience ratings, which categorize businesses by the number of injury claims paid to their employees to determine the amount of insurance premiums that will be assessed.

Depending on the state in which they are operating, an employer may provide workers' compensation insurance through a private insurance company, a state agency, or itself. If the state allows a self-insurance option, the security deposit required can be substantial since, under the self-insurance option, an employer might be solely responsible for the payment of large awards in the case of a serious accident.

Data Breach

Hospitality managers may have the mistaken belief that once they comply with the Payment Card Industry Data Security Standard (PCI DSS), as described in Chapter 10, they are protected from liability in the event of a breach of their data system. This reliance creates a false sense of security because hackers are constantly reinventing ways to breach systems. Insurance coverage can be purchased to protect the financial risks associated with someone hacking into an establishment's information technology systems and compromising customer data as well as its own. This type of coverage is also known as "cyber risk" or "data breach" insurance. Figure 15.1 provides more detail about the coverages you may want to include. Sometimes this type of coverage is provided under a professional liability insurance policy also known as "errors and omissions" insurance.

Network security and privacy is an enterprise risk management issue today. Technology and the "internet of things" pervades through any business organization with a myriad of ways a company can be impacted. One risk management tool is to transfer the risk to an insurance product, typically called Network security and privacy or Cyber.

The typical cyber policy has two sections of coverage: Network security – provides coverage for third party financial damage from a breach in your entity's network and Privacy – disclosure of privacy data, whether through a network breach or non-network breach. Included in this portion of the policy is coverage for expenses such as IT forensics, notification expenses, cost of engaging legal advisors, credit monitoring, and crisis management expenses; coverage for fines, penalties and assessments associated with PCI compliance; defense expense coverage for regulatory investigations.

Other coverages may be purchased as part of the cyber policy such as media errors and omissions, cyber extortion, data recovery and restoration, and business income loss. Please note, the purpose of the policy is to protect the balance sheet from the cost of responding to an incident. The onus of loss mitigation, response and remediation still resides with the business.

Limit and retention determination takes into account the industry (which determines exposure – credit cards, social security numbers, confidential business information, passwords, etc.), revenues, countries in which you operate, number of records, and risk appetite.

Provided by Sou Ford, insurance executive who can be reached at youngbrune@gmail.com.

FIGURE 15.1 **Cyber insurance.**

There are basically two types of risks involved in cyber security threats. One is "first-party liability." An example is the breach of a hospitality facility's computers and information systems compromising the data. This type of coverage will generally cover customer notification, crisis management, anti-fraud protection for customers, and cost of cyber extortion. The other type of risk is called "third-party liability" for guests or customers of the hospitality business who find that their data systems had been breached. Third-party liability insurance may cover attorneys' fees, settlement cost, and court-ordered damage if the business is found liable for the security breach.

As in all insurance coverage, the hospitality manager's responsibility is not to assume that a specific coverage exists under another type of coverage but to make sure that the specific coverage has been secured. Franchise businesses under a franchise relationship should also discuss coverage with the franchisor rather than assuming that their business is immune from such risks.

15.3 Selecting an Insurance Carrier

Most insurance companies sell their products through agents rather than directly to the public. Some companies use agents that represent them exclusively, while others use independent agents. These independent agents may represent several insurance companies and can be a real asset in selecting the best policy at the best price. The premium rate, however, is set by the insurance company and generally cannot be changed by the agent.

An insurance agent does not provide insurance. The agent merely represents the insurance company that **underwrites** the actual insurance policy. When you buy an insurance policy, it is critical that you purchase it from a credible insurance company, not just from an agent who is an effective salesperson.

If an insurance company is to protect against risk, it must have the financial capability to pay any and all claims you are held responsible for during the coverage period. The last thing you want is to buy an insurance policy, then relax, believing you have coverage, only to find out after a claim has been filed that your insurance company does not have the assets to pay the claim. It is important to remember that if your insurance company will not, or cannot, pay a claim, you will be held responsible for payment.

Insurance companies are rated based on their financial capability to pay claims. According to analysts, the stronger the rating, the more financially solvent the company is projected to be. Rating categories vary based on the organization doing the rating and generally use either an A1, A, A2, B1, and so on, system, or an AAA, AA, A, BBB, and so on system. Today, it would be difficult to justify purchasing an insurance policy from an underwriter with a rating of less than A2 or AA. It is best to buy from those companies that have achieved a rating of A1 or AAA.

Ratings can be verified by contacting the rating companies directly. A.M. Best and Standard & Poor's are two such companies. Alternatively, you can contact your state's insurance regulatory department. It can also provide you with a list of complaints filed against insurance companies for failure to pay claims in a timely fashion or to act in good faith. This is information you need to know before you buy your policy.

LEGALESE

Underwrite: To assume agreed-upon maximum levels of liability in the event of a loss or damages.

Search the Web 15.1

Log on to **www.insure.com**

1. Click: Additional Resources.
2. Select: Financial Strength Ratings.
3. Click: "What do the ratings mean?" and read the definitions of AAA through B insurance ratings at the bottom of the page.
4. Select: Access Ratings Lookup Tool.
5. Type: The name of your own automobile or life insurance company into the search box.
6. Click: OK to find the rating of your own automobile or life insurance company.
7. Find: Your insurance company's rating.
8. Find: Your insurance company's rank among the insurance companies in your state.

15.4 Selecting the Insurance Policy

Once you have found two or three companies that you feel are financially sound, the next step is to get quotes, or bids, to provide coverage from each of the companies.

Consider the case of Vasal Bakar. Mr. Bakar is seeking to add a dental plan to his employees' health coverage. He selects three companies, all of which are rated AA, and proceeds to request a bid from each. When he asks for dental insurance bids to cover his 240 employees, he gets the following response:

Dental Insurance Quote for Vasal Bakar

Insurance Company	Coverage Cost per Employee
Company One	$45.00/month
Company Two	$43.25/month
Company Three	$17.80/month

While at first glance it might appear that Company Three is offering the best policy price, it will be important to determine whether the level of dental coverage is the same for all three policies. When Mr. Bakar investigated further, he found that in the proposals of the first two companies, annual per employee maximum benefits were $3,000, and that in the case of Company Three, the per employee annual maximum was only $1,000. Under these circumstances, the price for each $1,000 of employee dental insurance provided was actually highest from Company Three. The decision of whether to pay for the higher amounts of coverage and whether the employees would be asked to contribute partial payments, is of course, left to Mr. Bakar.

To understand how much insurance you are actually purchasing for your premium dollar and to realize how much total insurance you have for the period of time covered by the policy, it is critical that you understand the terms used in marketing insurance products.

Tina Shulky, the owner of a bagel franchise, is seeking liability coverage for her business. She selects some potential insurance providers based on their financial ratings and then requests quotes on a **primary policy** with a **per occurrence** amount of $500,000, an **aggregate** of $1 million, and an additional **umbrella** policy of $1 million.

If the policy that Ms. Shulky ultimately selects states that she has $500,000 of coverage per occurrence, it means that for each and every incident that occurs for which Ms. Shulky could be held liable, her insurance company will pay up to $500,000 on her behalf less any **deductible**. If the judgment exceeds that amount, she would be responsible for anything over and above $500,000.

If her insurance policy has the term **aggregate** after the amount, it means that this is the total amount her insurance company will pay for all incidents and damages incurred during the coverage period. Thus, if she had a $500,000 per occurrence policy and $1 million aggregate, two claims of $500,000 would wipe out her total insurance coverage (as would four claims of $250,000).

It's also important to understand how a deductible affects your total insurance costs. The deductible is an amount of money you are responsible for paying on a claim before your insurance company will begin paying for it. If you choose a high deductible, your premium payments will be lower because you are assuming more risk by agreeing to pay a higher share of any claim filed against you. Managers must learn to factor the cost of the deductible into their insurance buying decision and to balance the needs of having a set amount of coverage that will be paid out by their insurance company with the amount of premium payments they are willing to make.

Basic coverage is referred to as "primary coverage." In addition, you can purchase an umbrella, or what is commonly referred to as "excess coverage." Be aware that umbrella coverage ordinarily pays only when and if your primary per occurrence coverage is completely exhausted from a single claim.

To illustrate this point, assume the following scenario: You have a $500,000 per occurrence policy with $500,000 aggregate and a $1 million umbrella, or excess coverage, plan. The policy period runs from January 1, 2012, to December 31, 2012. An accident occurs on January 20, 2012, and the claim is settled for $750,000. The primary coverage will pay the first $500,000 less any deductible you might have. Your umbrella policy will pay the remaining $250,000. However, if you have a subsequent claim from an incident that occurs on February 15, 2012, how much coverage do you have available to pay this claim? The answer is zero. You have depleted your coverage under your primary policy because it has a $500,000 aggregate. Your umbrella policy is not available because it pays only if you have exhausted your primary per occurrence amount on a given claim. If you do not have any primary per occurrence coverage left, the conditions for coverage of your umbrella policy cannot be met unless you are able to pay the first $500,000 out of your pocket. If you find yourself in this situation, you need to buy additional primary coverage.

15.5 Policy Analysis

Analyzing an insurance policy consists of determining both what is and what is not covered. You are responsible for knowing and understanding the types and amounts of coverage that are written into your insurance policy. A policy can be complicated, so no assumptions should be made about its coverage. You must verify that you have coverage. Additionally, be aware that when you purchase insurance, you ordinarily do not immediately receive a copy of the actual policy because it takes some time for the insurance company to put the formal policy together with your unique coverages and exclusions. Instead, you receive a one-page **face sheet**, which generally sets out the types and amounts of coverage; it does not contain detailed information on what is specifically included and excluded from the policy's coverage. The actual policy will contain this information, but usually, you will not receive it until 30 to 60

LEGALESE

Primary policy: The main insurance policy that provides basic coverage.

Per occurrence: The maximum amount that can or will be paid by an insurer in the event of a single claim.

Aggregate: The maximum amount that can or will be paid by an insurer for all claims during a policy period.

Umbrella: Insurance coverage purchased to supplement primary coverage. Sometimes referred to as "excess insurance."

Deductible: The amount of money the insured has to pay before the insurance coverage will begin to pay. Accordingly, the higher the deductible, the less risk to the insurance company, which should equal lower premiums.

Face sheet: A one-page document briefly describing the type and amount of insurance coverage contained in an insurance policy. Sometimes referred to as a "declaration page."

B. Limits of Liability

Regardless of the number of persons or entities insured or included in Part I.D. Covered Persons or Entities, or the number of claimants or Claims made:

1. The maximum liability of the Company for **Damages and Claim Expenses** resulting from each **Claim** first made against the Insured during the **Policy Period** and the Extended reporting Period, if purchased, shall not exceed the amount shown in the Declarations as each Claim:
2. The maximum liability of the Company for all **Damages and Claim Expenses** as a result of all **Claims** first made against the Insured during the **Policy Period** and the Extended Reporting Period, if purchased, shall not exceed the amount shown in the Declarations as Aggregate.

The Company shall not be obligated to pay any **Claim** for **Damages** or defend any **Claim** after the applicable Limit of Liability has been exhausted by payment of judgments, settlements, **Claim Expenses** or any combination thereof. **Claim Expenses** are a part of and not in addition to the applicable Limits of Liability. Payment of **Claim Expenses** by the Company reduces the applicable Limits of Liability.

The inclusion of more than one Insured, or the making of **Claims** by more than one person or organization, docs not increase the company's Limit of Liability. In the event two or more **Claims** arise out of a single negligent act, error or omission, or a scries of related negligent acts, errors or omissions, all such **Claims** shall be treated as a single **Claim.** Whenever made, all such **Claims** shall be considered first made and reported to the Company during the **Policy Period** in which the earliest **Claim** arising out of such negligent act, error or omission was first made and reported to the Company, and all such **Claims** shall be subject to the same Limit of Liability.

FIGURE 15.2 **Insurance policy language.**

days from the date of purchase. In other words, the face sheet contains the large print, or overview, while the actual policy, which you will not have until after you buy, contains the fine print. A thorough analysis of the fine print is important so that you know exactly what coverage is in place.

Figure 15.2 shows a segment of language taken from an actual insurance policy. It is important to remember that, despite the difficulty of reading documents such as this, the courts will hold an insured party responsible for reading and understanding his or her policy. If you are at all unclear about what your final insurance policy will and will not cover, have your attorney review a sample policy, which can be provided by the insurance company.

Because you will not receive the actual insurance policy until after you purchase the policy, it is imperative that you discuss any unclear issues with the insurance agent before you buy. Ask for written answers to your questions, and continue to request information until you are satisfied with your comprehension of the details. Once the policy arrives, read it and make sure you fully understand:

- The policy's language, and whether it is consistent with your agent's earlier explanations.
- The policy's coverage, **exclusions**, **exceptions**, and clarifying language.

LEGALESE

Exclusions: Liability claims that are not covered in an insurance policy.

Exceptions: Insurance coverage that is normally included in the insurance policy, but that will be excluded if the insured fails to comply with performance terms specifically mentioned in the policy.

Most insurance policies will have both exclusions and exceptions. The insurer will almost always retain the right to exclude certain types of liability claims. If, for instance, a restaurateur has purchased fire insurance but proceeds to intentionally set fire to his or her own restaurant, the insurance company would exclude, or refuse to cover, the cost of replacing the restaurant. Common exclusions include those involving intentional acts and fraud by the insured.

Exceptions are also common in insurance policies, and it is best to be well aware of all that apply. An exception is a statement by the insurer that it will not pay for an otherwise legitimate claim if certain conditions have not been met. For example, the insurance company may require a restaurant to have a valid license to serve food in order to protect that restaurant in the event a guest claims damages resulting from food poisoning. Likewise, a fire insurance policy may require that an operator purchase and install specific types of fire suppression equipment and that it be inspected and approved on a regular basis by a qualified inspector.

In most cases, your insurer will require you to notify the company immediately if you have made a claim or if you believe something has occurred that might lead to litigation. In addition, if an attorney serves you with notification of intent to sue you, you must contact your insurance carrier. Some insurance policies are "claims-made" policies. This term means that the coverage is available only if an actual claim is brought to the attention of the insurance company during the policy period. Most insurance policies, however, cover claims that occur during the policy period, even though they are not brought to the attention of the insurance company until after the coverage period has elapsed. Obviously, the claims made policy is preferable for the hospitality manager.

In spite of the problems and expense involved, not having insurance is not an option; it is a protection needed to operate your businesses with a sense of comfort and peace. You can avoid unpleasant surprises by taking the proper care when selecting insurance. This includes speaking and listening to your colleagues and asking those questions that will make it easier for you to purchase the right coverage in the right amount from the right insurance company.

Most policies are issued for a one-year period. Generally, new policies are issued annually, assuming that there is mutual satisfaction with the coverage, claim responsiveness by the carrier, and an agreement as to the premium (or cost) paid for the amount of insurance.

In Chapter 9, "Your Responsibilities as a Hospitality Operator," we examined how you can take steps to reduce insurance costs through the effective management and training of staff. Prevention of insurance claims, like the prevention of all legal claims, should be the goal of every hospitality manager.

International Snapshot

Hotels Operating Internationally Need to Think Globally

Often the marketing focus of a global hotel chain is to show its properties worldwide. Its selling point is to have a consistent value and quality no matter where you are in the world. Global brand loyalty causes customers in a new city to seek a brand name establishment because it is comfortable and familiar, and they know what to expect. For this reason, it is vitally important that the global hotel chain ensure a consistent approach to global safety, insurance, and claims.

International insurance claims and issues often are smaller than U.S. claims due to several factors, including:

- They are made in a less litigious claims environment.
- They have fewer claims.
- Punitive damages are not awarded.
- Social environment regarding claims.

Because of these factors, pricing for insurance internationally has remained lower than that in the United States—often by more than 50 percent—especially in markets where the majority of clientele is not from the United States. Multinational hotel chains in the United States place more emphasis on claims and risk control. Most hotels, especially those in chains with large properties, are fairly adept at the basics of risk management that will allow them to control claim costs, minimize litigation potential, and maximize safety and risk mitigation. Too often, these concepts do not cover overseas locations on a consistent basis due to cost or internal operational hurdles. However, for a hotel chain, the types of claims that are globally consistent and the fact that the costs are less should not reduce the attention to claims details.

With the hotel industry's primary focus on the expensive insurance market in the United States and its highly litigious culture, the international insurance market and global legal climate continues to change in ways that are critical to a hotel's operation. These developments drive the expense of the program, the success of claims management, and the brand's overall reputation.

The market selection and pricing in the international insurance industry have been a key driver in forcing multinational hotel chains to accept higher risk and to manage that risk in more countries.

Why Is This Happening?

A number of changes in the global insurance market and global legal climate are forcing underwriters and hotels alike to re-examine international insurance. These are:

Market capacity: Hotels have traditionally been loss leaders in the insurance marketplace, which reduces the number of insurance carriers that are willing to look at a hospitality risk to a much smaller footprint. Additionally, the number of carriers that can actually manage large multinational coverage with admitted policies remains small. More international carriers have to lower risk coverage of hospitality businesses. This puts fewer markets in play for a hotel risk and forces pricing and selectivity up.

Legal changes: The world legal climate still remains well behind the litigious environment in the United States. However, there have been significant increases in "claims awareness" in a number of countries. While the systems are not as developed, they are nevertheless making large strides and increasing claims for the hospitality industry. There is also a growth of global case law; that is, legal decisions in other countries, such as Australia, that have been based on California case law. Many hotels without centralized control of claims are now seeing precedent set for a U.S. claim by a settlement made in a foreign country for the same type of claim.

Claims counts: As awareness for the needs to have insurance is increasing internationally, sharp increases in claims around the world are being recorded in the hospitality business. Since underwriting pricing is traditionally much lower in international policies as compared to U.S. policies, increases in them will put an immediate strain on insurer profitability and insured's costs.

Risk changes: The world is becoming riskier as events in Istanbul, France, the United States, and Belgium can prove. Global hotel chains, restaurants, and airports must provide to inspectors their plans and procedures to prevent, mitigate, or stop losses from terrorist, other catastrophic events, and those that cannot be foreseen. The procedures examined relate to basic safety issues, for example, did the insured have a pool or lagoon with animals in it?

Brand risk changes: Many hotels manage brands in regard to licensees, owned locations, nonowned locations, and joint ventures. Often a hotel's global growth has a complex ownership structure. In a global media world, the brand damage in one location spreads globally, often in a viral manner.

Social change: More and more, we are becoming a global economy. People travel the world and expect the legal system to keep up with them. Legislation, such as the European Union's Tour Operators Liability is now globally accepted. Hotels need to protect every location they have in every country of the world.

(continued)

What Should Be Done?

Hospitality companies worldwide need to manage risk more aggressively and more consistently than ever before. Regardless of their ownership structure, all enterprises that operate globally must implement the minimum basics of risk management. Such strategies would involve:

Claims and litigation management: Hotel chains should settle claims worldwide in a consistent manner whether they are self-insured or are covered by insurance policies. A claim settled in Germany should be settled in the same way as a claim in California. This information should be centrally managed by a claims organization that reviews hotels' operational goals and guidelines. Instructions regarding claims worldwide should be customized for a hotel chain even if on a guaranteed cost program.

Program management: Many international programs stand apart from a domestic program and may or may not require participation from all locations. Compliance with local insurance regulations on admitted and nonadmitted insurance should be reviewed each year, and a centralized decision made on where policies should be utilized.

Brand-name protection: All locations bearing a company's name should be required to carry the same amount of insurance or have a documented exception. As more claims are being made internationally, companies need to ensure that their brand is protected in any court in the world. All franchises should be required to carry U.S.-based coverage no matter where they are in the world. Since that is not available in most countries, they should be required to purchase this as part of a program that the parent company sponsors.

Information management: The key to underwriting and managing insurance risk is information flow. Forms for information on property and liability risks should be standardized and collected annually. Although this is a burdensome administrative task, it is critical for managing the insurance. Claims that involve death or permanent disability should be reviewed at least quarterly. Hotels should consider claim causes, not claims dollars, to manage risk outside the United States.

Incident management: Managing safety and claims is the traditional tool to prevent global risk in the hospitality industry. In today's world, using the incident management tools to prepare locations for a loss is invaluable. Some useful tools would include:

Tabletop exercises: Many locations outside of the United States would not have dealt with hundreds of claims, especially catastrophic ones. Creating scenarios allows locations to plan what they would do during a crisis, for example, a terror attack that involves a hotel or its periphery. Experts in global risk management should provide instruction on the different steps to take.

- Global templates: Developing templates and checklists for what to do and how to do it is crucial to ensuring that risk-related behaviors are consistent. Failures happen when the global checklist includes items such as OSHA reports, U.S. legal requirements, and so on. Simple changes, like ensuring the templates, include postal codes vs. ZIP codes, will increase compliance worldwide, because the forms add value.
- CAT response team: Having a global CAT response team to assist a local hotel will be critical. Much of the support may be via phone but will improve communication, data, and response on any major claim.
- On-site visits: Many risk managers cannot travel extensively due to budget and time restrictions, yet site visits are a key tool. Using brokers, underwriters, and other hotel employees as the representative will add to your resources to get to all locations. Arming these people with the data and processes that a risk manager wants to implement globally will put out information faster and improve international relationships.
- Video, smartphone, and other technology: More than ever, positive global relationships are key to an enterprise's success. Using various technologies to create a personal relationship will improve the overall program outcomes tremendously. Instead of reading emails, asking for a picture from a smartphone on an item being discussed might create better and faster answers.

Insurance programs should help a hotel manage its risk: Historically, most international hotels have used insurance as a reason not to manage their risk because it did not cost them to have claims. As the changes evolve, a hotel chain must be a step ahead of its insurance carrier to allow it to control its own insurance destiny.

Provided by *Elizabeth F. Demaret, EVP International Development, Sedgwick Claims Management Services, Inc.*

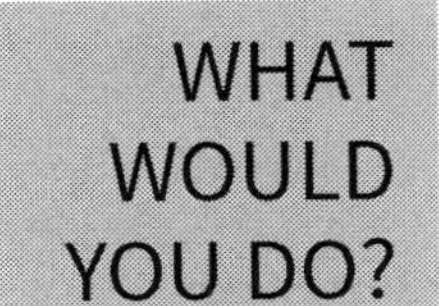

Assume that you are an insurance agent with the Arizona Business Insurance Company (ABIC), which specializes in the hospitality industry. You sell ABIC products exclusively. Your company, which is rated AA, offers insurance that covers a variety of risks, including workers' compensation.

You are approached by Ted Betz, the operational vice president of J-Town Smokies, a chain of pit barbeque restaurants. Mr. Betz would like to purchase workers' compensation insurance from your company because he will be opening five stores in the Southwest in the coming year. A review of his application and claim history indicates that J-Town Smokies has experienced a rather large number of worker injuries in its four years of existence. In fact, the rate of worker injury per employee hour worked is nearly twice that of the restaurant industry average. Further investigation indicates that most of these injuries resulted from cutting meat prior to or after the barbeque process.

	Employee Injuries in per Thousands	Accident Rate per Thousand This Year	Accident Rate per Thousand Last Year
Meat-packing plants	147.2	36.6	30.3
Ship building and repair	102.5	32.7	27.4
Steel foundries	26.6	26.4	26.4
Mobile home construction	68.0	24.3	26.2
Automotive stamping	117.7	23.8	23.2
Restaurants	250.0	16.1	16.6

A review of the U.S. Department of Labor statistics reveals the following highest injury rate industries for this year and last.

1. What type of information would you want to see from Mr. Betz before you offer to sell him a workers' compensation policy from your company?
2. Do you believe Mr. Betz's restaurants should pay the same amount for workers' compensation coverage as other restaurants, or should he be charged rates consistent with those in the meat-packing industry?

WHAT DID YOU LEARN IN THIS CHAPTER?

Insurance is a necessary and valuable tool to help protect a business and its owners from financial loss. There are many different types of insurance coverage, including property/casualty, liability, health/life, and that for injuries to workers. Not all insurance companies are the same, so an owner/operator should research a company's reputation, claims-paying record, and financial strength prior to purchasing the needed coverage for the business. A thorough understanding of the terms used in the insurance industry—such as "primary, umbrella, exclusions," and "exceptions"—is crucial for an owner/operator to make informed decisions about coverage and pricing.

Glossary

Abandoned property Personal property that has been deliberately put aside by the rightful owner with no intention of ever returning for it.

Acceptance Unconditional agreement to the precise terms and conditions of an offer.

Actuary A mathematician or statistician who computes insurance risks and establishes premium rates.

Adhesion contract A contract whose terms were not truly negotiated or bargained and, as a result, may be so one-sided in favor of the stronger party so that the contract is often deemed unenforceable by the courts.

Affirmative action A federally mandated requirement that employers who meet certain criteria must actively seek to fairly employ recognized classes of workers. (Some state and local legislatures have also enacted affirmative action requirements.)

Agent A person authorized to act for or to represent another, usually referred to as the principal.

Aggregate The maximum amount that can or will be paid by an insurer for all claims during a policy period.

Americans with Disabilities Act Federal legislation (law) that protects the rights of people with disabilities so that they may be treated fairly in the workplace and have access to places of public accommodation, such as hotels, restaurants, and airplanes.

Amusement park An entertainment facility featuring rides, games, food, and sometimes shows. Theme parks have rides, attractions, shows, and buildings that revolve around a central theme or group of themes. Examples include the Disney- and Universal Studios-owned amusement parks.

Annuity Fixed payments, made on a regular basis, for an agreed-upon period of time or until the death of the recipient.

Appeal A written request to a higher court to modify or reverse the decision of a lower-level court.

Arbitration A process in which an agreed-on, independent, neutral third party (the arbitrator) renders a resolution to a dispute. The decision of the arbitrator is known as the "award."

Attorney Any person trained and legally authorized to act on behalf of others in matters of the law.

Attrition Reduction in the number of projected participants or attendees.

At-will employment An employment relationship whereby employers have a right to hire any employee, whenever they choose, and to dismiss an employee for or without cause, at any time, so long as the employee's civil rights are not violated; the employee also has the right to work for the employer or not, or to terminate the relationship at any time.

Bailee A person or entity that receives and holds property in a bailment arrangement.

Bailment The delivery of an item of property for some purpose with the expressed or implied understanding that the person receiving it shall return it in the same or similar condition in which it was received, when the purpose has been completed. The property involved relates to coat checks, valet parking, safety deposit boxes, laundry, luggage storage, and delivery.

Bailor A person or entity that gives property to another in a bailment arrangement.

Bill of sale A document noting that personal property is transferred from a seller to a buyer.

Blood alcohol concentration (BAC) A measurement, expressed in a percentage, of the concentration level of alcohol in the bloodstream. Also known as "blood alcohol content" or "blood alcohol level" (BAL).

Bona fide occupational qualification A job qualification established in good faith and fairness that is necessary to safely or adequately perform the job.

Bond(ing) An insurance agreement in which the insurer guarantees payment to an employer in the event of financial loss caused by the actions of a specific employee.

Breach of contract Failure to keep the promises or agreements of a contract.

Capital improvement The purchase or upgrade of real or personal property that results in an increased depreciable asset base.

Caveat emptor A Latin phrase meaning "let the buyer beware." The phrase implies that the burden of determining the relative quality and price of a product falls on the buyer, not the seller.

Chattel Personal property, movable or immovable, that is not considered real property.

Civil law The body of law (usually in the form of codes or statutes) created by governmental entities that are concerned with private rights and remedies, as opposed to criminal matters.

Claim Demand for money, property, or repairs to property.

Class action lawsuit A lawsuit filed by one or more people on behalf of themselves and a larger group of people who were similarly affected by an event.

Clause (contract) A distinct contract provision or stipulation.

Collateral Property that is pledged to secure the repayment of a debt.

Collective bargaining agreement (CBA) A formal contract between an employer and a group of employees that establishes the rights and responsibilities of both parties in their employment relationship.

Commercial lease A lease that applies to business property.

Common carrier A company or individual that is in the regular business of transporting people and/or freight for a fee. Examples include airlines, cruise lines, trains, and buses.

Common law Laws derived from the historical customs and usage of a society and the decisions by courts when interpreting those customs and usages.

Comparative negligence Shared responsibility for the harm that results from negligence comparing the degree of negligence by the defendant with that of the plaintiff. Also known as *comparative fault*.

Compensatory damages Monetary amount awarded to restore an injured party to the position he or she was in prior to the injury (e.g., medical expenses, lost wages); also referred to as *actual damages*.

Condominium A multiple-unit complex (i.e., hotel, apartment house, office building), the units of which are individually owned with each owner receiving a recordable deed to the individual unit purchased, including the right to sell that unit and sharing in joint ownership of all common grounds, hallways, and on-site facilities.

Condominium homeowners' association (CHOA) A group of condo owners elected by all of the condo owners in a project to interpret, develop, and implement the policies and procedures required to effectively manage their condominium complex.

Conference services contract An agreement that details the space, products, and services to be provided to a group before, during, and after its meeting.

Confirmed reservation A contract to provide a reservation in which the provider guarantees the guest's reservation will be honored until a mutually agreeable time. A confirmed reservation may be either guaranteed or nonguaranteed.

Consideration The payment/value exchanged for the promise(s) contained in a contract.

Contingency fee A method of paying for a civil attorney's services as a percentage of any money awarded as a settlement in the case. Typically, these fees range from 20 to 40 percent of the total amount awarded.

Contract An agreement or promise made between two or more parties that the courts will enforce.

Contributory negligence Negligent conduct by the complaining party (plaintiff) that contributes to the cause of his or her injuries.

Copyright The legal and exclusive right to copy or reproduce intellectual property.

Copyright owner A person or entity that legally holds a right to intellectual property under the copyright laws.

Corporation A group of individuals granted a charter, legally recognizing them as a separate entity with rights and liabilities distinct from those of its individual owners.

Counteroffer Conditional agreement to the terms and conditions of an offer that includes a change to those terms, creating a new offer.

Course and scope The sum total of all common, job-related employee activities dictated or allowed by the employer.

Crisis An occurrence that holds the potential to jeopardize the health of individuals and or the business.

Cut-off date The date on which any rooms contracted, and thus held for sale, but not yet picked up (reserved) by the group are returned to the hotel's general rooms' inventory.

Damages Losses or costs incurred due to another's wrongful act or omission.

Deductible The amount of money the insured has to pay before the insurance coverage will begin to pay. Accordingly, the higher the deductible, the less risk to the insurance company, which should equal lower premiums.

Deed A written legal document for the transfer of land or other real property from one person to another.

Deed of trust Used in some states instead of a mortgage. A deed of trust places legal title to a real property in the hands of a trustee until the debtor has completed paying for the property. Some states use names such as trust deed or deed to secure debt for securing a loan.

Defamation False statements that cause someone to be held in contempt, lowered in the estimation of the community, or to lose employment status or earnings or otherwise suffer a damaged reputation.

Defendant The person or entity against which litigation is initiated, sometimes referred to as the respondent.

Demand letter Official notification, typically delivered to a defendant via registered or certified mail usually in advance of litigation that details the plaintiff's cause for impending litigation to seek a settlement between the parties.

Depositions Oral answers, given under oath, to questions asked during the discovery phase of a lawsuit. Depositions are recorded by a certified court reporter and/or by videotape.

Depreciation The decrease in value of a piece of property due to age and/or normal wear and tear.

Depressant A substance that lowers the rate of vital body activities.

Detained property Personal property held by a bailee until lawful payment is made by the bailor.

Disclosure To reveal fully and honestly.

Dividends A portion of profits received by a shareholder, usually in relation to his or her ownership (shares) of a corporation.

Dram shop A name given to a variety of state laws establishing a liquor licensee's third-party liability.

Dram shop acts Legislation passed in a variety of forms and in many states that imposes liability for the acts of others on those who serve alcohol negligently, recklessly, or illegally.

Duty of care A legal obligation that requires a particular standard of conduct.

Emergency plan A procedure or series of procedures to be implemented in response to a crisis.

Employee An individual who is hired to provide services to an employer in exchange for wages or a salary.

Employee evaluation A review of an employee's performance, including strengths and shortcomings; typically completed by the employee's direct supervisor.

Employee manual A document written to detail the policies, benefits, and employment practices of an employer.

Employer An individual or entity that pays wages or a salary in exchange for a worker's services.

Employment agreement The terms of the employment relationship between an employer and employee that specifies the rights and obligations of each party to the agreement.

Enforceable contract A contract recognized as valid by the courts and subject to the court's ability to compel compliance with its terms.

Ethics Choices of proper conduct made by an individual in his or her relationships with others.

Eviction The procedure that a lessor uses to remove a lessee from physical possession of leased real property, usually for violation of a significant lease provision, such as nonpayment of rent.

Exceptions Insurance coverage that is normally included in the insurance policy, but that will be excluded if the insured fails to comply with performance terms specifically mentioned in the policy.

Exclusions Liability claims that are not covered in an insurance policy.

Exculpatory clause (or contract) A contract, or a clause in a contract, that releases one of the parties from liability for his or her wrongdoings.

Express contract A contract in which the components of the agreement are explicitly stated, either orally or in writing, as opposed to an implied contract.

Face sheet A one-page document briefly describing the type and amount of insurance coverage contained in an insurance policy. Sometimes referred to as a "declaration page".

Fiduciary A relationship based on trust and the responsibility to act in the best interest of another when performing tasks.

Fiduciary responsibility The requirement that agents act in the best interest of their principals.

Financing statement A formal notice of a lien being held on personal property required under the Uniform Commercial Code in most cases. Also called a UCC-1 because of its form number in the UCC.

Fixture An article that was once a chattel but that has become a part of the real property because the article is permanently attached to the soil or to something attached to the soil.

Foodborne illness Sickness or harm caused by the consumption of unsafe foods or beverages.

Force majeure Greater force; a natural or human-induced disaster through no fault of the parties to the contract that causes a contract to not be performed.

Foreseeability The ability of a reasonable, prudent person to know or reasonably anticipate that harm, damage, or injury would occur or was likely to occur as a result of an action or omission.

Forum (venue) selection clause A statement in a contract identifying the agreed-on tribunal for resolving legal disputes related to the contract's terms.

Fractional ownership A purchase arrangement in which a condominium owner purchases the use of his or her unit for a portion (fraction) of a year. The fraction may be defined in terms of the number of days per year (e.g., 30, 60) or very specific days and/or months (e.g., January 1 through March 31). Individual units purchased under such an arrangement are commonly known as fractionals.

Franchise A contract between a parent company (franchisor) and an operating company (franchisee) to allow the franchisee to run a business with the brand name of the parent company, as long as the terms of the contract concerning methods of operation are followed.

Franchise agreement A special hospitality contract that details the responsibilities of both parties (franchisor and franchisee) involved in the operation of a franchise.

Franchisee The person or business that has purchased and/or received a franchise.

Franchisor The person or business that has sold and/or granted a franchise.

Gaming Legalized gambling.

Garnish A court-ordered method of debt collection in which a portion of a person's salary is paid to a creditor.

General (or managing) partner The entity in a limited partnership relationship who makes the management decisions and can be held responsible for all debts and legal claims against the business.

General partnership A business organization in which two or more owners agree to share the profits of the business but are also jointly and severally liable for its debts.

Global distribution system (GDS) An interconnected computer system that connects travel professionals worldwide to those companies selling travel services.

Gratuitous bailment One in which there is no payment (consideration) in exchange for the promise to hold the property.

Gross negligence The reckless or willful failure of an individual or an organization to use even the slightest amount of reasonable care.

Guaranteed reservation A contract to provide a confirmed reservation in which the provider guarantees the guest's reservation will be honored regardless of time of arrival but stating that the guest will be charged if he or she no-shows the reservation. Prepayment or payment authorization is required.

Guest A customer who lawfully utilizes a facility's food, beverage, lodging, or entertainment services.

Hospitality law Those laws that relate to the industry involved with the provision of food, lodging, travel, meetings, events and entertainment services to its guests, employees, vendors and clients.

Implied warranty An unwritten expectation that a product purchased is free of defects.

Improvements An addition to real estate that ordinarily enhances its value.

Indemnification To make one whole; to reimburse for a loss already incurred.

Independent contractor A person or entity that contracts with another to perform a particular task but whose work is not directed or controlled by the party retaining the person to do the task.

Infra hospitium A Latin term meaning "within the hotel."

In-house dispute resolution A program funded by employers that encourages the equitable settlement of an employee's claim of unfair employment, prior to or without resorting to litigation.

Insure (insurance) To protect from risk.

Insured The individual or business that purchases insurance against a risk.

Insurer The entity that provides insurance.

Intangible property Personal property that cannot be held or touched. Examples include patent rights, copyrights, and concept rights.

Intellectual property Personal property that has been created through the intellectual efforts of its original owner.

Intentional act A willful action undertaken with or without full understanding of its consequences.

Interdiction program An arrangement whereby citizens contact police to report suspected criminal activity before a crime is committed.

International travel law The ordinances, rules, treaties, and agreements used to regulate the international travel industry.

Interrogatories Questions that require written answers, given under oath, asked during the discovery phase of a lawsuit.

Interstate commerce Commercial trading or the transportation of persons or property between or among states.

Intoxication A condition in which an individual's BAC reaches legally established levels. These levels are not uniform across the United States. An intoxicated person may not sell or purchase alcohol, nor operate a motor vehicle.

Invitee An individual who is on a property at the expressed or implied consent of the owner.

Job description A written listing of a specific job's basic responsibilities and reporting relationships.

Job qualifications The knowledge or skill(s) required to perform the responsibilities and tasks listed in a job description.

Jurisdiction The authority given by law or treaty to a court to try cases and make decisions about legal matters within a particular geographic area and/or over certain types of cases.

Kickback A secret rebate of part of a purchase price given by the seller to the buyer in exchange for the buyer's influence in the purchasing decision.

Landlord The lessor in a real property lease.

Law The rules of conduct and responsibility established and enforced by a society.

Lease A contract that establishes the rights and obligations of each party with respect to property owned by one entity but occupied or used by another.

Lessee The entity that occupies or uses the property covered in a lease.

Lessor The entity that owns the property covered in a lease.

Liable To be legally responsible or obligated.

License Legal permission to do a certain thing or operate in a certain way.

Licensee One who is granted a license.

Licensing agreement A legal document that details the specifics of a license.

Licensor One who grants a license.

Lien A claim against property that gives the creditor (lien holder) the right to repossess and/or sell that property if the debtor does not repay his or her debt in a timely manner.

Limited liability company (LLC) A type of business organization that protects the owners from liability for debts incurred by the business without the need for some of the formal incorporation requirements. The federal government does not tax the profits of LLCs; however, some states do, but others do not.

Limited partner The entity in a limited partnership relationship who is liable only to the extent of his or her investment. Limited partners have no right to manage the partnership.

Limited partnership (LP) A business organization with two classes of owners. The limited partner invests in the business but may not exercise control over its operation, in return for protection from liability. The general or managing partner assumes full control of the business operation and can also be held liable for any debts the operation incurs.

Liquor license A permit issued by a state that allows for the sale and/or service of alcoholic beverages. The entity holding the license is known as the licensee.

Litigation The act of initiating and carrying on a lawsuit, often used to refer to the lawsuit itself.

Lost property Personal property that has been inadvertently put aside and then forgotten by the rightful owner.

Management agreement The legal agreement that defines the responsibilities of a business owner and the management company chosen to operate the owner's business. Also known as a *management contract*.

Management company An entity that, for a fee, assumes responsibility for the day-to-day operation of a business.

Management contract The legal agreement that defines the responsibilities of a business owner and the management company chosen to operate the owner's business.

Maritime law Also called "admiralty law" or "the law of admiralty," the laws, regulations, international agreements, and treaties that govern activities in navigable waters.

Master bill A single folio (bill) established for a group that includes specifically agreed-on group charges. Sometimes called a "master folio," "group folio," or "group bill."

Mediation A process in which an appointed, neutral third party (the mediator) assists those involved in a dispute to resolve their differences. The result of mediation, when successful, is known as the "settlement."

Medical Tourism The travel by patients who are residents of one country or region to another country or region for the purpose of obtaining health care benefits and general medical treatments.

Meeting planners A group of professionals that plan and organize meetings and events for their employers and clients.

Merchantable Suitable for buying and selling.

Minimum wage The lowest amount of wages that an employee covered by the FLSA or state law may be paid by his or her employer.

Mislaid property Personal property that has been put aside on purpose but then has been forgotten by the rightful owner.

Mortgage The pledging of real property by a debtor to a creditor to secure payment of a debt incurred to purchase the property.

Negligence per se Violation of a rule of law by the operator; such violation of a rule of law is considered to be so far outside the scope of reasonable behavior that the violator is assumed to be negligent.

Negligent (negligence) The failure to use reasonable care.

Negligent hiring Failure on the part of an employer to exercise reasonable care in the selection of employees.

Negligent retention Failure to terminate an employee after the employer becomes aware that an employee is a danger or threat to others and is unsuitable for the job.

Nondisturbance clause A clause in a contract that stipulates that leases or other ownership investments in the property will be allowed to continue uninterrupted in the event of a default or insolvency by the landlord/seller.

Nonguaranteed reservation A contract to provide a confirmed reservation where no prepayment or authorization is required.

Off the record An oral agreement between a reporter and an interviewee wherein the reporter promises not to quote the interviewee's comments for publication.

Offer A proposal to perform an act or to pay an amount that, if accepted, constitutes a legally valid contract.

Ombudsperson A company official appointed to investigate and resolve worker complaints.

Operating agreement A contract that details the areas of responsibilities of the owner of a business and the entity selected by the owner to operate the business. Also referred to as a "management contract."

Operating structure The relationship between a business's ownership and its management.

Organizational structure The legal entity that owns a business.

Overstay A guest who refuses to vacate his or her room when he or she has exceeded the number of nights originally agreed to at check-in; also known as a "hangover."

Owner–operator A type of operating structure in which the owners of a business are directly responsible for its day-to-day operation. Also known, in some cases, as an "independent."

Patent A grant issued by a governmental entity ensuring an inventor the right to exclusive production and sale of his or her invention for a fixed period of time.

Perfect a lien To make a public record of a lien, or to take possession of the collateral.

Per occurrence The maximum amount that can or will be paid by an insurer in the event of a single claim.

Personal injury Damage or harm inflicted upon the body, mind, or emotions.

Personal property Tangible and intangible items that are not real property.

Plaintiff The person or entity that initiates litigation against another, sometimes referred to as the claimant, petitioner, or applicant.

Policy (insurance) The contract for insurance agreed upon by the insurer and insured.

Post-traumatic stress disorder (PTSD) A severe reaction to an event that threatened an individual's physical or emotional health.

Premium The amount paid for insurance coverage; it can be paid in one lump sum or over time, such as monthly.

Press release An announcement made by an organization or individual distributed for use by the media.

Primary policy The main insurance policy that provides basic coverage.

Principal Employer, the person hiring and directing employees (agents) to perform his, her, or its business.

Progressive discipline An employee development process that provides increasingly severe consequences for continued violation of workplace rules.

Proximate cause The event or activity that directly contributes to (causes) an injury or harm.

Public accommodation A facility that provides entertainment, rooms, space, or seating for the use and benefit of the general public.

Public domain Property that is owned by all citizens, not an individual.

Punitive damages A monetary amount used as punishment and to deter the same wrongful act in the future by the defendant and others.

Quid pro quo Latin term for "giving one thing in return or exchange for another."

Quitclaim deed A deed that conveys only the rights that the grantor has, if any. This type of deed transfers the owner's interest to a buyer but does not guarantee that there are no other claims against the property or that the property is indeed legally owned by the seller.

Real estate Land, including soil and water, buildings, trees, crops, improvements, and the rights to the air above, and the minerals below, the land.

Real property Land and all the things that are permanently attached to it.

Reasonable care The degree of care that a reasonably prudent person would use in a similar situation.

REIT Short for "real estate investment trust," a very special form of business structure in which the owners of a business are generally prohibited from operating it.

Respondeat superior Literally; "let the master respond," a legal theory that holds the employer (master) responsible for the acts of the employee.

Right of first refusal A clause in a contractual agreement between two parties in a business relationship in which one party, upon termination of the business relationship, can exercise the right to buy the interest of the other party before those rights can be offered for sale to another.

S corporation A type of business entity that offers liability protection to its owners and is exempt from corporate taxation on its profits. Some restrictions limit the circumstances under which an S corporation can be formed.

Safety programs Those procedures and activities designed to ensure the physical protection and good health of guests and employees.

Security agreement A contract between a lender and borrower that states that the lender can repossess the personal property the borrower has offered as collateral if the loan is not paid as agreed.

Security interest A legal ownership right to property.

Segregate To separate a group or individual on any basis, but especially by race, color, religion, or national origin.

Service charge An amount added to a guest's bill in exchange for services provided.

Service mark(s) Similar to a trademark, a legally registered word, name, symbol, or combination of these used to indicate the source or producer of an organization's services.

Shares Fractional portions of a company in which the owner of the portion(s) has voting rights and rights to a respective fraction of the assets of the company.

Sharing economy An economic system in which assets or services are shared between private individuals for a fee, typically by means of a smartphone and the Internet.

Signatory An entity that signs and agrees to abide by the terms of a document.

Small claims court A court designed especially to hear lawsuits entailing relatively small sums of money. They can provide a speedy method of making a claim without the necessity of hiring a lawyer and engaging in a formal trial.

Sole proprietorship A business organization in which one person owns and, often, operates the business.

Standard of care The industry-recognized, reasonably accepted level of performance used in fulfilling a duty of care.

Stare decisis The principle of following prior case law.

Statute of limitations Various laws that set maximum time periods in which lawsuits must be initiated. If this suit is not initiated (or filed) before the expiration of the maximum period allowed, then the law prohibits the use of the courts for recovery.

Strict liability Responsibility arising from the nature of a dangerous activity rather than negligence or an intentional act. Also known as *absolute liability* or *liability without fault*.

Sublet To rent property one possesses by a lease, to another. Also called subleasing.

Subpoena A court-authorized order to appear in person at a designated time and place, or to produce evidence demanded by the court.

Tangible property Personal property that has physical substance and can be held or touched. Examples include furniture, equipment, and inventories of goods.

Tariff The agreement between an airline and its passengers. When purchasing a ticket, the passenger agrees to the terms of the tariff.

Tenant Anyone, including a corporation, who rents real property for an extended period of time with the intent of establishing a permanent occupation or residency.

Third-party liability The two areas of liability theory that a hospitality manager should be aware of focus on the duties of a host who holds a party where alcohol is served, and that of an establishment licensed to sell alcohol.

Timeshare A form of shared property ownership in which a buyer acquires the right to occupy a piece of real estate, such as a condominium in a resort area, for a specific period of time each year.

Tip credit The amount an employer is allowed to consider as a supplement to employer-paid wages in meeting the requirements of applicable minimum wage laws.

Tip pooling/sharing An arrangement whereby service providers share their tips with each other on a predetermined basis.

Tips A gratuity given in exchange for a service performed. Literally an acronym for "to insure prompt service."

Title The sum total of all legally recognized rights to the possession and ownership of property.

Title search A review of land records to determine the ownership and description of a piece of real property.

Tort An act or failure to act (not involving a breach of contract) that results in injury, loss, or damage to another (e.g., negligence is an unintentional tort, whereas battery, physically touching someone, is usually an intentional tort).

Tour operator A company whose primary activity is the planning, packaging, and marketing of travel services, including transportation, meals, accommodations, and activities.

Trade dress A distinct visual image created for and identified with a specific product.

Trade secrets Business information that is general not known or reasonably ascertainable by others that may provide another business organization or individual with an economic competitive business advantage over other businesses.

Trademark A word, name, symbol, or combination of these that indicates the source or producer of an item. Sometimes called a mark.

Transient guest A customer who rents real property for a relatively short period of time (e.g., few number of days with no intent of establishing a permanent residency).

Travel law The laws regulating business and individual behavior in the travel industry.

Truth-in-menu laws The collective name given to various laws and regulations that have been implemented to ensure accuracy in the wording on menus.

Umbrella Insurance coverage purchased to supplement primary coverage. Sometimes referred to as "excess insurance."

Underwrite To assume agreed-upon maximum levels of liability in the event of a loss or damages.

Unemployment benefits A benefit paid to an employee who involuntarily loses his or her employment without just cause.

Unemployment claim A petition, submitted by an unemployed worker to his or her state unemployment agency, which asserts that the worker is eligible to receive unemployment benefits.

Unemployment insurance A program, funded by employers, that provides temporary monetary benefits for employees who have lost their jobs.

Uniform Commercial Code (UCC) A model statute covering such issues as the sale of goods, credit, and bank transactions.

Vicarious liability A party's responsibility for the acts of another that result in an injury, harm, or damage. (See also *respondeat superior*.)

Warranty A promise about a product made by either a manufacturer or a seller that is a part of the sales contract.

Warranty deed A deed that provides that the person granting the deed agrees to defend the title from claims of others. In general, the seller is representing that he or she fully owns the property and will legally stand behind this promise.

Warsaw Convention Short for the Convention for the Unification of Certain Rules Relating to International Carriage by Air signed at Warsaw on October 12, 1929, this agreement set limits on the liabilities of airlines that follow established guidelines for the safe operation of international airline flights.

Whistle-blowers protection acts Laws that protect employees who have reported illegal employer acts from retaliation by that employer.

Workers' compensation A benefit paid to an employee who suffers a work-related injury or illness.

Wrongful termination An employer's violation of the employment relationship resulting in the unlawful firing of the employee.

Index

A

Abandoned property, 209, 210
Ability to pay, guest, 190
Acceptance
 contract, 62–64
 deposit, 63
 partial or full payment, 63
Accident response, 180–183
Accidents, guests, 200
Activity safety, amusement park operations and, 250
Actuary, 283
Adhesion contracts, 239
Admiralty law, 243
Admission, guest, 189–191
Advertisements, classified, 125, 126
Advertising, online travel sales and, 254
Affirmative action, 127
Affordable Care and Patient Protection Act (ACA), 287
Age Discrimination in Employment Act (ADEA), 129, 165–166
Agency relationship, 55–57
 agent-principal relationship, 56
 independent contractors, 57
 master-servant relationship, 55–56
Agency relationship clause, 84
Agent-principal relationship, 56
Agents, 56
Aggregate amounts, insurance and, 290
Agreement in writing, 63–64
Airline Deregulation Act of 1978, 241
Airlines
 Aviation Disaster Family Assistance Act, 246
 baggage responsibility and, 245
 overbooking and, 244–245
 service provider relationship and, 241
 tariffs and, 241
Alcohol and Tobacco Tax and Trade Bureau (TTB), 26–27
Alcoholic Beverage Commission (ABC), 29–30
Alcohol service
 blood alcohol concentration and, 222
 dram shop laws and, 224–226
 happy-hour laws and, 223
 intoxication and, 222
 liability associated with, 223–226
 licensing and, 29–30, 222
 privilege of, 221–223
 regulatory requirements for foreign producers, 228
 revoked license and, 223
 social host standards and, 224
 third-party liability and, 224
 training for responsible service, 226–228
Allegheny Airlines, 69
Allergic reactions, food service and, 215–216
Allowable attrition, 75–76
Alternative dispute resolution, 66, 179–180
American Hotel and Lodging Association (AH&LA), 2, 42, 226
American Society of Travel Agents (ASTA), 232
Americans with Disabilities Act (ADA), 3, 28, 127–129
Americans with Disabilities Act (ADA), Title III, 195–197
Amtrak, 242
Amusement park operations, 246, 249–251
 activity safety and, 25
 employee training litigation and, 251
 industry history and, 250
 performance expectations and, 250–251
 potential liability issues and, 250–251
Annuity, 284
Appeals, personal injury lawsuits and, 179
Applicant screenings, 119–125
 applications and, 119–121
 background checks and, 123–125
 classified advertisement wording and, 125, 126
 defamation cases and, 125
 interviews and, 122, 123
 negligent hiring and, 124
 preemployment testing and, 122, 123
 references and, 124
Applications, employee, 119–121
Arbitration, 66
Association of Corporate Travel Executives, 239
Attorney General, 30
Attorneys, 2
Attractions and activities, travel industry and, 233
At-will employment, 134–135
Authorization to modify contracts, 75
Automated external defibrillators, 195
Automobiles, guests', 208
Aviation Disaster Family Assistance Act, 246

B

Background checks, 123–125
Baggage, transportation industry and, 245
Bailee, 206
Bailments, 205–208
 bailment relationship, 206
 detained property and, 208
 innkeeper's lien and, 208
 liability under bailment relationship, 206–208
 types of, 206
Bailor, 206
Bedbugs, 194–195
Bill of sale, 98–99
Blackstone, William, 3
Blood alcohol concentration, 222
Bona fide occupational qualification, 118
Breach of contract
 alternative dispute resolution and, 66
 basics of, 65–66
 economic loss and, 66
 liquidated damages and, 66
 preventing, 68–70
 statute of limitations and, 66, 68
 suit for specific performance, 66
Broadcast rights, 114
Building and zoning agencies, 33
Bureau of Alcohol, Tobacco, Firearms, and Explosives (ATF), 26–27
Buses, 243–244
Business operating structures
 condo hotels/shared services, 54–55
 franchise, 51–53
 management contracts, 53–54
 owner-operator, 51
 REITs, 54
Business organization structures
 C corporations, 47–49
 general partnerships, 46–47
 importance of, 45–46
 limited liability companies, 49–51
 limited partnerships, 47
 operating structure, 45
 organizational structure, 45
 S corporations, 49
 sole proprietorships, 46
 summary chart, 50–51
Buy *vs.* lease decisions, 109–110

C

Caesar's Project 21, 248
Canadian employment laws, 137–138
Canadian innkeepers limited liability, 211
Cancellation policies, 75
Capacity and legality, 61–64
 acceptance and, 62–64
 consideration and, 62
 offer and, 61
Capital improvements, leasing property and, 110
Cardiac Arrest Survival Act, 195
Car rentals, 244
Carrier selection, insurance, 289
Caveat emptor, 64
C corporations, 47–49
Centers for Disease Control and Prevention (CDC), 35–36
Certified travel associate (CTA), 236
Certified travel industry executive (CTIE), 236
Chattel, 96
Checks
 fraudulent, 271
 verification of, 271
China, hotel industry entities and, 58
Civil law, 3
Civil Rights Act of 1964, Title VII, 126–127
Claims, insurance, 284
Class action lawsuits, travel agents and, 237
Classified advertisements, employee hiring and, 125
Clause (contract), 74
Codes of ethics, 8–12
Collateral, 102, 103
Collective bargaining agreements, 135–136
Commercial lease, 110
Committees, safety, 265

Common carriers, 240. *See also* Transportation and common carriers
Common law, 3
Common law liability, 203–205
Communicable diseases, guest, 190
Company property theft, 271, 272
Comparative negligence, 174–175
Compensation. *See* Employee compensation
Compensatory damages, 176
Competing tenants, leasing property and, 108
Complaint investigations, employee, 145–147
Complaint resolution, employee, 147
Complaint resolution form, 147
Completion dates, contractors and, 77–78
Con artists, 203
Condo hotels/shared services, 54–55
Condominium homeowners' association (CHOA), 54
Condominiums, 54
Coney Island, 250
Conference services contracts, 87–92
  cut-off dates and, 91
  group lodging contracts, 88, 91–92
  master bill and, 87
  meeting space contracts, 88–91
Confirmed reservation, 69
Consideration, contracts and, 62
Consolidated Omnibus Budget Reconciliation Act (COBRA), 28, 287
Consumer theft of services, 269–270
Contingency fee, 177
Contract parties, online travel sales and, 252–253
Contracts. *See also* Breach of contract
  allowable attrition and, 75–76
  business contracts, 59
  capacity and legality, 61–64
  clauses for providing products and services to guests, 75–77
  clauses for purchasing products and services, 77–80
  completion dates and, 77–78
  conference services contracts, 87–92
  defendants, 59
  delivery or start dates and, 77
  deposit and cancellation policies, 75
  dispute resolution terms and, 79–80
  educating and sharing information on, 68
  ensuring third party performance and, 68
  exculpatory clauses and, 80
  forecasting contract capacity, 68–69
  franchise-related contracts, 73, 80–84
  getting in writing, 67
  good faith and, 67
  group lodging contracts, 74–75
  identification who is authorized to modify contract, 75
  indemnification and, 76, 78–79
  international, 71
  keeping copies of, 67
  length of time the contract price term exists, 75
  licenses and permits and, 78
  management contracts, 84–87
  management operating agreements, 73–74
  meeting space contracts, 74
  nonperformance clauses, 79
  note and calendar time deadlines, 67–68
  payment terms and, 76–77
  performance standards and, 77, 78
  plaintiffs and, 59
  reading thoroughly, 67
  resolving ambiguities and, 68
  specific contract clauses, 73–80
  verbal and written contracts, 59–61
Contributory negligence, 174
Copyright, 111–112
Copyright Act of 1976, 111
Copyright owner, 111
Corporate travel, 239–240
Counterfeit money, 271
Counteroffers, 63
Courts, local, 33
Credit cards
  fraudulent use of, 270–271
  guidelines for handling of, 270
  lost, 198
Crimes against guests, 175–176
Crisis management, 260
Crisis management programs, 274–281
  crisis response and, 277–279
  emergency plan development, 274–275
  emergency plan practice, 275–277
  guest response and, 278–279
  management response and, 277
  media relations and, 279–280
  postcrisis assessment and, 280–281
  precrisis planning and, 274
  staff response and, 277–278
Cruise Lines International Association (CLIA), 243
Cruise ships, 242–243
Customs and Border Protection (CBP), 28
Cut-off dates, 91

D

Damages
  indemnification and, 76
  leasing property and, 108, 109
  liquidated, 66
Data breach, 288–289
Data interface issues, online travel sales and, 253
Data privacy, guest, 192–193
Data security, online travel sales and, 253–254
Deaths, guests, 200
Debtor and creditor relationships, property purchases and, 102–103
Deceptive advertising, online travel sales and, 254
Deceptive sales tactics, resort/timeshare operations and, 249
Deductibles, insurance, 290
Deeds, 97
Deeds of trust, 103
Defamation cases, applicant screenings and, 125
Default, resort/timeshare operations and, 249
Defendants, 59
Defibrillators, 195
Delaware business laws, 46
Delivery or start dates, 77
Deluxe motor coach, 243
Demand letter, personal injury lawsuits and, 177–178
Department of Commerce, 36
Department of Homeland Security (DHS), 28–29, 37–38, 130
Department of Interior (DOI), 36
Department of Justice (DOJ), 28
Department of Labor (DOL), 27–28
Department of Labor (DOL) records, 164–165
  on employee meals and lodging, 164–165
  on family and medical leave, 165
  for tipped employees, 165
Department of State, 36–37
Department of Transportation (DOT), 33, 38, 254
Deposit acceptance, 63
Deposit and cancellation policies, 75
Depositions, 179
Deposits, leasing property and, 108, 109
Depreciation, 110
Depressants, 221
Detained property, 208
Digital Millennium Copyright Act (DMCA), 111
Directorate for Management, 37–38
Disabled guests, 195–197
Discipline, employee, 158
Disclosure requirements, franchises and, 93
Discovery and disclosure, travel agents and, 237
Discovery phase, personal injury lawsuits and, 179
Discrimination in selection process, 126–129
  Age Discrimination in Employment Act, 129
  Americans with Disabilities Act, 127–129
  Civil Rights Act of 1964, Title VII, 126–127
Discrimination prevention, workplace, 142
Disneyland, 250
Dispute resolution programs, 161
Dispute resolution terms, 79–80
Disruptive guests, 199
Diversity management, 142–143
Dividends, 48
Domestic Nuclear Detection Office, 38
Dram shop insurance, 286–287
Dram shop laws, 29, 224–226
Drug screening tests, 122
Duties of care, 171–172

E

Economic impact, resort/timeshare operations and, 249
Economic loss, breach of contract and, 66
Economy buses, 243
EEOC v. Sage Realty Corporation, 148
Eligibility verification, employment, 129–134
  Fair Labor Standards Act of 1938, 130
  Immigration Reform and Control Act, 129–130
  qualifying documents and, 134
Embezzlement, 271–272
Emergency plan development, 274–275
Emergency plan practice, 275–277
Emergency telephone list, 275
Employee benefit security, 28
Employee compensation, 149–156
  minimum wage and overtime, 149–154
  taxes and credits, 155–156
  tipped employees and, 154–155
  tip pooling, 155
Employee consent form for background checks and application verification, 125
Employee consent form for drug testing, 124
Employee liability insurance, 286
Employee management
  compensation and, 149–156
  complaint investigations, 145–147
  complaint resolution, 147
  diversity management, 142–143
  employee manuals, 140, 141

employee records, 164–166
employment posting, 166, 167
employment relationships, 139–141
Family and Medical Leave Act, 148–149
liability insurance, 148
managing employees abroad, 168–169
offer letter and, 139–140
Patient Protection and Affordable Care Act of 2010, 156–157
performance management, 157–161
preventing discrimination and, 142
protection of trade secrets, 141
sexual harassment, 143, 144
third-party harassment, 148
unemployment claims, 161–164
Uniform Services Employment and Reemployment Rights Act, 149
vicarious liability and, 143
workplace surveillance, 166, 168
zero tolerance and, 144–145
Employee manual, 140, 141
Employee motivation, 6
Employee Polygraphy Protection Act of 1988, 28
Employee records
ADEA-required records, 165–166
Department of Labor records, 164–165
immigration-related records, 165
Employee Retirement Income Security Act (ERISA), 28
Employee selection
applicant screenings, 119–125
at-will employment, 134–135
discrimination in selection process, 126–129
eligibility verification, 129–134
job descriptions and, 118
job qualifications and, 118–119
labor unions and collective bargaining, 135–136
selection practices, 117–126
Employee training, amusement park operations and, 251
Employee working conditions, gaming industry and, 248
Employment Security Agency, 29
Entertainer nonperformance clause, 79
Environmental Protection Agency (EPA), 19
Equal Employment Opportunity Commission (EEOC), 25–26, 28, 122, 142, 147
Ethics, 6–12
codes of ethics, 8–12
free champagne example and, 7–8
guidelines and, 6
European Union Trade Mark (EUTM), 114
Evaluation, employee, 157–158
Evictions, 107, 199
Exceptions, insurance policy, 291
Exclusions, insurance policy, 291
Exculpatory clauses, 80
Executive motor coach, 243
Expectations, travel law and, 234
Express contract, 63
Eyster, James J., 85

F

Face sheet, insurance policy, 290
Facility evaluation steps, 196
Facility maintenance, 193–197
bedbugs and, 194–195
defibrillators and, 195
safe environment and, 193–194
spas/hot tubs, 194
swimming pools and, 193–194
workout and fitness areas, 194
Facility management, disabled guests and, 195–197
Facility modifications, safety and security and, 264
Fair Labor Standards Act (FLSA), 27, 130, 149–150
Fairness in Music Licensing Amendment, 113, 114
Family and Medical Leave Act (FMLA), 28, 148–149, 165, 167
Faragher v. City of Boca Raton, 143
Federal Aviation Act of 1958, 241
Federal Aviation Administration (FAA), 38
Federal Civil Rights Act of 1964, 189
Federal Emergency Management Agency (FEMA), 38
Federal Highway Administration (FHWA), 38
Federal Insurance Contribution Act (FICA), 155
Federal Law Enforcement Training Center (FLETC), 38
Federal Railroad Administration, 38
Federal regulatory and administrative agencies
Bureau of Alcohol, Tobacco, Firearms, and Explosives, 26–27
Department of Justice, 28
Department of Labor, 27–28
Environmental Protection Agency (EPA), 19
Equal Employment Opportunity Commission, 25–26
Food and Drug Administration, 25
Internal Revenue Service, 15–16
Occupational Safety and Health Administration, 16–25
U.S. Department of Homeland Security, 28–29
Federal Trade Commission (FTC), 35, 81, 255
Federal Unemployment Tax Act (FUTA), 155–156
Fiduciary responsibility, 56
Financing property purchases, 102–105
collateral and liens, 102–103
debtor and creditor relationship, 102–103
financing statements and, 103–105
Liens, 102–103
mortgages and deeds of trust, 103
security agreements and, 103
Financing statements, 103–105
Fire crisis emergency plan, 276
Fire departments, 34
Fixtures, 96
Food Allergen Labeling and Consumer Protection Act, 215
Food and beverages. *See also* Alcohol service; Truth in menu laws
allergic reactions and, 215–216
foodborne illness, 213, 215
foreign producers of alcohol, 228
general nutrition and obesity, 220–221
guest safety and, 214–216
merchantable food, 213
reasonable expectation test, 214
serving alcohol, 221–228
serving food, 213–216
truth in menu laws, 216–221
Uniform Commercial Code warranty and, 213–214
Food and Drug Administration (FDA), 25, 218, 219
Foodborne illness, 213, 215
Foodservices, travel industry and, 233
Force majeure, 65
Forum (venue) selection issues, online travel sales and, 254
Fractional ownership, 54
Franchise contracts, 80–84
agency relationship clause, 84
franchise agreements, 83
franchise offering circular, 82–83
the franchise rule, 81
franchise warning statement, 81
purchasing a franchise, 80–83
revised franchise rule, 81–82
right of first refusal clause, 84
selling a franchise, 84
Franchisee, 52
Franchise rule, 81
Franchises, 51–53
contracts and, 73, 80–84
international disclosure requirements and, 93
management contracts for, 86–87
offering circulars, 82–83
sales, 84
warning statements, 81
Franchising Trade Regulation Rule, 81–82
Franchisor, 52
Fraudulent payments, 270–271
cash and, 271
credit cards and, 270–271
personal checks and, 271
Full facilities, potential guests and, 191
Full payment acceptance, 63

G

Gaming industry, 246–248
employee working conditions and, 248
government approved, 246
history of, 246–247
Internet gambling, 248
potential liability issues and, 247–248
reckless gaming behavior and, 247–248
regulation and control and, 247
Garnishment, 33
General (or managing) partner, 47
General partnerships, 46–47
Global Business Travel Association, 239
Global distribution system, online travel sales and, 253
Government agency inquiries and complaints, 41–42
Government travel, 239–240
Gratuitous bailment, 206
Greytrails Bus Lines, 243
Gross negligence, 174
Group lodging contracts, 74–75, 88, 91–92
Guaranteed reservation, 70
Guards, safety and security, 264
Guest crisis response, 278–279
Guestroom lock policy, 266–267
Guests. *See also* Facility maintenance; Nonguest responsibilities
accidents and, 200
accommodating, 187–191
admitting, 189–190
crimes against, 175–176
deaths and, 200
definition of, 187–188

Guests (*continued*)
denying admission to, 190–191
food service safety and, 214–216
health emergency response and, 200
illness and, 200
inappropriate conduct and, 199
lack of payment and, 198–199
overstays and, 199–200
privacy and, 191–193
records privacy and, 191–192
registration cards and, 60
removal of, 198–200
tenant, 188
transient guest, 188
Guests of guests, 197
Guests' property
abandoned property, 209, 210
bailments, 205–208
common law liability and, 203–205
liability for, 203–205
lost-and-found ticket, 210
lost property, 209, 210
luggage replacement value limits and, 205
mislaid property, 209
negligence penalty and, 205
posting liability notice and, 204
property with unknown ownership, 209–210
required possession limits and, 205
secure safe and, 204–205
suitable locks on doors and windows and, 205
unclaimed property disposal, 210, 211

H

Happy-hour laws, 223
Health and sanitation agencies, 33
Health benefits, food laws and, 220
Health codes and regulations, 30–33
Health/dental/vision insurance, 287
Health emergency response, guests, 200
Historical preservation, 34
Hospitality manager
future and, 1–2
legal management and, 2–6
Hospitality operator
duties of care and, 171–172
standards of care and, 172
Hostile environment harassment, 143
Hotel and Motel Fire Safety Act of 1990, 40
Hotel room "walks," 270
House rules statement, 191
Human trafficking, 273–274
in hotel industry, 273
indicators, 273–274
labor trafficking, 273
sex trafficking, 273
Hyatt Corporation ethical standards, 8–12

I

Illness, guests, 200
Immigration, 42–43
Immigration and Customs Enforcement (ICE), 28
Immigration Reform and Control Act (IRCA), 129–130, 165
Immigration-related records, 165
Implied warranty, 101
Improvements, 96
Inappropriate conduct, guests and, 199
Incident reporting form, 182–183
Incident response, 180–183
Income tax, 155
Indemnification, 76, 284
Indemnification/insurance, 78
Independent contractors, 57
Indian Gaming Regulatory Act of 1988 (IGRA), 247
Infra hospitium, 207
Ingredients, food, 219
In-house dispute resolution, 160–161
Injury or accident, tour operators and, 239
Innkeeper's lien, 208
Inquiries, regulatory, 41–42
In-room videos or movies, 114
Inspection provisions (OSHA), 18
Insurance, 292–293
actuary and, 283
aggregate amount and, 290
annuity and, 284
carrier selection and, 289
claims and, 284
coverage types and, 285–289
data breach, 288–289
deductibles and, 290
dram shop insurance, 286–287
employee liability insurance, 286
exceptions and, 291
exclusions and, 291
face sheet and, 290
health/dental/vision insurance, 287
indemnification and, 284
insured and, 284
insurer and, 284
introduction to, 283–285
language and, 291
leasing property and, 106
liability insurance, 286
per occurrence maximums and, 290
policies and, 284
policy analysis and, 290–292
policy selection and, 289–290
premiums and, 284
primary policy and, 290
property-casualty/business interruption, 285–286
umbrella coverage and, 290
workers' compensation and, 287–288
Insured, 284
Insurer, 284
Intangible property, 96, 97
Intellectual property rights, 110–114
copyright, 112
international, 114–115
patents, 111
preventing infringement and, 112–114
public domain and, 112
trade dress, 112
trademarks, 110, 111
Intentional acts, 175
Interconnectivity, travel law and, 234
Interdiction programs, 266
Internal Revenue Service (IRS), 15–16
Internal theft of assets, 271–272
International Air Transport Association (IATA), 244
International Civil Aviation Organization (ICAO), 39
International contracts, 71
International disclosure requirements, franchises and, 93
International Franchise Association, 51–53
International trademark protection, 114–115
Internet
gambling, 248
online travel sales, 251–255
travel sales advertising checklist, 255
Interrogatories, 179
Interstate commerce, 100, 126
Interviews, applicant, 122, 123
Intoxication, 190, 222
Investigation consent forms, 146
Invitees, responsibility towards, 197–198
Itinerary changes, unplanned, 245

J

Job descriptions, 118
Job interviews, 122, 123
Job qualifications, 118–119
Jukeboxes, 114
Jurisdiction, travel law and, 234

K

Kickbacks, 86
Kroc, Ray, 53

L

Labor unions, 135–136
Landlord, 105
Landlord expenses, 108
Landlord representation and default, 107–108
Landlord rights, leasing property and, 108, 109
Law
civil law, 3
common law, 3
evolutionary nature of, 3–4
historical origins of, 2–3
Law enforcement
guest privacy and, 192
regulatory role and, 34
relationships with, 265–267
Leasing property, 105–110
buy-*vs.*-lease decision, 109–110
capital improvements and, 110
commercial lease, 110
competing tenants and, 108
deposits, damages, and normal wear and tear, 108, 109
depreciation and, 110
essential lease terms as a lessee, 107–108
essential lease terms as a lessor, 105–107
eviction and, 107
expenses paid by landlord, 108
insurance and, 106
landlord representation and default, 107–108
landlord rights and, 108, 109
length of lease and, 105–106
renewal terms and, 108
rent amount and, 106
subleasing rights of tenant and, 106
termination rights and, 106–107
Legal assistance for employees, 161
Legal damages, 176
Legal environment, 1–2
Legal jurisdiction, transportation industry and, 244
Lessee, 105
Lessor, 105
Liability
alcohol service and, 223–226
amusement park operations and, 250–251
under a bailment relationship, 206–208
Canadian innkeepers limited liability, 211
common law liability, 203–205
comparative negligence, 174–175

contributory negligence, 174
crimes against guests, 175–176
gaming industry and, 247–248
gross negligence, 174
guests' property and, 203–205
intentional acts, 175
liability insurance, 148, 286
medical tourism, 251
negligence, 173–174
negligence per se, 176
online travel sales and, 252–254
reasonable care and, 172–173
resort/timeshare operations and, 249
strict liability, 175
theories regarding, 172–176
third-party liability, 224
torts, 173
tour operators and, 238–239
transportation industry and, 244–246
travel agents and, 236–237
Liable, 5
License, 52
Licensee, 52
Licenses and permits, 78
Licensing agreements, 52
Licensor, 52
Limited liability, 211
Limited liability companies (LLC), 49–51
Limited partner, 47
Limited partnerships, 47
Liquidated damages, 66
Liquor bottles disposition, 27
Liquor liability, 286–287
Liquor licenses, 29–30, 222
Local economies, travel industry and, 234
Local regulatory and administrative agencies
building and zoning, 33
courts and garnishment, 33
fire department, 34
health and sanitation, 33
historical preservation, 34
law enforcement, 35
tax assessor/collector, 35
Lock policy, guestroom, 266–267
Locks on doors and windows, 205
Lodging, travel industry and, 232–233
Lost-and-found ticket, 210
Lost property, 210
Lottery control, 31–32
Luggage replacement values, 205

M

Madrid Protocol, 115
Management agreement, 84
Management companies, 53, 84–85
Management contracts, 53–54, 84–87
for franchised properties, 86–87
kickbacks and, 86
management agreements and, 84
management companies and, 84–85
types of, 85–86
Management crisis response, 277
Management operating agreements, 73–74
Manufacturer's warranty, 101–102
Maritime Administration, 243
Maritime laws, 243
Master bill, 87
Master-servant relationship, 55–56
McDonald's, 51–53
Media crisis relations, 279–280
Mediation, 66, 179–180
Mediators, 161
Medical field lessons, 4
Medical tourism, 251
history of, 251
potential liability issues, 251
Meeting expectations, 8
Meeting planners, 74
Meeting space contracts, 74, 88–91
Merchantable food, 213
Mexican Law, 281–282
Minimum wage, 149–154
Mislaid property, 209
Misrepresentation
tour operators and, 239
travel agents and, 236–237
Montreal Convention, 241
Mortgages, 103
Music rights, 113

N

Nader, Ralph, 69
Nader v. Allegheny Airlines, Inc., 69
National Highway Traffic Safety Administration (NHSTA), 38
National Labor Relations Board (NLRB), 28, 135
National Park Service, 36
National Protection and Programs Directorate, 37
National Railroad Passenger Corporation, 242
National Restaurant Association (NRA), 42, 213, 215, 226
National Tourism Policy Act of 1981, 36
Negligence
liability and, 173–174
negligence per se, 176
negligent hiring, 124
overseas, 184
penalties, 205
travel agents and, 237
Neighborhood business watch programs, 236
Noncompliance penalties (OSHA), 18
Nondisturbance clauses, 249
Nonguaranteed reservation, 69–70
Nonguest responsibilities, 197–198
guests of guests, 197
invitees, 197–198
trespassers, 198
Nonperformance clauses, 79
Nonverbal agreements, 63
North American Gaming Regulators Association (NAGRA), 247
No-show reservations, 70
Nutrient claims, food laws and, 220
Nutrition Labeling and Education Act (NLEA), 220

O

Obesity, general nutrition and, 220–221
Occupational Safety and Health Administration (OSHA), 16–25
inspection provisions, 18
penalties for noncompliance, 18
safety data sheet, 18–25
Offer letters, 139–140
Offers, 61
Office of Health Affairs (DHS), 38
Office of Intelligence and Analysis (DHS), 38
Office of Operations Coordination and Planning (DHS), 38
Office of Policy (DHS), 38
Off the record comments, media and, 279
Ombudspersons, 161
Omnibus Appropriation Act, 36
Online travel sales, 251–255
background of, 252
data interface issues and, 253
data security/ownership issues and, 253–254
forum (venue) selection issues and, 254
global distribution system and, 253
lawful advertising and, 254
legal issues and, 252–254
parties to the contract and, 252–253
Operating agreements, 73–74
Operating structure, 45
Operation Bet Smart, 247
Organizational structure, 45
Origin of product, food laws and, 219
Overbooking, transportation industry and, 244–245
Overstays, 199–200
Overtime pay, 149–154
Owner-operator, 51
Ownership issues, online travel sales and, 253–254

P

Partial payment acceptance, 63
Patents, 111
Patient Protection and Affordable Care Act of 2010, 156–157
Patriot Act, 200–201
Patrols, safety, 262–263
Payment, lack of, 198–199
Payment terms, 76–77
Perfecting a lien, 102
Performance expectations, amusement park operations and, 250–251
Performance management, 157–158
discipline and, 158
employee evaluation, 157–158
employee terminations, 158–160
in-house dispute resolution, 160–161
whistle-blowers protection acts, 159
Performance standards, 78
Permits, 78
Per occurrence maximums, insurance, 290
Personal checks. *See* Checks
Personal injury lawsuits, 176–180
alternative dispute resolution and, 179–180
demand letter and, 177–178
discovery phase and, 179
manager's role in, 180
personal injury, 177
petition filing and, 178–179
trial and appeal and, 179
Personal property, 95–97
bill of sale and, 98–99
purchasing, 98–102
stolen property, 99–100
warranty and, 100–102
Petition filing, personal injury lawsuits and, 178–179
Plaintiffs, 59
Plant closing and layoffs, 28
Policies, insurance, 284
Policy analysis, insurance, 290–292
Policy selection, insurance, 289–290
Polygraphs, 28
Postcrisis assessment, 280–281
Posting, employment, 166, 167

Posting notice, guests' property liability and, 204
Post-traumatic stress disorder (PTSD), 278
Prearranged services nonpayment, tour operators and, 238
Precrisis planning, 274
Preemployment testing, 123
Premiums, insurance, 284
Preparation style, food, 218–219
Preplanning services, travel industry and, 232
Press releases, crisis management and, 279
Preventative legal management, 4–6
  medical field lessons and, 4
  motivating techniques and, 5–6
  STEM process and, 4–6
Priceline.com, 253
Price terms, 75
Pricing agreements, travel agents and, 236
Primary policy, insurance, 290
Principal, 56
Privacy, guest, 191–192
Privacy policy, 166, 168
Product size, food and, 219–220
Progressive discipline, 158, 159
Progressive discipline form, 159
Promised services
  tour operators and, 239
  travel agents and, 236
Property. *See also* Guests' property; Personal property; Real property
  financing purchase of, 102–105
  fixtures and, 96
  intangible property, 96, 97
  intellectual property rights, 110–114
  leasing property, 105–110
  personal property, 95–102
  purchasing real property, 97–98
  real property, 95–96
  tangible property, 96, 97
Property-casualty insurance, 285–286
Protection of trade secrets, 141
Proximate cause, 173
Psychological tests, 122
Public accommodation, 189
Public domain, 112
Public Health Department, 30–33
Puffing, online travel sales and, 254
Punitive damages, 176

Q

Quantity, performance standards related to, 77
Quick-change artists, 271
Quid pro quo sexual harassment, 143
Quitclaim deeds, 97

R

Real estate investment trusts (REIT), 54
Real property
  deeds and, 97
  defined, 95
  purchasing, 97–98
  title and, 97
  title insurance and, 98
Reasonable care, 172–173
Reasonable expectation test, food service and, 214
Reckless gaming behavior, 247–248
Records, employee, 164–166
Records privacy, guests, 191–192
References, applicant screenings and, 124, 125
Regulation and control, gaming industry and, 247
Regulation conflicts, 40–41
Regulation, transportation industry and, 244
Regulation violation inquiries, 41–42
Regulatory agencies. *See* Federal regulatory and administrative agencies; Local regulatory and administrative agencies; State regulatory and administrative agencies
Regulatory change, monitoring, 42
Regulatory interaction impacting travel and tourism, 35–40
  Centers for Disease Control and Prevention, 35–36
  Department of Commerce, 36
  Department of Homeland Security, 37–38
  Department of Interior, 36
  Department of State, 36–37
  Department of Transportation, 38
  Federal Trade Commission, 35
  International Civil Aviation Organization, 39
  international organizations, 39–40
  Tourism Policy Council, 39
  Treasury Department, 38
  U.S. government agencies, 35–39
  World Health Organization, 39–40
  World Tourism Organization, 39
Regulatory structure
  tour operators and, 238
  travel agents and, 236
Renewal terms, leasing property and, 108
Rental cars, 244
Rent amount, 106
Request for no further action form, 146
Required possession limits, 205
Reservation policy, 69–70
  confirmed reservation, 69
  guaranteed reservation, 70
  nonguaranteed reservation, 69–70
  reducing no-show reservations, 70
Resort/timeshare operations, 246, 248–249
  deceptive sales tactics and, 249
  economic impact of, 249
  industry background, 248
  liability issues and, 249
  nondisturbance clauses and, 249
  rights in event of default, 249
  types of, 248
Respondent superior, 56
Revised franchise rule, 81–82
Right of first refusal clause, 84
Robbery, 203

S

Safes, guests' property and, 204–205
Safety and security. *See also* Crisis management programs
  areas of concern and, 263
  checklist for, 264
  consumer theft of services and, 269–270
  crisis management and, 260
  crisis management programs and, 274–281
  embezzlement and, 271–272
  establishing standard procedures and, 264
  facility, 193–197
  facility modifications and, 264
  four-step management method and, 262–268
  fraudulent payment and, 270–271
  guestroom lock policy and, 266–267
  hospitality business and, 268–272
  internal theft of assets and, 271–272
  law enforcement relationships and, 265–267
  management of, 259–260
  monitoring program results and, 267
  planning advantages and, 260–262
  program development and, 262–264
  program implementation and, 264–267
  safety and security departments, 264–265
  safety and security guards, 265
  safety committees, 265
  surveillance and/or patrols and, 262–263
  systematic inspections and, 264
  theft of company property, 271, 272
  threat prevention training and, 262
  threat recognition and, 262
Safety data sheets (SDS), 18–25
Sanitation agencies, 33
Science and Technology Directorate, 37
S corporations, 49
Security. *See* Safety and security
Security agreements, 103
Security interest, 103
Segregating guests, 189
Self-renewing contacts, 78
Service charge, 155
Service provider identification, travel law and, 234–235
ServSafe program, 215
Sexual harassment, 143, 144
Shares, 48
Signatory, 241
Sign permit ordinance, 34
Skills tests, 122
Small claims court, 199
Social host standards, alcohol service and, 224
Society of Government Travel Professionals, 239
Sole proprietorship, 46
Spas/hot tubs, 194
Specialty buses, 243
Staff crisis response, 277–278
Standards of care, 172
Stare decisis, 3
Start dates, 77
State of Ohio limitations on innkeeper liability, 204
State regulatory and administrative agencies
  Alcoholic Beverage Commission, 29–30
  Attorney General, 30
  Department of Transportation, 33
  Employment Security Agency, 29
  Public Health Department, 30–33
  Treasury Department/Controller, 30
Statute of limitations, 66, 68
STEM process, 4–6
Stolen property, 99–100
Strict liability, 175
Strikes, 136
Subleasing rights, 106
Sublet, 106
Subpoenas, 179
Suit for specific performance, 66
Surveillance activities, 262–263
Suspension, employee, 158
Swimming pools, 193–194
Systematic safety and security inspections, 264

T

Taft-Hartley Act, 28
Tangible property, 96, 97
Tariffs, 241
Tax accessor/collector, 35
Tax-exempt notice, 30
Telephone list, emergency, 275
Tenants, 105, 188
Termination, employee, 158–160
Termination rights, leasing property and, 106–107
Terrorist acts, 200–201
Testing, preemployment, 123
Theft, 204
Theft of internal assets, 271–272
Theft of services, consumer, 269–270
Third-party harassment, 148
Third-party liability, 224
Threat prevention training, 262
Threat recognition, safety and security and, 262
Threats, guest, 190
Timeshares. *See* Resort/timeshare operations
Tip credit, 155
Tip income, reporting, 17
Tipped employees, 154–155, 165
Tip pooling, 155
Tip-pooling consent form, 155
Title, 97
Title insurance, 98
Title search, 97
Title VII of the Civil Rights Act of 1964, 25
Torts, 173
Tourism, 246–251
  amusement park operations and, 246, 249–251
  gaming industry and, 246–248
  government support of, 255–256
  medical tourism, 251
  resort/timeshares and, 246, 248–249
Tourism Policy Council (TPC), 39
Tour operators, 237–239
  adhesion contracts and, 239
  liability for injury or accident and, 239
  misrepresentation and, 239
  nondelivery of promised services and, 239
  nonpayment for prearranged services and, 238
  potential liability issues and, 238–239
  regulatory structure and, 238
  service offerings and, 238
  travel agencies dual role, 237
Trade dress, 112
Trademarks, 110, 111, 114–115
Training for Intervention Procedures (TIPS), 226
Training programs
  alcohol service and, 226–228
  security, 267
  sexual harassment and, 144
Trains, 242
Transient guest, 188
Transportation and common carriers, 240–246
  airlines, 241
  baggage responsibility and, 245
  buses, 243–244
  car rentals, 244
  cruise ships, 242–243
  industry-specific issues and, 245–246
  legal jurisdiction and, 244
  overbooking and, 244–245
  potential liability issues, 244–246
  regulation and, 244
  tariffs and, 241
  trains, 242
  transportation industry and, 240–244
  travel industry and, 232
  unplanned itinerary changes and, 245
  Warsaw Convention and, 241
Transportation Security Administration (TSA), 38
Travel agents, 235–237
  class action lawsuits and, 237
  compensation and, 235–236
  failure to discover and disclose and, 237
  failure to honor agreed-upon pricing and, 236
  failure to provide promised services and, 236
  fiduciary responsibility and, 235–236
  misrepresentation and, 236–237
  negligence and, 237
  potential liability issues and, 236–237
  regulatory structure and, 236
  responsibilities and, 236
Travel and tourism. *See also* Regulatory interaction impacting travel and tourism
  attractions and activities and, 233
  corporate and government travel, 239–240
  economic breadth and impact, 233–234
  expectations and, 234
  foodservices and, 233
  interconnectivity and, 234
  jurisdiction and, 234
  legal issue complexity and, 234–235
  local economies and, 234
  lodging and, 232–233
  online travel sales, 251–255
  preplanning services and, 232
  service provider identification and, 234–235
  tourism, 246–251
  tour operators, 237–239
  transportation and common carriers, 232, 240–246
  travel agents, 235–237
  travel industry, 231–233
  uncontrollable forces and, 235
Travel and Tourism Promotion Advisory Board, 36
Travelers checks, lost, 199
Travel warnings, 37
Treasury Department, 30, 38
Trespassers, 198
Trial, personal injury lawsuits and, 179
Tribal Gaming Commissions (TGC), 247
Truth in menu laws, 216–221
  accuracy in menu, 216
  health benefit claims and, 220
  health benefits and, 220
  ingredients and, 219
  nutrient claims and, 220
  origin and, 219
  preparation style and, 218–219
  product size and, 219–220

U

Umbrella coverage, insurance, 290
Unclaimed property disposal, 210, 211
Uncontrollable forces, travel law and, 235
Underwriters, 289
Unemployment benefits, 29
Unemployment claims, 161–164
  claims and appeals and, 163–164
  criteria for granting or denying, 163
Unemployment insurance, 161
Uniform Commercial Code (UCC), 64–65, 78, 103–105, 213–215
Uniform Services Employment and Reemployment Rights Act, 149
USA PATRIOT Act, 200–201
U.S. Citizenship and Immigration Services (USCIS), 28, 38
U.S. Coast Guard, 38
U.S. Code Title 17, Section 504, 113
U.S. Customs and Border Protection, 38
U.S. Department of Homeland Security, 28–29
U.S. Immigration and Customs Enforcement, 38
U.S. legal system, 4
U.S. Patent and Trademark Office, 112
U.S. Secret Service, 38

V

Valet parking, 207
Verbal agreements, 63
Verbal contracts, 59–61
Verbal warnings, employee, 158
Vicarious liability, 143

W

Wage and hours standards, 27
Warnings, employee, 158
Warranty, 100–102
Warranty deeds, 97
Warsaw Convention, 241
Weapons policy, 190
Wear and tear, leasing property and, 108, 109
Whistle-blowers protection acts, 159
WIPO Performances and Phonograms Treaty, 111
Worker Adjustment and Retraining Notification Act (WARN), 28, 159
Workers' compensation, 29, 287–288
Workmen's Compensation Act of 1908, 287
Work Opportunity Tax Credit (WOTC), 156
Workout and fitness areas, 194
Workout areas, 194
Work permits, 168
Workplace surveillance, 166, 168
World Health Organization (WHO), 39–40
World Intellectual Property Organization (WIPO) Copyright Treaty, 111
World Tourism Organization (UNWTO), 39
World Travel and Tourism Council (WTTC), 231, 233
Written contracts, 59–61
Written warnings, employee, 158
Wrongful termination, 158

Z

Zero tolerance policies, 144–145
Zoning, 33

Made in the USA
Columbia, SC
28 June 2020